Dun & Bradstreet's Guide to

Doing Business Around the World

Revised

Dun & Bradstreet's Guide to

Doing Business Around the World

Revised

Terri Morrison · Wayne A. Conaway · Joseph J. Douress

Prentice
Hall Press

Library of Congress Cataloging-in-Publication Data

Morrison, Terri.
　　Dun & Bradstreet's guide to doing business around the world / Terri Morrison, Wayne
A. Conaway, Joseph J. Douress. — Rev.
　　　　p.　cm.
　　ISBN 0-7352-0108-0
　　　1. Export marketing—Handbooks, manuals, etc.　2. International trade—Cross-cultural
studies—Handbooks, manuals, etc.　3. International business enterprises—Cross-cultural
studies—Handbooks, manuals, etc.　4. Intercultural communication—Handbooks,
manuals, etc.　I. Title: Dun and Bradstreet's guide to doing business around the world.
II. Title: Guide to doing business around the world.　III. Conaway, Wayne A.　IV. Douress,
Joseph J.　V. Title.
　　HF1416.M78　2000
　　658.8'48—dc21
　　　　　　　　　　　　　　　　　　　　　　　　　　　　　　　　　　　00-059846
　　　　　　　　　　　　　　　　　　　　　　　　　　　　　　　　　　　CIP

Acquisitions Editor: *Tom Power*
Production Editor: *Eve Mossman*
Formatting/Interior Design: *Robyn Beckerman*

Printed in the United States of America

10 9 8 7 6 5 4 3 2 1

ISBN 0-7352-0108-0

Prentice Hall Press Paramus, NJ 07652

http://www.phdirect.com

Dedication

To *Nica* and *Alex*
Gifted, gorgeous, and gracious.
Thank you for keeping me from routines.
I love you.

—Terri Morrison

To my *Parents*
I hope I was a good long-term investment.

—Wayne A. Conaway

To *Maureen, Joseph, Megan, Amanda,* and *Sarah Catherine Ann*
You light up my world.

—Joseph J. Douress

Foreword

Globalization and technology have become the watchwords of U.S. industry. Americans are enjoying a period of unprecedented economic prosperity fueled by small business, the locomotive for growth. With most of the world's population and purchasing power residing outside of the United States, America's business, particularly energetic small and medium-sized firms, must fully participate in the global marketplace to ensure sustained economic growth and prosperity in the 21st century. *Dun & Bradstreet's Guide to Doing Business Around the World* offers an informative and resourceful gateway to international trade and its potential opportunities.

Businesspeople are not the only ones who will find this book valuable. Anyone who travels internationally or works with a culturally-diverse populace has use for this book. The data on how to communicate and negotiate with different cultures is useful whether one is in a another country or here at home. The information on how global politics, religions, and societies influence decision-making is highly relevant as well.

Change is a fact of life in international relations, carrying with it risks and opportunities. Recognizing the volatility of their information, and the need to manage change, the authors have included a unique feature which will insure this book's value for years to come. Much of the time sensitive data in *Dun & Bradstreet's Guide to Doing Business Around the World* can be updated online. This insures that this book will be an invaluable resource, both now and in times to come.

The judicious combination of cultural, political and trade data in this revised edition of an already excellent book makes it an effective tool for everyone—from the Fortune 500 executive to the individual entrepreneur.

Hans H. B. Koehler
Director, Wharton Export Network

Introduction

Great Britain reigned supreme in the 19th Century. Once Napoleon was defeated, the Pax Britannica made the world safe for British trade and commerce until the First World War began in 1914. A businessman (virtually all traders were male in those days) could make a good living without going outside the boundaries of the British Empire.

The 20th Century was often called the American Century. The United States of America turned the tide in two World Wars, and emerged from the Cold War as the last Superpower. By mid-century, any businessman who restricted his trade to the British Empire found himself without an Empire to trade with.

Now we are in the 21st Century. Will this be the Pacific Century? Can the U.S.A. maintain its economic, political, technological and military dominance? If power shifts to the world's most homogeneous and forward-looking nation, it will be the Japanese Century. Or it may go to the world's most populous nation, and give birth to the Chinese Century.

No one can say with certainty.

However, one *can* predict that globalization offers businesspeople their best chance to participate in the economy of the 21st Century. None of us wants to be like that British businessman who found himself without an Empire to trade with. Successful executives of the 21st Century will compete on a global scale.

Even if the 21st Century turns out to be the first E-Century, it will involve the shifting of goods and services across national borders. E-commerce may be decentralized, but nation-states are not going to disappear any time soon.

This book, *Dun & Bradstreet's Guide to Doing Business Around the World*, is designed to help you enter the global market. This expansive volume includes vital data and guidelines for conducting business with the top 40 trade partners of the U.S.A.

The information in *Dun & Bradstreet's Guide to Doing Business Around the World* is organized for ease of use by both new and experienced exporters. Each chapter is crammed with data on many topics which impact on exporting. This plethora of information is carefully broken down into category and type so as to remain accessible. If (for example) your only interest was whether or not each country is a member of the Berne Convention for the Protection of Intellectual Property Rights, this information is easily found (in this example, under each country's "Protection of Intellectual Property Rights," section).Of particular note is a section near the beginning of each chapter listed as "5 CULTURAL TIPS." Not all businesspeople have the time to read *Dun & Bradstreet's Guide to Doing Business Around the World* in its entirety. But even if you are too busy to read anything else, knowing these five need-to-know precepts can enhance your chances of success in these 40 target countries.Many of these tips cover the protocols for initial business contacts—which, like any first impression, can be difficult to overcome. A single cultural gaffe in an initial contact can eliminate the possibility of a second contact. In effect, a bad first impression can ruin any chance of a business deal. Some topics covered in the CULTURAL Tips include:

Techniques for selling to Australians (and why high-pressure sales won't work).

- Eye contact among Mexicans, and what it reveals about relationships.
- Why a Dutch executive may be preparing a complete dossier on you.
- How foreigners can run afoul of the Indonesian precept of "asal bapak senang" (which translates as "keeping father happy").
- Why a disregard for history will cause you problems in Poland.
- What to expect when you are invited to a South African braaivleis.
- Who a mudang is, and why this person can spoil your deal with South Koreans.
- In what everyday environment where the normally-smiling Thais lose their smiles.
- Why handshakes among the French are brief, and how to keep the French from considering you to be dull.

Failure to respond correctly to any of these cultural idiosyncrasies can result in the a loss of credibility. But forewarned is forearmed.

Each of the USA's 40 top trading partners is given a separate chapter. Each chapter begins with vital demographic data. Population figures are important, but less-commonly-provided data such as age breakdowns are equally important. If you're marketing products for retirees, you need to know the number of older people in a country—not just the overall population.

Of course, there are many other factors to be considered. Once the size of a market has been determined, you will need to know the per capita income. Can the people in your target country afford to buy your product? Is their economy growing or shrinking?

Dun & Bradstreet's Guide to Doing Business Around the World provides this data.

What about cultural factors? Will your product encounter opposition on political or religious grounds? Can such opposition be overcome? Opposition from religious leaders won't stop your product from selling in Sweden...but it may stop it in Saudi Arabia. Each chapter includes an evaluation of the religious and societal influences on business. And the religious breakdown of each nation is included, detailing what percentage of the population adheres to which religion.

Each country also has a general overview of its history and politics. Nothing is more insulting to natives of any country than being confused with natives of someplace else. These general overviews will enable you to pin down each nation's global identity. In addition, that country's relationship to the United States is noted. Is their government friendly and cooperative? By its nature, international trade is subject to the whims of governments. While the numbers may say that trade is worthwhile, a difficult government may make an otherwise-profitable deal more trouble than it's worth.

This book includes comparative data ratings for each country. On a scale of one-though-five, the country is judged as to the following:

- Gross Domestic Product growth
- Per Capita Income
- Trade Flows with the USA
- Risk Factors
- Monetary Policies
- Trade Policy
- Protection of Intellectual Property Rights
- Foreign Investment Climate

Along with these ratings, the country's imports and exports with the USA are detailed. The country's GDP, rate of growth, and per capita income are also listed.

In addition, we list the top US exports to each country, as well as the top prospects for export in the future.

Ratings are useful only if what they are measuring is clear. Dun & Bradstreet is well known for its ratings of companies worldwide. Dun & Bradstreet also provides an assessment of the risk associated with conducting business within specific countries through the D&B Economic Group in High Wycombe, United Kingdom.

The third section of each chapter (following the demographic and comparative data sections) explains in detail what is being measured in the following areas:

- Country Risk (compiled from D&B's International Risk and Payment Review providing a cross-border assessment of the risk of doing business in a specific country.)
- Monetary Policy
- Trade Policy, broken down into Tariffs, Import Licensing and Import Taxes
- Protection of Intellectual Property Rights
- Foreign Investment Climate

Since there is no substitute for experience, each chapter includes one or more observations from someone who has done business in that country. These comments could be from U.S. executives who trade there, or from natives of that country who work with visiting businesspeople.

In the hope that we can all profit by learning by our mistakes, many chapters contain a business error or gaffe. Listed under the title faux pas, these range from simple mistranslations to serious breaches of cultural etiquette. Each of these errors resulted in a serious cost to the businesspeople involved. The first executives to make these errors had an excuse: they didn't know any better. You won't have that excuse. But you won't have to suffer their consequences, either.

Finally, you might like to test your "Cultural I.Q. " on various topics at the end of seven different chapters. The questions are meant to entertain, as well as exercise your cultural knowledge in Taiwan, Italy, Saudi Arabia, Mexico, Japan, Spain and Venezuela.

From the first conception of a deal to the final consummation, we have endeavored to include all the information you might need. Whether you are a one-man or one-woman trading concern or an integral part of a vast trading empire, *Dun and Bradstreet's Guide to Commerce and Culture* will have many of the answers you need.

While the data in *Dun & Bradstreet's Guide to Doing Business Around the World* contains valuable statistics, trends, facts, commerce and culture, it is clearly a snapshot in time. A template of important information to be used over and over, as well as dynamic data to be updated as time goes by. Fortunately, we also direct readers to online web sites where the new trends, politicians, and trade data can be updated online. (Many of these websites can be found in the appendix.) Their inclusion makes *Dun & Bradstreet's Guide to Doing Business Around the World*, a truly valuable resource of current and future information for business travelers, researchers, educators, and tourists.

Of course, much of the information in this book (ranging from attitudes towards time to the cultural notes) will remain as useful decades from now as it is today.

We hope your international business and travels benefit from *Dun & Bradstreet's Guide to Doing Business Around the World*, and we would appreciate hearing from you. The authors welcome your input, and can be contacted through our website at getcustoms.com, or via email to TerriMorrison@getcustoms.com; telephone 610.725.1040; fax: 801.516.8774; or mailing address: Box 136, Newtown Square, PA 19073, USA.

Table of Contents

Argentina

Official Name:	Argentine Republic (República Argentina)
Official Language:	Spanish
Government System:	Federal republic
Population:	36.7 million (1999 estimate)
Population Growth Rate:	1.29% (1999 estimate)
Area:	2,766,890 sq. km. (1.1 million sq. mi.); about the size of the U.S. east of the Mississippi River
Natural Resources:	fertile plains of the pampas, lead, zinc, tin, copper, iron ore, manganese, crude oil, uranium
Major Cities:	Buenos Aires (capital), Cordoba, Rosario, La Plata, Mendoza

---

Cultural Note: Argentina is a country gifted with such abundant natural resources that it could be one of the world's wealthiest nations. In years past, Argentines often said that their country was "blessed by resources but cursed by politics." Poor leadership kept the Argentine economy in turmoil for much of this century. But, since 1989, the Argentine government has pursued a highly successful policy of economic restructuring. Argentina currently boasts a profitable and business-friendly environment for foreign investment.

Age Breakdown

0–14 = 27%   15–64 = 62%   65+ = 11% (1999 estimate)
Life Expectancy: 71.3 years, male; 78.56 years, female (1999 estimate)

Time

North American executives are expected to be punctual to business appointments, but do not be surprised if your Argentine counterpart is late.

Everyone—even visitors from the U.S.—is expected to be 30 to 60 minutes late for dinner or parties. It would be considered impolite to show up on time.

If you are confused about whether or not to be on time, ask "¿En punto?" ("on the dot?").

Argentina is 3 hours behind Greenwich Mean Time (GMT –3), which is 2 hours ahead of U.S. Eastern Standard Time (EST. +2).

Holidays

A web-based *World Holiday and Time Zone Guide* is available at www.getcustoms.com with updated official holidays, cultural tips, time zones, and tables that compare worldwide business hours.

The following list is a working guide. Dates should be corroborated before final travel plans are made. In cases where holidays fall on Saturday or Sunday, commercial establishments may be closed the preceding Friday or following Monday.

Jan 1	SA	New Year's Day
Apr 20	TH	Holy Thursday
Apr 21	FR	Good Friday
May 1	MO	Workers Day
May 25	TH	May Revolution (1810)
Jun 12	MO	Malvinas Islands Memorial
Jun 19	MO	Flag Day
Jul 9	SU	Independence Day
Aug 17	TH	General José de San Martin Day
Oct 12	TH	Columbus Day
Dec 8	FR	Immaculate Conception
Dec 25	MO	Christmas Day

Argentina has two Independence Days; each one celebrates a different historical event.

Argentines love holidays and may take off from work during additional minor holidays. The observances of official holidays may be shifted by a few days to provide a long weekend. Again, the days of observance should always be corroborated by local contacts.

Work Week

- The standard work week is Monday through Friday.
- Argentine executives may put in a very long day, often lasting until 10:00 P.M. An 8:00 P.M. business meeting is not at all unusual.

Observation: "A large city has a tempo, a rhythm with which the new arrival seeks to fall in step—but I could not gauge the rhythm of Buenos Aires. It seemed that there was no particular time at which people awoke, went to work, lunched, returned home, went to bed. Trying to reach someone at the office was a wasted effort. Invariably, the person you were looking for had not yet arrived and no one knew when he was due in. No matter what day it was, the advice was to 'ring back on Monday.' It took me several weeks to see that this was a stalling device: Monday was a fiction.

"Only gradually did I come to realize that life in Buenos Aires could not be subdued and contained by timetables—even if you set off with the best intentions, each day held in store its quota of disruptions. Meetings were habitually late, cancelled or skipped."

—From *Bad Times in Buenos Aires*. The author, British journalist Miranda France, received the Shiva Naipul Memorial Prize for travel writing.

Religious/Societal Influences on Business

Roman Catholicism is the official religion of Argentina, and about 92% of the population are members of the Catholic faith. However, freedom of religion is guaranteed, and Argentina has citizens who adhere to many belief systems.

Argentina remains a male-dominant culture. The Argentine dance called the *tango* is seen by many as the ultimate expression of indigenous popular culture. Certainly, the tango reflected male–female roles in Argentina: In its original form, the tango was a dance of complete male dominance over the female, with the woman clutching onto her partner as he drags her around. Putting lyrics to tango music broadened its popularity while it diminished its eroticism. The heyday of the tango has passed, but many Argentines remain fanatic admirers of it.

All Argentines must deal with the repercussions of the military dictatorship, the six years of the so-called "Dirty War." Some nine thousand Argentines were missing and are presumed dead. Few officials have been punished for the kidnappings, tortures and executions. Complicity with the dictatorship was widespread, even in the Church (some Catholic clergy offered council to torturers disturbed by their jobs). Most Argentines seem to want to forget those days. Notably, the group known as the Argentine Forensic Anthropology Team (which unearths the mass graves of anonymous victims of the Dirty War) is funded from outside Argentina. The junta was disgraced by

Argentina's defeat in the 1982 Falkland Islands War (remember, the Argentines call them the Malvinas Islands); which led to the return of a civilian government in 1983.

Interestingly, psychoanalysis is very popular among the upper-class residents of Buenos Aires.

5 Cultural Tips

1. Establishing a close social relationship is a prerequisite for conducting business. Meetings begin *and* end with polite small talk. You may insult your Argentine counterparts if you rush off without chatting at the end of a meeting.

2. Compared with other South Americans, Argentines—especially those from Buenos Aires—have a reputation for seriousness and melancholy. To call someone or something "not serious" is one of the most damning accusations an Argentine can make. A formal sober manner (with a firm handshake and good eye contact) is appropriate in Argentina.

3. On the other hand, when somber Argentines become humorous, you will know that they have become comfortable with you. Argentine banter is full of put-downs, from comments about your wardrobe to your weight. Don't be offended. You may respond in kind, but do not comment on Argentine institutions or traditions in an unfavorable manner, even in jest.

4. Expect long days. Executives may work irregular and extended hours, sometimes lasting until 10:00 P.M., so business meetings as late as 8:00 P.M. are not at all unusual. Argentines do not eat dinner until 10:00 P.M., so they break for a snack between 4:00 and 6:00 P.M. The food is usually pastries; the drink is tea, coffee, or *mate*. *Mate* (pronounced "mah-tay") is a caffeinated drink made from an indigenous herb. It is also called Paraguayan tea. If you are in a meeting during that time, you will be offered something. Accept something to drink, even if you don't want it.

5. Elegant clothes are very important. Argentines—particularly those in the capital, Buenos Aries—pride themselves on dressing as fashionably as refined Parisians or Milanese. (Businesspeople, however, tend more towards the conservative attire of London.) Many travelers from North America feel underdressed when they arrive in Argentina. In order to be taken seriously, executives must dress appropriately.

Observation: "Buenos Aires, in fact, was the first place I'd ever visited where I always felt underdressed: when I went to a tearoom, my first afternoon in town, at three o'clock on a weekday, every single male in the place—but me—was wearing a tie. Only a few years ago, men had been arrested for wearing shorts in the street."

> —Travel writer Pico Iyer, in a 1990 essay about Argentina. Arrests for improper public dress were not common, but did occur during the junta; women wearing trousers were also subject to arrest. This essay is reprinted in Pico Iyer's 1993 collection *Falling Off the Map*.

Economic Overview

Argentina, rich in natural resources, benefits also from a highly literate population, an export-oriented agricultural sector, and a diversified industrial base. Nevertheless, following decades of mismanagement and protectionist policies, the economy in the late 1980s was plagued with huge external debts and recurring bouts with hyperinflation.

Argentina's economic growth has been slowed by fluctuating commodity prices and economic turmoil elsewhere. The devaluation of the Mexican peso in late 1994 caused some dislocation, and the Brazilian crisis of 1998 caused even more damage.

In addition, unemployment remains a serious issue for the government. Despite the overall strength and high growth rate of the Argentine economy since 1991, unemployment has doubled. This is largely a result of layoffs in government bureaus and the privatization of inefficient state-owned industries. U.S and other foreign firms have continued substantial direct investment.

Argentina is a member of Mercosur, one of the largest and most successful trade groups in the developing world. However, the collapse of the Brazilian economy in 1998 hampered trade among Mercosur members.

All restrictions on foreign-owned banks were removed in 1994. Similar liberalization occurred in the insurance industry in late 1998.

5 Largest Businesses in Argentina

Electronica Ion S.R.L., Berazategui
   95,030 employees
Elira S.A., Escobar
   42,269 employees
Empresa Nacional de Correos y Telegrafos (ENCOTEL), Buenos Aires
   30,000 employees
Telegonica de Argentina S.A., Buenos Aires
   18,098 employees
Ferrocarriles Metropolitanos S.A., Buenos Aires
   15,000 employees

Comparative Data

Comparative Data Ratings
(Scale: 5 = Highest; 1 = Lowest)
Argentina: 3

   A. GDP Growth: 3
   B. Per Capita Income: 3
   C. Trade Flows with the U.S.: 3
   D. Country Risk: 3
   E. Monetary Policy: 4

F.   Trade Policy: 3
   • Tariffs
   • Import Licensing
   • Import Taxes
G.   Protection of Property Rights: 3
H.   Foreign Investment Climate: 2

GROSS DOMESTIC PRODUCT: $330 billion (1997) $374 billion (1998 estimate)

GDP GROWTH: 3.9% (1998)   –3.0% (1999 forecast)   4.0% (2000 forecast)

PER CAPITA INCOME: $8,900 (1997) $10,300 (1998 estimate)

Trade Flows with the U.S.

U.S. EXPORTS TO ARGENTINA: $5.9 billion (1998 estimate)

U.S. IMPORTS FROM ARGENTINA: $2.3 billion (1997)

TOP U.S. EXPORTS TO ARGENTINA: Electric power generation equipment; machinery; plastics; telecommunications equipment; oil and gas pipeline equipment; mineral oils and fuel; food-processing equipment

TOP U.S. PROSPECTS FOR EXPORT TO ARGENTINA: Mineral fuels and oils; animal and vegetable products (including fish, meat, fruits, nuts and sugar); petroleum; stones; iron and steel; leather; tobacco

Country Risk

Dun & Bradstreet rates Argentina as having sufficient capacity to meet outstanding payment liabilities. However, enough uncertainty warrants close monitoring of country risk. Bankruptcies surged in 1999.

Letters of credit are recommended for initial transactions, along with credit checks on individual firms. When open account terms are used, 30- to 60-day terms are the norm.

Monetary Policy

Thanks to the Menem administration's policies, Argentina's consumer price index for 1997 was an astonishingly low 0.3%. The 1998 estimate was for 0.5%, and inflation was forecast at 0% for 1999.

A Convertibility Plan that pegs the Argentine peso to the U.S. dollar and bans the printing of unbacked specie has helped keep inflation very low. Inflation is expected to remain below 1% through the year 2000.

MONETARY UNIT: peso

Trade Policy

TARIFFS   Tariff rates have been reduced. Argentina now has a tiered tariff schedule with a maximum rate of 20% ad valorem and an average rate of 10%.

The structure of tariffs is as follows: 10% on almost all capital goods; 2–14% on agricultural products; 2–16% on most industrial inputs and raw materials; 20% on consumer goods.

IMPORT LICENSING   Import licenses are not required for any import, except autos and auto parts which are subject to a special regime.

Permanent quotas remain on goods such as automobiles. Temporary quotas exist on paper, pulp, and a few other items. Other goods such as pharmaceuticals, foodstuffs, defense materials, and other particular items require the approval of the related government department.

IMPORT TAXES   A 0.5% statistics fee is charged on all imports except capital goods. A 21% value-added tax (VAT) is levied on all imports.

Protection of Intellectual Property Rights

Argentina officially adheres to most treaties and international agreements on intellectual property protection and belongs to the World Intellectual Property Organization (WIPO). A bilateral copyright treaty signed in 1934 between the U.S. and Argentina still exists, despite changes made to bring Argentine law into compliance with GATT/TRIPS. Argentina is still on the Section 301 U.S. Trade priority watch list. Copyright piracy remains a particular concern. *Pharmaceutical patents, which had been a major area of contention between the U.S. and Argentina, are allowed after October 23, 2000.*

The Argentina Constitution provides that the inventor is the exclusive owner of his work for the period established by law. Inventions must be novel, be inventive, and have industrial application. Protection is given to both utility models and patents made by employees. Patents are granted for a term of 20 years from application and utility models have a 10-year term. Individuals and legal entities may own patents. Companies may apply for patents for inventions. Patents may be assigned if ownership is recorded with NIIP. Foreign patents may be ratified for a maximum term of 10 years. Patents are subject to compulsory licensing after 3 years from grant for nonuse. Patent infringement is considered criminal in Argentina.

Trademark rights are obtained by registration. Both products and services are protected. The international classification system is followed. Color combinations and advertising slogans can be registered. Any interested party may file opposition. If the opposition is not withdrawn, the application is rejected and the applicant's only recourse is to appeal to court. Trademarks have 10-year renewable terms. Use is required for renewals and to defend a cancellation action. Trademark use in one class suffices to renew registrations in other classes. Cancellation may be initiated by a public or private action. Trademark rights are transferable if the assignment is properly recorded. Misuse of trademarks is criminal.

Argentina's copyright law was enacted in 1993. Nevertheless, Argentina joined the Berne Convention in 1967, some 20 years ahead of the U.S. To be copyrighted, three copies of the work must be deposited with the national Copyright Register. Copyrights belong to the author for life and to his heirs and assigns for 50 years after death. Copyrights for works by employees are good for 50 years. If there are no assigns or heirs, copyrights revert to the state. The state has the right to receive fees for performances and exhibitions for works in the public domain.

Foreign Investment Climate

Foreign direct investment is an essential element of Argentina's economic growth. Argentina's climate for foreign investment is one of the most favorable in Latin America. The Menem administration has encouraged foreign investment through national treatment under a free foreign exchange and capital movement regime.

Decree 1853 of September 8, 1993 governs foreign investment in Argentina. Foreign companies may invest in Argentina without registration or prior government approval on the same terms as investors domiciled in Argentina. A U.S.–Argentina agreement for reciprocal promotion and protection of investments entered into force in October 1994.

Investors are free to enter Argentina via the most convenient vehicle—merger, acquisition, or joint venture. Foreign firms are among the most prominent participants in Argentina's ambitious privatization program, which includes gas, oil, electric power, telecommunications, transportation, water, and sewer sectors.

There are very few sectors in which Argentina reserves the right to maintain exceptions to national treatment for U.S. investors: real estate in border areas, air transportation, shipbuilding, nuclear energy, uranium mining, insurance, and fishing. Foreign firms can enter the fishing and insurance industries by purchasing an interest in existing firms.

U.S. direct investment in Argentina has ballooned from US$2.7 billion in 1991 to US$14 billion in 1998. This growth is expected to continue in the foreseeable future.

Political Leaders, Parties, and International Organizations

The International Academy at Santa Barbara at http://www.iasb.org/cwl publishes *Current World Leaders*, an excellent resource for up-to-date data on political leaders, parties, demographics, etc., in Argentina. Tel: 1-800-530-2682 or (805) 965-5010 for subscription information to their database.

Head of State and the Government:
    President Fernando de la Rúa Bruno

Next Election:
    October 2003

Political parties and leaders:

Justicialist Party (PJ); Radical Civic Union (UCR); Union of the Democratic Center (UCD); Dignity and Independence Political Party (MODIN); Front for a Country in Solidarity or Frepaso (a four-party coalition); Action for the Republic; New Leadership; several provincial parties

Membership in international organizations:

G77, LAIA, NAM, OAS, SELA, UN and all of its specialized agencies and related organizations (including FAO, GATT, IAEA, IBRD, ICAO, IDA, IFAD, IFC, ILO, IMF, IMO, ITU, UNESCO, UNIDO, UPU, WHO, WIPO, WMO)

Political Influences on Business

The Menem Administration strongly encouraged private initiative through its privatization of state firms, deregulation of the economy, and encouragement of foreign direct investment, which it saw as a necessity to the country's continued growth. Foreign investors are welcome in virtually every economic sector.

The highly favorable investment climate notwithstanding, businesses continue to face occasional inconsistencies associated with governmental actions. A variety of cases exist in which U.S. companies that have invested in or traded with Argentina have been unfairly affected by what they consider to be the federal government's arbitrary and capricious enforcement of laws. Some cases endure from the old days of statist intervention by military juntas; others have occurred in the present environment, in which companies are buffeted by the sheer profusion of change. Although much has been achieved in such areas as deregulation and market opening, the government has been less successful in guaranteeing juridical security (*seguridad juridica*, or the rule of law). The government itself recognizes that the administration of justice could be improved as well, to speed up court cases; the U.S. government is providing assistance to promote the change.

Social stability is also a potential issue of the future. Despite the outward measures of success—a rate of economic growth second only to China's in the last three years—problems have cropped up in the model, such as a record-high serious unemployment rate, regional disparities in economic development, and the lack of adequate social services. All of these issues could erode popular support for the program and force the government to slow the pace of change or even roll back some reforms. On the other hand, the public's memory of decades of increasing economic chaos—which culminated in the hyperinflationary episodes of 1989–90—is still very fresh and was the key factor to Menem's reelection.

After serving as president since 1989, Carlos Saul Menem's second and final term in office ended in May 1999. While business-friendly policies are expected to continue under Menem's successor, President Fernando de la Rúa, there is some trepidation about what the future may bring. Nor should it be forgotten that the 1989 succession from President Raul Alfonsin to Carlos Menem was the first peaceful transfer of power between democratically elected Argentine leaders in more than sixty years. President Fernando de la Rúa's administration will hopefully prove to be a stable, enlightened one.

Contacts in the United States

THE EMBASSY OF THE ARGENTINE REPUBLIC
1600 New Hampshire Avenue, NW
Washington, D.C. 20009
Tel: (202) 939-6400
Fax: (202) 238-6471
www.embassyofargentina-usa.org

Passport/Visa Requirements

A passport is required. U.S. citizens do not need a visa for a three-month tourist stay. For current information concerning entry and customs requirements for Argentina, travelers can contact the Argentine Embassy.

U.S. citizens who wish to apply for a passport may visit Passport Services' well-organized website at http://travel.state.gov/passport_services.html.

ASSOCIATION OF AMERICAN CHAMBERS OF COMMERCE IN LATIN AMERICA
1615 H Street, NW
Washington, D.C. 20062
Tel: (202) 463-5485
Fax: (202) 436-3114
www.aaccla.org

Contacts in Argentina

THE EMBASSY OF THE UNITED STATES
OF AMERICA
4300 Colombia
1425 Buenos Aires
Tel: (54) (11) 4777-4533
Fax: (54) (11) 4511-4997
www.usia.gov/posts/baires_embassy

THE AMERICAN CHAMBER OF COMMERCE
IN ARGENTINA
Viamonte 1133, Piso 8
1053 Buenos Aires
Tel: (54) (11) 4371-4500
Fax: (54) (11) 4371-8400
www.amchamarg.com

DUN & BRADSTREET S.A.
Viamonte 570/72
1053 Capital Federal
Buenos Aires, Argentina
Tel: (54) (11) 4318-3100
Fax: (54) (11) 4318-3192

OFFICE OF THE PRESIDENT
Balcarce 50
1064 Buenos Aires, Argentina

Further contacts and websites can be found in Appendix A.

Communications

TELEPHONE: The country code for Argentine is 54.

MAIL: Business letters should be addressed as follows: (*Notes in parentheses*)

Office:	Secretaria de Agricultura, Ganaderia, Pesca y Alimentacion (*Secretariat of Agriculture, Livestock, Fisheries and Food*)
Title & Name:	Ing. Agr. Felipe Carlos Sola, Secretary (*Ing. is an abbreviation for Ingenero = Engineer*)
Street:	Av. Paseo Colon 982 (*The street number may precede or follow the name of the street.*)
Routing Code & City:	1063 Buenos Aires
Country:	Argentina

Unlike most Latin Americans, the majority of Argentines do not use both their father's and mother's surnames. However, there are exceptions. There are also many Argentine citizens with non-Hispanic surnames—including President Carlos Menem, who is of Syrian origin.

E-MAIL: E-mail addresses located in Argentina end with the code .ar

DATES: The date is written in this order: day, month, year (unlike the U.S. practice of writing month, day, year). Sometimes the month is given in Roman numerals, such as 2/XI/00 for November 2, 2000.

Cultural Note: Argentina's natural wealth has attracted immigrants from all over the world. Rags-to-riches stories were common, and the phrase "wealthy as an Argentine" entered the world's vocabulary late in the 1800s. Immigrants arrived from England, Ireland, Germany, Poland, and Russia. The parents of former Argentine President Carlos Menem came from Syria. Aside from Spain, the major country of origin for Argentines was Italy. As a result, the Spanish spoken in Argentina is heavily influenced by Italian. While it is comprehensible to most Spanish-speakers, it is quite unlike the Spanish spoken elsewhere.

Australia

Official Name:	Commonwealth of Australia
Official Language:	English
Government System:	Democratic, federal–state system
Population:	18,783,551 (July 1999 estimate)
Population Growth Rate:	0.9% (1999 estimate)
Area:	7,686,844 sq. km. (2.96 million sq. mi.); about the size of the continental U.S.
Natural Resources:	bauxite, coal, iron ore, copper, tin, silver, uranium, nickel, tungsten, mineral sands, lead, zinc, diamonds, natural gas, petroleum
Major Cities:	Canberra (capital), Sydney, Melbourne, Brisbane, Perth, Adelaide

Age Breakdown

0–14 = 21% 15–64 = 66% 65+ = 13% (1999 estimate)
Life Expectancy: 77.22 years, male; 83.23 years, female (1999 estimate)

Time

Australian executives expect promptness. Tardiness is seen as indicative of carelessness.
Australia spans three time zones. They are:

- Western Australia (including the city of Perth) is 8 hours ahead of Greenwich Mean Time (GMT +8). This is the part of Australia farthest away from the United States, and is 13 hours ahead of U.S. Eastern Standard Time (EST +13). Singapore and Hong Kong are also in this time zone.
- The Northern Territories (including Darwin) and South Australia (including Adelaide) are 9-1/2 hours ahead of Greenwich Mean Time (GMT +9-1/2). This is the middle section of Australia, and is 14-1/2 hours ahead of U.S. Eastern Standard Time (EST +14-1/2).
- Eastern Australia—which encompasses New South Wales (including Sydney and the capital territory, Canberra), Victoria (including Melbourne), Tasmania (including Hobart), and Queensland (including Brisbane)—is 10 hours ahead of Greenwich Mean Time (GMT +10). This is the part of Australia closest to the United States, and is 15 hours ahead of U.S. Eastern Standard Time (EST +15).

When traveling to Australia from the Americas, remember that you cross the International Date Line. When flying westward (U.S. to Australia), you lose a day. Flying eastward (Australia to the U.S.), you gain a day.

Holidays

A web-based *World Holiday and Time Zone Guide* is available at www.getcustoms.com with updated official holidays, cultural tips, time zones, and tables that compare world-wide business hours.

This list is a working guide. Dates should be corroborated before final travel plans are made. In cases where holidays fall on Saturday or Sunday, commercial establishments may be closed the preceding Friday or following Monday.

Jan 1	SA	New Year's Day
Jan 26	WE	Australia Day
Mar 1	WE	Labor Day—WA, Tas
Mar 13	MO	Labor Day—Vic
Mar 16	TH	Canberra Day—ACT
Apr 21	FR	Good Friday
Apr 22	SA	Holy Saturday—ACT, NSW, NT, Qld, SA, Tas
Apr 24	MO	Easter Monday
Apr 25	TU	ANZAC Day
May 1	MO	Labor Day—NT, Qld
May 15	MO	Adelaide Cup Day—SA
Jun 7	WE	Foundation Day—WA
Jun 12	MO	Queen's Birthday—ACT, NSW, Vic, Tas, SA, NT, Qld
Aug 2	WE	Bank holiday—NT
Aug 7	MO	Bank holiday—NSW
Aug 16	WE	Royal National Show—Qld
Sep 25	MO	Queen's Birthday—WA

Oct 2	MO	Labor Day—ACT, NSW, SA
Nov 7	TU	Melbourne Cup Day—Vic
Dec 25	MO	Christmas Day
Dec 26	TU	Boxing Day
Dec 26	TU	Proclamation Day—SA

Good Friday and Easter Monday are also official holidays. Each Australian state also celebrates additional holidays. The Queen's Birthday is currently celebrated, but not on the same day in each state!

Confirm your appointments with local representatives to avoid conflicts with regional festivities.

The best time to visit is from March through November, since the peak tourist season is December through February. Christmas and Easter are especially hectic; many executives will be on vacation.

Work Week

Business hours are 9:00 A.M. to 5:00 P.M., Monday through Friday; 9:00 A.M. to noon, Saturday. Banks are open 9:30 A.M. to 4:00 P.M., Monday through Thursday; 9:30 A.M. to 5:00 P.M. on Fridays.

Religious/Societal Influences on Business

Australia has no official religion. Most faiths are represented, while 13% of the population professes to follow no religion. Roman Catholics, with 27.3%, constitute the largest group, with Anglicans close behind at 23.8%.

5 Cultural Tips

1. As a general rule, Australians are friendly, informal, and easy to get to know. Although Australia is still part of the British Commonwealth, traditional British reserve is not widely seen. Unlike in England, foreigners are welcome to introduce themselves.

2. Australians do not respect people who go on about their education, qualifications, or achievements. Modesty is considered a virtue. "Cut down the tall poppy" is a common Australian aphorism, similar to "the nail that sticks out gets hammered down." Braggarts are considered fair game for ridicule or criticism.

3. Less is more among the Australian business community. Australians tend to be laconic; brevity is admirable. Keep your business presentation short and to the point; do not digress or go into too much detail. A verbose salesperson can easily talk himself out of a sale.

ACT = Australian Capital Territory; NSW = New South Wales; Vic = Victoria; Tas = Tasmania; SA = South Australia; NT = Northern Territory; Qld = Queensland; WA = Western Australia

4. High-pressure sales and hype are counterproductive down under. Australians prefer honesty and directness, and tend to fiercely resist pressure tactics. Present your case in a forthright manner, articulating both the good and the bad. Also, price your initial offer realistically, since the final price agreed upon will probably be close.

5. Argument is considered entertaining by many Australians. They tend to be very direct and open with their opinions. People who are afraid of candor and cannot frankly express themselves are not respected.

Economic Overview

The Australian economy is enjoying a period of sustained, moderate growth. To the surprise of many (including Australians), the 1997 Asian economic crisis did not halt Australia's economic growth. As exports to Asian markets fell, most Australian industries managed to sell products to Europe and the Americas.

Australia is well-positioned for continued solid economic growth, with very little in the way of unfavorable indicators. The nation's resources, proximity to the globe's largest population centers, privatization of utilities and continuing economic reform, indicate that Australia's trade and investment climate will be attractive for the foreseeable future.

Australia began a basic reorientation of its economy back in 1983. Since then, it has transformed itself from an inward-looking, import substitution country to an internationally competitive, export-oriented one. The government's economic development strategy focuses on continued economic reform to encourage expansion of value-added production in the minerals and agricultural sectors; manufacturing in high-technology products; and expansion of the services sector.

The United States is Australia's second largest trading partner, behind only Japan. The U.S. is Australia's largest source of merchandise imports. Indeed, Australia represents the United States'—only significant bilateral trade surplus in Asia.

The Australian economy displays many of the same features of the U.S. economy, such as a substantial growth in the service sector and a decline in union membership. Both countries share similar weaknesses, including low savings rates and major trade deficits. Unlike the U.S., Australia suffers from stubborn unemployment rates (estimated at 7% in 1999).

The U.S. and Australia have been close allies for more than 50 years, during which Australia has been the southern link in the structure of Asia–Pacific strategic alliances. Like the United States, Australia is a leading advocate of trade and investment liberalization.

Geographically, Australia is similar in size to the United States. Despite its small population and vast landmass, the country has well-developed nationwide air, road, port, and telecommunications infrastructure networks.

5 Largest Businesses in Australia

The Myer Emporium Ltd., Tooronga
    136,195 employees
Penneys Pty. Ltd., Silverwater
    135,000 employees
Coles Myer Ltd., Tooronga
    135,000 employees
G.J. Coles & Coy Pty. Ltd., Malvern
    135,000 employees
Coles Myer International Pty. Ltd., Tooronga
    135,000 employees

Cultural Note: Australians feel a strong impetus to deflate people who put on airs. Referred to as "cutting down the tall poppy," this habit is thought to have grown out of Australia's origin as a British penal colony. Naturally, the Australian prisoners hated their high-class British overseers and wished to insult them whenever possible. Furthermore, many Australian convicts were Irish—a people already looked down upon by the British at that time. This feeling is still so ingrained that many Australian politicians decline an offer of a British knighthood for fear of alienating their constituents.

Downplay your expertise/knowledge/skills. Try to let your accomplishments speak for themselves. More than one Australian has complained that eager young U.S. executives "sound like walking resumes," since they are so quick to list their accomplishments and qualifications.

Comparative Data

Comparative Data Ratings
(Scale: 5 = Excellent; 1 = Poor)
Australia: 4.5

   A.   GDP Growth: 4
   B.   Per Capita Income: 5
   C.   Trade Flows with the U.S.: 4
   D.   Country Risk: 5
   E.   Monetary Policy: 5
   F: Trade Policy: 4
        • Tariffs
        • Import Licensing
        • Import Taxes
   G.   Protection of Property Rights: 5
   H.   Foreign Investment Climate: 4

GROSS DOMESTIC PRODUCT: $393.9 billion (1998 estimate) $374.5 billion (1999 estimate)

GDP GROWTH: 4.6% (1998) 4.0% (1999 estimate)

PER CAPITA INCOME: $21,200 (1998 estimate)

Trade Flows with the U.S.

U.S. EXPORTS TO AUSTRALIA: $11.9 billion (1998 estimate) $12.3 billion (1999 estimate)

U.S. IMPORTS FROM AUSTRALIA: $5.15 billion (1998 estimate) $5.27 billion (1999 projection)

TOP U.S. EXPORTS TO AUSTRALIA: Aircraft and associated equipment, computers, office machinery, measuring and checking equipment, telecommunications.

TOP U.S. PROSPECTS FOR EXPORT TO AUSTRALIA: Computer software; computers and peripherals; medical equipment; automotive parts; telecommunications equipment; telecommunications services; defense equipment; security equipment; aircraft and parts; laboratory and scientific equipment

Country Risk

Dun & Bradstreet rates Australia as having excellent capacity to meet outstanding payment liabilities.

Generally, all common terms of payment are in use, but open account predominates. More secure terms are recommended for new customers. Credit terms of 30 to 60 days are the norm.

Monetary Policy

Inflation is predicted to remain relatively low, with only moderate upward pressure from wages and the effect of a weaker currency. Inflation actually dropped to a negative 0.2% in 1997; Dun & Bradstreet forecast that inflation would be under 2.5% in 1999 and 2000.

MONETARY UNIT: Australian dollar

Trade Policy

TARIFFS Australia initiated a program for progressive tariff reductions in 1988. This program is continuing, placing over 90% of Australian tariffs within WTO boundaries. The maximum tariff rate for most goods is 5%. Tariff rates do affect competitive pricing of imported goods.

Automobile and auto parts tariffs, pegged at 22.5% in June 1997, will be gradually reduced to 15% (the target date is January 2005).

The 25% tariff on textiles, clothing, and footwear will be gradually reduced to 10% (also with a target date of 2005).

IMPORT LICENSING   Australia has phased out its import licensing requirements. Effective March 1993, import quotas were ended, except for cheese and curd.

Restricted imports include drugs, steroids, weapons/firearms, heritage items, cordless telephones and CB radios (unless approved by the Department of Communications and the Arts), food, plants, animals, and protected wildlife.

IMPORT TAXES   There are no import taxes in Australia. The Australian government does, however, impose a tax on the sale of both domestically manufactured and imported goods. The general rate of this tax is 22% of the sale value. There are a large number of exempt goods set out in a schedule to the Sales Tax Act. There are also categories of goods subject to tax at 12% (household goods) and 32% (luxury goods).

Protection of Intellectual Property Rights

Australia is a member of the World Intellectual Property Organization (WIPO), the Paris Convention for Protection of Intellectual Property, the Berne Convention for Protection of Literary and Artistic Works, and the Universal Copyright Convention. It is also a party to GATT and a signatory to the Patent Cooperation Treaty. Patents, copyrights, trademarks, industrial designs, integrated circuits, and plant breeder rights are protected. Australia hosts the Summer Olympics in 2000, and passed the Olympic Insignia Protection Act in 1987 to protect designs and insignias associated with the Olympics. The government of the U.S. has two concerns with Australia's IP laws: Australia has failed to extend pharmaceutical patents to compensate for testing delays, and Australians have pending legislation that would remove protection for parallel imports.

The Patents Act of 1991 extends patent protection to all fields of technology. Patents are granted for useful inventions that are novel and inventive over prior disclosures worldwide. Application and examination are required. Pre-grant oppositions are permitted. The patent term is 20 years from application. Actions may be brought for contributory infringement. Registered designs protect the visual appearance of articles of manufacture. Assignments must be in writing and signed by both the assignor and assignee.

Trademark rights can be acquired two ways: either by use in association with goods or services or by registration. The Trade Mark Act of 1995 provides trademark and service mark protection. The common law action of passing off is preserved. Trademark rights acquired by use cannot be assigned or licensed separately from the goodwill of the business. Rights to trademark registrations, however, can be assigned independently of the goodwill. The term of trademark registration is 10 years, and registrations are renewable for additional 10-year terms. Infringement actions can be brought in federal or state court. Nonuse for a continuous period of three years in Australia is grounds for cancellation.

There are no common law copyrights. The Copyright Act of 1968, as amended, extends copyright protection to every Territory of the Commonwealth. Published and unpublished works are protected. In 1994, rental rights were granted to copyright owners of software and sound recordings. Fair use is not an infringement. The basic term of copyright is life of the author, plus 50 years. Performance rights are protected for 20 years. The Circuits Layout Act of 1989 protects integrated circuits. However, copyright enforcement in the courts is sometimes lax.

Foreign Investment Climate

The Australian government welcomes foreign investment, and the United States is the country's largest source of foreign capital. Total U.S. investment in Australia, including both direct and portfolio investment, exceeds $54 billion. The federal government and each state government vigorously encourages investment by offering incentives to multinational companies to set up regional headquarters for financial and other services and manufacturing operations. The government touts the benefits of Australia's safe, stable business environment, skilled work force, and lower facility, site and operating costs in comparison to other regional centers such as Singapore, Hong Kong, and Taiwan.

Australia's government generally does not interfere with takeovers of domestic firms by foreign investors. They are treated under the same guidelines as any other foreign investment.

The Federal Treasury regulates foreign investment with the assistance of the Foreign Investment Review Board (FIRB). The Board screens investment proposals for conformity with Australian law and policy.

Foreign investment in three sectors—media, civil aviation, and urban real estate—is severely limited.

Political Leaders, Parties, and International Organizations

The International Academy at Santa Barbara at http://www.iasb.org/cwl publishes *Current World Leaders*, an excellent resource for up-to-date data on political leaders, parties, demographics, etc., in Australia. Tel: (800) 530-2682 or (805) 965-5010 for subscription information to their database.

Chief of State:
   Queen Elizabeth II

Local Representative of the Chief of State:
   Governor-General Sir William Deane

Head of the Government:
   Prime Minister John Howard

Political Parties:
   Australian Labor Party (ALP), Liberal Party (LP), National Party (NP), Australian
      Democrats

Membership in international organizations:

Antarctic Treaty Consultative Group, ADB, APEC, Australia-US Pact (ANZUS), CP, C, EBRD, IEA, OECD, PECC, UN and most of its specialized agencies and related organizations (including FAO, ESCAP, GATT, IAEA, IBRD, ICAO, IDA, IFAD, IFC, ILO, IMF, IMO, ITU, UNESCO, UPU, WHO, WIPO, WMO)

Political Influences on Business

The United States and Australia have been close allies for over 50 years, during which time Australia has been the southern link in the structure of Asia–Pacific strategic alliances. The Australian government contributes to mutual security and regional stability by hosting key joint defense facilities and ship visits, participating in a range of exercises and exchanges with U.S. forces, and fostering regional security dialogue. In addition, the two governments cooperate in worldwide nonproliferation, arms control, and peacekeeping efforts.

Like the U.S., Australia is a leading advocate of trade and investment liberalization. Because of common interests and convictions, the two countries work together on many global issues (e.g., U.N. reform, promoting democracy and human rights, protecting the environment, and enhancing the multilateral trading system and the World Trade Organization).

U.S. export subsidies for wheat and other agricultural commodities have generated periodic friction. But these concerns were attenuated because of agreement during GATT's Uruguay Round on substantial worldwide reductions in agricultural–export subsidies.

There are no major political issues that detract from the business climate or the stability of the bilateral trading relationship with the United States. All of Australia's major political parties seek to promote growth and encourage investment, including investment from abroad.

Other policy directions that attract equally universal support include Australia's desire to define itself as a part of the dynamic Asia–Pacific region, as well as efforts to upgrade its mix of exports in order to reduce reliance on basic commodities and increase sales of value-added products. There is also broad political approval for federal and state government programs to privatize public services so as to reach world-quality standards, and for labor and work force reforms.

Australia has a federal system of government and a long history as a multiparty parliamentary democracy. There is no written Bill of Rights, but fundamental rights are ensured by law and respected in practice. Voting has been compulsory since 1924, although many Australians feel that mandatory voting is no longer necessary.

The Commonwealth (federal) government and the six state governments operate under written constitutions that draw on the British tradition of a Cabinet government, led by a Prime Minister, who is responsible to a majority in Parliament's lower house. The Federal Constitution, however, also contains some elements that resemble American practice (including a Senate, in which each state has equal representation).

The Head of State is Queen Elizabeth II, the reigning British monarch, but she exercises her functions through personal representatives who live in Australia (i.e., Australian citizens who serve as the Governor-General of Australia, and the Governors of the six states). Australians are debating whether their country should become a republic, give up ties with the Queen, revise the constitution, and adopt a new flag.

Members of the Federal House of Representatives are elected for three years. Members of the Senate are elected for six years. All major parties support the U.S.–Australia alliance and stress the importance of close relations between Australia and the United States. Thus, this longstanding and stable pattern is essentially unaffected by the outcome of national elections.

Contacts in the United States

THE EMBASSY OF AUSTRALIA
1601 Massachusetts Avenue, NW
Washington, D.C. 20036
Tel: (202) 797-3000
Fax: (202) 797-3168
www.austemb.org

Passport/Visa Requirements

Passport required. Persons traveling to Australia who are not holders of Australian or New Zealand passports require visas.

U.S. citizens who wish to apply for a passport may visit Passport Services' well-organized website at http://travel.state.gov/passport_services.html.

Visa Application Procedure

Applicants must forward or bring in the following to the appropriate Australian Consular Office; visa office hours vary from office to office.

1. Application Form 48 must be completed and signed by the applicant. A separate application form is required for each passport holder. For a visitor visa application form, please write to the nearest Australian Embassy or Consulate, requesting number of forms needed, and enclose a self-addressed, stamped envelope for return of the forms.
2. Valid passport of the applicant. The visa will be placed in the passport. (Applicants must make certain that their passport has two free pages facing each other for this purpose.)
3. Applications made in person are generally decided immediately, and, if approved, the visa is issued while you wait.

4. If applying by mail, applicants must enclose a stamped, self-addressed envelope large enough to enable return of passport(s). Applicants should also make appropriate arrangements with the postal service if they wish passports returned by certified, registered, express mail, or special delivery. (Mail marked insufficient postage will not be accepted. It is the applicant's responsibility to ensure that the self-addressed, stamped envelope submitted bears the necessary postage and markings. Metered stamps are not acceptable.) It is recommended that a secure form of postage be used for the mailing of passports.

5. A Business visitor must provide a company letter giving a description of proposed activities while in Australia and expected length of stay.

6. Fee: Australian visas and application forms for a stay of less than three months are issued free of charge. For a stay longer than three months and up to six months, or if a multiple-entry visa with a validity of greater than twelve months is required, a fee is charged.

7. Length of stay: Visitor and Business Visitor visas can authorize a maximum stay of three months in Australia.

8. Formalities on arrival: On arrival in Australia, visitors must produce their visa and passport.

9. Non-U.S. (and Non-Canadian) citizens: Applicants who are not a citizen of either of these countries should inquire at an Australian Consular office regarding any special requirements that may apply.

Important Note: Persons who travel to Australia as visitors are not permitted to engage in employment or formal studies. Those interested in entering Australia for either purpose should check Australian Consular offices to determine requirements and eligibility.

Departure Tax

Australian travelers and overseas visitors departing (Australia) for overseas destinations must purchase an A$25.00 departure tax stamp. There are some exceptions (e.g., children, one-day visitors, etc.).

Contacts in Australia

THE U.S. EMBASSY
Moonah Place
Yarralumla
Canberra
A.C.T 2600

MAILING ADDRESS: APO AP 96549
Tel: (61) (6) 6214-5600
Fax: (61) (6) 6214-5970
www.usis-australia.gov/embassy

THE AMERICAN CHAMBER OF COMMERCE
IN AUSTRALIA
Level 2, 41 Lower Street
Sydney, N.S.W. 2000
Tel: (61) (2) 241-1907
Fax: (61) (2) 251-5220

DUN & BRADSTREET (AUSTRALIA) PTY. LTD.
Postal Address: P.O. Box 7405, St. Kilda
Road, Melbourne, Vic. 3004

Street Address: 479 St. Kilda Road, Melbourne, Vic. 3004
Tel: (61) (3) 9828-3333
Fax: (61) (3) 9828-3300 (General); (61) (3) 9828-3162 (Head Office)

OFFICE OF THE PRIME MINISTER
Parliament House
Canberra ACT 2600, Australia

Further contacts and websites can be found in Appendix A.

Communications

TELEPHONE: The international country code for Australia is 61.

Australian phone numbers are undergoing a change. When the change is accomplished, all Australian numbers will be eight digits in length with a single-digit area code.

E-MAIL: E-mail addresses located in Australia end with the code .au

---

Three Ways in Which Australia Is Different from New Zealand

1. The European colonization of Australia began as a penal colony. New Zealand was never a penal colony.

2. New Zealand is a Nuclear Free Zone and prohibits ships that carry nuclear arms from entering its ports. Since the U.S. will not confirm which of its ships carry nuclear weapons, a de facto ban on virtually all U.S. military vessels in New Zealand waters was implemented and resulted in the suspension of the ANZUS (Australia/New Zealand/United States) mutual defense treaty.

3. The indigenous people of New Zealand, the Maoris, have not been as marginalized as the Aborigines of Australia. Maoris still occupy a substantial amount of the country's arable land, and Maori words are in common use. In part, this is because the Maori make up a larger proportion of New Zealand's population. About 10% of New Zealanders are Maori, while only about 1.5% of Australians are Aborigines.

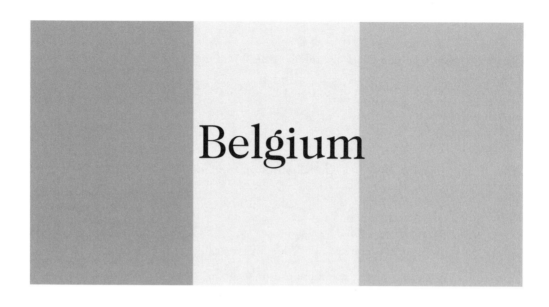

Belgium

Official Name:	Kingdom of Belgium; Koninkrijk België (Dutch); Royaume de Belgique (French)
Official Languages:	Dutch*, French, German
	*The Belgian dialect of Dutch is also known as Flemish.
Government System:	Parliamentary democracy under a constitutional monarch
Population:	10,182,034 (1999 estimate)
Population Growth Rate:	0.06%
Area:	30,518 sq. km. (11,780 sq. mi.); about the size of Maryland
Natural Resources:	coal, natural gas
Major Cities:	Brussels (capital), Antwerp, Ghent, Charleroi, Liège, Bruges

Cultural Note: Belgium may be small, but it nevertheless encompasses separate cultural and linguistic traditions that have threatened to divide the country into even smaller units. The majority (57%) of Belgians speak Dutch. They are known as the Flemish. (The term *Flemish* is also used to identify their dialect of Dutch.) Most of the remainder (42%) speak French. French-speaking Belgians are known as Walloons. (Their language is French, not Walloon; linguistically, *Walloon* refers to a specific French dialect, which is now almost extinct.) Finally, a small minority (1%) speaks German.

Age Breakdown

0–14 = 17%   15–64 = 66%   65+ = 17% (1999 estimate)
Life Expectancy: 74.31 years, male; 80.9 years, female (1999 estimate)

Time

Most Belgians expect punctuality in all business and social engagements. This is espe-cially true among Dutch and German-speaking Belgians. French-speaking Belgians tend to be a little more relaxed about punctuality, especially to social events.

Belgium is 1 hour ahead of Greenwich Mean Time (GMT +1), which is 6 hours ahead of U.S. Eastern Standard Time (EST +6).

Holidays

A web-based *World Holiday and Time Zone Guide* is available at www.getcustoms.com with updated official holidays, cultural tips, time zones, and tables that compare world-wide business hours.

This list is a working guide. Dates should be corroborated before final travel plans are made. In cases where holidays fall on Saturday or Sunday, commercial establish-ments may be closed the preceding Friday or following Monday.

The following holidays should be confirmed by local contacts—regional observa-tions of these and other festivals may vary.

Jan 1	SA	New Year's Day
Apr 24	MO	Easter Monday
May 1	MO	Labor Day
Jun 1	TH	Ascension
Jun 12	MO	Whit Monday
Jul 21	FR	Belgian National Day
Aug 15	TU	Assumption
Nov 1	WE	All Saints Day
Nov 11	Sa	Armistice Day
Dec 25	MO	Christmas

Most Belgians take a one-month vacation per year.

Work Week

- The length of the Belgian work week has varied; it now averages 37.5 hours.
- Businesses open at 8:30 A.M. and close at 5:30 P.M. for most of the week, although some stay open until 9:00 P.M. on Fridays.

Religious/Societal Influences on Business

Most Belgians—Dutch and French-speakers alike—are members of the Roman Catholic Church. There are small numbers of Protestants and Muslims.

Since they share the same religion, divisions in Belgian society run along linguistic lines. There are significant historical conflicts between the Dutch-speaking Flemish in the north and the French-speaking Walloons in the South. Political parties calling for the division of Belgium along linguistic lines have a small but notable representation in the Belgian parliament. Class differences contribute to the conflict, since French had become the language of the ruling and upper classes. The Second World War exacerbated these differences. Dutch-speakers hoped that Nazi rule would free them from their French-speaking overlords. (Despite Nazi collaboration by both Flemish and Walloons, the Belgian resistance helped half of Belgium's Jews to flee the country.)

Attempts to mollify both sides have led to a complex patchwork of legislation. Belgium is divided into three regions, three cultural communes, and four linguistic areas. Numerous laws deal with the use of language in different locales.

Brussels, the Belgian capital, is officially considered a multilingual area, although French-speakers predominate. The political importance of Brussels is a point of pride for the Belgians. As the seat of the European Council of Ministers, Brussels is the de facto capital of the European Union. Belgium is also the central headquarters for NATO. The NATO Council meets in Brussels.

Belgium is a kingdom, although the king has only ceremonial duties. The royal family is generally popular and seen as a unifying force.

5 Cultural Tips

1. Belgium has three recognized cultural groups, so it is important to know with whom you are working. The Flemish (Dutch-speakers) have different traditions from the Walloons (French-speakers) and Germans. As there is some rancor between the groups, never mistake a Flemish executive for a Walloon, etc.

2. Formerly a major industrial nation, Belgium has been shifting to a service economy. English is widely spoken and many Belgian executives have experience dealing with foreigners. However, your promotional materials should be translated into the main language of your Belgian counterpart—generally Dutch or French.

3. The Belgians (especially the Flemish and Germans) place a high value on privacy. Doors are kept closed, both at home and in the office. Always knock before entering an office—even after you have been told that your Belgian counterpart is ready for you.

4. Flemish executives are generally very linear and place great importance on planning. This contrasts strongly with the Walloons who tend to be more flexible and improvisational. Not surprisingly, the management styles of the two groups can clash.

5. Belgium is often used as a test market for new products. The multilingual and multicultural population of Belgium is seen as representative of the entire European

Union. The Belgians provide a highly sophisticated market, with consumers who consider both price and quality to be equally important. Many Belgians believe that their culture has the best of both worlds: They have the business acumen of the Dutch and the cultural sophistication of the French.

Observation: "In Belgium, with its dreary climate and its endless history of foreign occupation, people pull into themselves and are quietly tough. Food and eating have what seems to American eyes an incredibly important place in the lives and imaginations of Belgians.

"Every year, Jacqueline and I have Christmas dinner with her mother and another couple, she Belgian, he an American economist. All five of us are occupied in the long discussions of what will be eaten, where to get it, how to cook it, how to serve it, in what order. I learn to my astonishment that my mother-in-law believes any dinner party, especially one for a festive occasion, 'takes three days. One day to shop. One day to cook. One day to clean up.'

"As an American, at first I found these carryings-on amusing, as all such exaggerations seem amusing. When actually eating a meal, of course, my amusement turns to delight at the exquisiteness of each production . . ."

—From Stuart Miller's *Understanding Europeans*. An American, he wrote this book (in part) to better understand his Belgian wife, Jacqueline.

Economic Overview

Belgium is the ninth largest trading nation in the world. A long history of reliance on international trade has given its people a high awareness of global issues. Due to this global outlook and the lack of natural resources, Belgium is heavily engaged in both importing and exporting. Imports and exports are equivalent to nearly 70% of GDP, making Belgium one of the highest per capita exporters in the world. Belgium imports many basic and intermediate goods, adds value, and then exports the final products. About 75% of Belgium's foreign trade is with other European Union (EU) countries, pointing to the country's importance as a commercial axis in Western Europe.

Belgium and the United States have strong reciprocal trade relations. It is a major market for U.S. products.

Due to its history and location, Belgium is a true cultural microcosm of Europe with three linguistic communities: French, Dutch, and German. This diversity, combined with its small, manageable size, makes Belgium an excellent test market and subsequent launching pad for the European operations of U.S. businesses.

Overall, government leaders at all levels are very supportive of open trade and investment.

Belgium's agriculture suffered serious shocks in the Spring of 1999 when traces of dioxin were found in Belgian food. Other members of the European Union banned or destroyed Belgian food imports. The scandal was badly handled and contributed to the defeat of the ruling Christian Democratic Party in the general election of June 13, 1999.

5 Largest Businesses in Belgium

La Poste Enterprise Publique Autonome ets Util. Pub., Bruxelles
    46,935 employees
Belgacom SA, Bruxelles
    26,000 employees
KBC Bank NV, Bruxelles
    23,000 employees
Electrabel SA, Bruxelles
    16,605 employees
Commission des Communautes Eruopeennes, Bruxelles
    15,000 employees

Cultural Note: Multicultural Brussels has become a favorite locale for test marketing. There are few European cultures more different from the Dutch and the French, and both are represented in Brussels. A product that can appeal to both is likely to be a winner.

Comparative Data

Comparative Data Ratings
(Scale: 5 = Excellent; 1 = Poor)
Belgium: 4.4

    A. GDP Growth:　3
    B. Per Capita Income:　5
    C. Trade Flows with the U.S.:　4
    D. Country Risk:　5
    E. Monetary Policy:　5
    F. Trade Policy:　4
        • Tariffs
        • Import Licensing
        • Import Taxes
    G. Protection of Property Rights:　5
    H. Foreign Investment Climate:　4

GROSS DOMESTIC PRODUCT:　$236 billion (1998) $266 billion (1999 estimate)

GDP GROWTH:　2.8% (1998) 2.0% (1999 forecast) 2.4% (2000 forecast)

PER CAPITA INCOME:　$23,400 (1998) $25,576 (1999 estimate)

Trade Flows with the U.S.

U.S. EXPORTS TO BELGIUM: $13.9 billion (1998)

U.S. IMPORTS FROM BELGIUM: $8.4 billion (1998)

TOP U.S. EXPORTS TO BELGIUM: Machinery; tobacco and tobacco products; organic chemicals; plastics; precious stones; motor vehicles and auto parts; medical instruments; computer hardware and software; chemicals

TOP U.S. PROSPECTS FOR EXPORT TO BELGIUM: Automotive parts; travel and tourism services; computer services; telecommunication services and equipment; computer software; pollution-control equipment; building products; apparel; electric power systems; aircraft parts; seafood

Country Risk

Dun & Bradstreet rates Belgium as having excellent capacity to meet outstanding payment liabilities. It carries the lowest degree of risk when compared with other countries.

All types of payments terms are in use, including open account and letter of credit. Generally speaking, buyers show a preference for payment by cash against documents. The most common payments terms are net 30 days.

Monetary Policy

Inflation has remained low in Belgium for the past several years. Inflation ran 1.6% in 1997 and 1.2% in 1998. Dun & Bradstreet forecast inflation at around 1.4% in 1999, although increases in the price of petroleum may have caused it to rise.

MONETARY UNIT: Belgian franc, now being phased out in favor of the EU euro

Trade Policy

TARIFFS   As a member of the European Union, Belgium applies the EU common external tariff to goods imported from non-EU countries. There is a single duty among all EU members toward products coming from non-EU members. (Most manufactured goods are subject to rates of between 5 and 17%.) For goods imported into Belgium from other EU countries, no customs duties apply unless goods contain components imported from outside the EU upon which customs duties have not been paid in another EU country.

IMPORT LICENSING   Many products may be imported without any prior license, but products from certain countries and certain listed products are subject to an import license. These include textile and steel products, diamonds, and weapons. Strategic goods are also subject to an import and/or quota license.

IMPORT TAXES   Goods imported into Belgium or made in Belgium are normally subject to a value-added tax payable upon importation if Belgium is the destination of the goods being shipped into the EU. One of three rates will apply: 6% for daily necessities, foodstuffs, etc.; 12% for tobacco, fuel, etc.; 21% for the majority of commercial goods.

Value-added tax (VAT) is applied after all customs duties are added to the price of the goods. Since EU products do not pay customs duties, while those from the U.S. do, the effective VAT rate for non-EU goods is actually higher than the rates cited above.

Protection of Intellectual Property Rights

Belgium is a member of the Paris Union Convention, the Treaty of Rome, the Munich European Patent Convention, the Luxembourg European Patent Convention, the Hague Agreement (designs), and the Madrid Agreement (trademarks). Belgium has patent and copyright systems, but trademarks have been preempted by the Benelux Uniform Trademark Act (BUTA). Patent protection may be obtained by filing in Belgium or under the European Patent Convention.

The governing law for patents is the 1984 Act that took effect in 1987. Inventions require worldwide novelty, an inventive step, and industrial application. Software is precluded from protection. Examination is optional and is done for informational purposes; examination is not used as a basis for rejection. The statute of infringement is five years. Plant and animal varieties are protected under the Plant Varieties Protection Act of 1975.

Benelux trademarks are a bargain: protection in three countries (Belgium, the Netherlands, and Luxembourg) for the price of one! Trademark rights are acquired by registration. The term of trademark is 10 years and is renewable. The statute of limitations for bringing an infringement action is five years. Actions for infringement are brought locally under the court system of each country. Trademark assignments must be in writing. Occasionally, you may still encounter some pre-BUTA Belgium registrations.

The copyright law was updated in 1994. Copyrights protect original works of authorship expressed in tangible form. Computer programs are protected under a special statute. No filing or registration is required for protection and enforcement. The term of copyright is the life of the author plus 70 years, or 70 years after release to the public for works that do not designate an actual author. Designs and models are protected under the Hague Agreement.

Foreign Investment Climate

Belgium has traditionally maintained an open economy, highly dependent on imported inputs and international trade for its well-being. Since World War II, foreign investment has played a vital part in the Belgian economy, providing much technology and employment. Given the importance of trade and investment, Belgium generally discourages protectionism. The government actively encourages foreign investment on a national treatment basis. Foreign corporations in Belgium account for about one-third of the top 3,100 corporations.

While the total dollar amount of U.S. direct investment in Belgium has increased (reaching US$17.7 billion at the end of 1996), the total share of investment by U.S.

companies has fallen, from a 40% share in 1993 to just 13% in 1996. (Some of the booming foreign investment is due to the growth of the European Union; Belgium houses both the EU Parliament and the EU Council.) More than 1,300 U.S. companies are present, ranging from offices with one person to firms with thousands of employees.

Foreign companies investing in Belgium are generally eligible for the same tax-related investment incentives as domestic companies—and are subject to the same accounting requirements.

Any foreign company wishing to engage in trade or manufacture in Belgium can set up a subsidiary or branch. Belgian nationals are not required to own part of the equity of the enterprise, and the repatriation of capital and profits is unrestricted.

Certain restrictive rules do apply to investors. Belgian and foreign investors must obtain special permission to open department stores, provide transportation, produce and sell certain food items, cut and polish diamonds, and sell firearms and ammunition. Foreign interests may enter into joint ventures and partnerships on the same basis as domestic parties, except for certain professions such as doctors, lawyers, and architects.

Political Leaders, Parties, and International Organizations

The International Academy at Santa Barbara at http://www.iasb.org/cwl publishes *Current World Leaders*, an excellent resource for up-to-date data on political leaders, parties, demographics, etc., in Belgium. Tel: (800) 530-2682 or (805) 965-5010 for subscription information to their database.

Head of State:

King Albert II van Saksen Coburg-Gotha

Head of the Government:

Prime Minister Guy Verhofstadt

Political Parties:

Flemish Christian Democrats or CVP (Christian People's Party); Francophone Christian Democrats or PSC (Social Christian Party); Flemish Socialist Party or SP; Francophone Socialist Party or PS; Flemish Liberal Democrats or VLD; Francophone Liberal Reformation Party or PRL; Francophone Democratic Front or FDF; Volksunie or VU; Vlaams Blok or VB; National Front or FN; AGALEV (Flemish Greens); ECOLO (Francophone Greens); other minor parties

Membership in international organizations:

Belgium–Luxembourg Economic Union (BLEU), Belgium–Netherlands–Luxembourg Economic Union (Benelux), CE, EBRD, EU, INTELSAT, NACC, NATO, OECD, OSCE, UN and all of its specialized agencies and related organizations (including FAO, GATT, IAEA, IBRD, ICAO, IDA, IFAD, IFC, ILO, IMF, IMO, ITU, UNESCO, UNIDO, UPU, WHO, WIPO, WMO), WEU

Political Influences on Business

Belgium has been a constitutional monarchy since 1930. Albert II was invested as King in August 1993, after the death of his brother Baudouin. The King, Prime Minister, and Cabinet represent the executive branch of the federal government, with the newly-formed 71-member Senate and 150-member Chamber of Deputies representing the legislative branch.

The Cabinet must retain the support of a majority in the Chamber of Deputies to remain in power. Federal parliamentary elections are held every four years (or before that if the government loses the support of a majority in the Chamber and no alternative coalition can be formed). There is universal suffrage, with compulsory voting and proportional representation. Governments are always coalitions comprising two or three of the traditional parties—the Christian Democrats (center), the Socialists (left wing), and Liberals (right wing).

The most significant, long-term factor in Belgian politics is the gradual devolution of powers from the central authority to the regions. In the new federal structure, approved in July 1993, sovereignty is spread over three authorities: the central state, the regions, and the language communities. There is no hierarchy among these policy levels. Each of the three levels has its own exclusive powers and is not allowed to interfere in matters that are under the jurisdiction of the others.

The regions are Flanders (the northern, Dutch-speaking part of Belgium), Wallonia (the southern, French-speaking area), and Brussels (the capital regions, limited to 19 bilingual communes). Each region is responsible for a wide range of socio-economic matters for its own territory.

Elected regional assemblies for Flanders, Wallonia, and Brussels exercise legislative powers within their own regions and elect executive authorities. Under the evolving federal system, the responsibility for areas of interest to U.S. business—such as foreign trade, environment, and investment regimes and incentives—will increasingly become the responsibility for the regional governments. This devolution means that Americans wishing to do business in Belgium will eventually have more contact with regional officials than in the past.

Belgium is also a member of the European Union and Belgian businesses are subject to EU regulations. Belgium became one of the first tier of countries to begin using the EU's currency, the euro, on January 1, 1999.

Contacts in the United States

THE EMBASSY OF THE KINGDOM OF BELGIUM
3330 Garfield Street, NW
Washington, D.C. 20008
Tel: (202) 333-6900
Fax: (202) 333-3079
www.belgium-emb.org/usa

Passport/Visa Requirements

Note: European Union countries, including Austria, Belgium, Finland, Germany, Luxembourg, the Netherlands, Portugal, and Spain, have implemented the Schengen zone agreement to end all passport controls between the participating member states.

Italy and Greece are signatory to the agreement, but have not implemented the terms. France is signatory to the agreement, but for security reasons has suspended terms of the agreement.

A passport is required. U.S. citizens do not require a visa for a temporary visit not exceeding three months. For a stay exceeding three months, U.S. citizens should apply for a visa of provisional sojourn before their departure.

To engage in independent professional activities, the applicant should first apply for a Professional Card (Carte Professionnelle/Beroepskaart). To engage in professional activities on a salaried basis, you should apply for a Work Permit (Permis de Travail/Arbeidskaart) through the employer in Belgium. When either a Professional Card or a Work Permit has been obtained, the application for a temporary residency permit can be processed by the appropriate Belgian Consular Office.

For details on this and other documents pertinent to working in Belgium or residing there on a temporary basis (i.e., longer than three months), contact the Belgian Embassy.

U.S. citizens who wish to apply for a passport may visit Passport Services' well-organized website at http://travel.state.gov/passport_services.html.

THE BELGIAN–AMERICAN CHAMBER OF COMMERCE
1330 Avenue of the Americas, 26th Floor
New York, NY 10019
Tel: (212) 969-9940
Fax: (212) 969-9942
www.belcham.org

Contacts in Belgium

THE U.S. EMBASSY
27 Boulevard du Regent
B-1000
Brussels
Tel: (32) (2) 508-2111
Fax: (32) (2) 511-2725
www.usingo.bel

THE AMERICAN CHAMBER OF COMMERCE IN BELGIUM
Avenue des Arts 50
Boite 5, 1000 Brussels
Tel: (32) (2) 513-6770
Fax: (32) (2) 513-3590

DUN & BRADSTREET–EURINFORM S.A.–N.V.
Postal Address: Avenue des Pleiades 73, Plejadenlaan 73, B-1200
Bruxelles—Brussels
Street Address: Avenue des Pleiades 73, Plejadenlaan 73, B-1200
Bruxelles–Brussels
Telephone: (32) (2) 778-7211
Fax: (32) (2) 778-7272.

KING ALBERT II
Palais Royal
B-1000 Brussels, Kingdom of Belgium

OFFICE OF THE PRIME MINISTER
16 rue de la Loi
1000 Brussels, Kingdom of Belgium

Further contacts and websites can be found in Appendix A.

Communications

TELEPHONE: The country code for Belgium is 32.
Phone numbers are usually six digits in length.
City codes may be one or two digits long.

E-MAIL: E-mail addresses located in Belgium end with the code .be

---

Cultural Note: Some knowledge of Belgium's impressive artistic and cultural history will be appreciated. This includes such world-famous artists as Peter Bruegel (the Elder), Jan van Eyck, Peter Paul Rubens, and the Surrealist painter René Magritte.

Official Name:	Federative Republic of Brazil (República Federativa do Brasil)
Official Language:	Portuguese
Government System:	Multi-party federal republic
Population:	171.9 million (July 1999 estimate)
Population Growth Rate:	1.16% (1999 estimate)
Area:	8,511,965 sq. km. (3,286,473 sq. mi.); about the size of the U.S. excluding Texas and Louisiana
Natural Resources:	iron ore, manganese, bauxite, nickel, uranium, phosphates, tin, hydropower, gold, platinum, petroleum, timber
Major Cities:	Brasília (capital), São Paulo, Rio de Janeiro, Belo Horizonte, Recife, Porto Alegre, Salvador, Manaus

---

Cultural Note: The Portuguese language uses acute accent marks, cedillas, and tildes. Whereas in Spanish the tilde only appears over the letter n, in Portuguese it appears over several vowels. Accents and cedillas may usually be dropped without affecting understanding. However, the deletion of a tilde can change the meaning of a word.

Unfortunately, many typewriters and computer keyboards cannot place tildes over any letter except an n. If your keyboard can produce an umlaut, this can be substituted for the tilde. While not grammatically correct, it will at least make your typing comprehensible to a Brazilian.

Age Breakdown

0–14 = 30%   15–64 = 65%   65+ = 5% (1999 estimate)
Life Expectancy: 59.35 years, male; 69.01 years, female (1999 estimate)

Time

Punctuality often seems to be an alien concept to Brazil. In fact, prompt Brazilians are said to keep *tempo británico (British time).*

Brazil is large enough to have two time zones. Most of Brazil is 3 hours behind Greenwich Mean Time (GMT -3), which is 2 hours ahead of U.S. Eastern Standard Time (EST +2). Western Brazil is 4 hours behind Greenwich Mean Time (GMT -4), which is 1 hour ahead of U.S. Eastern Standard Time (EST +1).

Observation: "In some countries, making others wait is the essence of status. In a survey in Brazil, my colleagues and I asked people how much they thought punctuality for appointments was tied to success. To my surprise, Brazilians rated people who are always late for appointments as most successful and punctual people as least successful. Our data showed that Brazilians rated a person who was always late for appointments as more relaxed, happy, and likeable—all of which tend to be associated with being successful.

—From Robert Levine's *A Geography of Time*

Holidays

An up-to-date, web-based *World Holiday and Time Zone Guide* is available at www.getcustoms.com. It lists official holidays by country and by day of the year, cultural tips, a corruption index, and time zones with worldwide business hours.

This list is a working guide. Dates should be corroborated before final travel plans are made. In cases where holidays fall on Saturday or Sunday, commercial establishments may be closed the preceding Friday or following Monday.

Jan 1	SA	New Year's Day
Mar 6	MO	Carnaval Monday
Mar 7	TU	Carnaval
Mar 8	WE	Ash Wednesday
Apr 20	TH	Holy Thursday
Apr 21	FR	Good Friday
Apr 21	FR	Tiradentes Day
Apr 22	SA	Holy Saturday
May 1	MO	Labor Day

Jun 22	TH	Corpus Christi
Sep 7	TH	Independence Day
Oct 12	TH	Our Lady Aparecida
Nov 2	TH	All Souls Day
Nov 15	WE	Proclamation of the Republic
Dec 8	FR	Immaculate Conception
Dec 25	MO	Christmas Day

Most businesses will also be closed Christmas Eve and New Year's Eve.

There are many additional regional holidays, and business may be particularly difficult to conduct around Carneval, Easter, and Christmas. Some regional holidays (such as San Sebastian Day in Rio de Janiero) are religious; others (like the Anniversary of the Founding of the City in São Paulo) are secular. Again, the days of observance should always be corroborated by local contacts.

Work Week

- Business hours are generally advertised as 8:30 A.M. to 5:30 P.M., but decision makers usually begin work later in the morning and stay later in the evening. Try making appointments from 10:00 A.M. to noon, and 3:00 P.M. to 5:00 P.M. If your business runs into lunch, be prepared to spend at least two hours.

- The lack of punctuality is a fact of life in Brazil. Become accustomed to waiting for your Brazilian counterpart.

Religious/Societal Influences on Business

Brazil has no official church. About 70% of Brazilians are Roman Catholics. Protestant Churches, especially Evangelistic Sects, have experienced tremendous growth in Brazil in the past two decades. Virtually all religions are represented in Brazil, including Islam, Judaism, and Buddhism.

Religious beliefs in Brazil are not exclusive. People can hold seemingly contradictory beliefs. Brazilian Marxists, for example, can believe in Spiritualism; Catholic Bishops can preach Socialist Revolution.

A substantial number of Brazilians also follow the informal Afro–Brazilian beliefs known as Umbanda. When African slaves were brought to Brazil and forced to become Catholics, they transposed their native beliefs onto Christian ones. The sword-wielding African war god Ogum was disguised as the Christian Saint George; the sea goddess Yemanjá became the Virgin Mary. Such syncretic beliefs display the Brazilian ability to both absorb and adapt new cultures. Umbanda beliefs are pervasive enough to support the growth of anti-Umbanda churches, where former Umbanda clergy specialize in exorcising the various Umbanda deities.

The family and its associated responsibilities exert tremendous influence on Brazilians. It is the most important institution in their lives.

5 Cultural Tips

1. There are two Brazilian professionals you will probably need to hire to conduct business. A Brazilian contact (called a *despechante* in Portuguese) is invaluable for making introductions. Once the negotiation stage is reached, your contracts will need to be reviewed by a specialist called a *notario* (there is no direct equivalent in English, but *notarios* are somewhat similar to lawyers).

2. Brazilians are a physically active people, and their greetings can be effusive. Even a first encounter will involve extended handshakes. As the relationship deepens, this will advance to embraces and back-thumping between men; women may kiss each other on alternating cheeks. (Married women kiss twice, but single women kiss three times—that third kiss invokes good luck towards finding a spouse.) Shake hands with everyone present, both upon arrival and upon departure.

3. While Brazil is one of the most informal of countries, people still tend to address each other by their last names. Most people will be addressed as *Senhor* (Mr.) or *Senhora* (Mrs.) plus their surname. People with titles should be addressed as such. Note that some Brazilians sometimes introduce themselves using their titles and their *first* names (i.e., Doctor John).

4. The "hard sell" does not work well in Brazil. Brazilians do business with people they like, and must get to know potential business partners first. This takes time, and Brazilians do not proceed in a linear fashion. During the course of negotiations, they are likely to go back and reexamine the entire deal several times.

5. Brazil has a very open culture, capable of absorbing disparate trends into Brazilian society at large. Both fact and fiction can be interpreted as evidence, based upon their feelings for the people or issues involved. This is especially true when it appears on television. Much of Brazil's large illiterate population watches television (more homes in tropical Brazil have television sets than have refrigerators), and they often believe what they see.

Economic Overview

With the largest economy in Latin America, Brazil is a country with immense export opportunities. Although Brazil has experienced recent economic difficulties, it has continued to be an important trading partner. U.S. exports to Brazil nearly doubled between 1994 and 1998.

In addition, the stabilization plan introduced in mid-1994 successfully restrained Brazil's chronically high inflation. The plan, which included the introduction of a new currency, the *real*, has proven to be the most successful stabilization plan in the past 15 years.

The real has also created more buying power for many Brazilian consumers. Salaried workers realized a 15 to 30% increase in actual purchasing power after the real was introduced.

The Cardoso government has pursued a comprehensive economic liberalization agenda. The government is emphasizing increased economic opportunities for the private sector through privatization, deregulation, and the removal of impediments to competition. The engine of Brazilian economic growth is more and more the private sector.

Brazil responded to the 1997 Asian financial crisis by doubling interest rates and adopting a contractionary fiscal package. As a result, Brazil's growth slowed, affecting the economies of the entire region.

U.S. exporters are now able to expand and participate in new business opportunities that will make Brazil one of the strongest commercial partners of the United States. Nevertheless, the complexities of the Brazilian business environment still create formidable challenges for U.S. exporters. Doing business in Brazil is not easy and requires knowledge of local regulations and procedures.

The U.S. and Brazil have historically had close and cordial relations. This relationship encompasses a broad range of political and economic agendas on both a bilateral and multilateral basis. Commercial and trade issues occupy a significant position on these agendas. The U.S. exports $16 billion to Brazil and Brazil has consistently run a trade surplus with the United States. Economic stabilization is the major political issue affecting the business climate.

Cultural Note: Brazilians do business through personal connections and expect to have long-term relationships with individuals (not corporations). Your business relationship will need to be reaffirmed each time your Brazilian representative changes.

Be prepared to commit long-term resources of time and money to establishing strong relationships in Brazil. Without such commitments, there is no point attempting to do business there at all.

---

5 *Largest Businesses in Brazil*

Banco Bradesco SA, Osasco
 74,580 employees
Caixa Economica Federal, Brasilia
 65,000 employees
Empresa Brasileira de Correios e Telegrafos, Brasilia
 70,000 employees
Luguide Industria e Comercio de Confeccoes Ltda, Sao Paulo
 50,000 employees
Petroleo Brasileiro SA Petrobras, Rio de Janeiro
 51,399 employees

Comparative Data

Comparative Data Ratings
(Scale: 5 = Excellent; 1 = Poor)
Brazil: 2.75

A. GDP Growth: 3
B. Per Capita Income: 1
C. Trade Flows with the U.S. 4
D Country Risk: 3
E. Monetary Policy: 3
F. Trade Policy: 2
   - Tariffs
   - Import Licensing
   - Import Taxes
G. Protection of Property Rights: 3
H. Foreign Investment Climate: 3

GROSS DOMESTIC PRODUCT: $1.04 trillion (1998 estimate)

GDP GROWTH: 0.5% (1998 estimate)

PER CAPITA INCOME: $6,100 (1998 estimate)

Trade Flows with the U.S.

U.S. EXPORTS TO BRAZIL: $15.1 billion (1998 estimate)

U.S. IMPORTS FROM BRAZIL: $10.1 billion (1998 estimate)

TOP U.S. EXPORTS TO BRAZIL: Machinery; electrical components; organic chemicals; motor vehicles; medical and optical equipment; aircraft and parts; mineral fuel and oil; plastics and resins; beverages; fertilizers

TOP U.S. PROSPECTS FOR EXPORT TO BRAZIL: Franchising; computer hardware and peripherals; sporting goods and recreational equipment; telecommunications; aircraft and parts; automotive parts and service equipment; building products; mining equipment; metalworking equipment

Country Risk

Dun & Bradstreet rates Brazil as having significant uncertainty over expected returns. Risk-averse customers are advised to protect against potential losses.

A letter of credit is recommended. When open account terms are extended, 60- to 120-day terms are the norm.

Monetary Policy

Lower official interest rates coupled with cuts in bank reserve requirements are pushing down commercial bank-lending rates.

MONETARY UNIT: real

Trade Policy

TARIFFS   Tariffs, in general, are the primary instrument in Brazil for regulating imports. The average tariff in late 1997 was 13.8%. By contrast, the average tariff in 1990 was 32%.

These lower tariffs have increased the demand for imports from the United States. Tariffs on some items, however, remain high.

Brazil signed and ratified the Treaty of Asuncion establishing the Southern Common Market (MERCOSUL) in 1991. Brazil and its MERCOSUL partners concluded negotiations in August 1994 for a common external tariff (CET) which went into effect on January 1, 1995. The average tariff covered by the CET is 14.7%.

IMPORT LICENSING   The import permit, known as the *Guia de Importacao*, is the single most important document required for importing goods into Brazil. An import permit must be obtained by the importer for all but a very limited list of products. Import permit requests must be accompanied by the foreign manufacturer's catalogs or price lists covering the goods to be imported.

Import licensing is now automatic within five days of requesting a license with a few exceptions.

The Brazilian government has eliminated most import prohibitions. However, it places special controls on certain imports. Importation of used machinery, automobiles, clothing, and many consumer goods continue to be severely restricted.

IMPORT TAXES   Brazil levies numerous import taxes in addition to import duties. These include an *Industrial Products Tax* which ranges from zero to 15% depending on the product and the *Merchandise Circulation Tax*, a state government value-added tax, with the predominant rate of 17%.

As of 1998, other import taxes include a brokerage fee equal to 2% of the value of the import, a warehouse fee equal to 0.65% of the value of the import, terminal handling charges, merchant marine renewal tax, and additional port taxes.

Protection of Intellectual Property Rights

Brazil is a member of the World Intellectual Property Organization (WIPO), the Paris Convention for Protection of Intellectual Property, the Berne Convention for the Protection of Literary and Artistic Works, the Universal Copyright Convention, and the

Patent Cooperation Treaty. Brazil has a long history of passing legislation that limits or restricts the intellectual property rights of foreigners. Particularly subject to scrutiny were foreign technology licensors who licensed technology to local subsidiaries. However, IP protection has improved, and Brazil does not appear on the current U.S. Trade watch list. IP and technology agreements must be translated into Portuguese and registered with the National Institute of Industrial Property.

The 1996 patent law provides for patenting inventions that are novel, involve creative steps, and have industrial application. The law protects prior bona fide users. Patents are granted for 20 years from filing but never less than 10 years from the granting date. Industrial designs are registered for 10 years from filing and are renewable for three consecutive 5-year terms.

Trademark rights are obtained by registration. Protection of well-known marks registered in Brazil extends to all classes. Well-known international marks are also protected—in theory. Prior users have continuing usage rights. Registration is for a term of 10 years and is renewable. Cancellation can be brought after 5 years of nonuse. Franchising is regulated under a 1994 law. Trademark infringement is a criminal violation.

Copyrights are automatic on creation of a work. The exclusive right of use, reproduction, and publication resulting from copyright is transferable to heirs. Computer programs are protected for a 50-year period. Neither registration nor enrollment is required and deposit is optional. Foreign parties are protected if their country provides reciprocal protection. Parties who infringe the copyright of computer programs are subject to possible imprisonment.

Foreign Investment Climate

Brazil welcomes foreign investment with some restrictions. A wide ranging reform effort (which required constitutional reform) was undertaken by the Cardoso administration to expand the private sector, including foreign investment. These efforts included privatization, deregulation, and the encouragement of competition. U.S. investors have responded by increasing long-term investment, especially through joint ventures.

All foreign investment must be registered with the Central Bank.

Brazil has a privatization program in which foreigners have been allowed to participate, but are limited to 40% of the voting shares for sale.

Foreign and domestic private entities may establish, own, and dispose of business enterprises.

Unemployment rose in the latter half of the 1990s. Although the official unemployment rate in 1999 was 8%, the true figure is much higher. One 1999 estimate yielded an unemployment rate of 20% in São Paulo, Brazil's largest industrial metropolis. With such high levels of unemployment, foreign-owned businesses should have little trouble hiring employees in Brazil.

Political Leaders, Parties, and International Organizations

The International Academy at Santa Barbara at http://www.iasb.org/cwl publishes *Current World Leaders*, an excellent resource for up-to-date data on political leaders, parties, demographics, etc., in Brazil. Tel: (800) 530-2682 or (805) 965-5010 for subscription information to their database.

Head of State and the Government:

President Fernando Henrique Cardoso

Next election:

October 2002

Political Parties:

National Reconstruction Party (PRN), Social Democratic Party (PDS), Party of the Brazilian Democratic Movement (PMDB), Democratic Workers' Party (PDT), Workers' Party (PT), Brazilian Labor Party (PTB), Liberal Front Party (PFL), Popular Socialist Party, Brazilian Social Democratic Party (PSDB), Liberal Party (PL)

Membership in international organizations:

G77, ICCO, ICO, ISO, INTELSAT, LAIA, OAS, UN and all of its specialized agencies and related organizations (including FAO, GATT, IAEA, IBRD, ICAO, IDA, IFAD, IFC, ILO, IMF, IMO, ITU, UNESCO, UNIDO, UPU, WHO, WIPO, WMO)

Political Influences on Business

Brazil and the United States have historically had close and cordial relations. This relationship encompasses a broad political and economic agenda. Commercial and trade issues occupy a significant position on this agenda. Two-way trade exceeds US$16 billion, and Brazil has consistently run a trade surplus with the United States.

Education remains an important issue in Brazil. In the 1980s, many Brazilians averaged only five years of education. Since then, Brazil has made great strides in improving education. By the late 1990s, Brazil was spending 1.2% of its GNP on education (far more than most nations), but much remains to be done.

Economic stabilization is the major political issue affecting the business climate. Brazil has suffered from chronic inflation throughout much of its recent history. The initial success of the stabilization plan developed by Fernando Henrique Cardoso (when he was Finance Minister) was a significant factor in his election to the Presidency in October 1994. The Brazilian recession of the late 1990s is also hampering the economy.

Brazil is a federal republic with 26 states and a Federal District. The federal government is comprised of the executive, legislative, and judicial branches. The system is governed by the 1988 Constitution, which grants broad powers to the federal government. The President holds office for four years and appoints his own cabinet. There are 81 Senators (three for each state and the Federal District) and 513 Deputies. Senate terms are for eight years (with elections staggered so that two-thirds of the upper house is up for election at one time and one-third four years later). Chamber terms are for four years. Chamber elections are based on a complex system of proportional representation. Each state is eligible for a minimum of 8 seats; the largest state delegation (Sao Paulo's) is capped at 70 seats. The net result is a system heavily weighted in favor of geographically large, but sparsely populated states.

States are organized like the federal government, with three branches of government. Because of mandatory revenue allocation to states and municipalities provided for in the 1988 Constitution, Brazilian governors and mayors have exercised considerable power since 1989.

Contacts in the United States

The Embassy of the Federative Republic of Brazil
3006 Massachusetts Avenue, NW
Washington, D.C. 20008
Tel: (202) 745-0200
Fax: (202) 745-2827
http://www.brasilemb.org

Passport/Visa Requirements

A passport and visa are required.

1. A transit visa is valid for 10 days. Arrival and departure must be from the same port of entry. No extension of validity is granted.
2. A tourist visa is valid for 5 years, also valid for reentry or reentries during the permitted stay.
3. Business persons traveling to Brazil to visit agents or to take part in business discussions may enter the country as tourists, provided they do not sign legal documents, engage in financial or commercial transactions, perform work (paid or not), which involves taking tools or samples. (If they do not meet these conditions, they must, instead, obtain a business visa, as outlined in the next paragraph.)

BUSINESS TRIPS: Before applying for a visa of this type, subscribers should check the requirements under the preceding paragraph. Most executives will be able to travel on a tourist visa, as described, instead of complying with the following. If in doubt as to which visa to apply for, Brazilian officials should be consulted.

A Temporary Visa can be granted to a businessperson, upon the applicant meeting the following requirements and presenting the following documents to passport visa officials of Brazil:

1. Valid passport (valid for a minimum of six months);

2. Application form in duplicate;

3. Two passport-size photographs (2 × 2 inches) in color or black-and-white (vending machine prints and tinted photographs are not acceptable).

4. Letter from the applicant's company on the company's letterhead explaining the purpose of the assignment in Brazil and stating their financial responsibility for the applicant (must not be signed by person requesting visa); and

5. If children are accompanying the applicant, a Polio Vaccination Certificate for each child from three months to six years old. Fee: $60.00 payable in money order, certified check, or company check. Gratis to U.S. citizens.

6. Business visas for U.S. citizens are valid for 5 years, with a 90-day limit for each entry and a maximum 180-day (six-month) stay per year.

For current information concerning entry and customs requirements for Brazil, travelers can contact the Brazilian Embassy or the nearest Brazilian Consulate

U.S. citizens who wish to apply for a passport may visit Passport Services' well-organized website at http://travel.state.gov/passport_services.html.

BRAZILIAN–AMERICAN CHAMBER OF COMMERCE
22 West 48th St., Suite 404
New York, NY 10036
Tel: (212) 575-9030
Fax: (212) 921-1078

Contacts in Brazil

THE EMBASSY OF THE UNITED STATES OF AMERICA
Avenida das Nacoes, Quadra 801, Lote 3
Distrito Federal Cep 70403-900
Brasilia
APO AA Miami 34030, Unit 3500
Tel: [55] (61) 321-7272
Fax: [55] (61) 225-9136
http://www.embaixada-americana.org.br

AMERICAN CHAMBER OF COMMERCE FOR BRAZIL–RIO DE JANEIRO
Praca Pio X-15, 5th Floor
Caixa Postal 916
20.040 Rio de Janeiro
Tel: (55) (21) 203-2477
Fax: (55) (21) 263-4477

Dun & Bradstreet do Brasil Ltda.
Av. Bernardina de Campos 98
2 Andar
04004-040-Sao Paolo-SP
Tel: (55) (11) 888.6800
Fax: (55) (11) 888.6802

Office of the President
Palacio de Planalto
Praca dos Tres Poderes
70150 Brasilia, DF, Federative Republic
of Brazil

Further contacts and websites can be found in Appendix A.

Communications

TELEPHONE: The international country code for Brazil is 55.

At this writing Brazilian phone numbers vary in length. The most common lengths are six or seven digits long. In writing, the first two or three numbers are usually offset by a dash (for example, 433-9041 or 92-8771).

City codes also vary in length; they can be one or two digits long. City codes may be offset by a dash or by parentheses.

E-MAIL: E-mail addresses located in Brazil end with the code .br

---

Cultural Note: A normal conversation between two Brazilians generally takes place somewhere between 6 and 12 inches apart. This seems either an intimate or hostile distance to most executives from the U.S., and can be stressful if they are not prepared for such close encounters. However, if you are going to conduct business in Brazil, it is advisable to practice interacting with coworkers at close proximity before your trip. It is insulting to continually back away from your Brazilian counterparts, as they feel uncomfortable at the normal U.S. range of 2 feet or more.

Official Name:	Canada
Official Languages:	English and French*
Government System:	Federal multi-party parliamentary democracy
Population:	31 million (July 1999 estimate)
Population Growth Rate:	1.06% (1999 estimate)
Area:	9,970,610 sq. km. (3.8 million sq. mi.); second largest country in the world
Natural Resources:	nickel, zinc, copper, gold, lead, molybdenum, potash, silver, fish, timber, wildlife, coal, petroleum, natural gas
Major Cities:	Ottawa (capital), Toronto, Montreal, Quebec, Vancouver, Edmonton

Cultural Note: Canada has never invaded the United States of America. However, the U.S. has invaded Canada (unsuccessfully) several times. Every schoolchild learns about Canada's brave resistance to unprovoked U.S. aggression. Today, Canadians no longer fear a military invasion, but the economic and cultural influence of the U.S. continues to grow. The loss of Canadian culture and traditions remains a grave concern—although there is little unanimity as to what actually is that culture.

* While Canada is officially bilingual, French is rarely heard in most provinces. French is the official language of the province of Quebec, where most French-speaking Canadians reside. The province of New Brunswick is officially bilingual in English and French. The Inuit language Inukitut will probably be made an official language of the new territory of Nunavut.

Age Breakdown

0–14 = 20%   15–64 = 68%   65+ = 12% (1999 estimate)
Life Expectancy: 76.12 years, male; 82.79 years, female (1999 estimate)

Time

Canada's different cultures take different attitudes towards time. In general, English-speaking Canada follows U.S. patterns towards punctuality: Be on time to all business appointments, but be slightly late to social engagements.

French-speaking Canada follows the more polychronic French conception of time. Punctuality is expected from foreign business executives, but is not always practiced by French-speaking Canadians.

Canada is large enough to span *six* time zones. The following four correspond to the identically-named time zones in the contiguous 48 United States:

- Most of Quebec and Ontario are on Eastern Standard Time, which is 5 hours behind Greenwich Mean Time (GMT -5).
- Western Ontario, Manitoba, and eastern Saskatchewan (including Regina) are on Central Standard Time, which is 6 hours behind Greenwich Mean Time (GMT -6).
- Western Saskatchewan, Alberta, and easternmost British Columbia are on Mountain Standard Time, which is 7 hours behind Greenwich Mean Time (GMT. -7).
- Most of British Columbia is on Pacific Standard Time, which is 8 hours behind Greenwich Mean Time (GMT -8).

The remaining two Canadian time zones do not correspond to time zones in the contiguous United States:

- Atlantic Standard Time is 1 hour ahead of Eastern Standard Time, making it 4 hours behind Greenwich Mean Time (GMT -4). All the Maritime Provinces are on Atlantic Standard Time—except:
- Newfoundland Island, which reminds the world of its separate identity by maintaining a separate time zone called Newfoundland Standard Time, which is *30 minutes* ahead of Atlantic Time, making it 3-1/2 hours behind Greenwich Mean Time (GMT -3-1/2). Note that this 30-minute difference applies only to Newfoundland Island; Labrador, which is the mainland part of Newfoundland Province, is on Atlantic Standard Time. *Note:* Newfoundland is pronounced "new-fin-land," not "new-found-land."

Holidays

An up-to-date, web-based *World Holiday and Time Zone Guide* is available at www.getcustoms.com. It lists official holidays by country and by day of the year, cultural tips, a corruption index, and time zones with worldwide business hours.

This list is a working guide. Dates should be corroborated before final travel plans are made. In cases where holidays fall on Saturday or Sunday, commercial establishments may be closed the preceding Friday or following Monday.

Jan 1	SA	New Year's Day
Feb 21	MO	Family Day—Alberta
Feb 25	FR	Heritage Day—Yukon
Apr 21	FR	Good Friday
Apr 24	MO	Easter Monday
May 22	MO	Victoria Day
Jun 24	SA	St. Jean Baptiste Day—Quebec
Jun 24	SA	Discovery Day—Newfoundland, Labrador
Jul 1	SA	Canada Day
Aug 7	MO	Civic holiday
Aug 21	MO	Discovery Day—Yukon, Northwest Territories
Sep 4	MO	Labor Day
Oct 9	MO	Thanksgiving
Nov 11	SA	Remembrance Day
Dec 25	MO	Christmas Day
Dec 26	TU	Boxing Day

Note that while the United States and Canada share many holidays, the Canadian Thanksgiving comes over a month before the U.S. Thanksgiving.

Individual Canadian provinces and Territories also have specific holidays. For example, Quebec celebrates St. Jean Baptiste Day in June, and the Northwest Territories celebrate Discovery Day in August.

Good Friday and Easter Monday are also holidays in Canada. Again, the days of observance should always be corroborated by local contacts.

Work Week

- Business hours are generally 9:00 A.M. to 5:00 P.M. Monday through Friday.
- Banking hours are generally 10:00 A.M. to 3:00 P.M. Monday through Thursday, and 10:00 a.m. to 6:00 p.m. on Friday. Some banks have later hours and/or Saturday hours.
- Shop hours are generally 10:00 A.M. to 6:00 P.M. Monday through Saturday, although many shops are open to 9:00 P.M.
- Sunday shopping was prohibited under "The Lord's Day Act," but some provinces have changed the law, allowing local municipalities to decide if they want Sunday shopping.

Religious/Societal Influences on Business

Canada has become a truly multi-ethnic nation. Its citizens exhibit traditions of many backgrounds. This includes not just British and French, but Inuit, Amerindian, and

Métis (a mixture of French and Amerindian) as well. Canada has always been a country of immigrants, with large numbers from Germany, Italy, China, Ukraine, and the Netherlands. The recent influx from Hong Kong came when many well-off Chinese acquired Canadian citizenship in anticipation of Beijing's 1997 takeover of Hong Kong. At present, 17% of Canadian citizens are foreign born.

Most religions are represented in Canada. The largest group consists of Roman Catholics (45.7% of the population). Various Protestant denominations make up the next largest group (36.3%). Other religions include Eastern Orthodoxy, Judaism, Islam, Buddhism, and Hinduism. This diversity is acknowledged in the phrase "the Canadian *mosaic*" (as opposed to the United States's *melting pot*).

With such diversity, it is difficult to generalize about Canadians. Dividing Canadians into the two largest groups, English and French-speakers, allows some characteristics to be noted.

English-speaking Canadians tend toward British manners and reserve. Public displays of emotion are frowned upon. On the other hand, they are capable of great exuberance in sport and revelry (as befits a people living in an often-harsh, low-population environment). The influence of the United States is seen in several areas, including a preference for U.S. terminology over British terms. However, Canadian spelling tends to follow British guidelines. British-speaking Canadians are usually Protestant or Roman Catholic, but religion does not tend to have great influence on everyday life.

French-speaking Canadians exhibit the language and traditions of France. Most (but not all) live in the province of Quebec. The majority are Roman Catholic, and probably were educated in a Church-run school. The Church exerts a greater influence in Quebec than it does in France.

Since the future of united Canada is in doubt, Canadians of all ethnicity live with insecurity about their future. Quebec separatists continue to push for independence. First Nation people (Native Indian Cultures) demand the return of vast areas of territory. The Western Provinces resent rule from Ottawa, and find more commonality with the Northwest United States.

Canadians are, and expect others to be, relatively honest and open. Canada's low population sometimes requires services to be paid for "on the honor system." Services that would have attendants to enforce payment (such as parking lots) in the United States often just have a box, in which users are trusted to deposit payment.

5 Cultural Tips

1. Although many Canadians are quick to move to a first-name basis, it is best to wait for your Canadian counterpart to suggest doing so.

2. Gestures in Canada are similar to those in the U.S. However, note that the "V-for-Victory" sign is done with the palm facing out. It can be taken as an insult when done with the palm inward.

3. Respect the Canadian desire for "Canadian identity," even if the differences between Canadian and U.S. culture escape you. One difference is in how the two countries view the settlement of their Western regions. U.S. legend glorifies "taming the West," while Canadians celebrate *unifying* their country via their transcontinental railroad. (Of course, Canada is a much less violent country than the U.S.)

4. Many Canadians characterize U.S. businesspeople as purveyors of self-promotion and "hype." Avoid this image by sticking to the facts. Canadians expect to hear the truth.

5. Business gifts should be modest; ostentation is frowned upon by most Canadians. Gifts are usually given after the close of a deal. Wrapped gifts are usually unwrapped immediately and shown to all assembled. It is also customary to bring a gift of flowers, candy, or alcohol when visiting a Canadian home.

Economic Overview

The U.S.–Canada trading relationship is the largest in the world, with well over $300 billion in two-way trade taking place each year. Merchandise exports from the United States account for approximately 70% of the Canadian import market, and the U.S. remains by far Canada's largest export market.

Since implementation of the North American Free Trade Agreement (NAFTA) in 1994, U.S. exports to Canada have increased by more than 20%. Despite some well-publicized trade disputes, overall market conditions are unlikely to experience any significant changes, and U.S. companies will continue to find Canada an extremely attractive and easily accessible place to do business.

The sluggish Canadian economy has been showing signs of improvement in recent years. In 1998, the Canadian finance ministry balanced the budget for the first time in 28 years. Unemployment also fell to 8.6%, the lowest level it has reached in the 1990s. The Canadian export sector survived despite the loss of markets due to the Asian economic crisis. For the forseeable future, the Canadian economy is expected to continue its modest growth rate of about 3% per year.

Growth was fueled by exports, which reaped the benefits of the lower Canadian dollar and a strong U.S. economy. Canada is the world's seventh largest market economy. Production and services are predominantly privately owned and operated.

With a population of about one-tenth of that of the United States, the Canadian economy mirrors that of the U.S. in approximately the same ratio, and has developed in many ways along similar lines. This has made Canada an ideal export and investment destination for many U.S. companies who have found an environment and marketplace very similar to that of the domestic U.S. It also offers an ideal first stop for U.S. businesses seeking to begin export marketing, with business practices, attitudes, conditions, and environments more similar to those found in the United States than any other country in the world. Notwithstanding these similarities, however, significant cultural and linguistic differences, which vary across each of Canada's four distinctive regional markets, allow first-time U.S. exporters to develop an appreciation of the complexities of overseas marketing.

Business opportunities in Canada fall within the full spectrum of industry sectors and in virtually every business activity. Geographic proximity, cultural and historical ties, and strong awareness of business and other developments in the U.S. are key accelerators for the sale of U.S. goods and services in the Canadian market. Third-country competition tends to be far less prevalent in Canada than in most other international markets.

5 Largest Businesses in Canada

BCE Inc., Montreal
    122,000 employees
Weston George Ltd., Toronto
    83,000 employees
Laidlaw Inc., Burlington
    79,999 employees
Northern Telecom, Ltd., Brampton
    72, 896 employees
Hudson's Bay Company, Toronto
    70,000 employees

Cultural Note: As a general rule, Canadian businesspeople (especially English-speakers) respond well to direct eye contact and an open, friendly, honest manner.

Personal Observation: "(Living in Canada) has allowed me to see the US from the outside, as others see it. The US beat the Soviets with Levis and rock & roll. It wasn't anything the Pentagon did. The US has created a pop culture that the whole world wants. Now they're continuing this conquest with CNN and the Internet."

   —Best-selling author William Gibson coined the term "cyberspace" and foresaw the
     Internet, virtual reality, computer viruses, and electronic cash. Born in South Carolina,
     Gibson fled to Canada to avoid service in the Vietnam War.

Comparative Data

Comparative Data Ratings
(Scale: 5 = Excellent; 1 = Poor)
Canada: 4.5

   A.   GDP Growth: 3
   B.   Per Capita Income: 5
   C.   Trade Flows with the U.S.: 5
   D.   Country Risk: 5
   E.   Monetary Policy: 5

F. Trade Policy: 4
    - Tariffs
    - Import Licensing
    - Import Taxes
G. Protection of Property Rights: 5
H. Foreign Investment Climate: 4

GROSS DOMESTIC PRODUCT: $688.3 billion (1998 estimate)

GDP GROWTH: (1998 estimate)

PER CAPITA INCOME: $22,400 (1998)

Trade Flows with the U.S.

U.S. EXPORTS TO CANADA: $156 billion (1998)

U.S. IMPORTS FROM CANADA: $175 billion (1998)

RANK AS A SUPPLIER OF IMPORTS INTO THE U.S.: 1st

TOP U.S. EXPORTS TO CANADA: Machinery and equipment; automotive products; industrial goods; consumer goods; agricultural and fishing products; energy and forestry products

TOP U.S. PROSPECTS FOR EXPORT TO CANADA: Computer and peripherals; computer software; telecommunications equipment; automotive parts and equipment; building products; travel and tourism services; furniture; medical equipment; pollution-control equipment; apparel; sporting goods; and electronic components

Country Risk

Dun & Bradstreet rates Canada as having excellent capacity to meet outstanding payment liabilities.

Open account terms are generally common. Normal credit terms are 30 to 60 days.

Monetary Policy

Subdued growth prospects, pulling capacity utilization downwards, together with moderate wage growth are likely to keep a lid on price pressures. As in the U.S., inflation has been low. From a rate of 2.6% in 1996, inflation fell to 1.6% in 1997 and 1.4% in 1998.

MONETARY UNIT: Canadian dollar

Trade Policy

TARIFFS As a result of the 1988 U.S.–Canada Free Trade Agreement (FTA), many Canadian tariffs on U.S. products have been eliminated. NAFTA removed some remaining barriers and expanded specific provisions of the FTA.

The remaining tariffs, mostly agricultural products, textile, and apparel products, were phased out on January 1, 1998.

IMPORT LICENSING   There are no general licenses required for importing goods into Canada. There are, however, provisions related to a variety of prohibited, controlled, and restricted goods. The majority of U.S. products shipped to Canada enter the market free from any import restrictions. However, under the provisions of the Canadian Customs Tariff regulations, certain commodities cannot be imported such as oleomargarine, reprints of Canadian copyrighted work, and some game birds.

Other goods are controlled, regulated, or prohibited under legislation falling within the jurisdiction of other government departments. Examples of regulated goods include food products, clothing, drug and medical devices, hazardous products, some offensive weapons and firearms, endangered species, and motor vehicles.

IMPORT TAXES   Canada implemented a 7% goods and services tax in 1991. The tax does not apply to basic groceries, prescribed drugs, and medical devices; most agricultural and fish products; most educational services; most financial services; health and dental care services; and a variety of other services.

A separate excise tax of 10% applies to certain products such as watches or jewelry, when duty-paid value exceeds C$50. Other excise taxes are applied to tobacco, cigarettes, liquor, and wines.

Protection of Intellectual Property Rights

Canada subscribes to numerous treaties, conventions, and bilateral agreements pertaining to intellectual property matters. Canada has long been a member of the Berne Convention for the Protection of Literary and Artistic Works. Canada's obligations to the World International Property Organization (WIPO) were satisfied in 1996.

Inventions are limited to new and useful art, process, machine, manufacture, or composition of matter. Claims for foods or medicine are limited to process. During the period 1989–96, Canada switched from a first-to-use to a first-to-file system. Absolute novelty is required with a one-year grace period for disclosures attributable to the inventor. The term of patent is 20 years from application. It is abuse of trademark rights not to satisfy demand for the claimed products or services in Canada.

Canada has a combination system of common law marks and a national registration system. Registration gives the owner the exclusive right to use the mark in relation to the goods or services throughout Canada. A trademark, whether common law or registered, is transferable with or without goodwill. Applications may be based on use, intent to use, or on a registration in the applicant's home country. A unique feature concerning Canada is that it is the only country that does not have trademark classes. You can list as many goods and services as you desire in one application for one filing fee. Registrations have a term of 15 years and are renewable, but can be cancelled for nonuse. Use by a licensee is equivalent to use by the trademark owner.

Canada has long been at the forefront of copyright protection. For many years U.S. publishers did backdoor concurrent publications in Canada to qualify for protection under the Berne Convention. Copyrights in Canada are statutory. The current law is the Copyright Act of 1996. Amendments were added in 1997 to make the law compatible with the Rome Convention. Copyrights exist in every original literary, dramatic, musical, and artistic work. Computer programs are protected as literary works. Copyrights belong to their creators. The term of copyright is life of the author plus 50 years. Although registration is not required for protection, there is a means of registration. Criminal sanctions may be imposed on infringers.

Foreign Investment Climate

Canada has long been considered a stable and remunerative environment for foreign investment, and its economic progress has been made possible to a large extent by a sustained inflow of foreign capital. Since 1985, foreign investment policy in Canada has been guided by the Investment Canada Act which replaced the more restrictive Foreign Investment Review Act.

With few exceptions, Canada offers foreign investors full national treatment within the context of a developed open market economy operating with democratic principles and institutions. Canada is, however, one of the few OECD countries that still has a formal investment review process, and foreign investment is prohibited or restricted in several sectors of the economy.

While the Investment Canada Act provides the basic legal framework for foreign investment in Canada, foreign investment in specific sectors may be covered by special legislation. For example, foreign investment in the financial sector is governed by laws administered by the federal Department of Finance, and the Broadcast Act governs foreign investment in radio and TV broadcasting. Under provisions of Canada's new Telecommunications Act, foreign ownership of transmission facilities is limited to 20%; while in the case of holding companies that wish to invest in Canadian carriers, two-thirds of the holding company's equity must be owned and controlled by Canadians.

Canada's federal system of government subjects investment to provincial as well as national jurisdiction. Provincial restrictions on foreign investment differ by province, but are largely confined to the purchase of land and to certain types of provincially-regulated financial services.

Since the beginning of 1994, investment relations between the United States and Canada have been governed by the NAFTA negotiated by the U.S., Canada, and Mexico. The U.S.–Canada Free Trade Agreement (FTA), which entered into force at the beginning of 1989, has been suspended as long as the two countries remain parties to the NAFTA. The NAFTA builds on the investment relationship created in the FTA.

The FTA established a mutually beneficial framework of investment principles sensitive to the national interests of both countries, with the objective of assuring that investment flowed freely between the two countries and that investors were treated in a fair and predictable manner.

The FTA provided higher review thresholds for U.S. investment in Canada than for other foreign investors, but it did not exempt all U.S. investment from review nor did it override specific foreign investment prohibitions, notably in the cultural area. The

NAFTA incorporates the gains made in the FTA, expands the coverage of the Investment Chapter to several new areas and broadens the definition of investors with rights under the agreement, and creates the right to binding investor-State dispute settlement arbitration under limited circumstances.

Political Leaders, Parties, and International Organizations

The International Academy at Santa Barbara at http://www.iasb.org/cwl publishes *Current World Leaders*, an excellent resource for up-to-date data on political leaders, parties, demographics, etc., in Canada. Tel: (800) 530-2682 or (805) 965-5010 for subscription information to their database.

Chief of State:

Queen Elizabeth II

Local Representative of the Chief of State:

Governor-General Adrienne Clarkson

Head of the Government:

Prime Minister Jean Chrétien

Political Parties:

Progressive Conservative Party, Liberal Party, New Democratic Party, Reform Party, Bloc Quebecois

Membership in international organizations:

Agency for Cultural and Technical Cooperation, APEC, C, EBRD, G7, IEA, INTELSAT, NACC, North Atlantic Fisheries Organization, NATO, OAS, OECD, OSCE, PECC, UN and all of its specialized agencies and related organizations (including FAO, GATT, IAEA, IBRD, ICAO, IDA, IFAD, IFC, ILO, IMF, IMO, ITU, UNESCO, UNIDO, UPU, WHO, WIPO, WMO)

Political Influences on Business

Canada is a parliamentary democracy and a federal state composed of ten provinces and three territories. The United States and Canada share a range of fundamental values, such as a commitment to democracy, tolerance, and respect for human rights. It is no wonder that the two countries are close friends and allies. Both also have dynamic market economies with sophisticated industrial, agricultural, resource, and service sectors, and a commitment to high living standards for their citizens. These factors complement the obvious geographic facts and have combined to make each the other's best customer. Despite occasional frictions, the relationship—probably the most intensive and complex in the world—between the U.S. and Canada is positive and cooperative.

Unlike the United States, there are strong separatist influences within Canada. The Parti Quebecois (PQ), which advocates withdrawing Quebec from Canada, has run referendums on Quebec independence. Each time the referendum is held, the vote grows closer in favor of independence. However, it is understood that an independent Quebec would remain part of NAFTA, so the effect on U.S. trade would be minimal.

Separatist sentiment also exists between regions and Amerindian groups (most Canadian Indians prefer the term "First Nations" to "Native Americans"). People in the western provinces feel little commonality with Quebec or the Maritime provinces.

The most remarkable recent redrawing of the Canadian map occurred on April 1, 1999, when part of the Northwest Territories were turned over to the native Inuit (the people formerly called "Eskimos"). This new territory is called Nunavut, which means "Our Land" in Inukitut, the predominant Inuit language. This huge territory, comprising a fifth of Canada, has a total population of only about 25,000. With few exploitable natural resources, Nunavut is expected to depend indefinitely upon subsidies from the Canadian government.

Canada continues to face a debt crisis with very grave potential consequences. Per capita debt ratios are among the highest in the world, and with taxes already at very high levels, the government's margin of maneuver is severely constrained. Governments at all levels are struggling to contain costs while maintaining as much as possible of the social welfare programs Canadians value. A major effort to revamp such programs, including unemployment insurance, is underway but moving slowly. If successful, it could well reallocate premiums and benefits.

While Canada and the U.S. are allies in most political arenas, there are areas of disagreement. One such disagreement concerns the northern Pacific salmon fishery. Overfishing has severely depleted the salmon, and the Pacific Salmon Treaty of 1985 has failed to resolve the issue.

Contacts in the United States

THE EMBASSY OF CANADA
501 Pennsylvania Avenue, NW
Washington, D.C. 20001
Tel: (202) 682-1740
Fax: (202) 682-7726
www.cdnemb-washac.org

Passport/Visa Requirements

Proof of U.S. citizenship and photo identification are required for travel to Canada. Visas are not required for U.S. citizens and permanent residents entering from the United States for stays up to 180 days.

For current information concerning entry and customs requirements for Canada, travelers can contact the Canadian Embassy.

U.S. citizens who wish to apply for a passport may visit Passport Services' well-organized website at http://travel.state.gov/passport_services.html.

Contacts In Canada

THE EMBASSY OF THE UNITED STATES
100 Wellington Street
Ottawa, Ontario K1P 5T1
P.O. Box 5000, Ogdensburg, NY 13669-0430
Tel: (613) 238-5335 or 4470
Fax: (613) 238-5720
www.usembassycanada.gov

DUN & BRADSTREET CANADA
Postal Address: P.O. Box 6200, Station A, Mississauga, Ontario L5A 4G4
Street Address: 5770 Hurontario Street, Mississauga, Ontario L5R 3G5
Tel: (905) 568-6000
Fax: (905) 568-5794 (Finance & Administration); (905) 568-6320/6321 (Information Resources); (905) 568-6278/6279 (Business Information Services); (905) 568-6196/6197 (Duns Marketing Services); (905) 568-5815 (Dunstel); (905) 568-6360 (Human Resources); (905) 568-6051/6052 (Info. Tech. Svs.); (905) 568-6037 (RMS)

OFFICE OF THE PRIME MINISTER
Langevin Blk.
Ottawa, Ontario, Canada K1A OA2

Further contacts and websites can be found in Appendix A.

Communications

TELEPHONE: The Canadian phone system is virtually identical to that of the U.S.

Canada is divided into three-digit area codes, just like the U.S. No country code is needed to phone a Canadian number from the U.S.

Phone numbers are seven digits in length.

Canadian toll-free numbers use the 800 prefix.

At this writing, U.S. toll-free 800 numbers *cannot* be called from Canada. U.S. companies should be sure to include a toll number in their promotional material.

E-MAIL: E-mail addresses located in Canada end with the code .ca

Some Notes on French-Speaking Canadians

1. If English-speaking Canadians can be said to exhibit a traditional British reserve, French-speaking Canadians display French characteristics. Their gestures tend to be expansive, they may stand closer than the English when talking, and they are more likely to touch during a conversation.

2. French-Canadian businessmen shake hands more often than English-speaking Canadians. Both groups shake hands upon greeting, but French-Canadian men also shake hands at departures, even if the person has been greeted earlier that day. Women may decide whether or not to shake hands. In general, the French handshake is briefer and less hearty than the English handshake.

3. Only good friends and family members will be greeted with an embrace, and (sometimes) a series of kissing on the cheeks. French-Canadians do not end an embrace by thumping each other on the back.

4. A French-Canadian house is divided into "public" rooms (which visitors may enter) and "private" rooms (which one may only enter when asked). Be aware that the kitchen is often one of the private rooms.

5. Address French-Canadians by their title and surname until invited to do otherwise. While they often use first names over the telephone, French-Canadians usually revert to using surnames in person.

6. Of course, when working with French-Canadians, it is important to have all material written in French as well as English.

Chile

Official Name:	Republic of Chile (Républica de Chile)
Official Language:	Spanish
Government System:	Unitary multi-party republic
Population:	14.93 million (1999 estimate)
Population Growth Rate:	1.23% (1999 estimate)
Area:	756,626 sq. km. (292,058 sq. mi.); nearly twice the size of California
Natural Resources:	copper, timber, iron ore, nitrates, precious metals, molybdenum
Major Cities:	Santiago (capital), Viá del Mar, Valparaiso, Concepcion, Temuco

---

Cultural Note: Chile is isolated. During the days of the Spanish Empire, it was the most remote colony on this continent. The Andes cut Chile off from the rest of South America. Isolation is a fact of life even within Chile itself; the deserts of Northern Chile are a long way from the rainy hills of Southern Chile. From a marketing point of view, Central Chile is the most important region to focus upon. Approximately 90% of the population resides in Chile's Central Valley.

Age Breakdown

0–14 = 28%   15–64 = 65%   65+ = 7% (1999 estimate)
Life Expectancy: 72.33 years, male; 78.75 years, female (1999 estimate)

Time

Punctuality is expected from foreigners. However, do not be surprised if your Chilean counterpart is late.

Everyone—foreigners included—is supposed to be late to social functions. For a meal at a Chilean home, arrive about 15 minutes late. Be at least a half hour late to a party.

Chile is 4 hours behind Greenwich Mean Time (GMT -4), which is 1 hour ahead of U.S. Eastern Standard Time (EST +1).

Holidays

An up-to-date, web-based *World Holiday and Time Zone Guide* is available at www.getcustoms.com. It lists official holidays by country and by day of the year, cultural tips, a corruption index, and time zones with worldwide business hours.

Jan 1	SA	New Year's Day
Apr 21	FR	Good Friday
Apr 24	MO	Easter Monday
May 1	MO	Labor Day
May 21	SU	Battle of Iquique
Jun 29	TH	Sts. Peter and Paul
Aug 15	TU	Assumption
Sep 18	MO	Independence Day
Sep 19	TU	Armed Forces Day
Oct 12	TH	Columbus Day
Nov 1	WE	All Saints Day
Dec 8	FR	Immaculate Conception
Dec 25	MO	Christmas Day

In addition to the above, the Catholic celebration of Corpus Christi is a holiday. Again, the days of observance should always be corroborated by local contacts.

Work Week

- Business hours are 9:00 A.M. to 5:00 P.M. Monday through Friday. A two-hour lunch is usually eaten at 12:00. Government offices are open 9:00 A.M. to 4:30 P.M. Monday through Friday, and bank hours are 9:00 A.M. to 2:00 P.M.

- The best times to make appointments are from 10:00 A.M. to 12:00 noon and 2:30 to 5:00 P.M. Following-up a late morning appointment with a business lunch is a common occurrence (and key to developing a business relationship).

Santiago, the capital, is subject to severe air pollution, especially between the months of May and October.

Religious/Societal Influences on Business

The majority of Chileans (over 75%) are Roman Catholic. However, Chile has no official religion, and the Chilean Catholic Church has never achieved the degree of political influence that the Church has in some other Latin American nations. Protestantism is growing rapidly, and now counts 13% of Chileans among its followers.

Chile's traditional values center around the family. As a corollary, Chileans prefer to do business with their relatives. Nepotism does not generate any controversy in Chile. Chile remains a male-dominated society, and machismo is still strong.

In their isolation from the rest of the world, Chileans developed a sophisticated body of art and literature. Pablo Neruda is one of the best-known poets of the twentieth century. The first Nobel Prize in Literature awarded to a Latin American went to Chile's Gabriela Mistral in 1945. Novelist Isabel Allende, a very successful contemporary author, was related to former Chilean President Salvador Allende, the Marxist who was overthrown and slain in a C.I.A.-supported coup in 1973.

Chileans are also proud of their world-class wines. Due to Chile's isolation, its vineyards escaped the phylloxera mite that has periodically devastated the world's vineyards since the 1870s.

Observation: ". . . the Chilean Church had experienced a chronic inability to recruit priests throughout the century. In 1968, the worst year, only two had been ordained in the entire country. . . .

"However lukewarm many Chilean Catholics were about the faith, everyone I met, up and down the country, seemed to have a strong sense of the importance of the Church as a national institution, both historically and in their own time. It was different from faith. It was a sense, or an awareness, which had been bred into their ancestors. It had survived the arrival of the secular age, which by the mid-nineteenth century had dislodged the Church from the privileged position it had inherited from medieval Europe, and it had outlived the 1925 constitution, which officially separated Church and State after almost fifty years of political controversy on the subject."

—from *Travels in a Thin Country* by Sara Wheeler

---

5 Cultural Tips

1. Be wary about drawing parallels between Chile and other "Southern Cone" nations. Chile's relations with its neighbors are not always cordial. Chile and Argentina have had several border disputes, especially over the oil resources of Tierra del Fuego. To the north, Chile won the War of the Pacific in 1879 against Peru and Bolivia, after which Chile annexed the nitrate-rich Atacama desert. Peru and Bolivia still want this land back. Additionally, Chile lays claim to a large section of Antarctica—land also claimed by Argentina and the United Kingdom.

2. Chileans are very patriotic. Although Chile won the War of the Pacific, it lost the first sea battle of the war. At the Battle of Iquique, two small Chilean ships fought a huge Peruvian warship off the port city of Iquique. Badly outclassed, Chilean Captain Arturo Prat rammed the Peruvian ship and tried to board it. He and his men died in the attempt, but their never-say-die attitude inspired all of Chile.

3. Chile is a conservative country in several respects. The Spanish spoken in Chile is fairly "pure"—quite unlike the Italian-influenced Spanish of Argentina. Introductions are formal and business dress is conservative. Executives of both sexes generally wear blue or gray suits, without jewelry.

4. Chile and Argentina have been competitors for almost two centuries. Executives who do business in both countries should be aware of this rivalry.

5. Chile returned to economic and political stability during the eight-year rule of General Augusto Pinochet. The Chilean economy was so successful that other countries attempted (without success) to duplicate the "Chilean Model." However, General Pinochet's reign was accompanied by serious human-rights abuses. The 1998 arrest of General Pinochet in the United Kingdom brought the cruelties of his dictatorship to renewed attention. Curiously, some of the same Chileans who suffered under Pinochet's leadership protested his arrest, which they consider a violation of Chile's sovereignty.

Cultural Note: Chile is a major wine-producing country. Wine makes a good topic of conversation and is appreciated at many meals. In addition to wine, Chile produces several other varieties of alcohol. *Chicha* is made from grape juice that has not yet fully fermented into wine. The powerful, colorless liquor called *pisco* is made only in Chile and Peru; it is often mixed into a *pisco sour*. Another strong liquor is *Aguardiente*, used in a traditional Christmastime coffee drink. Legend has it that the eleven letters in the word *Aguardiente* gave the name for the daily Chilean snack, *las once*. Belying its name, *las once* is not served at 11 A.M., but in the late afternoon, like a British tea.

Economic Overview

Thanks to decades of market-oriented reforms, Chile's economy has expanded for the last 15 years. Chile now enjoys a prosperous, essentially free-market economy. Its growth averaged over 8% per year for most of the 1990s. This economic expansion was led by a boom in exports, concentrated in primary and processed natural resources—principally copper, fresh fruit, forestry, and fishery products.

However, in the late 1990s, the Chilean economy experienced problems and growth dropped below 5% per year. Chile is the world's largest producer and exporter of copper. Copper constitutes around 40% of Chilean exports and remains vital to the health of the economy. The downturn of world copper prices in the late 1990s seriously hurt Chile's economy. Success in meeting the government's goal of sustained annual growth of 5% depends on world copper prices, the level of confidence of foreign investors and creditors, and the government's own ability to maintain a conservative fiscal stance. In addition, one-third of all Chilean exports go to Asia, and the Asian financial crisis hurt exports to that region.

Since the return to democratic rule in 1990, Chilean–U.S. relations have flourished. The U.S. government has welcomed Chile's successful effort to regain its place in the international arena after years of political isolation, and views Chile's successful program of sustained economic reform and its peaceful transition to democracy as models for other countries. However, Chileans are disappointed that they have not been granted admission into the North American Free Trade Agreement (NAFTA). Chile already has free-trade agreements with Canada and Mexico; Chile's admission into NAFTA has been held up by the U.S. Congress since 1995, which has refused to give the Executive Branch "fast-track" negotiating authority.

Chile is also a member of the Southern Common Market (Mercosur). The other Mercosur members are Argentina, Bolivia, Brazil, Paraguay, and Uruguay.

5 Largest Businesses in Chile

P&O Alfin S.A., Santiago
   22,000 employees
Goulds Pumps, Inc., Santiago
   14,000 employees
Capital de Riesgo CMPC S.A., Santiago
   10,000 employees
Distribution y Servicio D&S S.A., Santiago
   8,868 employees
Compania Chilena de Tabacos S.A., Santiago
   8,700 employees
Chilean businesses may use the following abbreviations:
   S.A. = Sociedad Anónima is the most common designation for a corporation.
   Ltda. = Sociedad de Responsabilidad Limitada indicates a privately owned corporation; such businesses are usually small.

Cultural Note: About 40% of Chileans live in or around the capital, Santiago. Although Santiago was founded in 1541, the Chileans did not settle their Southern frontier until the 1880s—around the same time the United States was settling its Western frontier. As in the U.S., Chile's Southern region had been the domain of formidable Indian tribes. These Araucanian Indians defended their fjords and rain-drenched mountains from the Chileans in a war lasting 350 years!

Comparative Data

Comparative Data Ratings
(Scale: 5 = Excellent; 1 = Poor)
Chile: 2.75

A. GDP Growth: 3
B. Per Capita Income: 2
C. Trade Flows with the U.S.: 1
D. Country Risk: 4
E. Monetary Policy: 3
F: Trade Policy: 3
  - Tariffs
  - Import Licensing
  - Import Taxes
G. Protection of Property Rights: 3
H. Foreign Investment Climate: 3

GROSS DOMESTIC PRODUCT: $184.6 billion (1998 estimate)

GDP GROWTH: 3.5% (1998 estimate); 0.4% (2000 estimate)

PER CAPITA INCOME: $12,500 (1998)

Trade Flows with the U.S.

U.S. EXPORTS TO CHILE: $4.0 billion (1998)

U.S. IMPORTS FROM CHILE: $2.5 (1998)

TOP USA EXPORTS TO CHILE: Machinery; motor vehicles; electrical components; plastics; medical and optical equipment; aircraft and parts; mineral fuel; paper; fertilizers; organic chemicals

TOP U.S. PROSPECTS FOR EXPORT TO CHILE: Medical equipment; travel and tourism; telecommunications equipment; port and shipping equipment; pollution-control equipment; building materials; mining equipment and supplies; electrical power systems and equipment; plastics/resin production machinery; security equipment; computers and peripherals; construction equipment; fresh fruit and grains

Country Risk

Dun & Bradstreet rates Chile as having good capacity to meet outstanding payment liabilities.

Liberal credit terms now predominate on sales to Chile. Letters of credit account for only about 15% of shipments, but are still advised for initial transactions. Open account terms of 30 to 60 days are the norm.

Monetary Policy

Helped by an appreciating peso, inflation declined gradually since 1990, reaching 4.70% in 1998, and was expected to fall even further—to 4.3% in 1999. The Asian financial crisis and low world copper prices slowed GDP growth, from the 8% range in the mid-1990s to under 5% in 1998.

With a savings rate of almost 24%, Chile boasts the highest savings rate in the Western Hemisphere. These high savings have been achieved, in part, by mandatory retirement contributions administered by private pension funds. As a result, Chile is not dependent upon short-term foreign capital to finance investment.

MONETARY UNIT: Chilean peso

Trade Policy

TARIFFS   The Chilean tariff rate is currently 10% on nearly all products from most countries, although many products from Latin American countries with which Chile has trade arrangements enter with lower duties.

Chile maintains a price band system for wheat, wheat flour, edible oils, and sugar. This variable tariff system is designed to maintain domestic prices for these commodities within a predetermined band, which shields Chilean producers from price fluctuations in international market prices.

IMPORT LICENSING   Import licenses are granted as a routine procedure. Licenses are required for weapons and pharmaceuticals. Licensing requirements are maintained largely as a statistical gathering mechanism, not as a control or barrier.

The importation of used passenger and cargo transportation vehicles is prohibited, except in the following cases: used ambulances, armored cars, mobile homes, prison vans, street highway cleaning vehicles, and cement-making vehicles.

IMPORT TAXES   Imports are subject to the same 18% value-added tax (VAT) as are domestic goods.

Imported automobiles are subject to luxury taxes based on value and engine size. Other imported luxury goods such as yachts, some types of jewelry, and others are also subject to luxury taxes.

Protection of Intellectual Property Rights

Chile belongs to the intellectual property conventions, including the Berne Convention for Protection of Literary and Artistic Works, the Universal Copyright Convention, the Inter-American Convention for the Protection of Industrial Property, and the World Intellectual Property Organization (WIPO). However, even though Chile's IP rights are better than most countries in the region, they do not meet international standards.

Patents may be based on foreign patents or a new application may be submitted. An invention must be new, inventive, and have industrial application. Worldwide novelty is required. The term of patent is 15 years from filing. When the patent is based on a filing in another country, the term cannot exceed the lesser of 15 years or the remaining term of such patent.

Trademark rights result from registration instead of use. A trademark should be registered as soon as the exporter/investor has any intention of doing business in Chile. There are no trademark rights apart from the registrations. The term of registration is 10 years and is renewable. Both products and services are protected. Notice of registration is designated using the words *Marca Registrada* or the initials *MR* on the product or packaging.

Chile joined the Berne Convention in 1948, some 40 years before the U.S. The term of copyright is the life of the author plus 50 years for heirs and assigns. If the heirs are the author's wife and single or widowed daughter, the term is for a lifetime. However, at this writing computer programs are not protected.

Foreign Investment Climate

The U.S. is one of the largest foreign investors in Chile. In 1997, the United States ranked second as a source of foreign investment in Chile. The 1997 U.S. investment, at $913 million, was exceeded only by the $1.5 billion investment from Spain; Canada ranked third in 1997 with $679 million. The mining sector alone received $1.6 billion in foreign investment, but investment in mining is expected to fall due to declining copper prices on the world market.

A key feature of Chile's development strategy is a welcoming attitude toward foreign investors, which is embodied in the country's foreign investment law, known as D.L. 600.

D.L. 600 was promulgated in 1974 and has frequently been liberalized. Since 1991, nearly all foreign direct investment in Chile has taken place through D.L. 600. Under this law, foreign investment must be approved by the government's Foreign Investment Committee, but approval procedures are expeditious and not burdensome. Typically, applications are approved within a matter of days, and almost always within a month.

Under D.L. 600, investors sign standardized contracts giving them the rights to: receive nondiscriminatory treatment; participate in any form of investment; hold assets indefinitely; remit or reinvest earnings immediately and remit capital after one year; opt for either national tax treatment or a guaranteed rate for the first 10 years of an investment; and acquire foreign currency at the interbank rate of exchange.

Chile's welcoming attitude to foreign investment, along with the country's wealth of natural resources, has resulted in some $25 billion in foreign direct investment since 1974.

Despite Chile's generally positive attitude toward foreign capital, certain negative treatment of foreign capital persists. Profits may be repatriated immediately, but capital may not be repatriated until after one year. Other restrictions exist as well.

Businesses in Chile are predominantly owned and controlled by private interests. Although the military and democratic governments of the last 20 years have privatized many state corporations, the state retains holdings in several industries. The most important public corporation is CODELCO, the world's largest copper company, which the government has said it will not sell.

Political Leaders, Parties, and International Organizations

The International Academy at Santa Barbara at http://www.iasb.org/cwl publishes *Current World Leaders*, an excellent resource for up-to-date data on political leaders, parties, demographics, etc., in Chile. Tel: (800) 530-2682 or (805) 965-5010 for subscription information to their database.

Head of State and the Government:

Ricardo Lagos Escobar

Next Election:

December 2005

Political Parties:

Christian Democratic Party (PDC), Social Democratic Party, Socialist Party, Pro-Democracy Party (PPD), Centrist Alliance Party, National Renewal Party (RN), Independent Democratic Union (UDI), National Party, Radical Party (RP), Humane Party (PH)

Membership in international organizations:

G77, IADB, LAIA, OAS, Organization of Copper Exporting Countries (CIPEC), PECC, SELA, UN and all of its specialized agencies and related organizations (including FAO, GATT, IAEA, IBRD, ICAO, IDA, IFAD, IFC, ILO, IMF, IMO, ITU, UNESCO, UNIDO, UPU, WHO, WIPO, WMO)

Political Influences on Business

Chilean politics is marked by broad consensus among the major parties about the importance of a democratic political system and a free-market economic system. Key differences between the governing coalition and the rightist opposition involve strategies for, and the role of government in, addressing issues such as poverty eradication, health care, infrastructure, and education, as well as the degree to which the political system should be reformed to eliminate power-sharing arrangements created under the former military government which protect the interests of the armed services and the political right at the expense of those in the elected majority.

President Eduardo Frei, a Christian Democrat leading a coalition of four center–left parties, won an overwhelming victory in December 1993 elections and began his six-year term on March 11, 1994, when he succeeded Patricio Aylwin (also a Christian Democrat). An engineer by training, Frei was a successful businessman before entering politics in the 1980s. Many of his closest advisors were U.S.-trained and shared his commitment to Chile's successful free-market economic model. The next presidential election was scheduled for December 1999.

Chile's powerful executive branch and its coalition may have a majority of the elected seats in both the lower and upper houses of Congress (the Chamber of Deputies and the Senate). Nonetheless, under constitutional provisions promulgated during the period of military rule (1973–1990), the balance of power in the upper house is held by the eight living "institutional" senators appointed near the end of the Pinochet era. Thus, the government must negotiate with the conservative opposition to pass any of its legislative programs.

For much of this century, Chilean politics were marked by a three-way division among the political right, center, and left, with each holding roughly one-third of the vote. This division persists today with the important modification that, since the transition to democracy, the political center (including the center–right and center–left) has gained strength at the expense of the extremes. As a result, Chilean politics today revolve around two large political blocs: the center–left governing coalition and the rightist opposition which includes relatively modern center–right forces. The former includes the centrist Christian Democratic and Radical parties, and the moderate-leftist Party for Democracy and the Socialist Party. The latter includes the National Renewal Party, the Independent Democratic Union, and the populist center—Center Union. Chile also has several small fringe-left parties, including a largely unreconstructed Communist Party, which are not represented in the Executive Branch or the Congress, but which have elected representatives in local governments.

Contacts in the United States

THE EMBASSY OF THE REPUBLIC OF CHILE
1732 Massachusetts Avenue, NW
Washington, D.C. 20036
Tel: (202) 785-1746
Fax: (202) 887-5579
(no website as of this writing)

NORTH AMERICAN–CHILEAN CHAMBER OF
COMMERCE, INC.
220 East 81st Street
New York, NY 10028
Tel: (212) 288-5691
Fax: (212) 628-4978

Passport/Visa Requirements

Passport is required. No visa is required for U.S. citizens for a three-month stay. Those considering scientific, technical, or mountaineering activities in areas classified as frontier areas are required to obtain authorization from the Chilean government. Requests for authorization must be presented to Chilean authorities at least 90 days prior to the beginning of the expedition. Upon request, a round-trip ticket or a ticket to any boundary country must be shown.

For current information concerning entry and customs requirements for Chile, travelers can contact the Chilean Embassy or the nearest consulate.

U.S. citizens who wish to apply for a passport may visit Passport Services' well-organized website at http://travel.state.gov/passport_services.html.

Contacts in Chile

THE U.S. EMBASSY
Avenida Andres Bello 2800
Santiago
Tel: (56) (2) 232-2600
Fax: (56) (2) 330-3710
E-mail: usembl@rdc.cl
Website: http://www.usembassy.cl

CHILEAN–AMERICAN CHAMBER OF COMMERCE
Av. Americo Vespucio Sur 80
9 Piso
82 Correo 34
Santiago
Tel: (56) (2) 208-4140
Fax: (56) (2) 206-0911
E-mail: amcham@entelchile.net
Website: http://www.amcham.cl

DUN & BRADSTREET LTDA.
Postal Address: Casilla 19096 Vitacura, Santiago
Street Address: Av. El Bosque Norte 0177, Oficina 901, Santiago
Tel: (56) (2) 332-0800
Fax: (56) (2) 332-0810

OFFICE OF THE PRESIDENT
Palacio De La Moneda
Santiago, Republic of Chile

Further contacts and websites can be found in Appendix A.

Communications

TELEPHONE: The country code for Chile is 56.

At this writing Chilean phone numbers vary in length, from four to seven digits in length. A hyphen is usually included in longer numbers, but its placement varies.

City codes can be one or two digits in length.

City codes may be written in parentheses. Some Chilean companies that do business internationally include both the city code and country code within single parentheses.

Chile boasts one of the best telecommunications networks in the Western Hemisphere, including an up-to-date, all-digital telephone system.

E-MAIL: E-mail addresses located in Chile end with the code .cl

DATES: The date is written in this order: day, month, year (unlike the U.S. practice of writing month, day, year).

Faux Pas: A U.S. executive went to Chile for a final negotiating round with the owner of a major Chilean corporation. Unfortunately, the gentleman from the U.S.A. wore a heavy gold ring with a diamond, plus a gold watch. The Chileans interpreted this jewelry as proof that the American was in business to amass personal wealth, and furthermore had the poor taste to display it. The Chilean contract went to an Italian firm.

China

Official Name:	People's Republic of China (Chung-hua Jen-min Kung-ho-kuo)
Official Language:	Mandarin (Standard) Chinese
Government System:	Communist people's republic
Population:	1.25 billion (1999 estimate)
Population Growth Rate:	0.77% (1999 estimate)
Area:	9.57 million sq. km. (3.69 million sq. mi.); the U.S. is 9.51 million sq. km. (3.67 million sq. mi.)
Natural Resources:	coal, iron ore, petroleum, natural gas, mercury, tin, tungsten, antimony, manganese, molybdenum, vanadium, magnetite, aluminum, lead, zinc, uranium, hydropower potential
Major Cities:	Beijing (capital), Shanghai, Tianjin, Guangzhou, Shenyang, Wuhan, Chong Qing—and, since July 1997, Hong Kong

Cultural Note: China is the most populous nation on Earth. One in every fifth person in the world lives in the People's Republic of China. A strict one-child-per-couple policy (enforced more in the cities than in the countryside, and more among ethnic Chinese than among China's minorities) has reduced the growth rate to 0.77%.

Age Breakdown

0–14 = 26%   15–64 = 68%   65+ = 6%
Life Expectancy: 68.57 years, male; 71.48 years, female (1999)

Time

Foreigners are expected to be prompt to all business and social appointments. Making someone wait or canceling an appointment is a serious affront.

Despite its huge size, all of China is in the same time zone, 8 hours ahead of Greenwich Mean Time (GMT +8), which is 13 hours ahead of U.S. Eastern Standard Time (EST +13).

Holidays

An up-to-date, web-based *World Holiday and Time Zone Guide* is available at www.getcustoms.com. It lists official holidays by country and by day of the year, cultural tips, a corruption index, and time zones with worldwide business hours.

This list is a working guide. Dates should be corroborated before final travel plans are made. In cases where holidays fall on Saturday or Sunday, commercial establishments may be closed the preceding Friday or the following Monday.

Do not plan business trips during the Chinese Lunar New Year since many businesses close for a week before and after the festival. The date of the New Year varies according to the Lunar Calendar.

Jan 1	SA	New Year's Day
Feb 4	FR	Spring Festival (4–8)
Mar 8	WE	Women's Day
Apr 5	WE	Lantern Festival
May 1	MO	Labor Day
May 4	TH	Youth Day
Jun 1	TH	Children's Day
Jun 6	TU	Dragon Boat Festival
Jul 1	SA	Founding of the Communist Party
Aug 1	TU	Birthday of the People's Liberation Army
Sep 10	SU	Teacher's Day
Sep 12	TU	Mid-Autumn Festival
Oct 1	SU	National Day
Oct 2	MO	National Day

Holidays with variable dates include the Chinese New Year, the Spring Festival, the Dragon Boat Festival, and the Mid-Autumn Festival. In Hong Kong, Easter (Good Friday through Easter Monday) and Christmas (including Boxing Day) were once recognized as official holidays, and some people may take off then.

There are many local holidays celebrated in different regions. Check with your contact to insure your appointments will not conflict with these festivities.

The official work week runs Monday through Friday, 40 hours per week. Many people work Saturdays as well.

The best times to schedule a business trip are from April to June or September to October.

Many Chinese take a break between noon and 2:00 P.M. During this time everything stops, including manually operated elevators and switchboards.

Religious/Societal Influences on Business

Foreigners often refer to the People's Republic of China as Mainland China, Communist China, or Red China. In the presence of Chinese, only the term People's Republic of China or the abbreviation PRC is acceptable. The national language of the PRC is Mandarin Chinese, a northern dialect of Chinese. (Note that most Chinese–Americans speak Cantonese, a southern dialect. The two dialects are not mutually intelligible.) Never confuse the PRC with the Republic of China (Taiwan), which the PRC considers a rogue province temporarily out of its sovereignty.

The Chinese are proud of their history and lineage. Historically, China (often called the Middle Kingdom) was a country ruled by strong dynasties. The first recorded dynasty was founded around 2200 B.C., and the last dynasty, the Ching (Manchu), ended in 1911. During this time, China produced some of the most important innovations in the history of the world, including the compass, papermaking, gunpowder, and movable-type printing.

While the PRC is nominally a Communist country (and still tightly ruled by its Communist government), capitalism is on the rise.

Harmony is prized by the Chinese. Every person is entitled to respect, which is spoken of in English as *having face*. Showing respect for someone causes them to *gain face*. Embarrassing them in public causes a *loss of face*—a very serious breach of etiquette. Criticizing or upbraiding someone in front of others causes that person to *lose face*. A person who loses his or her temper in public has shamefully *lost face*, and causes *loss of face* to the person at whom the anger is directed.

Another important aspect of Chinese culture is *guanxi* (gwon-shee). Literally translated as "relationships," *guanxi* is better described as "relationships which incur obligations." Such relationships are crucial for conducting business. *Guanxi* is the way a Chinese executive performs his duty for his associates, and maintains their obligations to him as well. These relationships are the way issues are resolved and deals consummated. Every foreigner aspiring to do business in China needs to develop *guanxi*.

China's humiliation by foreign powers in the nineteenth and early twentieth centuries is an embarrassing memory. All Chinese (Communists and capitalists alike) are adamant that it must never happen again. This is one reason that the PRC is so deaf to foreign demands over human rights—such demands are seen as foreign interference in China's sovereignty. Foreign executives should always be aware of the Chinese determination to oppose all aggressors.

Since the average Westerner is physically bigger than the average Chinese, Westerners need to be careful not to intimidate them. (It is difficult to establish trust with someone who looms over you.) Tall people should take every opportunity to minimize the height differential. Sit rather than stand. When you must stand, try to stand on a lower level, such as a lower step on a staircase.

5 Cultural Tips

1. Always carry plenty of business cards; a foreigner without a business card in China is a non-person. One side of your card should be in English, and the other side should have a translation in Mandarin Chinese. Gold ink is the most prestigious color for the Chinese side. Although red is considered a lucky color in China, do not print your name in red ink. (Some Buddhists only print the names of the deceased in red.) Accept cards graciously and treat them with respect. Do not put a business card in your wallet if you keep your wallet in your back pocket.

2. China is a hierarchical society. Confucianism assigns a rank to every individual in society. Deference to those of a higher level is expected. Status is acquired through age, job, marriage, and wealth. When entering a business meeting, the senior member of your group should lead the way. Often, the senior executives in a delegation do the talking; junior members do not interrupt and only speak when spoken to. The guest of honor at a banquet is the last to arrive and the first to leave.

3. Conducting business in China takes time. If you deal with the government, expect the bulk of your first meeting to be taken up with a ritual introductory speech. A PRC official will usually detail the most general information about China and the state of your industry. (This introductory speech is typically so basic as to be useless, but it is part of the ceremonial process of doing business.)

4. Despite official disapproval from the Communist government, traditional Chinese beliefs are still followed. This includes not only Confucianism but folk beliefs (such as astrology and geomancy) as well. Many Chinese will consult the stars for an auspicious day and hour before concluding a business deal.

5. Above all else, patience is required to do business in China. U.S. executives have a reputation for impatience, and the Chinese will typically drag out negotiations well beyond your deadlines just to gain an advantage. They may try to renegotiate everything on the final day of your visit! If possible, do not let them know your departure date.

Observation: "In a Western culture such as Australia and the United States, it is likely that efficient use of time and money are important criteria for success. Western cultures have a tendency to view wealth and power as essential to the solution of most problems. . . .

"In communication style, the Westerner has a tendency to be reasonably aggressive and direct (at times), impatient, self-assured, and to regard business as the topic of major importance in most of his or her interactions, attaching a lesser value to discussion of family and personal matters.

"Depending upon the Asian's specific cultural background, it is likely they will have a different values and communication framework. For them, speed and efficiency in their day-to-day activities may be perceived as irrelevant or perhaps even negative. Material possessions, competition, and winning may be regarded with far less concern than by Westerners, and they may view extended family relationships as their main source of power and status. The family, school, work unit and local community are the basic social structure that give stability to one's life. The democratic model, technology, progress, and Western development may be viewed with cynicism and suspicion. . . . Work and leisure may well be blended, and they may have little concern for systematic or efficient organization or specialization. In discussions, they may well be relatively passive, indirect, and patient, and they will very likely place a much higher priority on family and friends than upon business as a topic."

—Turlough F. Guerin, a contributing writer for the *Asia Pacific Economic Review*. From an article in the December 1998–January 1999 issue.

Economic Overview

To date, the People's Republic of China has not suffered the full brunt of the Asian financial crisis. While China can no longer boast of one of the fastest growing economies in the world, its economic policies seem to have achieved the archetypal "soft landing."

China's gross domestic product posted an impressive 10.5% growth in 1995. By 1996, GDP growth slipped to 9.7%; in 1997, GDP growth was 8.8% and 7.8% in 1998.

Overall, the Chinese are becoming more prosperous, and a true middle class is emerging. Inflation has been kept to single digits. Unemployment, however, is growing. Inefficient state-owned industries continue to operate, since the government fears the destabilizing effect of increased unemployment. There are also wide income disparities between urban and rural Chinese. Rural Chinese continue to migrate to the cities in search of higher incomes. They often fail to find steady employment, and end up increasing the ranks of the urban unemployed.

After a 20-year hiatus, trade between the United States and China resumed in 1972 and developed rapidly after normalization of diplomatic relations in 1979. Two-way trade increased from $2.3 billion in 1979 to $85 billion in 1998. However, U.S. trade with China has been in deficit since 1983, exceeding even the U.S.–Japan trade deficit.

China's political leadership, characterized by group consensus rather than strong leadership by a single individual, generally supports foreign trade and business investment in China, and agrees on the need for continued economic reforms and for political stability. In February 1995, the U.S. and China signed a major agreement on protection of intellectual property which improved the atmosphere for bilateral economic relations.

Apart from macro factors affecting doing business in China, China's current state-controlled economic structure continues to erect roadblocks to doing business in China. These include:

- limitations on the right of foreign companies to directly access China's retail market,
- foreign exchange controls,
- an inefficient banking system,
- insufficient enforcement of intellectual property laws,
- very restricted access for foreign services,
- and an inadequate system for dispute resolution.

After 20 years of reform and opening, the government's role in the economy remains strong—and will be for the foreseeable future. The central government, however, continues to lack sufficient resources to carry out its programs. At times, the government appears to be more willing to use the traditional tools of a planned economy rather than pushing forward with deeper reforms. This more cautious attitude toward market-oriented economic reform is apparent in the stronger emphasis on state planning in industrial policy. It is likely to persist for some time.

U.S. licensing requirements for most exports to China continue to relax. At the same time the U.S. has tightened its enforcement of regulations prohibiting any type of export to Chinese end-users involved in the proliferation of missiles or weapons of mass destruction. Disagreement over weapons proliferation, human rights, and the status of Taiwan could continue to affect bilateral relations.

Actions on both sides harmed U.S.–China relations in 1999. The U.S. discovered that nuclear weapons and other defense technology was stolen by Chinese agents. And U.S.-led NATO forces accidentally bombed the Chinese Embassy in Belgrade, Yugoslavia, prompting serious protests against U.S. consular offices in China. As a result, the U.S. issued a travel advisory against travel by U.S. citizens to China.

5 Largest Businesses in the People's Republic of China

China National Petroleum Group
    1,570,000 employees
China National Nonferrous Metals Industry Company of Beijing
    1,246,422 employees
Jiangsu Xiao Xiang Group Company, Ltd., of Changzhou
    900,000 employees
China North Industries Company of Beijing
    780,000 employees
AVIC (Aviation Industry General Corporation)
    560,000 employees

5 Largest Businesses in the HKSAR
(Hong Kong Special Administrative Region)

Wah Mei Fashion & Trading Company Ltd.
  275,215 employees
Jardine Matheson Holdings Ltd.
  200,000 employees
Jardine Strategic Holdings Ltd.
  130,000 employees
Ming Sang Plastic & Metal Manufactory Ltd.
  101,000 employees
HSBC Holdings Plc.
  100,000 employees

Cultural Note: Revolutionaries have often made linguistic and cultural changes to signify a break with the past. After taking control of mainland China in 1949, the Communist Chinese made changes in their language, both written and verbal.

Outside of the People's Republic of China, many Chinese have been slow to incorporate these changes. To this day, Taiwan primarily uses pre-Revolutionary forms of written and spoken Chinese. When you have your written materials translated for use in the PRC, make sure your translator uses the appropriate, "reformed" Chinese.

Comparative Data

Comparative Data Ratings
(Scale: 5 = Excellent; 1 = Poor)
China: 2.75

  A. GDP Growth: 4
  B. Per Capita Income: 1
  C. Trade Flows with the U.S.: 5
  D. Country Risk: 3
  E. Monetary Policy: 2
  F. Trade Policy: 2
     • Tariffs
     • Import Licensing
     • Import Taxes
  G. Protection of Property Rights: 2
  H. Foreign Investment Climate: 3

GROSS DOMESTIC PRODUCT: $4.42 trillion (1998 estimate)

GDP GROWTH: 7.8% (1998 estimate)

PER CAPITA INCOME: $3,600 (1998 estimate)

Trade Flows with the U.S.

U.S. EXPORTS TO CHINA: $14.3 billion (1998)

U.S. IMPORTS FROM CHINA: $71.2 billion

TOP U.S. EXPORTS TO CHINA: Machinery; aircraft; fertilizers; electrical components; cotton/yarn/fabric; medical and optical equipment; motor vehicles; organic chemicals; plastics and resins; cereals

TOP U.S. PROSPECTS FOR EXPORT TO CHINA: Aircraft and parts; electric power systems; computers and peripherals; telecommunications equipment; agricultural chemicals; automotive parts; industrial chemicals; plastic materials and resins; pollution-control equipment; machine tools

Country Risk

Dun & Bradstreet rates China as having sufficient capacity to meet outstanding payment liabilities. However, there is enough uncertainty over expected returns to warrant close monitoring of country risk.

Letter of credit terms account for almost 80% of trade transactions. More liberal terms such as open account are increasingly being used, but not recommended without prior knowledge of the China market. When open account terms are extended, 60- to 90-day terms are generally given.

The deterioration of U.S.–China relations in 1999 is cause for concern. China's apparent theft of vital U.S. defense secrets increased U.S. suspicions. The accidental May bombing of the Chinese Embassy in Belgrade (resulting in several deaths) outraged both the Chinese government and populace. For days after the bombing, U.S. citizens in China were harassed and threatened, and the U.S. Embassy was besieged by protesters. While some of the protests were organized by the Chinese government, the incident also demonstrated a degree of genuine anti-U.S. sentiment among many Chinese citizens.

Monetary Policy

Since the beginning of China's efforts to stabilize its economy in mid-1993, Chinese authorities have been reluctant to pursue tight macroeconomic policies that might lead to a sharp economic contraction. At the core of the government's monetary and fiscal problems remains the issue of state enterprise reforms. Despite the crippling financial costs of support for state-owned enterprises, there is little to suggest that the central government is prepared to risk the labor unrest that might follow any serious effort to tackle the problem.

Strong inflationary pressures will continue to bedevil the economy unless the government introduces vital reforms required to address financial imbalances in the economy.

MONETARY UNIT: yuan

Trade Policy

TARIFFS   Import tariff rates are divided into two categories: the general tariff and the minimum (most-favored nation) tariff. Imports from the U.S. are assessed as the minimum tariff rate since the U.S. has concluded an agreement with China containing reciprocal preferential tariff clauses.

China has gradually reduced tariffs on selected products, though the overall tariff levels are still very high. Tariffs range from 3% on promoted imports to more than 150% on discouraged imports such as automobiles. The average tariff is 17%.

Preferential duty reductions or exemptions may be offered to firms located in Special Economic Zones, open cities, and foreign trade zones.

By adopting the harmonized system for customs classification and statistics, China indicated its interest in bringing its tariff system into conformity with international standards.

IMPORT LICENSING   China administers a complex system of nontariff trade barriers, including individual quotas on imports of machinery, electronic equipment, and general goods like grain, fertilizer, textiles and chemicals. While China is in the process of eliminating a great number of import licensing requirements, licenses will continue to be required for items like rubber products, wool, passenger vehicles, and hauling trucks. China's import licensing system still acts as an effective import barrier to many imported goods.

Numerous categories of commodities are affected by quotas, including watches, automobiles, motorcycles, machinery, electronic items, and carbonated beverages.

Under a bilateral Memorandum of Understanding (MOU) on Market Access signed in 1992, China agreed to reduce trade barriers and gradually open its market to U.S. exports.

IMPORT TAXES   In addition to the assessment and collection of tariffs, a value-added tax generally equal to 17% is also collected on imported items. Certain imports are also subject to a consumption (excise) tax.

Protection of Intellectual Property Rights

The U.S. and China signed a Memorandum of Understanding on the Protection of Intellectual Property (IPR/MOU) in 1992, pursuant to which China improved its laws governing intellectual property rights protection over the following two years and joined the Berne and Geneva Phonograms Conventions. The March 1995 extension of the IPR/MOU set out a plan for enforcing IPR and granted market access to certain products. The U.S. and China agreed to an extension of the 1992 MOU in 1995, and China agreed to open the market to companies with intellectual property rights products and rigorously enforce Chinese IPR regulations.

COPYRIGHTS   China and the U.S. established bilateral copyright relations in March 1992, and China subsequently acceded to several international conventions. U.S. owners of computer software, books, films, sound recordings, and other subject matter now enjoy protection under China's copyright legislation, the Berne Convention, the Universal Copyright Convention, and the Geneva Phonogram Convention. Computer software programs will be protected for 50 years without mandatory registration requirements.

PATENTS   China's Patent Law, enacted in 1984, was extended in 1993 to protect chemical inventions. The period of patent protection was also lengthened to 20 years. China acceded to the Patent Cooperation Treaty in 1994 and will perform international patent searches and preliminary examinations of patent applications. Under the Patent Law, foreign parties must utilize the services of a registered Chinese agent to submit the patent application.

TRADEMARKS   Trademark registration in China should be an integral part of any company's initial market entry. This is critical since China is a first-to-register system that requires no evidence of prior use or ownership. However, well-known trademarks are to receive protection even if there is no prior registration in China. Although problems remain with enforcement, China's trademark regime basically conforms to world standards. In 1989, China joined the Madrid Pact for the Protection of Trademarks, which grants reciprocal trademark registration to member countries. China amended its laws in 1993 to add special regulations allowing criminal prosecution for trademark infringement. Foreign companies must utilize the services of registered agents to submit the trademark application. Registered trademarks are valid for a 10-year period and are renewable for further 10-year periods.

Foreign Investment Climate

Since 1978, China has actively sought foreign manufacturing investment and technology. The government seeks to attract foreign investment to poorer inland provinces and may increase incentives in inland areas.

In China's partially reformed command economy, numerous restrictions are placed on foreign ownership and the establishment of business enterprises. Large sectors of the Chinese economy—particularly in services and infrastructure—remain largely or completely closed to foreign investment. China has been gradually relaxing some restrictions on ownership and establishment. Since 1992, for example, new services sectors were opened on an experimental basis, including retailing, insurance, and tourism.

China is now also encouraging, on a limited basis, foreign investment in other previously closed sectors such as Chinese airlines, goldmines, roads, railroads, and harbors.

The 1994 Foreign Trade Law provides for extension of national treatment on a reciprocal basis to contracting parties of international treaties to which China is also a party. In practice, however, China's restrictive foreign trade and investment regulations deny foreign companies national treatment in all service and many industrial sectors. The U.S. is working bilaterally and with other World Trade Organization (WTO) parties to encourage China to grant unconditional national treatment as part of its accession to the WTO.

In those sectors where foreign investment is allowed, foreign-invested enterprises (FIEs) can be established as holding companies, wholly foreign-owned enterprises, equity joint ventures, cooperative joint ventures, or, since January 1995, foreign-invested companies limited by share. Under China's 1994 Company Law, foreign firms can also now open branches in China.

Potential investment projects usually go through a multitiered screening process. The first step is approval of the proposed project. The central government has delegated varying levels of approval authority to local governments. Formerly, only the Special Economic Zones of Shenzhen, Shantou, Zhuhai, Xiamen, and Hainan, and *open cities* could approve projects valued at up to $30 million. This approval authority has now been extended to many provincial capitals and coastal cities. The inland cities and regions are limited to approving projects valued below $10 million. Projects exceeding these limits are approved by the Ministry of Foreign Trade and Economic Cooperation (MOFTEC) and the State Planning Commission (SPC), for greenfield projects, or the State Economic and Trade Commission (SETC) for projects involving existing enterprises. If an investment involves $100 million or more, it must also obtain State Council approval, after MOFTEC's review and approval.

Political Leaders, Parties, and International Organizations

The International Academy at Santa Barbara at http://www.iasb.org/cwl publishes *Current World Leaders*, an excellent resource for up-to-date data on political leaders, parties, demographics, etc., in China. Tel: (800) 530-2682 or (805) 965-5010 for subscription information to their database.

Head of Government:
> President Jiang Zemin. President Jiang is also General Secretary of the Central Committee of the Chinese Communist Party.

Head of State:
> Premier Zhu Rongji

Next Election:
> March 2003

Membership in international organizations:
> ADB, APEC, International Committee of the Red Cross, IMCO, INTELSAT, PECC, UN and most of its specialized agencies and related organizations (including FAO, IAEA, IBRD, ICAO, IDA, IFAD, IFC, ILO, IMF, IMO, ITU, UNESCO, UNIDO, UPU, WHO, WIPO, WMO)

Political Parties:
> Chinese Communist Party (CCP); eight registered small parties controlled by the CCP.

Political Influences on Business

China's top political leaders continue their strong commitment to foreign business investment in China. But disagreements over human rights, proliferation, and trade issues continue to affect bilateral relations.

Rapid price inflation, corruption, layoffs from state-run enterprises, the growing gap between coastal regions and the interior, and economic disparities between rural and urban areas have contributed to dissatisfaction among the populace. Northwestern China has been troubled by occasional unrest among minority ethnic and religious groups. Dissatisfaction has not often been translated into widespread political activity since 1989, in part because the government is working to minimize tensions over its economic policies, but also because it has acted swiftly to repress any potential political protests.

In practice, major decisions are made by a few key leaders of the Chinese Communist Party. Ministries and/or the Standing Committee of the National People's Congress (China's legislature) formulate policy on day-to-day issues. Some provincial governments, especially those in fast-growing coastal regions, actively adopt local policy variations. Senior political figures generally agree on the need for further economic reforms and the need for political stability, but there are differences over the content, pace, and ending point of reforms. The death of 90-year-old Party elder Deng Xiaoping has marked a gradual adjustment in the PRC's leadership.

Faux Pas: Numbers can have significant impact on the Chinese psyche. When the number 4 is pronounced in Chinese, it suggests the word for "death." No Chinese would live or work at a building with an address of "444."

Contacts in the United States

THE EMBASSY OF THE PEOPLE'S REPUBLIC OF CHINA
2300 Connecticut Avenue, NW
Washington, D.C. 20008
Tel: (202) 328-2500 or 2520
Fax: (202) 232-7855
http://www.china-embassy.org

CHINA CHAMBER OF INTERNATIONAL COMMERCE
4301 Connecticut Avenue, NW, Suite 139
Washington, DC 20008
Tel: (202) 244-3244

Passport/Visa Requirements

Passport and visa required.

For visitors/business F visa: A formal invitation/authorization letter or fax for visa processing is required from competent Chinese authorities or institutions, i.e., state commissions, ministries, provincial governments or government-authorized Chinese companies, corporations or institutions, etc., and a cover letter from your company.

Note that the validity of a single- or a double-entry visa is 1–3 months from the date of visa issuance; the passport should be valid for over six months and with blank visa pages. For double- or multiple-entry, within 3–6 months, the validity of the passport must be over 9 months; for one-year multiple-entry visa, the validity of the passport must be over 15 months, both with blank visa pages. Apply for visa one month before departure to avoid expiration of the visa.

For current information concerning entry and customs requirements for China, travelers can contact the Chinese Embassy.

U.S. citizens who wish to apply for a passport may visit Passport Services' well-organized website at http://travel.state.gov/passport_services.html

Contacts in China

THE EMBASSY OF THE UNITED STATES
OF AMERICA
Xiu Shui Bei Jie 3
Bieijing, PRC or
100600, PSC 461, Box 50,
Beijing
Mailing Address: FPO AP 96521-0002
Tel: (86) (10) 6532-3831
Fax: (86) (10) 6532-6422
usembassy-china.org.cn/

AMERICAN CHAMBER OF COMMERCE
Great Wall Sheraton Hotel
Room 318

NORTH DONGHUAN AVENUE
Beijing 100026
PRC
Tel: (86-10) 6500-5566, ext. 2378/2379
Fax: (86-10) 6501-8273
Email: amcham@public.bta.net.cn
(There are also offices in Guangdong
and Shanghai)

DUN & BRADSTREET INTERNATIONAL
CONSULTANT (SHANGHAI) LTD.
Unit 907-910A
Pidemeo Tower
318 Fu Zhou Road
Shanghai, 200001, P.R. China
Tel: + 86 21.6384.4636

PRESIDENT JIANG ZEMIN
Office of the President
Zhonganahai
Beijing, People's Republic of China

PREMIER ZHU RONGJI
Office of the Premier
Zhonganahai
Beijing, People's Republic of China

Further contacts and websites can be found in Appendix A.

Communications

TELEPHONE: The country code for the People's Republic of China is 86.

Chinese telephone numbers vary in length. When calling outside a local area, city codes are necessary. Beijing's city code is 1 (this is the only one-digit city code). Major cities have two-digit codes. Rural areas have three or even four digits.

The country code for Hong Kong is 852.

Current Hong Kong phone numbers are eight digits long, replacing older seven-digit ones. When given a seven-digit number which no longer works, try prefixing it with the number 2.

MAIL: The official language of the PRC is Mandarin Chinese, also called Standard Chinese. Chinese is written in a complex ideographical script, using thousands of characters. Although Chinese characters were traditionally written up and down in columns that were often read from right to left, the PRC has adopted the western format for envelopes. Consequently, envelopes are addressed horizontally and read left to right.

Letters may be addressed in either Chinese or English, using the Pinyin system of transliteration. Letters to the PRC may be addressed, in English, as follows: (*Notes in parentheses*)

Title & Name:	Chen Jianjie, Director of the Foreign Affairs Office (*Titles are important.*)
Company:	Agriculture Bank of China (*English abbreviations such as Ltd. are often used.*)
Street:	40 Fucheng Lu (*"Dajie," "Jie," and "Lu" are all terms for large streets, so "Fucheng Lu" means "Fucheng Street." Yuan is the term for square. When transliterated into English, all of these terms may become suffixes attached to the name of the street.*)
Additional Data:	Yulong Hotel 3/F #3008 (*Notable buildings are often named. 3/F = Third Floor, and #3008 would be the room number.*)
City and Postal Code:	BEIJING 100046 (*Chinese postcodes are 6-digit numbers.*)
Country:	People's Republic of China (*This may be abbreviated as PRC.*)

E-MAIL: E-mail addresses located in the People's Republic of China end with the code .cn

E-mail addresses located in Hong Kong end with the code .hk

DATES: In the PRC, the date is written in this order: year, month, day (which is very different from the U.S. practice of writing month, day, year). When written in English, the dates are usually separated by backslashes (00/10/11 indicates November 10, 2000). Although the Chinese have an ancient, traditional calendar, the PRC mandates the use of the Western (Gregorian) calendar for official purposes.

In Hong Kong, the date has traditionally been written in this order: day, month, year—the opposite of the practice in the PRC. When written in English, the dates are usually separated by backslashes (10/11/00 indicates November 10, 2000). Since Hong Kong has been returned to China, this practice may be dropped in favor of the PRC's format.

Eating in China

Food is extremely important in China. There are few better ways for a foreigner to ingratiate him- or herself than to express interest in the fine points of Chinese cuisine.

In addition to several business lunches, all business transactions require at least one evening banquet. In fact, there should be at least two banquets: the first one given by the host Chinese, the second one by you. It is vital for you to give a banquet in return for one given by your hosts. (Reciprocity is the way networks are built in China.)

1. Banquets range in size and price. Your banquet should appear to cost the same, per person, as the banquet given by your Chinese host. (Actually, as a foreigner without connections, you will probably pay more for the same banquet.) Never surpass your host in the degree of lavishness at your banquet—such one-upmanship will cause your host to lose face.

2. Most banquets start between 6:30 and 7:00 P.M. and last for about two hours. You should arrive about 30 minutes before your guests—they will arrive on time. Be prepared to sample every dish. The Chinese may even test your fortitude on purpose with exotic delicacies like marinated, deep-fried scorpions (intact with stingers) on a bed of rice.

3. The Chinese use chopsticks rather than a fork. Since the use of chopsticks takes time to learn, it is useful to practice this skill in advance. In fact, dropping your chopsticks is considered bad luck. Chinese chopsticks are generally both heavier and thicker than the chopsticks used in Japan. Chopsticks are called *kuaitzu*, a word that also means *hurry*. Most Chinese can eat very hurriedly indeed with chopsticks.

4. The Chinese also use a curved porcelain spoon. This is generally reserved for soup. However, when eating rice out of a small bowl, it is permissible to use the spoon *if one has added something to the rice* (say, meat or vegetables). But pure rice is eaten just with chopsticks—a task most Westerners find quite difficult to manage without spilling a lot of rice. Hold the rice bowl close to your mouth; this will catch some of the rice you drop. Fortunately, rice is traditionally served at the end of a meal. Since you want to display that you have eaten your fill, you will leave part of your last course uneaten.

5. A fine Chinese restaurant will provide a chopstick rest on which you may place your chopsticks. Traditionally, placing them parallel on top of your bowl was considered a sign of bad luck. Sticking your chopsticks straight up in your rice bowl was also frowned upon, since they then resembled the joss sticks used in religious ceremonies. But these traditions are no longer universally observed, especially in restaurants.

6. There is one other skill to learn with chopsticks: reversing them to use them as serving tongs. But again, a fine Chinese restaurant will provide a serving spoon with each dish, making this skill unnecessary.

7. Frequent toasts will be offered at a banquet. The host gives the first toast, and the ceremony continues all evening. It is acceptable to toast with a soft drink.

8. Never take the last bit of food from a serving dish. To do so would signify that you are still hungry.

9. The serving of fruit signals the end of the meal.

10. Where everyone sits has great significance in China. This is the traditional seating at a round Chinese table:

GUEST of HONOR (RANKED #1)

#2 RANKED PERSON   *#3 RANKED PERSON*

#4 RANKED PERSON   *#5 RANKED PERSON*

HOST
[DOOR]

The host will sit closest to the door, so that he or she may direct the waiters as they come in and out. Interestingly, this seating pattern results in the least-important people sitting next to the host.

Colombia

Official Name:	Republic of Colombia (República de Colombia)
Official Language:	Spanish
Government System:	Unitary multi-party republic
Population:	39.3 million (1999 estimate)
Population Growth Rate:	1.85% (1999 estimate)
Area:	1.14 million sq. km. (440,000 sq. mi.); about the size of Texas, New Mexico, and Arkansas combined
Natural Resources:	petroleum, natural gas, coal, iron ore, nickel, gold, copper, emeralds
Major Cities:	Bogotá (capital), Cali, Medellin, Barranquilla, Cartagena

Cultural Note: Colombia's rugged terrain has made it difficult for a strong central government to control the country. Colombia does have a tradition of democracy, but its governments have ranged from weak to ineffectual. It remains to be seen if that trend is being reversed. But the assassination of reformist candidates—usually narco-terrorists—makes the reform process more difficult.

Age Breakdown

0–14 = 33%   15–64 = 62%   65+ = 5% (1999 estimate)
Life Expectancy: 66.54 years, male; 74.54 years, female (1999 estimate)

Time

Foreign executives are expected to be prompt to all business appointments.

Colombians do not interpret time so literally as do North Americans. To most Colombians, they have arrived promptly to a meeting if they are within 15 or 20 minutes of the scheduled time. Do not expect an apology if your Colombian counterpart is 20 minutes late; the Colombian considers him- or herself to be on time.

Everyone is expected to arrive late to a social engagement. Foreigners should arrive between 15 and 30 minutes late. Colombians may be a full hour late to a dinner or party.

Deadlines are similarly flexible in Colombia. Continued contact with a Colombian firm is necessary to insure completion on time—as well as reminders as to why it is important that the deadline is met. Before going to pick up an item, don't trust assurances that it is completed. Ask also if now is a good time to pick up the item. Something that a Colombian considers "essentially completed" may not actually be ready for pickup.

Colombia is 5 hours behind Greenwich Mean Time (GMT -5), which is the same as U.S. Eastern Standard Time.

Holidays

An up-to-date, web-based *World Holiday and Time Zone Guide* is available at www.getcustoms.com. It lists official holidays by country and by day of the year, cultural tips, a corruption index, and time zones with worldwide business hours.

This list is a working guide. Dates should be corroborated before final travel plans are made. In cases where holidays fall on Saturday or Sunday, commercial establishments may be closed the preceding Friday or following Monday.

Jan 1	SA	New Year's Day
Jan 10	MO	Epiphany
Mar 20	MO	St. Joseph's Day
Apr 20	TH	Holy Thursday
Apr 21	FR	Good Friday
May 1	MO	Labor Day
Jun 5	MO	Ascension
Jun 26	MO	Corpus Christi
Jul 3	MO	Sacred Heart of Jesus
Jul 3	MO	Sts. Peter and Paul
Jul 20	TH	Independence Day
Aug 7	MO	Battle of Boyaca
Aug 21	MO	Assumption
Oct 16	MO	Columbus Day
Nov 13	MO	Independence of Cartegena
Dec 8	FR	Immaculate Conception
Dec 25	MO	Christmas Day

Local holidays may be observed in addition to those listed above.

The following Catholic feast days are observed as official holidays on varying dates each year in Colombia: the Epiphany, Saint Joseph's Day, Holy Thursday, Good Friday, Easter, the Ascension, Corpus Christi, Feast of the Sacred Heart of Jesus, Feast of Saints Peter and Paul, the Assumption, and All Saints' Day. These observances are usually held on Mondays to create three-day weekends.

The following secular celebrations are also observed on different dates each year: Columbus Day and the Independence of Cartagena. These observances are also usually held on Mondays.

Again, the days of observance should always be corroborated by local contacts.

Work Week

- Business hours are 9:00 A.M. to 5:00 P.M. Monday through Friday.
- Store hours vary, but are generally from 9:00 A.M. to 12:30 P.M., and then from 2:00 P.M. to 7:00 P.M. Monday through Saturday.
- Banking hours are from 9:00 A.M. to 3:00 P.M. Monday through Thursday, and until 3:30 on Friday.

Note: Unless you are traveling to the coastal lowlands, it is best to arrive a day early so you can adjust to the high altitude. This is especially true in the capital, Bogotá, which is 8,600 feet (2,600 meters) above sea level.

Religious/Societal Influences on Business

There is no official religion in Colombia, but the majority of people belong to the Roman Catholic Church. Most Colombians would cite their families and the Church (in that order) as the most important influences on their lives.

Social pressure is intense. "¿Que dirán?" ("What will people say?") is a question asked frequently in Colombian families whenever propriety is threatened. Appearances must be kept up, which includes wearing fashionable clothes. In order to be respected, foreigners also must have a refined wardrobe.

Colombians have strong traditions of hospitality. Foreign visitors usually find Colombian executives to be friendly, well-educated, and familiar with North American business practices. Many upper-class Colombians study in the United States.

The greatest strains on Colombia's relationship with the U.S. came over the extradition issue. The fight against extradition was supported by the drug traffickers—the late drug kingpin Pablo Escobar donated millions to his anti-extradition lobbying organization called *Los Extraditables*, which boasted the slogan "Better a grave in Colombia than a jail in the United States." But there was also genuine sentiment among Colombians against being dictated to by the United States. Colombians have not forgotten past U.S. intervention in their internal affairs, most notably over Panama. (In 1903, the U.S. recognized the breakaway Colombian province of Panama as an independent nation, so that the U.S. could build the Panama Canal.)

5 Cultural Tips

1. Regional differences are pronounced in Colombia. Expect a high level of formality in the interior, especially Bogotá. The coastal areas are far more relaxed. This is seen most clearly in the coastal preference for tú (the informal form of the pronoun *you* in Spanish) rather than the formal *usted*.

2. Greetings are very important in Colombia. Take the time to greet everyone formally. Give each person your undivided attention (sequentially). Businessmen shake hands with both men and women. Businesswomen usually shake hands with men; with other women, they may instead clasp each other's forearms. Friends are expected to hug and exchange kisses on the cheeks. When men hug each other, they often add a backslap or two.

3. Class consciousness is part of everyday life in Colombia. You must appear to be of the same level in society as your Colombian counterpart. Menial duties are delegated to others; the "hands-on-manager" is not part of local tradition. Most upper-class Colombians consider manual labor to be demeaning. Avoid any activity that would lower you in the eyes of Colombians.

4. As is common in class-conscious societies, many Colombians accept the basic inequality of their system as inevitable. A few people are rich and most people are poor; that is the way things are. Colombians find it puzzling when North Americans get upset over the plight of the poor.

5. Colombians are adaptable. They seem to have the ability to deal with any problem, no matter how disastrous. From earthquakes to terrorist bombings, they carry on. A foreigner who overreacts to a minor inconvenience will be treated with amusement or scorn. Colombians take care of themselves, and they do not depend on their government to do it for them.

Observation: ". . . Colombians attribute status to various types of work and resist doing work which they consider below their status. A foreigner who does manual labor may lose status in the eyes of Colombians. This is in sharp contrast to the gain in respect one merits in North America for being willing to 'get your hands dirty.' Similarly, planning and designing are considered high status jobs, while implementing the plans in all their detail connotes lower status."

— *Living in Colombia: A Guide for Foreigners* by Hutchison and Poznanski

---

Economic Overview

Colombia's long history of democratic governments, along with its steadily expanding economy, has made it one of Latin America's most attractive and stable markets for U.S. business. At the same time, the country has had to combat its international image as a narcotics producer, money launderer, human rights violator, and a place where street crime in the cities, guerrilla activity in the countryside, and violence often go unchecked.

Conscious of its need to improve its image, Colombia has worked to promote regional integration and security through active participation in regional and international organizations, and to reform its judicial and other institutions in an effort to stem the illicit drug trade.

Business links between Colombia and the U.S. are well-established. The United States is Colombia's main trading partner, supplying approximately 40% of Colombia's imports.

The U.S. also holds the largest share of direct foreign investment in Colombia—some 44% of total foreign direct investment. U.S. investment is diversified, covering the automotive, banking, chemical, communications, food, manufacturing, metal, paper, and pharmaceutical industries.

The Colombian economy has changed dramatically since the launching of the program of economic liberalization known as *apertura*, spearheaded by former President Cesar Gaviria. With the loosening of import and other controls and the privatization of many state-owned enterprises has come economic expansion, new domestic and foreign investment, and growing links with the U.S.

Colombia's rich energy and mineral resources and the improvement it is undertaking in infrastructure have attracted substantial new U.S. investment in recent years. The country should continue to draw U.S. capital and technology as the government adjusts its tax and regulatory regime, particularly in the oil and gas sector, and moves forward on privatization in the transport, utility, and telecommunications sectors.

4 Largest Businesses in Colombia

Caja de Credito Agrario Industrial y Minero, Santa Fe de Bogotá
    3,500 employees
Empresa Colombiana de Petroleos, Santa Fe de Bogotá
    11,000 employees
Almacenes Exito SA, Envigado
    8,500 employees
Gran Cadena de Almacenes Colombianos SA, Medellin
    7,425 employees

Cultural Note: Colombia's terrorist groups can cause serious problems for foreign businesses and their personnel. Most often, this occurs when they bomb oil pipelines and power or telephone networks. The far-left terrorist groups known as the *Revolutionary Armed Forces of Colombia (FARC)* and the *National Liberation Army (ELN)* remain active, although the *M-19* group has disbanded. Violent death in Colombia is roughly eight times as high as in the United States.

Kidnapping of business executives also continues, and foreign executives should consider themselves at risk. Never assume that you are safe because your company is small or your position is unimportant—criminals have frequently kidnapped the wrong people. Kidnap and ransom insurance is recommended; such policies not only pay ransom but the cost of security consultants to handle negotiations and the kidnap victim's loss of income. As the country with the most kidnappings in the world, insurance premiums Colombia are the most expensive.

Comparative Data

Comparative Data Ratings
(Scale: 5 = Excellent; 1 = Poor)
Colombia: 2.75

- A. GDP Growth: 2
- B. Per Capita Income: 2
- C. Trade Flows with the U.S.: 3
- D. Country Risk: 3
- E. Monetary Policy: 3
- F. Trade Policy: 3
  - Tariffs
  - Import Licensing
  - Import Taxes
- G. Protection of Property Rights: 3
- H. Foreign Investment Climate: 3

GROSS DOMESTIC PRODUCT: $254.7 billion (1998 estimate)

GDP GROWTH: 0.2% (1998 estimate)

PER CAPITA INCOME: $6,600 (1998 estimate)

Trade Flows with the U.S.

U.S. EXPORTS TO COLOMBIA: $4.8 billion (1998)

U.S. IMPORTS FROM COLOMBIA: $4.7 billion (1998)

TOP U.S. EXPORTS TO COLOMBIA: Machinery; electrical components; motor vehicles; organic chemicals; aircraft and parts; plastics; medical and optical equipment; cereals; woven apparel; paper

TOP U.S. PROSPECTS FOR EXPORT TO COLOMBIA: Telecommunications equipment and services; electrical power systems; oil and gas field machinery and equipment; computers and peripherals; automotive parts and accessories; financial services; plastic materials and resins; travel and tourism; construction and mining equipment; food processing and packaging; apparel; medical equipment

Country Risk

Dun & Bradstreet rates Colombia as having significant uncertainty over expected returns. In 1999, the prospects for economic recovery remained downbeat. A letter of credit is recommended. When open account terms are used, 60 to 90 days are the usual terms.

Monetary Policy

The government's goal of reducing inflation has been thwarted by continued public spending on the national economic development plan, by wage settlements that have been above the government's guidelines, and by high interest rates. Inflation was at 21.6% in 1996, 17.7% in 1997, and 16.7% in 1998.

MONETARY UNIT: Colombian peso

Trade Policy

TARIFFS   Colombia has initiated a tariff reduction program, lowering tariffs to a trade-weighted average of 12%, including duty-free entry for approximately 40% of tariff items. Colombia has a five-tier tariff system of 1, 5, 10, 15, and 20%.

Colombia has levied a surcharge of approximately US$1 per barrel on oil produced by foreign oil companies, but this is due to be phased out by December 31, 2000.

IMPORT LICENSING   Imports must be registered with the Colombian Foreign Trade Institute.

The Ministry of Agriculture must approve import licenses for products that could compete with domestically produced commodities including malting barley, wheat, palm oil, and sorghum.

The prohibited import list has been eliminated except for explosives and related raw materials and firearms.

IMPORT TAXES   Most imports are subject to a 15% value-added tax (VAT). Some exceptions apply as in the case of imported vehicles for which there is a 35% sales tax.

A few products (primarily food items, health care products, and some medicines) are exempt from the payment of the VAT.

Protection of Intellectual Property Rights

Colombia is an Andean Pact country, which means that key aspects of its intellectual property laws are prescribed to by treaty with other Andean Pact countries. Colombia also belongs to the Paris Convention for the Protection of Intellectual Property, the Berne Convention for the Protection of Literary and Artistic Works, the Universal Copyright Convention, the Inter-American Convention on the Rights of Authors, the Inter-American Agreement for Trademark and Commercial Protection, and the Marrakesh Agreement on Trade-related Aspects of Intellectual Property Rights.

Patents require novelty, inventiveness, and commercial application. The term of patent is 20 years from filing with a 10-year term for utility models. Medicines are non-patentable. Patent licenses must be in writing. Industrial designs are registered for 8 years and the law also protects trade secrets.

Trademark rights result from registration. Both trademarks and trade names are registerable. The term of trademark is 10 years and is renewable if use is shown in any Andean Group country within six months of the date of expiration.

Scientific, literary, and artistic works are copyrighted for the life of the author plus 80 years. Letters belong to the addressee, but the copyright belongs to the sender. Letters written by a deceased person cannot be published until 80 years after the person's death without the consent of the surviving spouse. Computer software is protected for 50 years.

Colombia has been on the U.S. government's Section 301 Priority Watch list for several years.

Foreign Investment Climate

Foreign investment policies are guided by two principles: equality (by which foreign and national investments receive the same legal and administrative treatment) and openness (meaning that few restrictions are applied regarding the amount of foreign investment or its destination).

Foreign investors are granted national treatment and are permitted 100% foreign ownership in virtually all sectors of the Colombian economy. Exceptions include national security, the disposal of hazardous waste products, and ownership of real estate and some real estate holding arrangements.

Liberalization of services has occurred in some sectors since 1991, especially in telecommunications, financial services, tourism, and television broadcasting.

All foreign investment in petroleum exploration and development in Colombia must be carried out by an association contract between the foreign investor and ECOPETROL, the state oil company.

Generally, foreign investors are allowed to participate in privatization efforts without restrictions. Colombia does not impose any investment restrictions on foreign investments that it does not impose on national investors. However, some investors may find the provisions of the Colombian law burdensome. For example, many investments require a commercial presence in-country.

Due in part to privatization, unemployment has been on the rise in Colombia, reaching almost 13% in 1997. In some manufacturing sectors, 80% of the labor must be Colombian citizens.

Political Leaders, Parties, and International Organizations

The International Academy at Santa Barbara at http://www.iasb.org/cwl publishes *Current World Leaders,* an excellent resource for up-to-date data on political leaders, parties, demographics, etc., in Colombia. Tel: (800) 530-2682 or (805) 965-5010 for subscription information to their database.

Head of State and of the Government:

President Andrés Pastrana Arango

Next Election:

May 2002

Political Parties:

Conservative Party, Liberal Party, Socialist Workers' Party, Patriotic Union Party (UP)

Membership in international organizations:

AG, G77, IADB, ICO, INTELSAT, LAIA, NAM, OAS, PAHO, SELA, UN and all of its specialized agencies and related organizations (including FAO, GATT, IAEA, IBRD, ICAO, IDA, IFAD, IFC, ILO, IMF, IMO, ITU, UNCTAD, UNESCO, UNIDO, UPU, WHO, WIPO, WMO)

Political Influences on Business

The foreign policy of the government of Colombia has focused on enhancing Colombia's image as a responsible global and regional player. In pursuing this overall strategy, Colombia has concentrated its resources in three major areas: regional integration and security, economic growth, and counternarcotics. In developing pragmatic means to further these interests, the government of Colombia has pursued a foreign policy that in some areas parallels that of the U.S.

To promote regional integration and security, the government of Colombia has taken an active part in regional and international organizations such as the Rio Group, the APEC, CARICOM, the OAS, and the UN and its specialized agencies, and has developed close bilateral relation with its neighbors, the EU, and the U.S. In international organizations, Colombia has taken an active role in seeking to limit the illegal transfer of arms and stop international narcotics trafficking.

In the area of trade, Colombia's foreign policy has created lasting effects for Colombian citizens. Former President Ernesto Samper, who led Colombia from 1994 to 1998, slowed the economic liberalization policy (known as *apertura*) of his predecessors. His successor, Andrés Pastrana Arango, is primarily concerned with achieving peace among Colombia's armed factions, and seems unlikely to press for economic reforms or privatization.

Conscious of its international image as a narcotics-producing country and a human rights violator, Colombia has implemented some reforms in the judiciary, police, and military designed to improve the situation. The Colombian Government ratified the UN Convention Against Illicit Traffic in Narcotic Drugs and Psychotropic Substances in 1993 (the Constitutional Court upheld the ratification in a 1994 decision) and the

Second Protocol to the Geneva Conventions regarding human rights safeguards in internal civil conflicts in 1994 (the Constitutional Court upheld the ratification in a 1995 decision).

The all-encompassing issue of narcotics will continue to affect nearly all aspects of Colombia's political and economic environment. Narcotrafficking has had a negative effect on Colombian society, with several congresspersons and politicians under investigation for illegal enrichment and/or other forms of corruption linked to the illicit drug trade. In addition to narcotraffickers, the high crime rate and guerrilla terrorism in Colombia adversely affect the business climate.

Notwithstanding Colombia's commitment to democratic institutions, its history has been plagued by violence. This situation has been exacerbated by the government's lack of a permanent presence in vast rural zones of the country. Guerrilla bands and narcotraffickers often have filled the resulting vacuum by establishing their own presence in these areas. At this writing, over one-third of Colombia is under the de facto control of a guerilla group, the Revolutionary Armed Forces of Colombia (FARC).

Contacts in the United States

THE EMBASSY OF THE REPUBLIC OF COLOMBIA
2118 Leroy Place, NW
Washington, D.C. 20008
Tel: (202) 387-8338
Fax:(202) 232-8643
www.colombiaemb.org

Passport/Visa Requirements

A passport and a return/onward ticket are required for stays up to three months. For current information concerning entry and customs requirements for Colombia, travelers can contact the Colombian Embassy.

U.S. citizens who wish to apply for a passport may visit Passport Services' well-organized website at http://travel.state.gov/passport_services.html.

Contacts in Colombia

THE EMBASSY OF THE UNITED STATES
Calle 22D-BIS, No.47-51, Apto. Aereo 3831
Bogotá
Mailing Address: APO AA 34038
Tel: (57) (1) 315-0811
Fax: (57) (1) 315-2197
www.usembassy.state.gov/posts/co1

COLOMBIAN–AMERICAN CHAMBER OF COMMERCE
Apto. Aereo 8008, Calle 35, No.6-16
Bogotá
Tel: (57) (1) 285-7800
Fax: (57) (1) 288-6434

Further contacts and websites can be found in Appendix A.

Communications

TELEPHONE: The country code for Colombia is 57.

E-MAIL: E-mail addresses located in Colombia end with the code .co

---

Faux Pas: Be careful when you measure height in Colombia! Colombians only measure *animals* by holding one hand *horizontally*, as if they were resting the hand on top of the animal's head. The height of a *person* is indicated by holding the hand *vertically* (palm out, thumb on top), as if it were resting on the *back* of the person's head. To describe someone's height by holding a hand horizontally is tantamount to calling that person an animal.

Costa Rica

Official Name:	Republic of Costa Rica (República de Costa Rica)
Official Language:	Spanish
Government System:	Unitary multi-party republic
Population:	3.67 million (1999 estimate)
Population Growth Rate:	1.89% (1999 estimate)
Area:	51,032 sq. km. (19,652 sq. mi.); slightly smaller than West Virginia
Natural Resources:	hydropower potential
Major Cities:	San José (capital), Alajuela, Cartago, Heredia, Limón, Puntarenas

Cultural Note: Because of its stability and tradition of democracy, Costa Rica (the name means *Rich Coast*) has long been known as the "Switzerland of Central America." The Costa Ricans (who call themselves *ticos*) are proud of their peaceful traditions. Costa Rica does not even have an army.

Age Breakdown

0–14 = 33%   15–64 = 62%   65+ = 5% (1999 estimate)
Life Expectancy: 73.6 years, male; 78.61 years, female (1999 estimate)

Time

Costa Ricans are generally the most punctual people in Central America. Foreigners are expected to be on time to all business appointments.

Costa Rica is 6 hours behind Greenwich Mean Time (GMT -6), which is 1 hour behind U.S. Eastern Standard Time (EST -1).

Holidays

An up-to-date, web-based *World Holiday and Time Zone Guide* is available at www.getcustoms.com. It lists official holidays by country and by day of the year, cultural tips, a corruption index, and time zones with worldwide business hours.

This list is a working guide. Dates should be corroborated before final travel plans are made. In cases where holidays fall on Saturday or Sunday, commercial establishments may be closed the preceding Friday or following Monday.

Jan 1	SA	New Year's Day
Apr 11	TU	National Heroes Day
Apr 20	TH	Holy Thursday
Apr 21	FR	Good Friday
May 1	MO	Labor Day
Jul 25	TU	Annexation of Guanacaste
Aug 2	WE	Our Lady of the Angels
Aug 15	TU	Assumption/Mother's Day
Sep 15	FR	Independence Day
Oct 12	TH	Columbus Day
Dec 25	MO	Christmas Day

The following Catholic feast days are observed as official holidays on varying dates each year in Costa Rica: Saint Joseph's Day, Holy Thursday, Good Friday, Easter, and the Feast of Saints Peter and Paul.

Local holidays may be observed in addition to those listed above.

Work Week

- Business hours are 8:00 A.M. to 5:00 P.M. Monday through Friday, and 8:00 to 11:00 A.M. Saturday. Businesses close for lunch from 11:00 A.M. to 1:00 P.M. daily.
- Government offices are open 8:00 A.M. to 4:00 P.M. Monday through Friday.
- Banks are open 9:00 A.M. to 3:00 P.M. Monday through Friday.
- Good times to do business in Costa Rica are February to March and September to November. The rainy season runs May through November (with rain heaviest on the Caribbean coast). Popular vacation times are December and January, and around Christmas and Easter holidays.

Religious/Societal Influences on Business

Roman Catholicism is the official religion of Coast Rica, but various Protestant groups have been making headway. A full 15% of the population follows an Evangelical Christian sect. Despite these inroads, the Catholic Church remains the most powerful organization (after the government) in Costa Rica.

Unlike other Latin American countries, race is not an issue in Costa Rica. Almost 97% of the population is European or *mestizo*, with virtually no difference between the two. Costa Rica's population is the lightest in color of any Central American nation. There are a miniscule number of African–Caribbeans, concentrated around the Atlantic port of Limón.

Although Costa Rica is not divided by race, class distinctions are important. Costa Rica had 44 Presidents between the years of 1821 and 1970, and 33 of those Presidents were descended from *three* of Costa Rica's original settlers! Despite the presence of this ruling oligarchy, Costa Rica has a larger middle class than many Latin American nations. Costa Rica cherishes its reputation as an egalitarian society of small independent farmers.

Costa Rica is pro-business and pro-United States. International trade is officially encouraged, promoted with the "Exportar es Bueno" ("It's Good to Export") campaign.

5 Cultural Tips

1. Costa Ricans have much to be proud of: their accomplishments, their egalitarian society, their growing interest in protecting the environment, and their history of stable government in turbulent Central America. As a result, Costa Ricans often consider themselves superior to their neighbors. (Many North Americans agree that Costa Rica is the best-run nation in the region.) Costa Ricans can be insulted if they are mistaken for Nicaraguans or Panamanians.

2. Costa Ricans tend towards more formality than their Central American neighbors. Styles of dress are conservative; for example, only foreigners wear shorts away from the beach. The public use of obscenity found in Nicaragua is rare in Costa Rica. Whereas most Latin Americans refer to citizens of the U.S. as *yanquis* or *norteamericanos*, some Costa Ricans prefer the more precise *estadounidense*—an adjective derived from *Estados Unidos de America*, Spanish for "United States of America." (Costa Ricans call themselves *ticos*.)

3. U.S. products sell well. Costa Ricans often feel isolated from their less-developed Central American neighbors, and feel comfortable associating themselves with the developed world.

4. Costa Rican manners tend to be "less Latin" than elsewhere in Central America. Men in Costa Rica greet each other with handshakes, not the back-thumping hug called an *abrazo*.

5. Even though almost all Costa Rican executives speak English (it seems to be a virtual second language), always translate your written material into Spanish.

Economic Overview

Costa Rica depends heavily on both agricultural and industrial imports. Although progress has been made in liberalizing its economy, promoting its domestic industry and enhancing its role as a global trading partner via bilateral and multilateral agreements, the strong role of state monopolies and the recent fiscal crisis are also significant factors in the economy.

While Costa Rica's industrial base is growing, it is still an agriculturally based economy where 47% of its economic base is food-related. However, in 1993 tourism surpassed banana exports as the nation's largest income producer. In the past few years, Costa Rica's economy has experienced modest growth after emerging from recession in 1997.

Costa Rica's commercial environment is user-friendly with widespread national receptivity to U.S. products and services. The bilateral relationship between the U.S. and Costa Rica has traditionally been and continues to be excellent. With the exception of the country's monopolies on some critical services (which include telecommunications, electricity, insurance, petroleum refining, banking services, etc.), and deficiencies in the intellectual property regime, there are no trade barriers that affect the importation of most goods to Costa Rica.

Due to its perennial spring climate, stability, and hospitable atmosphere, the country has attracted some 30,000 U.S. expatriates as well as immigrants from such countries as Spain, Israel, Germany, China, and Japan, all of whom play a role in creating competition for U.S. products and services.

Costa Rica has been the beneficiary of substantial foreign investment from the U.S., Japan, Germany, Spain, and Korea. Textile and electronic component *maquilas*, located in most cases in attractive free-trade zones, employ more than 70,000 Costa Ricans.

5 Largest Businesses in Costa Rica

Instituto Costarricense de Electricidad, San José
   10,800 employees
Corporation Mas por Menos S.A., San José
   6,500 employees
Banco Nacional de Costa Rica, San José
   3,800 employees
Instituto Costarricense de Acueductos y Alcantarillados, San José
   2,800 employees
Cooperativa de Productores de Leche R.L., San José
   2,400 employees

Cultural Note: Costa Rica is often promoted as a tropical paradise. Although the Costa Rican environment is still threatened, eco-tourism is encouraging protection of the rain forest. But a growing number of landless peasants (who are demanding land to farm) oppose the expansion of national parks.

Comparative Data

Comparative Data Ratings
(Scale: 5 = Excellent; 1 = Poor)
Costa Rica: 2.75

A. GDP Growth: 4
B. Per Capita Income: 2
C. Trade Flows with the U.S.: 2
D. Country Risk: 3
E. Monetary Policy: 3
F. Trade Policy: 3
   • Tariffs
   • Import Licensing
   • Import Taxes
G. Protection of Property Rights: 2
H. Foreign Investment Climate: 3

GROSS DOMESTIC PRODUCT: $24 billion (1998 estimate)

GDP GROWTH: 5.5% (1998 estimate)

PER CAPITA INCOME: $6,700 (1998 estimate)

Trade Flows with the U.S.

U.S. EXPORTS TO COSTA RICA: $2.3 billion (1998)

U.S. IMPORTS FROM COSTA RICA: $2.7 billion (1998)

TOP U.S. EXPORTS TO COSTA RICA: Woven apparel; machinery; aircraft; electrical components; paper/paperboard; plastics and resins; motor vehicles; knit apparel; cereals; mineral fuel

TOP U.S. PROSPECTS FOR EXPORT TO COSTA RICA: Paper and paperboard; computers and peripherals; plastic materials and resins; agricultural chemicals; automotive parts; telecommunications equipment; construction equipment; medical equipment

---

Cultural Note: Although Costa Rica technically has no army, the functions of the military have been taken over by the police forces (many of whom have received military training by U.S. advisors). The Costa Rican police are divided into numerous divisions, each accountable to a different branch of the government. This prevents the police from unifying and exerting undue influence—as the military often does in other Latin American nations.

Country Risk

Dun & Bradstreet rates Cost Rica as having sufficient capacity to meet outstanding payment liabilities.

Sight drafts and open account terms predominate, but letters of credit are recommended for new or small customers. When open account terms are used, 30- to 120-day terms are the norm.

Monetary Policy

Costa Rica's consumer price index (CPI) has been above 10% since 1993. Inflation hit 13.9% in 1996, fell to 11.1% in 1997, and rose slightly to 11.2% in 1998.

MONETARY UNIT: colón

Trade Policy

TARIFFS   Customs duties range from 0% to 28% ad valorem. Tariff reductions resulting from the GATT Uruguay Round implementation have lowered tariff rates, but most food tariffs are still between 14% and 19%.

Costa Rica is a member of the Central American Common Market (CACM), which also includes Guatemala, El Salvador, Honduras, and Nicaragua. The CACM members are working toward the full implementation of a Common External Tariff that ranges between 5 and 20% for most products.

IMPORT LICENSING   Import licenses are not required for most products. However, pharmaceuticals, drugs, cosmetics, and chemical products require an import permit from the Costa Rican Ministry of Health. Import permits from the Ministry of Health are valid for five years.

Food products that are new-to-market require a registration, and phytosanitary and animal health certification are required by the Agriculture Ministry's *Sanidad Vegetal* division. These permits must be obtained by the Costa Rican importer.

IMPORT TAXES   A selective consumer tax ranging from zero to 75% exists. This tax applies to about half of all products imported.

A sales tax of 13% is levied on all products and services not destined for official use by the government of Costa Rica. Certain essential items are exempt.

A 1% surcharge is imposed on all imports. Items exempt from this surcharge are medicines and raw materials for medicines for human use.

Protection of Intellectual Property Rights

Costa Rica belongs to the World Intellectual Property Organization (WIPO) and is a party to the Paris Convention for the Protection of Industrial Property, the Universal Copyright Convention, and the Pan American Convention on Copyrights. Costa Rica's general lack of interest in protecting the rights of foreign copyright holders is evident by the fact that it has failed to join the Berne Convention.

Worldwide novelty is required for patents. Foreign inventors may obtain patents for the remaining term of their foreign patent, but not to exceed 12 years. Patents on medicines are excluded. Patents are subject to compulsory licensing if not exploited. Industrial designs can be registered for 5 years. *Patent laws do not comply with international conventions.* Costa Rica has been placed on the U.S. Trade Representatives' Watch List because its patent law is deficient in several areas.

Trademarks can be industrial, commercial, or service. Industrial trademarks identify the manufacturer. Commercial trademarks represent the marks under which goods or products are sold. Service marks distinguish styles. Trademarks have a term of 15 years and may be renewed. The International Classification System is followed. Registration is mandatory for medicines and certain chemical substances.

In the past Costa Rica has been a haven for copyright piracy. In May 1994, Costa Rica amended its copyright law to strengthen sanctions for piracy and provide explicit protection of computer programs.

Enforcement of these laws, however, remains inconsistent. Copyrights are in force for life plus 50 years, except in cases where there are no heirs. Registration and deposit are required.

Foreign Investment Climate

In general, Costa Rica has a relatively open international trade and investment regime.

However, state monopolies in public utilities, insurance, bank-demand deposits, the production and distribution of electricity, hydrocarbon and radioactive minerals extraction, refining and the wholesale distribution of petroleum, and operation of ports and airports limit investment opportunities in these sectors.

In sectors not reserved to the state, there is widespread recognition in both public and private sectors that increased foreign investment is essential for increased exports and employment. Since mid-1982, the government has placed considerable emphasis on improving the investment climate, including the creation of the Ministry of Foreign Trade which is coordinating government efforts in the trade and investment areas.

The key to Costa Rica's attractiveness as a potential site for investment is the fact that Costa Rica is a beneficiary country of the U.S. Caribbean Basin Initiative (CBI) and Generalized System of Preferences (GSP). These programs grant Costa Rica duty-free access for some 4,000 products and have played a significant role in helping Costa Rica diversify its exports and increase two-way trade.

Laws governing private investment are identical for nationals and foreigners. Discrimination between these two groups is constitutionally prohibited. Foreign companies and persons may legally own equity in Costa Rican companies, including real estate, manufacturing plants and equipment, hotels, restaurants, and all kinds of commercial establishments.

In general, laws controlling investment by foreigners are fairly transparent.

Political Leaders, Parties, and International Organizations

The International Academy at Santa Barbara at http://www.iasb.org/cwl publishes *Current World Leaders*, an excellent resource for up-to-date data on political leaders, parties, demographics, etc., in Costa Rica. Tel: (800) 530-2682 or (805) 965-5010 for subscription information to their database.

Head of State and of the Government:

President Miguel Angel Rodríguez

Next Election:

February 2002

Political Parties:

National Liberation Party (PLN), Social Christian Unity Party (PUSC), Democratic Force Party (PFD), Agricultural Union Party of Cartago (PUAC), National Agrarian Party (PAN)

Membership in international organizations:

CACM, ICO, IDB, IPU, IWC, OAS, SELA, UN and most of its specialized agencies and related organizations (including FAO, IAEA, IBRD, ICAO, IDA, IFAD, IFC, ILO, IMF, IMO, ITU, UNESCO, UNIDO, UPU, WHO, WIPO, WMO)

Political Influences on Business

The bilateral relationship between the United States and Costa Rica has traditionally been and continues to be excellent. Although there have been and remain some bilateral irritants, these have been relatively minor in an otherwise superior relationship.

Expropriation cases (most of which involve undeveloped land)—long the main negative factor affecting U.S.–Costa Rican business relations—now appear on their way to resolution. However, a related problem has arisen with invasions of U.S. citizen-owned property by sometimes violent squatters that the Costa Rican police and judicial system have failed to deter.

Costa Rica is a democratic republic governed according to the Constitution of 1949. This charter established a system of checks and balances among the executive, legislative, and judicial branches. The 1949 Constitution abolished the Costa Rican Army and created a powerful independent body, the Supreme Electoral Tribunal (TSE), to oversee the impartiality and fairness of elections. A 1969 constitutional amendment limits the president to a single four-year term in office, although amendments allowing reelection or the extension of the presidential term to five years are currently under consideration by the Legislative Assembly.

The 57-member unicameral Legislative Assembly is elected concurrently with the President. Candidates for the legislature run on party slates in each province and not as individuals. The number of popular votes each party receives per province determines its quota of legislators in that jurisdiction. Deputies serve four-year terms and cannot be reelected for successive periods.

The Supreme Court has 22 magistrates who sit in four chambers, including the Constitutional review chamber.

Contacts in the United States

The Embassy of the Republic of Costa Rica
2114 S Street, NW
Washington, D.C. 20008
Tel: (202) 234-2945
Fax: (202) 265-4795
www.costarica.com/embassy

Passport/Visa Requirements

U.S. citizens travelling to Costa Rica on business or tourism do not require a visa. *Requirements:* A valid passport (or an original or certified birth certificate and a driver's license) and a roundtrip ticket. Length of stay is 90 days.

A tourist card will be issued at the boarding area by the airline company in which the passenger will be travelling to Costa Rica.

For current information concerning entry and customs requirements for Costa Rica, travelers can contact the Embassy for the Republic of Costa Rica.

U.S. citizens who wish to apply for a passport may visit Passport Services' well-organized website at http://travel.state.gov/passport_services.html.

Contacts in Costa Rica

The Embassy of the United States of America
Pavas Road
San José
Mailing Address: APO AA 34020
Tel: (506) 220 3939
Fax: (506) 220 2305
usembassy.or.cr

The Costa Rican–American Chamber of Commerce
Apdo 4946-1000
San José
Tel: (506) 220-2200
Fax: (506) 220-2300
E-mail: amchamcr@sol.racsa.co.cr
Website: http://www.magi.com/crica/amcham.html

CASA PRESIDENCIAL
Apdo 520, Zapote
San José
Republic of Costa Rica

Further contacts and websites can be found in Appendix A.

Communications

TELEPHONE: The international country code for Costa Rica is 506.

E-MAIL: E-mail addresses located in Costa Rica end with the code .cr

---

Faux Pas: Be sure to learn some highlights about the political history of Central America before your visit. Never get in a position like the U.S. executive who did not know anything about the Costa Rican President who won the Nobel Peace Prize in 1987 for authoring the Central American Peace Plan (President Oscar Arias Sanchez).

The Czech Republic

Official Name:	Czech Republic (Ceská Republika)
Official Language:	Czech
Government System:	Multi-party parliamentary republic
Population:	10.3 million (1999 estimate)
Population Growth Rate:	–0.01% (1999 estimate)
Area:	78,864 sq. km. (30,441 sq. mi.); about the size of Virginia
Natural Resources:	hard and soft coal, kaolin, clay, graphite
Major Cities:	Prague (capital), Brno, Ostrava, Plzen

Cultural Note: After four decades of authoritarian Communist rule, the Czech Republic moved faster towards democracy and capitalism than any other former Warsaw Pact nation. Still, the Czechs must deal with the legacies of the Communist regime. Besides massive environmental pollution, the Czechs need to overcome the "dependency mentality" of the Communist welfare state. They also have to deal with the former Communists within their midst. Former employees of the Secret Police and senior Communist Party officeholders were banned from public office until the year 2000.

Age Breakdown

0–14 = 17%   15–64 = 69%   65+ = 14% (1999 estimate)
Life Expectancy: 71.1 years, male; 77.88 years, female (1999 estimate)

Time

Punctuality is expected at both business appointments and social events.

The Czech Republic is 1 hour ahead of Greenwich Mean Time (GMT +1), which is 6 hours ahead of U.S. Eastern Standard Time (EST +6).

Holidays

An up-to-date, web-based *World Holiday and Time Zone Guide* is available at www.getcustoms.com. It lists official holidays by country and by day of the year, cultural tips, a corruption index, and time zones with worldwide business hours.

This list is a working guide. Dates should be corroborated before final travel plans are made. In cases where holidays fall on Saturday or Sunday, commercial establishments may be closed the preceding Friday or following Monday.

Jan 1	SA	New Year's Day
Apr 24	MO	Easter Monday
May 1	MO	Labor Day
May 8	MO	Liberation Day
Jul 5	WE	Sts. Cyril and Methodius
Jul 6	TH	Jan Hus Day
Oct 28	SA	Independence Day
Dec 24	SU	Christmas Eve
Dec 25	MO	Christmas Day
Dec 26	TU	St. Stephen's Day

Easter and Easter Monday are also official holidays.

While religion is not so important in the Czech Republic as in many other countries, Christian holidays are still observed. The days of observance should always be corroborated by local contacts.

Work Week

- Since the business day begins early and ends in mid-afternoon, expect to schedule your appointments between 9:00 A.M. and 12 noon or between 1:00 and 3:00 P.M.
- Most Czechs and Slovaks receive four weeks of vacation per year. The traditional vacation time runs from mid-July to mid-August, so do not expect to be able to conduct business during this period.
- Business hours: 8:00 or 8:30 A.M. to 4:00 or 5:15 P.M. Monday through Friday.
- Banking hours: 8:00 A.M. to 2:00 P.M. Monday through Friday. Some banks close later on certain weekdays, and open from 8:00 A.M. until noon on Saturdays.
- Store hours: 8:00 or 9:00 A.M. to 5:00 or 6:00 P.M. Monday through Friday. Some establishments will be open on Saturdays until noon. Note that small shops may close for lunch from noon to 2:00 P.M.

Religious/Societal Influences on Business

More Czechs identify themselves as *undenominational* (39.9%) than are members of the largest Church, the Roman Catholics (39.0%). The Czech Republic has no official religion, and organized religion plays a minor role in the daily lives of most citizens.

Most other religions are represented in the Czech Republic. Some local Protestant variations include: Czechoslovak Brethren Reformed (2.0%), Czechoslovak Hussite (1.7%), and Silesian Evangelical (0.3%).

Organized religion has little secular power in the Czech Republic. The Czech government had been offering restitution to churches for property seized by the Communist regime. But the leaders of the Czech Social Democratic Party (CSSD), which came to power in the 1998 elections, planned to halt such restitution to churches.

However, the Czech Republic has produced many profound thinkers and philosophers. Protestant reformer Jan Hus, who was burned as a heretic in 1415, remains a national hero to many Czechs. Writer Franz Kafka (1883–1924) was a native of Prague; the themes of isolation in his work were inspired by being a German-speaking Jew in a Christian, Czech-speaking city. Czech President Vaclav Havel, a playwright and essayist, is arguably the most profound chief of state in modern times.

Avoidance of violence is an important part of Czech philosophy. Czechs are proud of the way they endured two wrenching changes without violence: the 1989 Velvet Revolution in which the Communist regime gave way to democracy, and the peaceful separation of Czechoslovakia into the separate Czech and Slovak Republics in 1993.

Corruption and bribery have become a problem for foreigners doing business in the Czech Republic. Some of these habits evolved in the post-Communist dislocations, but some date back to older traditions. As one old Czech aphorism states: "Kdo neokrádá stát okrádá vlastní rodinu." ("He who does not steal from his company, steals from his family.")

The official language is Czech. Many businesspeople also speak either English or German.

5 Cultural Tips

1. Czech men shake hands both upon arrival and departure. Czech women may or may not shake hands, either with men or each other. Foreigners should wait to see if a Czech woman extends her hand for a handshake. Most Czechs studied manners at their local *Tanecni* (a dance-and-etiquette school).

2. Age is respected. When a single representative is sent to the Czech Republic, he or she should be at least 40 years old, and preferably over 50. Sending a young person will give the impression that your company is not serious about doing business. (This is especially true since Prague has become a favorite destination for Generation X Slackers. Czechs see thousands of young Americans tourists—few of whom appear to have serious ambitions.)

3. Czechs insist that paperwork be properly filed and complete. Even during the Communist regime, the Czech Secret Police would dutifully issue a receipt for contraband materials they seized.

4. Business dealings in the Czech Republic must still cope with frequently-changing regulations. Good legal advice from a Czech business lawyer is vital.

5. Czechs have a reputation as good hosts. Since business is conducted on a personal basis (Czechs must get to know you before they will do business with you), take advantage of social invitations. Business lunches are popular.

Observation: ". . . Czech society is characterised by egalitarian collectivism. Suppression of individual difference and personal autonomy engenders a strong egalitarian ethos ('We all have the same stomach'), which in socialist Czechoslovakia was realised in practice to a much greater degree than anywhere else in Eastern Europe.

"Although it would be foolish to deny that forty years of socialism in Czechoslovakia had played their part in strengthening the egalitarian ethos, it seems to me that the ideal of egalitarianism was the aspect of the socialist ideology to which Czechs objected least, precisely because it built upon Czech cultural values which, like individualism in England, had deep historical roots.

"A market in which entrepreneurs were perceived as active subjects and everyone else as a passive object offended the cultural ideal of equality . . ."

—From *The Little Czech Nation and the Great Czech Nation* by Ladislav Holy

---

Economic Overview

The Czech Republic is a small but growing market for U.S. products, and U.S. firms have had success selling computers and software, medical equipment, manufacturing technologies, energy and environmental technologies, and other industrial products. While the United States holds only a 3–4% share of the overall Czech import market, major investments by firms from the U.S. mean that their products and services will continue to enjoy a high profile and demand.

The Czech Republic is considered by many to be the most economically advanced reemerging market of the former Eastern Bloc. It has a stable currency with few foreign exchange controls, low unemployment, low national debt, and strong foreign currency reserves. A sweeping privatization program has moved the majority of state-owned assets to private hands, and the process of restructuring these firms has been underway. By all accounts, the economic and commercial pictures are bright.

Czech firms are plagued, however, by a lack of capital, marketing, and financial expertise. Many firms are insolvent. Czech firms that do have local currency to buy

U.S. goods and services are able to obtain U.S. currency to pay for them through the local bank with little difficulty.

European competition for the Czech market is quite fierce. More than half of the country's trade is conducted with its four neighboring countries—Germany, Austria, Slovakia, and Poland. For American firms, the key to success is price, delivery, and service terms to compete with strong German and other European competition.

Americans are among the most popular expatriates and visitors to the Czech Republic. U.S. firms enjoy broad acceptance and are welcomed by nearly all Czech firms looking for contacts with foreign firms. Bilateral relations between the Czech Republic and the U.S. are as good as they have ever been.

The Czech economy suffered due to the massive floods of July 1997. Although the flooding centered in Moravia, almost a third of the Czech Republic experienced flood damage. It was the worst flooding of the century. The infrastructure repairs alone have monopolized much of the available capital, and are projected to continue to do so for years.

5 Largest Businesses in the Czech Republic

Slovenske Energeticke Strojarne Akciova Spolecnost, Tlmace
  5,700 employees
Slovenska Armaturka Akciova Spolecnost, Myjava
  3,623 employees
Duslo Statny Podnik, Okr Galanta
  3,369 employees
Obuv Statni Podnik, Partizanske
  3,200 employees
Chemko Statny Podnik, Strazskke
  3,023 employees

Comparative Data

Comparative Data Ratings
(Scale: 5 = Excellent; 1 = Poor)
Czech Republic: 2.875

  A. GDP Growth: 2
  B. Per Capita Income: 3
  C. Trade Flows with the U.S.: 1
  D. Country Risk: 3
  E. Monetary Policy: 3
  F. Trade Policy: 4
      • Tariffs
      • Import Licensing
      • Import Taxes
  G. Protection of Property Rights: 3
  H. Foreign Investment Climate: 4

GROSS DOMESTIC PRODUCT: $116.7 billion (1998 estimate)

GDP GROWTH: 1.5% (1998 estimate)

PER CAPITA INCOME: $11,300 (1998 estimate)

Trade Flows with the U.S.

U.S. EXPORTS TO THE CZECH REPUBLIC: $568 million (1998)

U.S. IMPORTS FROM THE CZECH REPUBLIC: $672 million (1998)

TOP U.S. EXPORTS TO THE CZECH REPUBLIC: Machinery; electrical components; medical and optical equipment; motor vehicles; aircraft and parts; pollution-control equipment; pharmaceuticals; plastics and resins; franchising

TOP U.S. PROSPECTS FOR EXPORT TO THE CZECH REPUBLIC: Information technologies; electrical power systems; aircraft and parts; pollution-control equipment; medical equipment; travel and tourism services; franchising

Country Risk

The short-term outlook for the Czech Republic's Risk environment remains stable, although there are concerns about the slow pace of the economic recovery. There is enough concern to warrant close monitoring of the country risk situation.

Monetary Policy

The government is striving to keep the Czech rate of inflation below 10%. The rate of inflation for 1998 was 6.8% and was estimated to be 4.8% for 1999.

MONETARY UNIT: Koruna (crown)

Trade Policy

TARIFFS   The Czech Republic has adopted a GATT tariff code, which has an average tariff of 5 to 6%. Imports of raw materials and certain semifinished products that are processed before their reexport enter duty-free.

IMPORT LICENSING   Import licenses are required for certain classes of goods into the Czech Republic. These are listed in a special appendix to the trade law. *Appendix A* goods (in Czech trade law), for which a license is automatically granted after payment of an administrative fee, include uranium ore, scrap metals, and textile products, as well as certain agricultural products and food.

Appendices B, C, D, and E products, which include agricultural and food products, some minerals, chemicals, pharmaceuticals, raw hides and other hide products, poisonous and toxic substances, and military and dual-use items, are subject to license granted to a certain extent in relation to a limited value or quantity.

All licenses are issued by the Ministry of Industry and Trade.

IMPORT TAXES   A two-tiered value-added tax (VAT) is in effect. Basic articles such as fuel, energy, staple foodstuffs, and pharmaceuticals are subject to a 5% VAT. A 22% VAT is imposed on the remaining categories of goods and services.
Excise taxes are levied on gasoline, tobacco, alcohol, wines, and spirits.

Protection of Intellectual Property Rights

The Czech Republic belongs to the World Intellectual Property Organization (WIPO) and participates in numerous IP conventions. Conventions that it has joined include: the Berne Convention for Protection of Literary and Artistic Works, the Universal Copyright Convention, the Patent Co-operation Treaty, the Paris Convention for Protection of Industrial Property, the Madrid Convention on International Registration of Trademarks, and the Lisbon Convention for the Protection of Appellations of Origin.

Czech patent laws protect inventions and utility models. The term of patent is 20 years from application. Designs have an initial term of 4 years and 2 supplemental terms of 3 years each. Inventions must be new, be creative, and have industrial application. Priority rights result on filing. Applications are published in 18 months and a full examination is required within 36 months. The Czech Republic also has laws that protect semiconductor microcircuits and new varieties of plants and animals.

Trademarks protect both goods and services. Trademark rights result from registration with the Industrial Property Office. The term of the trademark is 10 years from application and is renewable. Trademarks can be licensed and assigned, subject to approval of the Industrial Property Office.

Copyrights are automatic on creation of a qualified work. No registration is required. Computer programs are copyrighted. The term of copyright is generally life of the author plus 50 years. For works where the author is unknown, the term is 50 years after publication. The problem is that enforcement is weak in some areas. Pirate CD plants are reported to operate and encrypted signals are retransmitted without authorization.

Foreign Investment Climate

An open investment climate has been a key element of the economic transformation of the Czech Republic. This transformation process has continued without disruption in the Czech Republic following the breakup of Czechoslovakia at the end of 1992.

The Czechoslovak government focused on improving the investment climate at the initial stages of economic reform in 1990. It was considered to be critical for attracting the foreign capital and investment much needed by undercapitalized state enterprises undergoing privatization. Additionally, the Czechoslovaks and Czechs set a high priority on economic integration with the world's advanced economies. The Czech government applied for membership in the European Union (EU) in 1996. It is now an associate member of the EU, but full membership in the EU is not expected until 2002 at the earliest.

In 1995, the Czech Republic became a member of the Organization of Economic Cooperation and Development (OECD)—the first former member of the Warsaw Pact to achieve that distinction. As such, the Czech government follows OECD guidelines towards equal treatment of foreign and domestic investors.

Foreign investors can, as individuals, establish sole proprietorships, joint ventures, and branch offices in the Czech Republic. Foreign and domestic investors are treated identically and both are subject to the same tax codes and other laws. The government does not screen foreign investment projects other than for those few industries that are considered sensitive. Industries considered sensitive include defense-related industries, national or cultural monuments, salt production, and companies involved in the distillation of pure alcohol. The government does, however, evaluate all investment offers for state enterprises undergoing privatization.

Foreign firms operating in the Czech Republic conduct business under the law as Czech firms. Foreign firms are able to repatriate profits and liquidate investments, and are protected from expropriation under both international and domestic law and under treaty.

Since 1990, direct investment in Czech Republic from the United States has totaled more than US$7 billion. The U.S. is the second-largest foreign investor in the Czech Republic. Germany remains the largest investor.

Political Leaders, Parties, and International Organizations

The International Academy at Santa Barbara at http://www.iasb.org/cwl publishes *Current World Leaders*, an excellent resource for up-to-date data on political leaders, parties, demographics, etc., in the Czech Republic. Tel: (800) 530-2682 or (805) 965-5010 for subscription information to their database.

Chief of State:
> President Vaclav Havel

Head of the Government:
> Prime Minister Milos Zeman

Next Election:
> January 2003

Political Parties:
> Civic Democratic Party, Christian Democratic Party, Civic Democratic Alliance, Liberal Social Union, Movement for Self-governing Democracy of Moravia and Silesia, Christian Democratic Union, Christian Social Union, Czech Social Democratic Party, Agrarian Party, Green Party, Assembly for the Republic, Czech Communist Party, Party of the Democratic Left

Membership in international organizations:

> CE, EBRD, NACC, OSCE, UN and many of its specialized agencies and related organizations (including FAO, GATT, IAEA, IBRD, ICAO, ILO, IMF, IMO, ITU, UNESCO, UNIDO, UPU, WHO, WIPO, WMO)

Political Influences on Business

Bilateral relations with the United States are as good as they have ever been. Since the establishment of the Czech Republic at the beginning of 1993, a series of high-level visits (including presidential visits to both countries, top-level military and cabinet contacts, and countless working-level meetings) have reaffirmed the breadth of cooperation and mutual interest. The United States has phased out its assistance programs to the Czech Republic—a clear indicator of the Czech Republic's role as emerging partner with the U.S. That partnership ranges from close bilateral military ties, cooperation in combating such transnational challenges as organized crime and narcotics, working together in the United Nations Security Council (where the Czechs occupied a seat from 1994–95), and working closely through a series of cultural, educational, and legal programs to deepen Czech progress in democratization and to ensure better U.S. understanding of the Czech achievement.

The political issues affecting the business climate are few. The Czech government is committed to entry into Western institutions. The Czech Republic is now a member of two major organizations: the Organization for Economic Cooperation and Development (OECD) and the North Atlantic Treaty Organization (NATO). It is currently an associate member of the European Union (EU) and hopes for full EU membership by 2002. Theirs is an export-driven economy, and European markets are the first priority. The U.S. has expressed concerns about some elements of the Czech business culture that are less than transparent, and sometimes too bureaucratic. Most problems of business representatives are also widely acknowledged by government officials, who are frequently cited as being open and available to listen to problems. The U.S. makes its concerns known to Czech officials and partners on a case-by-case basis, and while conflicts in some areas continue to exist, the seriousness with which the Czechs take foreign commercial concerns is encouraging.

The Czech Republic is a parliamentary democracy. Former Prime Minister Vaclav Klaus is credited as the architect of the country's economic reform. His Civic Democratic Party (ODS), a conservative secular free-market oriented party, lost its parliamentary majority in the 1996 general elections. President Vaclav Havel, the head of state, is an internationally recognized advocate of human rights and social justice. He was reelected in 1998 to a second five-year term, but severe health problems have limited his effectiveness.

The parliamentary Chamber of Deputies is elected every four years. Elections were held in 1998 (two years ahead of schedule). The center–left Czech Social Democratic Party (CSSD) won the most parliamentary seats, followed by the Civic Democratic Party (ODS). However, the coalition agreement gave the ODS considerable power, and Vaclav Klaus was elected chairman of the parliament. CSSD leader Milos Zeman became the new prime minister. The CSSD's platform includes support for economic reform and fighting bribery and economic corruption.

Contacts in the United States

THE EMBASSY OF CZECH REPUBLIC
3900 Spring of Freedom Street, NW
Washington, D.C. 20008
Tel: (202) 363-6315
Fax: (202) 966-8540
www.czech.cz/washington

Passport/Visa Requirements

For U.S. citizens, a passport is needed but a visa is not required for stays of up to 30 days. For stays of over 30 days, U.S. citizens must present their visa requests to the Czech Embassy in Washington, D.C. Except in an unusual case, processing of the visa application takes approximately three days. Applications presented in person are usually processed on the spot. The visa application form consists of three parts, all of which must be filled in.

The form is to be submitted to the Embassy with:

1. A travel document (passport, permit to reenter the U.S.) valid for at least another eight months from time of presentation.
2. Two photographs glued to the right side of the first and second pages (do not staple).
3. A money order or cashier's check, payable to the Czech Embassy, in the amount of $22.00 for each form to cover the visa fee for U.S. citizens. Personal checks are not accepted.
4. A stamped, self-addressed envelope with postage stamps for certified mail if the visa is to be returned by mail. For overnight mail, provide a prepaid self-addressed airbill for Express Mail, UPS, or Airborne Express and a telephone number. The Embassy cannot ship by Federal Express.

LENGTH OF STAY AND VALIDITY OF VISA   Visas can be granted by the Embassy for up to 30 days of stay. They may be extended at the local Passport and Visa Authorities for up to 6 months while the visitor is in the Czech Republic. A visa may be used any time within 6 months from date of issue. Bearers of the Czech Republic tourist visas must register their stay with the Czech Republic Passport Authorities within 48 hours after their arrival. Visitors staying in hotels are automatically registered with the authorities.

DOUBLE-ENTRY VISA   Special double-entry visas are available, allowing visitors to enter the Czech Republic twice. To obtain such a visa, two visa applications, four photographs, and a $33.00 fee by cashier's check or money order made payable to the Embassy must be presented.

MULTIPLE-ENTRY VISA   Multiple-entry visas for 90 days costs $51; for 180 days, $91.
For current information concerning entry and customs requirements for the Czech Republic, contact the Embassy of the Czech Republic.

U.S. citizens who wish to apply for a passport may visit Passport Services' well-organized website at http://travel.state.gov/passport_services.html.

Contacts in the Czech Republic

THE EMBASSY OF THE UNITED STATES
OF AMERICA
Trziste 15
118 01 Prague 1
Prague
Mailing Address: Unit 1330, APO AE
09213-5630
Tel: (42) (2) 5732-0663
Fax: (42) (2) 5732-0583
www.usembassy.cz

DUN & BRADSTREET SPOL S R.O.
Konevova St. 99
130 45 Prague 3
Tel: +42 2.7103.1500
Fax: +42 2.7103.1510

OFFICE OF THE PRESIDENT
119 08 Praha 1-Hrad
Czech Republic

OFFICE OF THE PRIME MINISTER
Nabr. E. Benese 4
125 09 Praha 1
Czech Republic

Further contacts and websites can be found in Appendix A.

Communications

TELEPHONE: country code for the Czech Republic is 42.

Czech city codes may be one, two, or three digits long.

MAIL: Czech is written in the Latin alphabet. A number of diacritical marks are used on both consonants and vowels (both capital and lower-case versions). The omission of the diacritical marks does not usually result in misunderstandings.

Letters to the Czech Republic may be addressed as follows: (*Notes in parentheses*)

Title & Name: Ing. Jiri Roudny, Director
(Titles are important, such as engineer = inženýr, doctor = doktor, abbreviated dr., and manager = magister, abbreviated mgr. The Czech equivalent of Mr. is Pan, abbreviated p., and Mrs. is paní, abbreviated pí. The Czech version of Miss, slečna has fallen out of contemporary usage. The English abbreviation Ms. has achieved some currency as a replacement.)

Office or Company:	Ministry of Finance
	(Large Czech corporations are usually called akciová společnost abbreviated a.s., while the smaller corporations are usually known as společnost s rucením omezeným, variously abbreviated as spol. s. r.o. or spol. s r.o.—note the lack of period after the s in s r.o.)
Street:	Letenska 15
	(Street numbers follow the name of the street. The Czech words for street = ulice, avenue = třída, abbreviated tř, or square = náměstí, abbreviated nám, are not always used.)
Postcode, City, and Postal District (if any):	118 00 PRAHA 1
	(Postcodes are 5-digit numbers that precede the name of the city. Czech postcodes have a space between the third and fourth digits. Large businesses may have their own postcodes. Praha is the Czech name for Prague; Prague is currently the only Czech city to add a postal district number. This number follows the name of the city.)
Country:	Czech Republic
	(The Czech name for the country is Česká Republika, which is abbreviated ČR.)

E-MAIL: E-mail addresses located in the Czech Republic end with the code .cz CS was also the automobile code for Czechoslovakia. After the 1993 division of Czechoslovakia, the automobile code for the Czech Republic was changed to CZ.

DATES: In the Czech Republic, the date is written in this order: day, month, year (unlike the U.S. practice of writing month, day, year). The dates are usually separated by periods (10.11.00 indicates November 10, 2000).

Cultural Note: "The Czech Republic has undergone two radical but nonviolent changes in recent years: the Velvet Revolution that removed the U.S.S.R.-backed Communists from power, and the peaceful separation of Czechoslovakia into two independent nations, the Czech and Slovak Republics. Even at their most angry moment, when protesters jammed Prague's Wenceslas Square demanding the removal of the Communists, the protesters admonished one another not to trample on the flower beds!"

—from *Kiss, Bow or Shake Hands: How to Do Business in Sixty Countries* by Morrison, Conaway, and Borden

---

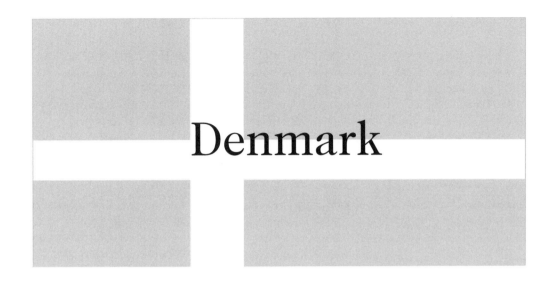

Denmark

Official Name:	Kingdom of Denmark (Kongeriget Danmark)
Official Language:	Danish
Government System:	Parliamentary state under a constitutional monarchy
Population:	5.36 million (1999 estimate)
Population Growth Rate:	0.38% (1999 estimate)
Area:	43,076 sq. km. (16,632 sq. mi.): slightly smaller than Vermont and New Hampshire combined. [This area does not include the Faroe Islands or the huge Arctic island, Greenland, which Denmark still controls.]
Natural Resources:	petroleum, natural gas, fish, salt, limestone, stone, gravel, sand
Major Cities:	Copenhagen (København) (capital), Århus, Odense, Ålborg, Frederiksberg

---

Cultural Note: The Danish language has three letters that do not appear in English. They are:

æ/Æ (pronounced like the *e* in *pet*)

ø/Ø (pronounced like the *e* in *err*)

å/Å (pronounced like the *o* in *core*)

If you have no way of printing these characters, substitute *ae* for *æ*, *oe* for *ø*, and *aa* for *å*.

These letters are placed at the *end* of the alphabet, so names beginning with these letters will be found at the end of a Danish telephone directory. There are pronunciation differences even in the letters shared by Danish and English. The most notable peculiarity is the Danish "soft d," which foreigners—even other Nordics—find difficult to duplicate. There is also a guttural "r" sound that English speakers have trouble imitating.

Age Breakdown

0–14 = 18%   15–64% = 67%   65+ = 15% (1999 estimate)
Life Expectancy: 73.83 years, male; 79.33 years, female (1999 estimate)

Time

Strict punctuality is expected in Denmark, both in business and social situations. Tardiness gives an impression of incompetence and poor time management.

Denmark is 1 hour ahead of Greenwich Mean Time (GMT +1), which is 6 hours ahead of U.S. Eastern Standard Time (EST 6).

Holidays

An up-to-date, web-based *World Holiday and Time Zone Guide* is available at www.getcustoms.com. It lists official holidays by country and by day of the year, cultural tips, a corruption index, and time zones with worldwide business hours.

This list is a working guide. Dates should be corroborated before final travel plans are made. In cases where holidays fall on Saturday or Sunday, commercial establishments may be closed the preceding Friday or following Monday.

Jan 1	Sa	New Year's Day
Apr 20	TH	Holy Thursday
Apr 21	FR	Good Friday
Apr 23	SU	Easter Sunday
Apr 24	MO	Easter Monday
May 1	MO	Workers' Day
May 19	FR	Common Prayer Day
Jun 1	TH	Ascension
Jun 5	MO	Constitution Day
Jun 11	SU	Whitsunday
Jun 12	MO	Whitmonday
Dec 24	SU	Christmas Eve
Dec 25	MO	Christmas Day
Dec 26	TU	Boxing Day
Dec 31	SU	New Year's Eve

The Christian celebrations of Maundy Thursday, Good Friday, Easter Monday, Ascension Day, and Whitmonday are all holidays. Denmark also observes a National Prayer Day, called *Store Bededag*, on the fourth Friday after Easter. (However, rather than spending the day in prayer, most Danes use it as a long weekend to enjoy the spring.)

Be sure to confirm your appointments with local representatives before taking your trip. Regional holidays may present a conflict.

- Many Danes take off from work the entire week preceding Easter.
- As in the rest of Scandinavia, summer is a time of leisure. It is both difficult and inconsiderate to try to conduct serious business during July and August. Many firms close for extended periods during these two months to allow their employees to take summer vacations. Danes have 5 weeks of paid vacation per year.

Again, the days of observance should always be corroborated by local contacts.

Work Week

- Business hours vary throughout Denmark. Opening times range from 8:00 to 9:00 A.M. and closing times from 4:30 to 5:30 P.M. Offices operate on a five-day schedule. Banks are open from 9:30 A.M. to 4:00 P.M. on weekdays with the exception of Thursday, when they stay open until 6:00 P.M.
- Danish workers average a work week of 37 hours, Monday through Friday.

Religious/Societal Influences on Business

Denmark's official religion is the Evangelical Lutheran Church, to which 87% of the population belongs. Generally, religion does not play a large part in the everyday lives of the Danes.

Fierce independence is a national characteristic of the Danes. (This should not be surprising; without it, tiny Denmark could never have maintained its independence in proximity to Germany.)

Social scientists have observed that the Danes have a highly nurturing culture. Both men and women are very concerned with social welfare and the quality of life. As one would expect in a country with a high proportion of women in business, Denmark offers generous child care and paternity leave.

The Danes consider truthfulness and modesty to be important virtues. Wealth is downplayed, and ostentation is frowned upon. Denmark is a meritocracy. Nepotism is not unheard of, but if relatives are hired, they are expected to be highly competent.

Cultural Note: It is not easy to be in a position of authority in Denmark. The egalitarian nature of Danish culture means each person has an opinion—an opinion that must be listened to. Danes do not simply take orders; they must be allowed their say and then convinced to go along with the program. But once a decision is made, everyone is expected to be supportive. Bosses are seen more like coaches than leaders, and they have to earn the respect of their employees.

5 Cultural Tips

1. While most Danes speak English, the greeting they traditionally give (which sounds like *hi*) is Danish, not English. This Danish word is *heij*, and it is used both upon greeting and farewell. A handshake accompanies the traditional greeting. Danes shake hands with both men and women.

2. Leadership among the independent-minded Danes requires consensus-building. There is a great deal of give-and-take among all levels of a Danish company. Strong negative input from even a minor member of a company could sink your proposal.

3. Since Danes are both slow to decide and independent-minded, the hard sell is the worst technique you can take. Present your pitch, supply all the follow-up data requested (no matter how extraneous this data may seem to you), and wait. The Danes cannot be rushed.

4. Work and homelife are kept separate in Denmark. Take an invitation to a Danish home as a great honor. Be sure to arrive on time. As a dinner guest, you may be led straight from the door to the dining table. In Denmark, drinks are served during and after a meal, but not before.

5. The fierce independence and individualism of the Danes has worked against the development of large corporations. The majority of Danish companies are small. More than half the population works in companies with fewer than 200 employees.

Observation: "You have to understand that the Danish way of life places more emphasis on leisure time than some other European cultures. Even more important, the state doesn't give you the encouragement to work longer hours or harder: the impact of the current taxation system is such that there is no personal financial incentive. It is impossible for a company executive to get rich in Denmark, unlike some other European countries. By the time you've paid your taxes, the differentials between one management grade and the next are marginal."

—From *EuroManagers & Martians* by Richard Hill

Economic Overview

The United States is Denmark's largest trading partner outside the European Union. There are approximately 250 American subsidiaries in Denmark representing about 12% of foreign direct investment. Direct investment from the U.S. totals about $2 billion.

Political and commercial relations with the United State are excellent. Denmark's standard of living, per capita GDP, and rate of personal taxation are among the highest in the world.

It is a good market and investment site for American companies. Denmark's central location, excellent infrastructure, and the skills of its labor force make it an attractive site for regional offices serving Scandinavia and the Baltics.

5 Largest Businesses in Denmark

Kobenhavns Amts Sygehus i Glostrup, Glostrup
   4,500 employees
Netto i/s, Ishoj
   2,000 employees
Gate Gourmet Copenhagen a/s, Kastrup
   1,000 employees
Danfloss Fluid Power a/s, Nordborg
   1,000 employees
Oresund Tunnel Contractors i/s, Kobenhavn
   1,000 employees

The numbers of employees are estimates; this information is not made public in Denmark.

Danish company abbreviations may be written in lower case or a combination of upper- and lower-case letters:

a/s = Aktieselskab (corporation, usually publicly traded—although the shares may be held by a small group of people)

ApS = Anpartsselskab (company, not publicly traded)

Cultural Note: Denmark has the highest percentage of women in business in the European Union. Be prepared to find women at all levels of Danish business and government.

Comparative Data

Comparative Data Ratings
(Scale: 5 = Excellent; 1 = Poor)
Denmark: 4.125

- A.   GDP Growth: 3
- B.   Per Capita Income: 5
- C.   Trade Flows with the U.S.: 2
- D.   Country Risk: 5
- E.   Monetary Policy: 5
- F.   Trade Policy: 4
  - Tariffs
  - Import Licensing
  - Import Taxes
- G.   Protection of Property Rights: 4
- H.   Foreign Investment Climate: 5

GROSS DOMESTIC PRODUCT: $124.4 billion (1998 estimate)

GDP GROWTH: 2.6% (1998 estimate)

PER CAPITA INCOME: $23,300 (1998 estimate)

Trade Flows with the U.S.

U.S. EXPORTS TO DENMARK: $1.79 billion (1998 estimate)

U.S. IMPORTS FROM DENMARK: $2.4 billion (1998 estimate)

TOP U.S. EXPORTS TO DENMARK: Aircraft and parts; computer parts; computers; military equipment; enzymes; pharmaceuticals; medical and scientific equipment; tobacco; motor vehicles; fruits and nuts; mineral fuel; forest products

TOP U.S. PROSPECTS FOR EXPORT TO DENMARK: Software; computers and electronic data-processing equipment; tourism; environmental-control equipment; electrical power systems; offshore oil machinery; medical equipment; telecommunications equipment; wine; animal (dog and cat) food; and fruit juices

Country Risk

Dun & Bradstreet rates Denmark as having excellent capacity to meet outstanding payment liabilities. It carries the lowest degree of risk. The terms for credit depend on the business sector and the size of transaction. Open accounts with payments due in 30 to 60 days are standard.

Monetary Policy

The Danish economy has experienced modest growth for several years. Inflation was estimated at 1.7% in 1998 and in 1999. It is expected to remain between 1.5% and 3% for the forseeable future. Inflation has averaged below 3% for the last five years.

MONETARY UNIT: Kroner

Trade Policy

TARIFFS   Because of its European Union membership, Denmark imposes common external tariffs on goods entering from non-EU countries, including the U.S. These duties run from 5 to 17% on manufactured goods.

Some agricultural products (including cereal grains, rice, milk and milk products, beef and veal, olive oil, and sugar) are governed by the common agricultural policy in which duties are supplemented by a system of variable levies. The purpose is to equalize prices of imported commodities with those produced within the EU. Because of these levies, some U.S.-processed food products are not competitive in the Danish market.

IMPORT LICENSING   With the exceptions of alcoholic beverages, weapons, and specified drugs and food products, Denmark requires no import licenses.

There are no special import restrictions or license requirements that constitute problems for U.S. industrial product exporters.

IMPORT TAXES   Although not an import tax, all goods imported into Denmark are also subject to a 25% value-added tax (VAT). The VAT is applied on a nondiscriminatory basis to all goods and most services, whether imported or locally produced.

Various consumer items are subject to additional taxes. These include tobacco, alcohol, oil and gasoline, and automobiles. Over two-thirds of Danish households own an automobile, despite a huge 180% tax on cars!

Protection of Intellectual Property Rights

Denmark is a signatory to various conventions and bilateral treaties relating to intellectual property. Conventions that Denmark has subscribed to include the Paris Convention for Protection of Industrial Property, the Patent Cooperation Treaty, the European Patent Convention, the Berne Convention for Protection of Literary and Artistic Works, and the Universal Copyright Convention. In 1997 the U.S. instituted an enforcement action against Denmark for failure to comply with TRIPS standards.

Denmark's patent laws were upgraded in 1993 and 1995. Patents have a term of 20 years from application. Patent rights result on registration. Maintenance fees are required. Patent marking is optional.

The Trademark Act was amended in 1991. Trademarks, service marks, and trade names are protected. Trademarks have 10-year renewable terms. Registrations are subject to cancellation if not used for five years. Rights in a trademark may be assigned with or without goodwill.

Denmark passed new copyright laws in 1995 that protect works that are independently created. Registration or copyright notation is not required. Copyrights have terms of 70 years. A compulsory license arrangement exists for libraries. An author can prevent lending of his works to the public. There is no fair-use clause. However, copying for personal use is permitted under specific exceptions.

Foreign Investment Climate

Because Denmark is heavily dependent on foreign trade and international cooperation, it follows liberal trade and investment policies and encourages increased foreign investment.

Denmark welcomes foreign investors on a nondiscriminatory, national treatment basis, including allowing them to benefit from national investment incentive programs. In the past few years, the Danish government has been actively seeking high-tech investors from the U.S. and Japan. As a general rule, foreign direct investment in Denmark may take place without restrictions and screening and there are no major foreign investment barriers.

Ownership restrictions apply to only a few sectors, including those subject to national security considerations.

There is a well-established system of commercial law and expropriation that is almost entirely limited to public construction purposes, in which case full compensation is paid. There are no restrictions on capital transfers and no foreign exchange restrictions. Worker productivity is high, inflation is low, and corporate taxation is one of the lowest in the EU.

Ownership restrictions apply in a few sectors including: hydrocarbon exploration, arms production, aircraft, and shipping.

Cultural Note: Danish executives are world-class experts at running meetings. Like the Danes themselves, their meetings are well organized. Their meetings always have specific, stated agendas. They start and finish at predetermined times. Participants prepare carefully, and everyone gets to express his or her opinion (as long as he or she is well informed on the matter). These meetings are an integral part of the Danish management style.

Political Leaders, Parties, and International Organizations

The International Academy at Santa Barbara at http://www.iasb.org/cwl publishes *Current World Leaders*, an excellent resource for up-to-date data on political leaders, parties, demographics, etc., in Denmark. Tel: (800) 530-2682 or (805) 965-5010 for subscription information to their database.

Head of State:

Queen Margrethe II

Head of the Government:

Prime Minister Poul Nyrup Rasmussen

Political Parties:

Social Democratic Party, Conservative People's Party, Socialist People's Party, Center Democratic Party, Christian People's Party, Liberal Democratic Party, Left Socialist Party, Progressive Party, Single Tax Party, Communist Party

Membership in international organizations:

CBSS, CE, EBRD, EU, INTELSAT, NACC, NC, NATO, OECD, OSCE, UN and all of its specialized agencies and related organizations (including FAO, GATT, IAEA, IBRD, ICAO, IDA, IFAD, IFC, ILO, IMF, IMO, ITU, UNESCO, UNIDO, UPU, WHO, WIPO, WMO)

Political Influences on Business

Although U.S.–Danish relations were strained in the early 1980s over security issues, the relations between the two countries have improved. NATO has been popular in Denmark, perhaps more so than in any other country in Europe. Denmark's membership in NATO was far more popular than its membership in the European Union. However, the 1999 bombing of Yugoslavia has been a matter of grave concern to the Danes.

While political issues rarely affect the Danish business climate, the business sector fears that the government's new series of environmental taxes imposed on business, pending introduction of similar taxes in Denmark's major competing countries, may jeopardize Danish competitiveness.

Denmark is a constitutional monarchy. The Parliament, known as the Folketing, is elected for a four-year term, but usually elections are held before the four years are up, either because the government is toppled in a vote of confidence, or because the Prime Minister calls an election (which he can do at any time) in an attempt to increase the government coalition's parliamentary position. Denmark has a history of minority governments.

With a few amendments (the latest and most comprehensive in 1953), the Constitution dates from 1849, when the King renounced absolutism (the "royal dictatorship"). Today Denmark is among the most politically stable democracies. The Monarch nominally rules through the Prime Minister and his Cabinet. As the Prime Minister is accountable to the Folketing (Denmark's unicameral parliament), the Monarch "chooses" him based on recommendations from the leaders of the political parties.

The Prime Minister works through Cabinet Ministers and their ministries. Cabinet Ministers need not be members of Parliament, although most usually are. Ministers have no political Deputy Ministers or Secretaries of State as in other parliamentary democracies. Rather, they have one or more Permanent Under Secretaries, who are the highest-ranking civil servants within the ministry. There are no political appointees among the civil servants, who remain unaffected by changes of government.

The parliament has 175 members, plus two each from Greenland and the Faroes, which are autonomous parts of the Danish realm.

Judicial power rests solely with the courts, although the Monarch on rare occasions grants pardons.

Political parties play a much greater role in Danish politics than in the United States for two major reasons. The first is the system of awarding seats on the basis of proportional representation. The second reason is the fact that Folketing members have no personal staff (nor, for that matter, do parliamentary committees). As a result, Danish parliamentarians rely on their parties for support and technical expertise, and party discipline is very tight.

Contacts in the United States

THE EMBASSY OF THE KINGDOM OF DENMARK
3200 Whitehaven Street, NW
Washington, D.C. 20008
Tel: (202) 234-4300
Fax: (202) 328-1470
www.denmarkemb.org

DANISH–AMERICAN CHAMBER OF COMMERCE
885 Second Avenue, 18th Floor
New York, NY 10017
Tel: (212) 980-6240
Fax: (212) 754-1904
E-mail: DACCNY@Interpart.net

Passport/Visa Requirements

A passport is required. U.S. citizens do not need a visa for a 3-month tourist stay, as long as they have not accumulated a total of 3 months' stay in any Nordic country within the past 6 months. For current information concerning entry and customs requirements for Denmark, travelers can contact Denmark's Embassy.

U.S. citizens who wish to apply for a passport may visit Passport Services' well-organized website at http://travel.state.gov/passport_services.html.

Contacts In Denmark

THE EMBASSY OF THE UNITED STATES
OF AMERICA
Dag Hammarskjolds Alle 24
DK-2100 Copenhagen O.
Mailing Address: PSC 73, APO AE 09716
Tel: (45) 35 55 31 44
Fax: (45) 35 43 02 23
www.usembassy.dk

DUN & BRADSTREET DANMARK A/S
Egegaardsvej 39, DK-2610 Rodovre
Tel: (45) 36 738.000
Fax: (45) 36 709.129

QUEEN MARGRETHE II
Office of the Queen
Amalienborg Palace
Copenhagen K., Kingdom of Denmark

OFFICE OF THE PRIME MINISTER
Christiansborg Palace
Prins Jorgens Gaard II
1218 Copenhagen K., Kingdom of Denmark

Further contacts and websites can be found in Appendix A.

Communications

TELEPHONE: The international country code for Denmark is 45.

Phone numbers are eight digits in length. They are usually read off in pairs of numbers (for example, 62 93 44 01). In writing, Danes do not separate the numbers by parentheses, dashes, or slashes.

The Danes eliminated their area and city codes in 1989. The eight-digit phone number is the only number currently needed to reach any phone in Denmark.

There is a charge for all calls in Denmark, including local calls.

Danish toll-free numbers begin with the digits 80. At this writing, these toll-free numbers *cannot* usually be called from outside Denmark.

Mobile phones begin with the digits 2, 3, or 4.

E-MAIL: E-mail addresses located in Denmark end with the code .dk

---

Faux Pas: A visitor from the U.S. was embarrassed when he attempted to chat with other patrons while waiting to be seated in a Danish restaurant. The Danes did not respond; they found it odd and intrusive that someone would try to strike up a conversation with total strangers.

Egypt

Official Name:	Arab Republic of Egypt (Jumhuriyah Misr al-'Arabiyah)
Official Language:	Arabic
Government System:	Republic
Population:	67.3 million (1999 estimate)
Population Growth Rate:	1.82% (1999 estimate)
Area:	997,739 sq. km. (385,229 sq. mi.); slightly smaller than Texas, Oklahoma, and Arkansas combined
Natural Resources:	petroleum, natural gas, iron ore, phosphates, manganese, limestone, gypsum, talc, asbestos, lead, zinc
Major Cities:	Cairo (capital), Alexandria, Aswan, Asyut, Port Said, Suez, Ismailia, Tanta

---

Cultural Note: Egyptians tend to have large extended families. They are rarely alone, and solitude is not often a chosen condition. As a result, Egyptians gravitate towards others in public. If you are sitting in an empty movie theater, an Egyptian will probably choose a seat next to you. If you are seated at one end of a bench, an Egyptian is likely to sit next to you, rather than at the other end of the bench. This is just force of habit—it does not mean that the Egyptian wishes to speak to you.

Age Breakdown

0–14 = 36%   15–64 = 61%   65+ = 3% (1999 estimate)
Life Expectancy: 60.39 years, male; 64.49 years, female (1999 estimate)

Time

Egyptians often find it amusing how dependent Westerners are on the clock. Punctuality does not have a high priority in Egypt. Your Egyptian counterpart may be late for an appointment or might not show up at all. You, as a Westerner, should try to be prompt. Everything will take longer in Egypt, including the decision-making process.

When asking "How long will a journey take?' in Egypt, the generic response is "10 minutes" . . . even if the travel time is closer to an hour. Gridlocked street traffic in cities like Cairo make any predictions of travel times problematical.

Egypt is 2 hours ahead of Greenwich Mean Time (GMT +2), which is 7 hours ahead of U.S. Eastern Standard Time (EST +7).

Holidays

An up-to-date, web-based *World Holiday and Time Zone Guide* is available at www.getcustoms.com. It lists official holidays by country and by day of the year, cultural tips, a corruption index, and time zones with worldwide business hours.

This list is a working guide. Dates should be corroborated before final travel plans are made. In cases where holidays fall on Saturday or Sunday, commercial establishments may be closed the preceding Friday or following Monday.

Remember that the Islamic calendar uses lunar months of 28 days, so an Islamic year of 12 months is only 354 days long. Holidays will thus be on different dates (by the Western calendar) every year. Muslim holiday dates are also approximations since they depend upon actual lunar observations. Paperwork should carry two dates, the Gregorian (Western) date and the Hijrah (Arabic) date. Be aware that Christian Egyptians (Coptics) have yet another calendar, different from both of the above.

Jan 7	FR	Christmas (Coptic)
Jan 8	SA	Ramadan Bairam (3 days)
Mar 15	WE	Wakfet Arafet
Mar 16	TH	Eid-al-Adha (4 days)
Apr 6	TH	New Year's Day
Apr 25	TU	Sinai Liberation Day
Apr 30	SU	Easter Sunday (Coptic)
May 1	MO	Sham El Nessim
May 1	MO	Labor Day
Jun 15	TH	Mawled El-Nabi

Jul 23	SU	Revolution Anniversary
Oct 6	FR	Armed Forces Day
Dec 23	SA	Victory Day
Dec 27	WE	Ramadan Bairam

- There are additional Islamic and Eastern Orthodox Christian holidays that vary in observance date from year to year. Confirm your appointments with local representatives to avoid conflicts with regional festivals.

- The lunar-based Muslim calendar is shorter than the solar Gregorian calendar. Consequently, with respect to the Gregorian calendar, Muslim holidays advance by some 10 days each year. Also, the posted dates of Muslim religious holidays are only approximations, since the start of the holiday depends upon actual lunar observations.

- From a foreigner's point of view, the most important Muslim observances in Egypt are:

  Ramadan: the Holy Month. During this month, observant Muslims abstain from all food, drink, tobacco, and sexual activity during daylight hours. Dusk is announced by a cannon shot. The faithful are awakened before sunrise by drummers who roam the streets, reminding them to eat before dawn. It is impolite for nonbelievers to eat, drink, or even smoke in the presence of those who are fasting; if you must do so, be discreet. Office hours may be curtailed.

  Ramadan Bayram: The three-day festival at the end of the Ramadan fast. Children go door-to-door asking for sweets; Muslims exchange greeting cards, feast, and visit one another. Banks and offices are closed for all three days.

  Courban Bayram: The Feast of the Sacrifice. Celebrating the traditional story of Abraham's near-sacrifice of his son Isaac, this is the most important religious and secular holiday of the year. The holiday lasts for four days, but many banks and businesses close for an entire week. Resorts and transportation will be booked solid.

As measured by the Western calendar, these holidays occur at different times each year.

Work Week

- Friday is the Muslim holy day; no business is conducted on Fridays. Most people do not work on Thursdays, either. The work week runs from Saturday through Wednesday.

- Working hours for businesses, banks, and government offices are truncated during the month of Ramadan.

- Government hours are 8:00 A.M. to 2:00 P.M. Offices are closed on either Thursday and Friday or Friday and Saturday (the variation is designed to reduce traffic on congested Cairo streets).

- Banking hours tend to be 8:30 A.M. to 1:30 P.M. Monday through Wednesday. Some banks keep Sunday morning hours from 10 A.M. to 12 noon. Most international hotels offer 24-hour banking services.
- Business hours vary widely. In the winter, many close for much of the afternoon and reopen for a few hours in late afternoon.
- A typical business schedule would be 8 A.M. to 2 P.M. in the summer; 9 A.M. to 1 P.M. and 5 P.M. to 7 P.M. in the winter.

Observation: "Egyptians undergo an odd personality change when behind the wheel of a car. In every other setting, aggression and impatience are frowned upon. The unofficial Egyptian anthem "Bokra, Inasha'allah, Malesh" ("Tomorrow, God Willing, Never Mind") isn't just an excuse for laziness. In a society requiring millennial patience, it is also a social code dictating that no one make too much of a fuss about things. But put an Egyptian in the driver's seat and he shows all the calm and consideration of a hooded swordsman delivering Islamic justice."

   —From *Baghdad Without a Map, And Other Misadventure in Arabia* by Tony Horowitz. He adds that Cairo was "the first city I'd seen where policemen stood at intersections simply to enforce traffic lights." Note also that the English spellings for Arabic words vary. For example, "insha'Allah" ("God willing") is often rendered as "inshallah."

Religious/Societal Influences on Business

Islam is the official religion of Egypt, and 90% of Egyptians are Sunni Muslims. The remaining 10% are primarily Coptic Christians. The Coptic religion predates the arrival of Islam in Egypt, but the Coptics feel that the majority of Muslims discriminate against them. In general, Coptics are not proportionately represented at the high levels of business or Egyptian government—although there are exceptions.

Egyptians are intensely nationalistic and are quick to take offense at foreign interference in their affairs. Sensitive areas include Egypt's former colonial overlords (France and Britain), economic and cultural influences from the U.S., Islamic fundamentalism, and Israel. After fighting (and losing) three wars with Israel, Egypt became the first Arab country to make peace with Israel. The Egyptian people might not have accepted a peace treaty had not the Egyptian Army "redeemed" itself in the Yom Kippur War. After being routed in the previous two wars, the Egyptian armed forces put up a stubborn fight in the Yom Kippur War. Even though they were defeated, this resistance allowed the military to "save face"—something that is always important in Egypt.

As in all Islamic countries, piety and decorum are valued. Alcohol and pork are prohibited to observant Muslims, but Islam in Egypt is not so strict as in Saudi Arabia (where foreigners are jailed for possessing alcohol). Most international hotels in Egypt serve alcohol. Beer and wine are even manufactured in Egypt, although the quality of both has not been high.

With the largest Arab population in the world, Egypt considers itself the leading Arab nation. Yet Egypt is essentially a poor country, with a growing population that still requires large amounts of foreign aid. Many poor Egyptians continue to get poorer.

Islamic fundamentalism has been a problem for Egypt's government, which has responded with forceful attacks against suspected fundamentalists. As part of this effort, the Egyptian Ministry of Religious Endowments is taking over control of the country's 65,000 mosques.

Fundamentalist influence seems to be decreasing in Egypt. At this writing, there have been no terrorist attacks against foreigners since 58 foreign tourists were slain in Luxor in 1997. Secular Egyptians now feel less threatened by the fundamentalists.

5 Cultural Tips

1. Egypt is one of the most Westernized nations of the Middle East. You will encounter some international executives who are very familiar with Western business customs. Other Egyptian executives may have traditional Arab manners. Be prepared for any extreme.

2. Adjustments foreigners must make include the work week (Friday is the Islamic Sabbath, so the work week runs Saturday through Wednesday) and Ramadan (the month of fasting, when no one eats during the day and many people may seem cranky!).

3. Exaggeration and Arabic go hand-in-hand. Acceptance is blown up to enthusiasm; disapproval becomes a dire threat. Learn to take this in stride. When you hear an Egyptian say *yes* in answer to a question, always consider the cultural context. A mild *yes* is probably a polite *no*; at best, it means *possibly*.

4. Saving face is always a consideration in Egypt. Never cause someone to be embarrassed in public. Be prepared to go to great lengths to protect someone's dignity.

5. Waiting Egyptians do not stand in neat lines. At (for example) a ticket window, everyone pushes their way towards the front. Unless you are aggressive, you will wait a long time to be served.

Observations: "One of the first questions I'm always asked is 'What is it like as a woman working in Egypt?' The answer is that it isn't very much different from the U.S.A. I wear the same business clothes (although skirts need to be below the knee and long sleeves are important) and do not have to cover my hair. About a third of the Egyptian business women dress the same way, another third wear European/U.S. clothing but cover their hair with a scarf and the remainder wear more traditional robes and scarves.

"The Egyptian people have a strong tradition of hospitality. Eating together and sharing information on family, friends and your life outside of work is important.

Egyptians are anxious to hear what Egyptian foods you had and which ones you like. Table manners will be familiar, although you should not expect alcohol to be served in a home or even some restaurants.

"Egyptians are concerned that Americans' knowledge of Egypt is not limited to ancient Egypt. They feel most Americans still think only 'camels, pyramids, desert.' The truth is that Cairo is a rapidly growing city with all the benefits and problems of large cities anywhere. Take the time to read about modern Egypt, learn about the key businesses and about the current government and political climate. Your efforts will be appreciated."

> —Clare Novak, Novak and Associates (novakc@earthlink.net). Her work, in Egypt and in the U.S.A., is in leadership development.

Economic Overview

Since launching an economic reform program in 1991, Egypt has opened its doors wider to foreign trade and foreign investment. Egypt is one of a handful of markets where the U.S. has a multibillion-dollar trade surplus.

Egypt boasts both the most central location in the Middle East and the largest population. Although much of the population of 67.3 million is poor, they are reasonably well educated, and English is the most popular foreign language. As many as 10 million Egyptians are wealthy enough to follow Western consumption patterns.

U.S. exporters enjoy a solid position with more than a quarter of the $14 billion import market. Egyptians like American goods and technology and the American image overall is quite positive. Although substantial progress has been made in liberalizing Egypt's trade regime, domestic industry remains protected by nontariff import barriers and relatively high tariff rates.

The relative poverty of the majority of the population limits the Egyptian consumer market. However, there is hope that the massive privatization which is taking place will raise the standard of living for many poor and middle-class Egyptians.

Cultural Note: Foreigners who inadvertently violate Egyptian taboos sometimes underestimate the seriousness of their transgression. But a single incident, when it gets out of hand, can ruin your reputation in Egypt. For example: A visiting British poetry professor, while lecturing at Ain Shams University in Cairo, unthinkingly displayed the sole of his foot to his audience. In Egypt, as in other Muslim countries, this is a serious insult. The professor's failure to respect Egyptian decorum resulted in a student protest, followed by newspaper headlines denouncing British arrogance.

Comparative Data

Comparative Data Ratings
(Scale: 5 = Highest; 1 = Lowest)
Egypt: 2.75

- A. GDP Growth: 4
- B. Per Capita Income: 2
- C. Trade Flows with the U.S: 2
- D. Country Risk: 3
- E. Monetary Policy: 3
- F. Trade Policy: 3
    - Tariffs
    - Import Licensing
    - Import Taxes
- G. Protection of Property Rights: 2
- H. Foreign Investment Climate: 3

GROSS DOMESTIC PRODUCT: $188 billion (1998 estimate)

GDP GROWTH: 5% (1998 estimate)

PER CAPITA INCOME: $2,850 (1998 estimate)

Trade Flows with the U.S.

U.S. EXPORTS TO EGYPT: $3.1 billion (1998)

U.S. IMPORTS FROM EGYPT: $660 million (1998)

TOP U.S. EXPORTS TO EGYPT: Cereals; motor vehicles; aircraft; machinery; arms and ammunition; electrical products; medical and optical equipment; mineral fuel (fuel from coal); paper and paperboard; plastics

TOP U.S. PROSPECTS FOR EXPORT TO EGYPT: Construction equipment and building materials; mining equipment; engineering services; packaging equipment; biotechnology laboratories; medical equipment; oil and gas field machinery; franchising; computers and peripherals; agricultural equipment; port development services; electrical power systems; paper and paperboard; telecommunications equipment

Country Risk

Dun & Bradstreet rates Egypt as having an adequate credit risk with a reasonable capacity to meet outstanding payment liabilities.

A letter of credit is recommended when doing business with Egyptian concerns. Only one-third of merchandise arrivals are conducted on open account.

Monetary Policy

Inflation has been in the low double digits during the first half of the 1990s. Since then it has fallen even lower; inflation was 3.9% in 1998 and estimated at 4% in 1999. Inflation is expected to remain below 10% for the foreseeable future.

MONETARY UNIT: Egyptian pound

Cultural Note: Generally, vendors will not offer you change in Egypt, so keep a large provision of one-pound notes with you.

Trade Policy

TARIFFS   Tariffs range between 5 and 50%. Egyptian tariff rates are considered relatively high compared to other developing countries. Certain higher rates still apply for luxury goods.

IMPORT LICENSING   Import licenses are no longer required.
Import bans apply to textiles, apparel, and poultry.
Approximately 130 items are inspected for quality control prior to admittance into Egypt. These include foodstuffs, spare parts, construction products, electronic devices, appliances, and many consumer goods.

IMPORT TAXES   Egypt assesses a 3–6% service fee on imports, depending on the tariff applied. Egypt has committed to the World Bank to reduce this service fee to a flat 2%.
A sales tax ranging between 5% and 25% is added to the final customs value of the imported item.

Protection of Intellectual Property Rights

Egypt belongs to the Paris Convention for Protection of Industrial Property, the European Patent Convention, the Madrid Trademark Agreements, the Berne Convention on Copyrights, and Patent Cooperation Treaty. Egypt is on the U.S. Trade Representatives Priority Watch List due to insufficient patent protection

Egypt has two types of patents—invention patents and patents of addition. *Invention patents* cover new inventions applied for in Egypt and meet with the prescribed novelty standards. *Patents of addition* are patents that are issued in another country and then are recorded in Egypt for their remaining term. Pharmaceuticals and food products cannot receive product patents under Egyptian Law.

Trademarks have terms for 10 years and are renewable. The first applicant is entitled to registration. Both trademarks and service marks are protected. Trademarks are classified according to the international system, but service marks are classified according to a local system. Prior users have rights for 5 years to object to registrations after which time the registrations become incontestable.

The copyright system favors local parties. The works must be published and the copyrights must be recorded to be valid. Copyrights to foreign works are lost if the works are not translated into Arabic within 5 years. It is not copyright infringement to make private copies or to display works privately for a nonpaying audience.

Foreign Investment Climate

The government of Egypt is open to foreign direct investment. The U.S. and Egypt implemented a Bilateral Investment Treaty in 1992.

Investments are automatically approved unless the sector is on a "negative list" of projects. Only two items are on the negative list—military products and related industries, and tobacco and tobacco products.

Most foreign investment is under Investment Law 230 which allows 100% foreign ownership of ventures and guarantees the right to remit income earned in Egypt and to repatriate capital. Under Law 230, enterprises may own land necessary for their objectives without obtaining the specific approval of the Prime Minister, regardless of the foreign ownership percentage.

Privatization guidelines clearly state that there shall be no discrimination against foreign investors, but the sale of sector assets to foreigners remains controversial.

Political Leaders, Parties, and International Organizations

The International Academy at Santa Barbara at http://www.iasb.org/cwl publishes *Current World Leaders*, an excellent resource for up-to-date data on political leaders, parties, demographics, etc., in Egypt. Tel: (800) 530-2682 or (805) 965-5010 for subscription information to their database.

Chief of State:

President Hosni Mubarak

Head of the Government:

Prime Minister 'Atif Muhammad 'Ubaid

Next Election:

October 2005

Political Parties:

National Democratic Party, Labor Socialist Party, Liberal Socialist Party, National Progressive Unionist Party, New Wafd Party, Al-Umma Party, Egyptian Green Party, New MISR Al-Fatah Party, Unionist Democratic Party, Nasserist Party, Social Justice Party, Egyptian Arab Party

Membership in international organizations:

EBRD, LAS, NAM, OAPEC, OAU, OIC, UN and all of its specialized agencies and related organizations (including FAO, GATT, IAEA, IBRD, ICAO, IDA, IFAD, IFC, ILO, IMF, IMO, ITU, UNESCO, UNIDO, UPU, WHO, WIPO, WMO)

Political Influences on Business

President Hosni Mubarak has supported a strong U.S.–Egyptian relationship based on shared interests in promoting regional peace and stability, revitalizing the Egyptian economy, and strengthening trade ties. Over the years, Egypt and the U.S. have worked closely to help further the Middle East peace process. Egypt has also facilitated negotiations between Israel and Syria.

Islamic fundamentalism has been a problem for the Egyptian government. Although the threat of terrorism remains an impediment to foreign business investment, actual terrorist attacks have declined. The Egyptian government has taken draconian action against Islamic fundamentalists; at this writing, the government seems to be winning.

Egypt has faced allegations of human rights violations in regard to its treatment of both Islamic fundamentalists and its Coptic Christian community.

The Egyptian political system has undergone significant liberalization since the Nasser era of a few generations ago. Today, citizens enjoy a substantial degree of freedom of expression and the judiciary regularly demonstrates its independence from the executive branch. Further progress on political reform has taken a back seat to meeting the challenge posed by terrorist groups. The government's antiterrorism campaign has raised serious allegations of such human rights abuses as torture, arbitrary arrest, prolonged detention without trial, and the use of military courts to try persons accused of terrorism. Moreover, the governing National Democratic Party (NDP) dominates the political scene to such an extent that, as a practical matter, people do not have a meaningful ability to change their government. Egypt remains under an official state of emergency, as it has since 1981.

The Egyptian Constitution provides for a strong president who is empowered to appoint one or more vice presidents, the prime minister, the cabinet, and the governors of Egypt's 26 provinces. In 1993, President Hosni Mubarak was endorsed in a national referendum, in which he ran unopposed, to serve a third six-year term as President by the People's Assembly.

The People's Assembly has 454 members, 444 of whom are popularly elected, with 10 appointed by the President. The constitution reserves 50% of the Assembly seats for workers and farmers. Assembly members sit for five-year terms. There is also a 210-member *Shura* (Consultative) Council that has an advisory role on public policy but little legislative power.

The NDP has been in power since its establishment in 1978 and commands large majorities in the Assembly and the Shura Council and effectively controls the local governments, mass media, organized labor, and the large public sector. The NDP is an umbrella political party containing within its ranks members who favor greater economic and political reform as well as those who advocate continued government ownership of the public sector and an active government role in "regulating" the economy.

There are 12 recognized opposition parties, but only one—the leftist Tagammu Party—has frequently been represented in the People's Assembly. The other parties have boycotted elections because of allegations of unfair election procedures. Some of the other opposition parties include the Wafd party (centrist), the Islamist-oriented Socialist Labor party, and the Nasserist Party (leftist).

Contacts in the United States

THE EMBASSY OF THE ARAB REPUBLIC OF EGYPT
3521 International Court, NW
Washington, D.C. 20008
Tel: (202) 895-5400
Fax: (202) 244-4319
or (202) 244-5131

Passport/Visa Requirements

A passport and visa are required. For those arriving by air, a renewable 30-day tourist visa can be obtained at airport points of entry. Those arriving overland and by sea, or those previously experiencing difficulty with their visa status in Egypt, must obtain a visa prior to arrival. Military personnel arriving on commercial flights are not exempt from passport and visa requirements.

Proof of yellow fever and cholera immunization is required if arriving from an infected area. Evidence of an AIDS test is required for everyone staying over 30 days. Tourists must register with local authorities (either through their hotels, at local police stations, or at the central passport office) within seven days of arrival.

To obtain a business visa, a letter is required from the company stating the purpose of the trip, duration of stay, and who's responsible for travel expenses.

- *Validity of Visas*: Tourist and Business Visas are valid for three months from date of issue.

- *Visa Fees/Tourist and Business Visas*: All visa fees are payable by certified check or money order payable to the Consulate General of Egypt. No personal checks are accepted.

For current information concerning entry and customs requirements for Egypt, travelers can contact the Embassy of the Arab Republic of Egypt.

U.S. citizens who wish to apply for a passport may visit Passport Services' well-organized website at http://travel.state,gov/passport_services.html.

Contacts in Egypt

THE EMBASSY OF THE UNITED STATES OF AMERICA
8 Kamal EL-Din Salah St.
Garden City, Cairo
U.S. Mailing Address: APO AE 09839
Tel: (20) (2) 355-7371
Fax: (20) (2) 357-3200
www.usis.egnet.net

AMERICAN CHAMBER OF COMMERCE IN EGYPT
Cairo Marriott Hotel, Suite 1541
P.O. Box 33 Zamalek
Cairo
Tel: (20) (2) 340-8888
Fax: (20) (2) 340-6667
www.amcham.org.eg

OFFICE OF THE PRESIDENT
Cairo
Arab Republic of Egypt

OFFICE OF THE PRIME MINISTER
Cairo
Arab Republic of Egypt

Further contacts and websites can be found in Appendix A.

Communications

TELEPHONE: The country code for Egypt is 20.

The Egyptian telephone system has been notoriously deficient. Phone service was apt to go out at any time. There was no guarantee that your phone would even have a dial tone when you picked up the receiver. Phone service has been improving in the past few years, however.

E-MAIL: E-mail addresses located in Egypt end with the code .eg

DATES: In Egypt, the date is written in this order: day, month, year (unlike the U.S. practice of writing month, day, year). The dates are usually separated by periods (10.11.00 indicates November 10, 2000). Although the majority of Egyptians are Muslim, the calendar used is the Western (Gregorian) calendar, not the Muslim (Hijra) one.

Faux Pas: Don't make assumptions about Egyptians not understanding English. A U.S. executive from an aircraft manufacturer, assuming his limo driver did not speak English, scoffed to a colleague about the inability of the Egyptians to fly the airplanes he was selling. Not only did the driver understand, but he reported the remark to his superiors. The information reached the Egyptian Minister of Defense, who asked the U.S. Ambassador to have this executive sent home. This incautious executive was gone within 48 hours.

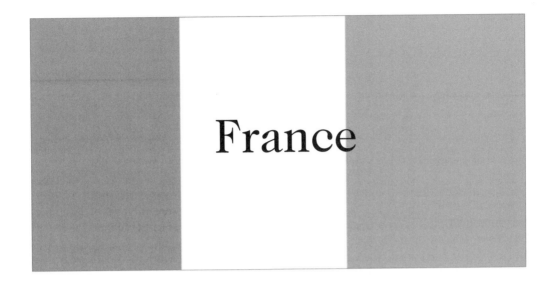

France

Official Name:	French Republic (République Française)
Official Language:	French
Government System:	Multi-party republic
Population:	58.978 million (1999 estimate)
Population Growth Rate:	0.27% (1999 estimate)
Area:	551,670 sq. km. (220,668 sq. mi.); the largest West European country, about four-fifths the size of Texas
Natural Resources:	coal, iron ore, bauxite, fish, timber, zinc, potash
Major Cities:	Paris (capital), Marseille, Lyon, Toulouse, Strasbourg, Nice, Bordeaux

Cultural Note: The French attitudes on money and sex are the reverse of those in the U.S. Unlike Americans, the French are almost impossible to embarrass about sex or nudity. On the other hand, money (and how you get it) is embarrassing to the French. Having money, or having the ability to make money, garners little respect in France. In fact, the simple question "What do you do?" is considered too personal to ask a stranger in France. To most French men and women, their jobs and their incomes are none of your business.

Age Breakdown

0–15 = 199%   15–64 = 65%   65+ = 16% (1999 estimate)
Life Expectancy: 74.76 years, male; 82.71 years, female (1999)

Time

Punctuality is treated very casually in France. People are often late, and no offense is taken. But the person in the subservient position is usually prompt. If you are trying to sell something to a French executive, you must be on time, while the executive is free to be late.

The rules for social events vary. People try to be punctual for lunch, since everyone will be returning to work afterwards (although lunch itself can easily span *two hours!*) At dinner, they can easily be a half-hour late.

In general, the French hate commitment. They will wait until the last minute before scheduling anything. Meetings and appointments will be rescheduled frequently.

France is 1 hour ahead of Greenwich Mean Time (GMT +1), which is 6 hours ahead of U.S. Eastern Standard Time (EST +6).

Holidays

An up-to-date, web-based *World Holiday and Time Zone Guide* is available at www.getcustoms.com. It lists official holidays by country and by day of the year, cultural tips, a corruption index, and time zones with worldwide business hours.

This list is a working guide. Dates should be corroborated before final travel plans are made. In cases where holidays fall on Saturday or Sunday, commercial establishments may be closed the preceding Friday or following Monday.

Jan 1	SA	New Year's Eve
Apr 24	MO	Easter Monday
May 1	MO	Labor Day
May 8	MO	Veterans' Day (WWII)
Jun 1	TH	Ascension Day
Jun 12	MO	Whitmonday
Jul 14	FR	Bastille Day
Aug 15	TU	Assumption
Nov 1	WE	All Saints Day
Nov 11	SA	Veterans' Day (WWI)
Dec 25	MO	Christmas Day

When a holiday falls on a Sunday, it is observed on Monday.

The Catholic observances of Good Friday, Easter Monday, Ascension Day, and the Assumption are also official holidays. Again, the days of observance should always be corroborated by local contacts.

Work Week

- Most French get four or five weeks' summer vacation, and take it in July and August. Indeed, except for the tourist industry, France virtually shuts down in August. Try to conduct business during other months.

- The fiscal year in the public sector runs on a calendar-year basis.

Religious/Societal Influences on Business

France has no official religion. Most religions are represented in France, but the majority of people (over 75%) are Roman Catholic. Recent immigrants from Algeria and other Mediterranean areas have increased the number of Muslims to 5.5%. An additional 3% of the French describe themselves as atheist.

Religion does not play a large part in the everyday lives of most French citizens. Anticlerical doctrines were made law during the French Revolution, and some of these survive to this day. Education, however, is the seminal event in the lives of most French citizens. French schools are rigorous, assigning so much homework that children have little time for other activities. Linguistic capability and wit are highly valued. Children are encouraged to develop their verbal skills from an early age. In order to discourage mundane topics of conversation, parents may respond to straightforward comments from children by saying "That's boring!"

France is a highly stratified society, with sharply-defined and competing classes. This "us against them" attitude is seen not only in politics, but in everyday interaction. Foreigners often find customer service in France to be below their standards and complain to the manager. Yet the manager nearly always sides with the employee. Manager and employee are part of a "family," and they unite against outsiders—even when it costs the company money! (But remember, earning money is not so high a personal priority in France as it is in the U.S.)

France remains a patriarchal country. Women's rights have come late to France; it wasn't until 1923 that women acquired the right to open their own mail! Sexual harassment has been illegal only since 1992.

5 Cultural Tips

1. The French handshake is brief—almost a hand clasp, accompanied by a short span of eye contact. There is good reason for this: French employees shake hands with each fellow employee every day . . . *twice*! When an employee arrives, he or she goes around the building shaking hands with everyone. When they leave, the process is repeated. Even in a small office, this can involve hundreds of handshakes every single day. While some French (of both sexes) kiss their friends on both cheeks, this is rarely done in a business setting.

2. The French have a great appreciation for art of conversation. However, be aware that the French frequently interrupt each other. *French conversation is not linear*. Instead, conversation is considered a dynamic process of give-and-take, where every possibility is articulated. Argument is a form of entertainment. Well-expressed opinions are appreciated, even if they are diametrically opposed to everyone else's. The French often complain that North Americans lecture rather than converse. Note that you do not have to answer every single objection to your proposal. The French want every opinion to be expressed—not necessarily refuted.

3. Food is important in France, and business always involves sharing meals. At a business lunch or dinner, show enthusiasm about the food before beginning a business discussion. Whoever initiates the meal is expected to pay. Reservations are necessary in most restaurants, except in brasseries and in hotels. In choosing a restaurant, stick to French rather than ethnic ones.

4. Respect privacy. The French close doors behind them; you should do the same. Knock and wait before entering.

5. Pay attention to voices. It is a sign of closeness in France to be able to recognize someone over the telephone by their voice alone. A friend is liable to be hurt if you have to ask "Who is this?" on the phone. Also be sensitive to the volume of your voice. It is no secret that U.S. executives are known to offend everyone in a restaurant, meeting, or on the street with their loud voices and braying laughter.

Observation: "I (a French person) call an office to ask for information. The phone is answered politely but rapidly, giving me the impression that if I do not hurry to ask all my questions, the party at the other end will hang up. I therefore have the impression of retaining that party against his or her will, and if I press him or her, I will be made to feel that I am going too far. . . . Perhaps the feeling here is that by telephoning, I am somehow cheating, since I am not waiting in line, I am not waiting my turn like everyone else.

—From *Cultural Misunderstandings: The French–American Experience* by Raymonde Carroll, translated from the French by Carol Volk

---

Economic Overview

France has the world's sixth largest economy and is the United States's eighth largest trading partner. The market for U.S. goods and services in France has been—and will continue to be—of major importance in industry, agriculture, and in the *invisibles* accounts, particularly in travel and franchising. As the economic recovery continues in France, there is expected to be improved demand for building materials, equipment related to air and surface transportation, and machine tools.

The French market is mature, sophisticated, and well-served by suppliers from around the world. Competition, both local and third-country, confronts American business at every corner in the coveted French market. With the increasingly free flow of goods and persons among European Union member nations, there is a natural tendency to buy within the community. U.S. businesses should keep this in mind so as to be competitive in shipping expenses and in timely delivery.

The French commercial environment is generally receptive to U.S. goods and services. It is dynamic and reflects consumer trends as well as the effect of comparative advantage in an interdependent world marketplace. The complex French society includes a strong market for high quality, high-tech consumer goods, particularly for its affluent cities where the distribution system still uses independent specialty stores as well as the more modern discount stores.

France and the U.S. are close allies. Despite occasional differences of view, the U.S. and France work together on a broad range of trade, security, and geopolitical issues.

Most U.S. companies face no major obstacles in doing business in France, with a few significant exceptions, namely, restrictions on the TV broadcast of non-European films and programs and the limitations on the performance of legal services by non-French lawyers. U.S. companies sometimes complain of France's complex technical standards and of unduly long testing procedures.

5 Largest Businesses in France

La Post, Boulogne Billancourt
    278,932 employees
Chemins de fer Francais, Paris
    175,012 employees
France Telecom, Paris
    144,025 employees
Ardouin Pierre, Marcillac
    139,733 employees
Electricite de France, Paris
    115,378 employees

Cultural Note: If you don't speak French, it is very important that you apologize for your lack of knowledge. The French are very proud of their language, and believe everyone should be able to speak it. (After all, for several hundred years, just about every Western diplomat *did* speak French.)

Observation: "On my speaking tour around America in 1990, I met many French professors teaching at Alliance Française centers in the U.S. They were cut off from their linguistic heartland. They suffered. They pined. You could feel their pulse quickening at the sight of another Frenchman.

"I said to one of them, 'It's amazing to Americans, the passion of the French for their language. I mean, we appreciate English, but we don't exactly think it's such an astonishing marvel—'

" 'Madame!' he cut me off. 'Not just a passion! A religion!' "

—Polly Platt, in her book *French or Foe?*

Comparative Data

Comparative Data Ratings
(Scale: 5 = Excellent; 1 = Poor)
France: 4.5

- A. GDP Growth: 3
- B. Per Capita Income: 5
- C. Trade Flows with the U.S.: 5
- D. Country Risk: 5
- E. Monetary Policy: 5
- F. Trade Policy: 4
  - • Tariffs
  - • Import Licensing
  - • Import Taxes
- G. Protection of Property Rights: 5
- H. Foreign Investment Climate: 3

GROSS DOMESTIC PRODUCT: $1.32 trillion (1998 estimate)

GDP GROWTH: 3% (1998 estimate)

PER CAPITA INCOME: $22,600 (1998 estimate)

Trade Flows with the U.S.

U.S. EXPORTS TO FRANCE: $17.7 billion (1998)

U.S. IMPORTS FROM FRANCE: $24 billion (1998)

TOP U.S. EXPORTS TO FRANCE: Machinery; electrical components; medical and optical equipment; aircraft and parts; precious stones and metal; organic chemicals; motor vehicles; plastics and resins; mineral fuel/oil; pharmaceutical products

Top U.S. Prospects for Export to France: Computer software; industrial chemicals; electronic components; computers and peripherals; security and safety equipment; electrical power systems; laboratory scientific equipment; aircraft and parts; pollution-control equipment; films/videos/records; telecommunications equipment; medical equipment

Country Risk

Dun and Bradstreet rates France as having excellent capacity to meet outstanding payment liabilities. France carries the lowest degree of risk.

Credit terms vary according to sector and size of transaction, but are usually between 60 and 90 days. Most transactions are on open account.

Monetary Policy

Inflationary pressures remain contained. The annual inflation rate for consumer process fell from 3.6% in 1989 to 0.7% in 1998, the lowest rate in France in 40 years. Inflation is expected to remain in the 2–2.5% range.

Monetary Unit: French franc

Trade Policy

Tariffs   Tariffs levied on imports from non-EU countries, including the U.S., are moderate. Most raw materials enter duty-free or at low rates, while most manufactured goods are subject to rates of between 5 and 17%. Most agricultural product imports are covered by the Common Agricultural Policy (CAP), under which many items are subject to variable levies designed to equalize the prices of imported commodities with those produced in the EU.

Import Licensing   Most products can be imported without an import license. Products subject to restrictive regulations include: poultry meat, enriched flour, genetic material, crayfish, and certain fruits and vegetables that are subject to seasonal price restrictions.

Import Taxes   In addition to the duties levied under the Common External Tariff, goods imported into France are also subject to a value-added tax (VAT). Currently, the VAT in France is generally charged at one of two rates: the standard rate of 20.6%; or the reduced rate of 5.5% applicable to most agricultural products and foodstuffs and certain medicines.

Most processed products entering the European Union and France are subject to additional import charges based on the percentage of sugar, milk fat, milk protein, and starch in the product. This situation should improve in the future because these charges will be converted to fixed tariff equivalents and reduced under the Uruguay Round Agreement.

Protection of Intellectual Property Rights

France abides by various intellectual property conventions and treaties, including: the Paris Convention for the Protection of Industrial Property, the Patent Cooperation Treaty, the European Patent Convention, the Madrid Convention on Trademarks, the Berne Convention for the Protection of Literary and Artistic Works, and the Universal Copyright Convention.

Patents protect novel industrial inventions and Certificates of Utility that cover minor improvements. Assignments and licenses involving French parties must be submitted for recording. Annual maintenance fees are required. Patents for inventions have a 20-year life span.

Trademark rights result on registration. Trademark registrations are good for 10 years and are renewable for similar periods. A six-month grace period is allowed for renewals. Trademarks and service marks are protected. Under previous French law there was no examination prior to registration or opposition. Under the new system opposition is permitted for six months after request for publication, and rights of registration may be challenged within 3 years of registration. Registrations may be challenged in courts if not used within the previous 5 years.

Copyrights cover artistic works, literary works, and software. In the French intellectual property rights regime, in order to qualify for a copyright, the language used to express the idea must be original, not the idea itself. Copyrights are valid for 50 years after the death of the author, with two major exceptions: music copyrights are valid for 70 years after the death of the composer, and software copyrights are valid for 25 years after creation.

Foreign Investment Climate

With its central location in a dynamic and unified European market, excellent infrastructure, productive and disciplined workforce, and high quality of life, France has become one of the most attractive potential locations for U.S. direct investment.

The French government actively courts foreign investment and has progressively liberalized its investment approval regime. Direct foreign investment is regarded as one of the best potential sources of new jobs.

However, U.S. investors still do not receive full national or EU treatment. The French state has a centuries-old tradition of extensive control of business and the economy. Today, even after a decade of rapid and comprehensive economic deregulation, and despite massive foreign investment by French companies, foreign investors in France occasionally face interference from government officials.

France offers a variety of financial incentives to foreign investors and its investment promotion agency, DATAR, provides extensive assistance to potential investors both in France and through its agencies around the world.

Political Leaders, Parties, and International Organizations

The International Academy at Santa Barbara at http://www.iasb.org/cwl publishes *Current World Leaders*, an excellent resource for up-to-date data on political leaders, parties, demographics, etc., in France. Tel: (800) 530-2682 or (805) 965-5010 for subscription information to their database.

Chief of State:
   President Jacques Chirac

Head of the Government:
   Prime Minister Lionel Jospin

Next Election:
   May, 2002

Political Parties:
   Socialist Party (PS), Leftist Radical Mov. (MRG), Communist Party (PCF), Rally for the Republic (RPR), Union for French Democracy (UDF), Green Party, Republican Party (PR), Center for Social Democrats (CDS), National Front (FN)

Membership in international organizations:
   CE, EBRD, EC, G7, INTELSAT, NACC, NATO, OECD, OSCE, UN and all of its specialized agencies and related organizations (including FAO, GATT, IAEA, IBRD, ICAO, IDA, IFAD, IFC, ILO, IMF, IMO, ITU, UNESCO, UNIDO, UPU, WHO, WIPO, WMO), WEU

Political Influences on Business

France and the U.S. are close allies. Despite occasional differences of view, the U.S. and France work together on a broad range of trade, security, and geopolitical issues.

France is a democratic republic whose political system is based on a written constitution approved by referendum in 1958. According to the French Constitution, the President of the Republic is elected by direct suffrage every seven years. The President names the Prime Minister, presides over the cabinet, commands the armed forces, and concludes treaties. He is also empowered to dissolve the National Assembly and, in certain emergency situations, may assume full power. France's political system is a hybrid of presidential and parliamentary systems, resulting occasionally in the President and Prime Minister being of opposing parties. From March 1993 to April 1995, for example, the Socialist President had a Prime Minister from a different party.

The Constitution provides for a bicameral parliament consisting of a National Assembly and a Senate. National Assembly deputies are directly elected by universal suffrage for five-year terms. Senators are indirectly elected for nine-year terms; one-third of the Senate is renewed every three years.

The French political spectrum includes five distinct political groups. From right to left, these are:

- the extreme right National Front (FN),
- the neo-Gaullist Rally for the Republic (RPR),
- the moderate Union for French Democracy (UDF),
- the Socialist Party (PS),
- and the Communists (PCF).

Numerous smaller parties have variable national political impact.

The late French President Francois Mitterrand, a Socialist, left office in May 1995, ending 14 years (two 7-year terms) in power. He was replaced by the former Mayor of Paris, Jacques Chirac, who edged out another Gaullist, Edouard Balladur (the former French Prime Minister), and Socialist Lionel Jospin for the Presidency. Jospin became Prime Minister in 1997.

In 1998, Prime Minister Lionel Jospin fulfilled a campaign promise by initiating a mandatory 35-hour work-week limit for most French employees. The measure was intended to relieve France's stubborn unemployment problem; the hope was that employers would be forced to hire more workers. To date, some 21,000 new jobs have been created since the imposition of the 35-hour mandate—far short of the 500,000 new jobs predicted. The French public sector is relatively unaffected by this regulation, because most French government employees already work less than 35 hours per week.

Contacts in the United States

THE EMBASSY OF THE FRENCH REPUBLIC
4101 Reservoir Road, NW
Washington, D.C. 20007
Tel: (202) 944-6000
Fax: (202) 944 6166
www.info-france-usa.org

Passport/Visa Requirements

A passport is required. For a stay not exceeding three months, the nationals of the countries listed do not need a visa to enter France, its overseas Departments (French Guyana, Guadeloupe, Martinique, Mayotte, Reunion, St. Pierre and Miquelon), and its overseas territories (French Polynesia, New Caledonia, Wallis and Futuna): Andorra,

Argentina, Austria, Belgium, Brunei, Canada, Chile, Croatia, Cyprus, the Czech Republic, Denmark, Finland, Germany, Great Britain, Greece, Hungary, Iceland, Israel, Ireland, Italy, Japan, Korea (ROK), Liechtenstein, Luxembourg, Malaysia, Malta, Monaco, Netherlands, New Zealand, Norway, Poland, Portugal, San Marino, Singapore, the Slovak Republic, Slovenia, Spain, Sweden, Switzerland, the United States, Uruguay, and the Vatican.

A visa is still required for a U.S. citizen for a short stay of less than 3 months if the individual is (a) intending to study in France, (b) a journalist on assignment, (c) member of a plane or ship crew on a mission, or (d) holder of diplomatic or official passports if on a mission.

Citizens of EU countries wishing to study or work in France do not need a visa. They need to go to the nearest Prefecture once in France. A visa is only required when the applicant wants to reside without working (retirement, for instance).

Citizens of the U.S. who intend to reside for more than three months must obtain a long-stay visa. These additional documents may also be needed: *carte de jour* (residency permit); a person intending to engage in business in France must apply for a *carte de commercant* (commercial card); and a person wishing to work there, a *carte de travail* (worker's card). For current information concerning entry and customs requirements for France, travelers can contact the French Embassy.

U.S. citizens who wish to apply for a passport may visit Passport Services' well- organized website at http://travel.state.gov/passport_services.html.

Contacts In France

THE EMBASSY OF THE UNITED STATES
OF AMERICA
2 Avenue Gabriel
75382 Paris Cedex 08
Paris
Mailing Address: PSC 116, APO AE
09777
Tel: (33) (1) 43 12 22 22
Fax: (33) (1) 42-66-97-83
www.amb-usa.fr

THE AMERICAN CHAMBER OF COMMERCE IN
FRANCE
21 Avenue George V
F-75008 Paris
Tel: (33) (1) 47 23 70 28
Fax: (33) (1) 47 20 18 62

DUN & BRADSTREET FRANCE S.A.
Postal Address: 345 avenue George
Clemenceau, Immeuble Defense
Bergeres, TSA 5003, 92882 Nanterre
CTC Cedex 9
Street Address: same
Tel: (33) (1) 41 35 1700
Fax: (33) (1) 41 35 1777

OFFICE OF THE PRESIDENT
Palais de l'Elysee
55-57 rue du Faubourg Sant Honore
75008 Paris, France

OFFICE OF THE PRIME MINISTER
57 rue de Varenne
75700 Paris, France

Further contacts and websites can be found in Appendix A.

Communications

TELEPHONE: The international country code for France is 33.

Phone numbers are eight digits in length. They are always read off in pairs of numbers (for example, 62.93.44.01).

There is currently only one regional code: The area around Paris uses a prefix of 1. The rest of France uses no prefix.

French toll-free numbers begin with the digits 05. At this writing, these toll-free numbers *cannot* be called from outside France. Toll-free numbers are colloquially known as *numéros verts* ("green numbers").

E-MAIL: E-mail addresses located in France end with the code .fr

---

Cultural Note: It is customary for the French to voice their opinions, even in business negotiations. However, it is not always necessary to respond to every comment or objection.

Germany

Official Name:	Federal Republic of Germany
Official Language:	German
Government System:	Democratic federal multi-party republic
Population:	82 million (1999 estimate)
Population Growth Rate:	0.01% (1999 estimate)
Area:	356,910 sq. km. (137,821 sq. mi.); about the size of Montana
Major cities:	Berlin (capital), Bonn (government seat), Hamburg, Munich, Frankfurt, Cologne, Leipzig, Dresden
Natural resources:	iron ore, coal, potash, timber, lignite, copper, natural gas, salt, uranium, nickel

Cultural Note: Keep your thinking linear in Germany. Thorough, methodical planning is how Germans have achieved their reputation for quality. Every aspect of every project will be examined in detail. This process can be very time-intensive.

Germans do not like the unexpected. Sudden changes—even if they may improve the outcome—are unwelcome.

Present your ideas in an organized manner. Be aware that the tendency of U.S. citizens to precede blunt criticism by first saying something positive is not done in Germany. A juxtaposition of good news/bad news may cause them to ignore your entire statement. In fact, Germans do not need or expect compliments. They just assume everything is satisfactory unless they hear otherwise.

Age Breakdown

0–14 = 27%   15–64 = 62%   65+ = 11% (1999 estimate)
Life Expectancy: 71.3 years, male; 78.56 years, female (1999 estimate)

Time

Punctuality is all-important in Germany. Arrive on time for every appointment, whether for business or social engagements. Being tardy—even by just two or three minutes—is very insulting to a German executive. Since planning is so important, appointments are made several weeks in advance. Do not expect to be able to wrangle an appointment on short notice.

Curiously, punctuality in Germany does not include delivery dates. Goods or services may be delivered late by Germans without either explanation or apology.

Germany is 1 hour ahead of Greenwich Mean Time (GMT +1), which is 6 hours ahead of U.S. Eastern Standard Time (EST +6).

Holidays

An up-to-date, web-based *World Holiday and Time Zone Guide* is available at www.getcustoms.com. It lists official holidays, cultural tips, time zones, and tables that compare worldwide business hours.

This list is a working guide. Dates should be corroborated before final travel plans are made. In cases where holidays fall on Saturday or Sunday, commercial establishments may be closed the preceding Friday or following Monday.

Jan 1	SA	New Year's Eve
Jan 6	TH	Epiphany[1]
Apr 21	FR	Good Friday
Apr 23	SU	Easter
Apr 24	MO	Easter Monday
May 1	MO	May Day
Jun 1	TH	Ascension
Jun 11	SU	Pentecost
Jun 12	MO	Pentecost Monday
Jun 22	TH	Corpus Christi
Aug 15	TU	Assumption[2]
Oct 3	TU	Day of German Unity
Oct 31	TU	Reformation Day
Nov 1	WE	All Saints Day

---

[1]Baden–Wuerttemberg, Bavaria Saxony–Anhalt

[2]Bavaria, Saarland

Nov 22	WE	Repentence Day[3]
Dec 25	MO	Christmas Day
Dec 26	TU	Second Day of Christmas

In addition to the above, the Christian observances of Good Friday, Easter, and Easter Monday are official holidays throughout Germany.

In many Catholic areas of Germany, Ascension Day, Pentecost, Pentecost Monday, Corpus Christi, and the Assumption are also official holidays.

The days of observance should always be corroborated by local contacts. There are also many regional holidays that are observed in addition to this list.

Work Week

- Business hours are generally 8:00 or 9:00 A.M. to 4:00 or 5:00 P.M. Monday through Friday.
- The preferred times for business appointments are between 11:00 A.M. and 1:00 P.M. or between 3:00 P.M. and 5:00 P.M. Late afternoon appointments are not unusual.
- Do not schedule appointments on Friday afternoons; some offices close by 2:00 or 3:00 P.M. on Fridays. Many people take long vacations during July, August, and December, so check first to see if your counterpart will be available. Also be aware that little work gets done during regional festivals, such as the Oktoberfest or the three-day Carnival before Lent.
- Banking hours: 8:30 A.M. to 1:00 P.M. and 2:00 to 4:00 P.M. Monday through Friday. *Except*: Closing time on Thursday is extended to 5:30 P.M.
- Store hours: 8:00 or 9:00 A.M. to 5:00 or 6:00 P.M. Monday through Friday. On Saturday, most shops close by 2:00 P.M., *except* for one Saturday per month when shops remain open into the evening.

Religious/Societal Influences on Business

Germany is evenly split between Roman Catholics (who are concentrated in the South) and Protestants (who are found in the North). With the exception of a few issues—such as abortion—there is little conflict between the churches.

Environmental consciousness approaches the level of religious belief in many Germans. Germany has some of the strictest packaging and recycling laws on Earth. Veneration of nature, especially forests, has deep historical roots.

Social factors are as important as religion towards regulating German behavior. There is a great desire for order and control. Every citizen has a responsibility to maintain order. This covers a huge range of behavior, from public deportment (which is

---

[3]Saxony

quiet and serious) to automobile maintenance (cars are kept amazingly clean). Life is considered serious, and humor confined to very specific times and places.

5 Cultural Tips

1. In business situations, most Germans shake hands at both the beginning and the end of a meeting. *Note that the handshake may be accompanied by a very slight bow—little more than a nod of the head.* Although this bow is subtle, it is important. Failure to respond with this nod/bow (especially to a superior) may get you off to a bad start.

2. Germans are sticklers for titles. Try to address people by their full, correct title—no matter how extraordinarily long that title may seem to foreigners.

   Most Germans expect to be addressed as Mr. or Mrs./Ms. followed by her/his surname (Mr. = *Herr*, Mrs./Ms. = *Frau*).

   Note that *Fraulein* (Miss) is no longer used except for women under age 18. A businesswoman should be addressed as *Frau*, no matter what her marital status.

   If someone has one or more titles, retain the Mr. or Mrs./Ms. but substitute the title(s) for the surname. Many professionals use their title, including engineers, pastors, politicians, and lawyers. Anyone with a doctorate is entitled to the title of *Doktor*. Teachers have the additional title of *Profesor*. A male teacher with a Ph.D. is addressed as *Herr Doktor Profesor*.

3. Germans reserve their smiles to indicate affection. In the course of business, Germans rarely smile, and laughter is certainly not considered appropriate.

4. While important business decisions are not made over the phone, expect many follow-up calls or faxes. However, Germans jealously guard their private lives, so do not phone a German executive at home without permission. Since reunification, great effort has been placed in bringing the poor phone system of the former East Germany up to West German standards.

5. In business encounters, age takes precedence over youth. In a delegation, the eldest person enters first. When two people are introduced, the younger person is introduced to an older person (if the eldest person has the highest rank).

Economic Overview

Germany remains the largest economy in Europe and one that U.S. companies must address. Unification of Germany made it all the more important for U.S. products—Germany is the fifth largest export market for U.S. products worldwide. The western German market is a wealthy one, whose population enjoys a very high standard of living. Long-term prospects are bright for the eastern states, but the road to prosperity will be rocky and tardy in reaching some corners of the region.

The top priorities of the German government are to maintain economic growth, reduce unemployment, and to continue fostering the development of eastern Germany.

The German economy is the world's third largest, behind only the U.S. and Japan. It accounts for approximately 25% of the European Union's GDP by itself. Germany's broadly diversified economy affords its citizens one of the highest standards of living in the world.

To a far greater degree than its European neighbors, Germany's population and industry are decentralized and evenly distributed. Major cities and businesses dot the countryside in a landscape that features no single business center. U.S. suppliers must ensure that their distributor, or own dealerships, have countrywide capability.

Success in the German market requires long-term commitment to market development and sales support.

5 Largest Businesses in Germany

Siemens Aktiengesellschaft, Berlin
 401,000 employees
Daimlerchrysler AG, Stuttgart
 295,514 employees
Deutsche Bahn AG, Frankfurt
 285,322 employees
Volkswagen Aktiensellschaft, Wolfsburg
 274,575 employees
Deutsche Post Aktiensellschaft, Bonn
 269,530 employees

Comparative Data

Comparative Data Ratings
(Scale: 5 = Excellent; 1 = Poor)
Germany: 4

- A. GDP Growth: 3
- B. Per Capita Income: 5
- C. Trade Flows with the U.S.: 5
- D. Country Risk: 5
- E. Monetary Policy: 5
- F. Trade Policy: 4
  - Tariffs
  - Import Licensing
  - Import Taxes
- G. Protection of Property Rights: 5
- H. Foreign Investment Climate: 4

GROSS DOMESTIC PRODUCT: $1.74 trillion (1997 estimate)

GDP GROWTH: +2.3% (1998), +1.3% (1999 estimate)

PER CAPITA INCOME: $20,800 (1997 estimate)

Trade Flows with the U.S.

U.S. Exports to Germany: $26.6 billion (1998)

U.S. Imports from Germany: $49.8 billion (1998)

Top U.S. Exports to Germany: Machinery; electronic components; medical and optical equipment; motor vehicles; aircraft; plastics; chemical products; pharmaceuticals; precious stones and metals; organic chemicals

Top U.S. Prospects for Export to Germany: Computer software; computer equipment and peripherals; information services; franchising; electronic components; telecommunications equipment; aircraft/parts; laboratory scientific equipment; industrial chemicals; automotive parts

Country Risk

Dun & Bradstreet rates Germany as having the highest creditworthiness with an excellent capacity to meet payment liabilities when compared with other countries. Germany carries the lowest degree of risk.

Most business is done on an open account basis with 30- to 60-day terms the norm. Closer scrutiny of creditworthiness is advised on eastern German companies, and moderately secure terms are recommended. Discounts are often expected for prompt payment.

Monetary Policy

Inflationary pressures remain firmly under control. Inflation is at very low levels and is expected to remain so in the short term.

Monetary Unit: Deutsche mark, currently being phased out in favor of the EU euro

Trade Policy

Tariffs   Most manufactured goods are subject to tariff rates of between 5% and 17%. Most raw materials enter either duty-free or at low rates. Most agricultural imports are covered by the Common Agricultural Policy (CAP) where many items are subject to variable levies designed to equalize the prices of imported commodities with those produced in EU member countries.

Import Licensing   Germany has one of the world's strongest market economies and one that poses few formal barriers to U.S. firms. Safety standards can at times complicate access to the market for many U.S. products. Firms interested in exporting to Germany should be well prepared to ensure they know precisely which standards apply to their product, and that timely testing and certification are obtained.

Import Taxes   Germany levies a 16% value-added tax (VAT) on industrial goods.

Protection of Intellectual Property Rights

Germany is a member of the EC, the Berne Convention for the Protection of Literary and Artistic Works, the Universal Copyright Convention, the Patent Cooperation Treaty, the European Patent Convention, the Paris Convention for the Protection of Industrial Property, and the Madrid Trademark Conventions. Patents and trademarks that were obtained either in the former East or West Germany are effective throughout the reunited German nation.

Inventors may file for a European or German patent.

German patent law provides for issuance of a basic patent for a period of 20 years following the effective filing date of application, subject to payment of required maintenance fees. Germany classifies inventions as free or bound. *Free* inventions are those that belong to the inventors. *Bound* inventions are those that belong to the inventor's employer.

Trademark rights derive from registration. Service marks and trademarks are registerable. Acoustic and three-dimensional marks (configurations) may be registered. Registrations have a term of 10 years from the application filing date and are renewable for similar periods. Interested parties may oppose the issuance of a registration. Cancellation actions may be brought for nonuse of a period of 5 years.

Copyrights result by operation of law and registration is unnecessary. Under the German Copyright Law, works of literature, music, and art are protected for the life of the author and 70 years after his or her death. Computer programs are subject to copyright protection. Laws were recently passed to protect databases.

Foreign Investment Climate

One hundred percent foreign ownership is permitted in almost all sectors open to private investment. Firms in certain sectors, such as the media, can only be owned up to 49% by any one individual or company, however.

Under German law, foreign-owned companies registered in Germany as a GmbH (limited liability company) or an AG (joint stock company) have domestic status.

The U.S. remains the single largest source of foreign investment in Germany, despite a maze of regulations that frequently baffle and anger foreign investors.

Political Leaders, Parties, and International Organizations

The International Academy at Santa Barbara at http://www.iasb.org/cwl publishes *Current World Leaders*, an excellent resource for up-to-date data on political leaders, parties, demographics, etc., in Germany. Tel: (800) 530-2682 or (805) 965-5010 for subscription information to their database.

Chief of State:

President Johannes Rau

Head of the Government:

Chancellor Gerhard Schröder

Next election:

May, 2004

Political parties:

Christian Democratic Union or CDU; Christian Social Union or CSU; Free
Democratic Party or FDP; Social Democratic Party or SPD; Alliance '90/Greens;
Party of Democratic Socialism or PDS; German People's Union or DVU

Membership in international organizations:

CBSS, CE, EBRD, EU, G7, IEA, INTELSAT, NACC, NATO, OECD, OSCE, UN and
all of its specialized agencies and related organizations (including FAO, GATT,
IAEA, IBRD, ICAO, IDA, IFAD, IFC, ILO, IMF, IMO, ITU, UNESCO, UNIDO,
UPU, WHO, WIPO, WMO), WEU

Political Influences on Business

The top priorities of the German government are to maintain economic growth and to
continue fostering the development of eastern Germany. The new states are now an
integral part of Germany, contain millions of voters, and are being brought up to the
economic standards of western Germany as quickly as possible. Accordingly, a high
priority continues to be placed on financing eastern development, implying the likeli-
hood of a flow of major project opportunities for years to come.

In addition, Germany's political leadership also wants to promote Germany's competitiveness and various proposals are being considered to modernize the country's
economic situation. Since unification on October 3, 1990 Germany has placed a high
priority on improving its relations with its neighboring states as well as strengthening
trans-Atlantic relations. Recognizing that political stability is nurtured by economic
prosperity, Germany has been one of the major sources of assistance to Central
European and CIS states.

The country continues to emphasize close ties with the United States, membership
in NATO, progress toward further European integration, and improved relations with
Central Europe. German–American political, economic, and security relationships
regardless of which administration has been in power in either country have been
based on close consultation and coordination at the most senior levels. High-level visits take place frequently, and the United States and the FRG cooperate actively in
international forums. U.S. government officials enjoy good access to policy- and decision-makers, and are able to raise issues directly affecting U.S. business active in
Germany.

Under the German Constitution, known as the Basic Law, the Federal Republic of
German (FRG) is a parliamentary democracy with a bicameral legislature, an inde-
pendent judiciary, and executive power exercised by a Prime Minister whose title is
Chancellor.

The lower house of Parliament, the *Bundestag*, currently consists of 672 deputies elected for 4-year terms. Members are elected through a mixture of direct constituency candidates and party lists. The Basic Law and the *Laender* (state) constitutions stipulate that parties must receive at least 5% of the national vote (or at least three directly-elected seats in federal elections) in order to be represented in the federal and state parliaments. One must be 18 years old to vote in Germany.

The president may be elected to two 5-year terms and his duties as chief of state are largely ceremonial. Executive power is exercised by the Chancellor who is elected by and responsible to the *Bundestag*. The Chancellor cannot be removed from office during a 4-year term unless the *Bundestag* has agreed on a successor.

The upper house, the *Bundesrat*, is composed of delegations from the 16 state governments and has a proportional distribution of its 68 votes, depending on the population of the state. The role of the *Bundesrat* is limited, but it can exercise substantial veto powers over legislation passed in the *Bundestag* when the proposed legislation would affect the numerous prerogatives of the *Laender*. Among these are matters relating to tax reform, law enforcement and the courts, culture and education, the environment, and social assistance.

The political parties represented in the *Bundestag* are:

- The Christian Democratic Union and its Bavarian sister party, the Christian Social Union (CDU/CSU). The CDU/CSU is generally conservative on economic and social policy.

- The Social Democratic Party (SPD), which abandoned the concept of a class party in 1959 while continuing to stress social welfare programs.

- The Free Democratic Party (FDP), which is composed of those who consider themselves "independents" and heirs to the European liberal tradition.

- The Party of Democratic Socialism (PDS), which is the successor party to the SED (the communist party of the former German Democratic Republic).

- The Alliance 90/The Greens (Bundnis 90/Die Gruenen), which has an environmentalist, pacifist platform.

Contacts in the United States

THE EMBASSY OF THE FEDERAL REPUBLIC OF GERMANY
4645 Reservoir Road, NW
Washington, D.C. 20007
Tel: (202) 298-4000
Fax: (202) 298-4249
www.germany-info.org

Passport/Visa Requirements

Citizens of the U.S. who plan to visit the Federal Republic of Germany as tourists or for business purposes for a period of up to three months during six months do not need a visa. A valid U.S. passport is sufficient. Citizens of other countries (except citizens of member states of the European Union) may require a visa.

All persons who wish to stay in the Federal Republic of Germany for a period of more than three months are required to obtain a residence permit in the form of a visa, which will be documented in the passport. Persons who wish to take up employment during their stay are required to obtain a work permit in addition to the residence permit.

For current information concerning entry and customs requirements for Germany, travelers can contact the German Embassy.

U.S. citizens who wish to apply for a passport may visit Passport Services' well-organized website at http://travel.state.gov/passport_services.html.

Contacts in Germany

THE EMBASSY OF THE UNITED STATES OF AMERICA
Deichmanns Ave
53179 Bonn 2
Bonn
Tel: (49) (228) 3392063
Fax: (49) (228) 334649
www.usembassy.de/

THE AMERICAN CHAMBER OF COMMERCE IN GERMANY
Rossmarkt 12, Postfach 100 162
D-6000 Frankfurt/Main 1
Frankfurt
Tel: (49) 28 34 01

DUN & BRADSTREET SCHIMMELPFENG GMBH.
Postal Address: Postfach 71 08 51, 60498 Frankfurt/M
Street Address: Hahnstr. 31-35, 60528 Frankfurt/M
Tel: (49) (69) 66303-0
Fax: (49) (69) 66303-175; (49) (69) 66303-624 (RMS)

OFFICE OF THE FEDERAL PRESIDENT
Schloss Bellevue
Spreeweg 1, 10557 Berlin
Federal Republic of Germany

OFFICE OF THE FEDERAL CHANCELLOR
Bundeskanzleramt
Adenauerallee 141
53113 Bonn, Federal Republic of Germany

Cultural Note: Germans keep a slightly larger personal space around them than most North Americans. Stand about 6 inches farther back than you would in the U.S. The position of office furniture follows this rule, too. Do not move your chair closer; a German executive could find that very insulting.

This expanded personal space extends to their automobiles. Expect a violent outburst from a German driver if you so much as touch his or her car. Never put a package down on any car except your own.

Further contacts and websites can be found in Appendix A.

Communications

TELEPHONE: The international country code for Germany is 49.

Phone numbers vary in length; most are six or seven digits in length. Six-digit numbers are usually divided into pairs of numbers (i.e., 25 49 01). When the number has seven digits, the first three numbers are grouped together (i.e., 813 70 33).

City codes may be two, three, or even more digits in length. The largest cities have two-digit codes.

The former East Germany is now included under the German phone system, and does not use its old country code of 37.

E-MAIL: E-mail addresses located in Germany end with the code .de (for Deutschland).

Faux Pas: A manufacturer of cabinet hardware was seeking a European distributor, and decided to approach a Frankfurt firm. They sent a bright young executive who was fluent in German to make their sales pitch. He was an accomplished speaker, and a past president of the local Toastmasters Club. The executive even had a connection, as his grandparents had immigrated from the Frankfurt region.

Despite these advantages, his presentation was not well received, and the Frankfurt firm did not become a distributor. The executive later discovered that the Germans had been put off by the start of his speech. Following American speaking customs, he opened with some humorous anecdotes. Germans find nothing funny about business, so his amusing opening caused them to immediately reject him as a serious prospect. Furthermore, he was too young to be sent alone to a country like Germany, where age conveys respect. The Germans assumed that if this was an important offer, an older executive would have been sent.

India

Official Name:	Republic of India (English), Bharat (Hindi)
Official Languages:	English and Hindi
Government System:	Multi-party federal republic
Population:	1 billion (1999 estimate)
Population Growth Rate:	16.8% (1999)
Area:	3,287,263 sq. km. (1,268,884 sq. mi.); about twice the size of Alaska
Natural Resources:	coal, iron ore, manganese, mica, bauxite, titanium ore, chromite, natural gas, diamonds, crude oil, limestone
Major Cities:	New Delhi (capital), Calcutta, Bombay, Madras, Bangalore, Hyderabad, Ahmedabad

Cultural Note: In the U.S., people think in terms of dominating or controlling the environment. For example, the West was "won," rivers are "tamed," and land is "developed." Most natives of India have an opposite viewpoint of nature. Perhaps because they are faced with the overwhelming power of yearly monsoons, Indians traditionally consider themselves to be at the mercy of their environment. In India, it is the *people* who are tamed by the land.

Age Breakdown

0–15 = 34%   15–64 = 61%   65+ = 5%
Life Expectancy: 62.54 years, male; 64.29 years, female (1999 estimate)

Time

As a foreign businessperson, you are expected to be relatively prompt. However, punctuality has not traditionally been considered a virtue in India. Your Indian counterpart may be late or may not show up at all.

India is 5-1/2 hours ahead of Greenwich Mean Time (GMT +5-1/2), which is ten-1/2 hours ahead of Eastern Standard Time (EST +10-1/2).

Holidays

An up-to-date, web-based *World Holiday and Time Zone Guide* is available at www.getcustoms.com. It lists official holidays by country and by day of the year, cultural tips, a corruption index, and time zones with worldwide business hours.

- The best time of year to visit India is between October and March (bypassing the seasons of extreme heat and monsoons).
- Business is not conducted during religious holidays, which are numerous throughout the many regions and states of India. Befitting a multicultural nation, India officially observes Hindu, Muslim, and Christian celebrations.
- This list is a working guide. In cases where holidays fall on Saturday or Sunday, commercial establishments may be closed the preceding Friday or following Monday.

Jan 9	SU	Eid-al-Fitr
Jan 26	WE	Republic Day
Mar 15	WE	Mahavir Jayanti
Mar 19	SU	Feast of the Sacrifice
Apr 16	SU	Muharram
Apr 21	FR	Good Friday
May 18	TH	Buddha Purnima
Jun 17	SA	Birth of the Prophet
Aug 15	TU	Independence Day
Oct 2	MO	Mahatma Gandhi's Birthday
Oct 7	SA	Dussehra Mela (2 days)
Oct 26	TH	Diwali
Dec 25	MO	Christmas
Dec 28	SA	Eid-al-Fitr

In addition to the above, India observes as official holidays the Hindu festivals of Janmashtami, Dussehra, and Diwali, plus the Muslim festival of Id Ul Fitr. The dates of these holidays vary from year to year. The dates for these holidays can be checked via the Indian Tourist Office, Consulate, or Embassy.

In addition to these national holidays, many local holidays are observed in different states in India.

Work Week

- Indian executives prefer late morning or early afternoon appointments, between 11:00 A.M. and 4:00 P.M.
- Business hours: 9:30 A.M. to 5:00 P.M. Monday through Friday (lunch is usually from 1:00 to 2:00 P.M.).
- Bank hours: 10:00 A.M. to 2:00 P.M. Monday through Friday, and 10:00 A.M. to 12:00 noon on Saturdays.
- Government office hours: 10:00 A.M. to 5:00 P.M. Monday through Saturday (closed for lunch from 1:00 to 2:00 P.M.). Note that government offices are closed the second Saturday of each month.

Religious/Societal Influences on Business

India has such a plethora of cultures, religions and castes, it would take several volumes to explain them all.

The majority of Indians are Hindu. Unlike many religions that are traced to a particular founder, Hinduism grew out of Indian mythology. Hinduism has many variants and lacks a single, authoritative text (like the Christian Bible or the Muslim Koran). It is a religion with multiple gods, and it teaches a belief in karma and reincarnation. To escape the cycles of reincarnation and achieve nirvana, one must stop committing both bad deeds and good deeds—a difficult process that requires virtual nonintervention with humanity. India's caste system is supported by most variants of Hinduism. Cows are venerated by many Hindus, who neither eat beef nor wear leather. Many Hindus are vegetarian. Although Hinduism focuses on the nonworldly, this does not prevent Hindus from being politically active. Indeed, Hindu nationalism—as manifested in the Bharatiya Janata Party (BJP)—became the dominant single political force in India in the 1990s.

A minority of Indians are Muslim. Islam is a monotheistic religion with ties to both Judaism and Christianity. Shiite Muslims outnumber Sunni Muslims by about three-to-one in India. Surrender to the will of Allah is a central belief. Pork and alcohol are prohibited to observant Muslims.

Since India's two major religions forswear beef and pork, it is not surprising that Indian cuisine uses mostly chicken, lamb, or vegetables. These religions also share an acceptance of fate, and have a fatalistic view of man's ability to change that fate.

About 2% of Indians are Sikhs. Sikhism combines tenets of both Hinduism and Islam.

Sikhs believe in reincarnation but do not recognize caste distinctions. Unlike Hindus, Sikhs reject nonintervention with the world as cowardly.

India also has Christians, Buddhists, Jains, and Zoroastrians.

Predominantly-Hindu India has been a rival of predominantly-Muslim Pakistan since the two countries achieved independence. The two countries have engaged in armed conflicts, and continue to compete for Indian-controlled Kashmir. In 1998, India detonated several nuclear devices—weapons designed primarily for defense against Pakistan. In response, Pakistan exploded its own nuclear weapons.

5 Cultural Tips

1. Business relationships in India are based on personal relationships. You must establish a relationship of mutual respect with Indian decision-makers. To do this, you may need to make your initial contacts with middle managers. While they do not make the final decision, they can bring your proposal to the attention of their supervisors. They will be much more accessible than the senior executives.

2. With 14 major languages and some 300 minor ones, English has become a unifying force in India. Generally, you will be able to conduct business in English, and it is not necessary to have your written materials translated.

3. Traditionally, Indians greet each other with a gesture called the *namaskar*. Upon meeting, each person raises his or her hands and holds them together—very much like Christians praying. The fingertips are raised approximately to the level of the chin. The entire motion is usually accompanied by a slight bow. Along with this gesture, a phrase of greeting is spoken by both persons. Hindus generally say the word *namaste*, which can be translated as "I salute the divine within you." Different ethnic and religious groups use different greeting phrases, but most use the same gesture. This gesture can be given both upon arrival and departure. Indian men who do business with foreigners may offer to shake hands with men. But public contact between the genders is rare, and men do not usually shake hands with women.

4. Body language in India is very different from North America. Head gestures for *yes* and *no* are virtually reversed. Indians show agreement by tossing their head from side to side, which Westerners can misinterpret as *no*. To show disagreement, Indians nod up-and-down . . . or rather toss their heads up and back. This is similar to the gesture Americans use to indicate *yes*.

5. Gift-giving is an important part of doing business in India. Remember that gifts are not opened in the presence of the giver. Wrap the gifts carefully, but avoid using black or white paper, which many people consider unlucky. If you have occasion to give money to an Indian, give an odd number, such as $11 rather than $10.

Faux Pas: At an appointment with a high-ranking Indian bureaucrat, a U.S. salesman of data-processing equipment was invited to give his pitch in the presence of a third person. The bureaucrat did not introduce this third man, nor did the third man speak. The presence of this man totally unnerved the salesman. He imagined worst-case scenarios, such as the third man being employed by his competitors. He became so distracted that he gave a poor presentation, and failed to make a sale.

In India (as in the Middle East), there is no guarantee that a business appointment will be private. Your Indian client may be joined by an advisor, a relative, or just an interested party. The silent person may be the real decision maker, observing you while you pitch to an underling. Do not become distracted by their presence.

Economic Overview

The United States is India's leading foreign investor and largest trading partner. The U.S. has identified India as one of the 10 "Big Emerging Markets" where future growth rates are poised to exceed those in the developed markets.

India's economy is a mixture of traditional village farming, modern agriculture, handicrafts, a wide range of industries, and a multitude of support services. Faster economic growth in the 1980s permitted a significant increase in real per capita private consumption.

Production, trade, and investment reforms since 1991 have provided new opportunities for Indian businessmen and an estimated 100 million to 200 million middle-class consumers. In 1998, India was hurt by a collapse in the stock market and a weak rupee. Nevertheless, India's dynamic entrepreneurial class is confident that their country's economy will recover and expand.

India has a dynamic private sector, a need for capital and technology that cannot be met domestically, a growing middle class hungry for opportunity, and a consensus favoring opening India to foreign trade and investment. Positive factors for the future include India's strong entrepreneurial class and the central government's recognition of the continuing need for market-oriented approaches to economic development. The progress of India's economic reforms offer investment and trade opportunities to U.S. firms willing and able to accept some measure of uncertainty as the process matures. Negative factors include the desperate poverty of some one billion Indians and the impact of the huge and expanding population on an already overloaded environment.

5 Largest Businesses in India
Banque Indosuez, Bombay
   850,000 employees
V.K. Verma & Co., New Delhi
   500,000 employees

Central Railways, Mumbai
    480,018 employees
Department of Telecommunications, New Delhi
    421,000 employees
Banque Nationale de Paris, Bangalore
    268,000 employees

Cultural Note: In a culture with a history of scarcity, complex traditions often develop. In India you will be offered refreshment (usually tea) at virtually every business meeting. Tradition requires you to turn down at least the first offer, and—if you wish—the second. However, you must accept the third offer, or risk insulting your host. The object of these refusals is not to be coy, but to avoid appearing greedy.

Comparative Data

Comparative Data Ratings
(Scale: 5 = Excellent; 1 = Poor)
India: 3.0

- A. Per Capita Income: 1
- B. GDP Growth: 5
- C. Trade Flows with U.S.: 3
- D. Country Risk: 3
- E. Monetary Policy: 4
- F. Trade Policy: 2
    - Tariffs
    - Import Licensing
    - Import Taxes
- G. Protection of Property Rights: 3
- H. Foreign Investment Climate: 3

GROSS DOMESTIC PRODUCT: $1.5 trillion (1997 estimate)

GDP GROWTH: 6.0% (1998 estimate), 6.5% (1999 estimate)

PER CAPITA INCOME: $1,600 (1997 estimate)

Trade Flows with the U.S.

U.S. EXPORTS TO INDIA: $3.5 billion (1998)

U.S. IMPORTS FROM INDIA: $8.2 billion (1998 estimate)

TOP U.S. EXPORTS TO INDIA:?   Machinery; aircraft; electrical products; organic chemicals; medical and optical equipment; fertilizers; iron and steel; precious stones and metals; plastic; copper

TOP U.S. PROSPECTS FOR EXPORT TO INDIA: Computers and peripherals; telecommunications equipment and services; aircraft and parts; oil and gas field machinery; electric power-generating and transmission equipment; plastic processing material and equipment; steel plant equipment and services; mining and mineral processing equipment; machine tools; amusement rides; games and machines

Country Risk

Dun & Bradstreet rates India as having sufficient capacity to meet outstanding payment liabilities.

Fully secured terms such as confirmed letter of credit are advised for initial transactions. Just 10% of all transactions in India are estimated to be concluded on open account terms.

Monetary Policy

Inflation has fallen from the double digits of the mid-1990s. Tightening of the monetary policy in April 1995 helped to bring inflation down under 9% in mid-1995. Inflation fell below 5% in the 1997–98 fiscal year, and forecast at 6% for 2000.

MONETARY UNIT: Indian rupee

Trade Policy

TARIFFS   The Indian government continues to reduce tariff rates. A 40% tariff ceiling was set in the 1997–98 budget, down from 300% in 1991. The import-weighted average tariff is 33%.

Despite reforms, Indian tariffs are still some of the highest in the world, especially for goods that can be produced domestically.

IMPORT LICENSING   The import licensing regime has been liberalized, but still limits many U.S. goods.

Importation of consumer goods is virtually banned except for some imports under the special import license (SIL) arrangement. Consumer goods are defined as goods that can directly satisfy human need without further processing. Thus, products of agricultural or animal origin must be licensed and are, in most cases, effectively banned.

India has liberalized many restrictions on the importation of capital goods.

IMPORT TAXES   India maintains a variety of additional duties and countervailing duties that raise the effective tariff rates well above the tariff ceiling for some products.

Protection of Intellectual Property Rights

India's intellectual property system is derived from Colonial British Law. India belongs to the World Trade Organization (WTO) and is a signatory to the Universal Copyright Convention and the Berne Convention on Protection of Literary and Artistic Works. In 1998 India joined the Paris Convention and the Patent Cooperation Treaty. Although

India's copyright laws are modern, its patent and trademark laws are outdated. No steps have been taken to conform its laws to Paris Convention standards.

Although India's patent laws were amended in 1972, patenting remains a problem because of high invention standards and subject matter restrictions. Chemical substances and pharmaceuticals cannot be patented. Also, under current law, compulsory licenses are exclusive rather than nonexclusive.

The Trademark Register is divided into Parts A and B. *Part A* registrations require distinctiveness and are equivalent to the Principal Registration in the U.S. *Part B* is like the U.S. Supplemental Registration and allows for registration for marks that may become distinctive. Registrations have terms of 7 years from application and are renewable. Nonuse for 5 years renders a mark subject to possible cancellation. Bona fide prior users have common law rights and cannot be sued. Registrations are assignable, with or without goodwill. Common law trademark and trade name rights exist irrespective of registration.

Copyright legislation is based on the British-Indian copyright law. Copyrights result on creation and registration is permissive. In addition to issuing registrations, the Copyright Register has court functions. There are stringent provisions covering audio and video piracy.

Foreign Investment Climate

After launching a concerted drive to modernize its economy, India is beginning to attract the attention of the international investment community. With its 200 million-strong middle class, vast pool of skilled labor, and relatively well-developed financial system, India offers both a rich market and tremendous potential productive capacity. However, nationalism, government restrictions, and a tradition of frugality limit the ability of foreign investors to tap this market.

The rush of foreign direct investment to India has been increasing rapidly, often doubling that of the previous year. The U.S. is the leading foreign investor in India.

Since July 1991 Indian government approvals for equity investments of up to 51% in most manufacturing industries have been automatic. Foreign equity investments in excess of 51%, or those that fall outside the specified "high priority" areas, must be approved by the Foreign Investment Promotion Board and approved by a Cabinet Committee. The only sectors of the Indian economy specifically excluded from foreign investment are the defense sector, railways, and atomic energy.

For investors, the crux of the 1991 economic reforms consisted of the deregulation of most domestic industries, removing licensing requirements, and permitting foreign and domestic firms far more independence in investment and marketing decisions. Regulatory reform has been accompanied by a far more positive attitude toward private enterprise and foreign investment on the part of regulators.

Political Leaders, Parties, and International Organizations

The International Academy at Santa Barbara at http://www.iasb.org/cwl publishes *Current World Leaders*, an excellent resource for up-to-date data on political leaders, parties, demographics, etc., in India. Tel: (800) 530-2682 or (805) 965-5010 for subscription information to their database.

Chief of State:

President Kocheril Raman Narayanan

Head of the Government:

Prime Minister Atal Bihari Vajpayee

Political Parties:

Bharatiya Janata Party or BJP; Congress (I) Party; Janata Dal Party; Janata Dal (Ajit); Rashtriya Janata Dal or RJD; Communist Party of India/Marxist or CPI/M; Tamil Maanila Congress; Dravida Munnetra Kazagham or DMK (a regional party in Tamil Nadu); Samajwadi Party or SP; Telugu Desam (a regional party in Andhra Pradesh); Communist Party of India or CPI; Revolutionary Socialist Party or RSP; Asom Gana Parishad; Congress (Tiwari); All India Forward Bloc or AIFB; Muslim League; Madhya Pradesh Vikas Congress; Karnataka Congress Party; Shiv Sena or SHS; Bahujan Samaj Party or BSP; Communist Party of India/Marxist-Leninist or CPI/ML; Akali Dal factions representing Sikh religious community in the Punjab; National Conference or NC (a regional party in Jammu and Kashmir); Bihar Peoples Party; Samata Party or SAP (formerly Janata Dal members); Indian National League; Kerala Congress (Mani faction); All India Anna Dravida Munnetra Kazhagam or ADMK; Biju Janata Dal or BJD; Trinamool Congress

Membership in international organizations:

ADB, CP, C, INTELSAT, NAM, SAARC, UN and all of its specialized agencies and related organizations (including FAO, GATT, IAEA, IBRD, ICAO, IDA, IFAD, IFC, ILO, IMF, IMO, ITU, UNESCO, UNIDO, UPU, WHO, WIPO, WMO)

Political Influences on Business

India continues to move from a state-controlled economy to a market economy. Somewhat mitigating this otherwise "business friendly" environment are India's stultifying (and still largely unreformed) bureaucracies; India's ongoing dispute with Pakistan (which has resulted in three wars); and caste and communal tensions that have worsened (sometimes exploding into violence) in recent years. Nevertheless, on balance, India is becoming an increasingly attractive business environment and most industrialized nations are rapidly expanding their commercial presence in the country. The progress of economic reform varies throughout India, and some individual states are increasingly seeking foreign investments on their own.

India is a multi-ethnic, multi-religious, federal republic composed of 25 states and 7 union territories. The country has a bicameral parliament—including the Upper House, the *Rajya Sabha* (government assembly), and the Lower House, the *Lok Sabha* (people's assembly). The judiciary is relatively independent and the legal system is based on English common law. National and state elections are ordinarily held every five years, although they may be postponed in an emergency and may be held more frequently if the government loses a confidence vote.

The Congress (I) Party has ruled India for most of its history as an independent nation. This is the party of the Nehru–Gandhi dynasty, which controlled the party until Rajiv Gandhi's assassination in 1991. In recent years, the Congress Party has taken second place to the Bharatiya Janata Party (BJP), a rightist, Hindu-centric party that emphasizes Indian nationalism. The BJP has generally supported market reforms and claims to favor closer relations between India and the United States. However, it was a BJP-led government that ordered the testing of three nuclear weapons in 1998, an action seen as destabilizing by foreign governments and investors. The United Front, a coalition headed by the Janata Dal Party, also held power in the 1990s.

Despite tremendous obstacles and the ever-present potential for disorder, India's recent elections displayed a degree of orderliness and honesty which would do any nation proud. Election sites had been set up even in remote mountain regions and accommodations were made for India's large numbers of illiterate voters. Once again, the world's most-populous democracy showed the world that it can manage its own affairs quite adeptly.

Contacts in the United States

THE EMBASSY OF THE REPUBLIC OF INDIA
2107 Massachusetts Avenue, NW
Washington, D.C. 20008
Tel: (202) 939-7000
Fax: (202) 483 3972
www.indianembassy.org

Passport/Visa Requirements

A passport and visa (obtained in advance) are required. Tourist, Entry, Business, Student, Research, Transit, and Missionaries visas are issued.

Passports should be valid for a period of at least six months from the date of application. Paste or staple two passport-size photographs at the specified location on the application form.

Persons entering India from, or through, a yellow-fever–infected area are required to be in possession of a valid certificate of vaccination against yellow fever. No other health certificates are obligatory (at present), but immunization against smallpox and cholera is recommended.

BUSINESS VISA   Valid for one year, multiple entry. A letter from the sponsoring firm or organization indicating the nature of the applicant's business, duration of stay, places and firms in India to be visited, and guaranteeing the applicant's expenses while in India and journey out of India is required.

If a passport is to be returned by mail, a self-addressed envelope with sufficient postage for certified mail should accompany applications for visa. Visa fee and mailing charges should be paid by personal check, cashier's check, or money order, payable to the Embassy of India, Washington, D.C. or to the Consulate General of India. In the case of applications presented in person, fee may also be paid in cash. Visa services requested at the Embassy are completed the same day. Applications sent by mail take approximately five working days to process.

For current information concerning entry and customs requirements for India, travelers can contact the Indian Embassy.

U.S. citizens who wish to apply for a passport may visit Passport Services' well-organized website at http://travel.state.gov/passport_services.html.

Contacts in India

THE EMBASSY OF THE UNITED STATES OF AMERICA
Shanti Path
Chanakyapuri 110021
New Delhi
Tel: (91) (11) 688-9033, 611-3033
Fax: (91) (11) 419-0017
www.usia.gov/posts/delhi.html

DUN & BRADSTREET INFORMATION SERVICES INDIA PTE LTD
Opp. Santogen Mills Saki Vihar Road
Powai, Mumbai 400 072
Tel: (91) (22) 857-4190
Fax: (91) (22) 857-2060

OFFICE OF THE PRESIDENT
Rashtrapati Bhavan
New Delhi 110004, Republic of India

OFFICE OF THE PRIME MINISTER
South Block
New Delhi 110011, Republic of India

Further contacts and websites can be found in Appendix A.

Communications

TELEPHONE: The country code for India is 91.

Indian phone numbers vary in length. Typically, they range from five to seven digits in length. A hyphen is usually included in longer numbers, but its placement varies.

Area/city codes—known as STD codes in India—also vary in length, from two digits to as many as six digits in rural areas.

E-MAIL: E-mail addresses located in India end with the code .in

DATES: The date is written in this order: day, month, year (unlike the U.S. practice of writing month, day, year). The dates may be separated by slashes (12/5/00 for May 12, 2000) or periods (12.5.00).

Observation: "The phone service in India is so slow that some businesses keep a boy on the payroll just to wait for a dial tone to put a call though. If the desired number is reached, he keeps it open under the possibility that someone might need it late in the day. A few years ago, the phone company crossed the line. P.C. Sethi, a member of Parliament, had spent most of the day trying to phone Bombay. When the call still hadn't been completed after several hours, Sethi took a gun, got an armed escort and stormed the telephone exchange. . . . Monopoly or not, Sethi had decided that the company had broken the rules by keeping a man of his importance waiting so long.

"Armed assault is admittedly an extreme reaction to frustration, but in this case it received considerable sympathy. . . ."

> —From A Geography of Time by Robert Levine. (While the state-controlled phone system remains antiquated and inefficient, the advent of private cellular and paging services has rapidly improved telecommunications in India.)

Names and Titles in India

Each ethnic group in India has different nomenclature patterns. All Indians, however, value professional titles. For someone who does not have a title, use Mr., Mrs., or Miss.

Historically, Hindus did not have family surnames. A Hindu man used the initial of his father's name first, followed by his own personal name. For example, for a man named *Thiruselvan* whose father was named *Vijay*, the everyday usage would be *V. Thiruselvan*. People would address him as *Mr. Thiruselvan*. On important documents, both names would be written out in full, separated by *s/o* (for *son of*). This same man would sign his name as *Thiruselvan s/o Vijay*. Note that long Indian names are often shortened. A man named *Thiruselvan* could shorten it to either *Mr. Thiru* or *Mr. Selvan*.

Hindu women's names follow the same pattern, except that instead of *s/o*, she would use *d/o* (for *daughter of*). When an Indian woman marries, she usually drops her father's initial; instead, she follows her personal name with her husband's name. For instance, if *S. Kamala* (female) marries *V. Thiru* (male), she will go by *Mrs. Kamala Thiru*.

Some Indians use Western-style surnames. Christian Indians often have Biblical surnames (*Abraham, Jacob,* etc.). Indians from the former Portuguese colony of Goa may have surnames of Portuguese origin, like *Rozario* or *DeSilva*. Such a person could be addressed as *Dr. Jacob* or *Mr. DeSilva*.

Sikh men use a given name followed by *Singh*. Sikh women follow their given name with *Kaur*. Address a Sikh by title and first name, not *Singh* or *Kaur*.

Indonesia

Official Name:	Republic of Indonesia
Official Language:	Bahasa Indonesia (modified form of Malay)
Government System:	Unitary multi-party republic
Population:	216.1 million (1999 estimate)
Population Growth Rate:	1.46% (1999 estimate)
Area:	2,027,665 sq. km. (782,000 sq. mi.); slightly smaller than Alaska and California combined
Natural Resources:	crude oil, tin, natural gas, nickel, timber, bauxite, copper, fertile soils, coal, gold, silver
Major Cities:	Jakarta (capital), Bandung, Semarang, Surabaya, Medan, Palembang, Ujung Pandang

Cultural Note: Status is very important in Indonesia, and every individual has a place on the "totem pole" of importance. In the native language (called Bahasa Indonesia) it is difficult to even converse with a person until you know if he or she is your superior, inferior, or equal. Even when the conversation is in English, Indonesians will not feel comfortable until they know your relative position. This is one reason why Indonesians will ask you very personal questions about your job, your education, and your salary.

Age Breakdown

0–14 = 30%   15–64 = 65%   65+ = 5% (1999 estimate)
Life Expectancy: 60.67 years, male; 65.29 years, female (1999 estimate)

Time

Indonesia spans three time zones. Java and Bali are in West Indonesia Standard Time, which is 7 hours ahead of Greenwich Mean Time (GMT +7). Central Indonesia Standard Time is 8 hours ahead of Greenwich Mean Time (GMT +8); Lombok and Nusatenggara are on Central Time. The East Indonesia Standard Time zone, which includes Maluku and Irian Jaya, is 9 hours ahead of Greenwich Mean Time (GMT +9).

Observation: "Remember a couple things while you're over there. . . . Indonesians just aren't precise about the same kinds of things we are. The Indonesian words for *science* and *magic* have the same root. *When* in future time is the same word as *if*. You'll ask someone when the boat is supposed to leave or the papers are supposed to be signed, and he'll say *besok*, but he won't mean literally *tomorrow*, like it says in the dictionary; he'll mean *maybe tomorrow or the day after*, or even *next week*."

—From The Wind Monkey by Leo Berenstain. The author spent two years as a field ecologist in the Borneo rain forests.

Holidays

An up-to-date, web-based *World Holiday and Time Zone Guide* is available at www.getcustoms.com. It lists official holidays by country and by day of the year, cultural tips, a corruption index, and time zones with worldwide business hours.

The holidays in Indonesia represent an attempt to accommodate the celebrations of Islam, Hinduism, Buddhism, and Christianity.

Jan 1	SA	New Year's Day
Jan 8	SA	Idul Fitri (end of Ramadan)
Jan 9	SU	Idul Fitri (end of Ramadan)
Mar 16	WE	Idul Adha
Apr 4	TU	Hindu New Year
Apr 6	TH	Moslem New Year
Apr 21	FR	Good Friday
May 18	TH	Waisak Day (Buddhist New Year)
Jun 1	TH	Ascension of Christ
Jun 15	TH	Birthday of Mohammad

Aug 17	TH	Independence Day
Oct 25	WE	Ascension of Mohammad
Dec 27	WE	Idul Fitri (end of Ramadan)
Dec 28	TH	Idul Fitri (end of Ramadan)

Observant Muslims fast from dawn to sundown during the month of Ramadan. Expect this to have a negative effect on business dealings. Also, do not eat or drink in front of fasting persons.

Three calendars are in common use in Indonesia. The Western (or Gregorian) calendar is the official calendar in use. Islamic holidays are dated via the Arabic calendar, which loses about 11 days each year against the Western calendar. Finally, there is a Hindu-influenced Javanese calendar.

Work Week

- Although the majority of Indonesians are Muslim, Indonesia does not follow the traditional Islamic work-week pattern (Friday is the Islamic Holy Day, so the traditional Muslim "weekend" is Thursday and Friday). Instead, the work week runs from Monday through Friday, plus a half-day on Saturday.

- Business hours are generally from 8:00 A.M. to 4:00 P.M. Monday through Thursday, with additional hours on Friday and Saturday mornings. Some businesses have a full workday on Fridays, although Muslim employees will take at least one hour off on Friday to pray. Saturday hours generally end by 1:00 P.M.

- Many Indonesians prefer to schedule business meetings early in the morning. On the island of Bali, where the tourist industry has yielded a plethora of hotels, breakfast meetings as early at 6:30 A.M. are not uncommon.

- The traditional lunchtime is from 12 noon (or 12:30 P.M.) to 1:30 P.M.; it is often the largest meal of the day.

- Most government offices keep an 8:00 A.M. to 4:00 or 4:30 P.M. schedule Monday through Friday, plus 8:00 A.M. to 1:00 P.M. on Saturday.

- Many Indonesian banks open from 8:00 A.M. to 4:00 P.M. from Monday to Thursday, with half days on Friday and Saturday. Other hours are possible; banks on Bali are often open only from 8:00 A.M. to 12 noon daily.

- Shop hours vary. Most shops will be open five or six days a week, beginning at 9 or 10 A.M. and closing at 6 or 7 P.M.

- Avoid trying to make appointments on Friday afternoons or on Saturdays.

Cultural Note: The Indonesian term *jam karet* ("rubber time") refers to the indigenous casual attitude towards time. Only a great emergency—such as a death or disaster—will impel many Indonesians to haste or punctuality.

Religious Influences on Business

In common with other multi-ethnic societies spread out over an archipelago, Indonesia must contend with divisiveness. Although the majority (87.2%) of Indonesians are Muslim, Islam has not been established as Indonesia's official religion. Instead, Indonesia has declared itself to be officially "monotheistic." The government has established an official doctrine called Pancasila, which affirms the existence of a single Supreme Being. This is in harmony with both Islam and Christianity, Indonesia's second largest religious grouping (9.6% of the population). It is, however, in opposition to Indonesia's minority Hindus (1.8%).

The five principles of Pancasila are:

- Belief in One Supreme God
- Belief in a just and civilized humanity
- Belief in the unity of Indonesia
- Belief in Democracy
- Belief that adherence to Pancasila will bring social justice to all the peoples of Indonesia

All Indonesian government employees and all students are indoctrinated in Pancasila.

Both Islamic and Hindu tradition call for modesty in dress. This applies to foreigners as well. Due to Indonesia's equatorial heat and humidity, business dress is often casual. The standard office wear for men is dark trousers and light-colored long-sleeved shirts and tie, without a jacket. Many businessmen wear a short-sleeved shirt with no tie. However, businesswomen must wear long-sleeved blouses with a skirt; their upper arms must be covered and their skirts should be knee-length or longer. (Indonesians manage to remain well-groomed despite the climate, often bathing several times a day.)

5 Cultural Tips

1. Appointments can be scheduled at relatively short notice. Be punctual; as a foreign businessperson, you are expected to be on time for all business appointments. However, it would be unrealistic to expect punctuality from all Indonesians, as promptness has not traditionally been considered a virtue. Furthermore, making people wait can be an expression of Indonesia' social structure. It is the prerogative of a person of higher standing to make a person of lower standing wait, and it is very poor manners for a person of lower rank to show anger or unhappiness towards a of higher position.

2. Even foreigners are expected to be late to social events. As a general rule, arrive about a half hour late. But be aware that there is a complex social interplay even at social events. When invited to a social event, Indonesians try to discover the guest list. They will then attempt to arrive later than lesser personages but earlier than more important ones. (For this reason, invitations to some events may state a time, but will add "please arrive fifteen minutes early." This is to insure that no one arrives after the most important guest.)

3. Indonesians show great deference to a superior. Consequently, superiors are often told what they want to hear. The truth is conveyed in private, "up the grapevine"—often by a friend of the superior. Indonesians honor their boss by shielding him from bad news in public. This Indonesian trait, called *asal bapak senang* (which translates as "keeping father happy") is instilled in Indonesians since childhood. A foreign executive must establish a network whereby he or she can be told the truth in private.

4. Since it is impolite to openly disagree with someone, Indonesians rarely say "No." The listener is expected to be perceptive enough to discern a polite "Yes (but I really mean No)" from an actual "Yes." This is rarely a problem when speaking in Bahasa Indonesia, since the language has at least 12 ways to say "No" and many ways to say "I'm saying 'Yes' but I mean 'No.' " This subtlety is lost in English.

5. Indonesians are comfortable with silence, in both business and social settings. A silent pause does not necessarily signal either acceptance or rejection. Westerners often find such pauses uncomfortable, but Indonesians do not "jump" on the end of someone else's sentences. Politeness demands that they leave a respectful pause (as long as 10 to 15 seconds) before responding. Westerners often assume they have agreement and resume talking before a Indonesian has the chance to respond.

Economic Overview

A few years ago, Indonesia was a marketplace that aggressive U.S. companies could not ignore. Indonesia's booming free-market economy experienced tremendous growth throughout most of the 1980s and 1990s. The country was designated as one of the 10 "Big Emerging Markets" by the U.S. Department of Commerce. Abundantly endowed with natural resources and a population approaching 200 million, Indonesia's wealth was trickling down to a growing middle. The World Bank classified Indonesia as an Asian growth tiger, and graduated the country to lower middle income status.

Then it all fell apart.

Nineteen ninety-seven was already shaping up to be a difficult year. World oil prices were depressed. Indonesia was afflicted by a severe drought attributed to El Niño. Smog due to widespread slash-and-burn agriculture choked much of the archipelago.

Separatist pressures were causing problems in various Indonesian islands. Then the Asian financial crisis (which began in Thailand in 1997) spread to Indonesia. The Indonesian government took some quick action, cutting the budget, allowing the rupiah to float, and requesting help from the International Monetary Fund. But none of these efforts kept the Indonesian economy from plummeting in 1998.

The long-simmering political discontent with the authoritarian rule of President Soeharto erupted into violence in May 1998. The minority ethnic Chinese, who run many of the small businesses throughout Indonesia, were targeted by rioters from Indonesia's ethnic majority (somewhat confusingly referred to as ethnic Malays). Many Chinese fled the country. Both Chinese and foreign investors took their money outside the country, further exacerbating the economic crisis.

Under pressure, President Soeharto resigned in May 1998, and Vice President B.J. Habibie took power. An election—the first free election in Indonesian history—was held in May 1999. Despite the advantages of money, experience, and control of the media, the long-ruling party of Habibie and Soeharto failed to win a majority in the election.

By 1999 the Indonesian economy appeared to have bottomed out, and a recovery was expected. But the failure of Jakarta to protect the people of the Indonesian state of East Timor after they voted for independence on August 30, 1999 led to worldwide outrage. It is possible that Indonesia will lose billions of IMF dollars and remaining foreign investment, stretching out the economic depression.

Eventually, Indonesia will recover. Its abundant natural resources are too valuable for the world to ignore. But that recovery may be some time off.

4 Largest Businesses in Indonesia

PT Astra International, Jakarta
    120,871 employees
PT Perusahaan Listrik Negara (PT PLN), Jakarta
    55,000 employees
PT Barito Pacific Timber, Jakarta
    53,249 employees
PT Perusahaan Rokok Tjap Gudang Garam, Jakarta
    49,000 employees

PT stands for *Perseroan Terbatas*, the Indonesian equivalent of Incorporated. PLN refers to *Penanaman Modal Asing*, which designates a joint venture with a foreign company.

Observation: "Indonesians negotiate virtually every aspect of their daily lives, from taxi rides to groceries, so you can expect considerable haggling over even the smallest point. Part of this is a cultural norm, but much of it is an attempt to wear down the opposition.

"Bribery is a standard form of getting things done, and the price goes up if the recipient has to ask. These bribes may extend to the lowest level of transaction (you often have to make payoffs just to get your car through an intersection), so be prepared to grease some wheels, both big and small. Failure to negotiate a reasonable payoff will mark your company for continuous shake-downs. If your home country has severe restrictions on bribery, you may find that a number of 'consultation' fees will be attached to your project. Budget accordingly."

—From the 1999 book A Short Course in International Negotiating by Jeffrey Edmund Curry. Small bribes (known as pungli in Bahasa Indonesian) are seen by many Indonesians as equivalent to the Western tradition of tipping service workers.

Comparative Data

Comparative Data Ratings
(Scale: 5 = Highest; 1 = Lowest)
Indonesia: 2.0

- A. GDP Growth: 1
- B. Per Capita Income: 2
- C. Trade Flows with U.S.: 3
- D. Country Risk: 2
- E. Monetary Policy: 1
- F. Trade Policy: 2
  - Tariffs
  - Import Licensing
  - Import Taxes
- G. Protection of Property Rights: 3
- H. Foreign Investment Climate: 2

GROSS DOMESTIC PRODUCT: $602 billion (1998 estimate)

GDP GROWTH: 13.7% (1998 estimate)

PER CAPITA INCOME: $2,830 (1998 estimate)

Trade Flows with the U.S.

U.S. EXPORTS TO INDONESIA: $2.3 billion (1998 estimate)

U.S. IMPORTS FROM INDONESIA: $9.3 billion (1998 estimate)

TOP U.S. EXPORTS TO INDONESIA: Household consumer goods; building products; architectural; construction and engineering services; electrical power systems; franchising; telecommunications equipment; pollution-control equipment; construction equipment; computer systems and peripherals; food-processing and packaging equipment

TOP U.S. PROSPECTS TO INDONESIA: Oil and gas equipment; telecommunications equipment; mining equipment; industrial pumps; forestry and woodworking machinery; medical equipment; hand and power tools; educational and training services; accounting and financial services; pollution-control systems and equipment

Country Risk

Considerable uncertainty is associated with expected returns. Dun & Bradstreet advises businesses to limit their exposure and/or select high-return transactions.

Monetary Policy

Even during the boom times, Indonesia had a fairly high rate of inflation, due largely to the inflow of foreign capital. Inflation topped 9% in 1994 and 1995, but fell to 6.5% in 1996.

When the Asian economic crisis broke, inflation rose as Indonesia's currency fell. Inflation hit 11.1% in 1997 and soared to around 80.0% in 1998. Inflation was 19.2% in 1999, and forecast at 7% in 2000.

MONETARY UNIT: rupiah

Trade Policy

TARIFFS   A May 1995 tariff reform package reduced import duties and taxes on most tariff categories by 5–10%. According to the Indonesian schedule for future tariff reform, tariffs below 20% will be reduced another 5% in 2000, and tariffs greater than 20% will be reduced to 10% by 2003.

The trade-weighted average tariff is 9.5%, but the effective tariff rate is much lower due to imported goods that are exempted from duty. Capital goods for approved investments, imports used to produce exported goods, and imports exempted by the Ministry of Finance are not subject to the duties.

IMPORT LICENSING   Nontariff barriers continue to protect a large share of both agricultural and manufacturing production. Major affected products are motor vehicles, rice, wheat, sugar, salt, soybean meal, alcoholic beverages, cloves, explosives, and petroleum products.

Importers of most goods must obtain a license from the Department of Trade.

Importers of food and drug-related products must be registered with the Department of Health. Importers of oil and gas products must also register with the appropriate department.

All ocean-borne imports valued at more than $5,000 must undergo a preshipment inspection.

IMPORT TAXES   Indonesia imposes import surcharges, or supplemental import duties, on approximately 200 tariff lines. These surcharges range from 5–30% with imports in the automotive sector subjected to surcharges of 75%.

Additionally, the government levies a 10% value-added tax (VAT) on the sale of all domestic and imported goods, and a luxury tax of 20–35% on a number of products. For imports, these sales taxes are collected at the point of import and are calculated based on the value of the product, including import duties.

Protection of Intellectual Property Rights

Indonesia belongs to the Paris Convention for Protection of Industrial Property, the Berne Convention for Protection of Literary and Artistic Works, the Patent Cooperation Treaty, and the Trademark Law Treaty. Bilateral treaties concerning various aspects of IP have been concluded with various countries, including the United States. The problem is that implementing laws and regulations haven't been passed in conformity with the conventions; and where laws and regulations exist, enforcement efforts are weak. Not surprisingly, Indonesia is on the Section 301 Priority Watch List.

Patents only require local novelty and have a term of 20 years from application; provided, however, that an extension for an additional two years can be obtained under certain circumstances. Utility models have 10-year terms. No patents are granted for medicines. Compulsory licenses by third parties may be sought 36 months after filing.

Trademark rights result from registration rather than use. Trademarks have terms of 10 years and are renewable. Acquisition of registrations for prominent foreign trademarks is accepted business practice. Applications must be filed separately in each class.

Copyrights result automatically on first publication. The term of copyright is life of the author plus 50 years or only 50 years if the work was for a corporation. Certain types of individual works have terms of 25–50 years from first publication. If a work is not translated into Indonesian and reproduced within three years of publication, the government may make its own arrangements for translation and publication.

Foreign Investment Climate

The Indonesian government has actively encouraged foreign investment. Foreign investment in industry, particularly in export-oriented and labor-intensive activities, is strongly encouraged. Although some sectors remain closed or restricted, the government periodically updates its negative investment list and list of sectors reserved for small business. Recently, several previously restricted sectors were opened to foreign investment, including harbors, electricity generation, telecommunications, shipping, airlines, railways, and water supply. However, foreign investment in many services remain restricted.

Foreign investors may purchase domestic firms except in sectors prohibited by the negative list. In June 1994 requirements for minimum equity in most foreign investments were eliminated. Foreign investors who open with 100% equity must divest some percentage of their holdings after 15 years. Foreign investors may not hold majority ownership in retail operations, although franchise, licensing, and technical service agreements are common. Foreign companies are also forbidden from providing domestic distribution services.

Most foreign investments must be approved by the Capital Investment Coordinating Board (BKPM). Investments in the oil and gas, mining, banking, and insurance industries are handled by the relevant technical government departments.

Of course, Indonesia's suitability as a place for foreign investment depends upon the country's stability. That stability remains in doubt ever since the violence in May 1998.

Political Leaders, Parties, and International Organization

The International Academy at Santa Barbara at http://www.iasb.org/cwl publishes *Current World Leaders*, an excellent resource for up-to-date data on political leaders, parties, demographics, etc., in Indonesia. Tel: (800) 530-2682 or (805) 965-5010 for subscription information to their database.

Head of State and the Government:
  President Abdurrahman Wahid

Next Election:
  2004

Political Parties:
  Indonesian Democratic Party (fusion of all nationalist and Christian parties),
    Golongan Karya (functional group), United Development Party (fusion of all
    Muslim parties)

Membership in international organizations:
  ADB, APEC, ASEAN, G77, IDB, INTELSAT, NAM, OIC, OPEC, PECC, UN and all of
    its specialized agencies and related organizations (including FAO, GATT, IAEA,
    IBRD, ICAO, IDA, IFAD, IFC, ILO, IMF, IMO, ITU, UNESCO, UNIDO, UPU,
    WHO, WIPO, WMO)

Political Influences on Business

The current leadership of Indonesia favors foreign investment. Business has been
growing, as has the standard of living for many Indonesians. However, human rights
concerns continue to hamper Indonesia's future. The Indonesian occupation of East
Timor is considered illegal by many nations. Note that politics and business are closely related; when a nation lodges protests against Indonesian actions, expatriate business executives from that country are liable to experience Indonesian disapproval.

Prompted by violent protests, the 32-year-long rule of President Soeharto ended
with his resignation in May 1998. His authoritarian reign lasted so long for two reasons:
the support of the Indonesian military and the willingness of the Indonesian people to
trade political freedom for prosperity. But the economic collapse of 1997 broke
Soeharto's compact with the people. Soeharto, his family, and cronies had become
tremendously wealthy during his three decades in power, and the Indonesian people
would not allow him to remain rich and powerful while their standard of living col-
lapsed. Much of the assets of the Soeharto family are expected to be seized.

The caretaker presidency of B.J. Habibie will soon give way to a new administration.
The new leaders of Indonesia are expected to be relatively business-friendly, but nothing definitive can be said until they take power.

Indonesia is one of the world's most important nonaligned nations (a distinction
that has less importance since the Cold War ended). Under the 1945 Constitution,
supreme governmental authority in Indonesia is vested in the 1,000-member People's
Consultative Assembly (MPR), which meets every five years to select the President and
Vice President and establish the broad outlines of government policy for the next five
years. Half of the MPR's members come from the partially elected Parliament (DPR)
and the other half are appointed by the government.

East Timor, the former Portuguese colony annexed by Indonesia in 1975, was allowed by the Habibie government to vote on its future in August 1999. The people of East Timor voted overwhelmingly for independence. Following the election, anti-independence militias taking orders from the Indonesian military killed and displaced hundreds of thousands of East Timorese. Whatever the outcome in East Timor, Indonesia will continue to be subject to separatist pressures. Many regions—including Aceh on the island of Sumatra and Irian Jaya on the island of New Guinea—are currently fighting to break free from Jakarta. It is not impossible that Indonesia will become the Yugoslavia of Southeast Asia, breaking up into several nations.

Contacts in the United States

THE EMBASSY OF THE REPUBLIC OF INDONESIA
2020 Massachusetts Avenue, NW
Washington, D.C. 20036
Tel: (202) 775-5200
Fax: (202) 775-5365
www.kbri.org

AMERICAN–INDONESIAN CHAMBER OF COMMERCE, INC.
711 Third Avenue, 17th Floor
New York, NY 10017
Tel: (212) 687-4505
Fax: (212) 867-9882
aicc.globalnetlink.com

Passport/Visa Requirements

Passports valid for a minimum of 6 months at time of admission and onward return tickets are required. Visas are not required for tourist/business stays of up to 2 months (nonextendable). Special permits are required for some areas of Indonesia.

BUSINESS AND SOCIAL VISAS   *Requirements:* (1) A valid passport (must be valid for at least 6 months from time visa application is submitted). Passport should contain one blank visa page. Amendments and endorsement pages cannot be used for visa purposes. (2) Immunization against smallpox, cholera, yellow fever, etc., are required for those who have visited infected countries prior to arrival in Indonesia (check with Indonesian officials regarding such countries and the immunization required). (3) Completed application form in duplicate with 2 photographs. (4) Letter in duplicate from employer or sponsor stating the purpose of the trip and guaranteeing sufficient funds for living expenses during stay in Indonesia; and transportation charges.

The visa is good for a single entry within 3 months from the date of issue. Processing time is three working days provided all requirements have been fulfilled.

SEMI-PERMANENT VISA　*Requirements:* (1) Valid passport (must be valid for at least 6 months from time visa application is submitted). Passport contains some blank visa pages. Amendments and endorsement pages cannot be used for visa purposes. (2) Completed application form in triplicate with 3 photographs attached. (3) Letter in triplicate from employer, sponsor, bank, etc., stating the purpose of the trip and guaranteeing sufficient funds for living expenses during stay in Indonesia; and transportation charges. (4) Applicant's curriculum—vitae in triplicate. (5) Police certificate of good conduct/behavior in triplicate. (6) Employee's agreement/contract and diplomas/degrees in triplicate. (7) Triplicate copies of marriage certificate and birth certificate of accompanying family. (8) Certificate of vaccination in triplicate.

Visa is good for any entry within 3 months from the date of issue. The semi-permanent visa must be collected within three months from the date of notification of authorization by the Indonesian Immigration Authority. Length of stay is over 3 months to 1 year.

For current information concerning entry and customs requirements for Indonesia, travelers can contact the Indonesian Embassy.

U.S. citizens who wish to apply for a passport may visit Passport Services' well-organized website at http://travel.state.gov/passport_services.html.

Contacts in Indonesia

THE EMBASSY OF THE UNITED STATES OF AMERICA
Jalan Medan Merdeka Selatan #5
Jakarta 10110
Mailing Address: Box 1, Unit 8129, APO AP 96520
Tel: (62) (21) 344-2211
Fax: (62) (21) 386-2259
www.usembassyjakarta.org

THE AMERICAN CHAMBER OF COMMERCE IN INDONESIA
World Trade Center, 11th Floor
Jalan Jendral Sudirman Kav. 29-31
Jakarta 12084
Tel: (62) (21) 526-2860
Fax: (62) (21) 526-2861
E-mail: amcham_indonesia@ibm.net
www.amcham.or.id

OFFICE OF THE PRESIDENT
Bina Graha
Jalan Veteran No. 17
Jakarta, Republic of Indonesia

Further contacts and websites can be found in Appendix A.

Communications

TELEPHONE: The international country code for Indonesia is 62.

Phone numbers may be six or seven digits in length.

Area codes for large cities are two digits in length; other areas have three digits.

The word for extension in Bahasa Indonesian is *pesawat*, which is abbreviated as *pes*.

E-MAIL: E-mail addresses located in Indonesia end with the code .id

---

Cultural Note: Numbers and symbols can have great significance in Indonesia. For example, when the 5th day of the Western (Gregorian) calendar's week coincides with the 5th day of the Javanese week (which is only 5 days long), it is an auspicious occasion.

Ireland

Official Name:	Éire (Irish), Ireland (English)
Official Languages:	Irish and English
Government System:	Parliamentary multi-party republic
Population:	3.6 million (1999 estimate)
Population Growth Rate:	0.38% (1999 estimate)
Area:	70,282 sq. km. (27,136 sq. mi.); slightly smaller than West Virginia
Natural Resources:	zinc, lead, natural gas, barite, copper, gypsum, limestone, dolomite, peat, silver
Major Cities:	Dublin (capital), Cork, Limerick, Galway, Waterford

---

Cultural Note: The Republic of Ireland joined the European Community in 1973, yielding favorable gains for Ireland. Trade with the EU took Ireland out from Britain's shadow. Multinational corporations have placed their headquarters in Ireland. As one of the poorest members of the EU, Ireland became eligible for EU loans and assistance.

EU influence is also helping women to achieve equality in Ireland. Historically a male-dominated society, Ireland now has many women in politics, including its former and current Presidents.

Age Breakdown

0–14 = 21%   15–64 = 67%   65+ = 12% (1999 estimate)
Life Expectancy: 73.64 years, male; 79.32 years, female (1999 estimate)

Time

Punctuality is expected for business appointments. The rules for social engagements—especially between friends—are more flexible.

Promptness has not historically been valued in Ireland. In order to encourage people to pay their bills on time, the Irish telephone and electric utilities automatically enter paid-on-time bills into a raffle! Even Irish schools have a fairly relaxed attitude about tardiness.

Irish attitudes towards time also extend to deadlines and delivery dates. Don't expect something to be executed at the time or date promised, unless you have been careful to explain *why* that deadline must be met.

In rural areas, everything shuts down at lunchtime from 1:00 P.M. to 2:00 or 2:30 P.M. for lunch. (For many people this includes a trip to the pub.) Shops and offices close down, and only food-service establishments remain open. In fact, one day a week, many rural businesses close for the day at 1:00 P.M., giving their employees an afternoon off.

In the cities, people take lunches in shifts, allowing businesses to remain open.

Ireland, like England, is on Greenwich Mean Time. This is 5 hours ahead of U.S. Eastern Standard Time (EST +5).

Holidays

An up-to-date, web-based *World Holiday and Time Zone Guide* is available at www.getcustoms.com. It lists official holidays by country and by day of the year, cultural tips, a corruption index, and time zones with worldwide business hours.

Jan 1	SA	New Year's Day
Mar 17	FR	St. Patrick's Day
Apr 21	FR	Good Friday
Apr 24	MO	Easter Monday
May 1	MO	May Day
Jun 5	MO	Summer holiday
Aug 7	MO	Summer holiday
Oct 23	MO	October holiday
Dec 25	MO	Christmas Day
Dec 26	TU	St. Stephen's Day

In addition to the above, Easter and Easter Monday are observed as official holidays. If New Year's Day, Saint Patrick's Day, Christmas Day, or Saint Stephen's Day fall on a weekend, the following Monday is a public holiday. The days of observance should always be corroborated by local contacts.

Work Week

- A 39-hour, 5-day work week is the norm for offices and factories. For offices, the customary working hours are 9:00 A.M. to 5:30 P.M. with lunch from 1:00 P.M. to 2:00 P.M. Banking hours are from 10:00 to 4:00 P.M., with banks having various evening hours posted. Most retail stores are open from 9:00 A.M. to 6:00 P.M. Monday through Saturday, although some have later hours to permit evening shopping.
- Because of vacations in July and August, many Irish executives may not be available except by appointment. Most businesses also close from December 24 through January 2 during the Christmas period.

Religious/Societal Influences on Business

It is not possible to define the Irish identity without reference to two seminal influences: the British Empire and the Catholic Church.

Ireland was invaded by the British many times. Subjugation began in earnest after Henry VIII changed England's official religion from Catholicism to Protestantism, which had the side effect of making wealthy Catholic monasteries into legitimate military targets. The Irish were dispossessed and Protestant gentry set up farms known as plantations. In the North of Ireland, even the plantations' tenant farmers were Protestant Englishmen. Southern Ireland was brutally subjugated by Cromwell the Protector in the 1650s. Catholic Irish lands were confiscated. By the eighteenth century, Catholics owned less than 15% of Irish lands.

The height of British misrule of Ireland occurred during the Potato Famine of the 1840s. The potato crop failed in 1842, then failed again in 1846. While a million Irish starved and another million fled Ireland, British-owned plantations in Ireland continued to export grain. By the time the Famine eased, the population of Ireland had dropped from over eight million to some six million. Emigration had become a way of life, and has continued to the present time.

The Irish pressed for reform. Aided by some English and Irish-Protestants, they sought first Home Rule, then outright independence for Ireland. The Republic of Ireland became a reality in 1921, but the Northern six counties remained part of Great Britain. (It is over the fate of Northern Ireland that the violence—which the Irish call *the troubles*—continues today.) *Not a single tourist has been killed or seriously injured by political violence since the troubles began in 1968.*

As in other occupied countries, the Church became a guardian of the national identity. While Ireland has no official religion, about 92% of the citizens of Eire are Catholic. The Church's influence can be seen in Ireland's legal obstacles to divorce, contraception, and abortion. Condoms were illegal until 1980; after that, they could only be sold to married couples—by prescription! Divorce and abortion are still essentially proscribed in Ireland.

Despite centuries of subjugation, the Irish are nevertheless proud of their history and heritage. Many consider the glory days of Ireland to be between the fall of the Roman Empire and the rise of Charlemagne. During this time span, Western scholarship and literacy was virtually isolated to Ireland. Once Charlemagne had restored stability to Europe, Irish scholars spread throughout the continent, reviving educational traditions that were lost in the Dark Ages.

5 Cultural Tips

1. The Irish character can seem complex and contradictory at times. (Sigmund Freud is alleged to have said that the Irish are the only people who cannot be helped by Psychoanalysis.) Ireland is a conservative Catholic country, yet the Irish people are inevitably described as rebellious by nature and sarcastic about authority. Ireland has the lowest rate of marriage per capita in the European Union, yet the highest fertility rate (2.1 children per woman)—plus an 18% illegitimacy rate. A poor country with high unemployment, Ireland often gives more per capita to charities than far wealthier nations.

2. Irish hospitality and friendliness are well known. Most Irish look forward to chatting with friends and strangers alike over a cup of tea or a pint of Guinness. It would be considered impolite not to talk to anyone (even a stranger) in whose company you found yourself, whether in a waiting room or a pub.

3. The Irish have an ambivalent attitude towards wealth. The founding father of the Irish Republic, Eamon De Valera, envisioned Ireland as a pastoral land of simple virtues. Moneymaking was not included as a virtue. People who have achieved financial success are not automatically respected. Ostentation is frowned upon, except in giving to charity.

4. In the 1990s, Ireland experienced unprecedented economic growth. Ireland's rates of employment and growth outstripped that of most other European Union nations. After decades of seeking work in other countries, Irish emigrants began returning home. This has brought the Irish a degree of satisfaction, but not the exuberance associated with a boom town in the U.S. The Irish continue to have a deep strain of pessimism. Many feel that success today is no guarantee of success tomorrow.

5. Leisure time is valued in Ireland. Only in sport is leisure highly structured. Most Irish enjoy simply chatting with their friends. (Naturally, in a country with such a changeable climate, the weather is a constant topic.) When encountering strangers, the favorite Irish pastime is to find out as much as possible about them while revealing as little as possible about oneself. In social situations, people quickly move to a first-name basis, but business acquaintances often retain the use of the surname.

Economic Overview

The commercial environment in Ireland is highly conducive for U.S. companies interested in trade and investment. The U.S. and Ireland enjoy longstanding political, economic, and commercial relations and a close cultural affinity.

The Irish economy continues to grow faster than that of any other Western industrialized nation, for which the country has earned the nickname the "Celtic Tiger." For much of the 1990s, Ireland achieved real economic growth of around 5% per year. Nineteen ninety-eight was even better, with a 8.9% growth rate. The outlook for the immediate future continues to be positive with GDP growth forecast at 8.2% in 2000 and 7.0% in 2001.

Ireland's economic miracle is attributed to its well-educated workforce, its economic policies (which include welcoming foreign investment), and the benefits of joining the European Union.

While the Irish market is small, many U.S. firms see Ireland as a gateway to the larger European market.

5 Largest Businesses in Ireland

Jefferson Smurfit Group, Plc., Dublin
    25,353 employees
C R H, Plc., Dublin
    22,708 employees
Allied Irish Banks, Plc., Dublin
    16,200 employees
Independent Newspapers, Plc., Dublin
    13,500 employees
Bord Telecom Eireann, Plc., Dublin
    13,000 employees

Cultural Note: The Irish propensity for talk is somewhat exaggerated; not all of the Irish chatter, nor do they all speak with great cleverness. But enough do to give foreigners this impression. Many Irish will take it upon themselves to talk to any foreigner they meet. A stranger's name, marital status, occupation, and reason for visiting is quickly ascertained, and this information is passed around from person to person. The contrast with cultures that ignore strangers is striking.

Comparative Data

Comparative Data Ratings
(Scale: 5 = Highest; 1 = Lowest)
Ireland: 4.375

A. GDP Growth: 5
B. Per Capita Income: 4
C. Trade Flows with the U.S.: 3
D. Country Risk: 5
E. Monetary Policy: 5
F. Trade Policy: 4
- Tariffs
- Import Licensing
- Import Taxes
G. Protection of Property Rights: 5
H. Foreign Investment Climate: 4

GROSS DOMESTIC PRODUCT: $67.1 billion (1998 estimate)

GDP GROWTH: 9.5% (1998 estimate)

PER CAPITA INCOME: $18,600 (1998 estimate)

Trade Flows with the U.S.

U.S. EXPORTS TO IRELAND: $5.7 billion (1998)

U.S. IMPORTS FROM IRELAND: $8.4 billion (1998)

TOP U.S. EXPORTS TO IRELAND: Machinery; electronic components; computers; medical and optical equipment; organic chemicals; pharmaceuticals; animal feed; plastics; telecommunications equipment; mineral fuels

TOP U.S. PROSPECTS FOR EXPORT TO IRELAND: Computers and peripherals; electronic components; travel and tourism services; computer software; industrial chemicals; electrical power systems; drugs and pharmaceuticals; medical equipment; building products; air conditioning and refrigeration equipment

Country Risk

Dun & Bradstreet rates Ireland as having the highest creditworthiness with an excellent capacity to meet outstanding payment liabilities. Ireland carries the lowest degree of risk when compared with other countries.

Usual credit terms are open account, 30 to 60 days.

Monetary Policy

Inflationary pressures remain subdued. Inflation in 1997 was 1.5%; in 1998 it was 2.4%. Dun & Bradstreet forecasts inflation to remain under 3.0% for the next several years.

MONETARY UNIT: Irish punt (pound)

Trade Policy

TARIFFS   As a member of the European Union (EU), Ireland applies EU tariffs. Duty rates on manufactured goods from the U.S. generally range from 5–8%. Most raw materials enter duty-free or at low rates. In accordance with EU regulations, agricultural and food items are often subject to import levies that vary depending on world market prices.

IMPORT LICENSING   Only a small number of goods of U.S. origin require import licenses, mostly agricultural and food items. Other items subject to licensing include coal and lignite fuel, a few products from the chemical and related industries, specified iron and steel products, various textiles and textile products, natural and synthetic precious and semi-precious stones, zinc, and controlled items such as arms and munitions.

Import licenses are generally granted quickly for goods of U.S. origin.

IMPORT TAXES   A 21% value-added tax (VAT) is charged on the import of goods and services into Ireland. The importer is liable for payment of the VAT at the time of customs clearance.

Excise taxes are levied on a limited number of products such as gasoline and diesel fuel, spirits, beer, wine, bottled water, cider, tobacco, motor vehicles, and liquid petroleum gas. Excise rates vary depending on the products.

Protection of Intellectual Property Rights

Ireland belongs to the European Union and is subject to its intellectual property regulations. Ireland has signed the Madrid Protocol on Trademarks. In 1997 the U.S. initiated dispute settlement proceedings against Ireland because it has not amended its copyright laws to comply with TRIPS, since, as a developed country, its laws should have been changed in 1996. New measures dealing with bootlegging and enhancing copyright owners are pending.

The Patent Act of 1992 put Irish patent law into conformity with EC requirements. Applications are published 18 months after filing. There is no novelty examination, but the applicant may request a search. It is up to the applicant to amend to avoid the references. The term of patent is 20 years from filing effective upon publication of acceptance. "Licenses of right" are permitted at the request of the patentee.

Trademarks can be national or European Union. The Irish trademark law was amended in 1996. Both marks for products and services are protected. Trademarks have a term of 10 years and are renewable. Trademarks are assignable with or without goodwill.

Copyrights are not registered. Copyright results automatically on creation of a work. Literary, artistic, musical, and dramatic works are protected for the life of the author plus 70 years (or 50 years in the case of sound recordings).

Foreign Investment Climate

Successive Irish governments for the last 30 years have actively sought to attract foreign private investment to Ireland. In recent years, Ireland's membership in the European Union, its reservoir of well-trained workers, its close access to the European marketplace, and significant investment incentives have been the primary attractions to foreign investors.

Central Bank of Ireland approval is required for investments by foreign companies in new projects and existing entities in Ireland.

One hundred percent foreign ownership is permitted in sectors open to private investment, except where restricted for national security purposes. Foreign ownership of land, however, is prohibited, except for stud farms and agricultural land associated with horses and horse racing.

The U.S. is the largest foreign investor in Ireland.

Political Leaders, Parties, and International Organizations

The International Academy at Santa Barbara at http://www.iasb.org/cwl publishes *Current World Leaders*, an excellent resource for up-to-date data on political leaders, parties, demographics, etc., in Ireland. Tel: (800) 530-2682 or (805) 965-5010 for subscription information to their database.

Chief of State:

President Mary McAleese

Head of the Government:

Taoiseach (Prime Minister) Bertie Ahern

Next Election:

November, 2004

Political Parties:

Fianna Fail; Labor Party; Fine Gael; Communist Party of Ireland; Sinn Fein; Progressive Democrats; The Workers' Party; Green Alliance

Note: Prime Minister Ahern heads a two-party coalition consisting of Fianna Fail and the Progressive Democrats; Democratic Left merged into the Labor Party on 1 February 1999

Membership in international organizations:

CE, EBRD, EU, INTELSAT, OECD, OSCE, UN and all of its specialized agencies and related organizations (including FAO, GATT, IAEA, IBRD, ICAO, IDA, IFAD, IFC, ILO, IMF, IMO, ITU, UNESCO, UNIDO, UPU, WHO, WIPO, WMO)

Political Influences on Business

Ireland and the United States enjoy uniformly good bilateral relations. The same language, similar values, frequent visits back and forth, and the presence of some 44 million Americans of at least partial Irish descent guarantee that they will continue to do so indefinitely.

There are no outstanding bilateral disputes. A few minor disagreements on specific trade issues (e.g., corn-gluten feed and malt-sprout pellets) occurred in the recent past but have been resolved. That is not to say that others could not arise, given Ireland's membership in the European Union (EU) and its support of the EU consensus on most issues. However, if any disagreement should arise, approval of the Uruguay Round of the GATT negotiations and the reservoir of goodwill built up on both sides should temper them.

Ireland, which has traditionally followed a policy of neutrality, has pledged to support the Common Foreign and Security Policy (CFSP) provided under the Maastricht Treaty on European Union. This commitment implies an eventual change in Irish neutrality. In any case, the end of the Cold War and the collapse of communism render the concept of neutrality largely perfunctory.

Ireland has on occasion been critical of some aspects of U.S. foreign policy (such as U.S. involvement in Central America in the 1980s and support for Israel), but recent world developments have practically eliminated any negative rhetoric. The only U.S. foreign policy stance that continues to draw Irish criticism is the maintenance of the U.S. embargo against Cuba. If anything, the Irish want the U.S.A. to play an even greater role in the resolution of critical international problems. During the 1990s, Irish relief workers were highly visible in the Balkans.

Although not an ally in technical terms, Ireland remains one of the United States' oldest and closest friends. Recent developments, such as the White House Conference for Trade and Investment in Ireland (convened in Washington in May 1995), together with President Clinton's 1995 visit to Ireland (under the aegis of the Presidential Economic Initiative for Ireland), have helped to reinforce these strong historical ties. Further enhancement of this relationship has been influenced by the active role the U.S. has taken in promoting the peace process and the economic confidence and stability.

Few major political issues significantly affect the business climate. The Irish economy is "on a roll," performing better than any other in Europe. The outlook is for continued strong growth of at least 5% per year, low inflation and interest rates, declining unemployment, and (thanks in part to European Union assistance) significant renovation and extension of the country's transportation and communications infrastructures. If the government continues the appropriate policies, the country will keep making steady progress in paying off the national debt, which now stands at 90% of GNP.

Despite continued high levels of taxation, consumer confidence and spending have shown strong growth in recent years. The strong performance of the Irish economy and the generally favorable economic climate in Europe have reinforced this growth. Although taxation is high, international companies enjoy significant tax breaks under government incentive programs.

Given Ireland's extensive social welfare system, employers often find the marginal cost of employing another worker excessively high. Strikes in the private sector are relatively rare, but unions strenuously oppose proposals to lay off or dismiss workers.

Ireland is a parliamentary democracy. Its president or head of state is a largely ceremonial figure elected to a 7-year term. According to the Irish Constitution, the president needs advance cabinet approval of speeches and travel.

The bicameral legislature is comprised of the *Seanad*, or Senate, with 60 members and the *Dail*, or House of Representatives, with 166 members. The 166 *Dail* representatives are elected by universal suffrage for a maximum of a 5-year term. Members of the Senate also hold office for a similar 5-year term; however, 11 Senate members are nominated by the Prime Minister and the remaining 49 are elected by local universities and from panels of candidates in the following five areas: Cultural and Educational, Agricultural, Labor, Industrial and Commercial, and Administrative. The *Dail* is the more powerful body. The electoral system features proportional representation in multicandidate constituencies.

Contacts in the United States

THE EMBASSY OF IRELAND
2234 Massachusetts Avenue, NW
Washington, DC 20008
Tel: (202) 462-3939
Fax: (202) 232-5593
www.irelandemb.org

Passport/Visa Requirements

A passport is required. Tourists are not required to obtain visas for stays under 90 days, but may be asked to show onward or return tickets. To reside in the country, U.S. citizens must satisfy the Immigration authorities that they can support themselves for the period of the proposed stay.

For current information concerning entry and customs requirements for Ireland, travelers can contact the Embassy of Ireland.

U.S. citizens who wish to apply for a passport may visit Passport Services' well-organized website at http://travel.state.gov/passport_services.html.

Contacts in Ireland

THE EMBASSY OF THE UNITED STATES OF
AMERICA
42 Elgin Road, Ballsbridge
Dublin
Tel: (353) 1-668-8777
Fax: (353) 1-668-9946
www.usembassy.ie

AMERICAN CHAMBER OF COMMERCE IN
IRELAND
20 College Green
Dublin 2
Tel: (353) 1-679-3733
Fax: (353) 1-679-3402

DUN & BRADSTREET LTD.
Postal Address: P.O. Box 455A, Dublin 2
Street Address: Holbrook House, Holles
Street, Dublin 2
Tel: (353) 1-676-4239
Fax: (353) 1-678-9301 Admin; (353) 1-676-4284 RMS; (353) 1-661-2795 Credit
Services; (353) 1-676-0770 Sales

OFFICE OF THE PRESIDENT
'Aras an Uachtaráin
Phoenix Park
Dublin 8, Ireland

PRIME MINISTER
Office of the Taoiseach
Government Buildings
Upper Merrion Street
Dublin 2, Ireland

Further contacts and websites can be found in Appendix A.

Communications

TELEPHONE: The international country code for Ireland is 353.

Phone numbers vary in length; most are five or six digits in length.

City codes may be one, two, or three digits in length. The largest cities have one or two digits; rural areas have three digit codes.

E-MAIL: E-mail addresses located in Ireland end with the code .ie

---

Cultural Note: The Irish frequently use the points of a compass to describe location. Not only will a site (such as a shop or office) be described as "East of here," but small objects within reach will be so located ("the directory is South of you on the table"). It is useful to know the cardinal points at all times while in Ireland. Curiously, *below* is used to mean *North*; "Dunmanway is the next village below" means "Dunmanway is the next village to the North."

Israel

Official Name:	State of Israel, Medinat Yisra'el (Hebrew), Isra'il (Arabic)
Official Languages:	Hebrew and Arabic
Government System:	Parliamentary multi-party democracy
Population:	5.7 million (including the population of the Golan Heights and East Jerusalem) (1999 estimate)
Population Growth Rate:	1.81% (1999 estimate)
Area:	20,320 sq. km. (7,846 sq. mi.); not including the Israeli-occupied Arab territories of the West Bank and Gaza Strip; about the size of New Jersey
Natural Resources:	copper, phosphates, bromide, potash, clay, sand, sulfur, asphalt, manganese, small amounts of natural gas and crude oil
Major Cities:	Jerusalem (capital), Tel Aviv, Haifa, Beersheba

Cultural Note: Israel has a diverse population. Jews make up only about 82% of the population, and almost half of the Israeli Jews were born outside Israel. The remainder includes Palestinians (who can be Muslim or Christian) and Druze (all of whom worship an offshoot of Islam).

Age Breakdown

0–14 = 28%   15–64 = 62%   65+ = 10% (1999 estimate)
Life Expectancy: 76.71 years, male; 80.61 years, female (1999 estimate)

Time

As a foreigner, you will be expected to be on time to business appointments. Many Israelis familiar with North American business customs will likewise be punctual. However, punctuality is not a custom in most Middle Eastern cultures.

Israel is 2 hours ahead of Greenwich Mean Time (GMT +2), which is 7 hours ahead of U.S. Eastern Standard Time (EST +7).

Observation: "Israel exists in a constant state of controlled chaos, which Israelis refer to as *balagan*. Punctuality and deadlines are demanded of foreigners but not of themselves. . . . Be prepared for late arrivals and a lack of urgency to get things done."

—From *A Short Course in International Negotiating* by Jeffrey Edmund Curry

---

Holidays

A web-based *World Holiday and Time Zone Guide* is available at www.getcustoms.com with updated official holidays, cultural tips, time zones, and tables that compare worldwide business hours.

Both Judaism and Islam use lunar calendars that are different from the Gregorian (Western) calendar. However, for official business purposes (and when dealing with foreigners), most Israelis will use the Gregorian calendar. If you feel the need to specify that you are using the Gregorian calendar, avoid using the Christian notations B.C. and A.D. Instead, use the initials C.E.. for *Common Era* and B.C.E. for *Before Common Era*, which have been adopted by many. (These initials usually follow the date.)

The following list of holidays is a working guide. The actual dates are computed by the Hebrew calendar and fall on a different date (by the Gregorian calendar) each year. In cases where holidays fall on Saturday or Sunday, commercial establishments may be closed the preceding Friday or following Monday.

> Passover (First and Last Days)
> Yom Ha'Atzma'ut (Independence Day)
> Shavuot (Pentecost)
> Rosh Hashanah (Jewish New Year)
> Yom Kippur (The Day of Atonement)
> Sukkot (Feast of Tabernacles)
> Simhat Torah (Celebration of the Law)
> Hanukkah (Festival of Lights; First and Last Days)

The variation between the Hebrew and Gregorian calendars is about a month. For example, the Jewish New Year (Rosh Hashanah) will generally fall within a span of one month, between mid-September to mid-October.

Muslims follow the Islamic calendar. In Islamic neighborhoods, the most important holidays are: the three-day feast celebrating the end of the fasting of the month of Ramadan (Id al Fitr), and the Feast of the Sacrifice (Id al Adha).

Work Week

- The Jewish holy day, the Sabbath, begins at sunset on Friday and ends at sunset on Saturday. In deference to the religious Jewish community, no business is conducted on the Sabbath. The work week runs from Sunday through Thursday.
- Government hours are generally 8:00 A.M. to 3:00 P.M., Sunday through Thursday. Many offices close at 2:00 P.M. during the summer.
- Banking hours vary. Main banks in commercial districts are open from 8:30 A.M. to 2:00 P.M. Sunday through Thursday; some extend their hours until 7:00 P.M. Branch banks that cater primarily to the public operate on a split schedule. They are usually open from 8:30 A.M. to 12:30 P.M. Sunday through Thursday, plus 4:00 to 5:30 P.M. on Sundays, Tuesdays, and Thursdays. Many banks close at noon on Fridays.
- Business hours vary widely. Even the days businesses are open depends upon the religion of the owner. Most Jewish businesses close on Fridays (especially in the afternoon) and Saturdays. Islamic-owned establishments will be closed all day on Fridays; Christian-owned ones will be closed Sundays. (Remember that Palestinians may be either Muslim *or* Christian.)
- A typical schedule for a Jewish-owned business would be 8:00 A.M. to 4:00 P.M. Sunday through Thursday, and 8:00 A.M. to 1:00 P.M. on Fridays.

Religious/Societal Influences on Business

Although Israel is the Jewish homeland, the State of Israel has no official religion. The Jewish population is divided into different groups. The Ashkenazi Jews came from Germany, Poland, and Russia. Most Jews in the U.S. came from this group. The native language of the Ashkenazim is Yiddish (although many also spoke the language of their country of residence).

The Sephardic Jews were exiled from Spain and Portugal in 1492. They spread throughout the Mediterranean, especially the Middle East. Before the Zionist movement encouraged Jews to move back to the Holy Land in the twentieth century, most Jews in Israel were Sephardim. The native language of the Sephardic Jews is Landino. After Israel's neighbors declared war on Israel, most Sephardim outside of Israel emigrated. The large Jewish communities in cities like Cairo and Baghdad left for Israel.

For years, Israel had approximately equal numbers of Ashkenazim and Sephardim. But the recent influx of Ashkenazim from the former USSR has irrevocably tipped the balance in favor of the Ashkenazim. Some Sephardim resent the dominant position of the Ashkenazi community.

The Yemeni and Ethiopian Jews are two smaller groups. They have been much less successful in Israel, and tension exists over their place in Israeli society. In January 1996 the Ethiopian community was outraged to discover that their blood donations were routinely destroyed. The black Ethiopians charged the government with racism, but the health service defended the practice, since the Ethiopian Jews come from an area of Africa where AIDS is endemic.

Aside from their ethnic origins, Israeli Jewry runs the gamut from fundamentalist belief to atheism. Many Jews consider themselves "secular" and rarely participate in their religion. In fact, some of the recent immigrants from Russia had never practiced Judaism and needed to study even the basics of Jewish belief. On the other hand, some very religious Jews want to make their beliefs part of daily life in Israel. Because of the Parliamentary system in Israel, small religious-oriented parties can have a disproportionate amount of power.

5 Cultural Tips

1. Jerusalem, the new capital of Israel, contains some of the most important shrines of Christianity and Islam, as well as Judaism. If this is your first trip, do not underestimate the tremendous impact these shrines may have on you. (The City of Jerusalem has one of the busiest asylums in the world, full of tourists who lost touch with reality after visiting the Holy Places.) Even the most logical and pragmatic businesspeople may be distracted.

2. The official work week in Israel runs from Sunday through Thursday, as the Jewish Sabbath begins at sunset on Friday and ends at sunset on Saturday. No business is conducted on the Sabbath, but many Jewish-owned business are open until 1:00 P.M. on Fridays. The Muslim holy day begins at dawn on Friday, and Muslims do not work on Thursday afternoons. Some Christian businessowners do not open on Sunday. So the only days that everyone in Israel works are Monday, Tuesday, Wednesday, and most of Thursday.

3. For many Orthodox and fundamentalist Jews, the Sabbath is devoted to God, and "not working" on the Sabbath is interpreted very broadly. Even turning on a light switch can be interpreted as work. Some will hire a non-Jew to do necessary chores on the Sabbath.

4. A large number of Israeli businesspeople speak English. If you have your materials translated into Hebrew, remember that Hebrew is read right-to-left (the opposite of English's left-to-right). Graphic design is also reversed; the back page of a booklet in the U.S. is the front page in Israel.

5. Most Israelis love to talk. Business meetings may begin with long discussions, during which the parties get to know each other. However, once the business discussion is underway, keep your presentation short and on track. The majority of Israeli businesspeople appreciate directness and clarity. Avoid exaggeration.

Economic Overview

The historic ties between the U.S. and Israel give distinct advantages to U.S. firms wishing to do business in Israel. A free-trade agreement between the U.S. and Israel, concluded in 1985, was fully implemented on January 1, 1995 and is a key factor in keeping the U.S. as Israel's largest trading partner. U.S. loan guarantees, a cheaper dollar, and programs that encourage joint research and development have helped maintain an advantage for U.S. firms.

Two major factors influencing Israel's economy in the 1990s are the influx of nearly 600,000 immigrants from the former Soviet Union and the peace process in the Middle East. Both have had positive effects on the Israeli economy. Remarkably, since Israel's massive immigration wave began in 1990, more jobs have been created than exist for the new labor market entrants.

Two main issues affect the business climate in Israel—regional instability and terrorism. These two issues have led some foreign business to move cautiously on investments in Israel. The assassination of Prime Minster Yitzhak Rabin in November 1995 underlines that there remains opposition from some Israelis to the Arab–Israeli peace process. Overall, however, it is believed that Rabin's assassination will actually serve to galvanize Israel's commitment to the Middle East peace process.

Israel has an increasingly open, modern, and sophisticated commercial environment with a well-educated population. The market for U.S. goods and services exists now and will continue to expand.

5 Largest Businesses in Israel

Kupat Holim Clalit, Tel Aviv
   30,000 employees
Clal (Israel) Ltd., Tel Aviv
   23,000 employees
Israel Corporation Ltd., Tel Aviv
   15,000 employees
Danel Adir Yehoshua Ltd., Tel Aviv
   15,000 employees
Israel Electric Corporation Ltd., Haifa
   13,372 employees

Cultural Note: All countries change, but few countries have had to deal with the changes Israel has seen in the past few years. The influx of Russian Jews, the peace agreement with the Palestinians, and the constant threat of terrorism have all changed Israel. Each of these have had unexpected effects.

Many of the Russian immigrants were highly educated, and Israel does not have enough high-level jobs to fully employ them. Israel is now the most "overeducated" nation in the world, with Russian engineers and musicians working as manual laborers.

As part of the peace agreement, Israel is disengaging from the Occupied Territories. Opposition to the "peace-for-land" policy has rent Israeli society, as reflected in the assassination of Prime Minister Rabin by an Israeli fundamentalist.

After every terrorist attack attributed to a Palestinian group (such as Hamas), the Israeli government closes the Israeli–Palestinian border. This punishes the many Palestinians whose economy depends upon Israel. But the frequent loss of Palestinian day-laborers also hurts their Israeli employers. To offset this, the Israelis have invited some Asians into Israel as replacement labor. (This is common in other Middle Eastern nations, where Filipinos and other Asians are brought in to supplement the work force.)

Observation:

"There really is no such thing as an Israeli culture. There are so many immigrants, even from cultural extremes. . . ."

—Shimon Alon, quoted in Richard Hill's *EuroManagers and Martians*

Comparative Data

Comparative Data Ratings
(Scale: 5 = Excellent; 1 = Poor)
Israel: 3.875

- A.   GDP Growth: 3
- B.   Per Capita Income: 4
- C.   Trade Flows with the U.S.: 4
- D.   Country Risk: 4
- E.   Monetary Policy: 3
- F.   Trade Policy: 4
  - Tariffs
  - Import Licensing
  - Import Taxes
- G.   Protection of Property Rights: 4
- H.   Foreign Investment Climate: 5

GROSS DOMESTIC PRODUCT: $96.7 billion (1998 estimate)

GDP GROWTH: 2.0% (1998); 1.5% (1999 estimate)

PER CAPITA INCOME: $17,500 (1997 estimate)

Trade Flows with the U.S.

U.S. EXPORTS TO ISRAEL: $7.0 billion (1998)

U.S. IMPORTS FROM ISRAEL: $8.6 billion (1998)

TOP U.S. EXPORTS TO ISRAEL: Aircraft; electronic components; machinery; precious stones and metals; motor vehicles; medical and optical equipment; cereals; ships and boats; tobacco; miscellaneous grain; seed and fruit

TOP U.S. PROSPECTS FOR EXPORT TO ISRAEL: Airport/ground support equipment; insurance services; pollution-control equipment; medical equipment and supplies; telecommunications equipment; franchising; electronic components; computers and peripherals; industrial process controls; information services

Country Risk

Dun & Bradstreet rates Israel as having good capacity to meet outstanding payment liabilities.

Open account terms are the dominant vehicle of payment, with 60- to 90-day terms the norm. A letter of credit for new accounts is required.

Monetary Policy

Israel has suffered from double-digit inflation rates throughout much of the 1990s. However, it dropped to 3.8% in 1999 and was forecast to be 3.4% in 2000.

MONETARY UNIT: new Israeli shekel

Trade Policy

TARIFFS   Under the U.S.–Israeli Free Trade Agreement, all remaining duties imposed on U.S.-made products were eliminated on January 1, 1995. Nontariff protection is still allowed on sensitive agricultural items; this portion of the agreement is due to be renegotiated in 2000.

IMPORT LICENSING   All import licensing requirements for U.S.-made consumer and industrial goods have been eliminated under the Free Trade Agreement. However, licensing requirements and quantitative restrictions still exist for a wide range of food and agricultural products. All medical devices and equipment are subject to supervision by the Ministry of Health.

Israel maintains extensive restrictions on agricultural imports ranging from quotas, licensing restrictions, and variable levies to outright prohibitions.

IMPORT TAXES   A value-added tax (VAT) of 17% is levied on almost all imported and domestically produced good and services. The exceptions are capital goods, exports, agricultural products, and food products.

Protection of Intellectual Property Rights

Israel is slowly making progress towards developing a viable intellectual property system. Comprehensive laws are being passed, and Israel has signed various international conventions and agreements. Israel is a member of the World Intellectual Property

Organization and GATT. However, laws notwithstanding, the general attitude in Israel is one of disrespect for IP rights. Software piracy is rampant and the U.S. has placed Israel on its Section 301 Priority Watch List.

The first user in Israel is entitled to apply for an invention except where application is made under international treaty. Worldwide novelty is required. Opposition may be made within three months of publication. Patent terms are for 20 years from application. Exploitation rights are reserved to prior users in Israel before the application date. Also, certain exploitation rights are reserved to the State and compulsory licensing may be ordered. Assignments must be recorded.

The International Classification system has been adopted for trademarks and service marks are recognized. Flexibility is provided to allow registration for honest concurrent users or other special circumstances. Oppositions may be filed within 3 months after a mark is advertised. Registrations are good for 7 years with 14-year renewals. There is a one-year bar against registering a lapsed mark. Registrations may be assigned with or without goodwill.

Israel's copyright laws are based on English law. Copyright rights in unpublished works exist only for Israeli citizens. Copying of audio recordings and videos is permitted for noncommercial use. Software is not expressly protected. As mentioned above, software piracy is endemic. (Israelis often joke that only one copy of software is needed for the entire nation of Israel.) Copyrights do not need to be registered. Copyright protection continues for the length of the author's life plus 50 years from the January first following the author's death.

Foreign Investment Climate

The Israeli government places a high priority on encouraging foreign investment in the Israeli economy. There are generally no restrictions for foreign investors doing business in Israel and, except in certain departments of the defense industry that are closed to outside investors, there are no restrictions on foreign investment in the private sector. Investments in regulated industries (e.g., banking and insurance) require prior government approval.

All benefits available to Israelis are available to foreign investors, and there is specific legislation to encourage foreign investment that gives the foreign investors certain advantages, such as reduced tax rates for longer periods of time than for residents.

Foreign investors are granted national treatment and are encouraged to participate in the ongoing Israeli privatization program.

Political Leaders, Parties, and International Organizations

The International Academy at Santa Barbara at http://www.iasb.org/cwl publishes *Current World Leaders*, an excellent resource for up-to-date data on political leaders, parties, demographics, etc., in Israel. Tel: (800) 530-2682 or (805) 965-5010 for subscription information to their database.

Chief of State:
President Moshe Katsav

Head of the Government:
Prime Minister Ehud Barak

Next Election:
March, 2003

Political Parties:
Likud, Labor, National Religious Party, Democratic Front (Communist), Shas, Moledet, Arab Democratic Party, Meretz, Tsomet, United Torah Judiasm, Yi'ud

Membership in international organizations:
EBRD, INTELSAT, UN and all of its specialized agencies and related organizations (including FAO, GATT, IAEA, IBRD, ICAO, IDA, IFAD, IFC, ILO, IMF, IMO, ITU, UNESCO, UNIDO, UPU, WHO, WIPO, WMO)

Political Influences on Business

Two main political issues affect the business climate in Israel: regional instability and terrorism. These two issues have led some foreign business to move cautiously on investments in Israel. It is expected that the recent agreements between Israel and its Arab neighbors will promote a climate conducive to business investment in the region.

Many aspects of Israeli life are governed by religious law. In observance of Shabbat (the Sabbath), most public transportation and Israel's national airline do not operate between sundown Friday and sundown Saturday. Most businesses and government offices are closed from Friday afternoon to Sunday morning. Laws of *Kashrut* (kosher requirements for food) also restrict the importation and selling of certain foods and beverages in Israel.

Israel is a parliamentary democracy. The president is elected by the *Knesset*, a unicameral parliament, for a five-year term. Traditionally, the president has selected the leader of the party most able to form a government to become prime minister. The prime minister exercises executive power.

The *Knesset*'s 120 members are elected to four-year terms, although the prime minister may decide to call for new elections before the end of the term or the prime minister's government can fall on a vote of no-confidence in the *Knesset*. The president then has the option of asking the current prime minister to form a new government. If he cannot, new elections take place for the *Knesset*. A total of eleven political parties are currently represented in the current *Knesset*. They include: Labor, Likud, Meretz, Tzomet, Shas, National Religious Party, United Torah Judaism, Hadash, Moledet, Yi'ud, and the Arab Democratic Party.

The political spectrum runs a wide gamut from the left-wing Hadash Party (which is mainly composed of former communists) to the liberal Meretz Party (which is a compendium of three separate parties), left–middle and ruling Labor Party, right–middle and chief opposition Likud Party, the right-wing libertarian Tsomet Party, the right-wing religious parties of National Religious Parties and United Tora Judaism (also a mix of two separate parties), and the ultra right-wing Moledet Party.

Three parties are difficult to categorize: Shas, a religious party that has been in and out of the ruling coalition with Labor and Meretz; Yi'ud, a breakaway party from Tsomet but which now votes with the Labor coalition; and the Arab Democratic Party, which is a vigorous defender of the rights of Arab Israeli citizens and the rights of Palestinians in the peace negotiations.

Contacts in the United States

THE EMBASSY OF THE STATE OF ISRAEL
3514 International Drive, NW
Washington, D.C. 20008
Tel: (202) 364-5500; 364-5590
Fax: (202) 364-5423
www.israelemb.org

AMERICA–ISRAEL CHAMBER OF COMMERCE
AND INDUSTRY, INC.
The Empire State Bldg.
350 Fifth Avenue, Suite 1919
New York, NY 10118
Tel: (212) 971-0310

Passport/Visa Requirements

U.S. citizens do not require a tourist or business visa to visit Israel provided they possess a passport valid for at least 9 further months of travel and that they have either a return (or onward) ticket or funds to purchase such a ticket. On arrival, U.S. passports are endorsed gratis for a three months' stay; this endorsement can be renewed.

For current information concerning entry and customs requirements for Israel, travelers can contact the Embassy of the State of Israel.

U.S. citizens who wish to apply for a passport may visit Passport Services' well-organized website at http://travel.state.gov/passport_services.html.

Contacts in Israel

THE EMBASSY OF THE UNITED STATES OF
AMERICA
71 Hayarkon Street
PSC 98, Box 100
Tel Aviv 63903
Mailing Address: APO AE 09830
Tel: (972) (3) 517-4338
Fax: (972) (3) 663449
www.usis-israel.org.il/

ISRAEL–AMERICAN CHAMBER OF COMMERCE
AND INDUSTRY
35 Shaul Hamelech Boulevard
P.O. Box 33174
Tel Aviv
Tel: [972] (3) 252-341

DUN & BRADSTREET (ISRAEL) LTD.
Postal Address: P.O. Box 50200, 61500
Tel Aviv
Street Address: City Palace, 27 Hamered
Street, Floor C-2, 68125 Tel Aviv
Tel: (972) (3) 510-3355
Fax: (972) (3) 510-3397;
(972) (3) 510-3398

OFFICE OF THE PRESIDENT
Beit Hanasi
3 Hanasi Street
92188 Jerusalem, State of Israel

OFFICE OF THE PRIME MINISTER
3 Kaplan Street
Kiryat Ben-Gurion
91919 Jerusalem, State of Israel

Further contacts and websites can be found in Appendix A.

Communications

TELEPHONE: The international country code for Israel is 972.

Phone numbers are currently six digits in length.

City codes may be one or two digits in length.

Israel plans to abolish the city codes and establish a nationwide system of eight-digit numbers.

E-MAIL: E-mail addresses located in Israel end with the code .il

---

Observation: " the Israeli economy lurched—or more accurately is still in the process of lurching—from monolithic, state-controlled monopolies to private-sector markets.

"Israelis generally want to please in business situations. They often promise what they might not be able to deliver. A culture of customer satisfaction—timeliness in meeting schedules, customer responsiveness, professional business ethics, reliability— is still in the formative stage."

—From *The Simple Guide to Customs and Etiquette in Israel* by David Starr-Glass

---

Italy

Official Name:	Italian Republic (Republica Italiana)
Official Language:	Italian
Population:	56.74 million (1999 estimate)
Population Growth Rate:	−0.08% (1999 estimate)
Area:	301,230 sq. km. (120,492 sq. mi.); about the size of Georgia and Florida combined
Natural Resources:	mercury, potash, marble, sulfur, dwindling natural gas and crude oil reserves, fish, coal
Major Cities:	Rome (capital), Milan, Turin, Naples

Cultural Note: The Italians—and their ancestors, the Romans—invented many of the business practices we use today. Their innovations included banking, insurance, and even double-entry bookkeeping. Do not let Italian friendliness and chatter lull you into forgetting that they are very astute businesspeople.

Age Breakdown

0–14 = 14%   15–64 = 68%   65+ = 18% (1999 estimate)
Life expectancy: 75.4 years, male; 81.82 years, female (1999 estimate)

Time

"Time is money" is not an Italian aphorism. Although foreign executives are expected to be relatively punctual for business appointments, Italians may not be. However, you should phone if you expect to be more than five minutes late.

Deadlines are considered flexible in Italy. If you must have something accomplished by a specific date, you must make that emphatically and repeatedly clear.

Italy is 1 hour ahead of Greenwich Mean Time (GMT +1), which is 6 hours ahead of U.S. Eastern Standard Time (EST +6).

Observation: "For the most part, Italians are quite punctual. Just go to church a half-hour before mass, or to a doctor's office a half-hour before appointments begin and note how many people are there waiting. For the theater or the opera, Italians are careful to arrive *puntualmente* (punctually) with sufficient time to chat and get comfortable to fully enjoy the performance.

"But *le persone importante si fanno aspettare* (important people arrive late). This is a common trend among young people. *Sono in ritardo, perciò sono importante* (I'm late, therefore I am important). Being late is an unspoken form of social status!"

—From *The Italian Way: Aspects of Behavior, Attitudes, and Customs of the Italians* by Mario Costantino and Lawrence Gambella

---

Holidays

An up-to-date, web-based *World Holiday and Time Zone Guide* is available at www.getcustoms.com. It lists official holidays by country and by day of the year, cultural tips, a corruption index, and time zones with worldwide business hours.

Jan 6	TH	Epiphany
Apr 24	MO	Easter Monday
Apr 25	TU	Liberation Day
May 1	MO	Labor Day
Jun 24	SA	St. John's Day (Florence, Genoa)
Jun 29	TH	St. Peter's Day (Rome)
Jul 15	SA	St. Rosalia's Day (Palermo)
Aug 15	TU	Assumption
Sep 19	TU	St. Gennaro's Day (Naples)
Nov 1	WE	All Saints Day
Dec 7	TH	St. Ambrogio's Day (Milan)
Dec 8	Fr	Immaculate Conception
Dec 26	TU	St. Stephen's Day

The Catholic observances of Easter Sunday, Easter Monday, Ascension Day, and Corpus Christi are also official holidays.

In addition, the observance of many regional holidays may close businesses. July and August are poor months for scheduling appointments as many firms close for vacation. The same is true during Christmas and New Year. Be sure to check with local contacts to confirm these and additional holidays.

When a holiday falls on a Tuesday or Thursday, Italians tend to extend their weekend to the holiday, giving themselves a four-day weekend.

Work Week

Normal business hours are from 8:00 or 9:00 A.M. to noon or 1:00 P.M. and from 3:00 to 6:00 or 7:00 P.M. Working hours for the various ministries of the government are normally from 8:00 A.M. to 2:00 P.M. without intermission. Bank hours are from 8:30 A.M. to 1:30 P.M. and 3:00 to 4:00 P.M.; they are closed on Saturdays.

Religious/Societal Influences on Business

The vast majority of Italians are raised Roman Catholic, although the Republic of Italy has no official religion. The Catholic Church remains influential in Italy, although it was unable to prevent the legalization of divorce and abortion in the 1970s.

If the Church has diminished in importance in Italy, so has that other icon of Italian culture, the family. Long before Italy was united into one country, the family was the institution that provided stability and order. Several generations lived under one roof, and most of the adults worked in the family business.

Today, both a falling birth rate and economics have changed the family. Currently, Italy's birth rate is not even sufficient to offset its death rate. Households now need two incomes, so more women work. Many Italians have moved away from their traditional homes in search of employment. Today the extended family with several generations under one roof is the exception, not the rule.

5 Cultural Tips

1. The Italian bureaucracy and legal system is notoriously slow. One reason for this is that Italy is burdened by over 2,000 years of law. New laws are added but old ones are rarely taken off the books—even laws dating back to the Roman Empire! The recent influx of EU regulations has only made things more difficult.

2. Sooner or later, everyone falls afoul of the extensive and sometimes contradictory Italian legal system. The tax codes are similarly hazardous. One Italian President claimed that if Italians paid all of their taxes, they'd owe 150% of their income! Get good local legal representation; you will need it.

3. Italian firms tend to have a fairly rigid hierarchy, with little visible fraternization between the ranks. This doesn't necessarily indicate a lack of communication. Even though you may be dealing with the top ranks of executives, the lower ranks of employees may also be evaluating your proposal.

4. Everyone tends to speak at once in Italian gatherings. This goes for business meetings as well as social events. It is possible for Italians to conduct a meeting in a more orderly fashion, but only if those rules are established in the beginning.

5. Italian executives often have more than one business card. One card will contain all important business information, including the person's educational degrees and/or professional titles, plus all contact information, phone and fax numbers, Internet address, etc. They may have a second card without the extensive professional titles. (Italians who lack this second card may instead cross out these titles on their card. This does not mean that those titles have been revoked! Instead, it means that the two of you have established a less formal relationship, and you do not have to address the Italian by his or her title.) Finally, there is a third card for social occasions—which some Italians may carry. This is a visiting card, and contains only the person's name—no titles, addresses, or phone numbers.

Economic Overview

Italy, representing the world's fifth largest economy, continues to transform itself. The government continues on a path of privatization and is reducing its role in the economy. As this rationalization of the economy moves forward, the economy is expected to offer even more opportunities to the U.S. as both a buyer of U.S. goods and for investment.

The Italian economy has recovered strongly from the recession and political scandals of the early 1990s. Growth slowed to 1.5% in 1997, but improved modestly since then. Inflation remains very low.

A strong export performance, driven by the weak lira, has been key to Italy's recovery.

5 Largest Businesses in Italy

Poste Italiane S.p.A., Rome
    203,126 employees
Ferrovie dello Stato Societa' di Trasporti e Servizi S.p.A., Rome
    117,700 employees
Enel S.p.A., Rome
    87,467 employees
Telecom Italia S.p.A., Rome
    82,317 employees
Fiat Auto S.p.A., Turin
    65,847 employees

Cultural Note: Italians appreciate the more refined aspects of life. They have a highly cultivated appreciation of art, science, history, literature, music, fine wines, beautiful clothes, excellent meals, the list goes on . . . They will respect the well-educated, civilized businessperson with accomplishments in more than just the workplace.

Comparative Data

Comparative Data Ratings
(Scale: 5 = Excellent; 1 = Poor)
Italy: 4.0

A. GDP Growth: 3
B. Per Capita Income: 5
C. Trade Flows with the U.S.: 4
D. Country Risk: 5
E. Monetary Policy: 4
F. Trade Policy: 4
    • Tariffs
    • Import Licensing
    • Import Taxes
G. Protection of Property Rights: 3
H. Foreign Investment Climate: 4

GROSS DOMESTIC PRODUCT: $1.181 trillion (1998 estimate)

GDP GROWTH: 1.5% (1998 estimate)

PER CAPITA INCOME: $20,800 (1998 estimate)

Trade Flows with the U.S.

U.S. EXPORTS TO ITALY: $9 billion (1998)

U.S. IMPORTS FROM ITALY: $21 billion (1998 estimate)

TOP U.S. EXPORTS TO ITALY: Machinery; computer software; electrical components; telecommunications equipment; computers and peripherals; medical and optical equipment; mineral fuel; organic chemicals; pharmaceuticals; automotive parts.

TOP U.S. PROSPECTS FOR EXPORT TO ITALY: Insurance services; telecommunications equipment and services; automotive parts and service equipment; franchising; electric power systems; computer services; computers and peripherals; sporting goods and recreational equipment; pollution-control equipment and services; computer software.

Country Risk

Dun & Bradstreet rates Italy as having excellent capacity to meet outstanding payment liabilities. It carries the lowest degree of risk.

Open account terms of 60 to 90 days is most commonly used, although letter of credit is advised for new customers.

Monetary Policy

Inflation fell below 4% for the first time in 25 years in 1994. It rose slightly in 1995 (due to tax increases and the devaluation of the lira), then fell again in the late 1990s. Inflation was only 1.8% in 1998 and was forecast to be 1.5% in 2000 and 1.7% in 2001.

To the surprise of many, Italy managed to bring its budget into line with the regulations of the 1992 Maastricht Treaty. This allowed Italy to enter into Europe's economic and monetary union in 1998. Italy qualified to be one of the first countries to use the euro as official currency in January 1999.

MONETARY UNIT: Italian lira, being replaced by the European Union's euro

Trade Policy

TARIFFS   Italy applies the European Union tariffs. Duty rates on manufactured goods from the United States generally range from 5–17%. Agricultural products face higher rates and special levies. Most raw materials enter duty-free or at low rates.

IMPORT LICENSING   With the exception of a small group of primarily agricultural goods, practically all goods originating from the U.S. can be imported without import licenses. Import licenses, when required, are generally granted quickly for goods of U.S. origin.

Various apparel and textile products and controlled items, such as arms and munitions, are the most frequently regulated items.

IMPORT TAXES   A 19% value-added tax (VAT) is applies to most goods and services. A 9% VAT applies to processed foods and a 4% rate applies to basic foods and medicines. A 38% rate applies to luxury goods.

Excise taxes are levied on a small number of products such as soft drinks, wine, beer, spirits, tobacco, sugar, and petroleum products.

Protection of Intellectual Property Rights

Italy belongs to the Universal Copyright Conventions, the Berne Convention for the Protection of Literary and Artistic Works, the Patent Cooperation Treaty, the European Patent Convention, the Madrid Trademark Agreement, and the Paris Convention for Protection of Industrial Property. Nevertheless, software piracy is a substantial problem in Italy.

Patents protect industrial inventions, utility models, industrial designs, new plant varieties, and semiconductor product topographies. Invention patents, utility models, and industrial designs must have industrial application, be novel, and have an inventive step. Patents of invention have a term of 15 years from application.

Trademark registration is permissive and unregistered marks that are in use can be protected. Trademarks may be registered by filing applications in Italy or with the EEC. Trademarks do not become incontestable until 5 years after registration. Registrations have renewable terms of 20 years.

Copyright protection applies only to Italian citizens and parties whose works are protected by convention or bilateral treaty. Copyrights are automatic on first publication. Copyrights are valid for 70 years. Computer software is recognized as subject to copyright. Although registration is permissive rather than compulsory, works are typically registered.

Foreign Investment Climate

Official Italian policy is to encourage foreign investment. For the most part, foreign investors will not find major impediments to investing in Italy. One hundred percent foreign ownership of corporations is allowed. The government does, however, have the authority to block mergers involving foreign firms for reasons essential to the national economy or if the home government of the foreign firm applies discriminatory measures against Italian firms.

There are several industry sectors that are either closely regulated or prohibited outright to foreign investors. These include domestic air transport and aircraft manufacturing. The government operates several monopolies, including petroleum, railroads, electrical generation and transmission, and production of cigars and cigarettes. A privatization program is reducing the state role in these sectors. Italy maintains restrictions and/or limits on foreign investment in banking, insurance, and shipping. Outside these sectors, there are no screening or blocking procedures directed solely at foreign investment.

Companies can bring in foreign workers only after certifying that no unemployed Italian is available to perform the expected duties.

Switzerland is the largest foreign investor in Italy, followed by the U.S. However, the combined investment from European Union countries dwarfs both at almost $50 billion in 1999.

On February 20, 1998 relations between Italy and the U.S. were damaged by an accident involving the U.S. military. A U.S. Marine jet out of the NATO airbase at Aviano in northern Italy inadvertently severed the cable supporting a ski-life gondola. The 20 people in the gondola plunged to their deaths. Italians were outraged both by the incident and the failure of U.S. courts to find the pilots criminally negligent, prompting many Italians to call for the withdrawal of U.S. forces on Italian soil. However, the usefulness of the NATO presence in Italy was underscored by the 1999 military effort in nearby Kosovo; many of the aircraft that bombed Serbian forces flew out of NATO bases in Italy.

Political Leaders, Parties, and International Organizations

The International Academy at Santa Barbara at http://www.iasb.org/cwl publishes *Current World Leaders*, an excellent resource for up-to-date data on political leaders, parties, demographics, etc., in Italy. Tel: (800) 530-2682 or (805) 965-5010 for subscription information to their database.

Chief of State:
  President Carlo Azeglio Ciampi

Head of the Government:
  Prime Minister Giuliano Amato

Next Election:

June, 2006

Political Parties:

Go Italy, Italian Popular Party, Christian Democratic Center, Democratic Party of the Left, National Alliance, Socialist Party, Democratic Alliance, Italian Socialist Movement, Northern League, Italian Republican Party (PRI), Union for Federalism, Centrist Union, People's Party, Radical Party, Union of Democratic Socialists, Green Party

Membership in international organizations:

CE, EBRD, EU, G7, INTELSAT, NACC, NATO, OECD, OSCE, UN and all of its specialized agencies and related organizations (including FAO, GATT, IAEA, IBRD, ICAO, IDA, IFAD, IFC, ILO, IMF, IMO, ITU, UNESCO, UNIDO, UPU, WHO, WIPO, WMO), WEU

Political Influences on Business

Italy is a republic whose government is divided into three spheres of power: the Parliament, the Government (which performs an executive function), and the Judicial. The President of the Republic (who has limited responsibilities in all three spheres) and the constitutional court help to maintain an equilibrium between these branches. The President of the Republic's most important functions are to nominate the prime minister and his cabinet, and to dissolve parliament.

Parliament consists of the Chamber of Deputies and the Senate. Over time, the Chamber of Deputies has become the leading body, but each is equivalent in power. A large part of the work of Parliament takes place in committees.

The executive functions are exercised by the Government, which consists of the Prime Minister and his Council of Ministers. The Prime Minister is the President of the Council and the leading figure in the government. His power is derived from the day-to-day running of the government, chairing the council and setting its agenda, as well as signing legislation. There are 22 ministers, including 4 without portfolio. The ministries form the basic structure of the state's public administration by implementing the policies and laws of the state.

The justice system consists of four branches (constitutional, common, administrative, and special), which are essentially independent of each other.

Although the power of the State is primarily centralized, the 20 regions have authority for the administration of some public functions and for enacting certain specific legislation (e.g., health care).

An important factor in the Government and the State is the power of the political parties. Because no party commanded a parliamentary majority for almost 45 years, coalition government was the norm.

Regionalism remains a major issue in Italy. Strong separatist movements exist both in the north and south of the country.

Contacts in the United States

THE EMBASSY OF THE REPUBLIC OF ITALY
1601 Fuller Street, NW
Washington, D.C. 20009
Tel: (202) 328-5500
Fax: (202) 483-2187
www.italyemb.org

Passport/Visa Requirements

U.S. citizens traveling to Italy as tourists, in possession of a valid U.S. passport, do not need a visa to enter Italy for a stay not exceeding 90 days. A visa is necessary for non-tourists or for tourists who stay longer than three months.

All persons or entities engaging in business in Italy in any capacity must be registered with the local Chamber of Commerce, Industry, and Agriculture, a quasi-governmental office operating essentially as a field office of the Ministry of Industry and Commerce. Depending on the kind of company, additional registrations may be necessary. For current information concerning entry and customs requirements for Italy, travelers can contact the Italian Embassy.

U.S. citizens who wish to apply for a passport may visit Passport Services' well-organized website at http://travel.state.gov/passport_services.html.

Contacts in Italy

THE EMBASSY OF THE UNITED STATES
OF AMERICA
Via Veneto 119/A
00187-Rome
Mailing Address: PSC 59, Box 100, APO
AE 09624
Tel: (39) (06) 46741
Fax: (39) (6) 488-2672
www.usis.it

THE AMERICAN CHAMBER OF COMMERCE IN
ITALY
Via Cantu 1
20123 Milano
Tel: (39) (2) 869-0661
Fax: (39) (2) 805-7737

DUN & BRADSTREET KOSMOS S.P.A.
Postal Address: Casella Postal 10052,
20100 Milan
Street Address: Via dei Valtorta 48,
20127 Milan
Tel: (39) (2) 284-551
Fax: (39) (2) 884-55500

OFFICE OF THE PRESIDENT
Palazzo del Quirinale
00187 Rome, Republic of Italy

OFFICE OF THE PRIME MINISTER
Palazzo Chigi
Piazza Colonna 370
00100 Rome, Republic of Italy

Further contacts and websites can be found in Appendix A.

Communications

TELEPHONE: The international country code for Italy is 39.

Phone numbers vary in length, but seven digits are the most common.

City codes vary in length from one to three digits.

A toll-free number is colloquially known as *Numero Verde* ("green number") and *cannot* be called from outside Italy.

E-MAIL: E-mail addresses located in Italy end with the code .it

---

Cultural I.Q. Question: Many people recognize the names of Italian musicians (Verdi, Puccini, and Vivalda . . .) or painters (Raphael, Michelangelo, Titian, Correggio . . .), but for what did Luigi Pirandello receive the Nobel Prize in 1934?

E-mail your answer to TerriMorrison@getcustoms.com. Each month a drawing will be held to award a correct respondent from all the questions within this book with a free copy of *The World Holiday and Time Zone Guide* (current electronic version).

Japan

Official Name:	Japan (Nihon)
Official Language:	Japanese
Government System:	Parliamentary democracy under constitutional monarch
Population:	126.2 million (1999 estimate)
Population Growth Rate:	0.2% (1999 estimate)
Area:	377,765 sq. km. (145,711 sq. mi.); slightly smaller than California
Natural Resources:	Negligible mineral resources, fish
Major cities:	Tokyo (capital), Yokohama, Osaka, Kyoto, Nagoya, Sapporo, Kobe

---

Cultural Note: Before a meeting begins, most Japanese executives already know what will be discussed, how everyone feels about it, and how it will affect their situation. To the Japanese, the purpose of a meeting is to reach some sort of consensus among the participants. A flexible agenda is necessary so that the discussions may flow more freely. When a foreigner tries to adhere religiously to an agenda, it inhibits the creation of consensus. Even worse, this implies that the foreigner's time in Japan is limited, which weakens the foreigner's bargaining position.

Age Breakdown

0–14 = 15%   15–64 = 68%   65+ = 17% (1999 estimate)
Life Expectancy: 77.02 years, male; 83.35 years, female (1999 estimate)

Time

Japan is 9 hours ahead of Greenwich Mean Time (GMT +9), or you can add 14 hours to U.S. Eastern Standard Time (EST +14).

Holidays

An up-to-date, web-based *World Holiday and Time Zone Guide* is available at www.getcustoms.com. It lists official holidays by country and by day of the year, cultural tips, a corruption index, and time zones with worldwide business hours.

When a national holiday falls on a Sunday in Japan, the following Monday is a compensatory day off. In addition, many Japanese companies and government offices traditionally close during the New Year's holiday season (December 28–January 3), "Golden Week" (April 29–May 5), and the traditional O-Bon Festival (usually August 12–15).

The following is a working guide. Dates should be corroborated before final travel plans are made.

Jan 1	SA	New Year's Day
Jan 2	SU	Bank Holiday
Jan 3	MO	Bank Holiday
Jan 10	MO	Adults' Day
Feb 11	FR	National Foundation Day
Mar 20	MO	Vernal Equinox Day
Apr 29	SA	Greenery Day
May 3	WE	Constitution Memorial Day
May 4	TH	National Holiday
May 5	FR	Children's Day
Jul 20	TH	Marine Day
Sep 15	FR	Respect for the Aged Day
Sep 23	SA	Autumnal Equinox Day
Oct 9	MO	Health-Sports Day
Nov 3	FR	Culture Day
Nov 23	TH	Labor Thanksgiving Day
Dec 23	SA	Emperor's Birthday
Dec 31	SU	Bank Holiday

- The exact dates of the Vernal and Autumnal Exquinoxes may vary by a day or two.
- While Christmas is celebrated as a gift-giving holiday by many Japanese, it is not officially observed as a holiday.

Work Week

- The standard work week is Monday through Friday 9:00 A.M. to 5:00 P.M.; many companies also work Saturday mornings, 9:00 A.M. to 12:00 noon.
- The official average of hours worked in 1998 was 43 hours, down from 42.9 per week in 1995. However, many executives work longer hours. These figures do not include after-hours socializing with coworkers and/or business clients, which are essentially mandatory to conduct business in Japan.

Religious/Societal Influences on Business

Many Japanese say that they are not religious. However, since the philosophy known as Shinto is so pervasive, Japanese behavior can be considered highly influenced by their belief systems.

As Confucianism is to China, so is Shinto to Japan.

Both Confucianism and Shinto are usually described as philosophies rather than religions. It is quite possible to adhere to Confucian or Shinto precepts while being a practicing Buddhist or Christian.

Shinto, or "the way of the gods," is deeply interwoven with Japanese tradition. It is so interconnected to the traditions of the Japanese State that the two cannot be entirely separated.

Shinto does not establish specific deities to be worshiped, as do most religions. However, it does detail numerous rituals and customs, which foreigners often perceive as religious ceremonies.

It is Shinto that maintained that the Japanese Emperor was a God . . . a concept that the U.S. Occupation Forces insisted be denied. The 1946 radio announcement by the late Emperor Hirohito that he was not divine was a traumatic event for the Japanese. Shinto was also dethroned as Japan's state belief system; Japan now has no official religion.

The Japan-centric beliefs of Shinto reinforce the Japan-first attitude that is so vexing to foreign negotiators.

Buddhism is the largest conventional religion in Japan. While officially followed by 38.3% of the population, many more Japanese will participate in occasional Buddhist observances. In fact, there is a saying that "Japanese are born Shinto but die Buddhist." This reflects the preference for Shinto celebrations at birth and for Buddhist ritual at funerals.

Only about 1.2% of Japanese describe themselves as Christian.

5 Cultural Tips

1. Do not expect to make Japan the headquarters for all your PACRIM/Asian operations. There are vast differences among cultures in Japan, China, Korea, Malaysia, etc. Neither is it generally wise to place an executive from any other Asian country in a management position in Japan.

2. It is important to view your company's objectives in a global, high-level manner, with an understanding of how all the pieces relate. Be prepared to communicate this big picture to the Japanese, and be ready to answer questions about any and all aspects of the presentation in depth, and in a nonlinear manner. While U.S. executives generally consider it logical to resolve each item one-by-one, and will "hammer" at a point of disagreement, the Japanese look at the overall picture. The Japanese believe that many issues may be explored (and resolved) simultaneously.

3. Emphasize and build on points of agreement with your Japanese counterparts. A persuasive, positive presentation is compatible with Japanese culture—a high-pressure, confrontational approach is not.

4. It is vital to deal with your Japanese contacts on their time frame. This includes:
   a. e-mailing your questions two weeks ahead of your meeting so you know they will be able to answer them comfortably in person;
   b. having your appointments confirmed by a third party (such as your interpreter) upon your arrival in Japan;
   c. waiting through what may seem an interminable amount of silence for a Japanese executive to respond to a question; and
   d. allowing the Japanese negotiating team weeks to reach its consensus. Never impose a U.S. concept of time on Japanese culture.

5. Do not be offended by the many personal questions the Japanese may ask you. Expect to be asked about your job, your title, your responsibilities, the number of employees that report to you, and so on. Japanese is a very complex language with many forms of address. The Japanese will need a lot of information in order to decide which form to use when speaking to you. (Most of this subtlety will be lost when translated into English, but it is important to the Japanese.)

Cultural Note: Do not be surprised if your Japanese interpreter translates Japanese-into-English almost simultaneously, but waits for you (the English speaker) to finish before translating your statements into Japanese. Unlike English, Japanese is a very predictable language. By the time a Japanese executive is halfway through a sentence, the translator probably knows how the sentence will end. Indeed, it would be very impolite for a Japanese to end a sentence with an unexpected choice of words.

Economic Overview

As the world's second largest economy and second largest export market for U.S. goods and services, Japan has offered large-scale opportunities and strategic benefits for U.S. firms. As an expensive, highly competitive and highly complex market, Japan remains a challenging place to do business. U.S. firms hoping to succeed in Japan must take a long-term approach to entering the market and building a market presence.

The Asian Economic Crisis hit Japan in 1997, resulting in a 0.7% fall in the country's economy. Japanese corporate earnings fell to levels not seen since the 1970s. At present, Japan is mired in a stubborn recession.

U.S. exports to Japan fell in 1998 by more than 10%. The weak value of the yen relative to the dollar had made U.S. goods less competitive in Japan. U.S. products will remain at a disadvantage as long as the yen remains weak.

One result of the Japanese recession is a collapse in land prices. The cost of premium retail space in Tokyo has fallen by as much as 70%. This has attracted the interest of large foreign chains and hyperstores.

However, although Japan's overall economic outlook remains cloudy, the long-term outlook is still good. Since the financial crisis forced Japanese regulators to loosen trade barriers, it is expected that U.S. exports will also increase.

Japan remains a highly homogenous society and business practices are characterized by longstanding, close-knit relations among individuals and firms. Regulatory processes and local business practices in Japan reflect systems designed for indigenous needs with little or no consideration given for potential participation by foreign companies. Even for Japanese businesspeople, it takes time to develop relationships and become an "insider." For the non-Japanese businessperson, the task is formidable, but not impossible.

The Japanese consumer has traditionally been conservative and brand conscious. However, during the recessionary environment of the past few years, opportunities are emerging for purveyors of "value." More fragmented buying habits are emerging among a new generation of more individualistic consumers. As a result of this, Japan's complex distribution system is now changing dramatically.

5 Largest Businesses in Japan

Nippon Telegraph & Telephone Corporation (NTT), Shinjuku-ku
    145,373 employees
Fujitsu Hokkaido Digital Technology Co. Ltd., Sapporo
    100,000 employees
Nippon Life Insurance Co., Osaka
    75,851 employees
Yamato Transport Co. Ltd., Chuo-ku
    74,193 employees
Hitachi Ltd., Chiyoda-ku
    71,160 employees

Observation: "(I wanted) to do some serious reporting on the Asianization of American fast food.

"... something we all noticed was that not just the flavor of the food but also the style of the stores has been adapted to Japanese tastes. That's why McDonald's in Japan has a uniformed staffer employed full-time to bow a greeting to cars entering the

Drive-Thru lane. That's why every take-out box of chicken at KFC . . . was personally signed by the cook—to convey that Japanese notion of a personal commitment to quality. . . . That's why, the one time we ran into Ronald McDonald prancing around outside one of his restaurants in Nagoya, he gave us his business card.

"Since fast food itself is considered a Western phenomenon, transactions in the fast-food trade must be carried out in English, or at least quasi-English. The first time I tried to order a small Coke . . . I had no doubt about how to do it; of course I knew how to say 'small' in Japanese. 'Coke,' I said. '*Chiisai* Coke." The friendly young woman behind the counter gave me one of those vacant looks that means communication is not taking place. 'Coke!' I repeated, somewhat louder. '*Chiisai!*' A few more repetitions ensued, and finally this Japanese person figured out what I wanted to say. 'Ahhhhh,' she said, with a bright smile of recognition. 'Coke, *essu.*' *Essu*! I should have known! *Essu* is the Japanese pronunciation of the English letter *S*. And as everybody in Japan knows, *S* stands for 'small' on American fast-food menus. So you jettison the perfectly good Japanese word for 'small' and use 'essu' instead. If you're too thirsty for a small Coke, you can order an 'emmu'—or even an 'erru,' which is the closest Japanese can come to saying *L*."

> —From *Confucius Lives Next Door: What Living in the East Teaches Us About Living in the West* by T.R. Reid, a Tokyo-based foreign correspondent for *The Washington Post* and commentator for National Public Radio

---

Comparative Data

Comparative Data Ratings
(Scale: 5 = Highest; 1 = Lowest)
Japan: 4.125

- A. GDP Growth: 3
- B. Per Capita Income: 5
- C. Trade Flows with the U.S.: 5
- D. Country Risk: 4
- E. Monetary Policy: 5
- F. Trade Policy: 4
  - Tariffs
  - Import Licensing
  - Import Taxes
- G. Protection of property Rights: 4
- H. Foreign Investment Climate: 3

GROSS DOMESTIC PRODUCT: $2.903 trillion (1998 estimate)

GDP GROWTH: –2.6% (1998 estimate)

PER CAPITA INCOME: $23,100 (1998 estimate)

Trade Flows with the U.S.

RANK AS EXPORT MARKET FOR U.S. GOODS & SERVICES: 2

U.S. EXPORTS TO JAPAN: $57.9 billion (1998 estimate)

U.S. IMPORTS FROM JAPAN: $122 billion (1998 estimate)

TOP U.S. EXPORTS TO JAPAN: Automobiles; auto parts and accessories; building materials; computers and peripherals; computer software; machinery; electronic components; aircraft; medical and optical equipment; pharmaceuticals; wood; cereals; meat; fish and seafood; tobacco

TOP U.S. PROSPECTS FOR EXPORT TO JAPAN: Electronic components; computers and peripherals; computer software; telecommunications equipment; automobiles; medical equipment and devices; auto parts and accessories; building products; electric power equipment; cosmetics; dietary supplements; machine tools and metalworking equipment

Country Risk

Dun & Bradstreet assigns a low degree of uncertainty associated with expected returns. However, countrywide factors may result in higher volatility of returns at a future date. Open account terms of 30 to 60 days are commonly used, with few cases of default reported.

Monetary Policy

Inflation remained very low throughout the 1990s. The rise in inflation to 1.9% in 1997 was considered high. However, as Japan imports virtually all its oil, a rise in crude petroleum prices in 1999 may have resulted in modest increases.

Japan's economy is still hampered by the high levels of debt accrued during the "bubble economy" of the late 1980s. The International Monetary Fund made several recommendations in 1998 to help Japan's economy. These measures, which included reductions in the consumption tax and other tax cuts, were rejected by the Japanese government.

Efforts made in 1999 to stimulate the economy, such as distributing almost $6 billion in government-issued vouchers to consumers, had mixed success. Public opinion in Japan is turning against large public works projects (such as airports and dams), which was a traditional method to stimulate the economy.

MONETARY UNIT: Yen

Trade Policy

TARIFFS   At 2%, tariff rates on industrial products entering Japan are among the lowest in the world. Almost all machinery imports are entered duty-free. However, import duties remain relatively high on some agricultural items and certain manufactured goods.

Goods with a value less than 10,000 yen are excluded from duty.

IMPORT LICENSING   Most goods qualify as freely importable and do not require an import license. The only exception are those commodities that fall under import quotas in which case the Japanese importer must apply for license approval. Rice, wheat, beef, and leather products are among the few remaining products subject to import quotas.

Use of chemicals and other additives in foods and cosmetics is heavily regulated.

IMPORT TAXES   In addition to customs duty, a 5% consumption tax is levied on all goods sold in Japan. Payment is required at the time of import declaration. Goods with a value of less than 10,000 yen are excluded from the consumption tax.

Protection of Intellectual Property Rights

Japan is party to the Patent Cooperation Treaty, the Agreement on Trade-Related Aspects of Intellectual Property, the Trademark Law Treaty, and the Berne Convention for Protection of Literary and Artistic Properties. Intellectual property rights include patents, utility models, design, trademarks, and copyrights.

Patent rights result from registration with the patent going to the first to file. Inventions publicly known or used in Japan or disclosed in publications anywhere before the date of application are a bar to registration. Patent applications are disclosed to the public 18 months after filing. Japan has recently switched from a pre-grant to a post-grant opposition system. The patent term is 20 years from filing for conventional patents and 6 years for utility models. Designs are valid for 15 years from registration.

Trademark rights result from registration. Service marks are now recognized, but retail store services are not yet considered to be services. The International Classification System is followed. Trademarks last for 10 years and are renewable. Supplemental filings are recommended in both Katakana and Kanji. *Multi-class coverage is now available. It is common practice for the Japanese to attempt to obtain all coverage in all classes.*

Copyrights result automatically upon creation of a qualifying work without registration or recording. Databases and compilations can also be copyrighted. Rights of the copyright owner include rights to copy, perform, broadcast, exhibit, screen, translate, lease, and adapt copyrighted works. Performance rights are granted to performers, phonorecord producers, and broadcasters, and publication rights are accorded to print publishers. Moral rights protect the author against unauthorized alteration and use of works not released to the public. The term of copyright is life of the author plus 50 years or 50 years after publication for works owned by an organization.

Foreign Investment Climate

Japan has progressively liberalized its foreign direct investment regime and is open to foreign investment, with certain exceptions. The level of foreign direct investment in Japan remains quite low when compared with its trading partners. In fact, Japan has 15 times as much direct investment abroad as foreign investment at home—U.S. external investment is 1.2 times the foreign investment within the country and Britain is 1.3.

Although most Japanese legal restrictions on foreign direct investment have been eliminated, considerable bureaucratic discretion remains. While Japan's foreign exchange laws have shifted to ex-post notification of planned investments in most cases, in numerous sectors (e.g., agriculture, mining, forestry, fishing) prior notification is still required.

In the sectors that still require prior notification, the Japanese government retains the right to restrict foreign direct investment if it determines that the investment would seriously and adversely affect the smooth performance of the national economy.

Recent changes have made it easier for foreign retailers to invest in Japan.

Political Leaders, Parties, and International Organizations

The International Academy at Santa Barbara at http://www.iasb.org/cwl publishes *Current World Leaders*, an excellent resource for up-to-date data on political leaders, parties, demographics, etc., in Japan. Tel: (800) 530-2682 or (805) 965-5010 for subscription information to their database.

Chief and Official Symbol of the State:

Emperor Akihito

Chief of the Government:

Prime Minister Yoshiro Mori

Political Parties:

Liberal Democratic Party (LDP), Social Democratic Party (SDPJ), Komei Party (KMP), Democratic Socialist Party (DSP), New Frontier Party, Communist Party (JCP), Progressive United Social Democratic Party Alliance (P/USDP), Rengo, Japan New Party

Membership in international organizations:

APEC, EBRD, G7, IEA, INTELSAT, OECD, PECC, UN and all of its specialized agencies and related organizations (including FAO, GATT, IAEA, IBRD, ICAO, IDA, IFAD, IFC, ILO, IMF, IMO, ITU, UNESCO, UNIDO, UPU, WHO, WIPO, WMO)

Political Influences on Business

Japan is a strong democracy in which basic human rights are well respected. Under the constitution and in practice, the Emperor's role is essentially symbolic. Japan has a parliamentary form of government. The head of government, the prime minister, is elected by Japan's parliament, the National Diet. Elections to the Lower House, the more powerful of the Diet's two chambers, are held at least once very four years.

Upper House elections are held every three years, at which time half of the membership is up for election. Most of Japan's political parties espouse moderate or conservative domestic and foreign policies.

Japan's entrenched bureaucracy is often blamed for Japan's slowness to liberalize its policies toward foreign trade. However, Japan is a highly insular culture. Protection of the Japanese homeland is ingrained, and protectionist policies have widespread support. Even a massive overhaul of Japan's bureaucracy would not guarantee a change in trade policy.

Contacts in the United States

THE EMBASSY OF JAPAN
2520 Massachusetts Avenue, NW
Washington, D.C. 20008
Tel: (202) 238-6700
Fax: (202) 328-2187
www.embjapan.org

U.S. DEPARTMENT OF COMMERCE
Office of Japan Trade Policy (OJTP)
Japan Export Information Center (JEIC)
International Trade Administration
Room 2320
Washington, D.C. 20230

OJTP
Tel: (202) 482-1820
Fax: (202) 482-0469
JEIC
Tel: (202) 482-2425
Fax: (202) 482-0469

Passport/Visa Requirements

Passports are required. Visas are not required for U.S. citizens' tourist/business stays of up to 90 days. However, anyone arriving under the terms of the 90-day visa waiver will not be allowed to extend his or her stay or adjust status. There are no exceptions to this rule. Onward/return tickets are required for visitors arriving on the visa waiver and may be requested for visitors arriving on other types of visas.

A visa is required for all travelers except those whose countries have reciprocal visa exemption arrangements with Japan.

The waiver of the visa requirement shall not apply to the nationals of the United States for the purpose of engaging in activities of the information media or seeking employment or permanent residence, of exercising a profession or other occupation or of engaging in public entertainment (including sports) for renumerative purposes, for the purpose of attending a deposition by a U.S. lawyer, and official government business.

The waiver of visa requirements does not exempt the nationals of the United States from complying with the laws and regulations of Japan concerning entry, stay, residence, and exit.

For current information concerning entry and customs requirements for Japan, travelers can contact the Japanese Embassy.

U.S. citizens who wish to apply for a passport may visit Passport Services' well-organized website at http://travel.state.gov/passport_services.html.

Contacts in Japan

THE EMBASSY OF UNITED STATES OF AMERICA
Akasaka 1-chome
Minato-ku
Tokyo 107-8420
Mailing Address: Unit 45004, Box 258, APO AP 96337-5004
Tel: (81) (3) 3224-5000
Fax: (81) (3) 3505-1862
www.usia.gov/posts/japan

THE AMERICAN CHAMBER OF COMMERCE OF JAPAN
Fukide Bldg.
No. 2, 4-1-21 Toranomon
Minato-Ku
Tokyo
Tel: (81) (03) 433-5381
www.accj.or.jp

DUN & BRADSTREET INFORMATION SERVICES JAPAN K.K.
Postal Address: 5F Aobadai Hills, 4-7-7 Aobadai, Meguro-ku, Tokyo 153
Street Address: 5F Aobadai Hills, 4-7-7 Aobadai, Meguro-ku, Tokyo 153
Tel: (81) (3) 3481-3561 (General); (81) (3) 3481-3576 (Mike Miyagawa);
    (81) (3) 3481-3562 (Sales & Marketing); (81) (3) 3481-3575 (RMS);
    (81) (3) 3481-3577 (TSR Alliance & Marketing/Planning);
    (81) (3) 3481-3573 (Finance)
Fax: (81) (3) 3481-3570

DUN & BRADSTREET SERVICES JAPAN K.K.
Postal Address: Toshin Tennosu Bldg., 1-2-5 Higashi-Shingawa, Shinagawa-ku, Tokyo 140
Street Address: Toshin Tennosu Bldg., 1-2-5 Higashi-Shinagawa, Shinagawa-ku,
Tokyo 140
Tel: (81) (3) 3740-5400
Fax: (81) (3) 3740-5420

OFFICE OF THE PRIME MINISTER
1-6-1, Nagata-cho
Chiyoda-ku
Tokyo 100, Japan

Further contacts and websites can be found in Appendix A.

Communications

TELEPHONE: The international country code for Japan is 81.

Phone numbers vary in length from four to eight digits in length. The final four digits are usually preceded by a hyphen.

City codes vary from one to three digits in length.

Japanese toll-free numbers begin with the digits 0120. At this writing, these toll-free numbers *cannot* usually be accessed from outside Japan.

E-MAIL: E-mail addresses located in Japan end with the code .jp

---

Cultural I.Q. Question: While suffering from a miserable cold, you travel to Japan. True or False: It is appropriate to use a handkerchief as discreetly as possible during your meetings.

Email your answer to TerriMorrison@getcustoms.com. Each month a drawing will be held to award a correct respondent from all the questions within this book with a free copy of The World Holiday and Time Zone Guide (current electronic version).

Malaysia

Official Name:	Malaysia
Official Language:	Bahasa Malaysia
Government System:	Federal parliamentary democracy with constitutional monarch
Population:	21.4 million (1999 estimate)
Population Growth Rate:	2.08% (1999 estimate)
Area:	329,749 sq. km. (127,316 sq. mi.); slightly larger than New Mexico
Natural Resources:	tin, petroleum, timber, copper, iron ore, natural gas, bauxite
Major Cities:	Kuala Lumpur (capital), Penang, Petaling Jaya, Ipoh, Malacca

Cultural Note: For the Pacific Rim, Malaysia has a relatively low population density (152.9 persons per square mile, compared with 258.2 per square mile in neighboring Indonesia). This low density has allowed Malaysia to keep large areas of its territory undeveloped. The Malaysian Timber Council estimates that as much as 75% of Malaysia's forests are protected (although many environmentalists would dispute this claim). Many forests are now being modified for recreation and eco-tourism. Environmental preservation has a high profile in Malaysia.

Age Breakdown

0–14 = 35%   15–64 = 61%   65+ = 4%
Life Expectancy: 67.62 years, male; 73.9 years, female (1999 estimate)

Time

Long-term planning is very big in Malaysia. The government continually announces goals to be met by specific dates. For example, Malaysia is building a new capital city, Putrajaya, to be completed by 2008. Prime Minister Mahathir Mohamad's ambitious "Vision 2020" program details the development of his country by the year 2020.

On a daily basis, however, time is more fluid. Foreigners are expected to arrive on time to business appointments, but Malaysians are not always prompt.

Arrival times at social events can involve complex rules of precedence. As a general guideline, however, foreigners should arrive about 15 minutes late.

Malaysia is 8 hours ahead of Greenwich Mean Time (GMT +8), which is 13 hours ahead of U.S. Eastern Standard Time (EST +13).

Holidays

An up-to-date, web-based *World Holiday and Time Zone Guide* is available at www.getcustoms.com. It lists official holidays by country and by day of the year, cultural tips, a corruption index, and time zones with worldwide business hours.

This list is a working guide. Dates should be corroborated before final travel plans are made. In cases where holidays fall on Saturday or Sunday, commercial establishments may be closed the preceding Friday or following Monday.

The scheduled Islamic holiday dates are approximations since they depend upon lunar observations; the actual celebrations could be a day or two off. Islamic holidays can be spelled different ways in English.

The holidays in Malaysia vary from state to state. The heavily Muslim states do not celebrate any non-Islamic holidays (including Easter, Christmas, and Western New Year's Day).

Jan 1	SA	New Year's Day
Jan 8	SA	Hari Raya Puasa
Jan 9	SU	Hari Raya Puasa
Jan 21	FR	Thaipusam
Feb 5	SA	Chinese New Year
Feb 6	SU	Chinese New Year
Feb 17	FR	Hari Raya Haji
Apr 6	TH	Awal Muharram
May 1	MO	Labor Day
Jun 3	SA	Birthday of Yang DiPertuan Agong
Jun 15	TH	Prophet's Birthday

Jun 18	SU	Wesak
Aug 31	TH	National Day
Oct 26	TH	Deepavali
Dec 25	MO	Christmas
Dec 27	WE	Hari Raya Puasa
Dec 28	TH	Hari Raya Puasa

Official holidays that fall on different dates each year include the Chinese New Year, Wesak Day (a Buddhist holiday), Birthday of the Prophet Mohammed, Hari Raya Puasa, Hari Raya Haji, and Deepavali.

The birthday of the current Malaysian king is celebrated in early June.

Work Week

Although most Malays are Muslim, not all of Malaysia follows the traditional Islamic work-week pattern (Friday is the Islamic Holy Day, so the traditional Muslim "weekend" is Thursday and Friday). In those areas where Friday is a workday, Muslim workers will take a two-hour break on Friday afternoons to attend a mosque.

Malaysia is divided into 13 states. Only the following 5 states follow the Islamic work week (Saturday through Wednesday): Perlis, Kedah, Kelantan, Terengganu, and Johor. All of these are in West (Peninsular) Malaysia. The Malaysian capital city, Kuala Lumpur, is in the state of Selangor, where the work week is Monday through Friday.

Business hours are generally from 8:00 A.M. to 5:00 P.M. Monday through Friday. Some offices will be open for a half day on Saturdays, generally in the morning. In the five states that follow the Islamic work week (Saturday through Wednesday), some people work a half day on Thursday.

The traditional lunchtime was from 12 noon (or 12:15 P.M.) to 2:00 P.M., but this generally has been reduced to a single hour, beginning at noon or 1:00 P.M. Nevertheless, many people will take longer than an hour for lunch. Friday is the Muslim Holy Day, and Muslims who work on Fridays will take a two-hour break at lunchtime.

Most government offices keep an 8:30 A.M. to 4:45 P.M. schedule, with a half day from 8:30 A.M. to noon on Saturday (on Thursday in the five aforementioned Muslim states).

Many Malaysian banks keep the traditional banking hours of 9:00 A.M. to 3:00 P.M., with a few hours on Saturday mornings (Thursday mornings in the five aforementioned Muslim states).

Shop hours vary. Most shops will open at 9:00 or 10:00 A.M., and will close at 6:00 or 7:00 P.M., five or six days a week.

Executives will often work far longer days than their subordinates. The ethnic Chinese, especially, have reputations as workaholics.

Religious/Societal Influences on Business

Malaysia is a multicultural nation. Ethnic Malays, known as the *Bumiputera*, make up over 60% of the population; they hold the political power in Malaysia. Ethnic Chinese constitute the next largest group, followed by ethnic Indians. The latter are well-represented in the professional arena (especially in law). The Chinese dominate the business spheres.

Most religions are represented in Malaysia. Ethnic Malays and many Indians are Muslims. When forced to choose, most Chinese will list themselves as "Buddhist," but they are quite capable of following several religious traditions simultaneously.

The strident defense of Asian traditions by Malaysian Prime Minister Mahathir Mohamad has been summarized in his 1996 book *The Voice of Asia*, coauthored by Shintaro Ishihara (Japanese politician and coauthor of *The Japan That Can Say No*). In this book, Mahathir proclaims:

". . . Westerners generally cannot rid themselves of (their) sense of superiority. They still consider their values and political and economic systems better than any others. It would not be so bad if it stopped at that; it seems, however, that they will not be satisfied until they have forced other countries to adopt their ways as well. Everyone must be democratic, but only according to the Western concept of democracy; no one can violate human rights, again according to their self-righteous interpretation of human rights. Westerners cannot seem to understand diversity. . . ."

Clearly, Malaysians are intent on maintaining their own cultural tradition, whether or not the West approves.

5 Cultural Tips

1. In multicultural Malaysia, it is good business to know something about each of the three main ethnic groups—Malay, Indian, and Chinese. The majority of Malaysian businesspeople are Chinese, and they share the habits of the "immigrant" Chinese in Singapore, Hong Kong, or Taiwan. Their native language will be a Southern Chinese dialect, but they will probably speak to you in English. Ethnic Malays, called *Bumiputera*, dominate Malaysia's government. Although many educated Malays speak English, the law mandates that official correspondence with the Malaysian government be written in the native language *Bahasa Malaysia*. Finally, while the native tongue of members of the Indian community could be one of several Indian languages, educated Indians speak English. Foreigners are most likely to encounter Indian Malaysians as lawyers or journalists.

2. Although the Chinese and Indians are immigrants to Malaysia, don't assume that they are newcomers. The Chinese began arriving in the fifteenth century! While many Indians came to Malaysia after World War I, it was Indian traders who brought Islam to Malaysia—over 400 years ago. There is a good chance that a Chinese or Indian's ancestors were in Malaysia long before the U.S. declared independence.

3. Historically, there has been animosity between the majority Malays and the Chinese who controlled Malaysia's wealth. As a result, the redistribution of wealth from Chinese to ethnic Malays has become official policy in Malaysia. This is done in several ways, including a law that requires that 30% of all new stock offerings

must go to *Bumiputera*. Although they must pay for the stock, the value of many stocks rises quickly from the initial offering price. (The official Anti-corruption Agency watches the government stock-allocation committees, preventing committee members from allocating promising stocks to themselves.)

4. Remember to follow the taboos typical of Islamic societies: eat only with your right hand (since the left hand is unclean), never expose the soles of your feet, dress modestly, and never touch anyone—even a child—on the head.

5. Malaysians are still recovering from the disastrous economic dislocations of 1998. As always, when things go wrong, scapegoats are blamed. As the primary holders of economic wealth in Malaysia, the Chinese merchant classes are often targeted. International currency speculators have also been singled out. Foreign executives who must deal with ethnic Malays (including government officials) should avoid being identified with either of these groups.

Economic Overview

Until the 1998 Asian economic crisis, the Malaysian economy averaged almost 7% growth per annum for the past three decades. Most sectors of the economy have been very open to international trade, and U.S. products have been successful in almost all of them. U.S.–Malaysian bilateral relations are close and productive across the board.

Malaysia has been transformed from a low income producer of commodities like tin, rubber, and palm oil into a middle income exporter of manufactured products. For example, Malaysia is the world's third largest producer (and largest exporter) of semiconductors. It is also the world's largest exporter of room air conditioners, color TV tubes, and VCRs.

Although the population of Malaysia is only 21 million, it is a more important market for U.S. exports than many countries of much larger size. This market continues to grow rapidly in line with the ongoing expansion and transformation of the economy. The United States is Malaysia's second largest trading partner, accounting for 19% of its total trade.

The U.S. was the largest foreign investor in Malaysia from 1991 through 1993, and third largest in 1994. The cumulative value of U.S. investments in Malaysia is more than $8 billion. The majority of foreign investment is in the oil and gas sector, with the rest in manufacturing, especially semiconductors and other electronic products.

5 *Largest Businesses in Malaysia*

Hume Concrete Marketing Sdn. Bhd., Kuala Lumpur
    301,000 employees
Mayban Securities (Holdings) Sdn. Bhd., Kuala Lumpur
    186,000 employees
ML Vijay Sdn Bhd., Kuala Lumpur
    100,000 employees

Sime Darby Sdn. Bhd., Kuala Lumpur
   40,000 employees
K T S Holdings Snd. Bhd., Sibu
   30,000 employees
Sdn. Bhd. is an abbreviation of *Sendirian Berhad*, which indicates a corporation.

Cultural Note: In the brave new world of Malaysia, there is no room for drug addiction. Draconian sentences are given for offenses. Any Malaysian citizen can be ordered to take a drug test, and failure to pass means a mandatory one- to three-year sentence in a rehabilitation camp.

Comparative Data

Comparative Data Ratings
(Scale: 5 = Excellent; 1 = Poor)
Malaysia: 3.875

- A. GDP Growth: 4
- B. Per Capita Income: 3
- C. Trade Flows with the U.S.: 4
- D. Country Risk: 3
- E. Monetary Policy: 5
- F. Trade Policy: 4
  - Tariffs
  - Import Licensing
  - Import Taxes
- G. Protection of Property Rights: 4
- H. Foreign Investment Climate: 4

GROSS DOMESTIC PRODUCT: $215.4 billion (1998 estimate)

GDP GROWTH: 7% (1998 estimate); 5.5% (1999 estimate); 6% (2000 estimate)

PER CAPITA INCOME: $10,300 (1998 estimate)

Trade Flows with the U.S.

U.S. EXPORTS TO MALAYSIA: $9.0 billion (1998 estimate)

U.S. IMPORTS FROM MALAYSIA: $19 billion (1998 estimate)

TOP U.S. EXPORTS TO MALAYSIA: Electronic components; machinery; aircraft and parts; medical and optical equipment; paper/paperboard; organic chemicals; plastics; ceramics; inorganic chemicals; iron and steel

TOP U.S. PROSPECTS FOR EXPORT TO MALAYSIA: Computer hardware; aircraft and parts; telecommunications services; architecture/construction management/engineering; pollution-control equipment; medical equipment; electrical power systems; computer software; franchising; industrial process control

Country Risk

Dun & Bradstreet rates Malaysia as having a fair capacity to meet outstanding payment liabilities.

Liberal credit terms such as open account are now widely acceptable, with letters of credit now accounting for just one-third of transactions. More secure terms (letter of credit) are still recommended on deals with smaller concerns and/or new accounts.

Monetary Policy

The government is aware of the inflationary potential of the economy's rapid development and expansion, and closely monitors fiscal and monetary policies to ensure low inflation. As a result, Malaysia's annual inflation rate has been below 5% for most of the 1990s. Inflation was estimated at 3.6% in 1997, 5.0% in 1998, and 3% in 1999.

MONETARY UNIT: Malaysian ringitt; it is often translated as the Malaysian dollar

Trade Policy

TARIFFS   Import duties range from zero to 300%, with the average duty rate being less than 10%. Higher rates apply to luxury goods.

Raw materials used directly for the manufacture of goods for export are exempted from import tariffs if such material is not produced locally or if local materials are not of acceptable quality and price.

IMPORT LICENSING   Import permits are required for arms and explosives, motor vehicles, dangerous drugs and chemicals, plants, soil, tin ore, and certain essential foodstuffs.

IMPORT TAXES   A sales tax of 10% is levied on most imported goods. The sales tax is not applied to raw materials and machinery used in export production.

Protection of Intellectual Property Rights

Malaysia has joined a selective core of intellectual property conventions. They include the Berne Convention for Protection of Copyright, the Paris Convention (relative to patents and trademarks), and the Patent Cooperation Treaty. Malaysia has managed to stay out of the spotlight while many of its neighbors (such as Indonesia, the Philippines, Hong Kong, and Thailand) have been targeted as pirates and counterfeiters. As a former colony of the United Kingdom, Malaysia carries vestiges of common law trademarks.

Trademarks can be registered for both goods and services. Malaysia's Trademark Register is divided into Parts A and B. *Part A* covers distinctive marks. *Part B* is for marks capable of becoming distinctive. Part A registrations become incontestable after 7 years. The initial term of trademark is 7 years, after which it can be renewed for successive terms of 14 years each. Actions can be brought under statute.

Copyright can be licensed either exclusively or nonexclusively. Assignments must be in writing. Rights extend to making reproductions, public performing, broadcasting, distributing, and preparing derivative works.

Foreign Investment Climate

The Malaysian government welcomes manufacturing investment, especially in high-tech areas. One hundred percent foreign ownership in manufacturing is permitted only in certain instances.

Investment approval depends on the size of the investment, whether or not it includes local equity participation, the type of financing required, the ability of existing and planned infrastructure to support the effort, and the existence of a local or foreign market for the output. The criteria are applied in a local nondiscriminatory manner, except in the rare case when a local and a foreign firm propose identical projects.

Domestic services industries are tightly protected, with foreign firms generally limited to 30% equity shares in new ventures. The government severely restricts establishment in the financial service industry with the notable exception of fund management firms. No banking or insurance licenses are being awarded.

On a manufacturing project approval basis, the U.S. has been one of the top foreign investors in Malaysia for the last several years. Only Japan and Taiwan rival the U.S. as foreign investors.

The Asian economic crisis has reduced foreign investment. With the 1998 arrest and removal of Deputy Premier Anwar Ibrahim (Dr. Mahathir's heir apparent as Prime Minister), the future of foreign investment is also in doubt. Anwar Ibrahim had favored such investment, whereas Dr. Mahathir is prone to blame foreign forces (especially "international monetary speculators") for Malaysia's problems.

Political Leaders, Parties, and International Organizations

The International Academy at Santa Barbara at http://www.iasb.org/cwl publishes *Current World Leaders*, an excellent resource for up-to-date data on political leaders, parties, demographics, etc., in Malaysia. Tel: (800) 530-2682 or (805) 965-5010 for subscription information to their database.

Chief of State:

Yang di-Pertuan Agong (Paramount Ruler) Salehuddin Abdul Aziz of Selangor

Head of the Government:

Prime Minister Dr. Mahathir Mohamad (full name: Dato Seri Mahathir bin Mohamad)

Political Parties:

National Front (BN), Democratic Action Party (DAP), Pan Malaysian Islamic Party (PAS)

Membership in international organizations:

ADB, APEC, ASEAN, C, INTELSAT, NAM, OIC, PECC, UN and most of its specialized agencies and related organizations (including FAO, GATT, IAEA, IBRD, ICAO, IDA, IFC, ILO, IMF, IMO, ITU, UNESCO, UNIDO, UPU, WHO, WIPO, WMO)

Political Influences on Business

The Malaysian political environment is strongly favorable to international and domestic business development. U.S.–Malaysian bilateral relations are close and productive across the board.

Malaysia is a constitutional monarchy with a parliamentary system of government. In practice, power is strongly concentrated in the Prime Minister. The Prime Minister has traditionally been head of UMNO (United Malays National Organization), the principal party in the governing coalition that has ruled Malaysia continuously since independence from the UK in 1957. The position of monarch, the *Yang di Pertuan Agong*, is rotated among the rulers of 9 of the 13 states of Malaysia. Over time, the role has become almost entirely ceremonial and symbolic.

The government has taken a strong proactive role in the development and industrialization of the Malaysian economy. This has included significant state sector investment, a close alliance between government and the private business community, and a variety of policies and programs to bolster the economic status of the Malay and indigenous communities, commonly referred to as *bumiputras*. Tensions between the Malay, Chinese, and Indian communities were serious in the past. However, with rapid economic growth over the past several decades (in which all groups in the country have shared), these tensions have been greatly reduced.

Malaysia enjoys friendly relations with the United States and has worked with the U.S. on many issues, including, for example, the U.N. peacekeeping operations in Somalia. Malaysia has also contributed forces to U.N. operations in Cambodia and Bosnia. Malaysia is a member of ASEAN (Association of South East Asian States), founded in 1967 with Indonesia, the Philippines, Singapore, Thailand, and Brunei. The U.S. has strongly supported ASEAN, and participates in an annual dialogue with ASEAN members at the level of Foreign Ministers. ASEAN is working to create AFTA (an ASEAN Free Trade Area), which, if successful, would create a single market of over 330 million people. If, as expected, Laos, Cambodia, and Myanmar (formerly Burma) also join ASEAN in the future, the group would include over 400 million people. Malaysia is also a member APEC (Asia–Pacific Economic Cooperation), which includes the U.S., China, Japan, and most of the other countries of the Pacific Rim.

Contacts in the United States

THE EMBASSY OF MALAYSIA
2401 Massachusetts Avenue, NW
Washington, D.C. 20008
Tel: (202) 328-2700
Fax: (202) 483-7661
www.undp.org/missions/malaysia

Passport/Visa Requirements

A passport is required. Visas are not required for stays of up to 3 months. Yellow fever and cholera immunizations are necessary if arriving from infected areas. On arrival in Malaysia, the Immigration Authorities will, usually, grant a 2 to 3 weeks' stay that may be extended up to a maximum period of 3 months. For purposes of employment, research, educational purposes, and other professional visits, visas are required.

International travelers from Ethiopia and Somalia or those who have visited these two countries within 14 days prior to entry into Malaysia are required to possess a valid international certificate against smallpox. Travelers from African and South American countries are also required to have valid documents against yellow fever. Travelers who come from cholera-infected areas should have a vaccination against cholera.

When visas are required, 3 application forms are to be filled in and 3 passport-sized photographs attached. A fee is required payable by postal money order (amount subject to change without notice) (no personal checks will be accepted). Passport should be sent to the Embassy or Consulate together with the application forms. Visa application will have to be referred to Malaysian Immigration Headquarters for clearance and approval.

A waiting period of between 6 to 8 weeks is required before the result of the visa application can be notified to the applicant.

Those wishing to enter the Borneo States of Sabah and Sarawak will need additional visa approval from the immigration authorities for visits involving a stay exceeding 3 months. Applicants are required to give the names of the sponsors or references in Malaysia in their application forms.

Visitors allowed to stay in Malaysia for more than a year are required to obtain National Registration Identity Cards from the nearest Registration office where they are staying.

For current information concerning entry and customs requirements for Malaysia, travelers can contact the Embassy of Malaysia.

U.S. citizens who wish to apply for a passport may visit Passport Services' well-organized website at http://travel.state.gov/passport_services.html.

Contacts in Malaysia

THE EMBASSY OF THE UNITED STATES OF AMERICA
376 Jalan Tun Razak
50400 Kuala Lumpur
Mailing Address:P.O. Box No10035, 50700 Kuala Lumpar, APO AP 96535-8152
Tel: (60) (3) 248-9011
Fax: (60) (3) 242-2207
usembassymalaysia.org.my

AMERICAN–MALAYSIAN CHAMBER OF COMMERCE
11.03 AMODA, 22 Jalan Imbi
55100 Kuala Lumpur
Tel: (60) (3) 248-2407
Fax: (60) (3) 242-8540

D&B INFORMATION SERVICES (M) SDN. BHD.
Postal Address: Suite 50D, 50th Floor, Empire Tower,
   Jalan Tun Razak, 50400 Kuala Lumpur
Street Address: Suite 50D, 50th Floor, Empire Tower,
   Jalan Tan Razak, 50400 Kuala Lumpur
Tel: (60) (3)262-7995
Fax: (60) (3) 264-4877 (General); (60) (3) 264-4853 (Operations)

OFFICE OF THE SUPREME HEAD OF STATE
Istana Negara
50500 Kuala Lumpur, Malaysia

OFFICE OF THE PRIME MINISTER
Jalan Dato Onn
50502 Kuala Lumpur, Malaysia

Further contacts and websites can be found in Appendix A.

Communications

TELEPHONE: The international country code for Malaysia is 60.

City codes are one or two digits in length. The major cities use the single-digit codes.

Malaysian phone numbers are seven digits in length.

E-MAIL: E-mail addresses located in Malaysia end with the code .my

---

Faux Pas: An expatriate American businessman who had rented a house in Kuala Lumpur was outraged to receive a municipal bill for *air* in the mail. He complained bitterly that no civilized country charged for air, let alone the polluted air of Kuala Lumpur. Eventually, a fellow expatriate explained that his "air bill" was actually a *water* bill. *Air* is the Bahasa Malaysian word for water (it is pronounced "ayer"). The Malays he complained to were too embarrassed to point out his error.

Official Name:	United Mexican States (Estados Unidos Mexicanos)
Official Language:	Spanish
Government System:	Federal republic
Population:	100.3 million (1999 estimate)
Population Growth Rate:	1.73% (1999 estimate)
Area:	1.972 million sq. km. (762,000 sq. mi.); about three times the size of Texas
Natural Resources:	petroleum, silver, copper, gold, lead, zinc, natural gas, timber
Major Cities:	Distrito Federal (Mexico City) (capital, colloquially known as "D.F."), Guadalajara, Monterrey, Tijuana, Juárez, León

Linguistic Note: Spanish commonly uses two diacritical marks: the acute accent over several vowels and the tilde over the letter *n*. (Umlauts are also seen over vowels in foreign loan-words.) In punctuation, questions are bracketed with question marks at both ends; the initial question mark is inverted. Exclamation points bracket sentences in a similar fashion. Inverted punctuation, accents, and umlauts can usually be deleted while retaining the meaning of the sentence. However, if you have no way of printing the tilde, be aware that the meaning of a word can change.

Faux Pas: Deleting the *tilde* over a Spanish word can change the word's meaning. A notorious example of this occurred when a U.S. company gave a holiday party for its Mexican affiliate. Executives ordered custom balloons that were intended to say "Happy New Year" in Spanish. But instead of reading "Bueno Año Nuevo," the tilde was deleted over the *n*, and they were printed as "Bueno Ano Nuevo." The word *año* means *year* in Spanish. Unfortunately, the word *ano* means *anus*.

Age Breakdown

0–14 = 35%   15–64= 61%   65+ = 4% (1999 estimate)
Life Expectancy: 68.98 years, male; 75.17 years, female (1999 estimate)

Time

Time is flexible in Mexico. Although foreign businesspeople are expected to be on time to business appointments, Mexican executives may be late—sometimes considerably late. Despite the advent of NAFTA, many Mexicans are not willing to give up the flexibility of their *hora mexicana* (Mexican time) for the Anglo rigidities of *hora inglesa* (English time). A traditional business meeting will probably start at least 15 minutes late and can start as much as an hour late.

When Mexican businesspeople hold meetings among themselves, the first person to arrive may be teased for being overly prompt with a comment like ¿Llegaste a barrer?" meaning "Did you arrive with the janitor?" It is not a compliment.

While foreigners are expected to be reasonably punctual for work, even *norteamericanos* (U.S. citizens; Canadians are *canadienses*) are expected to be late to social occasions. In general, arrive about 30 minutes late to social events such as parties. In Mexico City, guests often arrive as much as two hours late. When in doubt as to what time you are really expected, ask.

Be aware when you are told that something will be done mañana, this probably does *not* mean tomorrow (its literal translation). In this context, mañana refers to some indeterminate date in the near future. Deadlines are always flexible. Many foreigners recommend placing your contracted delivery date two weeks to a month ahead of the date you really need the product. With this much leeway, you stand a good chance of getting it on time.

Mexicans are well aware of U.S. attitudes towards time. Manipulating the use of time is one way they can gain the upper hand in the relationship.

Most of Mexico is 6 hours behind Greenwich Mean Time (GMT -6), which is 1 hour behind U.S. Eastern Standard Time (EST -1), or the same as U.S. Central Standard Time.

A portion of west–central Mexico is 7 hours behind Greenwich Mean Time (GMT -7), which is in the Mountain Time Zone (EST -2). The Mexican states of Sonora, Sinaloa, and Nayarit are in this time zone.

Finally, North and South Baja California are 8 hours behind Greenwich Mean Time (GMT -8), which places them in the Pacific Time Zone (EST -3).

Holidays

An up-to-date, web-based *World Holiday and Time Zone Guide* is available at www.getcustoms.com. It lists official holidays by country and by day of the year, cultural tips, a corruption index, and time zones with worldwide business hours.

This list is a working guide. Dates should be corroborated before final travel plans are made. In cases where holidays fall on Saturday or Sunday, most commercial establishments will be closed the preceding Friday or following Monday. Many people take off for three or more days when holidays occur near weekends. Such long weekends are known in Mexico as *puentes* (bridges).

Jan 1	SA	New Year's Day
Feb 5	SA	Constitution Day
Mar 21	TU	Juarez Birthday
Apr 20	TH	Holy Thursday
Apr 21	FR	Good Friday
May 1	MO	Labor Day
May 5	FR	Puebla Battle
May 10	WE	Mother's Day
Sep 16	SA	Independence Day
Oct 12	TH	Columbus Day
Nov 2	TH	All Souls Day
Nov 20	MO	Mexican Revolution
Dec 12	TU	Our Lady of Guadalupe
Dec 24	SU	Christmas Eve
Dec 25	MO	Christmas Day

In addition to the above, the Catholic celebrations of Holy Thursday and Good Friday are official holidays. Again, the days of observance should always be corroborated by local contacts.

- Avoid scheduling business trips around Easter, when many people take vacations.
- December 16 is an unofficial holiday marking the start of Christmas festivities, known as *posadas*.
- Many businesses close down entirely between Christmas and New Year's Day.

Work Week

- Business hours are generally 9:00 A.M. to 6:00 P.M. with lunch between 1:00 and 3:00 P.M. Monday through Friday. Banks are open 9:00 A.M. to 1:30 P.M. Monday through Friday. Government offices operate 8:00 A.M. to 2:30 P.M. Monday through Friday.
- The legal work week is 48 hours, including one paid day of rest—which, in essence, allows one to work 40 hours and be paid for 48.

Religious/Societal Influences on Business

The majority (89.7%) of Mexicans are Roman Catholic. Protestant sects (especially Evangelical) have enjoyed rapid growth in recent years, but they are still a small part of the population. Mexico has no official religion.

Mexico has been harsh on many of its inhabitants. Except for the elite, most Mexican families have experienced hardship and tragedy. By U.S. standards, most Mexican laborers work long hours for very low wages. Yet Mexicans are known for maintaining a positive outlook despite hardship. They maintain a zest for life and enjoy their numerous celebrations to the fullest.

The family is the most important institution in Mexico. Nepotism is an accepted practice. Mexican executives generally put a higher importance on the best interest of their families than on the company for which they work. Firing a high-ranking executive can be difficult, since he (Mexican business executives are overwhelmingly male) may have several relatives and friends working for the company, who feel great loyalty towards him.

While competence and achievement are appreciated in Mexico, they are by no means the most important consideration of an individual's worth. Mexicans find all people worthy of respect, regardless of their talents. Furthermore, each person is considered not only as an individual, but as a part of a family. Deference is shown to the elderly and to the status of one's family in the social hierarchy.

Mexico is a male-dominated society. But foreign female executives find few problems, since Mexican *machismo* requires male executives to be gentlemanly and polite. They may even grant a meeting to a female executive more quickly than a male one. Mexican women who find success in business have a reputation for toughness and efficiency while maintaining their femininity.

Crime had already become a problem before the 1995 economic crisis; since then, it has reached epidemic proportions. The risk of robbery, kidnapping, and murder has affected how most Mexicans live, and foreign visitors are also at risk. The Mexican authorities are making great efforts to restore order, but even the once-feared Mexican Army has become a victim of crime. In June of 1999 the Presidential Guard was robbed of its payroll just two blocks from the presidential residence.

5 Cultural Tips

1. Subordinates in Mexico do not make extended eye contact with their supervisors. Instead, they display respect by looking at the ground. This should not be interpreted as disinterest. As a foreign businessperson, you may engage in intermittent eye contact. Eye contact is yielded to the person talking, while the listener mainly looks away. Avoid intense, constant eye contact; it can be interpreted as aggression.

2. The handshake is the traditional greeting between men. Women have the option of shaking hands with men; men usually wait to see if a woman extends her hand. A man may include a slight bow while shaking hands with a woman. Good friends embrace. Women often kiss each other on the cheek while embracing.

3. Mexico has many resources but most Mexicans are poor, and this has engendered a sense of national thrift. While some wealthy Mexicans live very well indeed, ostentation is frowned upon. Foreigners should dress stylishly but avoid expensive jewelry. (Note that Mexican frugality does not include hospitality; Mexicans often spend lavishly to celebrate or entertain guests.)

4. Lunch is traditionally the largest meal of the day in Mexico, so business lunches tend to be expansive. Lunch usually lasts for two hours, from 2:00 P.M. to 4:00 P.M.. (However, near the U.S. border, some businesses have adopted 12 noon to 2:00 P.M. lunchtime.) Wine is often consumed with lunch; some executives will have some tequila as well. Foreigners in Mexico City (7,349-foot altitude) should remember that high altitudes increase the negative effects of alcohol.

5. Socializing is an integral part of doing business in Mexico. Accept invitations to social events, even though business will not be discussed. An invitation into a Mexican home is a great honor. Be assured that the phrase "Mi casa es su casa" ("My house is your house) is not uttered lightly. It means that you are being accepted as a friend of the family—a position of both honor and obligation.

Economic Overview

The economy of the nation of Mexico has always been inextricably linked to that of the United States. This has been even more true since Mexico entered into the *North American Free Trade Agreement (NAFTA)* with the U.S. and Canada.

Mexico has recovered steadily from the economic meltdown of 1995. Mexico's crisis occurred when an overvalued exchange rate and widening current account deficits created an unbalance that ultimately proved unsustainable. To finance the trade gap, the government became increasingly reliant on volatile portfolio investment.

"Poor Mexico—so far from God, so close to the United States."

—Attributed to Mexican Dictator Porfirio Díaz, who first came to power in 1876.

Despite Mexico's problems, there are still plenty of opportunities in this important market. Mexico, even after the peso devaluation, remains the third largest export for U.S. products, trailing only Canada and Japan. Mexico's economic fundamentals are still sound. Public finances are in balance. The private sector, not the government, is the driving force in an increasingly deregulated economy.

NAFTA has locked in many of the reforms in progress; there has been no turning back from the agreement on the part of the Mexican government. U.S. exporters should keep in mind that most U.S. goods now enter Mexico duty-free. During the first year of NAFTA, U.S.–Mexico trade increased by 23% to more than $100 billion. NAFTA is also bearing fruit in financial services.

While most Latin American economies grew slower than expected in 1998, the Mexican economy exceeded expectations. Mexico's Gross Domestic Product grew an estimated 3.7% in 1999, and was forecast to grow 4% in 2000.

5 Largest Businesses in Mexico

Delgado Lozano Martin Armando, Hermosillo
   41,991 employees
Grupo Carso S.A. de C.V., Ciudad de Mexico
   40,052 employees
Ferrocarriles Nacionales de Mexico, Ciudad de Mexico
   40,000 employees
Diblo S.A. de C.V., Ciudad de Mexico
   38,000 employees
Grupo Modelo S.A. de C.V., Ciudad de Mexico
   35,821 employees

Mexican businesses may use the following abbreviations:

S.A. = Sociedad Anónima is the most common designation for a corporation.

S.A. de C.V. = Sociedad Anónima de Capital Variable is another designation for a corporation

---

Cultural Note: Directness is not considered a virtue in Mexico. U.S. citizens used to being bluntly honest will not do well here. Courtesy and tact are valued more than truth; it is considered polite to tell someone what they (apparently) want to hear—even if that is untrue. Flattery is commonly used. While bargaining is enjoyed, arguing is not. Every effort is made to avoid a loss of face.

Observation: "I was working for Procter & Gamble in Mexico. We had this new detergent with enzymes in it, and we wanted to figure out a way to get people to stop buying the old heavy-duty detergents that they were used to and start buying ours. So we hired a local agency, and together we came up with the name Ariel and a package with an atom's symbol on it. Then they created this brilliant ad campaign.

"Now, in Mexico at this time, very few people had washing machines. Women did the laundry and they did it mostly by hand. For the wives of the laborers and the maids of the white-collar guys who wanted perfect, pristine white shirts, this was a real heavy-duty chore. A washing machine was the dream of millions of women. So the agency, Noble & Asociados, came up with a campaign that basically said 'Ariel makes any bucket into a washing machine.' It showed a bucket of clothes, and as the detergent started pouring in, the bucket began to agitate, turning left and right, just like the washing machine that every woman wanted. It offered a clear performance message, and it made the statement strongly. The brand took off like crazy.

"This experience sold me on advertising. . . ."

—From *The End of Marketing As We Know It* by Sergio Zyman, who is best known as the former Chief Marketing Officer for The Coca-Cola Company.

Comparative Data

Comparative Data Ratings
(Scale: 5 = Excellent; 1 = Poor)
Mexico: 2.75

  A. GDP Growth: 4
  B. Per Capita Income: 2
  C. Trade Flows with the U.S.: 5
  D. Country Risk: 3
  E. Monetary Policy: 2
  F. Trade Policy: 3
    • Tariffs
    • Import Licensing
    • Import Taxes
  G. Protection of Property Rights: 3
  H. Foreign Investment Climate: 4

GROSS DOMESTIC PRODUCT: $815.3 (1998 estimate)

GDP GROWTH: 4.8% (1998 estimate)

PER CAPITA INCOME: $8,300 (1998 estimate)

Trade Flows with the U.S.

U.S. Exports to Mexico: $79 billion (1998 estimate)

U.S. Imports from Mexico: $94.7 billion (1998 estimate)

Top U.S. Exports to Mexico: Electrical components; machinery; motor vehicles; plastics and resins; medical and optical equipment; paper/paperboard; iron and steel products; organic chemicals; mineral fuel/oil; cereals

Top U.S. Prospects for Export to Mexico: Automotive parts and service; franchising; pollution-control equipment; chemical production machinery; telecommunications equipment; building products; management consulting services; apparel; aircraft and parts; electronic components

Country Risk

Dun & Bradstreet rates Mexico as having reasonable capacity to meet outstanding payment liabilities.

Many U.S. companies sell to Mexico via open account. When open account terms are extended, 90- to 120-day terms are the norm. It is not at all unusual, and their experience indicates that, with prudent credit review practices, open account sales in Mexico need not be inherently risky. Dun & Bradstreet has an office in Mexico City to assist U.S. firms with this.

Monetary Policy

The 1995 economic dislocation caused inflation to jump from 7% in 1994 to 52% in 1995. Since then, inflation has dropped each year, from 28% in 1996 to 17% in 1997 and 12% in 1999. Forecasts called for a continued drop in inflation to 10% in 2000 and 2001.

The 1995 economic crisis occurred shortly after Mexican President Carlos Salinas de Gortari ended his term in office. His successor, Ernesto Zedillo, vowed to prevent a recurrence when he leaves the office of the Presidency in 2000. A package of financing and credits worth $23.7 billion was arranged through the International Monetary Fund to insure Mexico's economic stability during that period.

Monetary Unit: Mexican peso

Trade Policy

Tariffs With the entry into NAFTA, Mexico further lowered its tariffs on U.S. and Canadian origin goods. Mexico's average duty on U.S. goods is below 2%. The highest Mexican tariffs tend to be on agricultural products and finished motor vehicles.

Under NAFTA, tariffs on U.S. goods will be phased out over a maximum period of 10 years, varying by type of goods.

IMPORT LICENSING   Under NAFTA, Mexico abolished its import licensing requirements for U.S.-origin goods. Various agricultural products and finished motor vehicles,
however, remain subject to tariff rate quotas.

NAFTA provides that for the first 10 years of the agreement, Mexico may adopt or
maintain prohibitions or restrictions on the importation of certain used goods. These
are (primarily) construction machinery and heavy equipment, industrial machinery,
electronic data-processing equipment, motorcycles, motor homes and campers, and
most trailers and tankers.

IMPORT TAXES   Mexico imposes a 15% value-added tax (VAT) on most sales transactions, including foreign sales. Basic products such as food and drugs are exempt from VAT.
Mexican customs collects the VAT on imports upon entry of the merchandise into Mexico.

A 0.8% customs processing fee is also charged on the value of imports.

Protection of Intellectual Property Rights

Mexico is a member of most international organizations regulating the protection of
intellectual property rights. These include the Paris Convention for the Protection of
Industrial Property, the Patent Cooperation Treaty, the Agreement on Trade Related
Aspects of Intellectual Property, the Berne Convention, the Inter-American
Convention on Copyright and Literary Property, and the Universal Copyright
Convention. Although Mexico has implemented the highest level of intellectual prop-
erty laws, piracy and counterfeiting remain problems. Counterfeiting of trademarks is
evident on the goods for sale at any border town.

Patents must be novel, inventive, and have industrial application. Patents are granted for 20 years from application subject to payment of maintenance fees. Computer
programs are excluded from being patented. Industrial designs are protected for 10
years and vegetal species for 15 to 18 years. Patent licenses must be registered.
Compulsory licenses may be sought if the patents are not timely exploited.

Trademark, including commercial slogans, must be registered. Trademarks have
terms of 10 years and are renewable. In an apparent anticounterfeiting move, the law
has a provision that allows for cancellation of trademarks first used abroad by foreigners. Transfers of trademarks must be recorded. "Linked" marks of families or marks
must be transferred together.

Authors have both proprietary rights of copyrights and moral rights. Proprietary
rights remain in force for life plus 50 years. Performers and video producers' rights are
for 50 years. Moral rights are perpetual. Publishers are required to place a copyright
notice on published books. Proprietary rights can only be assigned for 15 years except
for publication rights for books and computer programs. Agreements transferring copyright rights must be in writing and recorded.

Although problems continue, Mexico actively enforces its intellectual property laws
and has seized and destroyed millions of dollars' worth of pirated merchandise. In an
effort to improve enforcement and put teeth into its intellectual property laws, the
Mexican government formed an intersecretarial commission in October 1993 to cut
through the bureaucratic obstacles hindering effective action.

Foreign Investment Climate

In December 1993 the government passed a foreign investment law that replaced a restrictive 1973 statute. The law is consistent with the foreign investment chapter of NAFTA and opened more areas of the economy to foreign ownership.

It also provided national treatment for most foreign investment; eliminated all performance requirements for foreign investment projects; and liberalized criteria for automatic approval of foreign investment proposals.

Most foreign investors operate in Mexico through corporations. Foreign-owned corporations are subject to the same laws as local companies as well as any special regulations governing foreign investment. A Mexican corporation must have at least five shareholders and, except in certain sensitive sectors, can usually be established in one or two months.

Non-Mexican citizens cannot own property within 50 kilometers of the sea coasts or within 100 kilometers of the Mexican border. Property within those areas can be leased through 30-year trusts held by Mexican banks. Foreign investors can acquire such property for commercial purposes by establishing a Mexican subsidiary.

Under NAFTA Mexico may not expropriate property, except for a public purpose on a nondiscriminatory basis. Expropriations are governed by international law and require rapid, fair market value compensation, including accrued interest. Investors have the right to international arbitration for violations of this or any other rights included in the investment chapter of NAFTA.

Political Leaders, Parties, and International Organizations

The International Academy at Santa Barbara at http://www.iasb.org/cwl publishes *Current World Leaders*, an excellent resource for up-to-date data on political leaders, parties, demographics, etc., in Mexico. Tel: (800) 530-2682 or (805) 965-5010 for subscription information to their database.

Head of State and the Government:

Dr. Ernesto Zedillo Ponce de Leon

Next election:

August 2000

Political Parties:

Institutional Revolutionary Party (PRI), Party of the Cardenista Front of National Reconstruction (PFCRN), National Action Party (PAN), Authentic Party of the Mexican Revolution (PARM), Party of the Democratic Revolution (PRD), Socialist Workers' Party (PST), Popular Socialist Party (PPS), Mexican Green Ecology Party

Membership in international organizations:

APEC, EBRD, IADB, INTELSAT, LAIA, OAS, OECD, PECC, SELA, UN and all of its specialized agencies and related organizations (including FAO, GATT, IAEA, IBRD, ICAO, IDA, IFAD, IFC, ILO, IMF, IMO, ITU, UNESCO, UNIDO, UPU, WHO, WIPO, WMO)

Political Influences on Business

Rarely have the vagaries of politics and economics been so well illustrated as in Mexico in the mid-1990s. Mexico was riding high until the end of 1994. Prosperity was increasing, and the signing of the North American Free Trade Agreement was augured to bring a golden age to Mexican trade. Newly-installed President Ernesto Zedillo and his predecessor, Carols Salinas, were heroes.

That all changed on December 20, 1994. On that date, a botched devaluation of the Mexican peso precipitated the collapse of the Mexican economy. Not all of this was Mexico's fault. The global investment market and instantaneous communications are relatively new phenomena. Some economists have called the Mexican collapse "the first crisis of the twenty-first century." Ernesto Zedillo and Carlos Salinas were discredited, weakening the long supremacy of their Institutional Revolutionary Party (PRI).

While trade has recovered, the standard of living of many Mexicans has not. Those who can buy Mexican goods or labor with foreign currency have made out well. Businesses that sell directly to the Mexican consumer have had a difficult time. Overall, however, the economy is stable and Mexico is exporting its way out of the financial crisis.

Mexico's current difficulties include the demand for debt relief by thousands of ordinary citizens. While international loans shored up big industrial debtors, thousands of small businesspeople found they were saddled with high-interest debts that they can never repay. The measures that were initiated to make it easier and quicker for creditors to attach the funds or properties of debtors outraged Mexican citizens. Yet the low savings and high debt levels of the Mexican people contributed to the crisis. If the Mexican government had discouraged debt and encouraged savings—as do many Asian governments—the Mexican economy would be much healthier.

It was international politics, not Mexican policymakers, that rescued the bond market. This came in the form of billions of dollars in guarantees from the U.S. and the International Monetary Fund. Mutual funds and bonds had superseded bank loans as Mexico's largest source of private financing. This is liable to be the last time, however, that such bond markets are rescued so easily.

Most international economists still view NAFTA as Mexico's best hope for revival. Thanks to the devalued peso and free trade, Mexican exports are booming. Continued privatization offers good long-term investment opportunities for investors.

Contacts in the United States

The Embassy of Mexico
1911 Pennsylvania Avenue, NW
Washington, D.C. 20006
Tel: (202) 728-1600
Fax: (202) 728-1718
www.embassyofmexico.org

U.S.–Mexico Chamber of Commerce
1730 M. Street, NW, Suite 112
Washington, D.C. 20036
Tel: (202) 296-5198
Fax: (202) 728-0768

Passport/Visa Requirements

Proof of citizenship is required for entry by U.S. citizens. A passport and visa are not required for a tourist/transit stay of up to 180 days. A tourist card issued by Mexican consulates and most airlines serving Mexico is required.

Evidence of U.S. citizenship (U.S. passport, birth certificate, naturalization certificate, or voter's registration certificate, if it shows place of birth) must be presented and carried during the trip.

In compliance with NAFTA, the Mexican government, through the National Immigration Institute (NII) of the Secretariat of the Interior, drafted and implemented the FM-N immigration form. This form may be used by businesspersons of U.S. or Canadian nationality who wish to enter Mexico under the protection of NAFTA.

For current information concerning entry and customs requirements for Mexico, travelers can contact the Mexican Embassy.

U.S. citizens who wish to apply for a passport may visit Passport Services' well-organized website at http://travel.state.gov/passport_services.html.

Contacts in Mexico

The Embassy of the United States of America
Street Address: Paseo de la Reforma 305, Colonia Cuauhtemoc, 06500 Mexico, D.F.
Mailing Address: P.O. Box 3087, Laredo, TX 78044-3087
Tel: (52) (5) 209-9100
Fax: (52) (5) 511-9980/208-3373
www.usembassy-mexico.gov

The American Chamber of Commerce in Mexico, A.C.
Lucerna 78
Colonia Juarez
06600 Mexico, D.F.
Tel: (52) (5) 724-3800
Fax: (52) (5) 703-2911

Dun & Bradstreet, S.A. De C.V.
Postal Address: Apartado Postal 40 BIS, 06700 Mexico, D.F.
Street Address: Durango 263, 4th & 5th Floors, Col. Roma,Delagacion Cuauhtemoc,
06700 Mexico, D.F.
Tel: (52) (5) 208-5066; (52) (5) 229-6900
Fax: (52) (5) 514-7502 (Carlos Blanco); (52) (5) 511-9640 (CSD Operations, Int'l &
Systems; (52) (5) 525-2002 (RMS Operations); (52) (5) 511-0065 (CSD), BMS, Sales,
Mktg, HR; (52) (5) 525-1050 (Trade Tape); (52) (5) 208-7972 (Finance)

Office of the President
Palacio Nacional
Patio de Hono, 20 Piso
Mexico City, D.F. 06067
Mexico

Further contacts and websites can be found in Appendix A.

Communications

TELEPHONE: The international country code for Mexico is 52.

At this writing Mexican phone numbers vary in length. The most common lengths are six or seven digits long. Six-digit numbers are usually read off in pairs of numbers (for example, 14 44 01).

Businesses that have multiple phone lines use the words *y* (and) or *al* (to) between the numbers.

City codes also vary in length; they can be one, two, or even three digits long. City codes are usually written in parentheses.

Mexican toll-free numbers begin with the digits 800. At this writing, these toll-free numbers *cannot* usually be called from outside Mexico.

E-MAIL: E-mail addresses located in Mexico end with the code .mx

---

Observation: Communications are hampered by the differences between literal translations and implied, culturally-specific meanings. Although Americans and Mexicans have lived in proximity for hundreds of years, they don't necessarily understand each other. Hispanic advertising executive Lionel Sosa examined such issues in his 1998 book *The Americano Dream*. The table shows his interpretations of some Spanish phrases and how they are heard by both Latinos and Anglos.

PHRASE	LITERAL TRANSLATION	MEANING TO LATINO	IMPLICATION TO ANGLO
A common expression by service personnel, such as waiters:			
Para servirle	Here to serve you	My pleasure	Wow! My valet!
A common response to "thank you":			
De nada	It's nothing	You're welcome	He/she must believe what I'm saying "thanks" for has little value
A standard response to a summons:			
Mándeme	Command me	Yes?	He/she must want me to tell him/her what to do
A common response to a complicated question:			
No sé de esas cosas.	I don't know about such things	It's not my place to have an opinion	Not a very smart person
A response to bad luck or unmet goals:			
Así lo quiere Dios	That's the way God wants it	It's not so bad; what could I expect?	This person has no initiative
Making a dinner date:			
Nos vemos a las seis para cenar	See you at six for dinner	I'll see you somewhere between 6:15 and 6:30, maybe 7:00	He's/she's late—but then, he's/she's always late

---

Cultural Note: At every first meeting, expect to be asked some variation of "What have you done (*or* seen) in Mexico?" This is a polite way of inquiring about your respect for Mexican culture and traditions. To establish your credentials as someone who cares about Mexico and its people, you are expected to see the sights and gain an appreciation of Mexican culture.

Cultural I.Q. Question: There is a tremendous font of ancient history in Mexico (the ruins of Chichén Itzá, etc.) as well as more modern treasures. One of Mexico's sons, Octavio Paz, contributed greatly to his country in many ways. What did he do?

E-mail your answer to TerriMorrison@getcustoms.com. Each month a drawing will be held to award 1 correct respondent from all the questions within this book with a free copy of *The World Holiday and Time Zone Guide* (current electronic version).

The ★Netherlands

Official Name:	Kingdom of The Netherlands (Koninkrijk der Nederlanden)
Official Language:	Dutch
Government System:	Multi-party parliamentary democracy under a constitutional monarch
Population:	15.8 million (1999 estimate)
Population Growth Rate:	0.47% (1999 estimate)
Area:	41,526 sq. km. (16,033 sq. mi.); about half the size of Maine
Natural Resources:	natural gas, petroleum, fertile soil
Major Cities:	Amsterdam (capital), The Hague (seat of government), Rotterdam, Utrecht

---

Cultural Note: *"True or False?* Holland and the Netherlands are the same. *Answer:* False. The Kingdom of the Netherlands is often incorrectly called Holland. Holland refers only to a specific area in the Netherlands, encompassing the major cities of Amsterdam, Rotterdam, and The Hague. It is no more correct to call all of the Netherlands Holland than it would be to call all of the U.S.A 'Dixie.' "

—From *Kiss, Bow or Shake Hands: How to Do Business in Sixty Countries* by Morrison, Conaway, and Borden

---

Age Breakdown

0–14 = 18%   15–64 = 68%   65+ = 14 (1999 estimate)
Life Expectancy: 75.28 years, male; 81.17 years, female (1999 estimate)

Time

Punctuality is vital. Be on time to both business and social engagements. The efficient use of time is considered an important virtue in the Netherlands. Tardiness is seen as indicative of other negative traits as well. People who cannot use their time wisely are not trusted!

The Netherlands is 1 hour ahead of Greenwich Mean Time (GMT +1), which is 6 hours ahead of U.S. Eastern Standard Time (EST +6).

Holidays

An up-to-date, web-based *World Holiday and Time Zone Guide* is available at www.getcustoms.com. It lists official holidays by country and by day of the year, cultural tips, a corruption index, and time zones with worldwide business hours.

This list is a working guide. Dates should be corroborated before final travel plans are made. In cases where holidays fall on Saturday or Sunday, commercial establishments may be closed the preceding Friday or following Monday.

Jan 1	SA	New Year's Day
Apr 21	FR	Good Friday
Apr 24	MO	Easter Monday
Jun 1	TH	Ascension
Jun 12	MO	Whitmonday
Dec 25	MO	Christmas Day
Dec 26	TU	Boxing Day

In addition to the above, the Christian holidays of Good Friday, Easter, Easter Monday, Ascension Day, and Whitmonday are official holidays. The days of observance should always be corroborated by local contacts.

Work Week

- Many Dutch executives take long vacations during June, July, August, and late December, so confirm that your counterparts will be available.
- Business hours: 8:30 A.M. to 5:30 P.M. Monday through Friday.
- Banking hours: 9:00 A.M. to 4:00 P.M. Monday through Friday. Some banks have Thursday night hours as well.

• Store hours: 8:30 or 9:00 A.M. to 5:30 or 6:00 P.M. Monday through Friday. Some shops will have extended evening hours on Thursday or Friday. Note that most shops will be closed for a half day each week.

Religious/Societal Influences on Business

Although the Netherlands has no official religion, the Calvinist ethics of the Dutch Reformed Church have a great influence over everyday life. Honesty is one such virtue. Not only do the Dutch dislike evasiveness and duplicity, they do not deal well with secrecy. They may even be uncomfortable when forced to conceal proprietary information.

Another Dutch virtue is frugality. Wealth is downplayed. Even the rich in the Netherlands display a lack of ostentation, often living in modest homes.

Planning is seen as important to success. This makes the decision-making process quite slow, since every aspect of a deal will be examined in detail. (This is a trait the Dutch share with their German neighbors.)

While there are many areas of commonality between the Netherlands and Germany, there are also substantial differences. Social Scientists use a scale called the *Uncertainty Avoidance Index*, which determines how far people will go to avoid uncertainty. Germany scores high on this scale. To try and eliminate as much uncertainty as possible, Germans generally legislate for every possibility (in their view, rules and regulations help give structure and stability to life). The Dutch feel no need to do this. (For example, in Germany everyone is required to carry their I.D. card. This is not the case in the Netherlands.)

The Netherlands has an extensive welfare system, which they are having increasing difficulty affording. But each Dutch citizen is considered valuable and worthy of respect. It is in this area—social welfare requirements—that U.S. corporations investing in the Netherlands report some of their greatest difficulties. A report issued by the Dutch Ministry of Economic Affairs found that U.S. management styles in general seemed ill-suited to the Netherlands, while Scandinavian managers report few problems at all.

As is common in small European countries, the Dutch do not expect foreigners to know their language. Most Dutch are multilingual and many speak English. An English-speaking person is usually close at hand in a business setting.

5 Cultural Tips

1. Since so many people in the Netherlands speak English, it is not necessary to translate business materials into Dutch. Be sure that your business cards note any advanced educational degrees, and keep your correspondence neat and formal. The Dutch feel that if they are going to the trouble of reading your correspondence in English, the least you can do is write a grammatically correct letter.

2. In keeping with Dutch egalitarianism, greet everyone in a small, enclosed space upon entering. They will respond in kind, then return to their work. This covers not only offices, but shops, waiting rooms, elevators, and railroad compartments as well. At a social event, if you have not been introduced to everyone, you should then go around the room and introduce yourself.

3. Data collection is very important to the Dutch. (Do not be surprised if, when you arrive for your first meeting, your Dutch counterpart has a complete dossier on you!) Be prepared to supply reams of information on every aspect of your deal. This is especially true for U.S. businesspeople, whose reputation for hyperbole engenders distrust among the pragmatic Dutch.

4. Never give the impression that you consider yourself superior in the Netherlands. The Dutch accord everyone a degree of respect, and respond badly to anyone who "puts on airs." This unwillingness to place oneself in a subservient position can result in poor customer service. Foreigners often complain that Dutch store clerks and waiters "act like they're doing you a favor to wait on you."

5. The Dutch value diversity and tolerance, which makes them well-suited to the international business arena. Curiously, they also exhibit a large degree of conformity of behavior. From its clockwork punctuality to its clean-swept streets, the Netherlands would not run so smoothly unless most of its citizens agreed on proper behavior.

Cultural Note: The Dutch have always been good businesspeople. They were the world's leading economic power during the seventeenth century. The modern conception of the limited-liability corporation was largely invented in the Netherlands.

Economic Overview

Historically, the Netherlands has been one of the world's leading trading nations. This tradition continues to this day; despite its small size and population, it is one of the top dozen trading countries. The Netherlands is ranked thirteenth in GNP, eighth in imports of goods and services from the United States, and third in foreign investment in the U.S. (behind only the United Kingdom and Japan). Of all the countries the United States trades with, the Netherlands offers its largest bilateral trade surplus.

After slow growth in the early 1990s, the economy of the Netherlands has surged. The Dutch now boast one of the strongest economies in Europe. To offset the possibility of slowing growth, the frugal Dutch government announced an increase in government spending in 1998.

The range of export potential for products and services in the Netherlands is amazingly broad-based. From high-tech to low-tech, all manner of goods coming into Europe can take advantage of Dutch distribution, warehousing, and value-added manufacturing.

American industrial goods, as well as consumer goods, are popular and have a reputation for quality.

An estimated 7,000 U.S. companies have appointed Dutch agents and distributors in the Netherlands. Of the top 500 U.S. companies, 105 have formed European Distribution Centers in the Netherlands. Approximately 1,100 American and American-affiliated companies have operations in the Netherlands. The country's strategic location—combined with the relative ease of doing business there—makes the Netherlands an ideal European operations location for American companies. The country's advanced transport and logistical infrastructure is second to none in Europe.

Historically, the U.S. and the Netherlands have had a close bilateral relationship, encompassing a full agenda of political, economic, military, and social issues.

At this writing, there is one cloud on the Dutch economic horizon: the 1999 adoption of the EU's currency, the euro, which has underperformed badly since its introduction.

5 *Largest Businesses in the Netherlands*

Mercury Signs Holding B.V., Hooge Zwaluwe
     111,998 employees
Polysoft B.V., Schiedam
     95,993 employees
Jacobs Family Card, Veenendaal
     81,998 employees
Abn Amro Bank N.V., Amsterdam Zuidoost
     80,091 employees
Europipeline Nederland B.V., Hoogerheide
     61,998 employees

Dutch corporations are usually either *B.V.* (*Beslote Vennootschapp*), designating a private limited company, or *N.V.* (*Naamloze Vennootschapp*), which is a public limited company.

Cultural Note: The Netherlands is a constitutional monarchy. Unlike the disdain in which some British hold their royal family, most Dutch like their royals.

Comparative Data

Comparative Data Ratings
(Scale: 5 = Excellent; 1 = Poor)
The Netherlands: 4.625

   A.   GDP Growth: 3
   B.   Per Capita Income: 5
   C.   Trade Flows with the U.S.: 4

D. Country Risk: 5
E. Monetary Policy: 5
F. Trade Policy: 5
  • Tariffs
  • Import Licensing
  • Import Taxes
G. Protection of Property Rights: 5
H. Foreign Investment Climate: 5

GROSS DOMESTIC PRODUCT: $348.6 billion (1998 estimate)

GDP GROWTH: 3.7% (1998 estimate)

PER CAPITA INCOME: $22,200 (1998 estimate)

Trade Flows with the U.S.

U.S. EXPORTS TO THE NETHERLANDS: $19.0 billion (1998 estimate)

U.S.A. IMPORTS FROM THE NETHERLANDS: 7.6 billion (1998 estimate)

TOP U.S. EXPORTS TO THE NETHERLANDS: Machinery; aircraft and parts; electrical components; medical and optical equipment; organic chemicals; plastics and resins; grain/feed/seed/fruit; motor vehicles; animal feed; mineral fuel/oil

TOP U.S. PROSPECTS FOR EXPORT TO THE NETHERLANDS: Computer software; telecommunications services; electronic components; computer services; computers and peripherals; telecommunications equipment; pollution-control equipment; aircraft and parts; building products; automotive parts and service equipment

Country Risk

Dun & Bradstreet rates the Netherlands as having excellent capacity to meet outstanding payment liabilities. It carries the lowest degree of risk.

Open account terms of 30 to 60 days are normally extended with few problems reported with payments.

Monetary Policy

Inflation has remained low for several years. Inflation rose slightly in 1997 to 2.75%, but fell to 2.0% in 1998. It was forecast to remain in the 2–2.5% range through 2000.

MONETARY UNIT: Dutch guilder, replaced by the EU euro as of 1999

Trade Policy

TARIFFS   Duty rates on manufactured goods from the United States generally range from 5–8%. Most raw materials enter duty-free or at low rates while agricultural products face higher rates and special levies.

IMPORT LICENSING   Only a small number of goods of U.S. origin require import licenses, mostly agricultural and food items. Other items subject to import licensing requirements include coal and lignite fuel, a few specified base metal products, various apparel and textile products, and controlled items such as arms and munitions. Licenses are generally granted quickly for goods of U.S. origin.

IMPORT TAXES   A value-added tax (VTA) is charged on the sale of goods and services within the country. A 6% rate applies to necessities of life such as food, medicines, and transportation. A 17.5% rate is the general or standard rate and applies to most goods.

Excise taxes are levied on a small number of products such as soft drinks, wine, beer, spirits, tobacco, sugar, and petroleum products. The EU plans to harmonize excise taxes.

Protection of Intellectual Property Rights

The Netherlands has national patent and copyright laws, but has forgone its national trademark system to use the BENELUX system along with Belgium and Luxembourg. The Netherlands belongs to the Berne Convention for Protection of Literary and Artistic Property, the Universal Copyright Convention, the European Patent Convention, the Patent Cooperation Treaty, the Madrid Agreement (trademarks), and the Paris Convention for Protection of Industrial Property. The Netherlands has a well-developed and comprehensive system of intellectual property. Piracy problems are minimal.

New and inventive industrial products and processes may be patented. Patents may be obtained by filing national applications or by making EC filings. National patents must be filed in Dutch and are not examined except for formalities. National and European patents cannot exist for the same subject matter. National and European patents have a maximum term of 20 years from application.

Trademarks must be registered. Unregistered marks are not protected. Registrations have a term of 10 years and are renewable. Both goods and services are protected. Trademark rights may be lost by acquiescence in infringement over a five-year period. Rights to trade names are required by local or foreign public use. Trade names cannot be conveyed separately from their businesses.

Copyrights do not require registration, marking, deposit, or other formalities. All original creative works are protected automatically, including computer programs. Neighboring rights are granted to performing artists, broadcasters, and producers of phonograms. The basic term of copyright is life of the author plus 70 years. Neighboring rights are protected for 50 years after performance, broadcast, or production.

Foreign Investment Climate

The Dutch government maintains liberal policies toward foreign direct investment. With the exception of public and private monopolies (military production; aviation; shipping; distribution of electricity, gas and water; railways; and radio and television broadcasting), foreign firms are able to invest in any sector and entitled under the law to equal treatment with domestic firms.

Provision of government incentives, rules of incorporation, access to the capital market, etc., are all nondiscriminatory. The Dutch actively recruit foreign investment through the Netherlands Foreign Investment Agency.

There are no apparent foreign investment screening mechanisms, and 100% foreign ownership is permitted in those sectors open to foreign private investment. All firms must conform to certain rules of conduct on mergers and takeovers. These are administered by the Socio-Economic Council, an official advisory board composed of representatives of business, labor, and government. Since 1993, anti-takeover measures have liberalized significantly. Draft legislation to further curtail corporate protective measures is under preparation.

The U.S. is the largest foreign investor in the Netherlands. During the last decade, the number of foreign companies with establishments in the Netherlands has grown to more than 6,300, employing close to 352,000 workers. Included are 1,680 U.S. companies accounting for 123,000 jobs. Foreign companies in the Netherlands account for a quarter of industrial production and about 20% of employment in industry. Close to one-third (29%) of foreign establishments in the Netherlands are of U.S. origin, with 5% Japanese, 51% from the EU, and 13% from other European companies.

Political Leaders, Parties, and International Organizations

The International Academy at Santa Barbara at http://www.iasb.org/cwl publishes *Current World Leaders*, an excellent resource for up-to-date data on political leaders, parties, demographics, etc., in the Netherlands. Tel: (800) 530-2682 or (805) 965-5010 for subscription information to their database.

Head of State:

Queen Beatrix van Oranje Nassau

Head of the Government:

Prime Minister Wim Kok

Political Parties:

Christian Democratic Alliance (CDA), Labor Party (PvdA), People's Party for Freedom and Democracy (VVD), Democrats '66 (D66), Reformational Political Federation (RPF), Calvinist Political Union (GPV), Centre Party (CP), Green Left (GL)

Membership in international organizations:

Benelux Economic Union, CE, EBRD, EU, ESA, IEA, INTELSAT, NACC, NATO, OECD, OSCE, UN and all of its specialized agencies and related organizations (including FAO, GATT, IAEA, IBRD, ICAO, IDA, IFC, IFAD, ILO, IMF, IMO, ITU, UNESCO, UNIDO, UPU, WHO, WIPO, WMO), WEU

Political Influences on Business

The Netherlands has an historically close bilateral relationship with the United States, encompassing a full agenda of political, economic, military, and social issues. The Netherlands and the United States work closely together in NATO, the United Nations, the GATT, the Organization on Security and Cooperation in Europe, the OECD, and other international organizations.

A three-party coalition consisting of the left-leaning Labor Party (PvdA), the right-leaning Liberal Party (VVD), and center–left Democrats (D66) has been in power for most of the latter half of the 1990s. In May 1999, D66 pulled out of the coalition when the other parties refused to heed its demand for referendums. Prime Minister Wim Kok tendered his resignation, but was persuaded to remain in office. Interestingly, this breakup of the ruling coalition caused no change in the Dutch economy.

In foreign affairs and defense policy, there is a strong consensus in the Netherlands in favor of continued close ties with the United States, support for NATO, and further European integration through the EU. Dutch forces were active in the 1999 operations against Serbia.

The Netherlands is a constitutional monarchy with a parliamentary form of government. The Monarch (Queen Beatrix) is the titular Head of State; however, the Council of Ministers (the Cabinet plus representatives of the Netherlands Antilles) is responsible for government policy. The Ministers, collectively and individually, are responsible to the Parliament, but do not serve in Parliament.

The Dutch Parliament (also known as the "States General") consists of two houses: the First and Second Chambers. The Second Chamber is the more influential of the two chambers. It consists of 150 members elected on party slates for four-year terms under a system of proportional representation. As a result, members represent the whole country rather than individual districts as in the United States. The difficulty of winning an absolute majority under this system has given rise to a tradition of coalition government.

The First Chamber, composed of 75 members, is elected by provincial legislatures for four-year terms. While it can neither initiate nor amend legislation, it must approve all legislation passed by the Second Chamber before it becomes law.

Contacts in the United States

THE EMBASSY OF THE KINGDOM OF
THE NETHERLANDS
4200 Linnean Avenue, NW
Washington, D.C. 20008
Tel: (202) 244-5300
Fax: (202) 362-3430
www.netherlands-embassy.org

THE NETHERLANDS CHAMBER OF COMMERCE
IN THE USA, INC.
One Rockefeller Plaza, 11th Floor
New York, NY 10020
Tel: (212) 265-6460
Fax: (212) 265-6402

Passport/Visa Requirements

A passport is required. A visa is not required for tourist or business stays up to 90 days. Possession of a return ticket or ticket to destination outside the Netherlands is required.

For further information concerning entry requirements for the Netherlands, travelers can contact the Embassy of the Netherlands or the nearest Dutch Consulate General.

U.S. citizens who wish to apply for a passport may visit Passport Services' well-organized website at http://travel.state.gov/passport_services.html.

Note: European Union countries—including Austria, Belgium, Finland, Germany, Luxembourg, the Netherlands, Portugal, and Spain—have implemented the Schengen zone agreement to end all passport controls between the participating member states.

Italy and Greece are signatory to the agreement, but have not implemented the terms. France is signatory to the agreement, but for security reasons has suspended terms of the agreement.

Contacts In the Netherlands

THE HAGUE
Lange Voorhout 102
2514 EJ The Hague
Tel: (31) (70) 310-9209
Fax: (31) (70) 361-4688
www.usemb.nl

AMERICAN CHAMBER OF COMMERCE IN THE NETHERLANDS
Carnegieplein 5
2517 KJ The Hague
Tel: (31) (70) 3-65-98-08/9
Fax: (31) (70) 3-64-69-92

DUN & BRADSTREET B.V.
Postal Address: P.O. Box 278, 3000 AG Rotterdam

Street Address: Westblaak 138, 3012 KM Rotterdam
Tel: (31) (10) 400-9400 (CDS), (31) (10) 400-9600 (RMS)
Fax: (31) (10) 414-7380 (International); (31) (10) 404-7463 (RMS)

OFFICE OF THE PRIME MINISTER
Binnenhof 20
P.O. Box 20001
2500 EA The Hague
Kingdom of The Netherlands

QUEEN BEATRIX WILHELMINA ARMGARD
Noordeinde 68
Postbus 30412
2500 GK The Hague
Kingdom of The Netherlands

Further contacts and websites can be found in Appendix A.

Communications

TELEPHONE: The international country code for the Netherlands is 31.

City codes for major cities are two digits; codes for other areas are longer.

Dutch phone numbers are six or seven digits in length.

E-MAIL: E-mail addresses located in the Netherlands end with the code .nl

---

Observation: "The Dutch are very like the English, . . . in the way they park their cars, in the way they set out their litter bins, in the way they dump their bikes against the nearest tree or wall or railing. There is none of the fastidiousness you find in Germany or Switzerland, where the cars on some residential streets look as if they were lined up by somebody with a yardstick and a spirit level. In Amsterdam they just sort of abandon their cars at the canalside, often on the brink of plunging in."

—From Bill Bryson's *Neither Here Nor There: Travels in Europe*

Nigeria

Official Name:	Federal Republic of Nigeria
Official Language:	English (English is a second language for most Nigerians; their first language is probably one of many indigenous languages, such as Yourba, Hausa, and Ibo.)
Government System:	Until May 1999: Military regime; since May 1999: Parliamentary democracy
Population:	113.8 million (1999 estimate)
Population Growth Rate:	2.92% (1999 estimate)
Area:	923,768 sq. km. (356,669 sq. mi.); approximately twice the size of California
Natural resources:	oil, natural gas, cocoa, cashew nuts, textiles
Major cities:	Lagos (largest city and former capital), Ibadan, Kano, Ogbomosho, Oshogbo, Ilorin. As of December 1991 the capital was moved to the Federal Capital Territory of Abuja, although the judiciary and some ministries remain in Lagos.

Age Breakdown

0–14 = 45%   15–64 = 52%   65+ = 3% (1999 estimate)
Life Expectancy: 52.55 years, male; 54.06 years, female (1999 estimate)

Cultural Note: Nigeria is one of the world's most challenging nations in which to do business. Fraud and corruption are endemic. Transparency International has consistently rated Nigeria as one of the most corrupt nations on their Corruption Perception Index. The first contact many North Americans have with Nigeria is an unsolicited fax offering a business deal yielding tremendous profit. Despite impressive-looking documentation, such deals are almost inevitably fraudulent. It is estimated that Canadians have lost over US$1 million to such frauds. Losses by U.S. citizens are far higher; a single U.S. investor lost $2 million.

The most common type of fraud is known as the 419 scam, in which a foreigner is coaxed into putting up money in advance to secure a much larger return. Needless to say, such advances disappear and the promised payoff never materializes. Foreigners who come to Nigeria to seek restitution have been threatened with arrest and physical violence.

The Nigerian government has been of little help in stopping this fraud. Such deals incite foreigners to violate Nigerian law. The Nigerian government's attitude seems to be that people who try to defraud the Nigerian government deserve whatever happens to them.

Observation: "The times had made beggars of men. You met the regular ones in the usual places—at street corners or in the snarled traffic—with begging bowls in their shriveled hands. The other variety turned up in offices or at airport lounges, good-looking, well-dressed, a tale of woe on their lips, a prayer for help in their eyes and empty pockets bulging with hope. . . . They had to be para-psychologists to identify a likely donor and they knew that unfailing element of a good story—surprise—which knocked you off your feet and sent your soft heart to your purse."

> —From "The New Beggars," an article by the late Nigerian author Ken Saro-Wira. The author goes on to tell how he was scammed by a Nigerian beggar with a good story (complete with photographic evidence!) at an airport. His observation that scam artists utilize the element of surprise is useful—once you have heard of a scam, you are unlikely to be conned by a similar fraud. Before traveling to Nigeria, a foreigner should learn about the types of scams in current use. Ken Saro-Wira was a minority rights activist who wrote in defense of Nigeria's Ogoni people. Despite strong international protests, Ken Saro-Wira was executed by the Nigerian military regime in 1995.

Time

Punctuality has not traditionally been considered a virtue in Nigeria. Nigerian executives who have been educated abroad are more likely to be on time. Foreign executives are expected to be prompt.

Nigeria is 1 hour ahead of Greenwich Mean Time (GMT +1), which is 6 hours ahead of U.S. Eastern Standard Time (EST +6).

Holidays

A web-based *World Holiday and Time Zone Guide* is available at www.getcustoms.com with updated official holidays, cultural tips, time zones, and tables that compare world-wide business hours.

This list is a working guide. Dates should be corroborated before final travel plans are made. In cases where holidays fall on Saturday or Sunday, commercial establishments may be closed the preceding Friday or following Monday.

The following holidays should be confirmed by local contacts—regional observations of these and other festivals may vary.

Jan 1	SA	New Year's Day
Jan 8	SA	Eid-El-Fitr (2 days)
Mar 16	TH	Eid-El-Kabir (2 days)
Apr 21	FR	Good Friday
Apr 24	MO	Easter Monday
May 1	MO	Labor Day
Jun 15	TH	Eid-El-Maulud
Oct 1	SU	National Day
Dec 25	MO	Christmas Day
Dec 26	TU	Boxing Day
Dec 28	TH	Eid-El-Fitr (2 days)

Nigeria observes both Christian and Muslim holidays as official holidays. In addition to the above, the Christian celebrations of Good Friday and Easter Monday are official holidays. The Muslim celebrations of Eid-El-Fitr and Eid-El-Kabir are two-day holidays; Eid-El-Maulud is an official one-day holiday. The dates of these holidays vary from year to year.

Work Week

- Standard business and government hours are around 7:30 A.M. to 4:00 P.M. Monday through Friday. A lunch break is taken from 1:00 to 2:00 P.M., during which no business is conducted. Some stores and businesses keep Saturdays hours as well.
- In Muslim areas all offices close for the day at 1:00 P.M. on Friday, when Muslims attend services at their local mosque. (Muslims are concentrated in Nigeria's north.)
- While mornings may be the best time for appointments, many Nigerian offices hold staff meetings on Monday and Friday mornings. Many executives and government officials will be unavailable during those times.

Religious/Societal Influences on Business

Nigeria was a British colony until 1965. To this day, Nigeria's civil service and common law remain patterned after those of the United Kingdom.

Around half of the population of Nigerians are Muslim. Approximately one-third of Nigerians consider themselves Christian, while the remainder adhere to traditional beliefs. (As with other data on Nigeria, these figures are subject to dispute. However, Islam is indisputably the majority religion in Nigeria.)

As they did elsewhere, the British ruled by designating one ethnic group as the local leaders. In Nigeria, the British set the Christian Ibo (also transliterated as Igbo) over Nigeria's other ethnic groups.

Nigeria's borders, like most former African colonies, were established by European colonizers without regard to the native populations. Consequently, Nigeria is a geographic entity encompassing numerous disparate tribal groups. English was chosen as the official language since Nigeria's peoples speak several different languages, most of which are not mutually intelligible.

The Ibo seceded from Nigeria in 1967 and tried to form the independent nation of Biafra. The Nigerian government was unwilling to let the Ibo (and their oil wealth) secede, and the bloody war that followed left hundreds of thousands dead. Violent clashes between the government and various ethnic groups continue to this day.

Muslim Nigerians place restrictions on the role of women in public. Among Christian Nigerians, women are often represented in business. In general, foreign businesswomen experience no more difficulties than foreign men in Nigeria.

Observation: "Christianity came with the white colonial powers which sought to transform traditional African societies and beliefs. Islam, by contrast, has been more of an indigenous phenomenon, since in sub-Saharan Africa it was spread largely by Africans. Islam is also more in accord with the African proclivity for the practical—a propensity for the present as opposed to the hereafter."

—From *Into Africa: Intercultural Insights* by Yale Richmond and Phyllis Gestrin

---

5 Cultural Tips

1. When conversing, Nigerians tend to stand more closely than most North Americans. However, this closeness is only acceptable with someone of the same sex. There is no physical contact in public between members of the opposite sex in Nigeria.

2. Since Nigeria's telephone network is in poor repair, do not expect to be able to make appointments or transact business by phone, fax, or e-mail. Telephone service can be problematical even in Nigeria's best hotels. (You might not even be able to contact the front desk from your room!) Nigeria's business culture works on face-to-face contact and hand-delivered messages.

3. Although the weather in Nigeria is often hot and humid (especially near the coast), foreign businessmen are expected to wear a suit and tie to business meetings. Foreign businesswomen should wear a suit. Nigerian executives may interpret casual dress as a sign of disrespect. Local businessmen may wear a European-style suit or their national dress (an embroidered robe called a *baban riga*). Nigerians often spend a substantial amount of their income on clothes.

4. Titles are considered important in Nigeria. Always use a Nigerian's title, especially traditional titles such as *Chief*. (*Chief* is standard English translation of several indigenous titles, which vary between ethnic groups.) Do not address someone by his or her first name unless invited to do so. Be especially careful when addressing persons older than yourself. The elderly are highly respected in Nigeria.

5. Although many African people tend to speak in polite circles, Nigerians have a reputation for being blunt and direct. This characteristic, along with their cosmopolitan outlook and aggressive business skills, have earned them the nickname "the New Yorkers of Africa."

Economic Overview

Nigeria, the most populous nation in Africa, has the resources to become the continent's major economy. Unfortunately, internal strife, corruption, and bad leadership have kept Nigeria from achieving its potential.

Oil reserves notwithstanding, most Nigerians work in agriculture. Almost 70% of the country's population are subsistence farmers, with minimal involvement in the cash economy.

The peaceful transfer of power from the military to a democratically-elected leader in May 1999 is an encouraging sign. However, Nigeria's problems have become so burdensome that no leader can turn the country around without years of reform. Nigeria's infrastructure is collapsing; the roads and railways are often impassable. The once-efficient civil service has been virtually destroyed by years of neglect and corruption. Even when all of these problems are overcome, the difficulties of tribal divisions will remain.

5 Largest Businesses in Nigeria

Nigerian National Petroleum Corporation, Abuja
    16,450 employees
First Bank of Nigeria PLC, Lagos
    10,910 employees
United Bank for Africa PLC, Lagos
    7,650 employees
U A C of Nigeria PLC, Lagos
    4,440 employees
Nigeria Airways Ltd, Lagos
    3,720 employees

Comparative Data

Comparative Data Ratings
(Scale: 5 = Highest; 1 = Lowest)
Nigeria: 2.375

- A.   GDP Growth: 3
- B.   Per Capita Income: 1
- C.   Trade Flows with the U.S.: 2
- D.   Country Risk: 5
- E.   Monetary Policy: 2
- F.   Trade Policy: 2
  - Tariffs
  - Import Licensing
  - Import Taxes
- G.   Protection of Property Rights: 2
- H.   Foreign Investment Climate: 2

GROSS DOMESTIC PRODUCT: $106.2 billion (1998 estimate)

GDP GROWTH: 1.6% (1998 estimate)

PER CAPITA INCOME: $960 (1998 estimate)

Trade Flows with the U.S.

U.S. EXPORTS TO NIGERIA: $820 million (1998 estimate)

U.S. IMPORTS FROM NIGERIA: $4.2 billion (1998 estimate)

TOP U.S. EXPORTS TO NIGERIA: Oil and gas machinery; cereals; iron and steel products; electrical machinery; plastics; motor vehicles and auto parts; medical instruments

TOP U.S. PROSPECTS FOR EXPORT TO NIGERIA: Oil and gas machinery; computers and computer software; telecommunication services and equipment; aviation services; medical equipment; cosmetics and toiletries; automotive parts and accessories; construction equipment; textiles and fabrics

Country Risk

Dun & Bradstreet rates Nigeria as having very high risk.

Cash in advance is recommended. Although credit risk is declining, it will remain significant for the foreseeable future outside of the oil and gas sectors.

Monetary Policy

Inflation has been in double digits in recent years, reaching 28% in 1996. Recently, inflation has settled in the 10%-per-year range.

MONETARY UNIT: Nigerian naira

Trade Policy

TARIFFS   Nigeria initiated a new tariff structure as of March 1, 1995. Tariff rates range between 5% and 60%. All imports must be accompanied by an Import Duty Report (IDR).

IMPORT LICENSING   In 1986 Nigeria stopped issuing licenses for importation of goods. Since then, importers must open an irrevocable letter of credit after receipt of an approved revised Form "M" processed through the importer's local bank. The importation of certain products is prohibited.

IMPORT TAXES   Nigeria assesses value-added taxes (VAT) on most imported goods, except some that are exempted. The value-added tax rate is 5%.

Protection of Intellectual Property Rights

Nigeria belongs to the Paris Convention for Protection of Industrial Property, the Berne Convention for Protection of Literary and Artistic Works, and the Universal Copyright Convention. Their trademark system is based on prior British law. A major effort will be required to revise their laws to current international standards. Copyright and trademark piracy is common and enforcement in the courts is tedious.

Patents extend for 20 years from application and require the payment of annual maintenance fees. Application may be made for a compulsory license three years after grant if the invention has not been sufficiently worked. Industrial designs are protected for 5 years and may be extended for two additional five-year terms.

The Trademark Register has Part A for regular marks and Part B for marks that are considered descriptive. Trademarks only protect goods; services cannot be registered. Conversion is being made to the international system of classification. Marks may be opposed within two months of publication. Registrations are for 7 years from application and renewals are for 14 years.

Copyrights protect literary works, musical works, motion pictures, sound recordings, and broadcasts. Included under literary works are computer programs. To be protected, works must be notified to the Nigerian Copyright Commission. Copyrights are granted for the life of the author plus 70 years.

Foreign Investment Climate

Nigeria has been a profitable if problematic area for foreign investment. While the peaceful election of Olusegun Obasanjo is encouraging for human rights and the advancement of democratic institutions, it is not necessarily encouraging for foreign investors, many of whom felt secure dealing with Nigeria's iron-fisted military juntas.

Political Leaders, Parties, and International Organizations

The International Academy at Santa Barbara at http://www.iasb.org/cwl publishes *Current World Leaders*, an excellent resource for up-to-date data on political leaders, parties, demographics, etc., in Nigeria. Tel: (800) 530-2682 or (805) 965-5010 for subscription information to their database.

Head of State/President:
   Olusegun Obasanjo

Next election:
   2003

Political Parties:
   People's Democratic Party (PDP), All People's Party (APP), Alliance for Democracy (AD)

Membership in international organizations:
   British Commonwealth, UN, World Bank, African Development Bank, OPEC, International Cocoa Organization, Economic Community of West African States (ECOWAS)

Political Influences on Business

Nigeria became an independent country in 1960. A former colony of the United Kingdom, it remains a member of the British Commonwealth.

Politically, Nigeria has experienced great turmoil since independence. It has spent more years under military dictatorship than a democracy. The military has ruled from 1966 to 1976, and again from 1983 to 1999.

Nigeria remains a developing country. The usual difficulties of such countries in sub-Saharan Africa—poverty, poor infrastructure, overpopulation, ethnic strife, AIDS, the remnants of colonialism, etc.—are magnified by the global interest in Nigeria's resources. Nigeria is no worse off than many of its neighbors. However, because so many foreigners seek Nigeria's oil wealth, the problems of Nigeria receive wider international attention.

Observation: "Previous episodes of civilian rule, and the opportunistic behavior of politicians under military governments, have inspired pervasive cynicism toward Nigeria's political class. Popular frustration is running high, and Nigerians expect serious attention to basic issues of governance."

   —From Peter Lewis's article "Nigeria: From Despair to Expectation" in the May 1999 issue of *Current History*

Contacts in the United States

THE EMBASSY OF THE FEDERAL REPUBLIC OF NIGERIA
1333 16th Street, NW
Washington, D.C. 20036
Tel: (202) 986-8400
Fax: (202) 775-1385
www.nigeria-consulate-atl.org

Passport/Visa Requirements

A passport and visa are required by U.S. and Canadian citizens. The visa must be obtained in advance of arrival in Nigeria. Foreigners who enter Nigeria without a visa are subject to arrest.

For details on this and other documents pertinent to working in Nigeria or residing there on a temporary basis (i.e., longer than three months), contact the nearest Nigerian Consular Office.

For current information concerning entry and customs requirements for Nigeria, contact the Nigerian Embassy.

U.S. citizens who wish to apply for a passport may visit Passport Services' well-organized website at http://travel.state.gov/passport_services.html.

NIGERIAN–AMERICAN CHAMBER OF COMMERCE
Consulate General of Nigeria
Nigeria House
828 Second Avenue
New York, NY 10017
Tel: (212) 808-0301
Fax: (212) 687-1476

Contacts in Nigeria

THE EMBASSY OF THE UNITED STATES OF AMERICA
2 Eleke Crescent
Victoria Island
Lagos
Mailing Address: P.O. Box 554, Lagos
Tel: (234) (1) 261-0097
Fax: (234) (1) 261-0257

At this writing, the U.S. Embassy remains in Nigeria's old capital of Lagos. Nigeria moved its capital to Abuja in 1991. The U.S. has opened a liaison office in Abuja to provide emergency consular services.

U.S. Embassy Liaison Office
9 Mambilla Street
Maitama District
Abuja
Federal Capital Territory
Tel: (234) (9) 523-0916

Nigerian–American Chamber of Commerce
Marble House, 8th Floor
1 Kingsway Road, Ikoyi
G.P.O Box 8508
Lagos
Tel: (234) (1) 269-2088
Fax: (234) (1) 269-3041

Further contacts and websites can be found in Appendix A.

Communications

TELEPHONE: The international country code for Nigeria is 234.

City codes are one or two digits in length.

Nigerian phone numbers are five or six digits in length.

E-MAIL: E-mail addresses located in Nigeria end with the code .ng

MAIL: At present, the Nigerian Postal Service is considered neither reliable nor secure. The use of courier services is recommended.

Warning: Travelers to Nigeria must have a valid, up-to-date visa. (Any invitation to enter Nigeria without a visa is indicative of illegal activity.) Between culture shock, the rigors of travel, and the tendency of some Nigerians (both in and out of uniform) to prey upon foreign travelers, it is important for the first-time traveler to be met at the airport in Nigeria by a trusted colleague who is known by sight. When careful precautions are taken, foreign travelers can expect to travel to Nigeria in relative safety. Remember that while only a minority of Nigerians are out to take advantage of foreigners, they will be the ones most likely to seek you out.

When arriving in Nigeria, U.S. citizens are advised to immediately register with the Americans Citizens Division of the Consular Section at the U.S. Embassy. The U.S. government also advises U.S. citizens to avoid public transportation. The Nigerian air fleet is currently aging and the U.S. Embassy in Lagos has serious concerns about its safety. As in other countries, foreign executives are sometimes kidnapped and held for ransom.

Official Name:	Republic of Peru (República del Perú)
Official Language:	Spanish, Quechua, Aymara
Government System:	Unitary multi-party republic
Population:	26.624 million (1999 estimate)
Population Growth Rate:	1.93% (1999 estimate)
Area:	1.285 million sq. km. (496,222 sq. mi.); three times larger than California
Natural Resources:	copper, silver, lead, zinc, gold, crude oil, timber, fish, iron ore, coal, phosphates, potash
Major Cities:	Lima (capital), Arequipa, Chiclayo, Piura, Cuzco, Huancayo, Trujillo

---

Cultural Note: Industry, ingenuity, and perseverance are considered part of the Peruvian heritage. These characteristics are necessary for survival in this harsh Andean nation. Much of Peru is mountainous and inhospitable, yet Indians scrape out a living there, often through subsistence agriculture. In the past decade, however, millions of poor people have left the countryside, fleeing the violent conflict between the Peruvian armed forces and various revolutionary groups—primarily the *Sendero Luminiso* (Shining Path). Some 25,000 Peruvian civilians have died in the conflict.

Age Breakdown

0–15 = 35%　15–65 = 60%　65+ = 5% (1999 estimate)
Life Expectancy: 68.08 years, male; 72.78 years, female (1998 estimate)

Time

The omnipresent historical sites—both pre-Columbian and Spanish Colonial—give Peru a sense of timelessness. Punctuality was never a part of this culture. However, foreign businesspeople are expected to be prompt.

Peru is 5 hours behind Greenwich Mean Time (GMT -5), which is the same as U.S. Eastern Standard Time.

Holidays

A web-based *World Holiday and Time Zone Guide* is available at www.getcustoms.com with updated official holidays, cultural tips, time zones, and tables that compare worldwide business hours.

This list is a working guide. Dates should be corroborated before final travel plans are made. In cases where holidays fall on Saturday or Sunday, commercial establishments may be closed the preceding Friday or following Monday.

Jan 1	SA	New Year's Day
Apr 20	TH	Holy Thursday
Apr 21	FR	Good Friday
May 1	MO	Labor Day
Jun 29	TH	Sts. Peter and Paul's Day
Jul 28	FR	Independence Day
Jul 29	SA	Independence Day
Aug 30	WE	St. Rosa of Lima
Oct 8	SU	Battle of Angamos
Nov 1	WE	All Saints Day
Dec 8	FR	Immaculate Conception
Dec 25	MO	Christmas Day

In addition to the above, the Catholic holidays of Holy Thursday, Good Friday, and Easter are observed as official holidays. These fall on different dates each year.

Confirm these dates as well as local holidays that may be celebrated regionally prior to scheduling appointments.

Again, the days of observance should always be corroborated by local contacts.

Work Week

- The work week is longer in Peru since businesses are often open six days a week. Business hours generally run from around 8:00 A.M. to 5:00 or 6:00 P.M. People may return home for lunch, so offices sometimes close between 1:00 and 3:00 P.M.

- Government offices and banks work different hours between summer (January to March) and winter (April to December).

- Many Peruvians go on vacation between January and March, and two weeks before and after Christmas and Easter. Therefore, try not to schedule major appointments then or during national holidays.

Religious/Societal Influences on Business

The overwhelming majority of Peruvians are Roman Catholic. Nevertheless, many of the Indians and mestizos retain their ancient Incan folk beliefs, as well as their native Quechua language. The sun festival of Inti Raymi each June is one remnant of Incan tradition. Another is stated in this Inca precept: *ama sua, ama qella, ama llulla* (meaning "do not steal, do not be idle, do not lie").

Peruvians are divided by geography, by ethnicity, and by class. Animosity exists between the majority poor (who are all or partially Indian) and the white oligarchy (who own the bulk of Peru's wealth and businesses). There is also friction between the residents of Lima (known as Limeños) and the rest of the country.

Peru's abundant natural resources make the plight of Peru's poor all the more bitter. Blessed with minerals, petroleum, fishing, and timber, Peru also has archaeological wonders for tourism. In the illegal economy, Peru produces billions in cocaine every year. It is no surprise that historically, the phrase *Vale un Perú* ("It's worth a Peru") became an expression of incalculable wealth throughout the Spanish-speaking colonial world.

5 Cultural Tips

1. Peru was the seat of the Spanish Colonial Empire in South America. Because of its mineral wealth, Spain held on to Peru as long as possible. Peruvians still maintain a higher level of formality than many other Latin Americans.

2. Blunt, frank speech is not valued. Politeness demands a less direct approach. When spoken to aggressively, many Peruvians will tell you what they think you want to hear. It is best to avoid questions that can be answered with *yes* or *no*.

3. The 1996 takeover of the Japanese Embassy in Lima by the Túpac Amaru Revolutionary Movement garnered worldwide publicity. This, along with media coverage of Peruvian earthquakes and cholera outbreaks, may exaggerate the dangers of traveling to Peru. Peruvians are, in general, friendly to foreigners. At this

writing, the average business traveler is safer in Peru than in some other Latin American countries (such as Colombia). In fact, the greatest risks to travelers are from petty theft and altitude sickness. (Lima is near sea level, but Cuzco is high enough for altitude sickness to strike.)

4. Historically, the role of women in Peruvian society was quite restricted. But the social and economic dislocations of the past few decades have forced women into public life. The need to feed their children led to the creation of all-women's organizations such as *Vaso de Leche* ("Glass of Milk"). Women have been elected to political office, especially at the local level.

5. The family (both nuclear and extended) is the cornerstone of relationships in every aspect of society. Peruvians commonly do business with people from their wide-reaching network of family and friends. Since relationships are so vital, never change your corporate negotiating team or local representatives during the sales process.

Economic Overview

The economic recovery brightened the commercial risk environment in 2000. According to the Peruvian government, real Gross Domestic Product grew by 6% in the first quarter, and should exceed the 5% target set for the year. At the same time, inflation was subdued at 3.8% through March. For these reasons, Peru should be an economic star in Latin America in 2000 and 2001.

U.S. products and services are well-regarded in the market and Peruvian companies are interested in expanding their business ties with the U.S.

4 Largest Businesses in Peru

Empresa Minera del Centro del Perú S.A., Lima
   7,960 employees
Telefónica del Perú S.A., Lima
   6,286 employees
Southern Peru Limited, Lima
   5,570 employees
Banco de Credito del Perú, Lima
   5,500 employees

Cultural Note: It is hard to exaggerate the changes President Fujimori brought to Peru. Just days after his accession to the Presidency in July 1990, he instituted an economic austerity program. (Ironically, this was virtually the same program proposed by the man Fujimori defeated for the Presidency, internationally-acclaimed author Mario Vargas Llosa.) The cost of living soared with the removal of price controls. The Peruvian poor and middle classes were hit hard. As one columnist put it, Peruvians faced "Japanese prices on African incomes." Yet the majority of Peruvians continued to support Fujimori for the same reason they elected him: Fujimori is *not* one of the white oligarchs who have ruled Peru since its inception. In racially-divided Peru, where the majority of citizens are poor and of mixed or Indian descent, the son of a Japanese grocer was seen as "one of us."

The economic austerity program—sometimes called "Fujishock"—successfully reduced inflation, which had reached a high of 7000% a year! Money from abroad once again flowed into Peru, and the budget has been balanced.

Two further events secured Fujimori's position. In April of 1992 he closed down the Peruvian Congress, a notoriously corrupt and useless body. This move was tremendously popular with the people. Just a few months later, the legendary leader of the Shining Path terrorist group was captured in Lima, crippling his organization. The constitution was amended to allow Fujimori to succeed himself as President, which he did for another term during the recent year 2000 election.

Comparative Data

Comparative Data Ratings
(Scale: 5 = Excellent; 1 = Poor)
Peru: 2.75

- A.   GDP Growth: 3
- B.   Per Capita Income: 2
- C.   Trade Flows with the U.S.: 2
- D.   Country Risk: 2
- E.   Monetary Policy: 4
- F.   Trade Policy: 3
  - Tariffs
  - Import Licensing
  - Import Taxes
- G.   Protection of Property Rights: 3
- H.   Foreign Investment Climate: 3

GROSS DOMESTIC PRODUCT: $111.8 billion (1998 estimate)

GDP GROWTH: 1.8% (1998 estimate)

PER CAPITA INCOME: $4,300 (1998 estimate)

Trade Flows with the U.S.

U.S. EXPORTS TO PERU: $2.1 billion (1998 estimate)

U.S. IMPORTS FROM PERU: $2.0 billion (1998 estimate)

TOP U.S. EXPORTS TO PERU: Machinery; mining equipment; oil and gas equipment; mineral fuel; electronic components; telecommunications equipment; cereals; motor vehicles; plastics; medical and optical equipment; pollution-control equipment; paper and paperboard

TOP U.S. PROSPECTS FOR EXPORT TO PERU: Mining industry equipment; telecommunications equipment; oil and gas equipment; pollution-control equipment; building products; computer software; auto parts and accessories; medical equipment; food processing/packaging equipment; hotel and restaurant equipment

Country Risk

There is significant uncertainty over expected returns. Secured terms are advised on initial deals. Only reputable banks should be used.

Monetary Policy

Inflation plummeted from 7650% in 1990 to 6.0% in 1998 as a result of tight monetary and fiscal policies. Inflation is expected to remain under 10% through the year 2000.

MONETARY UNIT: nuevo sol

Trade Policy

TARIFFS   Peru maintains 12% tariffs on 95% of the items on the tariff schedule. The remaining 5% of items (primarily textiles and footwear) have a 20% tariff. The trade-weighted average tariff is around 13%, down from 80% in the mid-1990s.

IMPORT LICENSING   The government has abolished import licenses for the vast majority of products. The only remaining products needing licenses are firearms, munitions and explosives imported by private persons, chemical precursors (used in cocaine production), and ammonium nitrate fertilizer, which has been used for terrorist car bombs.

IMPORT TAXES   Most imports are subject to an 18% value-added tax (VAT). Additionally, selective consumption taxes ranging from 10–50% are applied to certain luxury items.

Port fees have been reduced but are still relatively high for Latin America.

Protection of Intellectual Property Rights

Under the Fujimori administration, Peru has made significant improvements in its intellectual property rights protection. However, such protection is still not up to international standards and Peru remains on the Special 301 Watch List.

Peru is a member of the Andean Pact, which has regulations on the protection of patents and trademarks. In addition, Peru adheres to the Paris Convention, the Berne Convention, the Universal Copyright Convention, the Buenos Aires Convention, the Convention for Protection Against Unauthorized Reproduction of Phonograms, and the Agreement on Trade Related Aspects of Intellectual Property Rights.

Patents are valid for 20 years from application. Utility models are good for 10 years. Inventions must be novel, inventive, and have industrial application. Patents are subject to cancellation if not used or licensed in one of the Andean Pact countries.

Trademarks must be registered according to the international classification system. Services and slogans are registerable. Registrations have terms of 10 years and may be renewed.

Copyrights are automatic on creation of a work. Peruvian law protects computer programs and artistic performances. The term of copyright is the lifetime of the author, plus 70 years after death.

Foreign Investment Climate

The Fujimori government has sought to attract foreign investment in all sectors of the economy. Peru's liberal investment laws offer national treatment to all investors. An ambitious program of privatization has resulted in more than 90 privatizations since 1991. Many additional Peruvian companies and utilities—including oil, mining, and power—are scheduled for privatization.

However, the economic slowdown of 1998 resulted in unexpectedly low prices for state-owned industries. Consequently, President Fujimori decided to slow down the privatization program until prices recover. He opposed the sale of many of Peru's hydroelectric plants, including the giant Mantaro site. Mantaro, which has the capacity to generate one-fourth of Peru's electrical needs, is worth an estimated $850 million.

Foreign investors have the same rights as national investors and thus would benefit from any investment incentives such as tax exonerations. Foreign investors also have international arbitration rights to settle investment contract disputes.

Industries established in free trade zones are allowed to import manufacturing components free of all duties and fees. Zone users are also exempt from all taxes for a period of 15 years.

Political Leaders, Parties, and International Organizations

The International Academy at Santa Barbara at http://www.iasb.org/cwl publishes *Current World Leaders*, an excellent resource for up-to-date data on political leaders, parties, demographics, etc., in Peru. Tel: (800) 530-2682 or (805) 965-5010 for subscription information to their database.

Head of State and the Government:

President Alberto Fujimori (re-elected in 2000)

Next Election:

April 2005

Political Parties:

New Majority/Change 90 Party, Christian Popular Party, Renovation Movement, Leftist Democratic Movement, American Popular Revolutionary Alliance, Popular Action, United Left, Liberty Party

Membership in international organizations:

AG, G77, IADB, INTELSAT, LAIA, NAM, OAS, PECC, SELA, UN and all of its specialized agencies and related organizations (including FAO, GATT, IAEA, IBRD, ICAO, IDA, IFAD, IFC, ILO, IMF, IMO, ITU, UNESCO, UNIDO, UPU, WHO, WIPO, WMO)

Political Influences on Business

Peru is a republic with a dominant executive branch headed by President Alberto Fujimori, who was first elected in 1990 and won reelection by a landslide in 1995, and again in 2000. The President appoints a number of ministers to carry out and oversee the work of the executive branch. The legislative branch is a unicameral congress with 120 members elected at large. Like the president, they serve five-year terms.

Major political parties include President Fujimori's rather loosely organized "Cambio 90/Nueva Mayoria," which holds a majority in the congress; the equally loosely organized "Union por el Peru" whose leader is former U.N. Secretary General and presidential runner-up Javier Perez de Cuellar; and the quasi-socialist "American Popular Revolutionary Alliance" (APRA). There are a number of smaller parties with seats in the congress, including the socialist/marxist "United Left," centrist "Accion Popular," center–right "Partido Popular Cristiano," and the "Frente Independiente Moralizador." APRA and Accion Popular currently control most of the country's municipal governments.

U.S. policy in Peru reflects varied goals: the strengthening of democracy, fostering respect for human rights, the curtailment of illegal narcotics trafficking, supporting U.S. businesses and citizens, and encouraging sustainable development. The U.S. development and humanitarian assistance program is currently the largest in South America.

There has been considerable progress in Peru's human rights record during the last few years as the level of political violence has declined, The numbers of political disappearances and extrajudicial killings have dropped dramatically since 1992. Nonetheless, the U.S. government remains concerned about continued arbitrary detentions, lack of due process, reports of torture of detainees, and limited prosecution of those government and military officials accused of abuses.

Armed conflict broke out between Peru and Ecuador in January 1995 over a portion of the undemarcated border. Casualties for both sides were about 100–150 killed. A cease-fire was agreed to in February 1995, and is still respected. The U.S., along with Argentina, Brazil, and Chile, are guarantors of the Peru–Ecuador 1942 border treaty and are supporting Peruvian and Ecuadorian efforts to end the border conflict. An historic agreement between Peru and Ecuador on their borders was signed in October 1998.

The security situation has improved considerably since the September 1992 capture of terrorist leader Abimael Guzman. However, Peru's two terrorist groups, Sendero Luminoso and the Túpac Amaru Revolutionary Movement, although seriously debilitated by the capture of their top leaders, have not been defeated. Both groups continue to carry out terrorist activities, including attacks on foreign businesses and diplomatic missions.

Contacts in the United States

THE EMBASSY OF PERU
1700 Massachusetts Avenue, NW
Washington, D.C. 20036
Tel: (202) 833-9860 through 9869
Fax: (202) 659-8124
www.peruemb.org

Passport/Visa Requirements

A passport is required. Tourists who are U.S. citizens do not need a visa for a 90-day stay. A fully-paid onward or return ticket is required.

Travelers require a valid passport to obtain a business visa. This business visa is given by a Peruvian Consular official after presentation of the following: a letter of guaranty from the applicant's firm and copy of an onward or return trip ticket. Visa fee is $27.00 payable by cash or money order. All business transactions done in Peru must be reported, and the corresponding tax (if applicable) paid before leaving the country. Processing of this tax declaration takes approximately three days.

The U.S. Commerce Department recommends that citizens traveling to Peru avoid business visas. Travel as a tourist even if you are traveling on business, unless you expect to be reimbursed for services while inside Peru.

The importation of merchandise as baggage is prohibited.

For current information concerning entry and customs requirements for Peru, contact the Peruvian Embassy.

The United States government recommends that all U.S. citizens visiting Peru register upon arrival with the American Citizen Services Unit, Consular Section, of the U.S. Embassy. The American Citizen Services Unit is open from 8:00 A.M. to 12 noon on weekdays; it is closed on both U.S. and Peruvian holidays. Registrants should bring their U.S. passport and one photo. There is no charge for this service.

U.S. citizens who wish to apply for a passport may visit Passport Services' well-organized website at http://travel.state.gov/passport_services.html.

Contacts in Peru

THE EMBASSY OF THE UNITED STATES OF AMERICA
Avenida Encalada, Cuadra 17
Monterrico,
Lima, Perú
Mailing Address: P.O. Box 1995, Lima 1, APO AA 34031-5000
Tel: (51) (14) 434 3000
Fax: (51) (14) 434 3037
ekeko.rcp.net.pe/usa

AMERICAN CHAMBER OF COMMERCE
Av. Ricardo Palma 836 Miraflores
Lima 18
Tel: (51) (14) 47-9349
Fax: (51) (14) 47-9352

DUN & BRADSTREET S.A.
Postal Address: Apartado 3571, Lima 100
Street Address: Republica de Chile 388,
Piso 2, Edificio Sarmiento, Lima 11
Tel: (51) (1) 433-5533; (51) (1) 433-2948; (51) (1) 433-2989; (51) (1) 433-2994; (51) (1) 433-3070
Fax: (51) (1) 433-2897

OFFICE OF THE PRESIDENT
Palacio de Gobierno
Plaza de Armas S/N
Lima 1, Republic of Perú

PRESIDENT OF THE COUNCIL OF MINISTERS
Jr. Landa 535
Lima 1, Republic of Perú

Further contacts and websites can be found in Appendix A.

Communications

TELEPHONE: The international country code for Peru is 51.

Phone numbers vary in length.

Area codes also vary in length. The city code for Lima is 1.

E-MAIL: E-mail addresses located in Peru end with the code .pe

---

Cultural Note: Peru is the Southernmost nation in which bullfighting is still popular. In fact, Lima has the oldest bullfighting ring in the Americas. Peruvians consider bullfighting an art, not a sport. Whatever your feelings about bullfighting, do not speak disparagingly about it in Peru.

Faux Pas: In Lima, a recreation center for the national police requested a large number of Coca-Cola signs, which they placed on every outdoor wall surface. The local Coca-Cola representative was enthusiastic at this free advertising . . . until he discovered that the police were using the red Coca-Cola signs to obscure the graffiti on the walls! The Communist Shining Path group always painted their revolutionary slogans in red, which the red-and-white Coca-Cola signs disguised nicely.

The Philippines

Official Name:	Republic of The Philippines (Republika ng Pilipinas)
Official Language:	English, Pilipino (based on Tagalog, national language)
Government System:	Unitary republic
Population:	79.3 million (1999 estimate)
Population Growth Rate:	2.04% (1999 estimate)
Area:	300,000 sq. km. (117,187 sq. mi.); slightly larger than Arizona
Natural Resources:	timber, crude oil, nickel, cobalt, silver, gold, salt, copper
Major Cities:	Manila (capital), Quezon City, Davao, Cebu

Cultural Note: Due to years of foreign domination—by the Spanish, the Japanese, and the United States—most Filipinos are highly nationalistic. Slights against their country, even in jest, are the quickest way to poison a relationship. Avoid even backhanded comments, such as how efficiently something is done in the U. S. compared with the Philippines.

Age Breakdown

0–14 = 37%   15–64 = 59%   65+ = 4% (1999 estimate)
Life Expectancy: 63.79 years, male; 69.5 years, female (1999 estimate)

Time

Time is malleable. Foreign executives are expected to be on time to business meetings, but many Filipinos will not be punctual.

Everyone, even a foreigner, is expected to be late for social events. But the exact measure of the delay depends upon the status of each person. (The highest-ranking person should arrive last.) Rather than try to decipher the ranking of each party guest, foreigners should just ask their host (in private) what time they should actually arrive.

The Philippines is 8 hours ahead of Greenwich Mean Time (GMT +8), which is 13 hours ahead of U.S. Eastern Standard Time (EST +13).

Holidays

A web-based *World Holiday and Time Zone Guide* is available at www.getcustoms.com with updated official holidays, cultural tips, time zones, and tables that compare world-wide business hours.

This list is a working guide. Dates should be corroborated before final travel plans are made. In cases where holidays fall on Saturday or Sunday, commercial establishments may be closed the preceding Friday or following Monday.

Jan 1	SA	New Year's Day
Apr 9	SU	Bataan & Corregidor Day/Heroism Day
Apr 20	TH	Holy Thursday
Apr 21	FR	Good Friday
May 1	MO	Labor Day
Jun 12	MO	Independence Day
Jun 24	SA	Manila Day (Manila only)
Aug 19	SA	Quezon Day (Quezon City only)
Aug 27	SU	National Heroes Day
Nov 1	WE	All Saints Day
Nov 30	TH	Bonifacio Day
Dec 25	MO	Christmas Day
Dec 30	SA	Rizal Day

The Catholic observances of Holy Thursday, Good Friday, and Easter are official holidays.

In addition, each town and region has annual fiestas, during which normal business is suspended. Two of the most important regional holidays are:

Jun 24	Manila Day
Aug 19	Quezon Day

Work Week

• Mid-mornings or mid-to-late afternoons are usually best for appointments.

- Business hours are generally from 8:00 A.M. to 5:00 P.M. Monday through Friday. Most offices close during the lunch break, which is usually from 12:00 noon to 1:00 P.M. but can easily stretch for two hours. Some offices may open from 8:00 A.M. to 12:00 noon on Saturdays.
- Government offices keep an 8:00 A.M. to 5:00 P.M. schedule Monday through Friday. Many senior government officials work late, and some accept phone calls after hours—but only at their offices, never at home. (By contrast, many businesspeople can frequently be reached at home.)
- Banking hours are usually much shorter: from 9:00 A.M. to 2:30 or 3:00 P.M. Monday through Friday.

Religious/Societal Influences on Business

The Philippines has no official religion. The bulk of the population is (at least nominally) Roman Catholic, but various Protestant sects have experienced rapid growth. There are also breakaway sects of the Roman Catholic Church, such as the Philippine Independent Church. Islam is found in the south.

Thanks in part to the Catholic Church's opposition to birth control, the Philippines has a very high birth rate. (Former President Estrada himself has at least ten children.) The Philippines maintained a modest economic growth rate throughout the 1990s, but it will not be sufficient to raise the national standard of living unless population growth slows.

Social scientists have found that most Filipinos have a fairly low *Uncertainty Avoidance Index*. Societies that score high on this scale feel the need for creating rigid rules of behavior and extensive sets of laws to enforce them. At the opposite end of the scale, Philippine society and behavior exhibits flexibility and adaptability. The letter of the law is not strictly observed, nor are there regulations to cover every situation. This situation is probably ideal for a sprawling, geographically-divided, multicultural society, with technology levels that range from stone age to cutting edge. (Some 70 different languages and dialects are spoken within the Philippines.) But it has disadvantages for foreigners who assume that laws exist and are complied with. For example, one cannot assume that comprehensive building codes exist in all areas of the Philippines; and where they are extant, one cannot assume that they are strictly adhered to or enforced.

In fact, regulation enforcement is often used as a weapon among competitors. One party with government connections is allowed to flout regulations, while competitors are strictly held to the letter of the law. It is summed up in this Philippine expression: "For my friends—everything, for my enemies—the law."

Curiously, this does not prevent companies from adopting extensive in-house regulations for their employees. This reflects the difficulty that a boss has in disciplining an employee who is probably related to several company employees (or even related to the boss). By detailing punishments for various infractions, the boss gains a face-saving distance from any necessary disciplinary action.

Great inequalities exist in the Philippines. The majority of the population is poor, but mobility (or the hope of mobility) exists.

The most important influence on Filipinos is the family. Nepotism is common and is not considered to be detrimental.

5 Cultural Tips

1. Titles are important to the Filipinos—so important that many employees are rewarded with impressive-sounding titles (and little else). Address an executive by his or her title and surname, but do not expect to be able to tell much about a person's importance from the title.

2. Kinship is everything in the Philippines. You will be accepted more rapidly if you can explain your relationship to someone the Filipinos already know. Even if the relationship is distant (i.e., you are the friend of the brother of someone they know), that relationship helps establish you as a *real person* in Philippine eyes.

3. Philippine business operates at its own pace and it cannot be speeded up by outsiders. Most Philippine executives will not consider doing business with you until they feel they know you and like you. Extensive socializing will be necessary, both inside and outside the office. An extensive government bureaucracy slows down action even further. Be patient.

4. The avoidance of shame is vital in the Philippines. Unfortunately, bad news is often interpreted as a loss of face (shameful), so many Filipinos will tell you only good news (or what they think you want to hear). Filipinos will often smile and say *yes* when they really mean *no*. They do not intend to deceive; they are trying to save the feelings of everyone involved.

5. Groups of Filipinos do not arrange themselves in neat lines. Instead, they form a pushing, shoving crowd, with each person out for him- or herself. The only times that Filipinos have queued in neat lines was under the gun of armed soldiers, such as under the Japanese occupation army in World War II, so queues may have bad associations for Filipinos.

Economic Overview

In the past few years the Philippines has undergone a remarkable transformation. In the late 1980s and early 1990s, the Philippines was saddled with political instability and unrest, weak economic growth, a badly neglected infrastructure, and a slow pace of economic liberalization. Today, it is increasingly recognized by analysts that the Philippines has turned the corner economically, overcome several of its most pressing problems, and is heading for sustained economic growth and increased prosperity. GNP growth rates are up from near zero in the early 1990s to between 3% and 5%. Other economic indicators such as inflation and export growth also are positive. The Philippines even escaped the worst effects of the Asian financial crisis.

Democracy has taken secure hold in the Philippines. Under the Ramos Administration, the Philippine Congress took important, concrete steps toward economic liberalization, including reducing import duty reductions, opening up banking and telecommunications sectors, and liberalizing of investment laws.

These moves toward liberalization have created a more attractive climate to U.S. business, and strengthen an already very strong commercial relationship. Historically close bilateral ties and extensive people-to-people contacts have helped solidify the U.S. position as the Philippines's number-one trading partner and foreign investor. However, it remains to be seen if the subsequent administrations will continue these policies.

Trade with the U.S. accounts for almost a third of the Philippines's total trade turnover, and about one-fifth of Philippine imports come from the U.S., consisting chiefly of electronic components, telecommunications equipment, data-processing machines, and wheat.

U.S. direct investment in the Philippines is valued at about $2 billion, largely concentrated in manufacturing and banking. Gradual liberalization of Philippine foreign investment regulations have encouraged a growing number of U.S. companies to consider the country seriously as a new investment location. Relatively low costs of doing business, geographical location, and quality of the labor force have caused many companies to select the Philippines as a regional headquarters in Asia.

Deterrents to foreign trade and investment continue to exist including inadequate enforcement and slow adjudication of intellectual property rights, limitations on land ownership and on foreign investment in certain industries and activities, and customs barriers. In addition, the continuing Asian financial crisis and various natural disasters (such as the 1998 drought attributed to El Niño) have hampered Philippine growth.

5 Largest Businesses in the Philippines

Advanced Micro Device, Inc., Muntinglupa
  20,423 employees
EEI Corp., Manila
  19,000 employees
Philippine Long Distance Telephone Company, Makati
  16,473 employees
JG Summit Holdings, Inc., Mandaluyong City Corporate Center
  12,000 employees
Cebu Mitsumi, Inc., Cebu
  12,000 employees

Cultural Note: Filipinos grow up in extended families and are rarely alone. Indeed, solitude makes most Filipinos uncomfortable. A foreigner's desire for privacy is not understood. If you are sitting alone on a bus or in a cinema, a Filipino is likely to ignore all the empty seats and sit next to you. Such action is not about you; it is simply a cultural trait.

Observation: "Negotiations in the Philippines are conducted in a very formal manner. Company titles are very precise and are used to maintain the hierarchy. Locals will take on a very rigid manner when dealing with foreigners in an effort to preserve what they believe is a professional appearance.

"The Filipinos are strong believers in forging relationships and maintaining *pakiksama* (smooth relations) at all costs. Confrontation is unthinkable and a sign of disrespect. Part of this process is the *utang na loob* (reciprocity) system whereby one business (or political) connection leads to other, more lucrative, deals. Acceptance of a favor or reference will call for a larger one in return."

—From Jeffrey Edmund Curry's *A Short Course in International Negotiating*

Comparative Data

Comparative Data Ratings
(Scale: 5 = Highest; 1 = Lowest)
The Philippines: 2.88

- A.   GDP Growth: 3
- B.   Per Capita Income: 2
- C.   Trade Flows with the U.S.: 4
- D.   Country Risk: 3
- E.   Monetary Policy: 3
- F.   Trade Policy: 2
  - Tariffs
  - Import Licensing
  - Import Taxes
- G.   Protection of Property Rights: 3
- H.   Foreign Investment Climate: 3

GROSS DOMESTIC PRODUCT: $270.5 billion (1998 estimate)

GDP GROWTH: −0.5% (1998 estimate)

PER CAPITA INCOME: $3,500 (1998 estimate)

Trade Flows with the U.S.

U.S. EXPORTS TO THE PHILIPPINES: $6.7 billion (1998 estimate)

U.S. IMPORTS FROM THE PHILIPPINES: $11.9 billion (1998 estimate)

TOP U.S. EXPORTS TO THE PHILIPPINES: Telecommunications equipment; electrical components; machinery; cereals; plastics and resins; aircraft and parts; paper and paperboard; medical and optical equipment; organic chemicals; food-processing and packaging equipment

TOP U.S. PROSPECTS FOR EXPORT TO THE PHILIPPINES: Defense equipment; telecommunications equipment; computers and peripherals; aircraft and parts; electrical power systems; water resource equipment/services; building products; food-processing and packaging equipment; scientific and laboratory equipment; hotel and restaurant equipment

Country Risk

Dun & Bradstreet rates the Philippines as having sufficient capacity to meet outstanding payment liabilities.

Most business is conducted on letters of credit, although more liberal terms, including open account, are generally sufficient for repeat business. Credit terms of 60 to 90 days normally apply.

Monetary Policy

Average year-to-year consumer price inflation has been kept at single-digits since 1992. Dun & Bradstreet forecasts inflation to range between 7% and 9% throughout the year 2000.

MONETARY UNIT: Philippine peso

Trade Policy

TARIFFS The Philippines's average nominal tariff is 10%. Tariffs are grouped into four tiers of 5%, 7%, 15%, and 25%. A uniform 5% tariff for most items is planned beginning January 1, 2004.

IMPORT LICENSING Generally, all merchandise imports are allowed without a license. Several restricted and controlled items remain subject to quota restrictions for reasons of public health, morals, and national security.

Before any importation into the Philippines can be made, an importer must identify the product in the *Philippine Standard Commodity Classification Manual*. The Philippine government requires import permits for meat and meat products, fresh produce, planting seeds/plants, and all agricultural commodities that are officially prohibited for import.

IMPORT TAXES A value-added tax (VAT) of 10% is imposed on imports for resale or reuse. Firms located in export processing zones and free ports are exempt from VAT.

Protection of Intellectual Property Rights

The Philippines is a member of the Paris Convention for Protection of Industrial Property and the Patent Cooperation Treaty. By proclamation, copyright rights have been extended to citizens of the United States. However, enforcement of IP laws is lax and copyright piracy is commonplace.

Patent protection is for a term of 20 years from issue. Industrial designs are registered for 5 years and can be extended for an additional 5 years.

Trademarks, trade names, and service marks may all be registered for terms of 20 years. Affidavits of use are required every 5 years, but use is no longer necessary to obtain a registration. Trademark assignments must be in writing and be notarized.

The Philippines joined the Berne Convention in 1997. The term of copyright is life of the author plus 50 years.

Foreign Investment Climate

The Philippine government has taken important steps since 1990 to welcome foreign investment, despite occasional resistance by vested interests and *nationalist* groups. The 1991 Foreign Investment Act (FIA) lifted the 40% foreign ownership ceiling previously imposed on domestic enterprises, provided no incentives are sought and the activity does not appear on a foreign investment *negative list*. In 1994 amendments to the country's banking law allowed up to 10 foreign banks to establish branches in the Philippines. After decades of protection, the government is allowing additional foreign-owned companies to enter the insurance industry.

While investment liberalization has been substantial, barriers to foreign entry remain for a variety of reasons. Depending on the industry or activity, the FIA's foreign investment *negative list* fully or partially restricts foreign ownership under three broad categories:

List A restricts foreign investment in certain sectors because of constitutional or legal constraints. For example, industries such as mass media, retail trade, small-scale mining, private security agencies, and the practice of licensed professions are fully reserved for Philippine citizens. Land ownership is also constitutionally restricted to Philippine citizens or to corporations with at least 60% Filipino ownership.

List B restricts foreign ownership (generally to 40%) for reasons of national security, defense, public health, safety, and morals. This list also seeks to protect local small- and medium-sized firms by restricting foreign ownership to no more than 40% in nonexport firms capitalized at less than $500,000.

List C restricts foreign ownership (generally to 40%) in activities deemed *adequately served* by existing Philippine enterprises. This list has included sectors such as insurance, travel agencies, tourist lodging establishments, conference/convention organizers, and import and wholesale activities not integrated with production.

Political Leaders, Parties, and International Organizations

The International Academy at Santa Barbara at http://www.iasb.org/cwl publishes *Current World Leaders*, an excellent resource for up-to-date data on political leaders, parties, demographics, etc., in the Philippines. Tel: (800) 530-2682 or (805) 965-5010 for subscription information to their database.

Head of State and of the Government:

President Joseph Estrada

Next Election:

May 2004

Political Parties:

Lakas EDSA–National Union of Christian Democrats (Alliance of two parties), Nationalist Party, Filipino Democratic Party, Liberal Party, People's Reform Party, New Society Movement

Membership in international organizations:

ADB, APEC, ASEAN, CP, INTELSAT, PECC, UN and all of its specialized agencies and related organizations (including FAO, GATT, IAEA, IBRD, ICAO, IDA, IFAD, IFC, ILO, IMF, IMO, ITU, UNESCO, UNIDO, UPU, WHO, WIPO, WMO)

Political Influences on Business

U.S.–Philippine relations have improved substantially since the Philippine Senate's 1991 rejection of a treaty that would have permitted the continuation of U.S. bases at Clark and Subic Bay. In 1993 the administration of President Fidel Ramos came to an agreement with the U.S. on a new, post-bases partnership centering on expanded trade and investment ties as well as continued security cooperation under a Mutual Defense Treaty.

Although U.S. economic and assistance security levels to the Philippines have declined steeply in recent years, a modest aid program continues. The bilateral relationship is buttressed by longstanding historical and cultural links and extensive people-to-people interaction. The peaceful election of three successive presidential administrations has demonstrated that democratic stability has returned to the Philippines.

Of course much needs to be done. While the threat from communist insurgents and military rebels—which destabilized the Aquino administration—has greatly receded, armed Muslim separatists still threaten public order in the southern part of the country.

The Philippines has a presidential form of government patterned after that of the United States with a separation of powers among the Executive, Legislative, and Judicial branches. The Philippine Congress functions much like its U.S. counterpart and is the main arena for competition among the four principal political parties, all of which espouse moderate policies and appeal to similar constituencies.

In 1998, to the surprise of many outsiders, former film star Joseph Estrada was elected president. Estrada, who served as Vice President in the Ramos administration, won despite the opposition of the influential Roman Catholic Church and Fidel Ramos himself (the candidate supported by President Ramos won less than 16% of the vote). Although Estrada's lack of credentials dismayed many—he himself admitted that he knew little of economics—Estrada's law-and-order platform appealed to Filipinos who see their society as increasingly chaotic. Estrada also connected with the underclass in a way his opponents did not. After his election, he delivered his inaugural address in Pilipino (the national language), rather than in English (the language of the business elite).

Filipinos are not the only ones who are concerned about disorder. Expatriates and foreign-owned businesses in the Philippines have been the target of a rising crime rate. One reason for the failure of the authorities to stop crime is that Filipinos have been wary about giving the police increased powers. Memories of police abuse and martial law under former President Ferdinand Marcos still haunt the Philippines.

The Philippines has had a free and vigorous press ever since President Marcos was deposed. Shortly after his inauguration, President Estrada became displeased at his media coverage. In March 1999 he sued a Manila newspaper over a story about his connection to a business scandal (the paper apologized and he dropped the suit), and he has decided to limit reporters' access. But, to date, there has been no outright censorship—something that makes the Filipino media unique in Southeast Asia.

Contacts in the United States

THE EMBASSY OF THE REPUBLIC OF THE PHILIPPINES
1600 Massachusetts Avenue, NW
Washington, D.C. 20036
Tel: (202) 467-9300
Fax: (202) 328-7614
us.sequel.net/RpinUS

Passport/Visa Requirements

A passport is required. A visa is not required for tourists from the U.S. for a stay not exceeding 21 days. However, such travelers must have a valid passport and onward or return booking by sea or air.

Businesspersons require a visa no matter what the length of their stay.

Requirements for issuance of a visa are: (1) valid passport (validity must extend at least six months beyond the length of the proposed stay in the Republic of the Philippines); (2) one visa application form; (3) one recent (within 6 months) 2×2 photograph signed in front; (4) round-trip plane ticket or certification from travel agency; (5) extra documentation where required for business trips; (6) visa fee (variable).

For current information concerning entry and customs requirements for the Philippines, travelers can contact the Philippine Embassy.

U.S. citizens who wish to apply for a passport may visit Passport Services' well-organized website at http://travel.state.gov/passport_services.html.

Contacts In the Philippines

THE EMBASSY OF THE UNITED STATES OF
AMERICA
1201 Roxas Boulevard
Ermita, Manila 1000
Mailing Address: FPO 96515, APO AP
96440
Tel: (63) (2) 523-1001
Fax: (63) (2) 522-4361
www.usia.gov/posts/manilaemb

THE AMERICAN CHAMBER OF COMMERCE OF
THE PHILIPPINES, INC.
2nd Floor, Corinthian Plaza
Paseo de Roxas, Makati City
Tel: (63) (2) 811-3192
Fax: (63) (2) 811-3081
E-mail: amchamrp@mozcom.com
www.amchamphil.com.ph

OFFICE OF THE PRESIDENT
Malacanang Palace Compound
J.P. Laurel Sr. Street
San Miguel
Manila 1005, Republic of the Philippines

Further contacts and websites can be found in Appendix A.

Communications

TELEPHONE: The international country code for the Philippines is 63.

Phone numbers vary in length. They can be five, six, or seven digits in length.

Area codes also vary in length, from one to three digits.

E-*MAIL:* E-mail addresses located in the Philippines end with the code .ph

---

Faux Pas: Hosting visitors is an important tradition in the Philippines. Families have been known to impoverish themselves to provide an appropriate feast for a guest.

An American scientist was commissioned to improve poultry production in the Philippines. He imported several carefully-selected roosters and distributed one each to poor local farmers. When the time came to inspect the program's progress, the scientist arranged to visit one of the farmers. Arriving at the farm, the scientist was escorted to a feast table. The centerpiece of the feast was the imported rooster, fried! (The farmer felt that the only bird he owned that was good enough to serve to the distinguished scientist was the imported rooster.)

Poland

Official Name:	Republic of Poland (Rzeczpospolita Polska)
Official Language:	Polish
Government System:	Multi-party republic
Population:	38.6 million (1999 estimate)
Population Growth Rate:	0.05% (1999 estimate) (At present, the death rate and birth rate in Poland are almost equal.)
Area:	312,680 sq. km. (120,725 sq. mi.); about the size of New Mexico
Natural Resources:	coal, sulfur, copper, natural gas, silver, lead, salt
Major Cities:	Warsaw (capital), Lodz, Krakow, Wroclaw, Poznan, Gdansk

---

Cultural Note: Emigration has often been a solution to hard times in Poland. Thousands of Poles came to the U.S. in the past century. Today Poles are again emigrating, but this time it is the most educated Poles who are seeking opportunity abroad. In the 1990s one in five doctors and one in three mathematicians left Poland. This "brain drain" constitutes a serious problem for Poland.

On the other hand, much of the financial investment in post-Communist Poland has come from successful Polish expatriates.

Age Breakdown

0–14 = 20%   15–64 = 68%   65+ = 12% (1999 estimate)
Life Expectancy: 68.93 years, male; 77.41 years, female (1999 estimate)

Time

Under Soviet domination, punctuality was not expected. This behavior has changed significantly, but you still may encounter it.

As a foreign businessperson, you are expected to arrive on time to all appointments.

Poland is 1 hour ahead of Greenwich Mean Time (GMT. +1), which is 6 hours ahead of U.S. Eastern Standard Time (EST +6).

Holidays

An up-to-date, online *World Holiday and Time Zone Guide* is available at www.get-customs.com. It lists official holidays by country and by day of the year, business and cultural tips, a corruption index, and time zones with worldwide business hours.

This list is a working guide. Dates should be corroborated before final travel plans are made. In cases where holidays fall on Saturday or Sunday, commercial establishments may be closed the preceding Friday or following Monday.

Jan 1	SA	New Year's Day
Apr 24	MO	Easter Monday
May 1	MO	Labor Day
May 3	WE	Constitution Day
Jun 22	TH	Corpus Christi
Aug 15	TU	Assumption
Nov 1	WE	All Saints Day
Nov 11	SA	Independence Day
Dec 25	MO	Christmas Day
Dec 26	TU	Christmas holiday

The Catholic observances of Easter, Easter Monday, Corpus Christi, and the Feast of the Assumption are all official holidays. These observances fall on different days each year. Corroborate the days of observance through local contacts.

Work Week

- The Polish work day starts early. Appointments at 8:00 A.M. are not unusual.
- Business lunches are often held quite late, around 4:00 or 5:00 P.M.
- Requests for appointments should be made in writing when possible. Translating the request into Polish will make a good impression.

- Most businesses have a 5-1/2–day work week: 8:00 or 9:00 A.M. to 3:00 or 4:00 P.M. Monday through Friday, plus 8:00 A.M. to 1:30 P.M. on Saturdays. Other businesses work one full Saturday per month.

Religious/Societal Influences on Business

Catholicism is essentially the only religion in Poland today. Only 1.5% of the population is identified as belonging to another religion, although almost 10% of Poles are nonreligious (an atheist legacy of Soviet-dominated Poland).

During centuries of foreign domination, the national aspirations of the Polish people were sublimated into the Catholic Church. The Church was the single most important influence in preventing Poland's cultural absorption by Lutheran Prussia and Orthodox Russia. For preserving their cultural identity, the Polish people owe their Church a debt they can never repay.

With Poland free and independent at last, it is not surprising that the Catholic Church should want to collect on that debt by having a say in how Poland is run. Poland is now challenging Ireland for the honor of being "the most Catholic country in the world." As in Ireland, the major friction arises over the Church's prohibition of contraception and abortion. But, unlike Ireland, Poland had abortion on demand during the decades of Soviet domination. New restrictions on abortion have been passed, but are opposed by many Polish citizens. Businesses (including medical insurers) whose products or services touch on birth-control issues should be prepared for further changes in Poland.

While capitalism has been more successful in Poland than in any other former Warsaw Pact nation, it has also created a society of haves and have-nots. While most Poles are better off than they were under Communism, some (including farmers, miners, pensioners, and teachers) are not.

Despite the fact that virtually all of Poland's Jews were exterminated by the Nazis in World War Two, anti-Semitism is still extant in Poland.

5 Cultural Tips

1. Poland and Russia are locked into a complex historical relationship that colors all cross-border interactions. In brief: Poland was a civilized and sophisticated nation when the Russian city-states were still beating off Asiatic hordes. As Russia grew in stature, Poland's fortunes sank. To many Russians, Russia only became a great Western power after it humbled the proud Poles. Many Poles consider Russia the architect of Poland's misfortunes. Interactions that involve Poles and Russians will likely involve these beliefs.

2. Poland suffered greatly in World War Two, and most of its cities were devastated. The Polish love of history is evident in the way historic districts have been restored, using old photographs and prints as guides. Poles have a reverence for their past that is without equal in Europe.

3. Polish is one of the more difficult European languages for native speakers of English. It is complex, subtle, and formal. Certain sounds in Polish—notably the soft *s*, *sh*, *cz*, and *szcz*—are particularly hard for English-speakers to master. However, learning even a few phrases in Polish will endear a foreigner to the Polish people. Polish businesspeople often speak German or English.

4. In common with other Slavic groups, Poles give the appearance of being rather dour. Smiles are reserved for friends; they are rarely used in public. (When U.S. game shows were adapted to Polish television, the biggest problem was getting the serious Polish contestants to look happy and excited on camera!)

5. Poland is still a male-dominated society. Despite the equality of the sexes mandated under Soviet domination, traditional attitudes about women remain. International businesswomen report that Poland is one of the more difficult places in Europe to be taken seriously. Businesswomen must also deal with the prospect of socializing with Polish businessmen—a process that invariably includes large quantities of vodka.

Economic Overview

Opportunities for trade and investment exist across virtually all industrial and consumer sectors in Poland. U.S. firms lead investment in Poland, accounting for approximately one-third of all foreign investment. The prospect for real economic growth, the size of the Polish market, and political stability are the top reasons U.S. firms should consider the Polish market.

The U.S. Department of Commerce has designated Poland as one of the top 10 "Big Emerging Markets" in the world for U.S. exports.

Nineteen ninety-eight marked the seventh year in a row that the Polish economy experienced solid growth. A growth rate of 4–5% is expected throughout the year 2000. Other economic indicators, including balance of payments and unemployment, continue to improve.

Poland's economy has grown despite its government changing seven times in the past eight years. Although the successive post-communist governments have contributed greatly to Poland's economic recovery with their devotion to sound fiscal and monetary policies, frequent political changes limit consistency and momentum.

U.S. exports are faced with significantly higher customs duties than competitors from the European Union. This can also affect investors, as it adds costs to imported capital goods used in production.

4 Largest Businesses in Poland:

Lasy Panstwowe Gospodarstwo Lesne, Warsaw
   96,000 employees
Telekomunikacja Polska S.A., Warsaw
   72,500 employees

Nadwislanska Spolka Węglowa S.A., Tychy
  50,500 employees
Polskie Gornictwo Naftowe i Gazownictwo, Warsaw
  43,673 employees

Cultural Note: Although Polish businesspeople are anxious to modernize, they are still struggling with the legacy of a state-controlled economy. The decision-making process can be agonizingly slow. While Polish businesses are hierarchical, a consensus is nevertheless sought from all interested parties. Delays in the negotiating process may be caused by this need to achieve a consensus. Despite this, Poland has the highest economic growth of all the former Warsaw Pact nations.

Comparative Data

Comparative Data Ratings
(Scale: 5 = Highest; 1 = Lowest)
Poland: 3.0

  A. GDP Growth: 4
  B. Per Capita Income: 2
  C. Trade Flows with the U.S.A.: 2
  D. Country Risk: 3
  E. Monetary Policy: 3
  F: Trade Policy: 3
      • Tariffs
      • Import Licensing
      • Import Taxes
  G. Protection of Property Rights: 3
  H. Foreign Investment Climate: 4

GROSS DOMESTIC PRODUCT: $263 billion (1998 estimate)

GDP GROWTH: 4.0% (1999 estimate); 3.7% (2000 forecast)

PER CAPITA INCOME: $6,800 (1998 estimate)

Trade Flows with the U.S.

U.S. EXPORTS TO POLAND: $882 million (1998)

U.S. IMPORTS FROM POLAND: $783 million (1998)

TOP U.S. EXPORTS TO POLAND: Computers and peripherals; machinery; electronic components; computer software; motor vehicles; pollution-control equipment; medical and optical equipment; plastics; pharmaceuticals

TOP U.S. PROSPECTS FOR EXPORT TO POLAND: Computer software; computers and peripherals; electrical power machinery and equipment; construction materials and equipment; plastics in primary forms; automobile parts and accessories; pollution-control equipment; food-processing equipment; broadcasting; telecommunications

Country Risk

Dun & Bradstreet considers Poland to have sufficient capacity to meet outstanding payment liabilities. More than 75% of sales are now on open account terms, according to Dun & Bradstreet, with sight drafts widely used and cash-in-advance becoming less popular. Letters of credit are now used in approximately 10% of transactions, but are still recommended when dealing with new accounts. Usual terms are 60–90 days.

Monetary Policy

Poland's government won support from the international community in recognition of its commitment to disciplined financial policies. One important negative factor is inflation, which hovered around 30% annually in the mid 1990s. Inflation fell to 18.5% in 1996 and was estimated at just 13.0% in 1997. Inflation is expected to remain between 8% and 10% through the year 2000.

MONETARY UNIT: zloty

Trade Policy

TARIFFS   Tariff rates are subject to frequent change as Poland adjusts to becoming a market economy. Customs duties apply to all products imported into Poland. Tariffs range from zero to 45%, with the average rate being about 5%.

Refund of duty paid on raw materials, semi-finished goods, and products used in the manufacture of goods for export within 30 days are possible, contingent on documentation certifying customs duty was paid on the goods when they were imported.

Many categories of U.S. products face tariff disadvantages compared with European competitors.

IMPORT LICENSING   There are few formal trade barriers—that is, import quotas or import bans—in Poland. In some areas, including imports of strategic goods (such as police and military products, radioactive elements, weapons, transportation equipment, chemicals), a license or concession is required. Imports of beer and wine, gas, and certain agricultural and food products are also licensed.

Certain goods are subject to import quotas. These include gasoline, diesel fuel and heating oils; wine and other alcohol; and cigars and cigarettes.

Imports of all live plants require a phytosanitary import permit.

The list of products requiring import certification in Poland is always subject to change and appears to be growing. There are lengthy testing procedures required for import permits of certain products. U.S. exporters should ascertain whether their product requires import certification before shipping.

IMPORT TAXES   For some luxury and strategic products (including alcohol, cosmetics, cigarettes, sugar confectionery, video cameras, satellite antennas, cars, gasoline, and oil), excise tax is applied.

A value-added tax (VAT) is also assessed. There are three VAT rates: 0%, 7%, and 22% depending on the product.

Protection of Intellectual Property Rights

Poland is a party to various intellectual property conventions, including the Berne Convention, the Universal Copyright Convention, the Madrid Protocol, and the Paris Convention on Protection of Industrial Property. Poland has also entered into a number of bilateral Intellectual Property (IP) treaties. While the Polish IP laws are fairly comprehensive, enforcement remains a problem. In particular, piracy of sound recording is reported to be widespread.

Presentable inventions must be novel, unobvious, and useful. Computer programs are not patentable. Priority rights result on filing. Patents have terms of 20 years from filing. Patent assignments or licenses must be in writing. Design patents may be obtained for 5 or 10 years.

Trademarks may be visual or sonic and service marks are recognized. The first trademark applicant is entitled to registration. Trademark terms are for 10 years. Use is required for renewal. Unrelated parties cannot register an expired mark until 3 years have passed. Nonuse for 3 years will subject a mark to cancellation. Petitions may be filed to cancel registrations that infringe a well-known mark.

Copyrights result automatically when a protected work is created. Two types of copyright proprietorship are recognized: personal and proprietary. *Personal rights* include the right to publish first and may exist for an unlimited period of time. *Proprietary copyrights* are good for the life of the author plus 50 years.

Foreign Investment Climate

The Foreign Investment Act of 1991, and subsequent amendments to the Act, opened the Polish economy to foreign investment and established a level playing field between foreign and domestic investors. Under the law, any level of foreign ownership—up to 100%—is allowed. There is no screening of foreign investments.

Polish privatization efforts have been open to foreign investors and most of the largest transactions have involved sales to foreign firms.

The sale of land in former Communist countries (where most property was owned by the state) remains a contentious issue. This is especially true in Poland, where borders (and subsequent ownership of land) have often been shifted by Poland's conquerors and the majority of farms remained under the control of the peasants. While some land has been sold to foreigners, in 1999 the Polish government prohibited the sale of Polish farmland to foreigners for 18 years. If Poland intends to join the EU, this law may have to be amended.

Political Leaders, Parties, and International Organizations

The International Academy at Santa Barbara at http://www.iasb.org/cwl publishes *Current World Leaders*, an excellent resource for up-to-date data on political leaders, parties, demographics, etc., in Poland. Tel: (800) 530-2682 or (805) 965-5010 for subscription information to their database.

Chief of State:

President Aleksander Kwasniewski

Head of the Government:

Prime Minister Jerzy Buzek

Next Election:

November 2000

Political Parties:

Social Democratic Party, Polish Peasant Party (PSL), Democratic Union Party, Labor Union, Confederation for an Independent Poland, Union for Freedom, Solidarity, Non-partisan Bloc in Support of Reform, Christian National Union, Center Alliance, and several others

Membership in international organizations:

CBSS, CE, EBRD, Intl. Council for the Exploration of the Sea (ICES), Intl. Hydrographic Organization (IHO), IPU, ITC, NACC, OSCE, UN and most of its specialized agencies and related organizations (including FAO, GATT, IAEA, IBRD, ICAO, IDA, IFC, ILO, IMF, IMO, ITU, UNESCO, UNIDO, UPU, WHO, WIPO, WMO), WTO

Political Influences on Business

Poland's political leaders have repeatedly given strong public encouragement to western and specifically U.S. investment. There are nevertheless domestic political factors at play that can impinge on Poland's hospitality to foreign investment. Foreign investment is supported by most of the major political parties. However, the Polish Peasant Party (PSL) contains fiercely protectionist elements that occasionally prompt hostility toward foreign investors.

Trade union politics are also an element for foreign business to consider. The Polish trade union movement, the engine of communism's collapse in the 1980s, has occasionally been problematic for foreign investors, particularly when managers of newly-privatized state enterprises have instituted management changes.

Since 1989 Poles have enjoyed largely unfettered rights to free speech, press, and assembly as well as other commonly accepted Western human rights. Poland has a bicameral parliament, comprised of a lower house (*Sejm*) and upper house (Senate). Within the legislative branch of the government, the *Sejm* has more of the power; the Senate may only suggest amendments to legislation passed by the *Sejm* or delay it. Both bodies are democratically elected. The President may dissolve the parliament and call new elections before then if the government fails a vote of confidence or is unable to pass a budget.

The Polish Prime Minister, whom the President nominates to constitute a government and win a vote of confidence in the *Sejm*, chairs the Council of Ministers and serves as Poland's chief of government. There are 18 cabinet ministers, three of whom serve as deputy prime ministers, mostly drawn from the governing coalition parties. There are several ministers without any party affiliation.

Poland's president, who serves as the country's head of state, has a five-year term. If no candidate wins an absolute majority, the top two vote-getters must compete in a run-off election. The Polish president is the commander of the armed forces and may veto legislation passed by the parliament. Presidential vetoes can be overturned by a two-thirds vote in each parliamentary house.

The most influential political parties are:

- Democratic Left Alliance (SLD): A coalition comprised mostly of successor parties to the Communist Polish United Workers Party (PZPR). The party's leadership generally supports liberal economic policies, but stresses the importance of cushioning the harsher effects of economic reform.

- Polish Peasant Party (PSL): The PSL has grown from a communist subordinated party into a classic European agrarian party.

- Union of Freedom (UW): The most popular party with origins in the Solidarity movement, the UW pursues a mainly centrist course. Its membership is a diverse mix of liberal free-market thinkers, intellectuals, social activists, feminists, and Christian nationalists.

Other parties represented in the parliament are: the Union of Labor (UP), Non-Party Bloc in Support of Reform (BBWR), the Confederation for an Independent Poland (KPN), the Polish Socialist Party (PPS), and the Polish Right, a four-member parliamentary caucus consisting of breakaways from KPN.

Provincial and local governments can play an important role in facilitating or hindering trade and investment in Poland. Since 1998 political power has been decentralized, giving local governments more control.

There are some 2 million Poles engaged in farming (full or part time). Since they represent about 27% of the population, they have considerable political clout. When imported pork (subsidized by some EU countries) undercut their prices, they staged massive protests in early 1999, setting up roadblocks throughout much of the country. The government quickly gave in to some of the farmers' demands. Disturbingly, some of the farm leaders are also vocally anti-Semitic.

Poland joined NATO in 1999, just ten days before NATO forces began bombing Serbia to halt the ethnic cleansing of Kosovo. NATO remains popular in Poland, although many Poles are feeling less positive about joining the European Union. Poland still has a lot of unpopular regulatory changes to make before it can join the EU. Poland's target date for EU membership is 2003, but many observers predict that it will not be ready until 2005 at the earliest.

Contacts in the United States

THE EMBASSY OF THE REPUBLIC OF POLAND
2640 16th Street, NW
Washington, D.C. 20009
Tel: (202) 234-3800
Fax: (202) 328-6271
www.polishworld.com/polemb/

EASTERN EUROPE BUSINESS INFORMATION CENTER
International Trade Administration
Department of Commerce
Room 7412
Washington, D.C. 20230

Passport/Visa Requirements

A passport is required. A visa is not required for stays up to 90 days, depending upon the citizenship of the visitor. Visitors must register at a hotel or with local authorities within three days after crossing the Polish border. This requirement does not apply while the visitor is in transit. There is also a requirement to report the visitor's location, to be completed within 48 hours of arrival. An AIDS test is required for student visas; U.S. test results are accepted.

Three types of passport visas are obtainable from Polish Consular officials: (1) Regular Visa (issued for business purposes, cultural–educational or scientific matters, including conferences, for visit to relatives or friends, and for tourism); (2) Transit Visa (for transiting Polish territory to another nation within 48 hours); and (3) Visa with Permit to Work (is available if a work permit issued by the proper Polish authorities is submitted).

Requirements for obtaining a visa: valid passport (validity of passport must be valid for six months longer than the validity of a visa which is usually 12 months; passport must be signed); application form in three parts (all parts completely filled in); two signed passport-size photographs attached to back of first and third copies (Sections A & C); persons going on business, cultural–educational or scientific matters, including conferences, should submit a copy of an official invitation (letter or cable) from Poland.

Businesspeople, to expedite processing of their visas, can apply for a supporting letter from the Polish Commercial Counselor's Offices in New York, NY; Washington, D.C.; or Chicago, IL. The visa fee must accompany the documents.

Those applying for a transit visa must, before submitting their passport to a Polish Consulate, already have the visa of the onward country.

Further information on entry requirements may be obtained from the Embassy of the Republic of Poland, Consular Section.

U.S. citizens who wish to apply for a passport may visit Passport Services' well-organized website at http://travel.state.gov/passport_services.html.

Contacts in Poland

THE EMBASSY OF THE UNITED STATES
AmEmbassy Warsaw
Aleje Ujazdowskie 29/31
Box 5010, Unit 1340
Mailing Address: APO AE 09213-1340
Tel: (48) (2) 628-3041
Fax: (48) (2) 628-8298
www.usaemb.pl

AMERICAN CHAMBER OF COMMERCE IN POLAND
Plac Powstancow Warszawy 1
00-950 Warsaw
Tel: (48-22) 26-39-60
Fax: (48-22) 26-51-31

DUN & BRADSTREET POLAND SP. Z.O.O.
Ul.Jana Olbrachta 94
01-102 Warszawa
Tel: (48) (0) 22.533.2400
Fax: (48) (0) 22.533.2424

OFFICE OF THE PRESIDENT
Wiejska 10
00-902 Warszawa, Republic of Poland

OFFICE OF THE PRIME MINISTER
Council of Ministers
Aleje Ujazdowskie 1/3
00-950 Warszawa, Republic of Poland

Further contacts and websites can be found in Appendix A.

Communications

TELEPHONE: The international country code for Poland is 48.

Phone numbers vary in length.

Area codes also vary in length, from one to three digits. The area code for Warsaw is 22.

Cellular telephone numbers use a prefix of 90.

E-MAIL: E-mail addresses located in Poland end with the code .pl

---

Observation: "Poles have two codes of behavior, one public and the other private. In public, they can be pushy, demanding, distant, abrupt, and rude. In private, they are warm, generous, hospitable, and loquacious. Conversations are lengthy, and goodbyes never seem to end. As the poles say, "The English leave without saying goodbye. The Poles say goodbye but do not leave.' "

—Advice from Yale Richmond's 1995 book *From Da to Yes: Understanding the East Europeans*

Russia

Official Name:	Russian Federation (Rossiyskaya Federatsiya)
Official Language:	Russian
Government System:	Multi-party federal republic
Population:	146.4 million (1998 estimate)
Population Growth Rate:	−33% (1999 estimate) (Russia's birth rate has fallen far below the level needed to maintain the population.)
Area:	17,075,400 sq. km. (6,592,800 sq. mi.); larger than the U.S.
Natural Resources:	gold, crude oil, natural gas, coal, iron ore, hydropower, timber, diamonds, bauxite, copper, nickel, lead, tin, uranium
Major Cities:	Moscow (capital), St. Petersburg, Nizhny Novgorod, Voronezh, Volgograd, Vladivostok, Ekaterinburg, Saratov

Age Breakdown

0–14 = 19.0%   15–64 = 68%   65+ = 13% (1999 estimate)
Life Expectancy: 58.8 years, male, 71.7 years, female (1999 estimate)

Time

As a foreigner, you are expected to be on time. However, your Russian counterpart may be late . . . or not show up at all. Do not expect an apology from a tardy Russian.

For social events, even foreigners are expected to be from 15 to 30 minutes late.

Holidays

A web-based *World Holiday and Time Zone Guide* is available at www.getcustoms.com with updated official holidays, cultural tips, time zones, and tables that compare world-wide business hours.

This list is a working guide. Dates should be corroborated before final travel plans are made. In cases where holidays fall on Saturday or Sunday, commercial establishments may be closed the preceding Friday or following Monday.

As Russian governments change with startling rapidity, so do holidays. A day observed as an official holiday one year may be ignored the next.

Jan 1	SA	New Year's Day
Jan 7	FR	Christmas Day
Mar 8	WE	International Women's Day
May 1	MO	Labor Day
May 2	TU	Spring Day
May 9	TU	Victory Day
Jun 12	MO	Independence Day
Nov 7	TU	Revolution Day
Dec 12	TU	Constitution Da

Work Week

- Business hours are generally from 9:00 A.M. to 5:00 P.M. Monday through Friday.
- Banks and currency exchanges are usually open from 9:00 A.M. to 5:00 P.M. Monday through Friday; recently, some opened on Saturday. Some bank branches in tourist areas are open for currency exchanges until 7:50 P.M.
- Major stores are open from 9:00 or 10:00 A.M. to 8:00 or 9:00 P.M. Monday through Saturday. Smaller shops usually close by 7:00 P.M. Most close for an hour at lunchtime (usually between 1:00 and 2:00 P.M. for food stores, and from 2:00 to 3:00 P.M. for others). Food stores are also open on Sunday.

Religious/Societal Influences on Business

Due to the constant shortages under the Communist system, Russians grew accustomed to spending hours in lines. There were lines for virtually every product or service. Customers often had to stand in one line for goods and another line to pay for their purchases. The revered Soviet-era writer Anna Akhmatova actually wrote a poem about standing in line (although she was waiting outside a KGB prison for news about her imprisoned son).

People who wait endlessly are not always prompt. Under Communism it was almost impossible to fire employees. Many Russians arrived to work late, left early, or took overlong lunch breaks (during which they stood in line); after 70 years of this, it will take awhile to change Russian attitudes.

Western attitudes toward punctuality and prompt customer service are taught now from scratch to the Russian employees of foreign-owned companies. Managers find most Russians (especially younger ones) to be receptive.

5 Cultural Tips

1. Patience is a traditional virtue among Russians. Punctuality is not. Only the trains and theater performances begin on time in Russia. Do not be surprised if your business appointment begins one or even two hours late.

2. Russians have a reputation as great "sitters" during negotiations—able to wait out their opponents. In addition to their patience, many Russians regard compromise as a sign of weakness. To them compromise is, in and of itself, morally incorrect. Many Russians would rather out-sit the other negotiator . . . and gain more concessions from the other side.

3. Be aware that "Final Offers" are *never* final during initial negotiations. Be prepared to wait. The offer will usually be made more attractive if you can hold out.

4. Get emotional. If you (or your negotiators) have not walked out of the negotiating room in high dudgeon at least twice during the negotiations, you're being too easy. Russians *expect* walkouts and dire proclamations that the deal is off. Remember how often the Soviet delegation to the United Nations walked out in a huff? They always came back, sooner or later. Play hardball; they will.

5. Very little gets done in Russia without using *blat*—which is Russian for "connections" or "influence." *Blat* involves an exchange of favors; when you do something for someone, they owe you a favor. Gifts—monetary or otherwise—are often part of this exchange.

Economic Overview

A country with 150 million people with tremendous natural and human resources is not a market that U.S. business can afford to neglect for long. Demand exists in Russia across the board, from consumer goods to capital equipment. Foreign-made products are now common in Russia today—a sharp contrast to just a few years ago.

The Russian Federation is currently a country in economic, political, and social transition. Uncertainty, risk, and great opportunity characterize the commercial environment in Russia today. Doing business in Russia is not for the timid, but for the bold.

Russian firms and customers admire U.S. technology and know-how and generally want to do business with U.S. companies. There are few products or services that are not in demand in Russia. Numerous U.S. consumer goods manufacturers have already made Russia a major expansion market for their companies. In fact, consumer products is the second largest foreign investment sector in Russia, trailing only gas and oil exploration. The United States is the largest foreign investor in Russia with more than 850 establishments in Russia.

Russia's middle class is estimated at 20% of the total population. Conversely, one in every three Russians claims he has difficulty getting by on his income. The Russian economy has been up and down since 1991, with high fluctuations in inflation and the value of the ruble. The private sector now accounts for a 55–60% share of Russia's GDP.

The rise in violent organized crime—called "Mafia" in Russia—has become a problem for foreign, as well as Russian, businesses.

3 Largest Businesses in Russia

Gorki Automobile Plant Public Joint Stock Company, Nizhniy Novgorod
    97,100 employees
Lukoil Oil Company Public Joint Stock Company, Moscow
    95,000 employees
Concern Kamaz Public Joint Stock Company, Naberezhnyiye Chelny
    87,942 employees

Cultural Note: Don't overlook how large Russia is when you travel. (It's easy to forget after dealing with other European countries, most of which can be driven across in a day.) But the Russian Federation is so huge that it spans 11 time zones! Also, most of Russia's transportation systems are far below Western European standards, making transport even more time-consuming.

Comparative Data

Comparative Data Ratings
(Scale: 5 = Highest; 1 = Lowest)
Russia: 1.75

   A. GDP Growth: 1
   B. Per Capita Income: 2
   C. Trade Flows with the U.S.: 2
   D. Country Risk: 1
   E. Monetary Policy: 1
   F. Trade Policy: 2
       • Tariffs
       • Import Licensing
       • Import Taxes

G. Protection of Property Rights: 2

H. Foreign Investment Climate: 3

GROSS DOMESTIC PRODUCT: $593.4 billion (1998 estimate)

GDP GROWTH: –1% (1999 estimate); 1.5% (2000 forecast)

PER CAPITA INCOME: $4,000 (1998 estimate)

Trade Flows with the U.S.

U.S. EXPORTS TO RUSSIA: $3.5 billion (1998 estimate)

U.S. IMPORTS FROM RUSSIA: $5.7 billion (1998 estimate)

TOP U.S. EXPORTS TO RUSSIA: Telecommunications; computers and peripherals; pollution-control equipment; oil and gas machinery; building products; medical equipment; electric power systems equipment; consumer goods; food processing and packaging; forestry and woodworking equipment

TOP U.S. PROSPECTS FOR EXPORT TO RUSSIA: Oil and gas equipment; mining equipment; construction equipment; computers and software; medical equipment; telecommunications equipment; aircraft and airport equipment; cosmetics; food-processing and packaging equipment; chemicals; pharmaceuticals

Country Risk

Western businesses often request cash-in-advance terms when doing business with Russia. Dun & Bradstreet estimates that pre-payment terms are requested in 75% of business transactions.

When cash-in-advance is not an option, Dun & Bradstreet recommends using an irrevocable letter of credit. Open account terms should be reserved for only strong business relationships.

The payments climate remains poor in Russia with some remittances sometimes taking in excess of six months.

Monetary Policy

Russia has done a sporadic job of reducing the astronomical level of inflation. Inflation reached as high as 850% in 1993. By 1997 inflation was brought under control, falling to just 11%. But poor monetary policies caused inflation to rise to 84.4% in 1998. Each new Prime Minister seems to implement his own financial program—often with disastrous results.

U.S. currency is currently prized in Russia, more so than any other foreign currency. The US$100 bill is widely hoarded. Due to fears of counterfeiting, many Russians will accept only new, pristine bills. Even a faint bank stamp may cause Russians to reject a bill.

MONETARY UNIT: ruble

Trade Policy

TARIFFS Russia's tariffs range from 5–30%, with the average tariff 12.5%, up significantly from the 7–8% level in 1994.

IMPORT LICENSING Russia employs a liberal import licensing regime, generally free from quotas and licenses. Licenses are required for imports of medicines and chemical raw materials used for production of medicines, pesticides, and industrial waste.

Centralized importing has virtually been eliminated since most government-controlled firms have been privatized.

Many imports are subject to arbitrary certification requirements. However, Russia is establishing reciprocal standardization procedures with the U.S. and is reciprocally accepting foreign certification by accredited institutions.

IMPORT TAXES Taxes are continually in flux and are often applied not just to profits but also to revenue, making business operations at times uneconomical. Because taxes are so high and arbitrary, tax evasion is widespread.

Russia imposes a 10% value-added tax (VAT) and excise taxes range from 20–570% on alcohol, tobacco, automobiles, and some luxury goods.

Protection of Intellectual Property Rights

Russia assumed the Soviet Union's obligations under the Paris Convention for Protection of Industrial Property. Since 1991 Russia has entered into numerous Intellectual Property (IP) conventions and protocols. Russia belongs to the Berne Convention, the Universal Copyright Convention, and the Convention for Protection of Producers of Phonograms. Russia was an original signer of the Trademark Law Treaty.

Although Russia continues to take steps to enhance IP rights, because of its lack of experience in private ownership, enforcement mechanisms are nonexistent or ineffective. Russia remains on a special U.S. trade watch list and extensive piracy continues to take place for videos, movies, sound recordings, books, and software.

Inventions, utility models, and designs are patentable if they are novel, inventive, and have industrial application. Patents are valid for 20 years from application, utility models for 5–8 years, and designs for 10–15 years. Patent applications must be filed and enforced through a patent agent registered with the government Patent Agency.

Russia follows the international classification system for trademarks. Marks must be registered for terms of 10 years. Filings are made through the government Patent Agency. Trademark violations are both civil and criminal. Trademarks are only beginning to have importance in Russia as the private market system develops.

Copyrights extend for the life of the author plus 50 years and result on creation. Works are protected whether published or unpublished. Protection extends to computer programs, databases, and integrated circuits. The new laws and conventions notwithstanding, copyright piracy is a flourishing business in Russia.

Foreign Investment Climate

Few legal restrictions exist on foreign investment. The 1991 Investment Code guarantees foreign investors the same rights as those of Russian investors. Foreigners are not allowed to own land, but can take majority ownership in enterprises that own land. There are no restrictions on profit repatriation.

Joint venture agreements should include a clause requiring partners to submit to arbitration in a neutral country when they can't come to an agreement. Sweden is currently the most popular choice for third-country arbitration.

The absence of sufficiently developed civil, commercial, and criminal codes is a major constraint.

Political Leaders, Parties, and International Organizations

The International Academy at Santa Barbara at http://www.iasb.org/cwl publishes *Current World Leaders*, an excellent resource for up-to-date data on political leaders, parties, demographics, etc., in Russia. Tel: (800) 530-2682 or (805) 965-5010 for subscription information to their database.

President:

President Vladimir Vladimirovich Putin

Next election:

June 2004

Political Parties:

Liberal Democratic Party, Democratic Party of Russia, Russia's Choice, Communist Party of the Russian Federation, Agrarian Party, Russian Movement of Democratic Reforms, Party of Russian Unity and Accord, Yavlinsky–Boldyrev–Lukin Bloc, Women of Russia Party, Future of Russia Party, Constructive Ecology Movement of Russia, Dignity and Charity Party

Membership in international organizations:

CBSS, CIS, EBRD, INTELSAT, NACC, OSCE, UN and most of its specialized agencies and related organizations (including IBRD, IMF, UNESCO, WHO)

Political Influences on Business

With the end of the Cold War and the reemergence of a Russian State, U.S. relations with Moscow have evolved rapidly over the last few years. At meetings in Vancouver, Tokyo, and Moscow, Presidents Clinton and Yeltsin laid the basis for a U.S.–Russian partnership. Great strides have been made in a number of important fields, particularly arms control. While disagreements persist on individual issues, the U.S. and Russia now consult closely on major issues of mutual and international interest.

The United States firmly supports Russia's development into a democratic/market society, and Russia's further integration into the international community. The U.S. has made available substantial bilateral assistance—and has led international aid efforts. The U.S. has also taken steps to clear from the books Cold War-era legislation limiting contacts with Russia.

One of the most pressing issues that defines the business climate in Russia is the lack of legislation in most areas of economic activity. This is due primarily to the fact that there is no political consensus in the State Duma and the Government on how business activities should be regulated, whether private business should be promoted, and the role of foreign investment in Russian society. Not only does this make taxation and business regulation an unpredictable prospect at best, but there is no judicial basis for resolution of disputes between individuals and/or companies. In the absence of legislation, many government decisions affecting business have been taken by executive fiat—diminishing the prospects for their legitimacy and effectiveness, and often leading to inconsistent policy.

Russia has a bicameral legislative system. The Upper House is called the Federation Council and consists of two representatives from each subject of the Russian Federation. The Federation Council passes decrees on federation disputes and reviews legislation passed by the Lower House, including the federal budget. The Lower House, or State Duma, is made up of 450 deputies, one-half selected on the basis of geographic districts and one-half on the basis of party lists. The Duma passes most federal laws. Duma members are elected to four-year terms (after an initial two-year term that began in 1994).

There are over 20 parties and fractions represented in the Parliament. In addition to the fractiousness of the Russian Parliament, instability has been caused by Russia's merry-go-round of Prime Ministers. Former President Yeltsin appointed and fired no less than five Prime Ministers within 17 months. It is yet to be determined if the new President will have a more stabilizing effect on the economy and the Russian people.

Faux Pas: The Russian word *nyekulturny* (literally, "uncultured" or "bad mannered") signifies the wrong way to do something. Foreigners are often judged by the same standards Russians apply to themselves. Some *nyekulturny* behaviors are:

- Wearing your coat (and heavy boots) when you enter a public building—particularly the theater! You are expected to leave your coat in the *garderob* (cloakroom). One does NOT sit on one's coat at a concert or restaurant. Stadiums and cinemas generally do not have a *garderob,* but many office buildings do. HINT: To avoid the after-show waiting line at the theater, rent some opera glasses. Persons returning opera glasses to the *garderob* go to the front of the line.

- Entering a row of seats at the theater, cinema, or arena while facing the stage (which is standard behavior in the U.S.). It is impolite to squeeze past seated people with your back side to them.
- Standing with your hands in your pockets.
- Speaking or laughing loudly in public—Russians are generally reserved and somber.
- Not only is whistling indoors considered *nyekulturny,* but there is a superstition that it will cause a loss of money.

Contacts in the United States

THE EMBASSY OF THE RUSSIAN FEDERATION
250 Wisconsin Avenue., NW
Washington, D.C. 20007
Tel: (202) 628-7551
Fax: (202) 298-5735
www.russianembassy.org

Passport/Visa Requirements

A passport and visa are required. U.S. citizens may apply for the following visas: tourist, business, or a visitor or homestay visa (for a private visit to friends or relatives).

Different procedures must be complied with in order to register different kinds of documents in the Consular Division. All documents must be:

1. Acknowledged before a Notary Public.
2. Certified by the Central Authority in the traveler's state capable of issuing the Hague Convention APOSTILLE on documents intended for use in another convention country.
3. Registered by Consular Division of the Russian Embassy. There is a Consular fee for registration for each document. Only money orders payable to the Embassy of the Russian Federation are accepted.

All documents must be accompanied by a professional translation into Russian language, also notarized by a Notary Public. The translation must be properly attached to the original document. Documents and translations must be printed.

FOR ALL VISAS: After receiving the visa, check it for mistakes and, if necessary, return it to the Consulate for corrections. The Consulate will not be responsible for any mistakes in the visas that were not brought to its attention before departure from the U.S. If extending the validity of a business or tourist visa, obtain a new invitation or confirmation from the same organization mentioned on the visa, and submit it with the visa to the Consulate. There will be a charge for visa extensions, changes, and corrections if applicable. Return the original visa, money order, and information about the intended changes to the Consulate.

For the purposes of this book, we will cover requirements for a Business Visa. (Data for other visas can be obtained through the Embassy.)

BUSINESS VISA: The following paperwork must be submitted to the Embassy of the Russian Federation, Consular Division.

1. Completed visa application form (one per person) obtainable from the Consulate or from Travel Agencies and Visa Services.

2. A copy of the pages of the passport or any other travel document that contain personal data of the bearer. Diplomatic passport holders should submit original passport.

3. Three professional identical passport-size pictures of the applicant. Diplomatic passport holders on official business should submit only one picture. Pictures may be black-and-white or color, preferably on mat paper.

4. A letter of invitation from traveler's Russian counterpart, *not* from the representative of a foreign company there. The inviting organization must be duly registered in Russia and not a 100% foreign investment company. Traveler's name and the name of the inviting organization must be clearly shown on the invitation, as well as the dates of the visit and itinerary. If visiting representation of a foreign company, 100% foreign investment company, or a guest of an Embassy, the host should secure invitation through the Ministry of Foreign Affairs of the Russian Federation.

5. Cover letter from traveler's company or from the traveler, if travelling individually, explaining who is going, where, when, and for what purpose.

6. If applying by mail, attach return envelope or prepaid airbill of the mail chosen to return the visa. If this is not included, visa will be returned by regular mail. If applying personally or through a courier service, secure a pick-up slip from the visa officer.

7. Money order or company check, made out to Russian Embassy, for visa processing. Cash or personal checks are not accepted. A $20.00 fee is charged for bounced checks. There is a visa processing fee. As of this writing it is $20.00 for not less than two weeks' processing; $30.00 for not less than one week processing; $60.00 for not less than four days' processing; $100.00 for one to four days' processing; $120.00 for multi-entry visa processing (for business visas only).

Multi-entry visas can be issued within three working days only on authorization of the Ministry of Foreign Affairs of Russia.

The Consulate reserves the right not to issue next-day visas if it is not urged by the date of entry into Russia.

When applying by mail, add one day to the visa processing time.

Visas are processed by computer; one must follow a special pattern presentation. The copy of the passport page should be trimmed to the size of the original and stapled to the upper-left corner of the application form. Two pictures should be stapled to the copy of the passport page and one to the specially marked place at the upper-right corner of the application form. Paperwork not submitted in this manner will not be accepted.

U.S. citizens who wish to apply for a passport may visit Passport Services' well-organized website at http://travel.state.gov/passport_services.html.

Contacts in Russia

THE U.S. EMBASSY
Novinskiy Bulvar
19/23
Moscow
Mailing Address: APO AE 09721
Tel: (7) (095) 252-2451
Fax: (7) (095) 956-4261
Telex: 413160 USGSO SU
www.usia.gov/posts/moscow.html

AMERICAN CHAMBER OF COMMERCE IN RUSSIA
Kosmodamianskaya Nab., 52, Str.1, 8th floor
(Riverside Towers)
113054 Moscow
Tel: (7) (095) 961-2141
Fax: (7) (095) 961-2142
www.amcham.ru

DUN & BRADSTREET CIS
Postal Address: 3D Khoreshevski Proezd, Building 1/1, 4th Floor, 126007 Moscow
Street Address: same
Tel: (7) (095) 940-1816
Fax: (7) (095) 940-1702; (7) (095) 940-1708

OFFICE OF THE PRESIDENT
Government Offices
Moscow, Russian Federation

Further contacts and websites can be found in Appendix A.

Communications

TELEPHONE: The international country code for Russia is 7.

Phone numbers vary in length. They are usually six or seven digits in length.

Area codes also vary in length. Codes for major cities are three digits. Note that many city codes begin with 0. The area code for Moscow, for example, is 095.

E-MAIL: E-mail addresses located in Russia end with the code .ru

Faux Pas: Advertising in Russia can be a challenge to Western companies. While Russians have become familiar with advertising since the end of the Communist era, their cultural norms can make them react in unexpected ways. For example, when Camel cigarettes ran a television ad campaign, it showed a rugged, handsome man parachuting, canoeing, and driving a Jeep through the underbrush. The ads were meant to associate Camel cigarettes with an adventurous lifestyle. However, these activities are so alien to the average Russian citizen that they filled viewers with scorn. Russians viewed the man as an idiot for voluntarily engaging in such life-threatening activities. So why would anyone want to smoke a brand of cigarette endorsed by a fool?

Russian Names and Titles

- Russian names are listed in the same order as in the west, but the Russian middle name is a patronymic (a name derived from the first name of one's father). Thus, Fyodor Ivanovich Kuznetsov's first name is Fyodor (a Russian version of Theodore), his last name is Kuznetsov, and his middle name means "son of Ivan."

- Russian women add the letter "a" on the end of their surnames; Kuznetsov's wife would be Mrs. Kuznetsova. A woman's patronymic is also different, ending in "a." "Daughter of Ivan" would be "Ivanova," not "Ivanovich."

- Do not use first names until you are invited to do so. If a Russian has a professional title, use the title followed by the surname. If he or she does not have a title, just use Mr., Miss, Mrs., or Ms., plus the surname.

- Among themselves, Russians use a bewildering variety of diminutives and nicknames. First names and patronymics are also common in somewhat more formal situations (like Fyodor Ivanovich, from the previous example). This can be quite a mouthful. As you establish your relationship, you will be invited to use these. At that point, tell them your first name.

- Despite the length of their names, there are relatively few variations of first names and surnames in Russia. In fact, some names (e.g., Ivan, Ivanovich, Ivanov) are so common that additional information is needed to identify the correct person. In official circles, Russians use a person's birth date to differentiate between identically named persons.

Saudi Arabia*

Official Name:	Kingdom of Saudi Arabia (al Mamlakah al-`Arabīyah as-Sa`ūdīyah)
Official Language:	Arabic
Government System:	Monarchy with council of ministers and consultative council
Population:	21.5 million (1999 estimate)
Population Growth Rate:	3.39% (1999 estimate) (Many residents of Saudi Arabia are not—and cannot, by law, become—Saudi citizens. This figure relates to Saudi citizens only.)
Area:	2,248,000 sq. km. (868,000 sq. mi.); about one-fourth the size of the continental U.S.
Natural Resources:	petroleum, natural gas, iron ore, coal, copper
Major Cities:	Riyadh (capital), Jeddah, Makkah (Mecca), Madinah (Medina), Taif, Dammam, Tabuk

---

* What's wrong with this picture? Alone among the 40 national flags in this book, the above flag is *not* depicted with the name of the country emblazoned upon it. This is because Arabic script on the flag of Saudi Arabia incorporates the name of Allah. The name of Allah is considered sacrosanct by many Muslims; to obscure or trivialize it is considered blasphemy. Nor should the name of Allah be placed into contact with the foot (a part of the body considered unclean). Yet every time Saudi Arabia's soccer team is a finalist in the World Cup, someone manufacturers a soccer ball decorated with the flags of all participating nations—prompting protests from Saudi officials and observant Muslims.

Cultural Note: Westerners seem to have a particularly difficult time adapting to Saudi customs and traditions. Expats recommend these techniques: Learn the rules before you go to Saudi Arabia, follow them as best you can, and resign yourself to the fact that you aren't going to change the Saudis. Also remember that foreigners are fully subject to the draconian Saudi legal system. A Westerner caught with a prohibited substance (such as alcohol or pornography) can expect imprisonment and deportation.

Age Breakdown:

0–14 = 43%   15–64 = 54%   65+ = 3% (1999 estimate)
Life Expectancy: 68.67 years, male; 72.53 years, female (1999 estimate)

Time

As a foreigner, you are expected to be on time to all business appointments. However, Saudis view time very differently from Westerners. Saudis are not generally concerned with the clock, and they may or may not choose to be prompt. Often they will be very tardy; your appointment may start one or two hours after it was scheduled.

Muslims pray five times per day, which provides convenient ways of dividing the daylight hours. Saudis may make an appointment referring to a prayertime (i.e., "after the noon prayer"), even though this does not specify an exact time.

Saudi Arabia is 3 hours ahead of Greenwich Mean Time (GMT +3), which is 8 hours ahead of U.S. Eastern Standard Time (EST +8)

Holidays

An up-to-date, web-based *World Holiday and Time Zone Guide* is available at www.getcustoms.com. It lists official holidays by country and by day of the year, cultural tips, a corruption index, and time zones with worldwide business hours.

Jan 8	SA	Eid Al-Fitr
Mar 16	TH	Eid Al-Adha
Apr 6	TH	Islamic New Year
Apr 15	SA	Ashoura
Jun 15	TH	Birth of the Prophet
Sep 23	SA	Saudi National Day
Oct 26	TH	Ascension of the Prophet
Dec 28	TH	Eid Al-Fitr

- The dates for many Arabic holidays do not fall on the same day in the Western (Gregorian) calendar each year. This may be because Arabic holidays are dated using a calendar that does not correspond to the Western calendar (for example, the Arabic [Hijrah] calendar is only 354 days long). Or it may happen because the date of the holiday is computed from a variable occurrence, such as sightings of the phases of the moon.

- In cases where holidays fall on Saturday or Sunday, commercial establishments may be closed the preceding Friday or following Monday. Also remember that, in the Muslim world, the Sabbath is celebrated on Friday. Many Islamic nations have their "weekend" on Thursday and Friday, with Saturday as the start of the work week.

- No business is conducted on Friday, which is the Muslim holy day. Government employees (who make up a large proportion of the Saudi workforce) work Saturday through Wednesday. Banks and businesses are also open Saturday through Wednesday, but may also be open for a half-day on Thursday.

- Remember that the Islamic calendar uses Lunar Months of 28 days; an Islamic year of 12 months is 354 days long. Paperwork should carry two dates: the Gregorian (Western) date and the Hijrah (Arabic) date.

These are the three most important Islamic holidays in Saudi Arabia:

1. *Ramadan*, the Holy Month of Fasting. During Ramadan observers fast from dawn until dusk. Dusk is announced by a cannon shot. The faithful are awakened before sunrise by drummers who roam the streets, reminding them to eat before dawn. It is impolite for nonbelievers to eat, drink, or even smoke in the presence of those who are fasting; be discreet. Office hours may be curtailed. Efficiency tends to suffer during Ramadan.

   Business travel to the Kingdom during the holy month of Ramadan is best avoided. Office hours are shortened and shifted to the evening, and people may be affected by the fasting and customary late-night social gatherings. Hotels offer special daytime food services for their non-Muslim guests.

2. *Eid Al-Fitr*, the Festival of Breaking Fast. Also written in English as 'Aid-al-Fitr and Eid al Fitr, this festival occurs at the end of the holy month of Ramadan. During this period, children may go door to door asking for sweets; adult Muslims visit and exchange greeting cards. This is a three-day festival in many Muslim countries. It may last for ten full days in Saudi Arabia. The first and final days of the festival are the most important. Some businesses may be closed for the entire length of the festival.

3. *Eid Al-Adha*, the Feast of the Sacrifice. Also written in English as 'Aid-al-Adha and Eid al Adha, this holiday celebrates the traditional story of Abraham's near-sacrifice of his son Isaac. This is the most important religious and secular holiday of the Islamic year. Many businesses close for at least a week. Pilgrims from around the world come to the Holy City of Makkah (Mecca) at this time to perform their Hajj. Resorts and transportation will be booked solid during this festival.

Government entities observe these holidays assiduously and are generally closed for longer periods than the above dates.

There is also one civil holiday in Saudi Arabia—*Saudi National Day*—which commemorates the unification of the Kingdom. This holiday is celebrated each year on September 23. Almost all businesses and government offices remain open, with the notable exception of Saudi Aramco.

Work Week

- Saudi officials are prohibited by tradition from working more than six hours per day. Mornings are usually best for appointments.
- Friday is the Muslim holy day; no business is conducted. Most people do not work on Thursday, either. The work week runs from Saturday through Wednesday.
- Government hours are 7:30 A.M. to 2:30 P.M. Saturday through Wednesday.
- Banking hours tend to be 8:30 A.M. to 12 noon and 5:00 P.M. to 7:00 P.M. Saturday through Wednesday. Some banks keep Thursday morning hours as well.
- Business hours vary widely, but most close for much of the afternoon and reopen for a few hours in late afternoon.
- Because of the summer heat, some Saudi businesspeople work after dark. They may request an evening appointment at any time up to midnight.

Religious/Societal Influences on Business

Saudi Arabia is the home and point of origin for Islam, which is the country's official religion. The Saudi branch of Islam is a Sunni fundamentalist variant called *Wahabi* Islam. (There are a small number of Shiite Muslims.)

Wahabi Islam is even stricter and more fundamentalist than the Shiite Islam practiced in Iran. It is enforced in public by the religious police, the *Matawain*. They claim the right to enforce their religious precepts on everyone, including foreigners. Westerners who dress immodestly (by *Wahabi* standards) have often felt the sting of the *Matawain*'s camel-tail whips.

Saudi Arabia has changed enormously since World War Two. The majority of its inhabitants went from a near-medieval existence to a modern technological society. It is useful to remember that Saudi values and traditions are still those of a nontechnological society. For example, the renowned Saudi hospitality was vital in nomadic Bedouin society; travelers in the desert would die unless offered food and water by every household. No matter how many generations separate a town-dwelling Saudi from the nomadic life, he still considers himself a Bedouin at heart.

Bedouins are divided into tribes. Even today, a Saudi's loyalty belongs first to the family, then to the tribe, and only then to the State. If a Saudi is considering competing business offers, one from a foreigner and the other from a fellow tribe member, the Saudi will generally chose the latter—even if the deal is less advantageous.

The Saudi King is both head of state and chief of the government. The Kingdom of Saudi Arabia is very much a creation of the House of Saud. Tribal and religious differences still exist, and unity is provided only by allegiance to the King.

In some ways Saudi Arabia can be considered the ultimate male-dominated society. Women in Saudi Arabia do not have the right to interact with men (except relatives), drive a car, work outside the home except in a few occupations, and wear revealing or tight-fitting outfits.

Patience is the most important attribute for conducting business in Saudi Arabia. It takes a while for Saudis to get to know you, and a Saudi must like you before he will do business with you. At the beginning of their oil boom, Saudis were often duped by unscrupulous Westerners, so they are all the more determined to judge you before doing business.

5 Cultural Tips

1. Saudis speak at much closer quarters than do North Americans. Foreigners have sometimes claimed that a Saudi doesn't feel close enough until he (she) can feel your breath on his (her) face. This is only a slight exaggeration. Saudis feel uncomfortable being far away from others, even if they are among strangers. For example, in an empty elevator, a Saudi may elect to stand next to you rather than in an opposite corner (as a Westerner would). Eye contact is intense and constant (unlike the intermittent eye contact of North Americans).

2. Learning to decipher Saudi hyperbole is a major challenge for foreigners. This includes the pleasant *yes* which really means *maybe* or even *probably not*. It also is encountered when guests wish to leave but the host insists that they stay (generally, stay a few extra minutes, then leave).

3. Saudis generally keep their private life off-limits to foreigners. For example, a Saudi man might never mention his wife. On the other hand, many things Westerners would keep private are entirely public in Saudi Arabia. Business often falls in this category. A salesperson will be asked to give a pitch in a room full of extraneous people, including family members, friends, and unidentified strangers. Some of these people will pay attention; some will not. Be aware that the true decision-maker may not be your host—it may be an old man sitting quietly, observing you but never speaking. Information that would be confidential or proprietary in the West may be discussed among a Saudi's entire circle of friends.

4. Be prepared to remove your shoes before entering a Saudi home. (This may or may not be done at an office.) When ushered into a Saudi's office or home, expect to greet everyone of your sex in the room, while any persons of the opposite sex will probably be ignored.

5. Saudis usually greet foreigners with a brief but firm hand-clasp; there is no actual *shaking* of the hands. Sit where and when your host indicates, and stay there even when your host goes to talk to others. An office will have chairs to sit on, but in a home you may be sitting on the floor (there may be a cushion to sit on or simply

a low armrest called a *masnad*). Do not wander around, looking at the decorations. (Nor should you express your admiration for any object; your host may feel obliged to give it to you.) As you sit, be sure you do not expose the soles of your feet to any person—this is highly insulting. If your host stands when someone new enters the room, you should stand as well.

Observation: " 'I bring you a Koran, Missus,' says Manal, a Palestinian (one of the students). Then the girls quickly confer among themselves in Arabic.

" 'What are you saying? Say it in English,' I ask. It's my mantra with them.

"They look at me, reluctant to speak. 'Missus,' Jamila finally says, 'you must wash before reading the Koran. You must wash all body.'

"Even the most flighty-seeming girls are devout in word and in practice. Every college toilet stall is material evidence; all are equipped with spray hoses so that the faithful may wash private parts and feet before prayer. And every day the restrooms are flooded. We Western teachers, unaccustomed to our long skirts, curse to each other as we slosh through the wet restrooms."

—From "Bashfulness Is Required in the Kingdom," Christine Japely's memoir of teaching English at a women's college in Saudi Arabia

---

Economic Overview

The Saudi economy is the largest in the Near East–North Africa region. However, Saudi Arabia's economic health is inextricably linked to the price of oil. Oil revenues provide close to 75% of the revenues of the Saudi government.

After years of deficits, robust oil revenues in 1996 helped Saudi Arabia post a slight positive gain. Increased oil production in 1997 offset the effect of falling oil prices, marking the second consecutive year in which the Saudi GDP grew faster than the population. But those gains were erased in 1998 when oil prices plummeted to record lows. To deal with this shortfall, the Saudi government reduced expenses.

Saudi Arabia is a well-to-do oil based economy with strong government controls over major economic activities. About 35% of GDP comes from the private sector. The petroleum sector accounts for approximately 75% of budget revenues, 35% of GDP and almost all export earnings.

Although oil has brought rapid economic development, Saudi society remains strongly conservative and religious. The King supports modernization as long as it does not undermine the country's stability and Islamic heritage.

Despite the extreme philosophical differences between the U.S. and Saudi Arabia, the two countries continue to be vital to each other's economy. Consider the following:

- The U.S. is Saudi Arabia's leading trade partner.
- The U.S. leads all foreign countries investing in Saudi Arabia.

- The U.S. is the biggest supplier of military equipment to Saudi Arabia.
- U.S. companies lead in joint partnership with the Saudis.

4 Largest Businesses in Saudi Arabia

Dallah Al Baraka, Jeddah
    35,000 employees
Saudi Telecom Company, Riyadh
    30,000 employees
Saudi Arabian Airlines, Riyadh
    24,798 employees
Saudi Arabian Airlines Corporation, Jeddah
    24,000 employees

Comparative Data

Comparative Data Ratings
(Scale: 5 = Excellent; 1 = Poor)
Saudi Arabia: 3.0

- A.   GDP Growth: 3
- B.   Per Capita Income: 2
- C.   Trade Flows with the U.S.: 4
- D.   Country Risk: 4
- E.   Monetary Policy: 5
- F.   Trade Policy: 3
  - Tariffs
  - Import Licensing
  - Import Taxes
- G.   Protection of Property Rights: 3
- H.   Foreign Investment Climate: 3

GROSS DOMESTIC PRODUCT: $186 billion (1998 estimate)

GDP GROWTH: −10.8% (1998 estimate)

PER CAPITA INCOME: $9,000 (1998 estimate)

Trade Flows with the U.S.

U.S. EXPORTS TO SAUDI ARABIA: $7.3 billion (1996 estimate); $8.4 billion (1997 estimate)

U.S. IMPORTS FROM SAUDI ARABIA: $9.4 billion (1996 estimate); $10.1 billion (1997 estimate)

TOP U.S. EXPORTS TO SAUDI ARABIA: Motor vehicles; machinery; electrical components; aircraft and parts; tobacco; arms and ammunition; cereals; medical and optical equipment; furniture and bedding; plastics and resins

TOP U.S. PROSPECTS FOR EXPORT TO SAUDI ARABIA: Air conditioning and refrigeration equipment; oil and gas equipment and services; automotive parts and services equipment; pumps, valves, and compressors; computers and peripherals; computer software; mining industry equipment; chemical production machinery; franchising

Country Risk

Dun & Bradstreet rates Saudi Arabia as having good capacity to meet outstanding payment liabilities.

Sight drafts remain the most frequent method of payment, although letters of credit are also commonly used. When open account terms are extended, 30 to 90 days are the norm.

Monetary Policy

Inflation remains very low in Saudi Arabia. In 1995 the inflation rate was below 5% and it has been dropping ever since. The estimated rates for the next two years were 1% in 1996 and 0.4% in 1997. By 1998 prices had dropped enough to register a negative rate of inflation, estimated at –0.5%.

MONETARY UNIT: Saudi riyal

Trade Policy

TARIFFS   Saudi tariff protection is generally moderate, but has increased over the years. A number of Saudi industries, primarily new ones, now enjoy 20% tariff protection as opposed to the general rate of 12%.

IMPORT LICENSING   Only Saudi nationals are permitted to engage in trading activities. Non-Saudis are not permitted to register as commercial agents.

The importation of certain articles is either prohibited or requires special approval from competent authorities. In addition, import of the following products requires special approval by Saudi authorities: agricultural seeds; live animals and fresh and frozen meat; books, periodicals, movies, and tapes; religious books and tapes; chemicals and harmful materials; pharmaceutical products; wireless equipment; horses; products containing alcohol (e.g., perfume); and natural asphalt.

Importation of the following products is prohibited by law: weapons; narcotics; pork; pornographic materials; alcohol and alcohol distillery equipment; and certain sculptures.

IMPORT TAXES   Saudi Arabia has a liberal tax system and, as a result, no import taxes are levied beyond import tariffs.

Protection of Intellectual Property Rights

The Saudi legal system protects and facilitates acquisition and disposition of all property rights, including intellectual property. The Saudi Arabian government has acceded to the Universal Copyright Convention and implementation began July 13, 1994.

Saudi Arabia has had a Patent Law since 1989 and the Patent Office accepts applications, *but as of early 1995, it had yet to issue a patent.* Protection is available for product and product-by-process. Product-by-process protection is extended to pharmaceuticals. The term of protection is 15 years. The patent holder may apply for a five-year extension after the initial protection period is up.

Saudi Arabia's copyright law does not extend protection to works that were first displayed outside of Saudi Arabia, unless the author is a Saudi citizen. However, Saudi Arabia has acceded to the Universal Copyright Convention (UCC) and the Saudi government maintains that this is sufficient to extend protection to foreign works. The Saudi government has taken action to enforce copyrights of U.S. firms, and pirated material has been seized or forced off the shelves of a number of stores.

Trademarks are protected under the Trademark Law. Trade secrets are not specifically protected under any area of Saudi law; however, they are often protected by contract. While there is no specific protection for semiconductor chip layout design, it would nevertheless be protected under the Patent Law and the Copyright Law.

Foreign Investment Climate

The Saudi government generally encourages foreign direct investment. This is particularly true of foreign investment in joint ventures with Saudi partners, though Saudi Arabia allows wholly foreign-owned firms to operate. The government and the private sector actively promote investment opportunities in Saudi Arabia. The government hopes to attract investment in infrastructure, but has yet to make such investments financially attractive.

The foreign capital investment code specifies three conditions for foreign investments:

- The undertaking must be a development project.
- The investment must generate technology transfer.
- A Saudi partner should own a minimum of 25% equity (though this can be waived).

Foreign investors are denied national treatment in the following sectors: catering; cleaning; maintenance, and operations of facilities; power generation; trading; transportation; and businesses that affect national security.

Wholly foreign-owned firms are guaranteed the same protection accorded Saudi nationals in the Foreign Capital Investment Code. They are also eligible for a wide range of investment incentives, including advantageous utility rates, land in industrial estates at nominal rents, treatment as domestic producers for government procurement contracts, and custom duty exemptions on capital goods and raw materials.

One of the leading obstacles for foreign investors are restrictive Saudi visa requirements. *Investors or potential investors wishing to visit Saudi Arabia must have a Saudi sponsor to obtain the necessary business visa.*

Current Leaders, Parties, and International Organizations

The International Academy at Santa Barbara at http://www.iasb.org/cwl publishes *Current World Leaders*, an excellent resource for up-to-date data on political leaders, parties, demographics, etc., in Saudi Arabia. Tel: (800) 530-2682 or (805) 965-5010 for subscription information to their database.

Head of State, Prime Minister, and Custodian of the Two Holy Mosques:
   King Fahd bin Abdulaziz Al-Saud

Crown Prince, First Deputy Prime Minister, and Commander of the National Guard:
   Prince Abdullah bin Abdulaziz Al-Saud

Political Parties:
   not permitted

Membership in international organizations:
   Arab Satellite Organization (ARABSAT), GCC, IDB, INTELSAT, IWC, LAS, NAM, OAPEC, OIC, OPEC, UN and most of its specialized agencies and related organizations (including FAO, GATT, IAEA, IBRD, ICAO, IDA, IFAD, IFC, ILO, IMF, IMO, ITU, UNESCO, UNIDO, UPU, WHO, WIPO, WMO)

Political Influences on Business

The United States and Saudi Arabia have enjoyed a strong, close relationship since the establishment of diplomatic relations in November 1933. Saudi Arabia's huge oil reserves—one-quarter of the world's known supply—form one important basis for our close relationship. But U.S. geostrategic interests in Saudi Arabia are equally important. Saudi Arabia is situated between the Red Sea and the *Arabian Gulf* (don't call it the Persian Gulf in front of a Saudi!), which are two of the world's most critical waterways. Because of its location, Saudi Arabia is the key to controlling the movement of a major part of the world in oil trade plus a large amount of commercial and military traffic, both on the water and in the air. Saudi Arabia also represents a growing market for U.S. goods and services.

The Saudi government has relied heavily on the U.S. government and private U.S. organizations for technical expertise and assistance in developing its human and mineral resources. In addition to the U.S. Embassy in Riyadh, the U.S. has Consulates General in Jeddah and Dhahran.

The United States has a large Foreign Military Sales program in Saudi Arabia, including the F-15, AWACS, missiles, air defense weaponry, military vehicles, and other equipment. A U.S. Military Training Mission provides training and support for these weapons and other security-related services to the Saudi armed forces. A similar program assists the Saudi Arabian National Guard.

The U.S. benefits in the promotion of its interests from the leadership role Saudi Arabia plays in the Arab and Islamic communities. The Saudi government acts as a behind-the-scenes arbiter and partner in encouraging negotiating parties to move forward in the Middle East peace process. Saudi and American interests also coincide in support of moderate regimes and disapproval of destabilizing elements.

The United States and Saudi Arabia share a common concern about regional security and stable development. Military cooperation during the 1991 Gulf War was extensive. While supporting the Middle East peace process, the Saudi government has chosen to let the parties negotiating bilateral peace agreements with Israel take the lead in normalizing relations with Israel.

Despite rapid economic development, Saudi society remains strongly conservative and religious. The King supports modernization as long as it does not undermine the country's stability and Islamic heritage.

Saudi Arabia is a traditional monarchy. It is ruled by descendants of its founder, King Abdul Aziz al Saud, who unified the country in the early 1920s. The concept of separation of religion and state is foreign to Saudi society. The legitimacy of the royal regime depends to a large degree on its perceived adherence to *Wahabism*, a conservative form of Islam.

Saudi Arabia's legal system, Shari'a law, is based on the body of Islamic jurisprudence derived from the Koran and traditional sayings (*hadiths*) of the Prophet Mohammed, and interpreted by the Ulema, a body of religious experts. Shari'a law governs both civil and criminal law. In cases not covered by Shari'a law, civil officials make administrative decisions.

Judicial appeals are reviewed by the Justice Ministry, the Court of Cassation, or the Supreme Judicial Council to ensure that court procedures were correct and that judges applied the appropriate legal principles and punishments. In capital cases, the King acts as the highest court of appeal and has the power to pardon. There is no written constitution. There are no elected assemblies and political parties are not permitted.

In 1993 the King appointed a 60-member Consultative Council and 13 provincial councils. A 35-member Council of Ministers performs executive and legislative functions. The Council of Ministers advises and makes recommendations to the King, examines proposed royal decrees, and directs the government bureaucracy. The King promulgates his decisions by issuing royal decrees.

Political consensus is formed through traditional means of consultation and petition on an individual basis. Every citizen has the right to petition high officials and the King during public audiences. Political expression unfavorable to the government is not allowed.

Saudi Arabia is divided into 13 administrative provinces. The governors are appointed by the King, and are generally princes or close relatives of the royal family. The governors report to the Minister of Interior and often directly to the King.

Three independent bodies are charged with security duties. The Ministry of Defense and Aviation uses four uniformed services to protect against external military threats. The Saudi Arabian National Guard is responsible for defending vital internal resources (oilfields and refineries), internal security, and supporting the Ministry of Defense and

Aviation as required. The Ministry of Interior is charged with internal security, police functions, and border protection.

Contacts in the United States

THE EMBASSY OF THE KINGDOM OF
SAUDI ARABIA
601 New Hampshire Avenue, NW
Washington, D.C. 20037
Tel: (202) 342-3800
www.saudiembassy.net

NATIONAL U.S.–ARAB CHAMBER OF
COMMERCE
National Office
1100 New York Avenue, NW
East Tower, Suite 550
Washington, D.C. 20005
Tel: (202) 289-5920
Fax: (202) 289-5938
http://www.nusacc.org

Passport/Visa Requirements

Passports and visas are required. Tourist visas are not available for travel to Saudi Arabia.

Visitors to Saudi Arabia should obtain meningitis and cholera vaccinations prior to arrival. A medical report is required to obtain a work and residence permit. This includes a medical certificate stating that the individual is free of AIDS. Temporary visitors need not present an AIDS-free certification.

To obtain an entry visa for business purposes with a validity of normally one month, but which may be extended up to a maximum of three months, the applicant must meet the following requirements:

1. The white application form (completed and signed) with photo attached to copy.
2. A valid passport (must be valid for at least six months from the date of submitting application).
3. A letter from applicant's company or firm in the U.S. indicating the purpose of visit in detail, length of stay, and financial responsibility.
4. An original letter of invitation from the company in Saudi Arabia is requested including all passport details, and must be signed and notarized by the local chamber of commerce in Saudi Arabia.
5. A letter of invitation sent by the Ministry of Foreign Affairs in Saudi Arabia either by telex or by statement to the Royal Embassy of Saudi Arabia in Washington, D.C.
6. When applicable, a copy of the Green Card must be presented to the Saudi Arabian office.
7. If applying by mail, a self-addressed envelope with sufficient postage affixed must be presented.

For an employment block visa, present to Saudi Arabian visa officials:

1. The white visa application form (completed and signed) with photo attached to copy.
2. A valid passport (valid at least six months from the date of submitting application).
3. A letter from the company in Saudi Arabia sponsoring applicant must be attached and must indicate the Employment Block Visa No. and date.
4. A copy of the signed Contract attached.
5. A legalized copy of the university degree and academic transcript by the Saudi Cultural Office or a legalized copy of your technician's and professional licenses and diplomas by the U.S. State Department.
6. A letter of release attached if applicant has worked previously in Saudi Arabia.
7. A complete medical test must be completed in accordance with the medical form.

Exit visas are required for all foreigners with work visas who wish to leave Saudi Arabia. Latest details and regulations should be obtained from Saudi officials. *Remember that if you become involved in a legal dispute in Saudi Arabia, your exit may be barred until the dispute is settled.*

For current information on entry and customs requirements, travelers may contact the Royal Embassy of Saudi Arabia.

U.S. citizens who wish to apply for a passport may visit Passport Services' well-organized website at http://travel.state.gov/passport_services.html.

Contacts in Saudi Arabia

THE EMBASSY OF THE UNITED STATES OF AMERICA
Collector Road M
Riyadh Diplomatic Quarter
Unit 61307, RIYADH, 11693
Mailing Address: APO AE 09803-1307
Tel: (966) (01) 488-3800
Fax: (966) (01) 488-7360
www.usia.gov/posts/riyadh

KING FAHD BIN ABDULAZIZ AL-SAUD
Head of State, Prime Minister, and Custodian of the Two Holy Mosques
Royal Court
RIYADH 11111

Further contacts and websites can be found in Appendix A.

Communications

TELEPHONE: The country code for Saudi Arabia is 966.

MAIL: Although the official language is Arabic (which does not use the Roman alphabet), English is widely used in business and government. Business letters may be written in English, although Arabic is preferred. Letters may be addressed, in English, as follows: (*Notes in parentheses*)

Office:	Institute of Public Administration
Title & Name:	H.E. Dr. Hamad Ibraheem Al-Saloom, Director General
	(*H.E. stands for His Excellency*)
Street/P.O. Box:	P.O. Box 205
	(*Street addresses are rare, since there is no street delivery of mail. Most Saudi addresses will be Post Office Boxes.*)
City & Zone Code:	RIYADH 11411
	(*The name of the city should be in capital letters.*)
Country:	Saudi Arabia
	(*The U.S. Postal Service prefers "Saudi Arabia' to "The Royal Kingdom of Saudi Arabia" or its abbreviation "KSA."*)

Remember that Arabic is written from right to left, unlike English (which is written left to right). The last page of a magazine or proposal in English will be the first page of one written in Arabic. Even when printed matter is written in English, a native speaker of Arabic may instinctively begin by looking at the back cover. Consequently, the back cover should be as attractive as the front.

E-MAIL: E-mail addresses located in Saudi Arabia end with the code .sa

DATES: The preferred calendar of Saudi Arabia is the Muslim calendar. The Muslim calendar is a lunar calendar without corrections (such as leap days) to keep it in synchronization with the solar year. Consequently, the Muslim calendar "floats" in relation to the Western calendar. Muslim holidays generally advance about 10 days each year (reckoning by the Western calendar).

Eras in the Muslim calendar are reckoned by the date of the *Hijra* (called the *Hegira* in English)—the flight of the Prophet Mohammed from Mecca to Medina. This occurred in the Western year of 622 A.D.* Just as we use A.D. (for *Anno Domini*) or C.E. (for Common Era) to designate the date in the Western calendar, Muslims use the initial H (for *Hijra*; it is usually written without a period) to designate the Muslim year.

---

* In formal usage, the initials A.D. (which stand for *Anno Domini*, or the Year of our Lord, should precede the date. But in common business practice all such era designations now follow the year.

In the Muslim calendar, the date is written in this order: day, month, year (unlike the U.S. practice of writing month, day, year). The holy month of Ramadan (during which observant Muslims fast) is the ninth month of the Muslim calendar. The first day of Ramadan in the *Hijra* year 1421 would be written in this way: 1/9/21 H (the first day of the ninth month of the year 1421).

In the Western calendar, this religious holiday should fall on November 27, 2000 A.D. (The exact dates of Muslim holidays are approximate because they are determined by sightings of the moon.) In the following year, the first day of Ramadan will be: 1/9/22 H and since the shorter Muslim lunar year advances ten days in relation to the Western solar calendar, that holiday should fall upon November 17, 2001 A.D.

Saudis generally write Western calendar dates in the day-month-year order . . . but not always.

Cultural Note: The left hand is considered unclean in Saudi Arabia. People eat with the right hand only. If you must use your left hand in public for some reason, you may wish to say the phrase ". . . shimaalin ma tishnaak," which means "the left hand does not injure."

Cultural IQ Question: Beneath the desert sands of Saudi Arabia lies "Abu al-Hol" (literally, "The Father of Fear"). This natural phenomenon is:

A)   a massive oil field

B)   a cave

C)   an ancient burial site

Email your answer to TerriMorrison@getcustoms.com Each month a drawing will be held to award a correct respondent from all the questions in this book with a free copy of *The World Holiday and Time Zone Guide* (current electronic version).

Singapore

Official Name:	Republic of Singapore (English); Hsin-chia-p'o (Chinese); Republik Singapura (Malay); Singapore Kudiyarasu (Tamil)
Official Languages:	English, Mandarin Chinese, Bahasa Malaysia, Tamil
Government System:	Parliamentary democracy
Population:	3.5 million (1999 estimate)
Population Growth Rate:	1.15% (1999 estimate)
Area:	621 sq. km. (239 sq. mi.); about one-fifth the size of Rhode Island
Natural Resources:	fish, deepwater ports
Major Cities:	Singapore (capital)

Cultural Note: Since World War Two, Singapore has remade itself from a minor trading center to a booming entrepot of capitalism in Southeast Asia. For visitors, Singapore is considered very safe (even antiseptic). But be warned that Singapore's myriad laws apply to natives and foreigners alike. Before arrival travelers should become familiar with these laws; e.g., no littering, no chewing gum, no illegal drugs, no pornographic materials, no weapons, no jaywalking, no spitting, no smoking in most public places—and the fine for failing to flush a public toilet after use is $150!

Age Breakdown

0–14 = 21%   15–64 = 72%   65+ = 7% (1999 estimate)
Life Expectancy: 75.79 years, male, 82.14 years, female (1999 estimate)

Time

The different cultures of Singapore have different attitudes about time. Be on time for all business appointments; making a Singaporean executive wait is insulting. Most Singaporeans arrive on time or slightly late for social events. Some cultural traditions maintain that arriving on time to a dinner makes them appear greedy and impatient.

Singapore is 8 hours ahead of Greenwich Mean Time (GMT +8) or 13 hours ahead of U.S. Eastern Standard Time (EST +13).

Holidays

An up-to-date, online *World Holiday and Time Zone Guide* is available at www.get-customs.com. It lists official holidays by country and by day of the year, business and cultural tips, a corruption index, and time zones with worldwide business hours.

This list is a working guide. In cases where holidays fall on Saturday or Sunday, commercial establishments may be closed the preceding Friday or following Monday.

Singapore has no official religion. This is a wise policy, as Singapore's varied ethnic population observes widely different religious tenants—from the indigenous Malays (who are mostly Muslim) to the majority Chinese (who may profess to follow Buddhism, Confucianism, Taoism, none of these, or several simultaneously).

In many faiths, religious holidays are set via lunar calendars. Thus, the scheduled dates for the following religious holidays are approximations since they depend upon actual lunar observations.

Jan 1	SA	New Year's Day
Jan 8	SA	Hari Raya Puasa
Feb 5	SA	Chinese New Year (2 days)
Mar 16	TH	Hari Raya Haji
Apr 21	FR	Good Friday
May 1	MO	Labor Day
May 18	TH	Vesak Day
Aug 9	WE	National Day
Oct 27	FR	Deepavali
Dec 25	MO	Christmas Day

Again, the days of observance should always be corroborated by local contacts.

Work Week

- Business hours are generally 9:00 A.M. to 5:00 P.M. Monday through Friday. However, many offices stagger their work hours, with workers arriving any time from 7:30 A.M. to 9:30 A.M. Some offices will be open for a half day on Saturdays, generally in the morning.

- Many Singapore banks keep traditional banking hours: 9:30 A.M. to 3:00 P.M. Monday through Friday and 9:30 A.M. to 11:30 A.M. on Saturdays.

- Shop hours vary, with some shops staying open until 9:00 or 10:00 P.M. Monday through Saturday. Some have Sunday hours as well.

- The traditional lunchtime was from 12:00 noon to 2:00 P.M. Efforts have been made to reduce this to a single hour, from 1:00 P.M. to 2:00 P.M.; nevertheless, many people will take longer than an hour for lunch. Friday is the Muslim Holy Day and observant Muslims who work on Fridays will take a two-hour break at lunchtime.

- Remember that Singapore is a meritocracy. Few people get ahead, either in business or government, without hard work and long hours. Executives will often work far longer days than their subordinates.

Religious Societal/Influences on Business

Singapore has no official religion, since its varied ethnic population observes widely different religious tenants: the indigenous Malays are predominantly Muslim, the Indian community may be Hindu or Muslim, and the majority Chinese may follow Buddhism, Confucianism, Taoism, or Christianity (or several of these simultaneously). (For specifics on the influence of Islam, see the section on Malaysia; for notes on the Chinese, see China; for Hinduism, see India.)

The government of Singapore is known for its efforts at social engineering. In the name of its citizens' best interests, the government's actions have ranged from banning chewing gum to acting as a dating service (to encourage ethnic Chinese citizens to produce more children). The government also maintains an active propaganda department. The main thrust of this propaganda involves Singaporean unity. The disparate ethnic groups of Singapore have little in common, and—before Singaporean independence—violence sometimes broke out between them. To establish a sense of nationhood among these groups, Singapore's government produces slick television commercials (some of them using the skills of the best jingle writers in the United States).

As in neighboring Indonesia, the Singaporean government has established a national ethic of patriotism, hard work, thrift, and obedience to the law. (The latter has made Singapore one of the most graft-free places in Asia.) Since these largely reflect traditional Confucian values, they have been relatively easy to impose. Concomitantly, the civil liberties of the West are seen as excessive and corrupting. As long as Singapore's economy continues to rise, its citizens are likely to accept their intrusive government's guiding hand.

5 Cultural Tips

1. English is widely spoken. It is one of the country's four official languages and is used in most business transactions, and virtually all business or government correspondence. But be aware that the English spoken in Singapore often has native inflections, syntax, and grammar which can easily lead to misunderstandings. For example, in Chinese, it is polite to offer both the positive and negative options in virtually every question. Even when speaking in English, they are likely to add a "Yes/No" pattern to a question. Rather than asking "Would you like to have dinner?" they are likely to ask "You want dinner or not?" The phrases involved ("Want or not want?" "Good or not?" "Can or cannot?") are direct translations of Chinese phrases into English. They can sound oddly aggressive to Western ears.

2. Business cards are very important. Since most Singaporean businesspeople are Chinese, have one side of your card printed in English and the other in Chinese. The exchange of cards is quite formal: After being introduced, the visiting executive should offer his or her card to each person present. With both hands on your card, present it to the recipient with the print facing him or her. The recipient will receive the card with both hands and study it for a few moments before carefully putting it away in a pocket. You should do the same when a card is presented to you. Never put a card in your back pocket (where many men carry their wallets), and don't write on a business card.

3. Successful business relationships in Singapore require politeness. Keep your voice calm and quiet. Never display anger; a person who becomes angry in public has lost self-control and will not be trusted or respected. Avoid causing anyone to lose face—which means do not openly disagree with anyone! Politeness demands that you find a more subtle way of expressing your disagreement.

4. The word "No" is rarely heard in Singapore. The polite but evasive "Yes" is considered a valid technique to avoid giving offense. In Singapore, "Yes" can mean anything from "I agree" to "Maybe" to "I hope you can tell from my lack of enthusiasm that I really mean 'No.'" "Yes" really means "No" when there are any qualifications attached. (For example, "Yes, but . . ." probably means "No." "It might be difficult" is a clear "No.") Also, a clear way to indicate "No" is to suck in air through the teeth. This sound always indicates a problem, no matter what words are said. A true "Yes" will be followed by paperwork and documentation.

5. Show respect for age and seniority. In a group, the most important persons will be introduced first. If you are introducing two people, state the name of the more important person first (i.e., "President Smith, this is Engineer Wong").

Economic Overview

Singapore has one of the most developed industrial, commercial, financial, and consumer economies in the world and is an excellent market for U.S. products and services. Its role as the "Gateway to Southeast Asia" means that almost any American product can find an interested buyer.

Singapore buys a diverse variety of goods from the U.S. for both internal consumption within the country and for re-exports to other markets throughout Southeast Asia. Many U.S. companies use Singapore as a distribution center for Asia. Almost 40% of Singapore's imports are re-exported to other destinations.

Although the 1997 Asian economic crisis hurt the economy, Singapore weathered the crisis better than any of its neighbors. Despite the economic dislocations, Singapore managed to post a small increase (estimated at 1.3%) in economic growth in 1998.

5 Largest Businesses in Singapore

Dairy Farm International Holdings Ltd., Singapore
91,400 employees
Commodity International Trading Pte. Ltd., Singapore
49,884 employees
Singapore Airlines Ltd., Singapore
28,196 employees
Koninklijke Luchtvaart Maatschappij N.V., Singapore
25,000 employees
Natsteel Ltd., Singapore
18,658 employees

Corporations in Singapore are designated Limited (*Ltd.*), meaning a public corporation, or Private Limited (*Pte. Ltd.*), indicating a privately-held corporation. *N.V.* is a Dutch term for a publicly-traded corporation.

Cultural Note: The Republic of Singapore is a meritocracy. To get ahead in business or government, one has to work hard and put in long hours. Executives often work late into the night and on weekends. Many executives travel frequently, so appointments must be made at least two weeks in advance.

Comparative Data

Comparative Data Ratings
(Scale: 5 = Highest; 1 = Lowest)
Singapore: 4.5

- A. GDP Growth: 3
- B. Per Capita Income: 5
- C. Trade Flows with the U.S.: 5
- D. Country Risk: 4
- E. Monetary Policy: 5
- F. Trade Policy: 5
    - Tariffs

- Import Licensing
- Import Taxes

G. Protection of Property Rights: 4

H. Foreign Investment Climate: 5

GROSS DOMESTIC PRODUCT: $91.7 billion (1998 estimate)

GDP GROWTH: 2.5% (1999 estimate); 4.5% (2000 forecast)

PER CAPITA INCOME: $26,300 (1998 estimate)

Trade Flows with the U.S.

U.S. EXPORTS TO SINGAPORE: $15.7 billion (1998 estimate)

U.S. IMPORTS FROM SINGAPORE: $18.4 billion (1998 estimate)

TOP U.S. EXPORTS TO SINGAPORE: Electronic components; aircraft parts; industrial process controls; oil and gas field machinery; construction equipment; laboratory and scientific instruments; computer hardware and peripherals; medical equipment; telecommunications equipment; pumps/valves/compressors

TOP U.S. PROSPECTS FOR EXPORT TO SINGAPORE: Electronic industry production/testing equipment; aircraft and parts; electric power systems; franchising; construction equipment; industrial process controls; professional services; laboratory and scientific instruments; computer hardware and peripherals; building products

Country Risk

There is a low degree of uncertainty associated with expected returns.

The business environment in Singapore remains sound and liberal credit terms are used on most transactions. Open account 30- to 60-day terms are usually granted. More secure terms such as letter of credit or sight draft are advised for new or small and private accounts along with credit checks where available.

Monetary Policy

There is free movement of capital and profits in Singapore. Inflation is under control. The inflation rate in 1998 was 0.3% and is forecast at 1.0% in 2000. Despite the dislocations of the 1997 Asian economic crisis, inflation is expected to remain low for the foreseeable future.

MONETARY UNIT: Singapore dollar

Trade Policy

TARIFFS   Tariffs are minimal with 99% of goods entering Singapore duty-free. Significant tariffs remain on cigarettes, alcoholic beverages, automobiles, and gasoline. The average tariff in Singapore is well under 1%.

IMPORT LICENSING   Singapore maintains very few trade barriers. Most goods can be imported freely without import licenses. Generally, the import of goods that pose a threat to health, security, safety, and social decency is controlled. Import licenses are required for pharmaceuticals, hazardous chemicals, films, and arms and ammunition. Companies wanting to import controlled items into Singapore must apply for licenses from appropriate government agencies.

Companies must make an inward declaration for all goods imported into Singapore. Singapore prohibits the import of chewing gum, firecrackers, horns, sirens, silencers, toy coins, and currencies. A complete list of prohibited products can be obtained from the Trade Development Board.

IMPORT TAXES   A Goods and Services Tax (GST) of 3% is levied on all imports into Singapore. The GST is not levied on goods stored in free-trade zones.

Protection of Intellectual Property Rights

Singapore's Intellectual Property (IP) laws are based on the British, which means that common law rights are part of its legal heritage. Singapore belongs to the Paris Convention for Protection of Intellectual Property, the Patent Cooperation Treaty, and has committed to upgrade its IP laws and enforcement policies under TRIPS (Trade Related Intellectual Property Rights).

Inventions may be patented. Patent applications for inventions can be filed in accordance with Singapore law or filed under the Patent Cooperation Treaty in Singapore or any other receiving country. Patents have a term of 20 years from filing.

Trademark rights may be established both from common law usage and by registration. Both service marks and trademarks are protected. The Trademark Register is divided into Parts A and B. *Part A* is for distinctive marks and *Part B* is where marks are placed that are capable of becoming distinctive. Trademarks have a term of 10 years and are renewable.

Copyright protection results on creation of a protected work. Registration is permissive. Subject matter protected by copyright includes literary, artistic and musical works, sound recordings, films, broadcasts, and computer programs. The standard term of copyright is life of the author plus 50 years. Broadcasts are protected for 50 years from the broadcast. Criminal sanctions as well as civil remedies may apply.

Political Leaders, Parties, and International Organizations

The International Academy at Santa Barbara at http://www.iasb.org/cwl publishes *Current World Leaders*, an excellent resource for up-to-date data on political leaders, parties, demographics, etc., in Singapore. Tel: (800) 530-2682 or (805) 965-5010 for subscription information to their database.

Chief of State:
   President Sellapan Ramanathan (S.R. Nathan)

Head of the Government:
   Prime Minister Goh Chok Tong

Next Election:
   August 2005

Political Parties:
   People's Action Party, Workers' Party, Singapore Democratic Party, National Solidarity Party

Membership in international organizations:
   ADB, APEC, ASEAN, CP, C, G77, INTELSAT, NAM, PECC, UN and most of its specialized agencies and related organizations (including GATT, IAEA, IBRD, ICAO, ILO, IFC, IMF, ITU, UPU, WHO, WMO)

Political Influences on Business

Singapore is a parliamentary republic that prides itself on political stability and the predictability this offers to foreign investors and traders. Following independence in 1965, the country's basic economic strategy was molded by former Prime Minister Lee Kuan Yew, who stepped aside in November 1990 after 24 years on the job. The political succession was achieved with what some observers called "clockwork-like" precision.

Mr. Lee's policies have changed little under his successor, 54-year-old Goh Chok Tong. Moreover, Lee Kuan Yew continues to exercise considerable influence as head of the dominant People's Action Party (PAP) and as Senior Minister, a Cabinet position created expressly for him. Thus, Singapore's political leadership remains dedicated to free-market principles and to maintaining a first-rate infrastructure and labor force.

The PAP continues to remain the dominant party in Singapore's Parliament. The opposition is not expected to upset the PAP's dominance at any time in the foreseeable future.

The collapse of the Indonesian economy in 1997 led to political instability and widespread violence against ethnic Chinese. This has made the ethnic Chinese of Singapore all the more determined to maintain order in their country.

Contacts in the United States

THE EMBASSY OF THE REPUBLIC OF SINGAPORE
3501 International Place, NW
Washington, D.C. 20008

Tel: (202) 537-3100
Fax: (202) 537-0876
www.gov.sg/mfa/washington/

Passport/Visa Requirements

U.S. citizens need a valid passport (valid for six months or longer beyond the last day of stay) and return/onward tickets. A visa is not required for tourist/business stays of up to two weeks.

A visa is required to establish residence in Singapore either as a private citizen or in a business capacity.

U.S. citizens who wish to apply for a passport may visit Passport Services' well-organized website at http://travel.state.gov/passport_services.html.

Contacts in Singapore

U.S. EMBASSY
30 Hill Street
Singapore 0617
Mailing Address: FPO AP 96534-0006
Tel: (65) 338-0251
Fax: (65) 338-4550
www.usis-singapore.org.sg

AMERICAN CHAMBER OF COMMERCE IN SINGAPORE
1 Scotts Road
#16-07 Shaw Center
Singapore 0922
Tel: (65) 235-0077
Fax: (65) 732-5917
amcham.org.sg

DUN & BRADSTREET (SINGAPORE) PTE. LTD.
6 Temasek Boulevard #06/06
Suntec Tower Four
Singapore 038986
Tel: (65) 333-6388
Fax: (65) 434.9501

OFFICE OF THE PRESIDENT
Orchard Road
Istana, Republic of Singapore 0922

OFFICE OF THE PRIME MINISTER
Istana Annexe
Istana, Republic of Singapore 0923

Further contacts and websites can be found in Appendix A.

Communications

TELEPHONE: The international country code for Singapore is 65.

Phone numbers are seven digits in length.

There are no area codes in tiny Singapore.

E-MAIL: E-mail addresses located in Singapore end with the code .sg

Observation: "Singapore is the Manhattan of Southeast Asia, a long crowded island of soaring skyscrapers, lavish penthouses, and gridlocked streets. Like Manhattan, Singapore considers itself richer, trendier, more stylish, and all in all more important than any other place. . . . The autocrats who rule Singapore have created a sort of nanny state—a neat, clean enclave where nobody dares to do anything that might offend the governing clique. The island has been aptly called Disneyland with the death penalty.

". . . Singapore is also a world capital of the Confucian ethic, with Confucius' sayings taught in all schools and even set into the tile on the walls of subway stations."

—From *Confucius Lives Next Door: What Living in the East Teaches Us About Living in the West*. The author, T.R. Reid, has studied the influence of Confucianism on the cultures of Asia.

South Africa

Official Name:	Republic of South Africa
Official Languages:	English, Afrikaans, and nine African languages: Ndebele, Pedi (North Sotho), Sotho (South Sotho), Swazi, Tsonga, Tswana (West Sotho), Venda, Xhosa, Zulu
Government System:	Multi-party republic with bicameral parliament
Population:	: 43,426,386 (July 1999 estimate) (South Africa took a census October 10, 1996 that showed a population of 37,859,000 [after a 6.8% adjustment for underenumeration based on a post-enumeration survey]; this figure is still about 10% below projections from earlier censuses. Since the full results of that census have not been released for analysis, the numbers shown for South Africa do not take into consideration the results of this 1996 census.)
Population Growth Rate:	1.32% (1999 estimate)
Area:	1,233,404 sq. km. (472,359 sq. mi.); about twice the size of Texas
Natural Resources:	gold, chromium, antimony, coal, iron ore, manganese, nickel, lead, phosphates, tin, uranium, diamonds, platinum, copper, vanadium, salt, natural gas, titanium, zinc, asbestos, zirconium
Major Cities:	Pretoria (administrative capital), Cape Town (legislative capital), Bloemfontein (judicial capital), Johannesburg, Durban

Cultural Note: South Africans are big sports fans, and sports are always a good topic of conversation. Rugby is the most popular team sport among white South Africans. After rugby, the most popular sports in South Africa are football (soccer), squash, tennis, and golf. Jogging and bicycling are also very popular, as is swimming (many homes have swimming pools). The Afrikaans have an indigenous sport called *jukskei*, which is analogous to throwing horseshoes.

Age Breakdown

0–14 years = 34%   15–64 years = 61%   65+ = 5% (1999 estimate)
Life Expectancy: 54.76 years, total population; 52.68 years, male; 56.9 years, female (1999 estimate)

Time

South Africa's cultural groups have different attitudes towards time. Punctuality is highly emphasized among white South Africans. Be on time for all business appointments. Punctuality is not enforced for social events, but do not be more than a half hour late.

When working with native Africans, take your cues for the concept of time from them. They may consider time from a "polychronic" view: many activities going on concurrently, a flexible attitude towards schedule changes, and a constant information flow from many sources demanding many interruptions.

Due to the hot temperatures, the South African morning is often the most comfortable part of the day. As a result, most South Africans are early risers.

Holidays

An up-to-date, web-based *World Holiday and Time Zone Guide* is available at www.getcustoms.com. It lists official holidays by country and by day of the year, cultural tips, a corruption index, and time zones with worldwide business hours.

Jan 1	SA	New Year's Day
Mar 21	TU	Human Rights Day
Apr 5	WE	Family Day
Apr 21	FR	Good Friday
Apr 27	TH	Freedom Day
May 1	MO	Workers Day
Jun 16	FR	Youth Day

Aug 9	WE	National Women's Day
Sep 24	SU	Heritage Day
Dec 16	SA	Day of Reconciliation
Dec 25	MO	Christmas Day
Dec 26	TU	Day of Goodwill

In addition to the above, the Christian holidays of Good Friday and Easter are observed as official holidays.

South Africa's holidays have been changed since majority rule. Older South Africans may refer to Youth Day under its old name, Soweto Day. Similarly, the Day of Reconciliation used to be the Day of the Vow.

Again, the days of observance should always be corroborated by local contacts.

Work Week

- Official business hours are generally from 8:30 or 9:00 A.M. to 4:30 or 5:00 P.M. Monday through Friday.

- Government offices keep earlier hours, starting at 7:15 or 7:30 A.M. Monday through Friday. They may close anytime after 3:30 P.M.

- Banks hours vary, but most are open from 9:00 A.M. to 3:30 P.M. Monday through Friday. Some banks open for a few hours on Saturday mornings.

- Store hours also vary, but most are open from 8:30 A.M. to 5:00 P.M. Monday through Friday. Many shops are open for at least a half day on Saturdays. Until recently, most establishments were closed on Sundays due to Calvinist blue laws.

- In South Africa, a "cafe" is not a European-style bistro; rather, it is a local convenience store. They are open for long hours, 7 days a week.

Religious/Societal Influences on Business

South Africa's diverse population follows many religious beliefs. Most white South Africans are Christian, although there is a small Jewish population. Black South Africans may be Christian or follow traditional beliefs. The Hindu and Muslim minorities are concentrated in the Asian (Indian and Malay) population.

Ever since the discovery of mineral wealth, most immigrants have considered South Africa as a place to become rich. Consequently, South Africa is a place where drive and ambition are considered positive traits. In this respect, white South Africans are unlike their relatives in Britain or The Netherlands. As in the U.S., South Africans love a good rags-to-riches story.

On the other hand, South Africa is still emerging from its embargo period. South Africans view themselves as self-sufficient and are not willing to be bullied or cajoled by foreigners.

5 Cultural Tips

1. Once they get to know you, white South Africans usually begin talking about business after a very brief exchange of small talk, both in the office and at meals. South Africans of other races may spend more time on conversation. Many African traditions require long inquiries about your health and your family. Indian and Chinese businesspeople also may take more time in pre-business conversation.

2. Most (but not all) South African businesspeople have business cards. There is no formality involved in exchanging cards. Your card will not be refused, but you might not be given one in exchange. Don't be offended by this.

3. While businesspeople are respected in South Africa, they are not expected to be cutthroat. A businessperson who gloats over crushing his or her competitors is not appreciated. The ideal business deal (to white South Africans) will be a "win–win situation." Both parties should be seen to gain from the deal. On the other hand, the Indian and Chinese populations came to South Africa as merchants; they have generations of trading experience and are considered shrewd businesspeople. Their business dealings may be more aggressive than those of white South Africans.

4. White South Africans can often seem concerned that they might be taken advantage of by foreigners. The two-decade boycott left them somewhat out of practice in international negotiations. High-pressure tactics or emotion have little place in discussions with white South Africans. Most would rather let a deal fall through than be rushed.

5. Social events are important; most South Africans want to get to know you before doing business with you. South Africans often invite foreigners to a barbecue, which is called a *braaivleis* (Afrikaans for "roasted meat")—often shortened to *braai*. While business is not discussed at a *braai*, it is considered an important part of the business relationship. Guests usually bring something to a braai. Residents often bring one course of the meal, but foreign visitors need only bring something to drink or a dessert. Even if your host says you don't need to bring anything, it is good form to bring a bottle of wine or candy. (Large amounts of alcohol are often consumed at a *braai*.)

Observation: "South Africa, an ethnically diverse country of some 42 million, has eleven official languages including English and Afrikaans, the latter a creole spoken by descendants of the Dutch who settled in southern Africa more than three hundred years ago. Zulu is the most commonly spoken of South Africa's local languages, but many black South Africans without formal education are fluent in several languages which they need in order to communicate with other inhabitants of the multilingual black townships.

"... the basic rule is to be hospitable, says Lebo Chanza, a South African woman. 'When we have company at my house, we try to make them feel comfortable—all of them. So, my mother, when she summons them to eat ... she might say 'Avon tu, lali zheng,' which is both Suthu and Zulu. . . . She calls *avon tu*, which is 'eight people' in Zulu. *Lali zheng* is Suthu for 'come and eat' so that way, everybody feels equally welcome and equally . . . taken care of and sort of equally paid attention to."

—From *Into Africa: Intercultural Insights* by Yale Richmond and Phyllis Gestrin

Economic Overview

South Africa is the largest export market for U.S. goods and services in Sub-Saharan Africa. It offers immediate and long-term opportunities for many U.S. exporters and investors with the right products, resources, and ideas. As of 1996 new U.S. investments in South Africa surpassed the combined investments the U.K., Japan, Germany, and Malaysia.

While South Africa's profound political change and the lifting of international sanctions ushered in a new climate in which to build a stronger bilateral trade agenda, the attraction of South Africa for American companies to a large degree lies in the country's fundamentals. South Africa is the most advanced, broadly based, and productive economy in Africa, with a gross domestic product (GDP) nearly four times that of Egypt, its nearest competitor on the African continent. It possesses a modern infrastructure supporting an efficient distribution of goods to major urban centers throughout the region, and well-developed financial, legal, communications, energy, and transport sectors. *South Africa boasts a stock exchange that ranks among the top 10 in the world.*

Additionally, South Africa offers excellent potential in its long-term reconstruction and development efforts required to distribute economic benefits—traditionally enjoyed by only five or six million South Africans—to the 35 million people disenfranchised by apartheid.

South Africa has experienced modest economic growth each year since the initiation of majority democracy in 1994. The South African rand plunged 30% against the U.S. dollar in 1998, but recovered somewhat. Unemployment remains high, at over 20%, and is expected to remain at similar levels as inefficient industries face global competition.

South Africa's modest economic growth is not enough to make major dents in unemployment and poverty. The multiracial government inherited an economy whose structures were built in an era of isolation and that are not always congruent with those needed in an intensely competitive world economy.

Furthermore, violence has exploded. While the average visiting businessperson is not at extreme risk, robberies, thefts, and murders are an everyday occurrence in black neighborhoods. Today, violence is the most likely cause of death for a South African.

The AIDS epidemic has also hit South Africa particularly hard. In the gold mining industry, an estimated one-quarter of all miners are infected with the HIV virus.

5 *Largest Businesses in South Africa:*

Anglovaal Ltd., Johannesburg
 76,000 employees
Tiger Oates Ltd., Sandown
 63,113 employees
Iscor Ltd., Pretoria West
 53,400 employees
C.G. Smith Foods Ltd., Sandton
 52,000 employees
Murray and Roberts Holdings Ltd., Bedfordview
 49,754 employees

Cultural Note: Each of the many cultures of South Africa has its own traditions. While the majority of businesspeople in South Africa will still be from either the English or the Afrikaans ethnic groups, many new managers and CEOs are black.

An excellent, insightful viewpoint on South Africa's cultures, political struggles, and triumphs is found in the remarkable memoir of Nelson Mandela, the former president of the African National Congress and 1993 Nobel Prize recipient. *Long Walk to Freedom* should be required reading for everyone visiting or working in South Africa.

Comparative Data

Comparative Data Ratings
(Scale: 5 = Excellent; 1 = Poor)
South Africa: 2.75

- A. GDP Growth: 3
- B. Per Capita Income: 2
- C. Trade Flows with the U.S.: 2
- D. Country Risk: 3
- E. Monetary Policy: 3
- F. Trade Policy: 3
  - Tariffs
  - Import Licensing
  - Import Taxes
- G. Protection of Property Rights: 3
- H. Foreign Investment Climate: 3

GROSS DOMESTIC PRODUCT: $290.6 BILLION (1998 ESTIMATE)

GDP GROWTH: 0.5% (1998 ESTIMATE); 2.5% (1999 ESTIMATE)

PER CAPITA INCOME: $3,225 (1997 ESTIMATE); $6,800 (1998 ESTIMATE)

Trade Flows with the U.S.

U.S. EXPORTS TO SOUTH AFRICA: $3.6 billion (1998 estimate)

U.S. IMPORTS FROM SOUTH AFRICA: $3.1 billion (1998 estimate)

TOP U.S. EXPORTS TO SOUTH AFRICA: Machinery (computers, office machines, etc.); electrical goods; organic chemicals; aircraft; medical and optical equipment; motor vehicles; cereals; plastics; paper/paperboard; miscellaneous chemical products

TOP U.S. PROSPECTS FOR EXPORT TO SOUTH AFRICA: Airport and ground support equipment; telecommunications equipment; computer software; health care services and equipment; drugs and pharmaceuticals; security and safety equipment; computers and peripherals

Country Risk

According to Dun & Bradstreet, South Africa is considered to have sufficient capacity to meet outstanding payment liabilities. Letters of credit are used for an estimated 10% of total trade transactions and are recommended. Settlement by open account is common, with usual terms of 60 to 90 days.

Monetary Policy

South Africa's restrictive monetary policy has succeeded in keeping consumer inflation to under 10%, which is historically low for South Africa. The inflation rate averaged 8.6% in 1997 and fell to 7% in 1998. Continuing fiscal and monetary prudence have set the stage for sustained noninflationary growth.

However, the government faces strong demands for jobs and public works programs to reduce the high levels of unemployment, which was estimated at 22.9% in 1998.

MONETARY UNIT: South African rand

Trade Policy

TARIFFS   While many goods enter South Africa duty-free, those subject to duty generally pay a rate between 5% and 25%. However, rates of tariff protection can reach over 60%, with luxury goods tariffs as high as 60% and automobiles at 100%. The average tariff rate was reduced from 21% in 1993 to 12% in 1999. The South African government is in the process of simplifying the tariff system by consolidating categories of similar goods and lowering many tariff levels.

IMPORT LICENSING   Most goods may be imported into South Africa without restrictions. Import permits are required only for specific categories of goods and are obtainable from the Director of Import and Export. Importers must possess an import permit.

IMPORT TAXES   Import surcharges on luxury goods were abolished in March 1995.

A value-added tax (VAT) of 14% is payable on nearly all imports. However, goods used in manufacturing or resale by registered importers may be exempt.

Specific excise duties are levied on alcoholic and nonalcoholic beverages, tobacco and tobacco products, mineral waters, some petroleum products, and motor vehicles. *Ad valorem* excise duties are levied on office machinery, photographic film, and luxury consumer goods such as cosmetics, home entertainment products, and motorcycles.

Protection of Intellectual Property Rights

South Africa was removed from the watch list of countries with insufficient enforcement of intellectual property laws in 1996. However, counterfeiting of brand names and software piracy still occurs.

South Africa is a member of the Berne Convention and has adopted patent and trademark laws that follow the European Patent Convention and the European Directive on Trademarks. South Africa has entered into numerous bilateral treaties that have IP provisions. Because of its past connection with Great Britain, trademarks are protected both by statute and common law.

Inventions must have worldwide novelty, be unobvious, and have industrial application. The term of patents is 20 years. Applications are maintained in secret while pending. Patents rights to pharmaceuticals are now offered, although this has been the object of much controversy.

Trademarks must be capable of distinguishing goods and services of one party from another. The term of trademarks is 10 years and is renewable. Trademarks can be registered or action can be taken at common law.

Copyrights vest in the author, except for works made for hire and parties who have commissioned computer programs, in which case it vests in another. Copyright protection for literary, musical, and artistic works extends for the life of the author plus 50 years. For films, photographs, and sound recordings, protection extends for 50 years from the year the work is publicly released. Registration is not required.

Foreign Investment Climate

Foreign investors are permitted 100% ownership. The government encourages investments that strengthen, expand, and/or update various industries but does not require that new investments comply with specific requirements. Foreign firms are treated the same as domestic companies for various investment incentives such as export incentive programs and tariffs, and other trade regulations.

Foreign investors do face differences regarding access to domestic financing, and local borrowing restrictions imposed by exchange control authorities. Companies that are 25% or more owned or controlled by nonresidents face limits on local borrowing. Foreign-owned firms do not have unlimited access to local credit.

It is estimated that between 500 and 600 U.S. companies are located within South Africa, with more than 200 having direct investments.

Current Leaders, Parties, and International Organizations

The International Academy at Santa Barbara at http://www.iasb.org/cwl publishes *Current World Leaders*, an excellent resource for up-to-date data on political leaders, parties, demographics, etc., in South Africa. Tel: (800) 530-2682 or (805) 965-5010 for subscription information to their database.

Head of State and the Government:

President Thabo Mbeki

Political parties:

African Christian Democratic Party or ACDP; African National Congress or ANC; Democratic Party or DP; Freedom Front or FF; Inkatha Freedom Party or IFP; National Party (now the New National Party) or NP; Pan-Africanist Congress or PAC; United Democratic Movement or UDM

Membership in international organizations:

C, INTELSAT, NAM, OAU, SADC, UN and many of its specialized agencies and related organizations (including GATT, IAEA, IBRD, ICAO, IDA, IFC, IMF, ITU, WHO, WIPO, WMO)

Political Influences on Business

Just as South Africa underwent a historic transformation in 1994 from white minority rule to democratic nonracial government, so has its bilateral relationship with the United States changed. Under the Comprehensive Anti-Apartheid Act (CAAA) of 1986, the U.S. Congress enacted some of the most stringent economic sanctions imposed on South Africa during the apartheid years. Most CAAA economic and trade sanctions were lifted by Executive Order in July 1991.

The U.S.–South Africa relationship was strengthened even further in October 1994 when Presidents Clinton and Mandela signed an agreement in Washington D.C., which created the U.S.–South Africa Bi-National Commission. It was only the second one of its kind (the U.S.–Russia Binational Commission was the first).

Following the election of April 26–29, 1994 the international community normalized both its diplomatic and economic relations. Since the election, South Africa has not only resumed its full membership of the United Nations and rejoined the Commonwealth, but also became a member of the Organization of African Unity and the Nonaligned Movement.

South Africa's apartheid-era government, while preaching free-market economics, was essentially statist. The African National Congress, on the other hand, many of whose leaders were exiled for years in the Soviet Union and its satellite states, returned to South Africa firmly believing in centralized economic planning and nationalization of the means of production. However, as South Africa's Interim Constitution took shape at the multi-party negotiations, the African National Congress (ANC) began to see the merits of open and unfettered competition. For all practical purposes, the ANC has dropped its traditional nationalization plank from its policy framework.

As stipulated in South Africa's Interim Constitution, the country's parliament has two chambers: the National Assembly and the Senate. The 400 seats in the National Assembly are allocated to political parties on the basis of proportional representation in accordance with their share of the national vote.

Once elected, the members of the National Assembly elect the President who is vested with broad executive powers, including the power to appoint a 27-member cabinet. All parties that receive at least 20% of the national vote are guaranteed representation by a Deputy President, while all parties that receive at least 5% of the national vote are entitled to representation in the Cabinet proportional to their electoral strength.

Some 22 million voters participated in South Africa's first democratic, nonracial election. When South Africans went to the polls, they had 19 parties to choose from in the election for the National Assembly. An additional seven parties participated in one or more of the provincial elections only. The African National Congress won 62.6% of the national vote and, in addition, won controlling majorities in seven out of the nine provincial legislatures. The National Party won control of Western Cape province, and the Inkatha Freedom Party won control of Kwazulu/Natal province.

Seven parties are represented in the National Assembly. By far the largest, the African National Congress has a broadly based, predominantly black membership, although it enjoys growing support within the liberal white community. Representing the pre-election national liberation movement, the African National Congress is overwhelmingly preoccupied with the critical need to provide adequate health care, housing, education, and employment to the millions of black and "colored" South Africans whose standard of living was depressed under the old racist regime.

Second in size, the National Party ruled South Africa for 46 years prior to the recent election. It was responsible for creating the apartheid policy, but later, under F.W. de Klerk's leadership, abandoned it and entered into negotiations with the African National Congress. It has a right-of-center, still largely white membership, although it also enjoys majority support within the "colored" and Asian communities. In preparation for the election, the National Party worked hard to attract middle-class black voters, though with only limited success.

The third largest party is the mainly Zulu Inkatha Freedom Party whose support is heavily concentrated in Kwazulu/Natal. Inkatha made a strong appeal to Zulu ethnic pride, which proved effective especially in rural areas of the province. The party's policies have long favored federalism as a check on the powers of the central government; its economic policy is generally characterized as free-market oriented.

Contacts in the United States

THE EMBASSY OF THE REPUBLIC OF SOUTH AFRICA
3051 Massachusetts Avenue, NW
Washington, D.C. 20008
Tel: (202) 232-4400
Fax: (202) 265-1607
www.southafrica.net

Passport/Visa Requirements

For U.S. and Canadian citizens, and all EU countries, a valid passport is required; a visa is not required for passport holders on vacation, business, or in transit. Visas are required for extended stays for employment, study, diplomatic, and official passport holders. Evidence of a yellow fever vaccination is necessary if arriving from an infected area.

BUSINESS VISA REQUIREMENTS: (1) Letter from applicant's firm guaranteeing the applicant's expenses in South Africa, giving the names of South African businesses that will be approached, and stating the nature of the business to be conducted in South Africa. (2) Visa application form on which all questions must be answered. (3) No photographs for any visas are necessary.

Those applicants wishing to have visaed passports returned by mail should submit a stamped, self-addressed envelope with application. Metered postage is not acceptable. All passports are returned by certified mail; therefore, sufficient postage to cover this type of mail service must be placed in the envelope.

For current information concerning entry and customs requirements, travelers can contact the Embassy of South Africa.

U.S. citizens who wish to apply for a passport may visit Passport Services' well-organized website at http://travel.state.gov/passport_services.html.

Contacts in South Africa

THE U.S. EMBASSY
877 Pretorius Street
Arcadia 0083
Mailing Address: P.O. Box 9536, Pretoria, 0001
Tel: (27) (12) 342-1048
Fax (27) 342-2244
www.usia.gov/posts/pretoria

AMERICAN CHAMBER OF COMMERCE IN SOUTH AFRICA
P.O. Box 62280, 2107
Marshalltown
Tel: (27) (11) 788-0265
Fax: (27) (11) 880-1632

INFORMATION TRUST CORPORATION (PTY.) LTD.
(A Joint Venture with Dun & Bradstreet International and Trans Union Corporation)
Postal Address: P.O. Box 4522, Johannesburg 2000
Street Address: Information Trust House, 8 Junction Avenue, Parktown 2193
Tel: (27) (11) 488-2911 (General)
Fax: (27) (11) 499-2282 (General); (27) (11) 484-1308 (Management)

OFFICE OF THE PRESIDENT
Private Bag X83
Pretoria 0001
Republic of South Africa

Further contacts and websites can be found in Appendix A.

Communications

TELEPHONE: The country code for South Africa is 27.

South African phone numbers have six or seven digits.

Area codes can vary from two digits (major cities) to up to five digits (rural areas).

MAIL: All mail should be addressed using the Latin alphabet. If you have both a postal box and a street delivery address, use the post box for mail and the street delivery address for courier or air freight services.

Observation: ". . . the spelling of African names is another matter, since there seem to be no generally accepted rules of orthography. In some countries the familiar Muslim name will be Mohammed, and in others Muhammad or Mamedou. As one Englishman expressed his frustration, 'The problem of spelling African proper names has, over the years, substantially shortened my life."

—H.B. Thomas, quoted in *The White Nile* by Alan Moorehead (1960)

A postal box address may be either letters, numbers, or a mixture of letters and numbers, and can be referred to in any of the following ways:

English	*Afrikaans*
P.O. Box	Posbus
Private Box	Privaatbus
Private Bag	Privaatsak

Letters to South Africa may be addressed as follows: (*Notes in parentheses*)

Title & Name:	Mnr. C.A. de Buys
	(*Mnr. = Meneer is the Afrikaans equivalent of Mister*)
Company:	Rand Intermining Technologies Ltd.
	(*Larger, publicly-traded corporations are usually designated Ltd.=Limited; which is Bpk. in Afrikaans. Smaller, privately held businesses often use the term Pty.=Proprietary; in Afrikaans, this would be Edms.*)
Street:	Privaatsak X945
	(*Privaatsak=Private Bag usually indicates a larger volume of mail than a P.O. Box. This bag number mixes letters and numbers.*)
City and Postcode:	*Johannesburg 2000*
	(Postcodes are 4-digit numbers, and are usually written after the name of the city, although they can be placed elsewhere, such as on a separate line.)
Country:	*South Africa*

E-MAIL: E-mail addresses located in South Africa end with the code .za

DATES: Writing dates in South Africa can be confusing. English-speaking people usually write the date in this order: day, month, year (unlike the U.S. practice of writing month, day, year). The dates are usually separated by slashes or dashes (10/11/00 or 10-11-00 both indicate November 10, 2000).

However, the Afrikaans-speaking community often write the date the same way as U.S. citizens: month, day, year. And official government offices usually write year, month, day (under which pattern November 10, 2000 would be 00-11-10).

Faux Pas: While the boycott of South Africa during the Apartheid era may have been successful, most white South Africans resented what they saw as outside interference in their domestic affairs. It is important for a foreigner not to take any credit for changing South Africa's political system.

"I have fought against white domination and
I have fought against black domination.
I have cherished the ideal of a democratic and free society in which
all persons live together in harmony and with equal opportunity.
It is an ideal which I hope to live for and to achieve.
But if needs be, it is an ideal for which I am prepared to die."

—Nelson Mandela, Cape Town, February 11, 1990

South Korea

Official Name:	Republic of Korea (South) (Taehan Min'guk)
Official Language:	Korean
Government System:	Unitary multi-party republic
Population:	46.8 million (1999 estimate)
Population Growth Rate:	1% (1999 estimate)
Area:	99,173 sq. km. (38,031 sq. mi.); about the size of Indiana
Natural Resources:	coal, tungsten, graphite, limestone, molybdenum, lead
Major Cities:	Seoul (capital), Pusan, Taegu, Inch'ŏn, Kwangju, Taejŏn

Cultural Note: The Korean language is written in *Hangul*, a 40-character alphabet unique to Korea. There are three systems in current use for translating Korean into English. Expect variations in English spellings among the systems. Some translation systems use a few diacritical marks in English. However, Koreans are used to reading English translations without the diacritical marks.

Age Breakdown

0–15 = 22%   15–64 = 71%   65+ = 7% (1999 estimate)
Life Expectancy: 70.75 years, male; 78.32 years, female (1999 estimate)

Time

Just a generation ago, Korea was primarily an agricultural country, and there was no call for punctuality. Now that Korea has industrialized, promptness has more value. However, most Koreans consider themselves to be essentially on time if they are within a half hour of the scheduled meeting time (either before or after). A Korean will not usually apologize for being 30 minutes late, nor would they understand why a foreigner might be upset at the delay.

Since it is possible that a Korean will arrive 30 minutes early, a host needs to be ready early.

Of course, Koreans who deal with foreigners on a regular basis understand punctuality. These Koreans endeavor to be prompt, and they expect punctuality from foreigners.

South Korea is 9 hours ahead of Greenwich Mean Time (GMT +9), which is 14 hours ahead of U.S. Eastern Standard Time (EST +14).

Holidays

An up-to-date, online *World Holiday and Time Zone Guide* is available at www.get-customs.com. It lists official holidays by country and by day of the year, business and cultural tips, a corruption index, and time zones with worldwide business hours.

This list is a working guide. Dates should be corroborated before final travel plans are made. In cases where holidays fall on Saturday or Sunday, commercial establishments may be closed the preceding Friday or following Monday.

Jan 1	SA	New Year's Day
Jan 2	SU	New Year's holiday
Feb 4	FR	Lunar New Year's holiday (4–6)
Mar 1	WE	Independence Movement Day
Apr 5	WE	Arbor Day
May 5	FR	Children's Day
May 11	TH	Buddha's Birthday
Jun 6	TU	Memorial Day
Jul 17	MO	Constitution Day
Aug 15	TU	Liberation Day
Sep 11	MO	Harvest Festival holiday (11–13)
Oct 3	TU	National Foundation Day
Dec 25	MO	Christmas Day

In addition to the above, the Lunar New Year is observed as an official holiday.

Christmas is observed as a holiday, even though only a minority of Koreans are Christian.

The exact days of observance should always be corroborated by local contacts.

Work Week

- Business hours are generally from 8:30 or 9:00 A.M. to 5:00 or 6:00 P.M. Monday through Friday. Many businesses keep Saturday hours as well, from 9:00 A.M. to 12 noon or 1:00 P.M.

- Banking hours are 9:30 A.M. to 4:30 P.M. Monday through Friday, and 9:30 A.M. to 1:30 P.M. on Saturday.

- Most government offices are open 9:00 A.M. to 5:00 or 6:00 P.M. Monday through Friday, and 9:00 A.M. to noon on Saturday.

- The best times for business meetings are 10:00 to 11:00 A.M. and 2:00 to 3:00 P.M. Prior appointments are necessary. Business dinners are common, and meetings may take place in a local coffee shop. Business breakfasts are rare.

Religious/Societal Influences on Business

South Korea is a society run along Confucian precepts. In fact, Confucianism may have had a more profound effect on Korea than it has had even in China, where Confucianism originated. (Remember that Confucianism is not a religion in the classic sense of the word; rather, it is a philosophy and guide for living.)

Every person has a place and status in Korean society. The role is determined by Confucianism. Thus, the son must defer to his father, the wife defers to her husband, the younger sibling to the older sibling, the employee to the boss, etc. (Even identical twins have rankings: The younger twin must defer to the older one!) This ranking in society is all-important in Korea. Employees—and their salaries—are ranked by seniority. Foreign companies with Korean subsidiaries find it difficult to link pay with performance. Senior Korean executives are insulted if they are paid less than a junior executive (no matter how talented).

The only relationships of equality in Korea are between members of the same class. One's closest friends are drawn from this group.

Confucianism dictates an inferior position for women. Korea is defiantly a male-dominated society, where women are not expected to pursue lifelong careers in business. Only a few generations ago, women were completely isolated from society, kept in seclusion in a manner similar to Middle Eastern cultures.

Korea has no official religion. Buddhism has traditionally been the major Korean religion, but Buddhism has gone through periods where it has been repressed by Korea's Confucian rulers. Buddhism is Korea's most popular religion, although only 23.3% of Koreans identify themselves as Buddhist. (Over half of Koreans follow no formal religion at all.)

The Koreans are proud that Christianity did not reach Korea through missionaries. Instead, a Korean scholar studying in Beijing was baptized a Catholic in 1777. It was this scholar, on his return, who introduced Catholicism to Korea. Protestantism gained a foothold in 1884 via a Protestant physician who became the royal physician. Today, about 19.8% of Koreans identify themselves as Protestant; 6.7% are Roman Catholic.

Whatever their formal religion, most Koreans also follow traditional Shamanistic beliefs. These include a belief in spirits, the veneration of ancestors, and the usefulness of fortunetelling.

Education has always been highly prized in Korea. When the 1996 economic crisis resulted in layoffs and hiring freezes, many unemployed Koreans went back to school.

Cultural Note: Nepotism is common in Korea: securing jobs for relatives was traditionally a goal of the successful executive. This, like many traditions, may be changing. In April of 1999 South Korean President Kim Dae Jung denounced nepotism in the management of Korean Air—an airline with one of the world's worst safety records. "Korean Air is a typical case of management gone wrong with family members in its top managerial posts," noted President Kim. Although Korean Air is a private airline, President Kim believes that the airline's poor record reflects badly upon the Republic of Korea. At the time of this speech, Korean Air was the world's 13th largest airline.

---

5 Cultural Tips

1. Fortunetellers are consulted by Koreans in all walks of life—even executives consult them about business transactions. A negative report from a fortuneteller could ruin an entire deal. A fortuneteller is called a *mudang* in Korean.

2. The Korean boss is king of his (or, rarely, her) company. His employees defer to him and treat him with great respect. Bad news is never given to the boss at the start of the day; no one would want to start the day by upsetting the boss. Foreigners should attempt to show proper respect to Korean supervisors. This includes not putting anything on the boss's desk during a presentation. Korean executives are very territorial about their desks.

3. Koreans do not maintain so much eye contact as North Americans. As a general rule, Koreans of equal status will look at each other only half of the time during their conversation. When persons are of unequal status, the lower-ranking person will often avert his or her eyes during much of the conversation. Extended or intense eye contact is associated with anger. North Americans who try to maintain continuous eye contact may appear hostile or aggressive.

4. South Korea is one of the most crowded nations on Earth—even more densely populated than India or Japan. In such a crowded country, personal space is limited. Koreans are accustomed to standing or sitting close together. They compete aggressively on the street, bumping each other and treading on feet without apology. Since the contact is unintentional, Koreans do not feel the need to apologize for such behavior.

5. Never write a Korean's name in red ink. Korean Buddhists only write a dead person's name in red ink (either at the time of their death or at the anniversary of a death).

Cultural Note: If there is one classic Korean characteristic, it would be resiliency. Koreans seem to be able to survive almost any hardship. Sacrifice has been demanded of one generation after another of Koreans. The results of this sacrifice in South Korea are evident to any visitor: a poor, war-torn agricultural country with few resources has transformed itself into the world's 11th richest economy.

Faux Pas: In 1998, the Swedish automobile firm Volvo bought 85% of Samsung's construction equipment business. Volvo's corporate culture is very different from that of the average Korean firm. In particular, Volvo tried to institute its culture of transparency: sharing all its plans with its employees in the hope that they will offer useful suggestions. It was expected that Volvo's Korean employees would keep the corporation's plans secret. They did not. Male Korean executives, like Japanese executives, spend most nights drinking and singing karaoke with their friends. In Korea, these friends will be a cohort of people who graduated from the same college in the same year. Some of them may work for competing companies. Information that should be proprietorial tends to leak during these drinking sessions. Volvo is not the only foreign firm to have had problems in this arena.

Economic Overview

The Korea of the 1990s and 2000 is modern, cosmopolitan, fast-paced, and dynamic with abundant business opportunities for savvy American businesses. Since the devastation left behind from the Korean Conflict in the early 1950s, the Republic of Korea (ROK) has matured and expanded into a bustling and thriving economy buttressed by political and macroeconomic stability. Consumption spending, which accounts for more than half of South Korea's total GDP, is growing along with optimism about the economy.

South Korea did not escape the Asian Financial Crisis. Since 1996 it has been mired in its worst recession since the Korean War.

Despite the recession, South Korea still has the 11th largest economy in the world. As of 1998 Korea became the fifth largest market for U.S. exports. The U.S. provides over 20% of Korea's imports.

The domestic political situation in South Korea has been stable enough to permit remarkable growth over the last generation. While Americans planning to do business in Korea should continue to follow closely developments involving North Korea, they should also realize that the North Korean threat has yet to serve as a brake on South Korea's economic growth.

U.S.-manufactured goods related to infrastructure, consumables, and high-tech goods are expected to do well in the coming years.

The U.S. Department of Commerce has designated Korea as one of the 10 Big Emerging Markets (BEMs). The potential for business with Korea is immense. Not only is the Korean government spending billions to improve its infrastructure systems, it is also encouraging foreign investors.

The major question mark in South Korea's future remains North Korea. Reunification is a given, but no one can say when it will happen. The Communist government of North Korea could simply collapse—or, in a last-ditch attempt to retain power, declare war. Whatever happens, South Korea will be burdened with a reunification bill far greater than the one imposed on West Germany when it absorbed East Germany in 1988.

5 *Largest Businesses in South Korea*

Bumwoo Corporation, Songbuk-gu
    434,330 employees
Korea Industry Co., Ltd., Pusan
    336,508 employees
Samsung Life Insurance Co., Ltd., Chung-gu
    79,582 employees
Korea Telecommunication Authority, Chongno-gu
    60,058 employees
Samsung Electronics Co, Ltd., Kyongki-do
    59,086 employees

Cultural Note: Seperated by the language barrier, foreigners often are unaware of the scope of Korean humor. The Korean sense of humor has helped the Korean people survive centuries of hardship. Yet their humor is so untranslatable that Westerners often don't know it exists.

However, foreigners should know that not all smiles in Korea are happy ones. Embarrassment—even serious loss of face—is often responded to with a smile and a nervous giggle. The attentive foreigner can learn to distinguish between amused smiles and embarrassed ones.

Comparative Data

Comparative Data Ratings
(Scale: 5 = Excellent; 1 = Poor)
South Korea: 3.375%

A.	GDP Growth:	4
B.	Per Capita Income:	3
C.	Trade Flows with the U.S.:	5
D.	Country Risk:	3
E.	Monetary Policy:	4
F.	Trade Policy:	3
	• Tariffs	
	• Import Licensing	
	• Import Taxes	
G.	Protection of Property Rights:	3
H.	Foreign Investment Climate:	3

GROSS DOMESTIC PRODUCT: $631 billion (1997 estimate)

GDP GROWTH: 9.5% (1999 estimate)

PER CAPITA INCOME: $13,700 (1997 estimate)

Trade Flows with the U.S.

U.S. EXPORTS TO SOUTH KOREA: $16.5 billion (1998)

U.S. IMPORTS FROM SOUTH KOREA: $23.9 billion (1998)

TOP U.S. EXPORTS TO SOUTH KOREA: Electrical components; machinery; aircraft and parts; medical and optical equipment; organic chemicals; hides and skins; mineral fuel and oil; cereals; building products; plastics and resins

TOP U.S. PROSPECTS FOR EXPORT TO SOUTH KOREA: Electrical power systems; transportation services; travel and tourism; telecommunications equipment; aircraft and parts; architectural/construction/engineering services; computers and peripherals; computer software; pollution-control equipment; drugs and pharmaceuticals; medical equipment; education and training

Country Risk

There is enough uncertainty over expected returns to warrant close monitoring of country risk.

Unconfirmed letters of credit predominate on sales to South Korea, although more liberal terms are being used more and more. When open account terms are extended, 60 to 90 days are the norm.

Monetary Policy

Inflation has remained in single digits even during the Korean economic boom of the mid-1990s. The retail inflation rate was 4.5% in 1995 and 5.0% in 1996, and is expected to remain steady at around 5–6% for the foreseeable future.

The Korean won was hard hit by the Asian economic crisis, falling 54% against the U.S. dollar at the end of 1997. However, as the Korean economy regrouped in 1999, it had recovered over half of its previous value.

MONETARY UNIT: won

Trade Policy

TARIFFS   The average tariff rate on manufactured goods imported into South Korea is about 8%. However, tariffs on agricultural products range from 30–100%. Adjustment tariffs also exist that are used for balance of payment purposes.

Import duties are not assessed on capital goods and raw materials imported in connection with foreign investment projects. Additionally, certain raw materials used in the production of export goods are often exempt from duty, and certain machinery, materials, and parts used in design industries may enter South Korea either duty-free or at reduced rates.

Tariffs and taxes are payable in South Korean won before goods are permitted to clear customs.

IMPORT LICENSING   Under the system of licensing, all commodities may be freely imported unless included on a negative list, which includes commodities that are either prohibited or restricted. The negative list, known as the *Export and Import Notice*, is published by the Ministry of Trade, Industry and Energy, and remains effective until revised to meet changing economic conditions. Restricted items include firearms, illicit drugs, endangered species, etc.

IMPORT TAXES   South Korea has a flat 10% value-added tax (VAT) on all imports.

A special excise tax of 15–100% is also levied on the import of certain luxury items and durable consumer goods.

Protection of Intellectual Property Rights

South Korea is a member and signatory to the Paris Convention for the Protection of Industrial Property, the Patent Cooperation Treaty, and the Universal Copyright Convention.

Worldwide novelty and highly creative inventiveness are required for grant of patents. A lesser level of creativeness is necessary for utility models. The first party to file an invention prevails. Applications are published 18 months after filing. The term of patent is 20 years from application and the term of utility models is 15 years. A new design law was passed in 1998. Licenses and assignments have to be recorded in order to grant or transfer patent rights.

Trademark rights are established by registration. Revised trademark laws went into effect in 1996 and 1998. Applications for trademarks may be filed without proof of use—except on the 10-year renewal. Korea is one of the few countries with its own national classification system. Governmental approval is required for royalty-bearing licenses.

A new copyright act took effect in 1996 in which copyrights result on creation of the work. Copyrights have a term of 50 years from death (where the author is known), or 50 years from publication of anonymous or pseudonymous works. Stage performances and broadcasts are protected for 50 years as well. Computer programs are protected by a special act that provides rights equivalent to copyright.

Foreign Investment Climate

The South Korean government is making a concerted effort to reverse Korea's reputation as a difficult environment for foreign investment. A new program to attract foreign direct investment was begun in 1994. It was intended to offer a one-stop approval service for prospective investors, expanded land availability for factory sites, financing incentives for high-technology firms, and tax holidays.

In the past, South Korean law did not permit direct investment through merger with or acquisition of an existing domestic firm. Foreign and domestic investors were limited to 10% of the shares in a South Korean firm listed on the South Korea Stock Exchange. But the 1996 economic crisis increased the need for foreign capital. A restructuring drive in 1999 made possible the acquisitions of some of the largest Korean firms. Mergers and acquisitions were estimated to reach $15 billion in 1999. A few of Korea's largest banks have been bought by U.S., U.K., and German firms—something the government would have forbidden a few years ago.

Political Leaders, Parties, and International Organizations

The International Academy at Santa Barbara at http://www.iasb.org/cwl publishes *Current World Leaders*, an excellent resource for up-to-date data on political leaders, parties, demographics, etc., in South Korea. Tel: (800) 530-2682 or (805) 965-5010 for subscription information to their database.

Head of State and the Government:
President Kim Dae Jung

Next Election:
December 2002

Political Parties:
Grand National Party (formerly the New Korea Party), National Congress for New Politics, United Liberal Democrats

Membership in international organizations:

ADB, APEC, Asian People's Anti-Communist League, CP, EBRD, INTELSAT, IWhC, IPU, PECC, UN and most of its specialized agencies and related organizations (including ESCAP, FAO, GATT, IAEA, IBRD, ICAO, IDA, IFAD, IFC, ILO, IMF, IMO, ITU, UNCTAD, UNESCO, UNIDO, UPU, WHO, WIPO, WMO)

Political Influences on Business

South Korea's democratization, which began with free presidential elections in 1987, has led to a mature, bilateral relationship between South Korea and the U.S. The two countries consider themselves friends, partners, and allies. South Korea and the U.S. share common democratic values and practices and are working together, both in the region and in the rest of the world, to advance democratization and human rights.

The U.S. has a strong security relationship with South Korea and is committed to maintaining peace and stability on the Korean peninsula. The U.S. is obligated under the 1954 U.S.–Korea Mutual Defense Treaty to help South Korea defend itself from external aggression. In support of that commitment, the U.S. maintains about 37,000 uniformed men and women in the country, commanded by a U.S. four-star general who is also commander of the United Nations forces, including the Second Infantry Division and air force squadrons.

Spurred by the depression that began in 1996, the Republic of Korea's economy is undergoing a major restructuring. The government is insisting upon reform, efficiency, and greater transparency among Korean businesses. Nevertheless, there are parts of the government bureaucracy that cling to the old ways. Some foreign imports continue to be limited, and there is a nationalistic sentiment that colors popular attitudes against imports and foreign companies in South Korea.

Despite the country's amazing economic success, the prevailing attitude is that South Korea remains a poor country. For this reason, the South Koreans feel they should be exempt from the "level playing field" demanded by United States trade negotiators. Even though South Korea now has the world's 11th largest economy, in the minds of its citizens its success is still tenuous. The perception exists that South Korea still needs assistance and protectionist trade policies to survive.

South Korea is governed by a directly elected President and a unicameral National Assembly that is selected by both direct and proportional elections. The President serves five years and can serve only one term. National Assembly legislators are elected in a single election every four years.

Although nominally a democracy, most of South Korea's leaders following the Korean Conflict were authoritarian military leaders. In February 1993 Kim Young Sam became South Korea's first chief executive in three decades who did not come from the ranks of the military. He was succeeded in the 1998 elections by opposition politician Kim Dae Jung. Kim Dae Jung's election is especially significant as he was a political dissident who had been imprisoned under military rule.

Contacts in the United States

EMBASSY OF THE REPUBLIC OF KOREA (SOUTH)
2450 Massachusetts Avenue, NW
Washington, D.C. 20008
Tel: (202) 939-5600
Fax: (202) 387 0205
www.mofat.go.kr/usa

Passport/Visa Requirements

A passport is required. A visa is not required for tourist stays of up to 15 days. For longer stays and other types of travel, visas must be obtained in advance.

BUSINESS VISA: A valid passport; application for visa (form provided by Korean Consulate); letter from sponsoring organization indicating purpose of trip (contract number, if any), intended period of stay, and financial responsibilities; recent photograph. If a U.S. government contract is involved, include a copy of the government travel orders. Fee is $20.00.

For current information concerning entry and customs requirements for South Korea, travelers can contact the South Korean Embassy

U.S. citizens who wish to apply for a passport may visit Passport Services' well-organized website at http://travel.state.gov/passport_services.html.

Contacts in South Korea

THE EMBASSY OF THE UNITED STATES
82 Sejong-Ro
Chongro-Ku
Seoul
Mailing Address:American Embassy, Unit 15550, APO AP 96205-0001
Tel: (82) (2) 397-4114
Fax: (82) (2) 738-8845
www.usembassy.state.gov/seoul

THE AMERICAN CHAMBER OF COMMERCE IN KOREA
2/F Westin Chosun Hotel
87 Sokong Dong
Ghung-gu, Seoul
Tel: (82) (2) 753-6471
Fax: (82) (2) 755-6577
www.amchamkorea.org

OFFICE OF THE PRESIDENT
Chong Wa Dae
1 Sejong-no
Chongno-gu
Seoul, Republic of Korea

OFFICE OF THE PRIME MINISTER
77 Sejong-no
Chongno-gu
Seoul, Republic of Korea

Further contacts and websites can be found in Appendix A.

Communications

TELEPHONE: The international country code for South Korea is 82.

Phone numbers vary in length. They are usually six or seven digits in length.

Area codes also vary in length, from one to three digits. In writing, the area code is usually offset by parenthesis.

E-MAIL: E-mail addresses located in South Korea end with the code .kr

---

Observation: "Without question, the trait that sets Koreans apart from the Chinese, Japanese, and other Asians is their emotionalism. . . . They are quick to anger and just as quick to reconciliation. They are the only Asians among whom you will commonly see public tears or public displays of affection. . . .

"Korean men are very emotional even when making business decisions. If you strike the right emotional cord, the Korean decision-maker will often respond favorably simply on impulse. On the other hand, a Korean, unlike a Japanese, will not be polite when you get on his wrong side. Korean tempers can get awfully hot. . . ."

—From *The Asian Mind Game* by Chin-ning Chu

Faux Pas: A foreign manufacturer of dog food experienced delay after delay in his efforts to put dog food commercials on South Korean television. Only after months of fruitless effort did he discover the reason for the opposition: too many South Koreans still remember hunger and poverty. When people do not have enough food, South Koreans consider it shameful to promote a special food for dogs. Although there has been no famine in South Korea in decades, the memory of it is still present—and famine is still endemic in North Korea.

Spain

Official Name:	Kingdom of Spain (Reino de Espana)
Official Language:	Spanish
Government System:	Constitutional monarchy
Population:	39.2 million (1999 estimate)
Population Growth Rate:	0.1% (1999 estimate)
Area:	504,750 sq. km. (194,884 sq. mi.), including the Balearic and Canary Islands; about the size of Arizona and Utah combined
Natural Resources:	coal, lignite, iron ore, uranium, mercury, pyrites, fluorspar, gypsum, zinc, lead, tungsten, copper, kaolin, potash, hydropower
Major Cities:	Madrid (capital), Barcelona, Valencia, Seville, Zaragoza, Malaga, Bilbao

Cultural Note: The family always comes first in Spain. Nepotism is the rule rather than the exception. Given a choice between a mediocre offer from a relative and a lucrative offer from a stranger, many Spaniards would choose the relative's offer.

Age Breakdown

0–14 = 15%   15–64 = 68%   65+ = 17% (1999 estimate)
Life Expectancy: 73.97 years, male; 81.71 years, female (1999 estimate)

Time

Time seems to run slower in Spain. While foreigners are expected to be punctual, Spaniards do not consider themselves ruled by the clock. They generally consider deadlines an objective to be achieved, if possible, but do not become overly concerned with delays.

Spain is 1 hour ahead of Greenwich Mean Time (GMT +1), or 6 hours ahead of U.S. Eastern Standard Time (EST +6).

Holidays

An up-to-date, online *World Holiday and Time Zone Guide* is available at www.get-customs.com. It lists official holidays by country and by day of the year, business and cultural tips, a corruption index, and time zones with worldwide business hours.

This list is a working guide. Dates should be corroborated before final travel plans are made. In cases where holidays fall on Saturday or Sunday, commercial establishments may be closed the preceding Friday or following Monday.

Jan 1	SA	New Year's Day
Jan 6	TH	Epiphany
Mar 19	SU	St. Joseph's Day
Apr 20	TH	Holy Thursday
Apr 21	FR	Good Friday
Apr 22	SA	Holy Saturday
Apr 24	MO	Easter Monday
May 1	MO	Labor Day
Aug 15	TU	Assumption
Oct 12	TH	Spanish National Day
Nov 1	WE	All Saints Day
Dec 6	WE	Constitution Day
Dec 8	FR	Immaculate Conception
Dec 25	MO	Christmas Day
Dec 26	TU	St. Stephen's Day

Different cities have additional holidays, such as Las Fallas in Valencia, and St. Stephen's Day in Barcelona (December 26). Again, the days of observance should always be corroborated by local contacts.

Work Week

- The work week is 40 hours in Spain, but hours of operation may vary.
- In Madrid businesses are open from 9:00 A.M. to 1:30 P.M. and again from 3:00 P.M. to 6:00 P.M. Monday to Friday. In July and August, when most people take their vacations, hours may change to 8:30 A.M. to 2:30 P.M. Monday through Thursday, and 8:30 A.M. to 2:00 P.M. on Friday.

- Government offices are usually open to the public from 9:00 A.M. to 1:00 P.M. Monday through Friday.
- Banks are generally open from 9:00 A.M. to 1:00 or 2:00 P.M., although on Saturday they stay open from 9:00 A.M. to 3:00 P.M.

Religious/Societal Influences on Business

Although Spain has no official religion, the vast majority of Spaniards are raised in the Roman Catholic Church. The Church still wields great influence in Spain. The large size of Spanish families was attributed to the Church's opposition to contraception and divorce.

Children are still pampered in Spain, but the birth rate has been falling since the 1970s. Small children are taken everywhere. Foreigners can be disconcerted by the presence of noisy children at expensive restaurants, where the staff is more likely to indulge them than remonstrate them.

As a result of the social changes that followed the puritan Franco era, Spanish women have demanded more rights, both personally and professionally.

Machismo still defines the expected code of conduct for men; when one's honor is impugned, a response must be made. An ill-conceived joke can easily provoke a hostile response—or, in business, subvert a deal.

Related to *machismo* is the *yo primero* ("me first") attitude, evident in the Spanish reluctance to form queues. If you are doing business with multiple customers at a single site (such as a single sales counter) in Spain, provide a method of crowd control. Serving customers by number is a common technique. *Yo primero* can also be seen in the aggressive Spanish driving style, which endangers motorists and pedestrians alike.

Due to the prevalence of Catholicism in Spain, there are a number of movements based on Catholic spirituality and beliefs. The best known of these organizations is called *Opus Dei* ("The Work of God"). Its objectives of "sanctification of ordinary work and the accomplishment of professional duties" are taken very seriously by *Opus Dei* members. With its large membership, you may encounter its members at work, often among successful business executives.

Catholics must be baptized under the same given name as a Catholic Saint, and that Saint's yearly Feast Day is celebrated by the Saint's namesakes—like a second birthday.

5 Cultural Tips

1. While many Spanish businesspeople speak English, you should have all of your materials printed in Spanish. Your business cards should have English on one side and Spanish on the other. Present your card with the Spanish side facing your Spanish colleague.
2. Business in Spain is conducted via personal relationships. It takes time to establish such relationships. Take great care when selecting your Spanish representative, since once you have chosen him or her, it is difficult to switch to another person.

3. Get used to chaotic business discussions. It may seem like everyone is talking at once. Negotiations can be extended, laborious affairs.

4. Eating is part of establishing business relationships in Spain. However, never schedule a meal for the sole purpose of conducting business. Unless your Spanish counterparts bring up discussions of work, keep the conversation social.

   Your business associates may join you at all four meals: breakfast, lunch, the afternoon snack, and dinner. A business breakfast should be scheduled no earlier than 8:30 A.M. Lunch is the main meal of the day and doesn't start until 2 P.M. Many businesspeople go home for lunch every day. Around 5:00 or 6:00 P.M., Spaniards often go out for a drink and hors d'oevres, which are called *tapas*. Tapas are often eaten at more than one establishment; Spaniards stroll from one tapas bar to another, eating salted almonds in one place, potato omelets in another, etc. Dinner is never served before 9:00 P.M.

5. Although Spaniards have become more relaxed in recent years, they still dress more formally than many other Europeans. In Spain it is important to project an image of good taste and propriety. Wear well-made, conservative attire. Name brands are noticed in Spain!

Economic Overview

Although still faced with serious structural problems, Spain's economy has begun a slow but steady recovery. The government is moving ahead with major infrastructure projects and privatization in a number of key sectors. U.S. firms are responding to these changes and stepping up their activities in Spain.

Spain has been catching up economically with the rest of Western Europe. The economic recovery has shifted from export-led to investment-led growth. The U.S. is one of the top ten investor nations in Spain, with $1.3 billion in direct investment in 1997.

Although Spain maintains an open and transparent trading system and U.S. products and technologies are in demand, U.S. companies are disadvantaged vis-a-vis their European competitors by duties imposed on products from outside the EU, higher transportation costs, and the entrenched presence of EU firms in the Spanish markets.

U.S. firms should find increased opportunities for trade and investment as the Spanish government moves ahead with privatization in the telecommunications, power, and oil and gas sectors.

5 Largest Businesses in Spain

Telfonica S.A., Madrid
   65,663 employees
El Corte Ingles S.A., Madrid
   56,537 employees
Oganizacion Nacional de Ciegos de Espana, Madrid
   47,200 employees

Eulen S.A., Madrid
  28,611 employees
Banco Bilbao Vizcaya S.A., Bilbao
  24,811 employees

Cultural Note: Although Spanish is the official language of Spain, there are several regional variants of Spanish. *Catalán* is spoken in the east and *Gallego* in the northwest. Each has different pronunciations and spellings (such as using an *X* instead of a *J*). The native language of the Basque region, *Euskera*, is not Spanish at all—it is linguistically unrelated to any known language. *Castilian* is the version taught in schools.

Comparative Data

Comparative Data Ratings
(Scale: 5 = Highest; 1 = Lowest)
Spain: 3.5

A. GDP Growth: 3
B. Per Capita Income: 4
C. Trade Flows with the U.S.: 3
D. Country Risk: 4
E. Monetary Policy: 3
F. Trade Policy: 4
  • Tariffs
  • Import Licensing
  • Import Taxes
G. Protection of Property Rights: 3
H. Foreign Investment Climate: 4

GROSS DOMESTIC PRODUCT: $645.6 billion (1998 estimate)

GDP GROWTH: 3.9% (1999); 3.4% (2000 estimate)

PER CAPITA INCOME: $16,500 (1998 estimate)

Trade Flows with the U.S.

U.S. EXPORTS TO SPAIN: $5.5 billion (1998)

U.S. IMPORTS FROM SPAIN: $4.8 billion (1998)

TOP U.S. EXPORTS TO SPAIN: Pollution-control and water resources equipment; computers and peripherals; aircraft and parts; telecommunications services; miscellaneous grains/seeds/fruits; franchising; electric power systems; medical equipment; building products; architectural/construction/engineering services; telecommunications equipment; chemical machinery and equipment

TOP U.S. PROSPECTS FOR EXPORT TO SPAIN: Telecommunications services; pollution-control and water resources equipment; franchising; telecommunications equipment; electric power systems; medical equipment; automotive parts and accessories; architectural/construction/engineering services; organic chemicals for the pharmaceutical industry; paper and paperboard

Country Risk

Dun & Bradstreet rates Spain as a good creditworthy country with good capacity to meet outstanding payment liabilities. Credit terms vary according to sector and size of transaction, but are usually 60 to 120 days. Letter of credit is advised with new customers. Credit checks are advised especially for small or newly established businesses.

Monetary Policy

The Spanish peseta experienced strong fluctuations in the early 1990s, having been devalued five times between September 1992 and March 1995.

Stability returned with the economic prosperity of the second half of the decade. Inflation fell from between 4% and 5% in the mid-1990s to 2% in 1997 and 1998.

MONETARY UNIT: peseta; conversion to the European Union's euro started in 1999

Trade Policy

TARIFFS   For U.S. products, the tariff rate averages 5%. Spanish tariffs for European countries have been zero since January 1, 1993 while those from third-country goods, including those from the U.S., receive the EU's Common External Tariff. U.S. goods are taxed according to the standard EU duty rate.

While a few agricultural commodities are duty-free or subject to minimal duties, the great majority of agricultural products (those covered by the Common Agricultural Policy) and food products are subject to high duties or variable import levies that significantly restrict access into the Spanish market.

Most raw materials enter duty-free or at low duty rates.

IMPORT LICENSING   As a general rule, imports may be freely made into Spain.

An *Import Authorization* form is used to control imports that are subject to quotas. While Spain does not enforce any quotas on U.S.-origin manufactured products, this document may still be required if part of the shipment contains products or goods produced or manufactured in a third country.

Importers apply for import licenses at the Spanish General Register of Spain's Department of Commerce or any of its regional offices. The license application must be accompanied by a commercial invoice. Spanish customs accepts commercial invoices via fax. Import licenses, when granted, are usually valid for six months.

Spanish regulations ban the import of illicit narcotics and drugs. They also set up very restrictive regulations for imports of explosives, fire weapons, defense equipment and material in general, tobacco, and gambling material.

U.S. exporters should ensure, prior to making shipments, that the necessary licenses have been obtained by their importing party. Additionally, they should have their importer confirm with Spanish customs whether any product approvals or other special certificates are required for the shipment to pass customs.

IMPORT TAXES Spain has a 16% value-added tax (VAT), and a 7% reduced rate for food, water, books, newspapers, magazines, pharmaceutical products, and school supplies.

Protection of Intellectual Property Rights

Spain is a signatory to the Paris Convention for Protection of Industrial Property, the Madrid Trademark Agreements, the Universal Copyright Convention, the Berne Convention on Protection of Literary and Artistic Works, the Patent Cooperation Treaty, and the European Convention. Spain and the U.S. have signed a bilateral copyright treaty. Spain is the site of the European Trademark Office and recently executed the Trademark Law Treaty. Despite Spain's effort to upgrade and enforce its laws, however, software piracy continues.

Spain has two types of patents—patents of invention and patents of addition. *Patents of invention* require worldwide novelty and have terms of 20 years from application. *Patents of addition* cover improvements in the main patents and expire when the main patents expire.

Trademark protection extends to goods, services, and trade names. Trade names can only be registered if they are the names of the companies seeking registration. Trademark registrations have renewable terms of 10 years. The international classification system is followed. Cancellations based on prior use must be brought in 5 years of publication of the acceptance. Marks are subject to cancellation if not used within 5 years of grant.

Copyrights result automatically on creation of a work. Registration is permissive. Literary, artistic, and scientific works, including computer programs and databases, are protected by copyright. The term of copyright is life of the author plus 80 years.

Foreign Investment Climate

The Spanish government is interested in attracting new foreign investment to modernize the economy. Spanish law permits foreign investment up to 100% of equity, except in a small number of strategic sectors. Capital movements have been completely liberalized.

More than 550 U.S. firms have established subsidiaries in Spain. The U.S. ranks third among investor nations after The Netherlands and France.

The Spanish central, regional, and local governments all actively encourage foreign investment.

Political Leaders, Parties, and International Organizations

The International Academy at Santa Barbara at http://www.iasb.org/cwl publishes *Current World Leaders*, an excellent resource for up-to-date data on political leaders, parties, demographics, etc., in Spain. Tel: (800) 530-2682 or (805) 965-5010 for subscription information to their database.

Chief of State:

King Juan Carlos I

Head of the Government:

Prime Minister José María Aznar López

Political Parties:

Socialist Workers' Party (PSOE), Popular Party (PP), United Left (IU), Basque Nationalist Party (PNV)

Membership in international organizations:

CE, EBRD, EU, INTELSAT, NACC, NATO, OECD, OSCE, UN and all of its specialized agencies and related organizations (including FAO, GATT, IAEA, IBRD, ICAO, IDA, IFAD, IFC, ILO, IMF, IMO, ITU UNESCO, UNIDO, UPU, WHO, WIPO, WMO), WEU, World Tourism Organization

Political Influences on Business

Spain is a parliamentary monarchy based on its constitution of December 1978. Some observers feel that the choice of the term *parliamentary* monarchy rather than *constitutional* monarchy indicates that Spain is still in the process of inventing itself.

The last Prime Minister (a position technically known as President of the Government) was Felipe Gonzalez Marquez, the Secretary General of the PSOE. He was first elected to his position in 1982; his party governed with absolute parliamentary majorities from 1982–1993. After the June 1993 general election, Prime Minister Gonzalez won an unprecedented fourth consecutive term, although his Socialist Party presided over a minority government. The PSOE's chief ally in the coalition was the Catalan nationalist party CiU (which itself is a coalition). Continued party factionalism, high unemployment, a series of corruption scandals, and the GAL case involving extra-legal security force operations against ETA terrorists in the early 1980s led to a significant decline in Gonzalez's popularity. Also damaging was a scandal involving the phone-tapping (by the Spanish intelligence unit, CESID) of leading politicians, prominent businessmen, and even the King of Spain! But the CiU publicly committed itself to supporting Gonzalez through 1995, allowing Gonzalez to remain in office through the Spanish EU presidency (July–December 1995).

During the Gonzalez administration, the principal opposition party was the center–right Popular Party (PP). As a result of the continuing scandals of the Gonzalez administration, the Popular Party emerged the winner in the elections of March 1996. However, continued political infighting kept the Popular Party's choice for Prime Minister, Jose Maria Aznar, from taking office until May. Mr. Aznar's accession was supported by both the Catalan and the Basque regional parties. His support by the moderate Basque Nationalist Party has helped to end the bombing campaign waged against Spain by the Basque terrorist group ETA.

His administration has presided over strong economic growth in Spain. The economy has been helped by a massive privatization program. Spain was one of the initial EU members to adopt the euro as its currency in 1999.

The electoral term for national government is a maximum four years, but elections can be called before that term expires.

Contacts in the United States

THE EMBASSY OF THE KINGDOM OF SPAIN
2375 Pennsylvania Avenue, NW
Washington, D.C. 20037
Tel: (202) 452-0100
Fax: (202) 728-2317
www.spainemb.org/information/

Passport/Visa Requirements

A passport is necessary, but a visa is not required for tourist stays of up to 3 months; visitors may subsequently apply for an extension of stay at a Spanish immigration office.

Note: European Union countries—including Austria, Belgium, Finland, Germany, Luxembourg, the Netherlands, Portugal, and Spain—have implemented the Schengen zone agreement to end all passport controls between the participating member states.

Italy and Greece are signatory to the agreement, but have not implemented the terms. France is signatory to the agreement, but for security reasons has suspended terms of the agreement.

U.S. citizens who wish to apply for a passport may visit Passport Services' well-organized website at http://travel.state.gov/passport_services.html.

For further information concerning entry requirements, travelers may contact the Embassy of Spain.

Contacts In Spain

THE EMBASSY OF THE UNITED STATES OF AMERICA
Serrano 75
28006 Madrid

Mailing address: APO AE 09642
Tel: (34) (1) 577-4000
Fax: (34) (1) 577-5735
www.embusa.es

AMERICAN CHAMBER OF COMMERCE IN SPAIN
Avda. Diagonal 477, 8th Floor
08036 Barcelona
Tel: (34) (3) 405-1266
Fax: (34) (3) 405-3124

DUN & BRADSTREET, S.A.
Postal Address: Apartado de Correos
209, 28080 Madrid
Street Address: Salvador de Madariaga,
1,-2o, 28027 Madrid
Telephone: (34) (1) 377-9100
Fax: (34) (1) 377-9101

KING JUAN CARLOS I
Palacio de la Zarzuela
28071 Madrid, Kingdom of Spain

OFFICE OF THE PRIME MINISTER
Presidencia del Gobierno
Complejo de la Moncloa
28071 Madrid, Kingdom of Spain

Further contacts and websites can be found in Appendix A.

Communications

TELEPHONE: The international country code for Spain is 34.

Area codes may be one or two digits in length.

Phone numbers are six or seven digits in length. Six-digit phone numbers use two-digit area codes; seven-digit phone numbers are preceded by one-digit area codes. In other words, the total phone number will always be eight digits in length.

E-MAIL: E-mail addresses located in Spain end with the code .es

---

Faux Pas: Foreigners who buy or lease homes or offices in Spain sometimes fall afoul of Spain's "Ley de Propriedad Horizontal" (Law of Horizontal Property). This applies to anything that buildings share in common: electric or telephone lines, sewers, road frontages, etc.

The law holds all the tenants equally responsible for the shared item. You may find yourself paying a recalcitrant neighbor's share of a fee, just so you can have electric or sewer service!

Spanish Names and Titles

• First names are appropriate among close friends and young people only. Always wait for your Spanish counterpart to initiate the use of first names, or the use of the familiar form of address (*tú*) as opposed to the formal form (*Usted*).

- In Spain, the use of the familiar (*tú*) and formal (*Usted*) forms of address are different from their usage in Latin America. For example, Spaniards always speak to domestic servants in the formal (*Usted*) manner; they feel this confers dignity and shows respect for the servant as a person. Also, the informal (*tú*) form is more likely to be used by colleagues in a Spanish office than in a Latin American office. Sometimes employees even speak to their bosses using the *tú* (informal) form. This would border on insubordination in other Spanish-speaking countries.

- Most people you meet should be addressed with a title and their surname. Only children, family members, and close friends address each other by their first names.

- Persons who do not have professional titles should be addressed as Mr./Mrs./Miss + their surname. In Spanish, these are: Mr. = Señor, Mrs. = Señora, Miss = Señorita.

- Most Spaniards have two surnames: one from their father, which is listed first, followed by one from their mother. Only the father's surname is commonly used when addressing someone verbally, i.e., Señor Juan Antonio Martinez de García = Señor Martinez, Señorita Pilar María Nuñez de Cela = Senorita Nuñez.

  When a woman marries, she usually adds her husband's surname and goes by that surname. If the two people in the above example married, she would be known as: Señora Pilar María Nuñez Cela de Martinez.

  Most people would refer to her as: Señora de Martinez, or, less formally, Señora Martinez.

- As a general rule, use only one surname when speaking to a person, but use both surnames when writing.

- It is important to address individuals with any titles they may have, followed by their surnames. For example, teachers prefer the title "Profesor" while engineers go by "Ingeniero."

Cultural I.Q. Question: Spain has produced 5 Nobel Laureates for Literature, a multitude of artists, scientists, and philosophers. Who wrote the profound novel *Don Quixote*?

E-mail your answer to Terri Morrison@getcustoms.com. Each month a drawing will be held to award one correct respondent from all the questions in this book with a free copy of *The World Holiday and Time Zone Guide* (current electronic version).

Sweden

Official Name:	Kingdom of Sweden (Konungariket Sverige)
Official Language:	Swedish
Government System:	Parliamentary state under constitutional monarchy
Population:	8.91 million (1999 estimate)
Population Growth:	0.29% (1999 estimate)
Area:	449,964 sq. km. (173,731 sq. mi.); about the size of California
Natural Resources:	zinc, iron ore, lead, copper, silver, timber, uranium, gold, hydropower potential
Major Cities:	Stockholm (capital), Göteborg, Malmo, Örebro, Norrköping, Uppsala

---

Cultural Note: The Swedish language has three letters that do not appear in English—two versions of *a* and one of *o*, all with diacritical marks. They are:

å/Å (pronounced like the *oa* in *boat*)
ä/Ä (pronounced like the *e* in *pet*)
ö/Ö (pronounced like the *i* in *bird* or the *u* in *fur*)

If you have no way of printing these characters, substitute *ae* for *ä* and *oe* for *ö*. There is no acceptable substitute for *å*, although *aa* has sometimes been used.

In Swedish telephone books, names beginning with these letters are listed at the end of the alphabet, after the letter z.

Age Breakdown

0–14 = 19%   15–64 = 64%   65+ = 17% (1999 estimate)
Life Expectancy: 76.61 years, male; 82.11 years, female (1999 estimate)

Time

Swedes expect punctuality. Be on time for both business and social appointments. It is not appropriate to be "fashionably late" for any events. Swedes take most things seriously, including meals and recreational time. Many people go home for lunch every day between 11:30 and 1:30 P.M. The minimum vacation time for Swedish workers is five weeks per year. Most people take their vacations in July; it can be difficult to conduct business in midsummer. There is also a long Christmas holiday, extending from December 22 to January 6.

Sweden is 1 hour ahead of Greenwich Mean Time (GMT +1), which is 6 hours ahead of U.S. Eastern Standard Time (EST +6).

Holidays

An up-to-date, web-based *World Holiday and Time Zone Guide* is available at www.getcustoms.com. It lists official holidays by country and by day of the year, cultural tips, a corruption index, and time zones with worldwide business hours.

This list is a working guide. Dates should be corroborated before final travel plans are made. In cases where holidays fall on Saturday or Sunday, commercial establishments may be closed the preceding Friday or following Monday.

Jan 1	SA	New Year's Day
Jan 6	TH	Epiphany
April 21	FR	Good Friday
Apr 23	SU	Easter Sunday
Apr 24	MO	Easter Monday
May 1	MO	Labor Day
Jun 1	TH	Ascension Day
Jun 12	MO	Whitmonday
Jun 24	SA	Midsummer day
Nov 4	SA	All Saints Day
Dec 24	SU	Christmas Eve
Dec 25	MO	Christmas Day
Dec 26	TU	Boxing Day
Dec 31	SU	New Year's Eve

The Christian celebrations of Good Friday, Easter Monday, Ascension Day, and Whitmonday are all holidays. Again, the days of observance should always be corroborated by local contacts.

Offices usually close at 1:00 P.M. on the day preceding a holiday. On January 6 and December 31, banks and stores stay open for a half day, but other businesses are closed. Check with your local contact to review regional holidays, as well as those listed above.

Work Week

- The workweek is 8:00 or 9:00 A.M. to 4:00 or 5:00 P.M. Monday through Friday. One hour is usually set aside for lunch, which most people take sometime between 11:30 and 1:30 P.M.
- Banks are open Monday through Friday, 9:30 A.M. to 3:00 P.M. In large towns, many banks open one or more evenings from 4:30 to 6:00 P.M.
- Unlike many other countries in the European Union, most Swedes work a 40-hour work week.

Religious/Societal Influences on Business

The Lutheran Church of Sweden has been the official church for over 450 years. In the past, all Swedish citizens were enrolled as members and a portion of their taxes were donated to the Church of Sweden. However, since 1996, Swedish citizens are no longer automatically enrolled. Citizens only become members voluntarily after age 17. Today, although some 85% of Swedes are members of the Church of Sweden, only 4% of Swedes regularly attend Lutheran church services.

Sweden today has complete religious freedom, and many religions are observed by minority groups. Before 1860, only the Lutheran pastors could legally hold services in Sweden—even private religious meetings without a Lutheran minister were outlawed. In the nineteenth century, thousands of Swedes emigrated to North America. While economic betterment was the main impetus for emigration, religious freedom was also a factor.

Some aspects of the Lutheran Church, such as the importance of work and sharing, have become part of secular Swedish culture. Today, societal pressures probably exert more pressure on the average Swede than religious strictures. The state also intrudes into the lives of its citizens more than in other countries. For example, it is illegal in Sweden to discipline a child by spanking. Also, as many couples live together without marrying, Sweden has laws (*sambolagen*) delineating the rights of unmarried couples.

Cultural Note: U.S. citizens may be surprised to hear a Swede introduce his mate as his *sambo*. This is not a racial epithet; the term *samboende* refers to unmarried couples who live together, so one's mate is often called one's *sambo*.

---

5 Cultural Tips

1. Swedes place great value on punctuality and time management. After a bit of perfunctory small talk, Swedes often get right down to business.

2. Swedes generally avoid conflict. They are particularly keen on achieving a consensus with all parties before making a major decision or deal. (You may find management in favor of your proposal, but opposed by a labor representative.) Swedes believe that an ideal proposition, once crafted to the benefit of all parties, will leave little room for further negotiation. A win–win situation is always sought in negotiations.

3. Keep your presentation precise and factual. Have data to back up all your claims. Avoid hyperbole, but do not leave anything to the imagination.

4. Business lunches and dinners are popular in Sweden. Make reservations in advance at formal restaurants. Spouses should be invited to dinner, but not to lunch. When spouses attend a dinner or party, they are generally not seated together.

5. Women are accepted as equals to men in Sweden. It is not unusual for a businesswoman to pick up the check in Sweden, especially if she has an expense account.

Economic Overview

Sweden, which joined the European Union in January 1995, is an advanced, industrialized country with an elevated standard of living. Sweden is an excellent market for U.S. products and services. U.S. exports to Sweden will continue to grow as Sweden's economy and foreign trade expand. While Sweden imports a wide range of manufactured and agricultural products from the U.S., high-technology products are experiencing the fastest growth.

U.S. products are favorably regarded in the Swedish market.

The U.S. is Sweden's third largest foreign supplier after Germany and the U.K. The U.S. has a 9% share of the Swedish import market.

Sweden's economy has been experiencing an export-led recovery. Sweden recently pulled out of the deepest and most protracted recessionary period since the depression years of the early 1930s.

Foreign trade is vital to Sweden's economy. About 35% of Sweden's manufactured goods are exported. Because trade is so important to the economy, Sweden has traditionally maintained a policy favoring trade liberalization.

With stable political conditions, a skilled workforce, educated population, well-developed infrastructure, and relatively low corporate tax rates, Sweden is an attractive location for foreign investment.

5 Largest Businesses in Sweden

Postverket, Stockholm
   62,100 employees
Televerket, Stockholm
   34,052 employees

Scandinavian Airlines System (SAS), Stockholm
   18,710 employees
Foreningssparbanken AB, Stockholm
   10,568 employees
Astra AB
   6,614 employees

One other Swedish company worthy of mention is Stora-Great . . . not because of its size, but because it is the oldest known company in the world. Formerly known as Stora Kopparberg, its copper mining operations have records dating back to the year 1288.

Cultural Note: While discussing business, be serious and avoid jokes. Swedes often appear overly serious in their business dealings, but don't misinterpret this for being devoid of humor. Swedish humor tends towards the dry and sarcastic—more like British humor than American. Americans have been known to have difficulty comprehending the Swedish sense of humor.

Also, Swedes traditionally do not display emotion in public. Speaking voices are kept low. Exaggerating or boasting about personal accomplishments is considered poor form.

Some aspects of public behavior are codified in an unofficial law called the *Jantelagen*, which admonishes people to conform, be serious, and be satisfied with one's lot in life. One reason Swedes accept their heavy tax burden is because individuality and ambition are generally disliked; the tax structure reduces almost everyone to economic equality.

Comparative Data

Comparative Data Ratings
(Scale: 5 = Highest; 1 = Lowest)
Overall Rating: 3.8

   A. GDP Growth: 3
   B. Per Capita Income: 5
   C. Trade Flows with the U.S.: 3
   D. Country Risk: 5
   E. Monetary Policy: 4
   F. Trade Policy: 4
       • Tariffs
       • Import Licensing
       • Import Taxes
   G. Protection of Property Rights: 3
   H. Foreign Investment Climate: 4

GROSS DOMESTIC PRODUCT:　$175 billion (1998 estimate)

GDP Growth: 2.9% (1998 estimate)

Per Capita Income: $19,700 (1998 estimate)

Trade Flows with the U.S.

U.S. Exports to Sweden: $3.8 billion (1998)

U.S. Imports from Sweden: $7.8 billion (1998)

Top U.S. Exports to Sweden: Machinery (office machines, computers, etc.); electrical goods (telecommunications equipment, semiconductors/integrated circuits, etc.); aircraft; optical and medical equipment; motor vehicles; pharmaceutical products; miscellaneous chemical products

Top U.S. Prospects for Export to Sweden: Computers; computer services; computer software and peripherals; travel and tourism; telecommunications services and equipment; electronic components; medical equipment; aircraft and parts; automotive parts and accessories; safety and security equipment; pollution-control equipment; sports and leisure products; pharmaceuticals

Country Risk

Dun & Bradstreet rates Sweden as having both the highest creditworthiness and an excellent capacity to meet outstanding payment liabilities. Compared with other countries, Sweden carries the lowest degree of risk.

All normal methods of payment may be used, but Swedish buyers are not always willing to accept bills of exchange and suppliers are often forced to deal on open account terms, usually 30 to 60 days.

Monetary Policy

Inflation has remained low in Sweden throughout the late 1990s. Inflation fell to 0.5% in 1999 and was estimated at 1.6% for 2000. Inflationary pressures in the economy are forecast to remain subdued.

Sweden's currency, the krona, was de-linked from the ECU in 1992. Trade has increased and the economy has regained its strength. Although a member of the European Union, Sweden decided not to adopt the euro on January 1, 1999.

Monetary unit: krona

Trade Policy

Tariffs   Sweden now applies external European Union tariffs to imports from the U.S. Most industrial products are charged between 5% and 14% duty.

Certain agricultural products are subject to import duties and/or fees, which are imposed in accordance with EU rules and regulations. Among the products subject to these duties and fees are cereals, flour, certain fats and oils, fishery products, butter, cheese, eggs, poultry, meat, and some cattle and hogs.

IMPORT LICENSING   Import licenses are required for only a few goods, including live animals.

Certain goods, such as weapons, explosives, drugs, poisons, etc., may be imported by authorized persons and institutions only.

IMPORT TAXES   Goods imported into Sweden are subject to a value-added tax (VAT) of 25%.

Certain goods such as food and some services are subject to a lower 12% VAT rate effective 1996.

Protection of Intellectual Property Rights

Sweden is a member of the Paris Union International Convention for the Protection of Intellectual Property. American inventors are thus entitled to receive national treatment in Sweden under laws regarding the protection of patents and trademarks. Sweden is also a member of the Universal Copyright Convention and the Berne Union Copyright Convention.

Patent protection in all areas of technology may be obtained for 20 years. Protection of copyrights is governed by Law No. 729 of 1960 as amended. The term copyright protection of a work is for the author's life plus 50 years after the author's death. Sweden protects trademarks under the Trademark Act, effective January 1, 1961. Trademark registrations are valid for 10 years from the date of registration and are renewable for like periods.

Foreign Investment Climate

Until the mid 1980s, Sweden's approach to direct investment from abroad was quite restrictive and governed by a complex system of laws and regulations. Foreigners were restricted from acquiring shares of Swedish firms and laws required foreigners to obtain permission to transact business in Sweden.

Today, Swedish authorities have implemented reforms to improve the business regulatory environment that will benefit investment inflow. Foreign exchange transactions have been decontrolled, the law requiring foreigners to obtain permission to acquire shares or holdings in Swedish firms has been abolished, and real estate regulations have been changed so that foreigners can now acquire commercial real estate and land for mining in Sweden.

Political Leaders, Parties, and International Organizations

The International Academy at Santa Barbara at http://www.iasb.org/cwl publishes *Current World Leaders*, an excellent resource for up-to-date data on political leaders, parties, demographics, etc., in Sweden. Tel: (800) 530-2682 or (805) 965-5010 for subscription information to their database.

Head of State:

King Carl XVI Gustaf

Head of the Government:

Prime Minister Göran Persson

Political Parties:

Social Democratic Party, Center Party, Christian Democratic Party, Moderate Party, Left Party, Liberal Party, Green Party, New Democracy

Next election:

2002

Membership in international organizations:

ADB, AFDB, CBSS (The Council of Baltic Sea States), CE, EBRD, EFTA, EU, IDB, ICO, INTELSAT, IWC, NC, OECD, OSCE, UN and all of its specialized agencies and related organizations (including FAO, GATT, IAEA, IBRD, ICAO, IDA, IFAD, IFC, ILO, IMF, ITU, UNESCO, UNIDO, UPU, WHO, WIPO, WMO)

Political Influences on Business

Sweden is a constitutional monarchy and a multi-party parliamentary democracy. The King is the Head of State. All executive authority is vested in the Cabinet, which is formed through direct parliamentary elections every 4 years (until the 1994 elections, this was only 3 years) and consists of the Prime Minister (Head of Government) and some 20 Ministers. The Social Democrat Party has held power throughout the latter half of the 1990s, in coalition with the Left Party and the Environment (Green) Party.

Swedes tend to be politically cautious. Sweden did not become a member of the European Union until 1995. The Swedes did not join the European Monetary Union in 1999. Sweden's major foreign policy concerns focus on its immediate neighborhood, especially Russia and the former Soviet States of Lithuania, Latvia, and Estonia. As a leading member of the Council of Baltic Sea States, Sweden strives for cooperation and development in this region.

The Social Democratic Party regained power after the 1994 elections and barely hung on after the 1998 vote. The party has strong ties to the trade union movement and has made combating unemployment its top priority. It has its strongest support among blue-collar workers and public-sector employees. The party has abandoned many of its former socialist ideas but resists all attempts to concentrate power in the hands of the few.

The Moderate Party (conservative) stands for individual freedom with a minimum of involvement by the government, low taxes, and a strong defense. However, it supports government efforts to stimulate business and private industry.

The Center Party has support from agrarian groups but also from a significant environmental faction. The party wants an economy based on free enterprise, competition, and widespread ownership.

To the Liberal Party, liberalism's economic system is a socially oriented market economy. The party wants an economy that does not lead to concentration of power, economic gulfs, and over-exploitation of the environment. It favors unrestricted immigration and generous aid to developing countries.

The Left Party seeks to organize socialists, communists, and others prepared to support its policies. Traditionally, it always supports a Social Democratic government. The party is strongly against EU membership. The most populist party in Sweden's political system, its members include many former communists.

The Environment Party, also known as the Greens, has a vision of a society in ecological balance with nature. They believe that the economy must be subordinated to the ecological system. The party has a strong anti-EU stance and backs the political left.

The Christian Democratic Party stands for a Christian philosophy and wants greater support for homes and families in order to reduce youth problems, alcoholism, crime, and other social problems. They want society to actively work to prevent abortions. Like the Liberals, the party works for more aid to developing countries and for unrestricted immigration.

Cultural Note: Nowadays one major rule for toasting is to look the person you are toasting in the eye. Once the toast is given, everyone says "Skål" ("Cheers") and drinks. The host gives the first toast, then others—in order of seniority—may toast. The other major rule is to take a taxi if you've had too many toasts. Sweden has strict rules prohibiting drinking and driving.

Contacts in the United States

The Embassy of the Kingdom of Sweden
1501 M Street, NW
Washington, D.C. 20005-1702
Tel: (202) 467-2600
Fax: (202) 467-2699
www.swedenemb.org

Swedish–American Chamber of Commerce
599 Lexington Avenue
New York, NY 10022
Tel: (212) 838-5530
Fax: (212) 755-7953
business services@saccny.com
www.sacc-usa.org

Passport/Visa Requirements

A passport is required. A tourist or business visa is not required for U.S. citizens for stays up to 3 months (the 90-day period begins when entering the Nordic area: Sweden, Norway, Denmark, Iceland, or Finland). A visit longer than 3 months requires a special residence permit that is granted by the National Immigration and Naturalization Board and applied for at the nearest Consulate General or Embassy of Sweden. A foreigner who wishes to accept employment must first obtain a work permit.

For further information concerning entry requirements, travelers can contact the Embassy of Sweden.

U.S. citizens who wish to apply for a passport may visit Passport Services' well-organized website at http://travel.state.gov/passport_services.html.

There are also Swedish–American Chambers of Commerce in Atlanta, Chicago, Seattle, and San Francisco.

Contacts in Sweden

THE EMBASSY OF THE UNITED STATES OF
AMERICA
Strandvagen 101
S-115 89 Stockholm
Tel.: (46) (8) 783-5300
Fax: (46) (8) 661-1964
www.usis.usemb.se/

STOCKHOLM CHAMBER OF COMMERCE
Box 16050
S-103 22 Stockholm
Tel: (46) (8) 613-1800
Fax: (46) (8) 411-2432
stock@chamber.se
www.chamber.se

DUN & BRADSTREET SVERIGE AB
Frejgatan 1
114 20 Stockholm
Tel: + 46 (o) 8.5190.1350
Fax: + 46 (o) 8.5190.1359

OFFICE OF THE KING
King Carl XVI Gustaf
Kungliga Slottet
S-111 30 Stockholm
Kingdom of Sweden

OFFICE OF THE PRIME MINISTER
Rosenbad 4
S-103 33 Stockholm
Kingdom of Sweden

Further contacts and websites can be found in Appendix A.

Communications

TELEPHONE: The international country code for Sweden is 46.

Phone numbers and area codes vary in length. Area codes may be one digit (Stockholm = 8) or two (Malmo = 40) or even three in rural areas. Phone numbers are usually six or seven digits in length. In writing, Swedes often separate the area code from the phone number with a dash. Dashes are often used to separate digits within a phone number.

E-MAIL: E-mail addresses located in Sweden end with the code .se

---

Observation: "The Swedes themselves admit that they suffer from *titelsjuka*, by which they mean an unwholesome predilection for titles. In all fairness, titles do aid in identification. As included in the names in telephone directories they facilitate the search for a number, especially when the name is a common one. But one must know by which title the person is listed. In a long line of Anderssons, for instance, it helps if you know that the person in question is a lawyer, in Swedish *advokat*, the titles being listed alphabetically. Going down the lists of Anderssons with titles from *a* to *ö* (being the last letter of the Swedish alphabet), one finally comes to occupations like *överste*—colonel—or perhaps *ölutkörare*, meaning "beer truck driver." After all the *ö* jobs are exhausted, there follows a listing of Anderssons with street addresses only."

—From *Of Swedish Ways* by Lilly Lorénzen

Switzerland

Official Name:	Swiss Confederation (Confederation Suisse—French) (Schweizerische Eidgenossenschaft—German) (Confederazione Svizzera—Italian)
Official Languages:	French, German, Italian (A fourth language, Romansch, is protected but not official.)
Government System:	Federal state
Population:	7.3 million (1999 estimated)
Population Growth Rate:	0.2% (1999 estimated)
Area:	41,288 sq. km. (15,941 sq. mi.); about twice the size of New Jersey
Natural Resources:	hydropower potential, timber, salt
Major cities:	Bern (capital), Zurich, Basel, Geneva, Lausanne

---

Cultural Note: Switzerland has four distinct cultures, which are usually identified by their native languages: French, Italian, German, and Romansch. (Romansch is spoken by less than 1% of the Swiss, but it is accorded protected status as Switzerland's only indigenous language.) German-speakers are in the majority with about 70% of the population. French account for approximately 19%, and Italian for 10%. Most Swiss are multilingual, and the majority of businesspeople include English as one of their languages.

Age Breakdown

0–14 = 17%   15–64 = 68%   65+ = 15% (1999 estimate)
Life Expectancy: 75.3 years, male; 81.7 years, female (1994–1995 estimate)

Time

Punctuality is very important in Switzerland. Everyone and everything is expected to be on time: people, deadlines, and transportation. Be prompt for all business and social events.

Switzerland is 1 hour ahead of Greenwich Mean Time (GMT +1), which is 6 hours ahead of U.S. Eastern Standard Time (EST +6).

Holidays

An up-to-date, online *World Holiday and Time Zone Guide* is available at www.get-customs.com. It lists official holidays by country and by day of the year, business and cultural tips, a corruption index, and time zones with worldwide business hours.

This list is a working guide. Dates should be corroborated before final travel plans are made. Unlike in many other countries, when holidays fall on Saturday or Sunday, the following Monday is not a holiday.

Jan 1	SA	New Year's Day
Jan 2	SU	Berchtoldstag Day[1]
Jan 6	TH	Epiphany[1]
Mar 8	WE	Ash Wednesday[1]
Mar 16	SU	Palm Sunday[1]
Apr 21	FR	Good Friday
Apr 23	SU	Easter Sunday
Apr 24	MO	Easter Monday
May 1	MO	Labor Day[1]
Jun 1	TH	Ascension
Jun 12	MO	Whitmonday
Jun 22	TH	Corpus Christi[1]
Aug 1	TU	National Day
Aug 15	TU	Assumption[1]
Nov 1	WE	All Saints' Day[1]
Dec 8	FR	Immaculate Conception[1]
Dec 24	SU	Christmas Eve[1]
Dec 25	MO	Christmas Day
Dec 26	TU	Boxing Day
Dec 31	SU	New Year's Eve[1]

[1]Some cantons (states) only; some cantons half day only.

Some additional holidays are observed by individual Swiss cities. Again, the days of observance should always be corroborated by local contacts.

Work Week

- The work week is generally Monday through Friday from 7:30 A.M. to 5:30 P.M., with a one- or two-hour lunch break.
- Banks are open from 8:30 A.M. to 4:30 or 5:00 P.M. Monday through Saturday.
- Stores are open from 8:00 A.M. to noon, and 1:30 to 6:30 P.M. Monday through Saturday. Some close on Saturday or Monday mornings. Larger stores do not close for lunch.

Religious/Societal Influences on Business

Switzerland's four cultures—German, French, Italian, and Romansch—encompass a variety of religious traditions. Roman Catholics, at 46%, constitute the majority, with various Protestant denominations making up 40%. But most religions are represented in Switzerland, including Islam, Judaism, Buddhism, and Mormon.

Switzerland was at the center of the Protestant Reformation. Reformer Ulrich Zwingli (1484–1531) lived in Zurich; Jean Calvin (1509–1564) was French but was exiled to Geneva. Years of warfare between Protestant and Catholic devastated Switzerland. As a result, the Swiss today consider religion to be a private concern. Religion is rarely discussed in public. The doomsday cult known as the Order of the Solar Temple came to international prominence when 53 members were found dead in October 1994, the victims of murder and mass suicide. The Swiss were aghast at these events, which served to drive religion even further out of public discourse. Nevertheless, the Swiss consider themselves privately devoted to religious principals.

The Swiss believe they have developed a fair and beneficent society, and exert strong social pressures on their citizens to conform to Swiss patterns of behavior.

Divided by language and religion, the Swiss find unity in their devotion to their families, their work, and their country. The Swiss are patriotic and deeply involved in their country's politics. Their political system, which involves strong local government, allows each citizen's vote to have great effect on their everyday lives. Referendums are frequent, and the Swiss constitution can be challenged by a system called the People's Initiatives. Even basic institutions—such as whether or not to maintain a Swiss Army—can be challenged by a People's Initiative.

The Swiss are intensely concerned about the environment. They recycle most consumer products, and are second only to Germany in environmental restrictions.

5 Cultural Tips

1. Since Switzerland has four native cultures, try to find out the primary language of the people with whom you will do business. German cultural traditions are quite differ-

ent from those of the French or Italians. Fortunately, as most Swiss executives speak English, it is not vital to translate your business cards or promotional literature.

2. Age and seniority are important. Avoid sending a young executive alone to Switzerland; he or she will not be taken seriously. Expect to defer to the elderly. Also, if your company has a long lineage, the year it was established should appear on your business card and/or letterhead.

3. Bring plenty of business cards. You will need at least two for each appointment. You will give your business card to the secretary when you arrive, and she will keep that card for her file. You will need to present another card when you meet the executive.

4. Business in Switzerland is serious business, especially among the German-speaking populace. *Humor is out of place during negotiations.* Keep your posture erect and your body language formal. Slouching back in a chair or propping up one's feet would convey the wrong impression in Switzerland.

5. Swiss executives dress conservatively, but they are often quite fashionable. Exclusive brand names are recognized and respected. Invest in elegant clothing. (Remember that Switzerland has the highest standard of living in Europe, so it is an expensive country in which to do business.)

Economic Overview

Switzerland is a small, highly developed, multilingual market located at the crossroads of Europe. Its population of seven million people is diversified, well-educated, and affluent. It has a strong and stable economy, low inflation, relatively low unemployment, and a highly qualified workforce—all factors that contribute to making the Swiss Confederation a desirable market environment. Per capita income is the highest in Europe and spending power for foreign goods and services is thus extremely high.

Trade and prosperity are synonymous in Switzerland. The country is dependent upon export markets to absorb its production and sustain its wealth, but is also equally dependent upon imports for raw materials and to expand the range of goods and services available in-country. The U.S. ranks fourth as a source of Swiss imports and third as a destination for Swiss exports.

Switzerland is known for liberal trade and investment policies. Fiscal policy is moderate and cautious. The Swiss franc is one of the world's soundest and most stable currencies. The country is famous for its high standard of banking, ensuring rapid and reliable processing of business transactions.

After six years of stagnation, the Swiss economy finally showed measurable growth in the late 1990s.

U.S. relations with Switzerland are very good. The Swiss feel comfortable doing business with Americans. U.S. promotional themes are popular at stores, shopping centers, and restaurants, and many social functions feature American activities. U.S. products have a favorable reputation, particularly high technology and labor-saving capital goods and consumer products.

5 Largest Businesses in Switzerland

Micasa AG, Zurich
    71,964 employees
Die Schweizerische Post, Berne
    59,661 employees
Office des Nations Unies, Geneva
    52,000
Roche Chemische Unternehmungen AG, Basel
    10,568 employees
Cern, Meyrin
    8,000 employees

Cultural Note: The Swiss attribute much of their success to their work ethic. They work hard (and play hard). Punctuality is required and planning is done in advance. Everything is kept clean (this also applies to the country as a whole). Perhaps the only negative is that the Swiss are not usually good at improvising. But if everything follows the plan, they don't *need* to improvise.

Comparative Data

Comparative Data Ratings
(Scale: 5 = Highest; 1 = Lowest)
Switzerland: 4.375

- A. GDP Growth: 2
- B. Per Capita Income: 5
- C. Trade Flows with the U.S.: 4
- D. Country Risk: 5
- E. Monetary Policy: 5
- F: Trade Policy: 4
  - Tariffs
  - Import Licensing
  - Import Taxes
- G. Protection of Property Rights: 5
- H. Foreign Investment Climate: 5

GROSS DOMESTIC PRODUCT: $191.8 billion (1998 estimate)

GDP GROWTH: 1.3% (1999); 2.3% forecast for 2000.

PER CAPITA INCOME: $26,400 (1998 estimate)

Trade Flows with the U.S.

U.S. Exports to Switzerland: $7.3 (1998 estimate)

U.S. Imports from Switzerland: $8.7 billion (1998 estimate)

Top U.S. Exports to Switzerland: Computer software; computers and peripherals; telecommunications equipment; aircraft and parts; medical equipment; pollution-control equipment; laboratory scientific equipment; industrial process controls; security and safety equipment; sporting goods and recreational equipment

Top U.S. Prospects for Export to Switzerland: Telecommunications equipment; travel and tourism services; computer software; computers and peripherals; drugs and peripherals; telecommunications services; pollution-control equipment; sporting goods; medical equipment; analytical process-control instruments

Country Risk

Dun & Bradstreet rates Switzerland as having excellent capacity to meet outstanding payment liabilities. It carries the lowest degree of risk.

Credit terms vary according to sector and size of transaction, but are usually between 30 and 60 days. Open account terms are most common and letters of credit are rarely used.

Monetary Policy

The high value of the Swiss franc hurt the country's economy during much of the 1990s. Switzerland's economy has shown modest growth since the franc was devalued in 1997.

Swiss inflation remains very low. It is estimated to remain below 2% through 2001.

Monetary Unit: Swiss franc

Trade Policy

Tariffs   Import duties are generally low, averaging under 3% in the industrial goods sectors. Switzerland's tariff policy favors the development of trade.

Imports of virtually all agricultural products are subject to import and supplementary duties and to variable import quotas.

Import Licensing   Import licenses are required only for a limited number of products, and generally fall into two categories—measures for the protection of the country's agriculture and measures of state control. With minor exceptions, imports into Switzerland may be made freely.

Products subject to quota may not be imported without an import license, and licenses are granted only to importers established in Switzerland. Most quotas vary from year to year according to the size of harvests, volume of stocks, and market requirements.

IMPORT TAXES   In addition to customs duties, the Swiss customs administration levies a 3% statistical tax on the total customs duty payable.

A value-added tax (VAT) is levied on all imports of goods and services. The standard VAT rate is 7.5%, although there is a reduced rate of 2.3% for certain goods and services such as food and drinks (excluding alcoholic beverages and prepared meals), meats of all kinds, cereals, plants, seed and flowers, some basic farming supplies, medicine and drugs, newspapers, magazines, and books.

Protection of Intellectual Property Rights

Switzerland is a member of the World Intellectual Property Organization and the World Trade Organization, including TRIPS (Trade Related Aspects of Intellectual Property Rights). Switzerland adheres to a number of conventions including the Patent Cooperation Treaty, the Paris Convention on Protection of Industrial Property, the Berne Convention on the Protection of Literary and Artistic Works, the Madrid Conventions (trademarks and false designations of origin), the Universal Copyright Convention, and the European Patent Convention.

Cultural Note: The Swiss Patent Office was made famous because Albert Einstein worked there as an examiner.

Patents are granted even though an invention is not new. It is left to the Swiss courts to invalidate a patent for not being an invention. An interested party may bring an annulment action. The term of patents is 20 years from filing and is not renewable. Periodic maintenance fees are required.

Trademarks must be registered to have standing. Both goods and services are protected. Famous marks are protected for all categories. Trademarks have terms of 20 years from the date of application. There is a six-month grace period on renewals.

Copyrights automatically protect works of literature, art, photography, and computer programs. The term of protection is the author's life plus 70 years (except for software, for which the term is 50 years).

Foreign Investment Climate

The Swiss welcome foreign investment and accord it national treatment. Foreign investment is neither actively encouraged nor unduly hampered by barriers. The federal government adopts a relaxed attitude of benevolent noninterference toward foreign investment, confining itself to creating and maintaining the general conditions that are favorable both to Swiss and foreign investors. Such factors include economic and political stability, a firmly established legal system, a reliable infrastructure, and efficient capital markets. The government does not offer large-scale incentives to prospective investors, and those that exist are open to foreign and domestic investors alike.

With the exception of national security areas—such as hydroelectric and nuclear power, operation of oil pipelines, transportation of explosive materials, and operation of airlines and marine navigation—national treatment is granted to foreign investors.

A major law affecting foreign investments is the 1993 Federal Law on Authorization of Acquisition of Real Estate by Persons with Residence or Headquarters Abroad. This law limits the freedom of foreigners to purchase real estate in Switzerland and makes such purchases subject to local government approval. A modified law that would have removed the necessity for foreigners to have an authorization to acquire property for residential and commercial activity purposes was rejected by the Swiss electorate in June 1995.

Political Leaders, Parties, and International Organizations

The International Academy at Santa Barbara at http://www.iasb.org/cwl publishes *Current World Leaders*, an excellent resource for up-to-date data on political leaders, parties, demographics, etc., in Switzerland. Tel: (800) 530-2682 or (805) 965-5010 for subscription information to their database.

Federal President:

President Adolf Ogi

Next Election:

Yearly (The President is elected to a one year term.)

Political Parties:

Radical Democrats, Social Democrats, Christian Democrats, Volkspartei (People's Party), Liberal Party, Independent Party, Green Party, Coalition of Progressive Organizations and Greens, Swiss Democrats, Evangelical People's Party

Membership in international organizations:

ADB, Bank for International Settlements, CE, EBRD, EFTA, IADB, INTELSAT, OECD, OSCE, UN and most of its specialized agencies and related organizations (including ECE, FAO, GATT, IAEA, IBRD, ICAO, IFAD, ILO, IMF, IMO, ITU, UNESCO, UNICEF, UNIDO, UPU, WHO, WIPO, WMO)

Political Influences on Business

Switzerland has a relatively weak federal government and no recent tradition of executive leadership wielded by one individual. Many executive and administrative powers are vested in the 26 cantonal governments rather than in the federal government in Bern. Federal executive decision-making is undertaken by the seven-member Federal Council (cabinet). Its members head the various federal ministries: Treasury, Foreign Affairs, Justice, Economics, Interior, Transportation and Energy, and Defense. The entirely ceremonial position of President of the Federal Council (head of government) is rotated annually among the councilors according to seniority. The Federal Council strives to present a collegial image and to govern by consensus. Its deliberations are private. Contentious issues that cannot be decided by consensus are determined by majority vote, results of which are not released.

The composition of the Federal Council reflects the so-called "magic formula" coalition that has governed Switzerland since 1959. Under this informal arrangement, the four largest political parties, which generally receive 70–75% of the popular vote in federal parliamentary elections held every four years, fill the seven positions on the Federal Council. The three bourgeois parties in the coalition (Free Democrats, Christian Peoples' Party, and Swiss Peoples' Party) reflect center–right constituencies. The left-of-center Social Democrats are the fourth coalition party. The three largest parties in terms of popular vote (Free Democrats, Christian Peoples', and Social Democrats) each receive two Federal Council seats; the Peoples' Party receives one. In addition, it is understood that there will always be at least two members from French-speaking cantons on the Federal Council. According to the Constitution, no canton may have more than one representative on the Federal Council. Federal Councilors are elected by Parliament for life, but political tradition dictates that they retire in their 60s.

The presence of left- and right-wing elements in the governing coalition has allowed it to co-opt more extreme parties in the spectrum. The coalition's ideological diversity has brought prolonged political and social peace.

Treaties, agreements, and legislation approved by the Parliament are subject to challenge by popular vote in Switzerland's unique system of initiative and referendum procedures. These votes allow unusually intense popular involvement in the legislative process and keep the federal government under pressure and scrutiny. Most of the interesting moments in Swiss politics occur during these initiative and referendum campaigns.

Switzerland has, to date, refused to join either the United Nations or the European Union. (It is, however, a member of many UN agencies, such as the World Health Organization.) U.S. companies already acclimated to EU business practices and regulations should experience no difficulties in Switzerland, as the underlying Swiss goal is not to reject EU trade, but rather to make its trading environment as compatible as possible with that of the EU while still maintaining Swiss political and economic integrity.

Long a banking center, Switzerland's reputation was tarnished by its acceptance of assets from the Nazis in World War Two, as well as its refusal to return funds to the heirs of persons executed by the Nazis. Under threat of a U.S. boycott initiated by the World Jewish Congress, Swiss banks agreed in 1998 to disburse $1.25 trillion in funds, most of it to the heirs of Jewish victims of Nazi atrocities.

As a prosperous, neutral nation, Switzerland remains a magnet for refugees. Thousands of would-be refugees are turned back at the borders, but many manage to enter the country, legally or otherwise. During the Kosovo crisis of 1998–99, Switzerland sheltered some 40,000 refugees.

Contacts in the United States

THE EMBASSY OF SWITZERLAND*
2900 Cathedral Avenue, NW
Washington, D.C. 20008-3499
Tel: (202) 745-7900
Fax: (202) 387-2564
www.swissemb.org

Passport/Visa Requirements

A passport is required. U.S. citizens do not need a visa for a 3-month business or tourist stay.

For current information concerning entry and customs requirements for Switzerland, travelers can contact the Embassy of Switzerland.

U.S. citizens who wish to apply for a passport may visit Passport Services' well-organized website at http://travel.state.gov/passport_services.html.

Contacts in Switzerland

THE EMBASSY OF THE UNITED STATES
OF AMERICA
Jubilaeumstrasse 93
3005 Bern
Tel: (41) (31) 437-011
Fax: (41) (31) 437-344
www.us-embassy.ch

SWISS–AMERICAN CHAMBER OF COMMERCE
Talacker 41
CH-8001 Zurich
Tel. (41) (1) 211-2454
Fax: (41) (1) 211-9572
www.amcham.ch

DUN & BRADSTREET NOVINFORM AG
Postal Address: P.O Box, CH-8010 Zurich
Street Address: In der Luberzen 1,
CH-8902 Urdorf
Tel: (41) (1) 735 61 11
Fax: (41) (1) 735 61 61

OFFICE OF THE PRESIDENT
Federal Chancellery
Bundeshaus Nord
3003 Berne

Further contacts and websites can be found in Appendix A.

---

* Note that the Swiss Embassy in Washington also hosts the "Cuban Interests Section," the de facto Cuban Embassy to the U.S.

Communications

TELEPHONE: The international country code for Switzerland is 41.

Phone numbers and area codes vary in length.

E-MAIL: E-mail addresses located in Switzerland end with the code .ch

---

Observation: "In contrast to the French and Italians, the Swiss shun any form of theatricality. By dint of their earnestness in such matters, they have earned a reputation as Europe's most exasperating negotiators, either grinding down the opposition or bringing everything to a standstill. The Belgian general manager of a U.S. multinational even goes so far as to say that 'the German Swiss are so straightforward that you don't even have to see through them. You can easily guess their negotiating strategy.' Even the Italian Swiss are so meticulous in their attention to detail that they drive the average Italian mad."

—From Richard Hill's 1994 book *Euro Managers & Martians*

Taiwan

Official Name:	Republic of China (Chung-hua Min-kuo)
Official Language:	Mandarin Chinese
Government System:	Unitary republic
Population:	22.1 million (1999 estimate)
Population Growth Rate:	0.93% (1999 estimate)
Area:	35,981 sq. km. (14,000 sq. mi.); about the size of West Virginia
Natural Resources:	some coal, natural gas, limestone, marble, asbestos
Major Cities:	Taipei (capital), Kaohsiung, Taichung, Tainan, Keelung

---

Cultural Note: The Chinese phrase that describes so much of Taiwanese life is *re nau,* which means "hot and raucous." This describes not just Taiwan's lively nightlife, but the aggressive nature of daytime Taiwan as well. The streets are jammed and the noise is overwhelming; everyone has something to do and is in a hurry to get there. It is this energy that developed Taiwan into a major industrial power in half a century. Foreigners may find it unbearably noisy. But the Taiwanese know that death is the ultimate silence—as long as they can make noise, they're still alive.

Age Breakdown

0–14 = 22%   15–64 = 70%   65+ = 8% (1999 estimate)
Life Expectancy: 74.38 years, male; 80.85 years, female (1999 estimate)

Time

Far more important than punctuality is the preservation of one's public image, or dignity (often referred to as "face"). When you make a higher-ranking person wait for you, both of you have lost face.

As a general rule, foreigners should try to be on time to all business appointments. This is not easy in Taiwan's congested traffic. However, do not get upset if your Taiwanese counterpart is late.

Taiwan is 8 hours ahead of Greenwich Mean Time (GST +8), which is 13 hours ahead of U.S. Eastern Standard Time (EST +13).

Holidays

An up-to-date, online *World Holiday and Time Zone Guide* is available at www.getcustoms.com. It contains official holidays by country and by day of the year, business and cultural tips, a corruption index, and time zones with worldwide business hours.

Jan 1	SA	Founding Day
Feb 4	FR	Chinese Lunar New Year (4–8)
Feb 28	MO	Peace Memorial Day
Apr 5	WE	Ching Ming (Tomb-Sweeping) Festival
Jun 6	TU	Dragon Boat Festival
Sep 12	TU	Mid-Autumn Festival
Oct 10	TU	National Day
Nov 12	SU	Birthday of Dr. Sun Yat Sen

Three of Taiwan's major holidays—Chinese New Year, the Dragon Boat Festival, and the Mid-Autumn Festival—are calculated by the Chinese lunar calendar, so they fall on different days in the Western (Gregorian) calendar each year.

Work Week

- Business hours are generally 8:30 A.M. to 12 noon and 1:00 to 5:00 P.M. Monday through Friday, and 8:30 A.M. to 12 noon on Saturday.
- Banking hours are 8:30 A.M. to 3:30 P.M. Monday through Friday, and 8:30 A.M. to 12 noon on Saturday.

- Government offices are open 8:30 A.M. to 12:30 P.M. and 1:30 to 5:30 P.M. Monday through Friday, and 8:30 A.M. to 12 noon on Saturday.
- Many businesspeople nap after lunch (between 1:30 and 2:00 P.M.). They may not be fully awake for a 2:00 P.M. appointment.
- Plan a visit to Taiwan between April and September. Many people vacation from January through March.

Religious/Societal Influences on Business

A Taiwanese citizen does not have to wonder about the meaning of life. The Mandarin term *shengyi* translates as "meaning of life." It also means "business." There could be no greater work ethic than this: The purpose of life in Taiwan is to work hard, be successful in business, and accumulate wealth for one's family.

Confucian ethics form the backbone of Taiwan society. Confucianism is not a religion in the Western sense, but it does provide guides for living. Unlike the People's Republic of China (where the Communists preached loyalty to one's work group), the family in Taiwan remains the central unit of society.

Taiwan has no official religion, reflecting the ability of the Taiwanese to simultaneously follow more than one religion. Aside from Confucianism and traditional folk beliefs, Taiwanese are likely to be Buddhist, Taoist, or Christian. (To make matters more complicated, many Taiwanese follow Taoist philosophy while ignoring the Taoist priesthood.)

5 Cultural Tips

1. During the Cold War, no major policy could be executed in Finland without considering its dominating neighbor, the USSR. Today, a similar relationship exists between Taiwan and the People's Republic of China. For years, the government of Taiwan considered itself the legitimate government of all of China. The PRC considered Taiwan a rogue province that would one day be reabsorbed. The Taiwanese no longer claim to be the legitimate rulers of all of China, and some Taiwanese are ready to declare their island an independent nation. The PRC threatens to invade and occupy the island if Taiwan ever declares its independence. Relations between Taiwan and the PRC remain strained.

2. Companies wishing to do business in both Taiwan and the PRC are in a difficult situation. It is a challenge to keep citizens of both locations happy. One common error is to forget that the two locales use slightly different forms of written Chinese. The PRC instituted reforms to the Chinese writing system; the Taiwanese rejected these reforms. Use the appropriate form of writing for the respective country.

3. Western men who wear beards can be at a disadvantage in Taiwan. Taiwanese men are usually clean-shaven except after the death of their father or brother (they stay unshaven during the traditional seven-week mourning period). In fact, one of the Taiwanese terms for foreigners is *ang mo*, meaning "red beard." The term can be used for bearded or clean-shaven foreigners of any hair color, and it is not complimentary. It plays into the stereotype of Westerners as hairy, unkempt barbarians. Westerners can fight this characterization by being beardless and well-groomed.

4. While nepotism is a fact of life in Taiwan, foreign companies are advised to avoid hiring multiple members of the same family. Since loyalty to the family is one of the basic tenets of Taiwanese life, when you have several family members working in one office, they may begin to work for their family's interest rather than the company's. Furthermore, if they learn how to run your business, they may all quit and form their own competing firm.

5. The Taiwanese are generally smaller in stature than the average Westerner. This difference can be intimidating to the Taiwanese. If you can find a way to compensate for the height and weight differential (such as standing on a lower level so you and your Taiwanese counterpart are at eye level), do so. Large Westerners should also expect everything from furniture to clothing to be made on a smaller scale.

Cultural Note: Executives in the health care and medical supply industries must face the Taiwanese reluctance to discuss illness. People in Taiwan do not even like to give health warnings, nor do they comment on illness to a sick person. The insurance industry has gotten around this reluctance by speaking of insurance as if it were a bet (most Taiwanese love gambling). A life insurance salesperson will explain a policy by saying, "We will bet that you will live to age sixty and, if we lose, we will pay your beneficiaries."

Economic Overview

Through 40 years of hard work and sound economic management, the people of Taiwan have built the island into the world's 19th largest economy. Taiwan is an economic powerhouse with more than $175 billion in two-way trade. Until the Asian financial crisis, Taiwan's economy was expanding at almost 7% a year with full employment and low inflation. An expanding democratic government, strong economic performance, and economic liberalization shape the Taiwan market.

The island's ambition to transform itself from an export platform to a high-tech production center is proceeding on schedule. In 1994 the percentage of Taiwan's exports accounted for by high-tech and capital-intensive products for the first time exceeded labor-intensive exports.

As in other developed economies, the service sector is experiencing rapid growth. Services accounted for 47% of GDP in 1986, 59% in 1994, and 63% in 1996. Many new private banks, insurance companies, and securities firms have emerged. New financial services, such as automatic tellers machines and credit cards, have become common.

Taiwan is an excellent market for U.S. firms. Taiwan firms and consumers have money, are not afraid to spend, and are receptive to foreign products. The economy of Taiwan has largely escaped the Asian financial crisis of the late 1990s.

5 Largest Businesses in Taiwan

Southeast Travel Service Co., Ltd., Taipei
54,035 employees
Cathay Life Insurance Co., Ltd., Taipei
35,572 employees
Directorate General of Telecommunications, Taipei
35,526 employees
Chunghwa Telecom Co., Ltd., Taipei
34,748 employees
Taiwan Power Co., Taipei
30,044 employees

Cultural Note: The founders of the Republic of China considered themselves to be the legitimate rulers of all China. After the Communist victory on the mainland, the Nationalists retreated to Taiwan, where they have remained ever since.

To underscore its claim as true ruler of all China, the Taiwanese government chose traditional Mandarin Chinese as its official language. Initially, Taiwan used the old forms of written Chinese, rejecting the improved, simplified Chinese characters developed by the Communists. Over the years, though, Taiwan adopted some (but not all) of the Communists' most successful reforms to written Chinese. Executives having materials translated into Chinese should make sure the Taiwanese variant is used in Taiwan.

Westerners who wish to speak Chinese should be thankful that Mandarin was chosen as Taiwan's official language. Mandarin, with four different tones, is difficult enough to learn. The native Taiwanese language (imported from southern Fukien province) has six tones, which change depending upon the position of a word in the sentence!

Observations: "To North American eyes, some of the (Taiwanese) business practices seem rather Japanese. China Steel Corporation has a gym, a library, tennis courts, a post office, etc., for the workers, even a contemplation pond, made from one of the slag-heaps and stocked with goldfish (a second generation of them now). A dormitory capable of housing a thousand unmarried workers charges only about US$20 a month. . . . The site takes up 220 hectares. As late as 1971, the land was still a cane brake.

—From the 1995 book *The Other China: Journeys Around Taiwan* by Canadian author Douglass Fetherling. Taiwan's rapid industrialization has been accompanied by massive environmental damage. The capital, Taipei, is choked with smog much of the year. However, some observers argue that the Japanese influence on Taiwanese businesses is only superficial

"Business in Taiwan has no term comparable to (the Japanese) *keiretsu* or (the Korean) *chaebol* because it has no comparable economic structure. Taiwan does have a few large firms with international scope. . . . But these are unrepresentative features on the country's economic landscape. . . .

"The archetypical Taiwanese firm is still a small manufacturing business run by an individual entrepreneur with his extended-family members, which concentrates on a few niche products and scrambles to survive. . . . The great divide in the business cultures of East Asia is between Japanese-style and Chinese-style management. The Japanese-style system, most closely approximated in Korea, involves large organizations with skilled, bureaucratized management. The Chinese-style system features small family-run enterprises. Taiwan represents the Chinese model on a national scale.

"This difference has made Taiwan stronger in many ways. Its little firms can adapt very quickly and strike up deals around the world, and the business environment as a whole seems less monolithic and forbidding to outsiders than Japan's or Korea's has."

—From the 1994 treatise *Looking at the Sun: The Rise of the New East Asian Economic and Political System* by James Fallows. The author acknowledges that Taiwan has many Japanese influences, but maintains that the organizational structure of Taiwanese businesses are quite different.

Comparative Data

Comparative Data Ratings
(Scale: 5 = Highest; 1 = Lowest)
Taiwan: 4.0

    A.   GDP Growth: 4

B. Per Capita Income: 4
C. Trade Flows with the U.S.: 5
D. Country Risk: 4
E. Monetary Policy: 5
F. Trade Policy: 4
  • Tariffs
  • Import Licensing
  • Import Taxes
G. Protection of Property Rights: 3
H. Foreign Investment Climate: 3

GROSS DOMESTIC PRODUCT: $308 billion (1997 estimate)

GDP GROWTH: 5.7% (1999 estimate); 5.4% (2000 forecast)

PER CAPITA INCOME: $14,210 (1997 estimate)

Trade Flows with the U.S.

U.S. EXPORTS TO TAIWAN: $18.2 billion (1997 estimate)

U.S. IMPORTS FROM TAIWAN: $33.1 billion (1997 estimate)

TOP U.S. EXPORTS TO TAIWAN: Electrical components; machinery; aircraft and parts; insurance services; motor vehicles; organic chemicals; cereals; medical and optical equipment; plastics; miscellaneous grain, seeds, and fruit

TOP U.S. PROSPECTS FOR EXPORT TO TAIWAN: Insurance services; laboratory scientific instruments; electrical power equipment; electronics industrial production/testing equipment; computer software; travel and tourism services; drugs and pharmaceuticals; computers and peripherals; medical equipment; pumps, valves, and compressors

Country Risk

Dun & Bradstreet rates Taiwan as having good capacity to meet outstanding payment liabilities. Most transactions are undertaken on open account terms, although more secure letters of credit are still widely used. Credit terms of 30 to 90 days are common, although longer terms may be requested. A letter of credit is still recommended until good business relations have been established.

Monetary Policy

Despite robust economic growth, Taiwan's inflationary pressures remain subdued. Inflation fell from 3.1% in 1996 to 2.0% in 1998, to 0.4% in 1999.

The value of Taiwan's currency fell in 1997 but recovered in 1998.

MONETARY UNIT: yuan, better known in English as the New Taiwan dollar

Trade Policy

TARIFFS   The average nominal tariff rate is 8.3%, with the trade-weighted rate at 3.2%. Taiwan has made significant progress in reducing its tariff level on products of interest to the U.S. New legislation in 1995 resulted in the reduction of import duties on 758 industrial and agricultural products by an average of 2.8%.

IMPORT LICENSING   The number of items requiring import licenses is being gradually reduced. The import licensing system was replaced in 1993 with a "negative list," thus reducing the number of items subject to licensing. The majority of the 9,350 items in Taiwan's tariff schedule can be imported without an import license.

Approximately 240 items—including arms, munitions, and several important agricultural products (including rice)—are banned from import.

IMPORT TAXES   Importers must pay a 0.4% harbor construction fee and a 5% value-added tax (VAT). Air shipments are exempt from the harbor fees.

A commodity tax ranging from 2–60% is charged on imported products that fall into any of the following seven categories: rubber tires, cement, beverages, oil and gas, electric appliances, flat glass, and automotive products.

Protection of Intellectual Property Rights

Taiwanese international copyright rights are piecemeal and variable. Nevertheless, Taiwan's new IP laws are both comprehensive and enforced. In 1997 Taiwan was admitted to GATT/WTO. Taiwan was placed on the U.S trade watch list in 1988 and 1999 due to concerns about enforcement of IP laws.

In 1997 Taiwanese patent law was amended to qualify for GATT. A first-to-file system is followed. Three types of patents may be obtained: patents of invention, utility model patents, and design patents. The first two—inventions and utility models—require absolute novelty, industrial application, and an inventive step. Designs require creativeness. Patent applications are not opened until they are examined and approved. Patent infringement is both civil and criminal. Mask works (integrated circuits) are protected under a special law. Patent terms are 20 years for investment, 12 years for utility, and 10 years for new designs.

Trademark rights result from registration. Trademarks have a 10-year term that is renewable one term at a time. Associated trademarks may be obtained for use on similar goods and services. Defensive trademarks may be sought for use in connection with goods and services that are differentiated but related. Protective rights are accorded to owners of famous marks. Trademark infringement is criminal and may include imprisonment.

Copyright rights differ for nationals and foreigners. For Taiwanese nationals, rights result on completion of the works. Foreign rights are protected on creation. Rights of copyright include rights of reproduction, adapting a work to create a derivative work, leasing a work, publicly performing, publicity reciting, and publicly exhibiting an unpublished work. These rights extend to the copyright owner. Additionally, there are European-type moral rights that are restricted to the author. Protection is afforded for computer programs, sound recordings, and architectural works. Copyright protection is life of the author plus 50 years.

Foreign Investment Climate

Taiwan has long encouraged and facilitated direct foreign investment. Regulations affecting foreign-invested enterprises are thus generally transparent and nondiscriminatory. In its negotiations to enter the World Trade Organization as a developed economy, Taiwan has committed to bring its trade and investment regimes into full compliance with all international standards. Most ownership restrictions in the securities, trading, insurance, and banking industries have been removed.

The vast majority of industrial categories are open to foreign investment. A "negative list" adopted in 1990 specifies industries closed to foreign investment. These include agriculture, cigarette manufacturing, liquor distilling, petroleum refining, basic telecommunications, broadcasting, and electricity distribution. Foreign ownership is restricted in such industries as general construction, shipping, mining, legal, and accounting services.

Taiwan has a comprehensive legal system to protect foreign investments and property rights and ensure fair competition.

Political Leaders, Parties, and International Organizations

The International Academy at Santa Barbara at http://www.iasb.org/cwl publishes *Current World Leaders*, an excellent resource for up-to-date data on political leaders, parties, demographics, etc., in Taiwan. Tel: (800) 530-2682 or (805) 965-5010 for subscription information to their database.

Chief of State:
   President Chen Shui-bian

Head of the Government:
   Premier Vincent Siew

Next Election:
   2004

Political Parties:
   Kuomintang (KMT), Democratic Progressive Party (DPP), New Party, Young China Party (YCP), China Democratic Socialist Party (CDSP), Labor Party

Membership in International Organizations:
  Afro, Asian Rural Reconstruction Organization, ADB, APEC, Asian Productivity
  Organization, International Commerce of Military Medicine, International
  Cotton Advisory Commerce, International Criminal Police Organization
  (INTERPOL), International Union for Publication of Customs Tariffs, PECC,
  Permission Court of Arbitration

Political Influences on Business

Over the past few years Taiwan has made significant progress in its transition from a
single-party, authoritarian policy to a democratic, multi-party political system. Martial
law, which had been in force since the 1940s, was lifted in 1987. Taiwan's first democratically elected legislature was chosen in December 1992. The democratization process continued with the first direct elections of the mayors of Taiwan's two largest
cities (Taipei and Kaohsiung) and the governor of Taiwan Province in December 1994.
These officials were previously appointed by the central authorities.

  Taiwan's constitutional system divides the government into five branches, or Yuans.
The five branches are the Executive Yuan, the Legislative Yuan, the Judicial Yuan, the
Control Yuan, and the Examination Yuan. At the top of this structure is the President,
who has been chosen by the National Assembly. Taiwan held its first popular election
for President in March 1996. Since the People's Republic of China remains a one-party
state, the Taiwanese election of 1996 was the first time in 4,000 years of recorded history that a Chinese nation held a free and fair election.

  Although Taiwan has progressed rapidly toward full democracy, the Kuomintang
(KMT, or Nationalist Party), which ran the previous authoritarian government on
Taiwan, still holds most of the key political posts on the island. As of the 1998 elections, the KMT had a small majority in the law-making Legislative Yuan. The President,
who has been chosen by the KMT-controlled National Assembly, is also the Chairman
of the KMT and appoints the heads of the Yuans, including the head of the Executive
Yuan, the Premier. Factional fighting and weak party discipline within the KMT limits
the party's ability to take full advantage of its numerical superiority in the legislature,
but when push comes to shove the KMT has been able to muster the votes to achieve
its most important goals.

  The KMT, which brought its political power and two million people over from
Mainland China in 1949, was historically associated with the Mainlanders (i.e., people
who fled to Taiwan with the KMT and the descendants of those people). The DPP has
sought to identify itself with the Taiwanese (ethnic Chinese who immigrated to Taiwan
during the past 300 years, mostly from Fujian Province). Yet a majority of the officials
and members in the KMT, including the President, are now ethnic Taiwanese.

  The main opposition party is the Democratic Progressive Party. The Party's most
salient policy difference with the KMT has been the controversial issue of Taiwan independence. Currently the second largest party, the DPP has matured and gained a sig-

nificant role in the Legislative Yuan. Several other important Taiwanese elective positions are also held by DPP members. The DPP has modified its demand for immediate Taiwan independence and now calls for the people to decide Taiwan's future through a plebiscite. The DPP has also staked out generally populist positions of concern for the environment and for working people.

The third largest opposition party is the Chinese New Party, which consists mainly of second-generation "mainlanders" who have grown up in Taiwan. The New Party supports the eventual reintegration of Taiwan into the People's Republic of China (PRC).

The defining characteristic of Taiwan's international relationships is its lack of diplomatic ties with most nations of the world. The ruling authorities on Taiwan call their administration the "Republic of China," and for many years claimed to be the legitimate government of all China. Foreign nations wishing to establish diplomatic relations with a government of China had two choices: to recognize the "Republic of China" or to recognize the People's Republic of China (PRC). Most chose to recognize the PRC. The PRC was admitted to—and Taiwan left—the United Nations and most related organizations in the early 1970s. The U.S. switched diplomatic recognition to the PRC in 1979.

The Taiwan authorities several years ago backed away from their stance of insisting that they are the legitimate rulers of all of China. While still admitting that Taiwan is part of China, they now seek recognition as one of two "legitimate political entities" in China, the other being the PRC. Under this policy, the Taiwan authorities are seeking to join various international organizations, including the United Nations. Taiwan has been able to join the Asia–Pacific Cooperation (APEC) dialogue as an "economy" and is applying to join the World Trade Organization (WTO) as a "customs territory."

Although the United States does not have diplomatic relations with Taiwan, the U.S.–Taiwan relationship is generally excellent. The American Institute in Taiwan (AIT), a private, nonprofit institution, was established in 1979 to maintain the unofficial relations between the people of the United States and Taiwan.

Contacts in the United States

In an effort to strengthen economic and commercial ties, President Clinton approved the first adjustment in U.S. policy towards Taiwan in 15 years (September 1994). Taipei's de facto embassy in the United States, the Coordination Council for North American Affairs, had been upgraded to a representative office and will now be known as:

TAIPEI ECONOMIC AND CULTURAL REPRESENTATIVE OFFICE
4201 Wisconsin Avenue, NW
Washington, D.C. 20016
Tel: (202) 895-1800
dc.roc-taiwan.org

Passport/Visa Requirements

A passport and visa are required. (*Note*: Taiwan eased its visa regulations in early 1994, allowing citizens from 12 countries, including the United States, to enter Taiwan without a visa for a stay of up to 14 days.) Visas for stays of up to two months are issued without charge.

U.S. citizens who plan to visit Taiwan (ROC) for less than 180 days may apply for a visitor visa. (Initial duration of stay is 60 days; however, this can be extended twice to the maximum of 120 days subject to the approval of authorities.)

Applicants may apply for a resident visa if duration of stay in Taiwan (ROC) is more than 180 days.

U.S. citizens who wish to apply for a passport may visit Passport Services' well-organized website at http://travel.state.gov/passport_services.html.

Contacts in Taiwan

AMERICAN INSTITUTE IN TAIWAN (AIT)
Commercial Section
Suite 3207, 333 Keelung Rd.
Sec. 1, Taipei
Tel: (886) (2) 720-1550
Fax: (886) (2) 757-7162
www.ait.org.tw

AMERICAN CHAMBER OF COMMERCE IN TAIPEI
Rm. 1012, 96 Chungshan N. Rd.
Sec. 2, Taipei
Tel: (886) (2) 581-7089
Fax: (886) (2) 542-3376
www.amcham.com.tw

DUN & BRADSTREET INTERNATIONAL, LTD.
TAIWAN BRANCH
Postal Address: 12/F, National Enterprises Centre, No. 188 Nanking E. Road, Sec. 5 Taipei
Street Address: same
Tel: (886) (2) 756-2922
Fax: (886) (2) 749-1936 (General Line/Sales/RMS); (886) (2) 749-1937 (G.M./Financial Dept./Human Resources); (886) (2) 749-1938 (Operations Dept.)

OFFICE OF THE PRESIDENT
Chieh-Shou Hall
Chung-King South Road
Taipei, Republic of China

Further contacts and websites can be found in Appendix A.

Communications

TELEPHONE: The country code for Taiwan is 886.

City codes may be one or two digits in length. Phone numbers are six or seven digits in length.

E-MAIL: E-mail addresses located in Taiwan end with the code .tw

DATES: The Western (Gregorian) calendar is used in business. The date is written in this order: day, month, year.

Cultural I.Q. Question: Feng Shui is a combination of mystical beliefs, astrology, and folklore. In Taipei, Taiwan, many corporate headquarters incorporate **Feng Shui** features to generate auspicious flows of Chi. Which of these is an inauspicious structure?

A.   Square pillars

B.   Revolving doors

C.   Rounded corners

Email your answer to TerriMorrison@getcustoms.com. Each month a drawing will be held to award one correct respondent from all the questions within this book with a free copy of *The World Holiday and Time Zone Guide* (current electronic version).

Thailand

Official Name:	Kingdom of Thailand (Muang Thai)
Official Language:	Thai
Government System:	Constitutional monarchy
Population:	60.6 million (1999 estimate)
Population Growth Rate:	0.93% (1999 estimate)
Area:	513,115 sq. km. (198,114 sq. mi.); about the size of Texas
Natural Resources:	tin, rubber, natural gas, tungsten, tantalum, lead, fish, gypsum, ignite, fluorite, gemstones, crude oil, iron ore
Major Cities:	Bangkok (capital), Chiang Mai, Hat Yai, Nakon Ratchasima

Cultural Note: The royal family of Thailand is considered a strong unifying influence. Faced with a fractious parliament and a strong military, the Thai people turn to their constitutional monarch for leadership. Never make fun of the royal family.

The high standing of the Thai royal family stems in part from history: Thailand was the only nation in Southeast Asia that never became a European colony. By playing France and England off against each other, the Thai kings kept their country free.

Observation: "It is extremely difficult for Americans to understand the deep loyalty, respect, and love that Thais have for their king because there is no personage that occupies a similar position in their own frame of reference. Comparing the king to the president is inadequate. . . . Americans feel free to criticize, caricature, and even vilify their president if they believe his actions so warrant.

"Such denigration of the king would be unthinkable to a Thai, and no greater cultural sin could be committed by an American in Thailand than to insult or even speak of the king in any but the most respectful terms.

"Thais themselves do not criticize the king, particularly in public settings. Such an offense is punishable by law. Recently, a Thai politician was speaking before a village group far from Bangkok. He made some negative remarks about the royal family which, in the U.S., would have been considered tame. But in Thailand word of his disrespect got back to Bangkok and the politician was charged with *lèse majesté* and sent to jail."

—From *A Common Core: Thais and Americans* by John Paul Fieg

Age Breakdown

0–14 = 24%   15–64 = 70%   65+ = 6% (1999 estimate)
Life Expectancy: 65.58 years, male; 73.01 years, female (1999 estimate)

Time

Punctuality is expected from foreigners for business appointments. However, promptness is not a universal habit in Thailand.

Thailand is 7 hours ahead of Greenwich Mean Time (GMT +7), which is 12 hours ahead of U.S. Eastern Standard Time (EST +12)

Holidays

An up-to-date, web-based *World Holiday and Time Zone Guide* is available at www.getcustoms.com. It lists official holidays by country and by day of the year, cultural tips, a corruption index, and time zones with worldwide business hours.

This list is a working guide. Dates should be corroborated before final travel plans are made. In cases where holidays fall on Saturday or Sunday, commercial establishments may be closed the preceding Friday or following Monday.

For many countries, such as those in the Moslem world, holiday dates are approximations since they depend upon actual lunar observations. Moslem holidays also vary in spelling. Many businesses in Moslem countries are closed on Fridays.

Jan 1	SA	New Year's Day
Feb 5	SA	Chinese New Year
Feb 19	SA	Macha Bucha Day
Apr 6	TH	Chakri Day
Apr 13	TH	Songkran Festival (3 days)
May 1	MO	National Labor Day
May 5	FR	Coronation Day
May 18	TH	Visakha Bucha Day
Jul 1	SA	Bank holiday
Jul 17	MO	Aslahapuja Day
Jul 20	TH	Khao Phansa Day
Aug 12	SA	H.M. the Queen's Birthday
Oct 23	MO	Chulalongkorn Day
Dec 5	TU	H.M. the King's Birthday
Dec 11	MO	Constitution Day
Dec 31	SU	New Year's Eve

- Be certain to confirm your appointments with local representatives to avoid conflicts with regional festivities.
- The best time to schedule a visit to Thailand is between November and March. Most businesspeople vacation during April and May. Avoid the weeks before and after Christmas, and the month of April. Thailand's Water Festival is held in April and businesses close for an entire week.

Work Week

- Business hours: 8:30 A.M. to 5:00 P.M. Monday through Friday.
- Bank hours: 8:30 A.M. to 3:30 P.M. Monday through Friday.
- Government hours: 8:30 A.M. to 4:30 P.M. Monday through Friday.
- Shops: 10:00 A.M. to 6:30 or 7:00 P.M. Monday through Saturday. Smaller shops open earlier and close later.

Religious/Societal Influences on Business

Thailand's official religion is Buddhism. Almost 95% of Thais follow the Theravada form of Buddhism. Other religions are also represented, including Islam and Christianity.

Adherents to the Theravada school consider themselves followers of the form closest to Buddhism as it was originally practiced. The spiritual liberation of the individual is a main focus of the Theravada school. Each individual is considered responsible for his or her own actions and destiny.

Each person in Thai society has a specific place. It is every person's job to fulfill his or her role with a minimum of fuss. Failure to do so involves a loss of dignity, credibility, and face. The Thai phrase *mai pen rai* (meaning "never mind," or "no worries") is frequently invoked as a reminder not to risk embarrassment opposing the unopposable.

5 Cultural Tips

1. Thailand advertises itself as "The Land of Smiles," and the Thai people are genuinely friendly and polite. But their extreme politeness vanishes as soon as they get behind the wheel of a car. Driving is aggressive, and pedestrians seem to be fair game. Be very cautious every time you cross a street; use an overhead walkway if possible.

2. Because of travel difficulties in large Thai cities, many foreign executives plan on making only two meetings per day. The gridlock in Bangkok is so bad that many Thai businesspeople conduct business from their cars with cell phones and mobile fax machines. (Remember that Bangkok and other Thai cities have passenger service on canals. When the street traffic is stalled, consider commuting by boat.)

3. English is often spoken by Thai executives. For those who do not speak English, a translator is usually close at hand. Note that taxi drivers do not usually speak English. To arrive at your destination, have the street address written down in Thai, plus the name of the nearest major cross street.

4. Business entertaining is part of developing business relationships. Thais place great value on enjoyment (*kwam sanuk*). Laughter comes easily to Thais, and a foreigner can minimize his or her inevitable errors by laughing with them. Laughter can also be used to cover embarrassment.

5. Giving gifts will help create a good first impression. A bottle of imported liquor (especially scotch) is a good gift. Have the gift wrapped locally, and do not be surprised if the gift is immediately set aside—Thais do not open gifts in the presence of the giver. Some executives recommend giving a small gift to the office receptionist or secretary as well. In this case, food that can be shared with the rest of the office staff is recommended, such as cookies or candy.

Economic Overview

For much of the past two decades, Thailand was one of Asia's fastest growing, most attractive markets for U.S. exporters and investors. It succeeded in developing an open market economy based on a free enterprise system. Thai leaders pursued consistently conservative fiscal and monetary policies that have benefited the private sector.

Thailand underwent a period of political unrest in May 1992, but quickly recovered, posting a 7.8% growth rate in 1993 and 8% in 1994. But as the economy continued to boom, the seeds of economic collapse appeared. Thai and foreign banks made huge, undercollateralized loans. In 1996 it was revealed that the Bangkok Bank of Commerce had engaged in criminal lending practices. Other banking scandals followed. Loans went unpaid, businesses failed, consumer confidence fell, and by 1997 Thailand's currency plunged in value. Similar collapses occurred in neighboring countries. But the Asian financial crisis *began* in Thailand.

Thailand has been slowly recovering since the 1997 crisis. One of the more advanced developing countries in Asia, Thailand depends on exports of manufactured goods and the development of the service sector to fuel the country's rapid growth. While its growth is still far less than it was during the boom, Thailand is once again on the upswing. Growth will exceed 5% in 2000, and is predicted to reach 6% in 2001.

Thailand is not the only Asian nation with a thriving sex industry. Unfortunately, prostitution in this day and age yields a large numbers of AIDS patients. Thailand has the highest percentage of AIDS cases in Southeast Asia, and the cost of dealing with this disease will drain health-care dollars for years to come.

5 *Largest Businesses in Thailand*

Charoen Pokphand Group Co., Ltd., Bangkok
   80,000 employees
Seagate Technology (Thailand) Ltd., Samutprakarn
   39,000 employees
Miracle International Co., Ltd., Bangkok
   30,035 employees
Power Electronics of Minebea Co., Ltd., Bangkok
   30,030 employees
Electricity Generating Authority of Thailand, Nonthaburi
   30,000 employees

Cultural Note: Thai is a complex language with five different tones. While this makes it difficult for Westerners to speak, Thais will appreciate a foreigner who takes the time to learn even a few phrases in Thai.

There are only eight possible consonants that a word in Thai may end with: p, t, k, m, n, ng, w, and y. Consequently, when Thais speak English, they have trouble with words that end in other sounds. English words ending in l tend to be shifted to the n sound; for example, the word "Oriental Hotel" is pronounced "Orienten Hoten." Since the s sound is not used in endings, Thais tend to leave the s off plural words.

The Thai alphabet is similar to the alphabets used in Burmese and Laotian scripts. Thai is written from left to right. Adding to the difficulty for Westerners, there are no spaces between individual words.

Comparative Data

Comparative Data Ratings
(Scale: 5 = Highest; 1 = Lowest)
Overall rating: 3.5

A. GDP Growth: 4
B. Per Capita Income: 2
C. Trade Flows with the U.S.: 4
D. Country Risk: 3
E. Monetary Policy: 5
F. Trade Policy: 3
  • Tariffs
  • Import Licensing
  • Import Taxes
G. Protection of Property Rights: 3
H. Foreign Investment Climate: 4

GROSS DOMESTIC PRODUCT: $369 billion (1998 estimate)

GDP GROWTH: −8.5% (1998)

PER CAPITA INCOME: $6,100 (1998 estimate)

Trade Flows with the U.S.

U.S. EXPORTS TO THAILAND: $5.2 billion (1998 estimate)

U.S. IMPORTS FROM THAILAND: $13.4 billion (1998 estimate)

TOP U.S. EXPORTS TO THAILAND: Computer software; telecommunications equipment; electric power systems; airport/ground support equipment; pumps/valves/compressors; computers and peripherals; pollution-control equipment; food processing/packaging equipment; medical equipment; franchising

TOP U.S. PROSPECTS FOR EXPORT TO THAILAND: Airport and ground support equipment; electronic components; water resources equipment and services; packaging; food-processing equipment and machines; business services; electric power systems; telecommunications equipment; aircraft and aircraft parts; pollution-control equipment

Country Risk

Dun & Bradstreet rates Thailand as having fair capacity to meet outstanding payment liabilities. There is enough uncertainty to warrant close monitoring of country risk. Less than 50% of sales to Thailand are conducted on letters of credit, while about 25% of goods are shipped on open account. A confirmed irrevocable letter of credit is still advised for new and/or small accounts. Credit terms are usually 60 to 90 days.

Monetary Policy

Inflation rose slowly from 3% in 1993 to 5% in 1995. It remained between 5% and 6% in 1996 and 1997. Following the Asian economic crisis, inflation jumped to 8% in 1998, but has dropped below 2% since then.

MONETARY UNIT: Thai baht

Trade Policy

TARIFFS   The Thai government has endeavored and committed to reduce import duties as part of its obligations as a founding member of the World Trade Organization. There will be a phased implementation of the new tariffs. There is a special tariff rate of 30% maximum, down from 100%, for locally produced goods in need of special protection.

Tariff categories have been reduced from 39 to 6.

Duty exemptions are routinely granted to firms with investment promotion privileges, and rebates of import duties on raw materials are granted upon export of the finished product.

IMPORT LICENSING   In 1995 Thailand began the process of converting import licensing restrictions for many items to tariff rate quotas and tariffs under its World Trade Organization obligations. Import licenses are still required on industrial products.

Most goods can be freely imported, although some import licensing requirements remain to protect Thai industries for wealth, security, and other reasons.

IMPORT TAXES   A 7% value-added tax (VAT) was introduced in 1992.

Imported alcoholic beverages are assessed a separate excise duty with rates varying from 10–48%. Separate excise duties are also assessed on a number of other products such as tobacco and some electrical and petroleum products.

Protection of Intellectual Property Rights

Thailand belongs to the Berne Convention. Thailand has recently taken a number of steps to rid itself of its reputation as a violator of intellectual property rights. New intellectual property laws took effect on March 21, 1995 and enforcement has been improved. A court specializing in intellectual property matters has been established.

In order to be patented in Thailand, inventions must be novel, inventive, and have industrial application. Patent protection is 20 years from filing.

Trademarks and service marks can be registered, although there is often a time lag. Rights are transferable in writing. When a trademark is registered, it gives the applicant an exclusive right of use. Trademarks receive protection for a term of 10 years. Registrations can be extended for an unlimited number of 10-year periods.

The term of copyrights is the life of the author plus 50 years. Copyrights result automatically on creation. Excluded from copyright are ideas, discoveries, and mathematical theories. There is no requirement of registration.

Foreign Investment Climate

The Thai government maintains an open, market-oriented economy and encourages foreign direct investment as a means of promoting economic development, employment, and technology transfer.

The U.S.–Thai Treaty of Amity and Economic Relations of 1966 allows U.S. citizens and businesses incorporated in the U.S. or in Thailand that are majority-owned by U.S. citizens to engage in business on the same basis as Thais, exempting them from most of the restrictions on foreign investment imposed by the Alien Business Law of 1972. Under the Treaty, Thailand restricts American investment only in the fields of communications, transport, fiduciary functions, banking, the exploitation of land or other natural resources, and domestic trade in agricultural products.

Political Leaders, Parties, and International Organizations

The International Academy at Santa Barbara at http://www.iasb.org/cwl publishes *Current World Leaders*, an excellent resource for up-to-date data on political leaders, parties, demographics, etc., in Thailand. Tel: (800) 530-2682 or (805) 965-5010 for subscription information to their database.

Head of State:

King Bhumibol Adulyadej

Head of the Government:

Prime Minister Chuan Leekpai

Political Parties:

Chart Thai Party, Solidarity Party, Prachakorn Party, Social Action Party, Democratic Party, New Aspiration Party, Siam Democratic Party, Puangchon Chaothai, Samakkhi Tham Party, Palang Dharma, Chart Pattana Party

Membership in international organizations:

ADB, APEC, ASEAN, INTELSAT, PECC, UN and most of its specialized agencies and related organizations (including FAO, GATT, IAEA, IBRD, ICAO, IDA, IFAD, IFC, ILO, IMF, IMO, ITU, UNESCO, UNIDO, UPU, WHO, WMO)

Political Influences on Business

Recent civil administrations have devoted much effort to nurturing democratic institutions and working with the military (an important factor in Thai politics) to identify an appropriate role in the post-Cold War world. Other priorities included meeting basic economic needs and developing rural areas.

The U.S. government successfully pressed Thailand to improve its intellectual property regulations. The U.S. has also sought improvements in Thailand's protection of internationally recognized worker rights. Other concerns are child labor abuse, workplace safety, and restrictions on public sector employees' freedom of association and collective bargaining rights.

Of course, the major concern of all parties is the restoration of the Thai economy. Since the 1997 economic meltdown, Thailand has received some $17.2 billion from the International Monetary Fund. To qualify for this bailout, the Thai government had to institute harsh economic reforms. These cutbacks included the layoffs of 200,000 state employees (out of a total of 1.5 million), raising unemployment to 6% in 1998. Thai students studying abroad lost their government funding. Under IMF prodding, the Thai government has promised to privatize 59 state enterprises, including telecommunications and electric utilities. These unpopular measures have been largely accepted by the Thai populace. In 1998 government investigators revealed corruption in the Ministries of Agriculture, Education, Forestry, Health, and Transport. Such revelations demonstrated to the Thai people that the government itself will be held accountable.

Thailand is a constitutional monarchy with a Westminster-style parliament. Elections must be held every four years, but may be called more frequently. The Prime Minister must be an elected member of parliament. Political parties are not usually ideologically oriented. In nearly every case, they are formed around a key figure, usually the party leader. Thailand's political orientation is moderate to conservative, and all political parties support a free market system.

Contacts in the United States

THE EMBASSY OF THE KINGDOM OF THAILAND
1024 Wisconsin Avenue, NW, Suite 103
Washington, D.C. 20007
Tel: (202) 944-3625
Fax: (202) 944-3627
www.thaiembdc.org

Passport/Visa Requirements

Passport and onward/return tickets are required. Visas are not needed for stays of up to 30 days. However, without a visa, entry is permitted only when arriving at international airports in Bangkok, Phuket, or Chiang Mai.

Requirements for a Thai Visa

1. A valid passport (valid for at least six months and endorsed for travel to Thailand).
2. One completed visa application form for each passport. *Note:* All visa application forms must be signed regardless of the category of visa requested. The Attention for Tourist statement applies only to applicants whose stated purpose of visit is tourism. The signature on applications for minors should correspond with the sig-

nature in the applicant's passport. Submit two black-and-white or color passport-size photographs. Machine and photocopies of photographs are not acceptable.

3. Applications for visas, submitted in person and not requiring referral to Thailand, are usually processed within 48 hours.

Applicants should call the Thai Embassy for additional information about requirements for holders of U.S. passports or reentry permits for those who were born in Laos, Vietnam, or Cambodia.

Visa Fees

Transit Visas: $10.00 for each entry (maximum stay 30 days).
Tourist Visas: $15.00 for each entry (maximum stay 60 days).
Non-Immigrant Visas: $20.00 for each entry (maximum stay 90 days).

Note: The fee for a Thai visa may be paid by cash or U.S. Postal Money Order. Personal and company checks are not acceptable. Nationals of the following countries are exempt from paying a fee for a Thai visa: Denmark, Republic of Korea, Malaysia, Philippines, Norway, Singapore, Sweden, and Tunisia.

Travelers are required by Thai law to have in hand foreign currency or financial document transferable into cash as follows: (1) at least $250.00 per person or $500.00 per family for travelers with transit visas or without visas; (2) at least $500.00 per person or $1,000.00 per family for travelers with tourist or business visas.

For more current information, travelers may contact the Royal Thai Embassy.

U.S. citizens who wish to apply for a passport may visit Passport Services' well-organized website at http://travel.state.gov/passport_services.html.

Contacts in Thailand

THE U.S. EMBASSY
120 Wireless Road
Bangkok 10330
Mailing Address: APO AP 96535
Tel: (66) (2) 252-4000
Fax: (66) (2) 254-2990
www.usa.or.th

THE AMERICAN CHAMBER OF COMMERCE IN THAILAND
Kian Gwan Building.
140 Wireless Road, 7th Floor
Bangkok 10330
Tel: (66) (2) 251-9266/7
Fax: (66) (2) 651-4472
amcham-th.org

KING BHUMIBOL ADULYADEJ
Office of the King
Bangkok, Kingdom of Thailand

OFFICE OF THE PRIME MINISTER
Government House
Nakhon Pathom Road
Bangkok 10300, Kingdom of Thailand

Further contacts and websites can be found in Appendix A.

Communications

TELEPHONE: The country code for Thailand is 66.

City codes may have one or two digits. Phone numbers in Bangkok are seven digits in length. Elsewhere in Thailand, phone numbers are generally six digits long.

E-MAIL: E-mail addresses located in Thailand end with the code .th

DATES: In Thailand the date is usually written in this order: day, month, year (unlike the U.S. practice of writing month, day, year). While the Western (Gregorian) calendar is usually used in international correspondence, the Thais also have their own calendar.

Observation: "In Thai education, the idea is inculcated that mother is the most important of persons. She has given life to the child, suffering for and feeding it at great psychological and physical cost, and she gives it all freely. This tide of goodness results in a moral debt on the side of her child, a debt that it is never able to repay.

"This way of thinking may shed light on a curious phenomenon, the vast production of mother-centred literature. When I first ran across the collection *Mother Dear*, I was truly amazed at finding some sixty short stories and poems devoted to 'Mother,' written by all kinds of notables, such as army officers, medical doctors, government ministers, well-known nobility, and so on and so forth. Soon I found out that almost all Thai authors write one or more short stories, and sometimes whole novels, about mothers, presumably their own.

—From *Inside Southeast Asia* by Niels Mulder

Official Name:	Republic of Turkey (Turkiye Cumhuriyeti)
Official Language:	Turkish
Government System:	Multi-party republic
Population:	65.6 million (1999 estimate)
Population Growth:	1.57% (1999 estimate)
Area:	780,580 sq. km. (301,382 sq. mi.); slightly larger than Texas
Natural Resources:	antimony, coal, chromium, mercury, copper, borate, sulfur, iron ore
Major Cities:	Ankara (capital), Istanbul, Izmir, Adana, Konya, Bursa

Cultural Note: Tenacity is considered an important trait in Turkey. This characteristic is exemplified by the founder of the modern Turkish State, Kemal Ataturk. The venerated Ataturk—whose stern picture is everywhere in Turkey—is to Turkey what Chairman Mao Tse-Tung was to China. Ataturk's many accomplishments include:

- Forging a new Turkish State out of the ruins of the old Ottoman Empire.
- Replacing Arabic Script with the easier-to-master Roman Alphabet.
- Suppressing the influence of Islam and making Turkey a secular nation.
- Changing age-old patterns of dress; he outlawed the fez on men and denounced the head scarf on women.

Age Breakdown

0–14 = 30%   15–64 = 64%   65+ = 6% (1999 estimate)
Life Expectancy: 70.81 years, male; 75.88 years, female (1999 estimate)

Time

Foreigners are expected to be on time for appointments. However, punctuality has not traditionally been considered important in Turkey. Your Turkish counterpart could easily be an hour late. (The usual excuse for lateness is the unpredictable traffic in urban areas.) Younger Turkish executives are more likely to be on time.

The pace of everything in Turkey tends to be slower than in the United States. However, there is a great difference between attitudes towards time in the public and private sectors. Many Turkish businesses now operate as quickly and efficiently as any in the U.S. Substantial business deals can even be completed in a single day.

On the other hand, the Turkish civil service remains slow-moving and hampered by red tape. Simple transactions can take hours to complete, requiring paperwork from several different departments.

Speed is a prerequisite for driving in Turkey. Outside the gridlocked cities, Turkish drivers often ignore the rules and zoom about at a lethal pace. The rate of traffic accidents (and fatalities) is very high.

Turkey is 2 hours ahead of Greenwich Mean Time (GMT +2), which is 7 hours ahead of U.S. Eastern Standard Time (EST +7). Clocks are moved forward one hour in late March and moved back an hour in late September.

Holidays

An up-to-date, online *World Holiday and Time Zone Guide* is available at www.get-customs.com. It lists official holidays by country and by day of the year, business and cultural tips, a corruption index, and time zones with worldwide business hours.

This list is a working guide. Dates should be corroborated before final travel plans are made. In cases where holidays fall on Saturday or Sunday, commercial establishments may be closed the preceding Friday or following Monday.

Jan 1	SA	New Year's Day
Jan 8	SA	Ramazan Feast (3 days)
Mar 16	SU	Kurban Bairam (4 days)
Apr 23	SU	National Sovereignty and Children's Day
May 19	FR	Youth and Sports Day
Aug 30	WE	Victory Day
Oct 29	SU	Republic Day
Dec 28	TH	Ramazan Feast (3 days)

- Business appointments can rarely be made during the months of June, July, and August; most Turkish businesspeople take extended vacations during this time.

- Obviously, you cannot expect to conduct business on a Turkish holiday. Be aware, however, that many people will begin the holiday around noon the day before.

- The lunar-based Muslim calendar is shorter than the solar Gregorian calendar. Consequently, with respect to the Gregorian calendar, Muslim holidays advance by some 10 days each year. Also, the posted dates of Muslim religious holidays are only approximations, since the start of the holiday depends upon actual lunar observations.

From a foreigner's point of view, the most important Muslim observances in Turkey are:

- *Ramazan* (called *Ramadan* in other Muslim countries): the Holy Month. During this month, observant Muslims abstain from all food, drink, tobacco, and sexual activity during daylight hours. Dusk is announced by a cannon shot. The faithful are awakened before sunrise by drummers who roam the streets, reminding them to eat before dawn. It is impolite for nonbelievers to eat, drink, or even smoke in the presence of those who are fasting; if you must do so, be discreet. Office hours may be curtailed. Not surprisingly, fasting people may be short-tempered, especially when Ramazan falls during the sweltering days of summer. This is called *Ramazan kafasi* (Ramazan irritability, literally, "Ramazan head").

- *Sheker Bayram:* The three-day festival at the end of the Ramazan fast. Children go door-to-door asking for sweets. Muslims exchange greeting cards, feast, and visit one another. Banks and offices are closed for all three days.

- *Kurban Bayram:* The Feast of the Sacrifice. Celebrating the traditional story of Abraham's near-sacrifice of his son Isaac, this is the most important religious and secular holiday of the year. The holiday lasts for four days, but many banks and businesses close for an entire week. Resorts and transportation will be booked solid.

Work Week

- Business and banking hours: 9:00 A.M. to 12 noon and 2:00 P.M. to 5:00 P.M. Monday through Friday. (Note that business executives often arrive between 9:30 and 10:00 A.M.; they return from lunch around 2:30 P.M.)

- Store hours: 9:00 A.M. to 1:00 P.M. and 2:30 P.M. to 7:00 P.M. Monday through Friday; 9:00 A.M. to 12 noon and 1:30 P.M. to 8:00 P.M. Saturday.

- Observant Muslims attend a mosque on Fridays at noon. Unlike most countries with Muslim majorities, Turkey is officially secular, so the work week runs from Monday through Friday. Sunday is the government mandated "day of rest."

Religious/Societal Influences on Business

The majority of Turks (about 80%) are Sunni Muslims. Except for a few thousand Christians, the rest of the population are Shiite Muslims, mostly of a nonorthodox sect called Alevi. Since its founding in 1923, the Turkish Republic has been a secular state with no official religion. While there is considerable pressure to change this, other forces—including Turkey's powerful military—are determined to keep Turkey officially secular. The political victories of the Islamic political parties (such as the Welfare Party and the Virtue Party) notwithstanding, Turkey remains a secular state.

Every Turkish citizen, religious or not, is familiar with the basic precepts of Islam. The word "Islam" literally means "submission" (to the will of Allah). Consequently, both success and misfortune are attributed to the will of Allah. Destiny is not under the control of man.

Most Turkish children are trained to be self-reliant, to care for others, and to be satisfied with one's lot in life.

The official language is Turkish. Many businesspeople speak either English, German, or French. Many executives receive their degrees in colleges outside of Turkey.

5 Cultural Tips

1. All meetings will begin with extensive small talk. Expect to be asked about your journey, your lodgings, and how you like Turkey. (Be sure to have good things to say. Turks can say negative things about Turkey, but foreigners may not.) Sports and family are good topics of conversation, but avoid asking a man about his wife or daughters unless he brings them up first. The current rate of inflation is a constant topic of conversation. The Turks have had high inflation for so many years that they consistently compare and discuss inflation rates. Know the inflation rate in your country.

2. Age is respected. Defer to elders in all circumstances. Elders are served first, introduced first, and allowed to go through doors first. Since most Turkish businesses are family owned, the decision-maker is probably an elder.

3. Politeness is very important in Turkey. To disagree openly with someone in public would be insulting and undignified, so Turks rarely say *no* (except, of course, while bargaining). Foreigners often have difficulty recognizing when a *yes* is just a polite way of saying *no*. Turks may even let someone make a error rather than correct them, if the correction would result in a public embarrassment.

4. Although the majority of Turks are Muslim, the government and the military are determined to keep Turkey a secular state. While Muslim theocracies like Iran and Saudi Arabia insist that women cover their hair in public, the Turkish government has actually *prohibited* women from wearing head coverings in some locales, such as universities. Most women in Turkey do not live under harsh religious restrictions. In fact, Turkish women are well represented in business.

5. Historical enmities in the region remain strong. Try to avoid being associated with (or even discussing) Turkish minority groups, which include Greeks, Armenians, and Kurds. The Turkish government does not even wish to recognize Turkish Kurds as a culturally distinct people. Armed opposition to Ankara continues from the Kurdish Workers' Party (abbreviated as PKK).

Observation: "I found the Turks very pleasant and very proud of their country. The country and its social customs are changing very rapidly. For example, the old prohibition about not crossing your legs (so as not to insult someone by showing the sole of your foot) isn't strictly followed by the educated young people. When I asked about it, they said it doesn't offend them . . . but that they wouldn't do it around their fathers."

—Michael Landau, Executive Vice President of HLC Industries, Bala Cynwyd, PA

Economic Overview

Turkey remains unexplored territory for most American companies outside the *Fortune* 500 and defense suppliers.

Until the early 1980s Turkey was an insulated, state-directed economy. In the 1980s the country began an economic turnaround based on increased reliance on market forces, export-led development, lower taxes, integration with the world economy, and privatization.

A much-needed austerity and stabilization program in April 1994 cooled down the economy. GNP fell 6% in 1994, setting a post-war record. Unemployment jumped and real wages fell. The economy in 1995 began to show signs of recovery. Driven by a dynamic private sector and the prospect of eventual customs union with the European Union, Turkey's future looks bright.

The Turkish market now offers excellent growth prospects for U.S. exports. Increased spending on infrastructure projects and private sector investment will generate strong demand for a wide range of capital goods.

Turkey's young population of 64 million is growing rapidly, both in numbers and purchasing power. Turkey's outstanding growth prospects led to its designation by the U.S. Department of Commerce as one of the world's 10 Big Emerging Markets.

Cultural Note: *Yok* is a commonly heard Turkish phoneme, somewhat analogous to *nu* in Yiddish or *ayah* in Chinese. The exact meaning of *yok* depends upon the context and tone of voice. However, you can be sure that *yok* is—to one degree or another—negative. (The formal Turkish word for "no" is *hayir*.)

Comparative Data

Comparative Data Ratings
(Scale: 5 = Highest; 1 = Lowest)
Turkey: 2.75

A. GDP Growth: 3
B. Per Capita Income: 2
C. Trade Flows with the U.S.: 2
D. Country Risk: 2
E. Monetary Policy: 1
F. Trade Policy: 3
    • Tariffs
    • Import Licensing
    • Import Taxes
G. Protection of Property Rights: 2
H. Foreign Investment Climate: 4

GROSS DOMESTIC PRODUCT: $425.4 billion (1998 estimate)

GDP GROWTH: 1.5% (1999); 4.0% (2000 forecast)

PER CAPITA INCOME: $6,600 (1998 estimate)

Trade Flows with the U.S.

U.S. EXPORTS TO TURKEY: $3.5 billion (1998)

U.S. IMPORTS FROM TURKEY: $2.5 billion (1998)

TOP U.S. PROSPECTS FOR EXPORT TO TURKEY: Electrical power systems; telecommunications equipment; building products; telecommunications services (especially cellular phone service); medical equipment; textile machinery and equipment; automotive parts; architectural/construction/engineering services; pollution-control equipment; food-processing and packaging equipment

Country Risk

There is considerable uncertainty associated with expected returns. Businesses are advised to limit their exposure and/or select high-return transactions only. The financial impact of the 1999 earthquake, in conjunction with the economic slowdown, necessitates caution when extending credit.

Monetary Policy

Turkey's principal economic problem remains inflation, fueled by large public sector deficits. Annual consumer price inflation has averaged 74% since prices began to escalate in 1988. Inflation in 1999 was estimated at 60%.

Years of inflation have made small coins valueless in Turkey. Rather than give out small coins as change, neighborhood merchants instead give an item of small value, such as chewing gum or a book of matches.

MONETARY UNIT: Turkish lira

Trade Policy

TARIFFS   Turkey began to align its tariff system with that of the European Union in 1994. This was completed on January 1, 1996. This facilitated trade with not only the European Union but with other countries as well. As a result of this tariff reform, the Turkish government claims that the average duty rate for imports from the United States fell from 10.8% to 3.6%. The Turkish government estimates the average duty rate for all third-country imports at 5%. The EU tariff system also simplifies the calculation of duties of U.S. goods.

IMPORT LICENSING   In the past, all importers had to obtain a general import license valid for one year from the Undersecretaries of Foreign Trade. Importers were also required to obtain an import permission certificate for each type of item to be imported.

As a result of the 1996 trade revisions, an importer only needs to have a tax number for most imports. Some imports remain on the restricted list, such as hazardous materials, narcotics, and firearms.

Some items may only be imported by designated companies or the government monopoly enterprise, TEKEL. Alcohol may only be imported by TEKEL. The importation of tobacco products is limited to TEKEL and designated cigarette producers.

IMPORT TAXES   Imports are subject to a value-added tax (VAT). Most industrial products are charged a rate of 15%; however, some products can incur a rate as high as 23%. The VAT is also applied to goods produced in Turkey. Capital goods, some raw materials, and imports by government agencies and enterprises are exempt from import fees.

Protection of Intellectual Property Rights

Turkey lacks adequate, modern laws concerning intellectual property protection. Since 1992 the United States has listed Turkey on the priority watch list of countries that fail to protect American firms' intellectual property rights.

There has been progress on the legislative front driven primarily by Turkey's desire to enter into a customs union with the European Union. The agreement with the EU requires Turkey to meet EU standards for intellectual property protection.

Turkey amended its 1951 copyright law in June 1995. The amended law significantly improves protection for books, videos, sound recording, computer programs, and other copyright-protected media.

Turkey enacted a new patent law in June 1995, and introduced patent protection for pharmaceuticals in January of 1999. Turkey is a member of the Paris Convention for the Protection of Industrial Property. Patent terms are for 15 years from date of filing.

A trademark law has been drafted but not yet enacted. Counterfeiting of foreign trademarked products is currently widespread. Trademark registrations are effective for 10 years from date of registration and can be renewed for similar periods.

Foreign Investment Climate

Turkey has a liberal investment regime in which foreign investments receive national treatment. Almost all areas open to the Turkish private sector are also open to foreign participation and investment.

Screening mechanisms are routine and nondiscriminatory. Foreign companies established in Turkey are considered Turkish businesses. Apart from aviation, maritime transportation, insurance, and broadcasting (where equity participation by foreign shareholders is limited to 49%), there are no major sectors in which foreign investors do not receive national treatment. Foreign investors receive national treatment in privatization programs, too.

U.S. direct investment in Turkey is largely concentrated in manufacturing, petroleum, and banking. Since 1993 direct investment in Turkey from the United States has been over $1 billion per year.

Turkey also receives enormous amounts of economic and military assistance from the U.S.

Political Leaders, Parties, and International Organizations

The International Academy at Santa Barbara at http://www.iasb.org/cwl publishes *Current World Leaders*, an excellent resource for up-to-date data on political leaders, parties, demographics, etc., in Turkey. Tel: (800) 530-2682 or (805) 965-5010 for subscription information to their database.

President:
   Ahmet Necdet Sezer

Prime minister:
   Bülent Ecevit

Next Election:
   May 2007

Political Parties:
   Democratic Left Party, Nationalist Movement Party, Virtue Party, Motherland Party, True Path Party, Republican People's Party, Democratic People's Party, Grand Unity Party

Membership in international organizations:

AsDB, BIS, BSEC, CCC, CE, CERN (observer), EAPC, EBRD, ECE, ECO, ESCAP, FAO, IAEA, IBRD, ICAO, ICC, ICFTU, ICRM, IDA, IDB, IEA, IFAD, IFC, IFRCS, IHO, ILO, IMF, IMO, Intelsat, Interpol, IOC, IOM (observer), ISO, ITU, NATO, NEA, OECD, OIC, OPCW, OSCE, PCA, UN and some of its specialized agencies and related organizations (UNCTAD, UNESCO, UNHCR, UNIDO, UNIKOM, UNMIBH, UNOMIG, UNPREDEP, UNRWA, UPU, WEU (associate), WFTU, WHO, WIPO, WMO), WToO, WTrO

Political Influences on Business

The 1923 creation of the Turkish Republic out of the ruins of the Ottoman Empire was a remarkable achievement. However, one of the legacies of the founders was an insular, state-directed economy. The inefficiencies of such an economy gradually led to economic stagnation. This changed in 1980 with economic and legal reforms. Turkey joined the global economy and became a dynamic market for exports and imports.

Although Turkey has posted remarkable gains, the economic reforms are not yet complete. Government-directed industries still need to be downsized. Large deficits have yielded high levels of inflation. Turkey suffered a financial crisis in 1994, which resulted in post-war records in inflation (150%) and declining GDP (–6%). Fortunately, an austerity program succeeded in restoring the economy. Inflation is still high, but the GDP is again rising each year, despite recent political uncertainty.

The continued hostilities between Allied military forces and Iraq are of great concern to the Turks. Turkey—a member of NATO—allows the U.S. the use of its airfields to patrol the no-fly zones in Iraq. However, the accidental bombing by U.S. warplanes of an Iraqi oil pipeline that leads through Turkey strained this relationship.

Contacts in the United States

THE EMBASSY OF THE REPUBLIC OF TURKEY
1714 Massachusetts Avenue, NW
Washington, D.C. 20036
Tel: (202) 659-8200
www.turkey.org

EUROPEAN COUNCIL OF AMERICAN CHAMBERS
OF COMMERCE
5309 Burling Terrace
Bethesda, MD 20814
Tel: (301) 215-9076
Fax: (301) 215-9076

Passport/Visa Requirements

Valid passport and visa required. U.S. citizens with regular passports may obtain visas at Turkish border crossing points for tourist/business visits up to 3 months or through overseas Turkish consular offices (one application form is required).

Visas must be obtained in advance for visits lasting longer than 3 months, for study/research purposes, or for employment purposes.

U.S. citizens holding diplomatic or official passports must acquire their visas from Turkish Embassies prior to departing for Turkey. A gratis visa will be assigned for those traveling on official business or assigned to a U.S. mission in Turkey on a permanent/temporary basis upon submission of a letter of assignment.

For further information on entry requirements to Turkey, travelers can contact the Embassy of the Republic of Turkey or the nearest Turkish Consulate.

U.S. citizens who wish to apply for a passport may visit Passport Services' well-organized website at http://travel.state.gov/passport_services.html.

Contacts in Turkey

THE EMBASSY OF THE UNITED STATES OF
AMERICA
110 Ataturk Blvd.
ANKARA
PSC 93, Box 5000
Mailing Address: APO AE 09823
Tel: (90) (4) 468-6110
Fax: (90) (4) 467-0019
www.usis-ankara.org.tr

OFFICE OF THE PRESIDENT
Cumhurbaskanligi Kosku
Cankaya
ANKARA, Republic of Turkey

OFFICE OF THE PRIME MINISTER
Basbakanlik
Bakanliklar
ANKARA, Republic of Turkey

Further contacts and websites can be found in Appendix A.

Communications

TELEPHONE: The country code for Turkey is 90.

Turkish phone numbers were changed in 1993 to a U.S.-style system of seven-digit numbers.

MAIL: Turkish was formerly written in Arabic script, even though the Turkish language is not closely related to Arabic. In 1928 the Latin alphabet was adopted by decree. Many diacritical marks are used when writing Turkish with the Latin alphabet. However, Turks are accustomed to the limitations of foreign keyboards, and are not confused or insulted when these diacritical marks are omitted.

Letters in Turkey may be addressed as follows: (*Notes in parentheses*)

Title & Name: Mr. Ahmet Ozturk
  (*English honorifics such as Mr., Mrs., and Ms. are often used.*)
Company: Denet Mali Danismanlik A.S.
  (*The names of corporations are usually followed by
  A.S. = Anonim Sirket or Ltd. S. = Limited Sirket.*)

Street:	Buyukdere Cad. No:121
	(Buyukdere is the name of the street. Cad.=Caddesi=street. No:121 means Building Number 121)
Additional Data:	Ercan Han, K:4-6
	(Han = building, so Ercan Han = Ercan Building. Building names do not necessarily correspond with the principal tenant; the name could refer to the builder or owner.
	K = Kat = floor, so K:4-6 means Floors 4 through 6.)
Postcode, Locality, and City:	80300 Gayrettepe, ISTANBUL
	(Postcodes are 5-digit numbers, the "80" code indicates the central business district of Istanbul. Gayrettepe is a locality within Istanbul. Neither postcodes nor localities are universally used. The city name should be written all in capital letters. A locality name may be connected to the city name; this could be written Gayrettepe-ISTANBUL or even Gayrettepe/ISTANBUL.)
Country:	Turkey

E-MAIL: E-mail addresses located in Turkey end with the code .tr

DATES: In Turkey the date is written in this order: day, month, year (unlike the U.S. practice of writing month, day, year). The dates are usually separated by periods (10.11.00 indicates November 10, 2000). Although the majority of Turks are Muslim, the calendar used is the Western (Gregorian) version, not the Muslim (Hijra) calendar.

Faux Pas: Two foreigners traveling about Turkey on their motorbike decided to spend the night at a small hotel. They brought their motorcycle through a narrow door into the hotel courtyard for safekeeping. The next morning, they were surprised to find that they couldn't get their motorcycle out of the courtyard—it wouldn't fit through the door. A crowd gathered, giving fruitless advice. Finally, the travelers dismantled the motorcycle and took it through the doorway, piece by piece. One of the travelers angrily observed that the motorcycle fit through the door last night, and it should've fit in the morning. Only then did one of the crowd point out that they were using the wrong door—last night they had used an almost-identical (but slightly larger) door across the courtyard!

The Turks had been constrained by their standards of politeness. If the foreign travelers wanted to get their motorbike through a too-small door, they were entitled to. (Foreigners do many strange things.) To publicly point out the existence of a larger door might have embarrassed the travelers. Only when one of the foreigners articulated their error could someone politely correct them.

United Kingdom

Official Name:	United Kingdom of Great Britain and Northern Ireland
Official Language:	English (additionally, Welsh and Gaelic)
Government System:	Constitutional monarchy
Population:	*59.1 million (1999 estimate)*
Population Growth Rate:	0.24% (1999 estimate)
Area:	244,820 sq. km. (97,928 sq. mi.); slightly smaller than Oregon
Natural Resources:	coal, crude oil, natural gas, tin, limestone, iron ore, salt, clay, chalk, gypsum, lead, silica
Major Cities:	London (capital), Birmingham, Glasgow, Leeds, Sheffield, Liverpool, Bradford, Manchester, Edinburgh, Bristol
Official Language:	English (additionally, Welsh and Gaelic)

Cultural Note: The United Kingdom consists of four distinct regions: England, Wales, Scotland, and Northern Ireland. The Scots, Welsh, and Irish are *not English* and are offended when referred to as such. Use the correct terminology. Furthermore, most citizens of the United Kingdom do not consider themselves *European*, even though their nation is a member of the European Union.

Age Breakdown

0–14 = 19%   15–64 = 65%   65+ = 16% (1999 estimate)
Life Expectancy: 74.7 years, male; 80.2 years, female (1999 estimate)

Time

Punctuality is expected for both business appointments and social events.

The U.K. is in Greenwich Mean Time, which is 5 hours ahead of U.S. Eastern Standard Time (EST + 5).

Holidays

An up-to-date, online *World Holiday and Time Zone Guide* is available at www.getcustoms.com. It lists official holidays by country and by day of the year, business and cultural tips, a corruption index, and time zones with worldwide business hours.

Jan 3	MO	New Year's Day observed
Jan 4	TU	Bank holiday
Mar 17	FR	St. Patrick's Day[1]
Apr 3	MO	Bank holiday[2]
Apr 21	FR	Good Friday
Apr 24	MO	Easter Monday[3]
May 1	MO	May Day
May 15	MO	Victoria Day[2]
May 29	MO	Spring bank holiday[3]
Jul 12	WE	Orangeman's Day[1]
Aug 7	MO	Bank holiday[2]
Aug 28	MO	Summer bank holiday[3]
Sep 18	MO	Autumn holiday[2]
Dec 25	MO	Christmas Day
Dec 26	TU	Boxing Day

It is advisable to check with your local representatives for additional regional holidays and vacations during July, August, and September.

Work Week

- The work week is 9:00 A.M. to 5:00 P.M. Monday through Friday, although government offices close from 1:00 to 2:00 P.M. and stay open until 5:30 P.M.
- Executives leave their offices by about 5:30 P.M.

---

[1] Northern Ireland; [2] Scotland; [3] England and Wales

Religious/Societal Influences on Business

Technically, there are no *official* religions in the United Kingdom; instead, some parts of the U.K. have *established* churches. These are:

England: Church of England (Anglican Church)
Scotland: Church of Scotland (Presbyterian Church)
Wales: None
Northern Ireland: None

The majority (about 80%) of people in the U.K. are Christian. Roman Catholics have a slight numerical majority at 21% of the population, followed by Anglican (Church of England) 20%, Presbyterian (Church of Scotland) 14%, Methodist 5%, and Baptist 3%. Of non-Christian religions, Muslims form the largest group at 11% of the population, followed by Sikhs at 4%, Hindus at 2%, and Jews at 1%.

While most Britons would assert that they live in a Christian nation, religion plays a relatively small part in their day-to-day lives. Many people find age-old religious precepts to be ineffectual in the modern world. Secular activities and societal pressures exert more influence on behavior than do religious beliefs. Church attendance continues to fall, and many of Britain's great churches and cathedrals would have a hard time financially were it not for tourism.

The influence of the royal family has also lessened significantly, although Queen Elizabeth II, is still held in respect. As the sovereign, she is Chief of State of the United Kingdom. Anti-Royalists (also called Republicans) desire the dissolution of the monarchy, partially based upon the expense of financing the royalty versus their usefulness.

The British seem to apologize often, even over seemingly inconsequential events or for things over which they have no control. This is considered simple politeness, and should not be interpreted as a sign of weakness or insecurity.

The stiff-upper-lip stereotype of the British has some basis in fact. Most English are unemotional in public and downplay situations that would cause noisy outbursts in other cultures. There are considerable differences between the various regions of the United Kingdom. Stereotypes are risky; not all Welsh are romantic and not all Scots are parsimonious. A self-deprecating sense of humor can be said to be common to most natives of the United Kingdom. As the butt of a joke, nothing is sacred—from the royal family to the Church.

One downside of British reserve is a hesitancy to complain about poor customer service.

This can tend to aggravate problems; if more complaints were articulated, such situations might improve.

The British are enthusiastic gamblers, and buy more lottery tickets than any other people on the globe. An estimated 75% of British adults purchase at least one lottery ticket per week.

5 Cultural Tips

1. The British are a private and traditional people. Violating conventions will not make you any friends. The standard U.S. conversation-starter "What do you do?" is considered too personal. Avoid other invasive questions as well, including "What part of England are you from?"

2. Introductions are important for conducting business. The best way to make contact with British businesspeople is via a third-party introduction. (Note that after the introduction, the third party's responsibilities are over. It would be inappropriate to ask this same third party to intervene later.)

3. Don't underestimate British wherewithal in entering new markets. The Gillette company developed a new stainless steel blade that lasted *too long*; it was so superior to other blades that it would need far fewer replacements. Gillette decided not to market razor blades using the new technology. Instead, they offered the technology to the British Wilkinson company—then a manufacturer of garden tools. Gillette never imagined that Wilkinson would enter the disposable razor blade business, so they placed no restrictions on Wilkinson's use of the technology. But Wilkinson *did* enter the razor blade market, and did so well that they nearly supplanted Gillette as the market leader.

4. British consumers look for different things than U.S. consumers. British advertisements for Goodyear tires proclaim the product's safety. (In contrast, the same tire was advertised for its mileage and durability in the U.S., and for its performance and agility in Germany.)

5. Provide as many objective facts as possible during presentations and negotiations. To the English, scientific evidence is the truth, and interjecting your opinions, feelings, or ideologies into a business transaction muddies the waters.

Economic Overview

The United Kingdom remains solidly entrenched as the United States's largest European market and fourth largest worldwide. Given just its size and growth potential, the U.K. represents a uniquely important overseas market. Over the next few years, new and established U.S. exporters can expect to find exceptional trading opportunities.

The U.K. market is based on a commitment to the principles of free enterprise and open competition. International trade is vital to its economy. The absence of major trade barriers and the relative ease of doing business ensure that the U.K. will remain an attractive market. Demand for U.S. goods and services is growing as the sustained recovery in the U.K.'s industrial sector strengthens and as corporate investment is stepped up to meet competitive challenges of an integrated European Union.

The U.K. shares a long cultural heritage with the U.S. The great sense of affinity the British generally feel toward Americans translates into a high level of receptivity to U.S. goods, services, and investment.

5 Largest Businesses in the United Kingdom

British Telecommunications Plc., London
   1,292,000 employees
National Health Service (Executive Headquarters), Leeds
   1,000,000 employees
Tesco Plc., Waltham Cross
   309,752 employees
Unilever Plc., London
   287,000 employees
The Post Office, London
   193,633 employees

Cultural Note: Seemingly minor differences in nomenclature between U.K. and U.S. English can cause major business headaches. For example, what British mechanics refer to as a *right-handed motor* is considered a *left-handed motor* in the United States. To *table* a subject in England usually means to *begin* a discussion of it, while in the U.S. it means to *postpone* the discussion. The term *ground floor* in England refers to what an American would call the *first floor*. The English *first floor* is the *second floor* in the U.S.

Observation: "The . . . sense of the past defends the individual by orienting, informing, and limiting his character, in ways that must often remain incomprehensible to us Americans, who often love to tear up our pasts. A dry English woman in a gray London square complains to an American visitor: 'We had a great opportunity to set this city up in a logical way, but we didn't.' 'You mean after the Blitz?' 'Oh, no! After the Great Fire, you remember—in 1666.' Living with that much behind you is just different."

   —From *Understanding Europeans* by Stuart Miller. There is also an aphorism that illustrates the differences between Britons and Americans: "Americans think that 100 years is old; Britons think that 100 miles is far."

Comparative Data

Comparative Data Ratings
(Scale: 5 = Excellent; 1 = Poor)
United Kingdom: 4.625

   A.   GDP Growth: 3
   B.   Per Capita Income: 5
   C.   Trade Flows with the U.S.: 5

D. Country Risk: 5
E. Monetary Policy: 5
F. Trade Policy: 4
    • Tariffs
    • Import Licensing
    • Import Taxes
G. Protection of Property Rights: 5
H. Foreign Investment Climate: 5

GROSS DOMESTIC PRODUCT: $1.24 trillion (1998 estimate)

GDP GROWTH: 1.7% (1999 estimate); 2.7% (2000 forecast)

PER CAPITA INCOME: $21,200 (1997 estimate)

Trade Flows with the U.S.

U.S. EXPORTS TO THE U.K.: $39 billion (1998 estimate)

U.S. IMPORTS FROM THE U.K.: $35 billion (1998 estimate)

TOP U.S. EXPORTS TO THE U.K.:   Machinery; computer software; electrical components; aircraft and parts; medical and optical equipment; motor vehicles; plastics and resins; organic chemicals; books and newspapers; pharmaceuticals

TOP U.S. PROSPECTS FOR EXPORT TO THE U.K.:   Aircraft and parts; apparel; building products; computer hardware; computer software; defense equipment; drugs and pharmaceuticals; hotel and restaurant equipment; medical equipment; oil and gas field machinery

Country Risk

Dun & Bradstreet rates the United Kingdom as having excellent capacity to meet outstanding payment liabilities. It carries the lowest degree of risk.

Open account terms are common. Normally terms are between 30 and 60 days, although they vary according to the sector and type of transaction.

Monetary Policy

From a high of 10.9% at the beginning of the recession in September 1990, the underlying rate of inflation dropped under 2% by 1999. Steep declines in domestic demand early in the recession drove down inflation. Inflation has remained modest, reaching 1.7% in 1999. It is expected that unemployment and restrained wage growth should keep the underlying inflation rate from going over 3% through 2001.

MONETARY UNIT: United Kingdom pound sterling

Trade Policy

TARIFFS   The U.K. is a member of the European Union, which provides for a common external tariff. Rates on most manufactured goods fall within a range of 5–7%, while most raw materials enter duty-free or at low rates of duty. Duties on textiles can range up to 15% and some electronic products reach 14%.

IMPORT LICENSING   Only a very limited range of goods is subject to import licenses. These include firearms and explosives, controlled drugs, and controlled military equipment.

There are monitoring measures that apply to certain sensitive products. The most important of these measures is the automatic import license for textiles. This is granted to U.K. importers when they provide the requisite forms.

IMPORT TAXES   The U.K. applies a value-added tax (VAT) on most goods and services. The standard current rate is 17.5%. Certain items such as most foods, medicines, children's clothing and shoes, and books are exempt from VAT.

Protection of Intellectual Property Rights

U.K. intellectual property laws apply across the board to England, Wales, Scotland, and Northern Ireland. A system of common law similar to that in the U.S. is followed for trademarks. These laws are strict, comprehensive, rigorously enforced and conform to the harmonized approach to intellectual property rights adopted by the European Union.

The U.K. belongs to the Universal Copyright and Berne Conventions and the usual international patent and trademark conventions, including the Paris Convention for the Protection of Industrial Property and the Patent Cooperation Treaty.

Patent protection can be obtained by applying to the European or British Patent Offices. In order to be patented in the U.K., inventions have to have industrial application, be new, and exhibit inventiveness. Excluded subject matter for patents includes computer programs. Patents have a term of 20 years from application. Actions on patents can only be taken after issuance, but relate back to publication for purposes of damages.

Trademarks and trade names (called *tradenames* in the U.K.) are protected by common law. Trademarks can be registered, but trade names cannot. Even though the U.K. now has a service mark system, registrations still cannot be obtained for retail store services. Trademark registrations can be obtained based on Community, EC, and U.K. trademark applications. Registrations are for 7-year terms and are renewable for 14-year terms. Contrary to the U.S., registered marks can be assigned with or without goodwill.

Copyrights result automatically on creation of a work. Registration is optional. As is typical in Europe, moral rights are extended to the author. Various other rights are also granted. Performance and recording rights are granted to performers and studios. The term of copyright is life plus 70 years. Designs are good for 10-year terms.

Foreign Investment Climate

The U.K. does not discriminate between nationals and foreigners in the formation and operation of British companies. There are no restrictions on the repatriation of earnings, and foreign companies are treated the same as domestic companies for tax purposes. There are no requirements for joint ventures or local management participation or control. The Mergers and Industry Act of 1986 prohibits the takeover by nonresidents of certain manufacturing operations that might be deemed vital to national interests.

Foreign-owned companies now own 20% of the country's manufacturing facilities.

The United States is by far the largest foreign investor in the U.K. There are 3,500 branches, subsidiaries, and affiliates of U.S. firms, compared with 1,000 from Germany and approximately 250 from Japan. The U.S. and Japan invest more in the U.K. than in any other country in the European Union.

Political Leaders, Parties, and International Organizations

The International Academy at Santa Barbara at http://www.iasb.org/cwl publishes *Current World Leaders*, an excellent resource for up-to-date data on political leaders, parties, demographics, etc., in the United Kingdom. Tel: (800) 530-2682 or (805) 965-5010 for subscription information to their database.

Chief of State:

Queen Elizabeth II

Head of Government:

Anthony Charles (Tony) Blair

Political Parties:

Conservative Party, Labour Party, Social and Liberal Democrats, Social Democratic Party, Scottish National Party, Plaid Cymru (Welsh Nationalists), Ulster Unionist (Northern Ireland), Democratic Unionists (Northern Ireland), Social Democratic and Labour (Northern Ireland), Ulster Popular Unionist (Northern Ireland), Sinn Fein (Northern Ireland), Green Party, Communist Party

Membership in international organizations:

CE, EBRD, EU, G7, INTELSAT, NACC, NATO, OECD, OSCE, UN and most of its specialized agencies and related organizations (including FAO, GATT, IAEA, IBRD, ICAO, IDA, IFAD, IFC, ILO, IMF, IMO, ITU, UNIDO, UPU, WHO, WIPO, WMO), WEU

Political Influences on Business

The Anglo–American partnership is one of the most enduring of bilateral relationships. It remains securely anchored in historical traditions, common political systems and values, compatible security interests, and a shared cultural heritage. At the government level, the closeness of the relationship ensures a remarkable degree of cooperation on a very broad range of issues.

The U.S.–U.K. alliance continues to be a key one for both countries, and this pattern of productive cooperation is expected to continue. The two nations share very similar, if not identical, views on such priority issues as extending security to Eastern Europe, promoting political and economic reform in the former Soviet Union, and furthering peace in the Middle East.

The United Kingdom of Great Britain and Northern Ireland is comprised of four national entities: England, Scotland, Wales (together making Great Britain), and Northern Ireland. The United Kingdom is a constitutional monarchy.

The constitution is largely unwritten, and almost all political power is vested in one chamber of the bicameral Parliament—the House of Commons. The other chamber, the House of Lords—consisting of hereditary and life peers, as well as senior officials of the Church of England—has limited legislative powers. (The current Prime Minister, Tony Blair, is working to remove the hereditary peers from the House of Lords.) The House of Commons consists of 651 members—524 from England, 72 from Scotland, 38 from Wales, and 17 from Northern Ireland. Members are elected from specific geographic constituencies, each representing about 60,000 voters.

The government, a cabinet headed by a Prime Minister, is formed by whichever party, or coalition of parties, can command a majority in the Commons. Legislation is passed by majority vote.

Administratively, the United Kingdom acts as a centralized state. The national government, consisting of some 17 cabinet-level departments, plus smaller entities, is staffed by career, nonpartisan civil servants. Only the three or four senior policy positions in each department (the Secretary of State, the Minister of State, and the junior ministers) are occupied by political appointees. They are drawn from the ranks of the ruling party in the House of Commons or the House of Lords. Scotland and Wales now have their own parliaments.

After many years of Conservative government, the Labour Party won a majority in 1997. Fortunately for businesspeople, Prime Minister Tony Blair has continued to support the pro-business agenda of his Conservative predecessors. Blair's new Labour Party has reduced its traditional support of trade unions and has not sought to renationalize privatized industries and utilities.

British leaders continue to express deep concern over the effects that full European integration will have on the country's sovereignty. Britain opted out of the "social chapter" of the Maastricht Treaty and deferred a decision on joining the European Monetary Union in 1999.

Contacts in the United States

THE EMBASSY OF THE UNITED KINGDOM OF GREAT BRITAIN AND NORTHERN IRELAND
3100 Massachusetts Avenue, NW
Washington, D.C. 20008
Tel: (202) 462-1340
Fax: (202) 898-4255
www.britain-info.org

Passport/Visa Requirements

A passport is required. U.S. citizens are not required to obtain a visa for stays up to six months for business or tourism purposes provided the immigration officer (at the point or place of entry) is satisfied that they do not intend to settle or to work there, can support themselves and any dependents without working, and are able to meet the cost of their onward journey.

A person given permission to enter should read carefully the endorsement placed in his/her passport by the immigration officer, which may restrict the period allowed to stay and certain other conditions.

No visa is required for U.S. citizens (citizens of other nations should check with British officials regarding their position).

A person admitted as a visitor is normally prohibited from taking employment and may not remain longer than six months (maximum) on this basis. Special provisions apply to nationals of member states of the EU, of Austria, of Liechtenstein, of Monaco, and of Switzerland.

For current information concerning entry and customs requirements for the United Kingdom, travelers can contact the British Embassy.

U.S. citizens who wish to apply for a passport may visit Passport Services' well-organized website at http://travel.state.gov/passport_services.html.

Contacts in the United Kingdom

THE EMBASSY OF THE UNITED STATES
OF AMERICA
24/31 Grosvenor Square
London
W1A 1AE
England
Tel: (44) (171) 499-9000
Fax: (44) (171) 499-4022
usembassy.org.uk

THE AMERICAN CHAMBER OF COMMERCE IN
THE UNITED KINGDOM
75 Brook Street
London
W1Y 2EB
England
Tel: (44) (171) 493-0381
Fax: (44) (171) 493-2394

Dun & Bradstreet Europe Ltd.
Postal Address: Holmers Farm Way, High
Wycombe, Bucks HP12 4UL, England
Street Address: same
Tel: (44) (149) 442-2000
Fax: (44) (149) 442-2260

Queen Elizabeth II
Buckingham Palace
London, SW1A 1AA
United Kingdom of Great Britain and
Northern Ireland

Office of the Prime Minister
10 Downing Street
London, SW1A 2AA
United Kingdom of Great Britain and
Northern Ireland

Further contacts and websites can be found in Appendix A.

Communications

Telephone: The country code for the United Kingdom is 44.

Phone numbers in the UK now have seven digits.

City codes in major cities have three digits; Other areas have four digits. Since 1995, all city codes begin with the numeral 1. City codes were formerly called STD codes; they are now referred o as dialing codes.

E-mail: E-mail addresses located in the U.K. end with the code .gb (for Great Britain). Remember that Northern Ireland is part of the United Kingdom, *not* the Republic of Ireland. Curiously, even though Northern Ireland is *not* technically part of Great Britain, it uses the email code .gb

Dates: In the U.K., the date is written in this order: day, month, year (unlike the U.S. practice of writing month, day, year). Consequently, 3/5/02 in the U.K. refers to May 3, 2002.

Faux Pas: Confusing a Northern Irishman with an Englishman, a Welsh, or a Scot is highly offensive. Learn something about each country's specific history, and pick several good conversational topics to bring up at business or social occasions. When in doubt, ask about rugby or soccer.

Venezuela

Official Name:	Republic of Venezuela (República de Venezuela)
Official Language:	Spanish
Government System:	Federal multi-party republic
Population:	23.2 million (1999 estimate)
Population Growth Rate:	1.71% (1999 estimate)
Area:	912,050 sq. km. (353,841 sq. mi.); about the size of Texas and Oklahoma combined
Natural Resources:	crude oil, natural gas, iron ore, gold, bauxite, other minerals, hydropower, diamonds, marble, timber
Major Cities:	Caracas (capital), Maracaibo, Valencia, Barquisimeto, Maracay, Menda

Cultural Note: Venezuela is a highly class- and status-conscious country. Power flows from the top down, and bosses expect compliance. Employees do not contradict their bosses in Venezuela. Teams of foreigners in Venezuela should be careful not to argue with each other in public, since Venezuelans will interpret this as demonstrating poor leadership.

Age Breakdown

0–14 = 33%   15–64 = 62%   65+ = 5% (1999 estimate)
Life Expectancy: 69.97 years, male; 76.16 years, female (1999 estimate)

Time

Unlike in many parts of Latin America, Venezuelans tend to be prompt. Foreigners are expected to be on time to all business appointments. Social engagements also tend to begin on time.

Venezuela is 4 hours behind Greenwich Mean Time (GMT -4), which is 1 hour ahead of U.S. Eastern Standard Time (EST +1).

Holidays

An up-to-date, online *World Holiday and Time Zone Guide* is available at www.get-customs.com. It lists official holidays by country and by day of the year, business and cultural tips, a corruption index, and time zones with worldwide business hours.

This list is a working guide. Dates should be corroborated before final travel plans are made. In cases where holidays fall on Saturday or Sunday, commercial establishments may be closed the preceding Friday or following Monday.

Jan 1	SA	New Year's Day
Mar 6	MO	Carnival (2 days)
Apr 19	WE	Constitution Day
Apr 20	TH	Holy Thursday
Apr 21	FR	Good Friday
May 1	MO	Labor Day
Jun 24	SA	Battle of Carabobo
Jul 5	WE	Firma Acta de Independencia
Jul 24	MO	Simon Bolivar's Birthday
Oct 12	TH	Columbus Day
Nov 1	WE	All Saints Day
Dec 25	MO	Christmas Day

There are also regional holidays and many bank holidays, when banks are closed but most businesses remain open.

Work Week

- The work week is Monday through Friday, 8:00 A.M. to 5:00 P.M. with at least an hour break for lunch (many executives take a two-hour lunch).
- Stores are open from 9:00 A.M. to 12 noon and again from 2:00 or 3:00 P.M. to 6:00 P.M. or later. Shopping malls stay open later.
- Banks generally are open Monday through Friday, 8:30 to 11:30 A.M. and 2:00 P.M. to 4:30 P.M. Post offices stay open through lunch, except in small towns.
- Avoid scheduling appointments two or three days before a holiday.

Religious/Societal Influences on Business

There is no official religion in Venezuela, but over 92% of the population belongs to the Roman Catholic Church. While most Venezuelans derive a sense of stability from the Church, it does not have a great influence on their daily lives.

The family is the single most important institution in Venezuela. Extended families are the norm, and relatives often go into business with each other. When deciding between competing offers, a Venezuelan may ignore the better offer in favor of an offer coming from a relative—even a distant relative.

Venezuela is also a male-dominated society. Sociologists who rank cultures along a *Masculinity Index* rank Venezuela as one of the "most Masculine" in Latin America.

Another sociological finding puts Venezuela at the far end of the *Individuality Index*. This places the individual as the *least*-important person in a decision-making scenario. The best interests of one's family are considered first. Not surprisingly, the United States ranks at the other end of this scale, with the individual decision-maker considering his or her self-interest above all.

In politics as in business, Venezuelans tend to follow strong leaders. Leadership styles tend to be authoritarian rather than inclusive.

5 Cultural Tips

1. Nepotism is common and respected in Venezuela as "good for the family." Don't be judgmental about hiring practices.

2. Business attire in Venezuela is conservative, but quality and fashion are important. A poorly-dressed person cannot command respect. Dark-colored suits are preferred.

3. Business decisions involve far more than the bottom line. They may depend upon what is perceived as best for one's family, one's company, even Venezuelan society as a whole. What is best for the individual decision-maker may come last.

4. The decision-making process will probably involve emotional reactions. It is quite acceptable for a Venezuelan to "go with his (or her) instincts." Even if all the paperwork would indicate a favorable decision, he or she may decline on the basis of "feelings."

5. Venezuelan executives establish business relationships with individuals, *not* with companies. Changing your company's representative in Venezuela may have serious consequences. At the very least, the old representative should personally introduce the new representative.

Economic Overview

The government of Venezuela faces continued economic policy challenges. There has been a return to government intervention throughout the economy, reversing the 1989–93 trend toward loosening of government controls. The government's measures originated in response to the economic and financial crisis of early 1994.

The effects of the economic crisis that struck Venezuela in 1993 and 1994 are still felt. A recession began in 1993 and deepened with the failure of many banks. In mid-1994 the government instituted tight exchange controls to stop capital flight, and fixed the exchange rate. Price controls were decreed on a basket of basic commodities. Additional government measures, including utility rate controls, new checks on government spending, an anti-inflation pact, and delays in exchange approvals for private debt and dividend remittances have cut into free-market advances of the past decade. Raising gasoline prices (which were heavily subsidized) had caused riots in 1989, but a 400% rise in the cost of gas was grudgingly accepted by the public in 1996.

Over the long term, however, Venezuela's strong fundamentals should assure a return to robust growth. It is rich in natural resources, enjoys relatively cheap skilled labor, has extraordinary advantageous energy costs, and is geographically located to take advantage of several major markets, including the United States.

The U.S. has traditionally been Venezuela's most important trading partner. It exported $6.5 billion worth of merchandise to Venezuela in 1998, representing more than 50% of the country's total imports. The short-term outlook for U.S. exports is mixed. In the aggregate, private sector demand is expected to remain somewhat depressed.

The investment climate has been depressed due to a range of unfavorable factors. Recent memory of 1992–93 instability, debt service concerns, the reintroduction of exchange controls, and skepticism over the government's ability to manage the economy translate into falling international investor confidence. At this writing, it is too soon to tell what long-term effects the government of President Hugo Chávez will have on the Venezuelan economy. However, his assumption of emergency powers and his supporters' end-run around the Venezuelan Congress worried many investors. In April of 2000, Unilever closed three of its plants. Similar decisions were also made by Owen-Illinois and Honda.

The key sector for foreign investment is petroleum. In July 1995 the Venezuelan Congress approved foreign participation in light and medium oil exploration and development. Some government-owned aluminum companies may also be opened to private investment.

5 Largest Businesses in Venezuela

Corporacion Venezolana de Transporte Silva C.A., Caracas
  333,333 employees
Petroleos de Venezuela S.A., Caracas
  50,000 employees
Muebleria Casa Abelardo S.R.L., Los Teques
  35,526 employees
C.A. Nacional Telefonos de Venezuela, Caracas
  19,290 employees
Moore de Venezuela S.A., Maracay
  19,000 employees

Cultural Note: In general, Venezuelans display much of the easy-going informality of their Caribbean neighbors. Venezuelans tend to be outgoing and friendly. Their honor, however, must be defended against any slight, and a single ill-chosen comment can quickly anger most Venezuelan men. Sensitive topics include the family, women (especially mothers), honesty, and politics.

Comparative Data

Comparative Data Ratings
(Scale: 5 = Highest; 1 = Lowest)
Venezuela: 2.375

- A. GDP Growth: 2
- B. Per Capita Income: 2
- C. Trade Flows with the U.S.: 3
- D. Country Risk: 2
- E. Monetary Policy: 2
- F. Trade Policy: 2
  - Tariffs
  - Import Licensing
  - Import Taxes
- G. Protection of Property Rights: 3
- H. Foreign Investment Climate: 3

GROSS DOMESTIC PRODUCT: $194.5 billion (1998 estimate)

GDP GROWTH: −4.5% (1999 estimate); 2.0% (2000 forecast)

PER CAPITA INCOME: $8,500 (1998 estimate)

Trade Flows with the U.S.

U.S. EXPORTS TO VENEZUELA: $6.5 billion (1998)

U.S. IMPORTS FROM VENEZUELA: $9.3 billion (1998)

TOP U.S. EXPORTS TO VENEZUELA: Telecommunications services; telecommunications equipment; oil and gas field machinery and service; automobiles and light trucks; automobile parts and services equipment; computers and peripherals; medical equipment; electrical power systems; computer software and services; pumps/valves/compressors

TOP U.S. PROSPECTS FOR EXPORT TO VENEZUELA: Telecommunications services; telecommunications equipment; oil and gas field machinery and service; automobiles and light trucks/vans; automobile parts and services equipment; medical equipment;

electrical power systems; computers and peripherals; computer software and services; pumps/valves/compressors

Country Risk

Added caution is recommended in dealings with Venezuelan businesses. The recession has led to a severe deterioration in credit risk, with deficiencies exceeding 7% of all bank loans.

Liberal trading terms, such as open account and sight drafts, continue to decline in usage in response to the financial crisis. Secure terms, such as confirmed irrevocable letters of credit, are strongly recommended and credit checks are advisable. Only reputable banks should be used.

Monetary Policy

Since 1993 inflation has not dropped below 22%, and it has often gone above 25%. Inflation soared from 46% in 1993 to 103% in 1996. Since then, it has been falling. Inflation was at 29% in 1998 and 22% in 1999. It is forecast at 30% in 2000.

Venezuela has been under pressure to devalue its currency. The bolivar depreciated 1.5% per month during most of 1998.

MONETARY UNIT: bolivar

Trade Policy

TARIFFS   Venezuela generally adheres to the Andean Pact's Common External Tariff, which has four tariff levels: 5%, 10%, 15%, and 20%. Automobiles carry a duty of 35%.

Venezuela's average tariff is about 10%. Import duties remain at a maximum of 20% in almost all categories.

IMPORT LICENSING   Import licenses are rarely required, but there are a number of products that still require permits. These include arms and explosives, which require an import permit from the Ministry of the Interior.

Import certificates are required for certain products subject to special supervision. Almost all foods and agricultural imports must have sanitary or phytosanitary import certificates issued by the Ministry of Agriculture.

Medicines, foods, and cosmetics require registration with the Ministry of Health.

Imports of used autos, used clothing, and used tires are prohibited. Pork from most countries and poultry from the United States are also banned.

Some products can only be imported by the government, such as cigarette paper, bank notes, weapons of war, and certain explosives. Weapons for private use—such as shotguns, sporting rifles, air rifles, non-military pistols, and commercial explosives—can only be imported with authorization of the Interior Ministry's National Office of Arms and Explosives.

IMPORT TAXES   All imports are assessed a 2% customs handling charge. A 16.5% value-added tax (VAT) is also applied. A luxury tax, on a sliding scale of up to 20%, will also apply to some goods, including certain alcoholic beverages and luxury cars.

Protection of Intellectual Property Rights

Although intellectual property protection in Venezuela has improved over the last year or two, U.S. companies continue to express concern about inadequacies in enforcement of patent, trademark, and copyright protection, particularly as applied to pharmaceuticals, computer software, and motion pictures. Venezuela remains on the U.S. trade representative's special 301 watch list.

Venezuela is an active member of the World Intellectual Property Organization (WIPO) and a signatory to the Berne Convention for the Protection of Literary and Artistic Works, the Geneva Phonograms Convention, and the Universal Copyright Convention. It has ratified its membership in the Paris Convention for the Protection of Industrial Property.

Venezuela's legal framework for patent and trademark protection is currently provided by Andean Pact Decision 344, superseding Venezuela's national Patent and Trademark Law which dates from 1955. Decision 344 provides for patentability of pharmaceutical products, except those listed on the World Health Organization list of essential medicines. Invention and improvement patents are issued for five to ten years after grant at the owner's request.

Venezuela's 1993 Copyright Law is modern and comprehensive and extends copyright protection to all creative works, including computer software. Andean Pact Decision 351 is complimentary to Venezuela's national law for copyrights. The Venezuelan government announced in June 1995 that it established a national Copyright Office for the registration and protection of copyrights.

The first person to register a trademark obtains the rights to it. Registrations are valid for 15 years from registration date, renewable for similar periods. Care should be taken to use the registered trademark. *Venezuelan regulations allow for cancellation of the registration if the trademark is not used in at least one of the Andean Pact countries for three consecutive years.*

Since Venezuela does not automatically recognize foreign patents, trademarks, or logos, *foreign investors should be sure to register patents and trademarks appropriately.* It is necessary to register with the Autonomous Service of the Industrial Property Registry of the Ministry of Development.

Foreign Investment Climate

The Venezuelan government has eliminated legal barriers to foreign investment in most sectors. Presently, disincentives to invest in Venezuela stem principally from government economic policies, including its management at the macroeconomics level and the imposition of price and foreign exchange controls.

Venezuela's main legal framework for foreign investment is provided in Presidential Decree 2095 of 1992. Decree 2095 expanded foreign investment opportunities in Venezuela by lifting most restrictions on foreign participation. All sectors of Venezuela's economy, except those specifically noted, are open to 100% foreign participation. Since 1992 foreign companies have been able to operate in certain sectors formerly reserved to companies with a Venezuelan majority interest, including retail sales, export services, telephone and telecommunication services, electrical services, and water and sewage services. Decree 2095 does not cover investments in the petroleum, petrochemical, coal, mining, banking, and insurance sectors, which are regulated by special laws.

The process for making a foreign investment in Venezuela was also simplified. Decree 2095 eliminated the requirement to obtain prior government authorization for foreign investments in sectors covered by Decree 2095. The decree only requires that investors register with the Superintendent of Foreign Investment within 60 days of the date the new investment is realized.

Decree 2095 guarantees foreign investors the right to repatriate 100% of profits and capital, including proceeds from the sale of shares or liquidation of the company, and allows for unrestricted reinvestment of profits. However, Venezuela's current exchange control system does establish certain procedures and documentary requirements for investors wishing to remit dividends, capital, and royalty payments.

President Hugo Chávez, who was elected in November 1998, has promised to continue the privatization of Venezuelan industries.

Political Leaders, Parties, and International Organizations

The International Academy at Santa Barbara at http://www.iasb.org/cwl publishes *Current World Leaders*, an excellent resource for up-to-date data on political leaders, parties, demographics, etc., in Venezuela. Tel: (800) 530-2682 or (805) 965-5010 for subscription information to their database.

Head of State and of the Government:
 President Hugo Chávez

Next Election:
 December 2003

Political Parties:
 Patriotic Pole coalition, Democratic Action Party, Social Christian Party, Radical Cause Party, Movement Toward Socialism, Venezuelan Communist Party, Democratic Republic Union Party

Membership in international organizations:

AG, GATT, G77, ICO, IADB, INTELSAT, IWC, Latin American Energy Organization, LAIA, OAS, OPEC, SELA, UN and most of its specialized agencies and related organizations (including FAO, IAEA, IBRD, ICAO, IFAD, IFC, ILO, IMF, IMO, ITU, UNESCO, UNIDO, UPU, WHO, WIPO, WMO)

Political Influences on Business

Venezuela is a republic with an active multi-party democratic system and a long-standing commitment to democracy.

Since 1958 Venezuelan politics has been mostly dominated by two large parties: the Democratic Action Party (AD), associated with the Socialist International, and the Social Christian Party (COPEI) which is affiliated with the Christian Democratic movement. In recent years, other political parties have challenged the political dominance of AD and COPEI. These parties include: the Movement Towards Socialism (MAS), consisting of democratic-leftists; the Radical Cause Party (Causa R), a working-class oriented group; and the Convergence Party (Convergencia), a new party established in 1993 by Rafael Caldera.

Venezuela held presidential and congressional elections in December 1993 and President Caldera began his current five-year term in February 1994. President Caldera represented a coalition of political factions, incorporating most of the political spectrum from left to right, distinct from the two parties—AD and COPEI—that have dominated Venezuela's 40-year democratic history. As a result of the 1993 national elections, the congress evolved from a bi-party system dominated by AD and COPEI to a more diverse five-party system. This complicated the legislative process, causing considerable frustration among the Venezuelan people, who desperately wanted major reforms.

After completing his one term in office (all that the then-current Constitution allowed), President Caldera was replaced by Hugo Chávez in November 1998. Chávez was a former paratroop officer who attempted a coup against the government in 1992. As the Venezuelan economy sagged, he skillfully rode the wave of public discontent against the corruption and cronyism of the Caldera government. Chávez promised Venezuelans "Tony Blair-style Third Way policies."

Marshalling the votes of his supporters (who are known as *Chavistas*), Chávez packed the Congress with his own people. In a move of dubious legality, in August 1999 they declared Venezuela to be "in emergency," set up a Constituent Assembly, and granted themselves unprecedented powers. In essence, Chávez's supporters in his Patriotic Pole coalition have marginalized the legally elected Congress and all its opposition representatives.

At this writing, Chávez and his Patriotic Pole coalition retain popular support. The majority of Venezuelans are poor, and enjoy seeing the upper classes and corrupt politicians discomfited. Certainly, if Chávez can reduce Venezuela's endemic corruption, he will have done a service to every foreigner who does business in the country. His radical methods and unpredictability, however, have frightened off many foreign investors.

Contacts in the United States

The Embassy of the Republic of Venezuela
1099 30th Street, NW
Washington, D.C. 20007
Tel: (202) 342-2214
Fax: (202) 342-6820
www.embavenez-us.org

Venezuelan–American Chamber of Commerce and Industry
1615 L Street, NW, Suite 430
Washington, D.C. 20036-5619
Tel: (202) 822-0711; 463-7215
Fax: (202) 429-3231
www.venamcham.org/

Passport/Visa Requirements

A passport and a visa or tourist card are required. Tourist cards can be obtained from airlines serving Venezuela.

Tourist Cards

When arriving by plane, citizens of those countries who have signed special treaties with Venezuela, including the U.S., can obtain tourist cards from carriers. The tourist card is valid for one entrance and 90 days of stay in Venezuela.

Tourist Visas

Applicants must present the following at Venezuelan Consulates when applying for this type of visa:

1. One completed application form.
2. Passport with minimum validity of six months.
3. Certification of employment, specifying length of employment, position, and salary.
4. Original bank reference letter on business letterhead (bank statement will not be accepted), specifying opening date, number and type of account, and current balance.
5. One photograph (2 × 2).
6. Non-U.S. citizens need a copy of both sides of their green card.
7. The visa fee is $30.00 payable by money order or company check.

Business Visas

1. One completed application form.
2. Passport with minimum validity of six months.
3. Original letter from employer written on business letterhead stating position, purpose of trip, name and address of company to be contacted in Venezuela, and length of stay.
4. One photograph (2 × 2).
5. Non-U.S. citizens need a copy of both sides of their green card.
6. The visa fee is $60.00 payable by money order or company check.

Important Note: When visas are submitted and need to be returned by mail, a self-addressed, stamped envelope is required.

All visitors must pay a departure tax in bolivares at the Venezuelan airport or port.

All persons holding a business visa must obtain an income declaration (Declaracion de Rentas) at the offices of the Ministry of Finance (Ministerio de Hacienda), 8 A.M. to 4 P.M. Monday through Friday, required at time of departure.

Visas and current information concerning entry, tax, and customs requirements for Venezuela can be obtained from the Venezuelan Embassy, or the nearest consulate in Miami, Chicago, New Orleans, Boston, New York, Houston, or San Juan.

U.S. citizens who wish to apply for a passport may visit Passport Services' well-organized website at http://travel.state.gov/passport_services.html.

Contacts in Venezuela

THE AMERICAN EMBASSY
Avenida Francisco de Miranda and
Avenida Principal de la Floresta
P.O. Box 62291, Caracas 1060A
Mailing Address: APO AA 34037
Tel: (58) (2) 285-2222
Fax: (58) (2) 285-0366
usembassy.state.gov/posts/ve1/

VENEZUELAN–AMERICAN CHAMBER OF
COMMERCE AND INDUSTRY
Torre Credival, Piso 10
2da Avenida de Campo Alegre
Apartado 5181
Caracas 1010-A
Tel: (58) (2) 263-0833
Fax: (58) (2) 263-1829
www.venamcham.org

DUN & BRADSTREET C.A.
Postal Address: Apartado Postal 2111
Caracas 1010-A

c/o AEROCAV No. 1292
P.O. Box 02 5304
Miami, Florida 33102-5304

STREET ADDRESS: MAIN OFFICE
Avenida Principal Colinas de Bello Monte
Edificio Centro Cristobal, Pisos 8 y 9
Caracas
Tel: (58) (2) 752-9322
Fax: (58) (2) 752-2178

RMS DIVISION
Avenida Francisco de Miranda
Centro Seguros La Paz, Piso 6, Ofic. 065
Caracas
Tel: (58) (2) 238-3517; (58) (2) 238-5196;
(58) (2) 238-8244; (58) (2) 238-4655;
(58) (2) 238-1740
Fax: (58) (2) 238-8007

OFFICE OF THE PRESIDENT
Palacio de Miraflores
Caracas 1010, Republic of Venezuela

Further contacts and websites can be found in Appendix A.

Communications

TELEPHONE: The international country code for Venezuela is 58.

Phone numbers and area codes vary in length.

E-MAIL: E-mail addresses located in Venezuela end with the code .ve

---

Cultural I.Q. Question: One of Venezuela's marvels is the highest waterfall in the world. What is its name?

Email your answer to TerriMorrison@getcustoms.com. Each month a drawing will be held to award one correct respondent from all the questions within this book with a free copy of *The World Holiday and Time Zone Guide* (current electronic version).

Appendix A
Further Contacts and Websites

There are vast informational resources on the Internet, which change and expand daily. One of our goals for this book was to provide you with options for updating the dynamic data online.

Embassies

- http://www.embpage.org/index.html
  This site has a searchable database with over 50,000 addresses, phone numbers, and e-mail addresses of diplomatic posts worldwide.
- www.embassy.org/
  This site contains information on foreign embassies in Washington, D.C.

Department of State

- http://travel.state.gov
  The Bureau of Consular Affairs is a key site. It lists information on obtaining passports and visas (if required), posts travel warnings and consular information sheets, and links to many resources.
    Bureau of Consular Affairs
    American Citizen Services (worldwide caution announcements and travel advisories)
    Tel: (202) 647-1488
    Tel: (202) 647-5225

- http://travel.state.gov/passport_services.html
  This is Passport Services' well-organized website.
    Visa information
    Tel: (202) 663-1225

- www.stat-usa.gov
  The National Trade Data Bank (NTDB) is a compilation of over 130 government databases. For a fee, you can access market research studies, Industry Sector Analysis reports, and trade-related information. The NTDB telephone Helpline is (202) 482-1986.
- http://www.state.gov/www/background_notes/
  The U.S. State Department's Background Notes offers data on U.S. relations with each country, its history, economy, political conditions, and political parties.

Department of Commerce

- www.ita.doc.gov
  The International Trade Administration's site contains a wealth of information for U.S. exporters and importers. It provides trade and marketing data by country and by industry segment, directories of export assistance centers and overseas commercial service offices, and much more.

Central Intelligence Agency

- http://www.odci.gov/cia/publications/factbook/index.html
  The CIA's World Factbook contains maps, demographics, and data on each country's government, economy, etc.

The Centers for Disease Control and Prevention

- www.cdc.gov
  The Centers for Disease Control and Prevention is the hub of valuable global medical information and data on any outbreaks of virulent infections.

The U.S. Chamber of Commerce

- http://www.uschamber.org
  From here you can link to the international chambers worldwide.

The U.S. Census Bureau

- http://www.census.gov/
  There is a very large store of valuable data available here from the U.S. Census Bureau. The Foreign Trade Division is particularly interesting.

The Library of Congress

- http://www.loc.gov
  This is the definitive repository of knowledge in Washington, D.C.

International Electrical Adaptors and Telephone/Modem Adaptors, Magellans' Travel Supplies

- http://magellans.com/getcustoms   Magellan's has an excellent selection of worldwide electrical and telephone adaptors, along with other important supplies, for the international traveler.

Like all websites, the preceding Internet addresses are subject to change, and there is no guarantee that they will continue to provide the data we list here.

If you would like to contact us for updates on websites, we will be happy to help you find the data you require. Our website is http://www.getcustoms.com.

Appendix B
Documents Used in International Trade

Proper documentation is vital for success in international trade. Inaccurate or incomplete paperwork can result in delays and fines. The fines for false or incorrect declarations of weight and measure, as well as simple description of the merchandise itself, can be severe. When in doubt, contact an international trade expert. Aside from commercial firms like Dun & Bradstreet, such experts can be found at the U. S. Department of Commerce and at the commercial offices of U.S. Embassies abroad.

Bill of Lading

One of the most important shipping documents, the *Bill of Lading* has several functions:

1. It represents a contract between the shipper and the ocean carrier.
2. It serves as a receipt.
3. It conveys title to the merchandise.

A Bill of Lading may be *straight* (meaning nonnegotiable) or a *Shipper's Order* Bill of Lading (meaning negotiable). Some countries permit a third type, called a *To Order* Bill of Lading, which is made out to the order of a consignee or a foreign bank. But even in those countries which permit the use of the To Order Bill of Lading, it does not always offer the legal protection of the other types of Bills of Lading.

The Bill of Lading is filled out by the shipper on forms provided by the ocean carrier. Styles of forms vary. A typical straight Bill of Lading follows.

Air Waybill

When the shipper is an air carrier instead of an ocean carrier, an *Air Waybill* (also called an Air Consignment Notice) is used. However, unlike a Bill of Lading, an Air Waybill does not convey title.

473

As with Bills of Lading, the shipper fills out an Air Waybill form provided by the air carrier. Remember that air carriers (of necessity) have stricter shipping regulations for merchandise than do ocean carriers. Some items which safely go aboard a ship may not withstand the sudden changes in temperature and air pressure in an airplane's cargo hold.

An Air Waybill can also be used between a shipper and a freight consolidator (or freight forwarder). In this case the Air Waybill will be issued by the consolidator/forwarder rather than the airline.

Air Waybills are, by design, nonnegotiable.

Certificate of Origin

Trade treaties have made the *Certificate of Origin* increasingly more important. The same item imported from one country may be subject to a tariff; from another country, there may be no tariff at all. Sometimes a Certificate of Origin is required, and sometimes not. In some countries, a *Statement of Origin* will suffice. At times, a Certificate of Origin contains the same information as the Commercial Invoice.

Certificates of Origin vary from destination to destination. A few countries require a special form (which, in some cases, is only available through that nation's Consulate). Two Certificates of Origin, which would be used by a U.S. exporter are on following pages. The first would be used for shipment within the North American Free Trade Agreement (thus, from the U.S. to Canada or Mexico), the second is for a shipment from the U.S.A. to Israel.

Commercial Invoice

With or without a Certificate of Origin, each shipment generally needs a *Commercial Invoice*. This document is used for clearance through customs at the shipment's destination.

This form requires the listing of the sale price of each item in the shipment. Follow each country's regulations carefully, especially with regard to the prices you list on the forms.

Three Commercial Invoices follow. The first is a generic form.

In most British Commonwealth Countries, the Commercial Invoice is called a Customs Invoice. The following is a Canadian Customs Invoice, in English and French is included.

The final form is a Mexican Commercial Invoice, in English and Spanish.

Dock Receipt

Depending upon the agreement, the shipper's responsibility may end when the merchandise arrives at the port in the country of destination. In this case, it becomes someone else's responsibility to get the goods from port to distributor or destination. The *Dock Receipt* is a document which attests that the merchandise has arrived at a pier or warehouse. It is issued by the carrier or a carrier's agent after delivery. Dock Receipts are non-negotiable.

If the merchandise does not arrive complete in one shipment, a temporary receipt is issued for each partial shipment. Upon completion of the full shipment, the temporary receipts are exchanged for a Dock Receipt:

Shipper's Export Declaration

The United States Commerce Department requires this form to be filled out when an export shipment is valued at more than U.S. $2,500 (or more than U.S. $500 for a postal shipment).

Packing List

A *Packing List* has several uses:

1. It allows an exporter (or forwarder) to know the total shipping weight and volume of the shipment; information required to reserve shipping space.
2. It is used as a check-off list at the port of export.
3. It is also used as a check-off list at the port of import.
4. It is used by the buyer to inventory the merchandise upon receipt.
5. Finally, it is used if an insurance claim is filed.

However, for small shipments, the data on the Packing List can be incorporated into the Commercial Invoice, provided that no party has requested a Packing List. Some countries require the use of a Packing List.

Packing lists are available from commercial stationers. A sample Packing List follows.

Proforma Invoice

The *Proforma* Invoice is a form of preliminary, provisional invoice. It notifies an importer (and, if needed, an importer's government) of the main details of a planned shipment.

Some countries require a Proforma Invoice to be filled out before they will issue a Foreign Exchange Permit or an Import License.

Because a Proforma Invoice is prepared long before the merchandise is actually ready to ship, all parties understand that it will not be completely accurate. Data such as shipping charges, weight, and values are subject to change.

(SPACES IMMEDIATELY BELOW ARE FOR SHIPPERS MEMORANDA—NOT PART OF DOCK RECEIPT)

DELIVERING CARRIER TO STEAMER:	CAR NUMBER—REFERENCE
FORWARDING AGENT—REFERENCES	EXPORT DEC. No.

BILL OF LADING
(Conditions Continued from Reverse Side Hereof)

SHIPPER

CONSIGNEE: ORDER OF

ADDRESS ARRIVAL NOTICE TO	ALSO NOTIFY

SHIP	VOYAGE NO.	FLAG	PIER	PORT OF LOADING

FOR. PORT OF DISCHARGE (Where goods are to be delivered to consignee or on-carrier) | For TRANSSHIPMENT to (If goods are to be transshipped or forwarded at port of discharge)

PARTICULARS FURNISHED BY SHIPPER OF GOODS

MARKS AND NUMBERS	No. of PKGS.	DESCRIPTION OF PACKAGES AND GOODS	MEASURE-MENT	GROSS WEIGHT

FREIGHT PAYABLE IN

........@........PER 2240 LBS........ $............	(CONDITIONS CONTINUED FROM REVERSE SIDE HEREOF)	
........@........PER 100 LB........ $............	IN WITNESS WHEREOF, THERE HAVE BEEN EXECUTED........	
......FT........IN. @........PER 40 CU. FT........ $............	BILLS OF LADING, ALL OF THE SAME TENOR AND DATE, ONE OF WHICH BEING ACCOMPLISHED, THE OTHERS TO STAND VOID.	
......FT........IN. @........PER CU. FT........ $............		
.... $............		
.... $............	BY........................	
.... $............	FOR THE MASTER	
.... $............	ISSUED AT........................	
TOTAL........ $............	(DATE)	
	B/L No........................	

Form 35-084 ©, 1986 *UNZ&CO* 190 Baldwin Ave., Jersey City, NJ 07306 • (800) 631-3098 • (201) 795-5400

DEPARTMENT OF THE TREASURY
UNITED STATES CUSTOMS SERVICE

NORTH AMERICAN FREE TRADE AGREEMENT
CERTIFICATE OF ORIGIN
19 CFR 181.11, 181.22

Approved through 12/31/96
OMB No. 1515-0204
See back of form for Paper-
work Reduction Act Notice.

1. Exporter Name and Address	2. Blanket Period *(DD/MM/YY)*		
	FROM		
Tax I.D. Number	TO		
3. Producer Name and Address	4. Importer Name and Address		
Tax I.D. Number	Tax I.D. Number		

5. Description of Good(s)	6. HS Tariff Classifi- cation Number	7. Prefer- ence Criterion	8. Producer	9. Net Cost	10. Country of Origin

I Certify that:

- The information on this document is true and accurate and I assume the responsibility for proving such representations. I understand that I am liable for any false statements or material omissions made on or in connection with this document;

- I agree to maintain, and present upon request, documentation necessary to support this certificate, and to inform, in writing, all persons to whom the certificate was given of any changes that would affect the accuracy or validity of this certificate;

- The goods originated in the territory of one or more of the parties, and comply with the origin requirements specified for those goods in the North American Free Trade Agreement, and unless specifically exempted in Article 411 or Annex 401, there has been no further production or any other operation outside the territories of the Parties;

- This certificate consists of ⬚ pages, including all attachments.

11a. AUTHORIZED SIGNATURE	11b. Company:
11c. NAME	11d. Title:
11e. DATE *(DD/MM/YY)*	11f. TELEPHONE NUMBER ▷ *(Voice)* *(Facsimile)*

Form No. 16-765 Printed and Sold by *UNZCO* 700 Central Ave., New Providence, NJ 07974 ● 800-631-3098

Customs Form CF434 (121793)

This is a Certificate of Origin for a shipment from the U.S. to Israel:

● Copyright 1993 UNZ & CO.

U.S. CERTIFICATE OF ORIGIN
FOR EXPORTS TO ISRAEL

1. Goods consigned from exporter's business (name, address):	Reference No.
	U.S.—ISRAEL FREE TRADE AREA
	CERTIFICATE OF ORIGIN (Combined declaration and certificate)
2. Goods consigned to (consignee's name, address)	
	(See notes over leaf)
3. Means of transport and route (as far as known)	4. For official use

5. Item number	6. Marks and numbers of packages	7. Number and kind of packages, description of goods	8. Origin criterion (see notes over leaf)	9. Gross Weight or other quantity	10. Number and date of invoices

11. CERTIFICATION

The _____
a recognized chamber of commerce, board of trade, or _____
_____ under the laws of the State of _____
_____ has examined the manufacturer's invoice or shipper's affidavit concerning the origin of the merchandise and, according to the best of its knowledge and belief, finds that the products named originated in the United States of America.

_____
Certifying Official

EXPORTER AS PRODUCER:

The undersigned hereby declares that he/she is the producer of the goods listed in this invoice and that they comply with the origin requirements specified for those goods in the U.S.—Israel Free Trade Area Agreement for goods exported to Israel.

_____
Signature of Exporter

12. DECLARATION BY THE EXPORTER

The undersigned hereby declares that the above details and statements are correct; that all the goods were produced in the United States of America and that they comply with the origin requirements specified for those goods in the U.S.—Israel Free Trade Area Agreement for goods exported to Israel.

_____
Signature of Exporter

Sworn to before me this _____
day of _____ 19_____

_____
Signature of Notary Public

Form 10-388 *UNZCO* 190 Baldwin Ave., Jersey City, NJ 07306 • (800) 631-3098

COMMERCIAL INVOICE

SELLER (Name, Full Address, Country)	INVOICE DATE AND NO.	CUSTOMER'S ORDER NO.
	OTHER REFERENCES	
CONSIGNEE (Name, Full Address, Country)	BUYER (If Other Than Consignee)	
	PRESENTING BANK	
	COUNTRY OF ORIGIN OF GOODS	
PORT OF LADING	TERMS AND CONDITIONS OF DELIVERY AND PAYMENT	
COUNTRY OF FINAL DESTINATION / SHIP / AIR / ETC.		
OTHER TRANSPORT INFORMATION	CURRENCY OF SALE	

MARK AND NUMBERS DESCRIPTION OF GOODS	GROSS WEIGHT (Kg.)	CUBIC METRES

NO. AND KIND OF PACKAGES SPECIFICATION OF COMMODITIES (IN CODE AND/OR IN FULL)	NET WEIGHT (Kg.)	QUANTITY	UNIT PRICE	AMOUNT
	PACKING			
	FREIGHT			
	OTHER COSTS (Specify)			
IT IS HEREBY CERTIFIED THAT THIS INVOICE SHOWS THE ACTUAL PRICE OF THE GOODS DESCRIBED, THAT NO OTHER INVOICE HAS BEEN OR WILL BE ISSUED AND THAT ALL PARTICULARS ARE TRUE AND CORRECT.	INSURANCE			
_____ _____ _____ SIGNATURE AND STATUS OF DATE PLACE AUTHORIZED PERSON	TOTAL INVOICE AMOUNT			

Form 10-466 Printed and Sold by UNZCO 190 Baldwin Ave., Jersey City, NJ 07306 • (800) 631-3098 • (201) 795-5400

CANADA CUSTOMS INVOICE
FACTURE DES DOUANES CANADIENNES

| Revenue Canada | Revenu Canada |
| Customs and Excise | Douanes et Accise |

Page ___ of ___ de ___

1. Vendor (Name and Address)/*Vendeur (Nom et adresse)*

2. Date of Direct Shipment to Canada/*Date d'expédition directe vers le Canada*

3. Other References (Include Purchaser's Order No.) *Autres références (Inclure le n° de commande de l'acheteur)*

4. Consignee (Name and Address)/*Destinataire (Nom et adresse)*

5. Purchaser's Name and Address (If other than Consignee) *Nom et adresse de l'acheteur (S'il diffère du destinataire)*

6. Country of Transhipment/*Pays de transbordement*

7. Country of Origin of Goods *Pays d'origine des marchandises*

IF SHIPMENT INCLUDES GOODS OF DIFFERENT ORIGINS ENTER ORIGINS AGAINST ITEMS IN 12 / *SI L'EXPÉDITION COMPREND DES MARCHANDISES D'ORIGINES DIFFÉRENTES, PRÉCISER LEUR PROVENANCE EN 12*

8. Transportation: Give Mode and Place of Direct Shipment to Canada *Transport: Préciser mode et point d'expédition directe vers le Canada*

9. Conditions of Sale and Terms of Payment (i.e. Sale, Consignment Shipment, Leased Goods, etc.) *Conditions de vente et modalités de paiement (p. ex. vente, expédition en consignation, location de marchandises, etc.)*

10. Currency of Settlement/*Devises du paiement*

11. No. of Pkgs *N°ᵇʳᵉ de colis*	12. Specification of Commodities (Kind of Packages, Marks and Numbers, General Description and Characteristics, i.e. Grade, Quality) *Désignation des articles (Nature des colis, marques et numéros, description générale et caractéristiques, p. ex. classe, qualité)*	13. Quantity (State Unit) *Quantité (Préciser l'unité)*	Selling Price/*Prix de vente*	
			14. Unit Price *Prix unitaire*	15. Total

18. If any of fields 1 to 17 are included on an attached commercial invoice, check this box ☐
Si les renseignements des zones 1 à 17 figurent sur la facture commerciale, cocher cette boîte

16.	Total Weight/*Poids Total*		17. Invoice Total *Total de la facture*
	Net	Gross/*Brut*	

Commercial Invoice No. *N° de la facture commerciale* _____

19. Exporter's Name and Address (If other than Vendor) *Nom et adresse de l'exportateur (S'il diffère du vendeur)*

20. Originator (Name and Address)/*Expéditeur d'origine (Nom et adresse)*

21. Departmental Ruling (If applicable)/*Décision du Ministère (S'il y a lieu)*

22. If fields 23 to 25 are not applicable, check this box ☐
Si les zones 23 à 25 sont sans objet, cocher cette boîte

23. If included in field 17 indicate amount: *Si compris dans le total à la zone 17, préciser:*

(i) Transportation charges, expenses and insurance from the place of direct shipment to Canada *Les frais de transport, dépenses et assurances à partir du point d'expédition directe vers le Canada*

$ _____

(ii) Costs for construction, erection and assembly incurred after importation into Canada *Les coûts de construction, d'érection et d'assemblage après importation au Canada*

$ _____

(iii) Export packing *Le coût de l'emballage d'exportation*

$ _____

24. If not included in field 17 indicate amount: *Si non compris dans le total à la zone 17, préciser:*

(i) Transportation charges, expenses and insurance to the place of direct shipment to Canada *Les frais de transport, dépenses et assurances jusqu'au point d'expédition directe vers le Canada*

$ _____

(ii) Amounts for commissions other than buying commissions *Les commissions autres que celles versées pour l'achat*

$ _____

(iii) Export packing *Le coût de l'emballage d'exportation*

$ _____

25. Check (If applicable): *Cocher (S'il y a lieu):*

(i) Royalty payments or subsequent proceeds are paid or payable by the purchaser *Des redevances ou produits ont été ou seront versés par l'acheteur* ☐

(ii) The purchaser has supplied goods or services for use in the production of these goods *L'acheteur a fourni des marchandises ou des services pour la production des marchandises* ☐

DEPARTMENT OF NATIONAL REVENUE—CUSTOMS AND EXCISE

MINISTÈRE DU REVENU NATIONAL—DOUANES ET ACCISE

Printed and Sold by UNZ&CO 190 Baldwin Ave., Jersey City, NJ 07306

©Unz & Co. 1993

Factura Comercial Para México

Commercial Invoice for Mexico

Número de Factura *(Invoice No).*	Lugar y Fecha de Emisión de la Factura *(Place and Date of Issuance of Invoice)*	Orden de Compra Número *(Customer P.O. No.)*

Exportador/Vendedor *(Exporter/Vendor)*	Fabricante *(Producer)*

Destinatario Final *(Ultimate Consignee)*	País de Origen de la Mercancía *(Country of Origin of mdse)*	¿Certificación NAFTA? ☐ Si *(yes)* ☐ No

Términos de Pago *(Terms of Payment)*

Destinatario Intermedio *(Intermediate Consignee)*

Términos de Venta *(Terms of Sale)*

Agente de Transporte de Carga *(Freight Forwarder)*

Otras Referencias e Instrucciones para Consignación
(Other References, Consignment Instructions)

Transportista *(Carrier)*

Puerto de Exportación *(U.S. Port of Export)*	Puerto de Descarga *(Port of Unloading)*

Número y clase de Bultos *(Number & kinds of pkgs)*	Descripción Detallada de la Mercancía (incluyendo clase, tipo, número de serie, marcas, cantidades parciales/a granel); número de fracción arancelaria, primeros 6 dígitos. *(Detailed Commercial Description of Merchandise (include class, type, serial numbers, trademarks, partial/bulk quantities), 6-digit HS number.)*	Cantidad de Unidades *(Quantity, units)*	Peso Bruto, en kilos *(Gross weight in kg)*	Precio por Unidad *(price per unit)*	Valor Total en Dólares de los EUA *(Total Value, U.S. Dollars)*

Nota: La Descripción Deberá Ser en Espanõl
(Note: Description must be in Spanish!)

Dictamen Anticipado *(Advanced Ruling)* Fecha *(Date)*	Valor Comercial, LAB *(Commercial Value, FOB)*	

Identificación de Empaque *(Package Marks)*	Costos de Transporte, Seguro, Empaque, y Otros *(Transportation, Insurance, Packing, Other Costs)*	

Valor Total de la Factura *(Total Invoice Value)*

"Declaro bajo protesta de decir la verdad, que el valor y las declaraciones contenidas en esta factura son verdaderas y correctas." *("I declare under oath that the value and specifications contained in this Invoice are true and correct.")*

Firma del Declarante *(Signature of Preparer)*

Form No. 10-525 Printed and Sold by *UNZ&CO* 190 Baldwin Ave., Jersey City, NJ 07306 • *(800)* 631-3098
Forma No. 10-525 Impreso y Vendido por *UNZ&CO*

(SPACES IMMEDIATELY BELOW ARE FOR SHIPPERS MEMORANDA—NOT PART OF DOCK RECEIPT)

DELIVERING CARRIER TO STEAMER:	CAR NUMBER—REFERENCE
FORWARDING AGENT—REFERENCES	EXPORT DEC. No.

DOCK RECEIPT
NON-NEGOTIABLE

SHIPPER- -

SHIP	VOYAGE NO.	FLAG	PIER	PORT OF LOADING

FOR. PORT OF DISCHARGE *(Where goods are to be delivered to consignee or on-carrier)*	For TRANSSHIPMENT TO *(If goods are to be transshipped or forwarded at port of discharge)*

PARTICULARS FURNISHED BY SHIPPER OF GOODS

MARKS AND NUMBERS	No. of PKGS.	DESCRIPTION OF PACKAGES AND GOODS	MEASURE-MENT	GROSS WEIGHT

DIMENSIONS AND WEIGHTS OF PACKAGES TO BE SHOWN ON REVERSE SIDE

DELIVERED BY:

LIGHTER }
TRUCK } . . . .

ARRIVED— DATE . . . . TIME . . . .

UNLOADED— DATE . . . . TIME . . . .

CHECKED BY . . . .

PLACED IN SHIP / ON DOCK LOCATION . . . .

RECEIVED THE ABOVE DESCRIBED MERCHANDISE FOR SHIPMENT AS INDICATED HEREON, SUBJECT TO ALL CONDITIONS OF THE UNDERSIGNED'S USUAL FORM OF DOCK RECEIPT AND BILL OF LADING. COPIES OF THE UNDERSIGNED'S USUAL FORM OF DOCK RECEIPT AND BILL OF LADING MAY BE OBTAINED FROM THE MASTER OF THE VESSEL, OR THE VESSEL'S AGENT

AGENT FOR MASTER

BY . . . .
RECEIVING CLERK

DATE . . . .

U.S. DEPARTMENT OF COMMERCE—BUREAU OF THE CENSUS—INTERNATIONAL TRADE ADMINISTRATION

FORM **7525-V** (1-1-88)

SHIPPER'S EXPORT DECLARATION

OMB No. 0607-0018

1a. EXPORTER (Name and address including ZIP code)			
	ZIP CODE	2. DATE OF EXPORTATION	3. BILL OF LADING/AIR WAYBILL NO.

b. EXPORTER EIN (IRS) NO.

c. PARTIES TO TRANSACTION
☐ Related   ☐ Non-related

4a. ULTIMATE CONSIGNEE

b. INTERMEDIATE CONSIGNEE

5. FORWARDING AGENT

6. POINT (STATE) OF ORIGIN OR FTZ NO.   7. COUNTRY OF ULTIMATE DESTINATION

8. LOADING PIER (Vessel only)

9. MODE OF TRANSPORT (Specify)

10. EXPORTING CARRIER

11. PORT OF EXPORT

12. PORT OF UNLOADING (Vessel and air only)

13. CONTAINERIZED (Vessel only)
☐ Yes   ☐ No

14. SCHEDULE B DESCRIPTION OF COMMODITIES,
15. MARKS, NOS., AND KINDS OF PACKAGES   } (Use columns 17-19)

D/F (16)	SCHEDULE B NUMBER (17)	CHECK DIGIT	QUANTITY— SCHEDULE B UNIT(S) (18)	SHIPPING WEIGHT (Kilos) (19)	VALUE (U.S. dollars, omit cents) (Selling price or cost if not sold) (20)

21. VALIDATED LICENSE NO./GENERAL LICENSE SYMBOL

22. ECCN (When required)

23. Duly authorized officer or employee

The exporter authorizes the forwarder named above to act as forwarding agent for export control and customs purposes.

24. I certify that all statements made and all information contained herein are true and correct and that I have read and understand the instructions for preparation of this document, set forth in the "Correct Way to Fill Out the Shipper's Export Declaration" (available Bureau of Census, Wash., DC 20233). I understand that civil and criminal penalties, including forfeiture and sale, may be imposed for making false or fraudulent statements herein, failing to provide the requested information or for violation of U.S. laws on exportation (13 U.S.C. Sec. 305; 22 U.S.C. Sec. 401; 18 U.S.C. Sec. 1001; 50 U.S.C. App. 2410).

Signature

Confidential—For use solely for official purposes authorized by the Secretary of Commerce (13 U.S.C. 301 (g)).

Title

Export shipments are subject to inspection by U.S. Customs Service and/or Office of Export Enforcement.

Date

25. AUTHENTICATION (When required)

Form No. 15-795 Printed and Sold by *UNSCO*   700 Central Ave., New Providence, NJ 07974 • (800) 631-3098

UNZ & CO., 190 BALDWIN AVE., JERSEY CITY, N.J. 07306 N.J. (201) 795-5400. (800) 631-3098

PACKING LIST

© Copyright 1990 UNZ & CO.

_____ 19 _____

Place and Date of Shipment

To

Gentlemen:

     Under your Order No. _____ the material listed below

was shipped   via

To

Shipment consists of:	Marks
_____ Cases _____ Packages	
_____ Crates _____ Cartons	
_____ Bbls. _____ Drums	
_____ Reels	

*LEGAL WEIGHT IS WEIGHT OF ARTICLE PLUS PAPER, BOX, BOTTLE, ETC., CONTAINING THE ARTICLE AS USUALLY CARRIED IN STOCK.

PACKAGE NUMBER	WEIGHTS IN LBS. or KILOS			DIMENSIONS			QUANTITY	CLEARLY STATE CONTENTS OF EACH PACKAGE
	GROSS WEIGHT EACH	*LEGAL WEIGHT EACH	NET WEIGHT EACH	HEIGHT	WIDTH	LENGTH		

PROFORMA INVOICE

S H I P P E R	**PRO FORMA INVOICE NO.** DATE ISSUED
	TERMS AND CONDITIONS OF SALE
S O L D T O	**MODE OF TRANSPORT** CARRIER
	AIR/OCEAN PORT OF EMBARKATION LOADING PIER
	AIR/OCEAN PORT OF UNLOADING CONTAINERIZED ☐ Yes ☐ No
S H I P T O	**MARKS:**
	GROSS WEIGHT:

QUANTITY	U/M	DESCRIPTION OF MERCHANDISE	UNIT PRICE	AMOUNT
			FREIGHT	
			EXPORT PACKING	
			INSURANCE	
			MISC	
			TOTAL	

WE HEREBY CERTIFY This Invoice Is True and Correct and that the merchandise described is origin of the United States of America.

Authorized Signature

Title

Form 10-080 Printed and Sold by UNZCO 190 Baldwin Ave., Jersey City, NJ 07306 • (800) 631-3098 • (201) 795-5400

Appendix C

Abbreviations
of International Organizations

A	ABEDA	Arab Bank for Economic Development in Africa
	ACC	Arab Cooperation Council
	ACCT	Agence de Cooperation Culturelle et Technique; see Agency for Cultural and Technical Cooperation; changed name in 1996 to Agence de la francophonie or Agency for the French-Speaking Community
	ACP Group	African, Caribbean, and Pacific Group of States
	AfDB	African Development Bank
	AFESD	Arab Fund for Economic and Social Development
	AG	Andean Group; see Andean Community of Nations (CAN)
	AL	Arab League
	ALADI	Asociacion Latinoamericana de Integracion; see Latin American Integration Association (LAIA)
	AMF	Arab Monetary Fund
	AMU	Arab Maghreb Union
	Ancom	Andean Common Market; see Andean Community ofNations (CAN)
	ANZUS	Australia-New Zealand-United States Security Treaty
	APEC	Asia Pacific Economic Cooperation
	Arabsat	Arab Satellite Communications Organization
	AsDB	Asian Development Bank
	ASEAN	Association of Southeast Asian Nations
B	BAD	Banque africaine de developpement; see African Development Bank (AfDB)
	BADEA	Banque Arabe de Developpement Economique en Afrique; see Arab Bank for Economic Development in Africa (ABEDA)
	BCIE	Banco Centroamericano de Integracion Economico; see Central American Bank for Economic Integration (BCIE)

487

	BDEAC	Banque de Developpment des Etats de l'Afrique Centrale; see Central African States Development Bank (BDEAC)
	Benelux	Benelux Economic Union
	BID	Banco Interamericano de Desarrollo; see Inter-American Development Bank (IADB) Biodiversity Convention on Biological Diversity
	BIS	Bank for International Settlements
	BOAD	Banque Ouest-Africaine de Developpement; see West African Development Bank (WADB)
	BSEC	Black Sea Economic Cooperation Zone
C	C	Commonwealth
	CACM	Central American Common Market
	CAEU	Council of Arab Economic Unity
	CAN	Andean Community of Nations
	Caricom	Caribbean Community and Common Market
	CBSS	Council of the Baltic Sea States
	CCC	Customs Cooperation Council
	CDB	Caribbean Development Bank
	CE	Council of Europe
	CEAO	Communaute Economique de l'Afrique de l'Ouest; see West African Economic Community (CEAO)
	CEEAC	Communaute Economique des Etats de l'Afrique Centrale; see Economic Community of Central African States (CEEAC)
	CEI	Central European Initiative
	CEMA	Council for Mutual Economic Assistance; also known as CMEA or Comecon
	CEPGL	Communaute Economique des Pays des Grands Lacs; see Economic Community of the Great Lakes Countries (CEPGL)
	CERN	Conseil Europeen pour la Recherche Nucleaire; see European Organization for Nuclear Research (CERN)
	CG	Contadora Group
	c.i.f.	cost, insurance, and freight
	CIS	Commonwealth of Independent States
	CITES	see Endangered Species
	CMEA	Council for Mutual Economic Assistance (CEMA); also known as Comecon
	COCOM	Coordinating Committee on Export Controls
	Comecon	Council for Mutual Economic Assistance (CEMA); also known as CMEA
	Comsat	Communications Satellite Corporation
	CP	Colombo Plan

	CSCE	Conference on Security and Cooperation in Europe; see Organization on Security and Cooperation in Europe (OSCE)
D	DC	developed country
E	EADB	East African Development Bank
	EAPC	Euro-Atlantic Partnership Council
	EBRD	European Bank for Reconstruction and Development
	EC	European Community; see European Union (EU)
	ECA	Economic Commission for Africa
	ECAFE	Economic Commission for Asia and the Far East; see Economic and Social Commission for Asia and the Pacific (ESCAP)
	ECE	Economic Commission for Europe
	ECLA	Economic Commission for Latin America; see Economic Commission for Latin America and the Caribbean (ECLAC)
	ECLAC	Economic Commission for Latin America and the Caribbean
	ECO	Economic Cooperation Organization
	ECOSOC	Economic and Social Council
	ECOWAS	Economic Community of West African States
	ECSC	European Coal and Steel Community; see European Union (EU)
	ECWA	Economic Commission for Western Asia; see Economic and Social Commission for Western Asia (ESCWA)
	EEC	European Economic Community; see European Union (EU)
	EFTA	European Free Trade Association
	EIB	European Investment Bank
	EMU	European Monetary Union
	ESA	European Space Agency
	ESCAP	Economic and Social Commission for Asia and the Pacific
	ESCWA	Economic and Social Commission for Western Asia
	EU	European Union
	Euratom	European Atomic Energy Community; see European Community (EC)
	Eutelsat	European Telecommunications Satellite Organization
	Ex-Im	Export-Import Bank of the United States
F	FAO	Food and Agriculture Organization
	f.o.b.	free on board
	FRG	Federal Republic of Germany (West Germany); used for information dated before 3 October 1990 or CY91
	FSU	former Soviet Union
	FYROM	The Former Yugoslav Republic of Macedonia

G	GATT	General Agreement on Tariffs and Trade; subsumed by the World Trade Organization (WTrO) on 1 January 1995
	GCC	Gulf Cooperation Council
	GDP	gross domestic product
	GDR	German Democratic Republic (East Germany); used for information dated before 3 October 1990 or CY91
	GNP	gross national product
	GWP	gross world product
I	IADB	Inter-American Development Bank
	IAEA	International Atomic Energy Agency
	IBEC	International Bank for Economic Cooperation
	IBRD	International Bank for Reconstruction and Development (World Bank)
	ICAO	International Civil Aviation Organization
	ICC	International Chamber of Commerce
	ICEM	Intergovernmental Committee for European Migration; see International Organization for Migration (IOM)
	ICFTU	International Confederation of Free Trade Unions; see World Confederation of Labor (WCL)
	ICJ	International Court of Justice
	ICM	Intergovernmental Committee for Migration; see International Organization for Migration (IOM)
	ICRC	International Committee of the Red Cross
	ICRM	International Red Cross and Red Crescent Movement
	IDA	International Development Association
	IDB	Islamic Development Bank
	IEA	International Energy Agency
	IFAD	International Fund for Agricultural Development
	IFC	International Finance Corporation
	IFCTU	International Federation of Christian Trade Unions
	IFRCS	International Federation of Red Cross and Red Crescent Societies
	IGAD	Inter-Governmental Authority on Development
	IGADD	Inter-Governmental Authority on Drought and Development
	IHO	International Hydrographic Organization
	IIB	International Investment Bank
	ILO	International Labor Organization
	IMCO	Intergovernmental Maritime Consultative Organization; see International Maritime Organization (IMO)
	IMF	International Monetary Fund
	IMO	International Maritime Organization
	Inmarsat	International Mobile Satellite Organization
	InOC	Indian Ocean Commission
	Intelsat	International Telecommunications Satellite Organization

	Interpol	International Criminal Police Organization
	Intersputnik	International Organization of Space Communications
	IOC	International Olympic Committee
	IOM	International Organization for Migration
	ISO	International Organization for Standardization
	ITU	International Telecommunication Union
L	LAES	Latin American Economic System
	LAIA	Latin American Integration Association
	LAS	League of Arab States; see Arab League (AL)
	Law of the Sea	United Nations Convention on the Law of the Sea (LOS)
	LDC	less developed country
	LLDC	least developed country
	London Convention	see Marine Dumping
	LORCS	League of Red Cross and Red Crescent Societies; see International Federation of Red Cross and Red Crescent Societies (IFRCS)
	LOS	see Law of the Sea
M	Marecs	Maritime European Communications Satellite
	Marine Dumping	Convention on the Prevention of Marine Pollution by Dumping Wastes and Other Matter
	Marine Life Conservation	Convention on Fishing and Conservation of Living Resources of the High Seas
	MARPOL	see Ship Pollution
	Medarabtel	Middle East Telecommunications Project of the International Telecommunications Union
	Mercosur	Mercado Comun del Cono Sur; see Southern Cone Common Market
	MINURSO	United Nations Mission for the Referendum in Western Sahara
	MINUGUA	United Nations Verification Mission in Guatemala
	MIPONUH	United Nations Civilian Police Mission in Haiti
	MONUA	United Nations Observer Mission in Angola
	MTCR	Missile Technology Control Regime
N	NACC	North Atlantic Cooperation Council; see Euro-Atlantic Partnership Council (EAPC)
	NATO	North Atlantic Treaty Organization
	NC	Nordic Council
	NEA	Nuclear Energy Agency
	NIB	Nordic Investment Bank
	NIC	newly industrializing country; see newly industrializing economy (NIE)
	NIE	newly industrializing economy
	NSG	Nuclear Suppliers Group
	Nuclear Test Ban	Treaty Banning Nuclear Weapons Tests in the Atmosphere, in Outer Space, and Under Water

	NZ	New Zealand
O	OAPEC	Organization of Arab Petroleum Exporting Countries
	OAS	Organization of American States
	OAU	Organization of African Unity
	ODA	official development assistance
	OECD	Organization for Economic Cooperation and Development
	OECS	Organization of Eastern Caribbean States
	OIC	Organization of the Islamic Conference
	ONUMOZ	see United Nations Operation in Mozambique (UNOMOZ)
	ONUSAL	United Nations Observer Mission in El Salvador
	OPANAL	Organismo para la Proscripcion de las Armas Nucleares en la America Latina y el Caribe; see Agency for the Prohibition of Nuclear Weapons in Latin America and the Caribbean
	OPCW	Organization for the Prohibition of Chemical Weapons
	OPEC	Organization of Petroleum Exporting Countries
	OSCE	Organization on Security and Cooperation in Europe Ozone Layer Protection Montreal Protocol on Substances That Deplete the Ozone Layer
P	PCA	Permanent Court of Arbitration
	PDRY	People's Democratic Republic of Yemen [Yemen (Aden) or South Yemen]; used for information dated before 22 May 1990 or CY91
	PFP	Partnership for Peace
R	RG	Rio Group
S	SAARC	South Asian Association for Regional Cooperation
	SACU	Southern African Customs Union
	SADC	Southern African Development Community
	SADCC	Southern African Development Coordination Conference; see Southern African Development Community (SADC)
	SELA	Sistema Economico Latinoamericana; see Latin American Economic System (LAES)
	SFRY	Socialist Federal Republic of Yugoslavia; dissolved 5 December 1991
	Ship Pollution	Protocol of 1978 Relating to the International Convention for the Prevention of Pollution From Ships, 1973 (MARPOL)
	Sparteca	South Pacific Regional Trade and Economic Cooperation Agreement
	SPC	South Pacific Commission
	SPF	South Pacific Forum
U	UAE	United Arab Emirates
	UDEAC	Union Douaniere et Economique de l'Afrique Centrale; see Central African Customs and Economic Union (UDEAC)

UEMOA	Union economique et monetaire Ouest africaine; see West African Economic and Monetary Union (WAEMU)
UK	United Kingdom
UN	United Nations
UNAMIR	United Nations Assistance Mission for Rwanda
UNAVEM III	United Nations Angola Verification Mission III
UNCRO	United Nations Confidence Restoration Operation in Croatia
UNCTAD	United Nations Conference on Trade and Development
UNDOF	United Nations Disengagement Observer Force
UNDP	United Nations Development Program
UNEP	United Nations Environment Program
UNESCO	United Nations Educational, Scientific, and Cultural Organization
UNFICYP	United Nations Peace-keeping Force in Cyprus
UNFPA	United Nations Fund for Population Activities; see UN Population Fund (UNFPA)
UNHCR	United Nations High Commissioner for Refugees
UNICEF	United Nations Children's Fund
UNIDO	United Nations Industrial Development Organization
UNIFIL	United Nations Interim Force in Lebanon
UNIKOM	United Nations Iraq-Kuwait Observation Mission
UNITAR	United Nations Institute for Training and Research
UNMIH	United Nations Mission in Haiti
UNMIBH	United Nations Mission in Bosnia and Herzegovina
UNMOGIP	United Nations Military Observer Group in India and Pakistan
UNMOP	United Nations Mission of Observers in Prevlaka
UNMOT	United Nations Mission of Observers in Tajikistan
UNOMIG	United Nations Observer Mission in Georgia
UNOMIL	United Nations Observer Mission in Liberia
UNOMOZ	United Nations Operation in Mozambique
UNOMSIL	United Nations Mission of Observers in Sierra Leone
UNOMUR	United Nations Observer Mission Uganda-Rwanda
UNOSOM II	United Nations Operation in Somalia II
UNPREDEP	United Nations Preventive Deployment Force
UNPROFOR	United Nations Protection Force
UNRISD	United Nations Research Institute for Social Development
UNRWA	United Nations Relief and Works Agency for Palestine Refugees in the Near East
UNSMIH	United Nations Support Mission in Haiti
UNTAC	United Nations Transitional Authority in Cambodia
UNTAES	United Nations Transitional Administration in Eastern Slavonia, Baranja, and Western Sirmium

	UNTSO	United Nations Truce Supervision Organization
	UNU	United Nations University
	UPU	Universal Postal Union
	US	United States
	USSR	Union of Soviet Socialist Republics (Soviet Union); used for information dated before 25 December 1991
	USSR/EE	Union of Soviet Socialist Republics/Eastern Europe
W	WADB	West African Development Bank
	WAEMU	West African Economic and Monetary Union
	WCL	World Confederation of Labor
	WCO	World Customs Organization; see Customs Cooperation Council
	WEU	Western European Union
	WFC	World Food Council
	WFP	World Food Program
	WFTU	World Federation of Trade Unions
	Whaling	International Convention for the Regulation of Whaling
	WHO	World Health Organization
	WIPO	World Intellectual Property Organization
	WMO	World Meteorological Organization
	WP	Warsaw Pact
	WTO	see WToO for World Tourism Organization or WTrO for World Trade Organization
	WToO	World Tourism Organization
	WTrO	World Trade Organization
Y	YAR	Yemen Arab Republic [Yemen (Sanaa) or North Yemen]; used for information dated before 22 May 1990 or CY91

Appendix D
Corruption & Bribery Index

1999 TI Corruption Perceptions Index (CPI)

The Transparency International Corruption Perceptions Index (CPI) ranks countries in terms of the degree to which corruption is perceived to exist among public officials and politicians. The 1999 CPI ranks 99 countries. It is a composite index, drawing on 17 different polls and surveys from 10 independent institutions carried out among business people, the general public and country analysts.

1999 TI Bribe Payers Perceptions Index (BPI)

The Transparency International Bribe Payers Index (BPI) ranks the leading exporting countries in terms of the degree to which their companies are perceived to be paying bribes abroad.

The BPI is the result of a special international survey conducted for Transparency International by the Gallup International Association in 14 leading emerging market economies.

How to Read the Corruption Perceptions Index

The rank relates solely to the results drawn from a number of surveys and reflects only the perceptions of business people that participated in these surveys.

The column 1999 CPI Score relates to perceptions of the degree of corruption as seen by business people, risk analysts and the general public, and ranges between 10 (highly clean) and 0 (highly corrupt).

Standard Deviation indicates differences in the values of the sources for the 1999 index: the greater the variance, the greater the differences of perceptions of a country among the sources.

495

The number of surveys used refers to the number of surveys that assessed a country's performance. Seventeen surveys were used and at least 3 surveys were required for a country to be included into the 1999 CPI.

The 1999 Corruption Perceptions Index

The Transparency International 1999 Corruption Perceptions Index (CPI)

Country Rank	County	1999 CPI Score	Standard Deviation	Surveys Used
1	Denmark	10.0	0.8	9
2	Finland	9.8	0.5	10
3	New Zealand	9.4	0.8	9
	Sweden	9.4	0.6	10
5	Canada	9.2	0.5	10
	Iceland	9.2	1.2	6
7	Singapore	9.1	0.9	12
8	Netherlands	9.0	0.5	10
9	Norway	8.9	0.8	9
	Switzerland	8.9	0.6	11
11	Luxembourg	8.8	0.9	8
12	Australia	8.7	0.7	8
13	United Kingdom	8.6	0.5	11
14	Germany	8.0	0.5	10
15	Hong Kong	7.7	1.6	13
	Ireland	7.7	1.9	10
17	Austria	7.6	0.8	11
18	USA	7.5	0.8	10
19	Chile	6.9	1.0	9
20	Israel	6.8	1.3	9
21	Portugal	6.7	1.0	10
22	France	6.6	1.0	10
	Spain	6.6	0.7	10
24	Botswana	6.1	1.7	4
25	Japan	6.0	1.6	12
	Slovenia	6.0	1.3	6
27	Estonia	5.7	1.2	7
28	Taiwan	5.6	0.9	12

Country Rank	County	1999 CPI Score	Standard Deviation	Surveys Used
29	Belgium	5.3	1.3	9
	Namibia	5.3	0.9	3
31	Hungary	5.2	1.1	13
32	Costa Rica	5.1	1.5	7
	Malaysia	5.1	0.5	12
34	South Africa	5.0	0.8	12
	Tunisia	5.0	1.9	3
36	Greece	4.9	1.7	9
	Mauritius	4.9	0.7	4
38	Italy	4.7	0.6	10
39	Czech Republic	4.6	0.8	12
40	Peru	4.5	0.8	6
41	Jordan	4.4	0.8	6
	Uruguay	4.4	0.9	3
43	Mongolia	4.3	1.0	3
44	Poland	4.2	0.8	12
45	Brazil	4.1	0.8	11
	Malawi	4.1	0.5	4
	Morocco	4.1	1.7	4
	Zimbabwe	4.1	1.4	9
49	El Salvador	3.9	1.9	4
	Jamaica	3.8	0.4	3
50	Lithuania	3.8	0.5	6
	South Korea	3.8	0.9	13
53	Slovak Republic	3.7	1.5	9
54	Philippines	3.6	1.4	12
	Turkey	3.6	1.0	10
56	Mozambique	3.5	2.2	3
	Zambia	3.5	1.5	4
	Belarus	3.4	1.4	6
	China	3.4	0.7	11
58	Latvia	3.4	1.3	7
	Mexico	3.4	0.5	9
	Senegal	3.4	0.8	3
	Bulgaria	3.3	1.4	8
	Egypt	3.3	0.6	5
63	Ghana	3.3	1.0	4
	Macedonia	3.3	1.2	5
	Romania	3.3	1.0	6
68	Guatemala	3.2	2.5	3
	Thailand	3.2	0.7	12

Country Rank	County	1999 CPI Score	Standard Deviation	Surveys Used
70	Nicaragua	3.1	2.5	3
71	Argentina	3.0	0.8	10
72	Colombia	2.9	0.5	11
	India	2.9	0.6	14
74	Croatia	2.7	0.9	5
	Ivory Coast	2.6	1.0	4
	Moldova	2.6	0.8	5
75	Ukraine	2.6	1.4	10
	Venezuela	2.6	0.8	9
	Vietnam	2.6	0.5	8
80	Armenia	2.5	0.4	4
	Bolivia	2.5	1.1	6
82	Ecuador	2.4	1.3	4
	Russia	2.4	1.0	13
	Albania	2.3	0.3	5
84	Georgia	2.3	0.7	4
	Kazakhstan	2.3	1.3	5
	Kyrgyz Republic	2.2	0.4	4
87	Pakistan	2.2	0.7	3
	Uganda	2.2	0.7	5
	Kenya	2.0	0.5	4
90	Paraguay	2.0	0.8	4
	Yugoslavia	2.0	1.1	6
93	Tanzania	1.9	1.1	4
94	Honduras	1.8	0.5	3
	Uzbekistan	1.8	0.4	4
96	Azerbaijan	1.7	0.6	5
	Indonesia	1.7	0.9	12
98	Nigeria	1.6	0.8	5
99	Cameroon	1.5	0.5	4

Bribe Payers Perceptions Index

Transparency International (TI) released a new Bribe Payers Perceptions Index (BPI) ranking 19 leading exporting countries in terms of the degree to which their corporations are perceived to be paying bribes abroad.

The BPI reveals that on a scale of 0 - 10, where 10 represents a corrupt- free exporting country, the best score among 19 leading exporting countries was 8.3, while the worst score, representing a great propensity to use bribes, was 3.1. China (including Hong Kong) was seen as having the greatest willingness to pay bribes abroad, followed by South Korea, Taiwan, Italy and Malaysia. Sweden, Australia and Canada achieved the most favourable results.

The new survey involved detailed questions to more than 770 senior executives at major companies, chartered accountancies, chambers of commerce, major commercial banks and law firms. These respondents did include foreign nationals and executives at international firms. The questions concerned the propensity to bribe senior public officials by corporations.

The 1999 Bribe Payers Perceptions Index

1999 Transparency International
Bribe Payers Perceptions Index (BPI)
Ranking 19 Leading Exporters

Rank	Country	Score
1	Sweden	8.3
2	Australia	8.1
	Canada	8.1
4	Austria	7.8
5	Switzerland	7.7
6	Netherlands	7.4
7	United Kingdom	7.2
8	Belgium	6.8
9	Germany	6.2
	United States	6.2
11	Singapore	5.7
12	Spain	5.3
13	France	5.2
14	Japan	5.1
15	Malaysia	3.9
16	Italy	3.7
17	Taiwan	3.5
18	South Korea	3.4
19	China (including Hong Kong)	3.1

Notes: The questions related to leading exporters paying bribes to senior public officials. The standard error in the results was 0.2 or less. In the scoring: 10 represents a perceived level of negligible bribery, while 0 represents responses indicating very high levels of bribery.

Appendix E
Conversion Factors

To Convert From	To	Multiply by
acres	ares	40.468 564 224
acres	hectares	0.404 685 642 24
acres	square feet	43,560
acres	square kilometers	0.004 046 856 422 4
acres	square meters	4,046.856 422 4
acres	square miles (statute)	0.001 562 50
acres	square yards	4,840
ares	square meters	100
ares	square yards	119.599
barrels, US beer	gallons	31
barrels, US beer	liters	117.347 77
barrels, US petroleum	gallons (British)	34.97
barrels, US petroleum	gallons (US)	42
barrels, US petroleum	liters	158.987 29
barrels, US proof spirits	gallons	40
barrels, US proof spirits	liters	151.416 47
bushels (US)	bushels (British)	0.968 9
bushels (US)	cubic feet	1.244 456
bushels (US)	cubic inches	2,150.42
bushels (US)	cubic meters	0.035 239 07
bushels (US)	cubic yards	0.046 090 96
bushels (US)	dekaliters	3.523 907
bushels (US)	dry pints	64
bushels (US)	dry quarts	32
bushels (US)	liters	35.239 070 17
bushels (US)	pecks	4

To Convert From	To	Multiply by
cables	fathoms	120
cables	meters	219.456
cables	yards	240
carat	milligrams	200
centimeters	feet	0.032 808 40
centimeters	inches	0.393 700 8
centimeters	meters	0.01
centimeters	yards	0.010 936 13
centimeters, cubic	cubic inches	0.061 023 744
centimeters, square	square feet	0.001 076 39
centimeters, square	square inches	0.155 000 31
centimeters, square	square meters	0.000 1
centimeters, square	square yards	0.000 119 599
chains, square surveyor's	ares	4.046 86
chains, square surveyor's	square feet	4,356
chains, surveyor's	feet	66
chains, surveyor's	meters	20.116 8
chains, surveyor's	rods	4
cords of wood	cubic feet	128
cords of wood	cubic meters	3.624 556
cords of wood	cubic yards	4.740 7
cups	liquid ounces (US)	8
cups	liters	0.236 588 2
degrees Celsius	degrees Fahrenheit	multiply by 1.8 and add 32
degrees Fahrenheit	degrees Celsius	subtract 32 and divide by 1.8
dekaliters	bushels	0.283 775 9
dekaliters	cubic feet	0.353 146 7
dekaliters	cubic inches	610.237 4
dekaliters	dry pints	18.161 66
dekaliters	dry quarts	9.080 829 8
dekaliters	liters	10
dekaliters	pecks	1.135 104
drams, avoirdupois	avoirdupois ounces	0.062 55
drams, avoirdupois	grains	27.344
drams, avoirdupois	grams	1.771 845 2
drams, troy	grains	60
drams, troy	grams	3.887 934 6
drams, troy	scruples	3
drams, troy	troy ounces	0.125
drams, liquid (US)	cubic inches	0.226
drams, liquid (US)	liquid drams (British)	1.041

To Convert From	To	Multiply by
drams, liquid (US)	liquid ounces	0.125
drams, liquid (US)	milliliters	3.696 69
drams, liquid (US)	minims	60
fathoms	feet	6
fathoms	meters	1.828 8
feet	centimeters	30.48
feet	inches	12
feet	kilometers	0.000 304 8
feet	meters	0.304 8
feet	statute miles	0.000 189 39
feet	yards	0.333 333 3
feet, cubic	bushels	0.803 563 95
feet, cubic	cubic decimeters	28.316 847
feet, cubic	cubic inches	1,728
feet, cubic	cubic meters	0.028 316 846 592
feet, cubic	cubic yards	0.037 037 04
feet, cubic	dry pints	51.428 09
feet, cubic	dry quarts	25.714 05
feet, cubic	gallons	7.480 519
feet, cubic	gills	239.376 6
feet, cubic	liquid ounces	957.506 5
feet, cubic	liquid pints	59.844 16
feet, cubic	liquid quarts	29.922 08
feet, cubic	liters	28.316 846 592
feet, cubic	pecks	3.214 256
feet, square	acres	0.000 022 956 8
feet, square	square centimeters	929.030 4
feet, square	square decimeters	9.290 304
feet, square	square inches	144
feet, square	square meters	0.092 903 04
feet, square	square yards	0.111 111 1
furlongs	feet	660
furlongs	inches	7,920
furlongs	meters	201.168
furlongs	statute miles	0.125
furlongs	yards	220
gallons, liquid (US)	cubic feet	0.133 680 6
gallons, liquid (US)	cubic inches	231
gallons, liquid (US)	cubic meters	0.003 785 411 784
gallons, liquid (US)	cubic yards	0.004 951 13
gallons, liquid (US)	gills (US)	32
gallons, liquid (US)	liquid gallons (British)	0.832 67

To Convert From	To	Multiply by
gallons, liquid (US)	liquid ounces	128
gallons, liquid (US)	liquid pints	8
gallons, liquid (US)	liquid quarts	4
gallons, liquid (US)	liters	3.785 411 784
gallons, liquid (US)	milliliters	3,785.411 784
gallons, liquid (US)	minims	61,440
gills (US)	centiliters	11.829 4
gills (US)	cubic feet	0.004 177 517
gills (US)	cubic inches	7.218 75
gills (US)	gallons	0.031 25
gills (US)	gills (British)	0.832 67
gills (US)	liquid ounces	4
gills (US)	liquid pints	0.25
gills (US)	liquid quarts	0.125
gills (US)	liters	0.118 294 118 25
gills (US)	milliliters	118.294 118 25
gills (US)	minims	1,920
grains	avoirdupois drams	0.036 571 43
grains	avoirdupois ounces	0.002 285 71
grains	avoirdupois pounds	0.000 142 86
grains	grams	0.064 798 91
grains	kilograms	0.000 064 798 91
grains	milligrams	64.798 910
grains	pennyweights	0.042
grains	scruples	0.05
grains	troy drams	0.016 6
grains	troy ounces	0.002 083 33
grains	troy pounds	0.000 173 61
grams	avoirdupois drams	0.564 383 39
grams	avoirdupois ounces	0.035 273 961
grams	avoirdupois pounds	0.002 204 622 6
grams	grains	15.432 361
grams	kilograms	0.001
grams	milligrams	1,000
grams	troy ounces	0.032 150 746 6
grams	troy pounds	0.002 679 23
hands (height of horse)	centimeters	10.16
hands (height of horse)	inches	4
hectares	acres	2.471 053 8
hectares	square feet	107,639.1
hectares	square kilometers	0.01
hectares	square meters	10,000

To Convert From	To	Multiply by
hectares	square miles	0.003 861 02
hectares	square yards	11,959.90
hundredweights, long	avoirdupois pounds	112
hundredweights, long	kilograms	50.802 345
hundredweights, long	long tons	0.05
hundredweights, long	metric tons	0.050 802 345
hundredweights, long	short tons	0.056
hundredweights, short	avoirdupois pounds	100
hundredweights, short	kilograms	45.359 237
hundredweights, short	long tons	0.044 642 86
hundredweights, short	metric tons	0.045 359 237
hundredweights, short	short tons	0.05
inches	centimeters	2.54
inches	feet	0.083 333 33
inches	meters	0.025 4
inches	millimeters	25.4
inches	yards	0.027 777 78
inches, cubic	bushels	0.000 465 025
inches, cubic	cubic centimeters	16.387 064
inches, cubic	cubic feet	0.000 578 703 7
inches, cubic	cubic meters	0.000 016 387 064
inches, cubic	cubic yards	0.000 021 433 47
inches, cubic	dry pints	0.029 761 6
inches, cubic	dry quarts	0.014 880 8
inches, cubic	gallons	0.004 329 0
inches, cubic	gills	0.138 528 1
inches, cubic	liquid ounces	0.554 112 6
inches, cubic	liquid pints	0.034 632 03
inches, cubic	liquid quarts	0.017 316 02
inches, cubic	liters	0.016 387 064
inches, cubic	milliliters	16.387 064
inches, cubic	minims (US)	265.974 0
inches, cubic	pecks	0.001 860 10
inches, square	square centimeters	6.451 600
inches, square	square feet	0.006 944 44
inches, square	square meters	0.000 645 16
inches, square	square yards	0.000 771 605
kilograms	avoirdupois drams	564.383 4
kilograms	avoirdupois ounces	35.273 962
kilograms	avoirdupois pounds	2.204 622 622
kilograms	grains	15,432.36
kilograms	grams	1,000

To Convert From	To	Multiply by
kilograms	long tons	0.000 984 2
kilograms	metric tons	0.001
kilograms	short hundredweights	0.022 046 23
kilograms	short tons	0.001 102 31
kilograms	troy ounces	32.150 75
kilograms	troy pounds	2.679 229
kilometers	meters	1,000
kilometers	statute miles	0.621 371 192
kilometers, square	acres	247.105 38
kilometers, square	hectares	100
kilometers, square	square meters	1,000,000
kilometers, square	statute miles	0.386 102 16
knots (nautical mi/hr)	kilometers/hour	1.852
knots (nautical mi/hr)	statute miles/hour	1.151
leagues, nautical	kilometers	5.556
leagues, nautical	nautical miles	3
leagues, statute	kilometers	4.828 032
leagues, statute	statute miles	3
links, square surveyor's	square centimeters	404.686
links, square surveyor's	square inches	62.726 4
links, surveyor's	centimeters	20.116 8
links, surveyor's	chains	0.01
links, surveyor's	inches	7.92
liters	bushels	0.028 377 59
liters	cubic feet	0.035 314 67
liters	cubic inches	61.023 74
liters	cubic meters	0.001
liters	cubic yards	0.001 307 95
liters	dekaliters	0.1
liters	dry pints	1.816 166
liters	dry quarts	0.908 082 98
liters	gallons	0.264 172 052
liters	gills (US)	8.453 506
liters	liquid ounces	33.814 02
liters	liquid pints	2.113 376
liters	liquid quarts	1.056 688 2
liters	milliliters	1,000
liters	pecks	0.113 510 4
meters	centimeters	100
meters	feet	3.280 839 895
meters	inches	39.370 079
meters	kilometers	0.001

To Convert From	To	Multiply by
meters	millimeters	1,000
meters	statute miles	0.000 621 371
meters	yards	1.093 613 298
meters, cubic	bushels	28.377 59
meters, cubic	cubic feet	35.314 666 7
meters, cubic	cubic inches	61,023.744
meters, cubic	cubic yards	1.307 950 619
meters, cubic	gallons	264.172 05
meters, cubic	liters	1,000
meters, cubic	pecks	113.510 4
meters, square	acres	0.000 247 105 38
meters, square	hectares	0.000 1
meters, square	square centimeters	10,000
meters, square	square feet	10.763 910 4
meters, square	square inches	1,550.003 1
meters, square	square yards	1.195 990 046
microns	meters	0.000 001
microns	inches	0.000 039 4
mils	inches	0.001
mils	millimeters	0.025 4
miles, nautical	kilometers	1.852 0
miles, nautical	statute miles	1.150 779 4
miles, statute	centimeters	160,934.4
miles, statute	feet	5,280
miles, statute	furlongs	8
miles, statute	inches	63,360
miles, statute	kilometers	1.609 344
miles, statute	meters	1,609.344
miles, statute	rods	320
miles, statute	yards	1,760
miles, square nautical	square kilometers	3.429 904
miles, square nautical	square statute miles	1.325
miles, square statute	acres	640
miles, square statute	hectares	258.998 811 033 6
miles, square statute	sections	1
miles, square statute	square kilometers	2.589 988 110 336
miles, square statute	square nautical miles	0.755 miles
miles, square statute	square rods	102,400
milligrams	grains	0.015 432 358 35
milliliters	cubic inches	0.061 023 744
milliliters	gallons	0.000 264 17
milliliters	gills (US)	0.008 453 5

To Convert From	To	Multiply by
milliliters	liquid ounces	0.033 814 02
milliliters	liquid pints	0.002 113 4
milliliters	liquid quarts	0.001 056 7
milliliters	liters	0.001
milliliters	minims	16.230 73
millimeters	inches	0.039 370 078 7
minims (US)	cubic inches	0.003 759 77
minims (US)	gills (US)	0.000 520 83
minims (US)	liquid ounces	0.002 083 33
minims (US)	milliliters	0.061 611 52
minims (US)	minims (British)	1.041
ounces, avoirdupois	avoirdupois drams	16
ounces, avoirdupois	avoirdupois pounds	0.062 5
ounces, avoirdupois	grains	437.5
ounces, avoirdupois	grams	28.349 523 125
ounces, avoirdupois	kilograms	0.028 349 523 125
ounces, avoirdupois	troy ounces	0.911 458 3
ounces, avoirdupois	troy pounds	0.075 954 86
ounces, liquid (US)	cubic feet	0.001 044 38
ounces, liquid (US)	centiliters	2.957 35
ounces, liquid (US)	cubic inches	1.804 687 5
ounces, liquid (US)	gallons	0.007 812 5
ounces, liquid (US)	gills (US)	0.25
ounces, liquid (US)	liquid drams	8
ounces, liquid (US)	liquid ounces (British)	1.041
ounces, liquid (US)	liquid pints	0.062 5
ounces, liquid (US)	liquid quarts	0.031 25
ounces, liquid (US)	liters	0.029 573 53
ounces, liquid (US)	milliliters	29.573 529 6
ounces, liquid (US)	minims	480
ounces, troy	avoirdupois drams	17.554 29
ounces, troy	avoirdupois ounces	1.097 143
ounces, troy	avoirdupois pounds	0.068 571 43
ounces, troy	grains	480
ounces, troy	grams	31.103 476 8
ounces, troy	pennyweights	20
ounces, troy	troy drams	8
ounces, troy	troy pounds	0.083 333 3
paces (US)	centimeters	76.2
paces (US)	inches	30
pecks (US)	bushels	0.25
pecks (US)	cubic feet	0.311 114

To Convert From	To	Multiply by
pecks (US)	cubic inches	537.605
pecks (US)	cubic meters	0.008 809 77
pecks (US)	cubic yards	0.011 522 74
pecks (US)	dekaliters	0.880 976 75
pecks (US)	dry pints	16
pecks (US)	dry quarts	8
pecks (US)	liters	8.809 767 5
pecks (US)	pecks (British)	0.968 9
pennyweights	grains	24
pennyweights	grams	1.555 173 84
pennyweights	troy ounces	0.05
pints, dry (US)	bushels	0.015 625
pints, dry (US)	cubic feet	0.019 444 63
pints, dry (US)	cubic inches	33.600 312 5
pints, dry (US)	dekaliters	0.055 061 05
pints, dry (US)	dry pints (British)	0.968 9
pints, dry (US)	dry quarts	0.5
pints, dry (US)	liters	0.550 610 47
pints, liquid (US)	cubic feet	0.016 710 07
pints, liquid (US)	cubic inches	28.875
pints, liquid (US)	deciliters	4.731 76
pints, liquid (US)	gallons	0.125
pints, liquid (US)	gills (US)	4
pints, liquid (US)	liquid ounces	16
pints, liquid (US)	liquid pints (British)	0.832 67
pints, liquid (US)	liquid quarts	0.5
pints, liquid (US)	liters	0.473 176 473
pints, liquid (US)	milliliters	473.176 473
pints, liquid (US)	minims	7,680
points (typographical)	inches	0.013 837
points (typographical)	millimeters	0.351 459 8
pounds, avoirdupois	avoirdupois drams	256
pounds, avoirdupois	avoirdupois ounces	16
pounds, avoirdupois	grains	7,000
pounds, avoirdupois	grams	453.592 37
pounds, avoirdupois	kilograms	0.453 592 37
pounds, avoirdupois	long tons	0.000 446 428 6
pounds, avoirdupois	metric tons	0.000 453 592 37
pounds, avoirdupois	quintals	0.004 535 92
pounds, avoirdupois	short tons	0.000 5
pounds, avoirdupois	troy ounces	14.583 33
pounds, avoirdupois	troy pounds	1.215 278

To Convert From	To	Multiply by
pounds, troy	avoirdupois drams	210.651 4
pounds, troy	avoirdupois ounces	13.165 71
pounds, troy	avoirdupois pounds	0.822 857 1
pounds, troy	grains	5,760
pounds, troy	grams	373.241 721 6
pounds, troy	kilograms	0.373 241 721 6
pounds, troy	pennyweights	240
pounds, troy	troy ounces	12
quarts, dry (US)	bushels	0.031 25
quarts, dry (US)	cubic feet	0.038 889 25
quarts, dry (US)	cubic inches	67.200 625
quarts, dry (US)	dekaliters	0.110 122 1
quarts, dry (US)	dry pints	2
quarts, dry (US)	dry quarts (British)	0.968 9
quarts, dry (US)	liters	1.101 221
quarts, dry (US)	pecks	0.125
quarts, dry (US)	pints, dry (US)	2
quarts, liquid (US)	cubic feet	0.033 420 14
quarts, liquid (US)	cubic inches	57.75
quarts, liquid (US)	deciliters	9.463 53
quarts, liquid (US)	gallons	0.25
quarts, liquid (US)	gills (US)	8
quarts, liquid (US)	liquid ounces	32
quarts, liquid (US)	liquid pints (US)	2
quarts, liquid (US)	liquid quarts (British)	0.832 67
quarts, liquid (US)	liters	0.946 352 946
quarts, liquid (US)	milliliters	946.352 946
quarts, liquid (US)	minims	15,360
quintals	avoirdupois pounds	220.462 26
quintals	kilograms	100
quintals	metric tons	0.1
rods	feet	16.5
rods	meters	5.029 2
rods	yards	5.5
rods, square	acres	0.006 25
rods, square	square meters	25.292 85
rods, square	square yards	30.25
scruples	grains	20
scruples	grams	1.295 978 2
scruples	troy drams	0.333
sections (US)	square kilometers	2.589 988 1
sections (US)	square statute miles	1

To Convert From	To	Multiply by
spans	centimeters	22.86
spans	inches	9
steres	cubic meters	1
steres	cubic yards	1.307 95
tablespoons	milliliters	14.786 76
tablespoons	teaspoons	3
teaspoons	milliliters	4.928 922
teaspoons	tablespoons	0.333 333
ton-miles, long	metric ton-kilometers	1.635 169
ton-miles, short	metric ton-kilometers	1.459 972
tons, gross register	cubic feet of permanently enclosed space	100
tons, gross register	cubic meters of permanently enclosed space	2.831 684 7
tons, long (deadweight)	avoirdupois ounces	35,840
tons, long (deadweight)	avoirdupois pounds	2,240
tons, long (deadweight)	kilograms	1,016.046 909 8
tons, long (deadweight)	long hundredweights	20
tons, long (deadweight)	metric tons	1.016 046 908 8
tons, long (deadweight)	short hundredweights	22.4
tons, long (deadweight)	short tons	1.12
tons, metric	avoirdupois pounds	2,204.623
tons, metric	kilograms	1,000
tons, metric	long hundredweights	19.684 130 3
tons, metric	long tons	0.984 206 5
tons, metric	quintals	10
tons, metric	short hundredweights	22.046 23
tons, metric	short tons	1.102 311 3
tons, metric	troy ounces	32,150.75
tons, net register	cubic feet of permanently enclosed space for cargo and passengers	100
tons, net register	cubic meters of permanently enclosed space for cargo and passengers	2.831 684 7
tons, shipping	cubic feet of permanently enclosed cargo space	42
tons, shipping	cubic meters of permanently enclosed cargo space	1.189 307 574
tons, short	avoirdupois pounds	2,000
tons, short	kilograms	907.184 74
tons, short	long hundredweights	17.857 14
tons, short	long tons	0.892 857 1
tons, short	metric tons	0.907 184 74

To Convert From	To	Multiply by
tons, short	short hundredweights	20
townships (US)	sections	36
townships (US)	square kilometers	93.239 572
townships (US)	square statute miles	36
miles, square statute	acres	640
miles, square statute	hectares	258.998 811 033 6
miles, square statute	square feet	27,878,400
miles, square statute	square meters	2,589,988.110 336
miles, square statute	square yards	3,097,600
yards	centimeters	91.44
yards	feet	3
yards	inches	36
yards	meters	0.914 4
yards	miles	0.000 568 18
yards, cubic	bushels	21.696 227
yards, cubic	cubic feet	27
yards, cubic	cubic inches	46,656
yards, cubic	cubic meters	0.764 554 857 984
yards, cubic	gallons	201.974 0
yards, cubic	liters	764.554 857 984
yards, cubic	pecks	86.784 91
yards, square	acres	0.000 206 611 6
yards, square	hectares	0.000 083 612 736
yards, square	square centimeters	8,361.273 6
yards, square	square feet	9
yards, square	square inches	1,296
yards, square	square meters	0.836 127 36
yards, square	square miles	0.000 000 322 830 6

Note: At this time, only three countries—Burma, Liberia, and the US—have not adopted the International System of Units (SI, or metric system) as their official system of weights and measures. Although use of the metric system has been sanctioned by law in the US since 1866, it has been slow in displacing the American adaptation of the British Imperial System known as the US Customary System. The US is the only industrialized nation that does not mainly use the metric system in its commercial and standards activities, but there is increasing acceptance in science, medicine, government, and many sectors of industry.

About the Authors

Terri Morrison is President and Owner of Getting Through Customs (getcustoms.com), a software, training and research firm for international business travelers. Ms. Morrison is co-author of six books, including *Kiss, Bow or Shake Hands: How to Do Business in Sixty Countries*.

Wayne A. Conaway works in the publishing industry, writes for many publications, and is co-author of five books, including *Kiss, Bow or Shake Hands: How to Do Business in Sixty Countries*. He resides in West Chester, PA.

Joseph J. Douress is the former publisher of the *Exporter's Encyclopedia*, and former Director of Global Trade Services for Dun & Bradstreet. He is presently Director of Business Development of Reed Elsevier. His email is joseph.douress@renp.com

The authors of this book wish to express their appreciation to Getting Through Customs of Newtown Square, Pennsylvania. Getting Through Customs produces the PASSPORT System, the leading online database of global business, religious & social practices; cognitive styles & cultural overviews; medical & travel information; political data & contacts. The authors augmented their own research and experience with Getting Through Customs' online PASSPORT database. A demo of the database is available at www.getcustoms.com.

The study of intercultural communications and trade represents a lifelong interest for the authors of *Dun & Bradstreet's Guide to Doing Business Around the World*. By way of continuing that research, the authors invite your comments. Whether your experience confirms or diverges from the data in this book, they would like to hear from you. Please send your comments to:

Email: TerriMorrison@getcustoms.com
Tel: 610.725.1040
Fax: 801.516.8774

About Dun & Bradstreet

Dun & Bradstreet, a company of The Dun & Bradstreet Corporation (NYSE: DNB), is the world's leading provider of business-to-business credit, marketing and purchasing information and receivables management services. Companies of all sizes in all industries around the world use D&B information in their supply and demand chains. By integrating D&B information into business systems and processes, companies can better manage their customers and suppliers and achieve a direct and seamless link between back-office and front-office operations. The Dun & Bradstreet Corporation based in Murray Hill, N.J., employs approximately 11,500 people in 37 countries with majority-owned company entities, and generated 1999 revenue of $1.97 billion. Additional information about Dun & Bradstreet is available at www.dnb.com.

For information on D&B's global capabilities, please contact the D&B International Solutions Center at 1-800-923-0025, or access D&B's website at www.dnb.com

D&B International Business Information Reports

The D&B International Business Information Report provides background information about a company's payments, finances, history and operations. The report mirrors the content and style of the U.S. Business Information Report. However, the amount and type of information varies by country, due to local commercial practices, government restrictions on the use of company information, and differences in the availability of public and private information.

D&B International Risk & Payment Review

D&B International Risk & Payment Review prepares corporations and investors for the risks associated with doing business around the world. This monthly periodical and Internet service tracks the economic, political and commercial risk factors that affect trade. It also includes key data such as payment terms and delays, currency fluctuations and the unique D&B Country Risk Indicator which rates the overall risk of doing business with a specific country. Each country assessment also includes a two-year forecast that can help to facilitate the management of ongoing business risk. D&B's International Risk and Payment Review covers 131 countries.

D&B Country Reports

Provide in-depth, critical information and analysis on the trade environment of a single country. Available on individual countries, each D&B Country Report (85 countries available) provides up to 60 pages of analysis on key aspects associated with country risk - from political risk to economic risk to commercial risk. Analysis includes economic forecasts and the D&B Country Risk Indicator rating which provides a cross-country comparison of the risks of doing business around the globe. You can use the Country Reports to:

- Research new global markets
- Assess country risk
- Expand your global business opportunities
- Reduce your exposure to risk

D&B Exporters' Encyclopaedia

Exporters' Encyclopaedia is a guide to global market and export information on more than 220 countries. With this directory, you can understand a country's trade regulations, documentation requirements, and key contacts, so as to: Successfully enter global markets and minimize payment delays by understanding country requirements.

Index

Index

O